HBJ HARCOURT BRACE JOVANOVICH, INC.

CONCEPTS IN SCIENCE

A comprehensive program in science for the learning levels from kindergarten through junior high school

TEXTBOOKS

Primary and Intermediate Levels

CONCEPTS IN SCIENCE with accompanying *Teacher's Edition* including Answer Keys to *Teaching Tests: Concepts in Science*

Junior High School Levels

LIFE: ITS FORMS AND CHANGES
MATTER: ITS FORMS AND CHANGES
ENERGY: ITS FORMS AND CHANGES

Each of these books is accompanied by a *Teacher's Manual*

LABORATORY EQUIPMENT AND MATERIALS

CLASSROOM LABORATORY Sets with accompanying *Teacher's Manual* for each of the primary levels, and *Pupil's Manuals* and *Teacher's Editions* for each of the intermediate levels

LABORATORY EXPERIENCES with accompanying *Student's Manual* and *Teacher's Edition* for each of the junior high school levels

EXPERIENCE BOOKS AND SEARCHBOOKS

SEARCHBOOKS (individualized activities, investigations, and searches) for intermediate and junior high school levels with accompanying *Teacher's Editions* (intermediate) and *Answer Keys* (junior high)

TESTS

TEACHING TESTS for intermediate and junior high school levels

INDIVIDUALIZED PROGRAM FOR THE INADEQUATELY PREPARED READER

ON MY OWN, a boxed classroom supply of individual investigation leaflets

INVESTIGATION CARDS

100 INVITATIONS TO INVESTIGATE, a box of 100 nongraded, open-ended investigations on individual cards for easy access and use

TEACHING SCIENCE SERIES

Elementary Years

A BOOK OF METHODS
A SOURCEBOOK FOR ELEMENTARY SCIENCE

Junior High School Years

A BOOK OF METHODS
A SOURCEBOOK FOR THE BIOLOGICAL SCIENCES
A SOURCEBOOK FOR THE PHYSICAL SCIENCES

Monographs

ELEMENTS IN A STRATEGY FOR TEACHING SCIENCE IN THE ELEMENTARY SCHOOL
SUBSTANCE, STRUCTURE, AND STYLE IN THE TEACHING OF SCIENCE

To provide more flexible use of the *Concepts in Science* Series, grade-level designations have been replaced by a system of levels indicated by a color key on the spine, the front cover, the title page, and on pages F-16-F-17 of the Teacher's Editions. For average classes, the level of the book will probably be the same as the grade level. The sequence of levels is shown below. Please use color designations in placing orders and in all correspondence concerning a specific volume in the series.

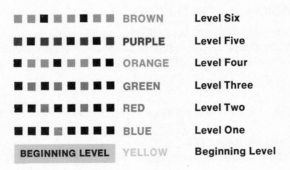

BROWN	**Level Six**
PURPLE	**Level Five**
ORANGE	**Level Four**
GREEN	**Level Three**
RED	**Level Two**
BLUE	**Level One**
BEGINNING LEVEL YELLOW	**Beginning Level**

We do not include a Teacher's Edition automatically with each shipment of a classroom set of textbooks. We prefer to send a Teacher's Edition only when it is part of a purchase order or when it is requested by the teacher or administrator concerned or by one of our representatives. A Teacher's Edition can be easily mislaid when it arrives as part of a shipment delivered to a school stockroom, and, since it contains answer materials, we would like to be sure it is sent *directly* to the person who will use it, or to someone concerned with the use or selection of texbooks.

If your class assignment changes and you no longer are using or examining this Teacher's Edition, you may wish to pass it on to a teacher who may have use for it.

■■■■■■■■PURPLE

TEACHER'S EDITION

CONCEPTS IN SCIENCE

THIRD EDITION

AUTHORS

PAUL F. BRANDWEIN

ELIZABETH K. COOPER

PAUL E. BLACKWOOD

ELIZABETH B. HONE

THOMAS P. FRASER

CONSULTING SPECIALISTS IN THE SCIENCES

HERMAN R. BRANSON, *Physics*

LAWRENCE P. EBLIN, *Chemistry*

GARRETT HARDIN, *Biology and Ecology*

RICHARD C. LEWONTIN, *Biology and Genetics*

ALISTAIR McCRONE, *Geology and Earth Science*

FRANKLIN MILLER, Jr., *Physics*

LLOYD MOTZ, *Astronomy and Space*

HBJ HARCOURT BRACE JOVANOVICH, INC.

NEW YORK CHICAGO SAN FRANCISCO ATLANTA DALLAS

AUTHORS

Paul F. Brandwein, Adjunct Professor, University of Pittsburgh, Pittsburgh, Pennsylvania; formerly Director, The Pinchot Institute for Conservation Studies, Milford, Pennsylvania; formerly chairman of department and teacher, now consultant to elementary, junior, and senior high schools; President, Center for the Study of Instruction, San Francisco; Vice President and Director of the School Department, Harcourt Brace Jovanovich, Inc.

Elizabeth K. Cooper, formerly Director of Elementary Education, Santa Monica Public Schools, Santa Monica, California; Coordinator of Teacher Training, University of California at Los Angeles; formerly teacher and supervisor in elementary schools in Ohio, New York, and California; author of children's books about science.

Paul E. Blackwood, Chief, Southeast Programs Operations Branch, U.S. Office of Education;* formerly head of Science, the University Schools, Ohio State University, Columbus, Ohio; Professor of Science, Central Washington College, Ellensburg, Washington.

Elizabeth B. Hone, Professor of Education, San Fernando Valley State College, Northridge, California; formerly elementary school teacher; formerly research assistant, Conservation Foundation; Coordinator of elementary student teachers, San Fernando State College; consultant in elementary science education.

Thomas P. Fraser, Professor of Science Education and Director of Summer Institute in Science for Secondary School Teachers, Morgan State College, Baltimore, Maryland; past President, National Association for Research in Science Teaching; formerly Interim President, Morgan State College.

*The work of Paul E. Blackwood on the *Concepts in Science* Series was done in his private capacity, and no official endorsement by the U.S. Office of Education is intended or should be inferred.

CONSULTING SPECIALISTS IN THE SCIENCES

Herman R. Branson, President, Lincoln University, Lincoln University, Pennsylvania; formerly Head of Department of Physics, Howard University, Washington, D.C.

Lawrence P. Eblin, Professor of Chemistry, Ohio University, Athens, Ohio.

Garrett Hardin, Professor of Biology, University of California, Los Angeles.

Richard C. Lewontin, Professor of Biology, The University of Chicago, Chicago, Illinois.

Alistair W. McCrone, Academic Vice President and Professor of Geology, University of the Pacific, Stockton, California; formerly Professor of Geology, Chairman, Department of Geology, and Associate of the Graduate School, New York University.

Franklin Miller, Jr., Chairman, Department of Physics, Kenyon College, Gambier, Ohio.

Lloyd Motz, Professor of Astronomy, Columbia University, New York, New York.

Cover Photographs: Front, Harbrace; Back, Mortimer Abramowitz. *Illustrations:* Pg. T-129; Reproduced from *Matter—Its Forms and Changes* by Paul F. Brandwein, et al, © 1972, 1968 by Harcourt Brace Jovanovich, Inc.; Pg. T-342; Reproduced from *Life—Its Forms and Changes* by Paul F. Brandwein, et al, © 1972, 1968 by Harcourt Brace Jovanovich, Inc.

ISBN 0–15–366130–5

Printed in the United States of America

CONTENTS

PART ONE: CONCEPTS IN SCIENCE—THE PROGRAM

PART TWO: CONCEPTS IN SCIENCE PURPLE

TEACHING SUGGESTIONS

APPRENTICE INVESTIGATIONS AND SEARCHES ON YOUR OWN

Concepts in Science PURPLE contains 31 Apprentice Investigations that are basic to concept-seeking. Each Apprentice Investigation together with additional investigations at the end of lesson clusters in the textbook and in this Teacher's Edition offer many opportunities for children to design investigations in which they use processes of science and develop behaviors in the art of investigation. In addition, the textbook contains 14 Searches On Your Own, one a long-term Search, initiating investigations that are individual and completely independent and open-ended.

All investigations can be performed with relatively simple and usually readily available materials. However, much equipment and many materials are supplied in conveniently packaged form in the CLASSROOM LABORATORY that is correlated with this textbook. Their availability is indicated at appropriate times in this Teacher's Edition. A listing of the textbook and Teacher's Edition pages follows for all Apprentice Investigations and Searches On Your Own. The Searches are indicated by •

PART ONE: CONCEPTS IN SCIENCE—THE PROGRAM

By Way of Beginning

The teacher is in many ways the key to *what* happens in the classroom, *how* it happens, and *why* it happens. Teaching style remains a personal invention. The teacher is at the heart of what Jerome Bruner has called "instructed learning."

In instructed learning (the kind of learning experience which is part of schooling), experiences do not occur at random. Experiences are carefully planned to help children fulfill their growth; to advance in developing their aptitudes, to seek out their opportunities and destinies. Instructed learning is learning that is non-randomized; it is experience in search of meaning. Children build upon their past, probing the future. They build upon their "knowns," probing what is not yet known—that is, what is unknown or even presently unknowable.

Teacher and child meet each other in the classroom. The teacher, knowing the relative growth and readiness of children, is the one who often determines to *whom* the experience happens, and *when*, and *how*, and *why*. Thus a teacher will often decide when a child—or the children—is ready for a given experience. Or the teacher, observing a child, sets her plans aside and takes the plans of the child, sharing with the child his search and his meaning. However, the goal of experience in instructed learning, whether initiated by the teacher or the child for a child, a group, a class, or a school, is growth.

The *Concepts in Science* (CIS) program in the teaching of science is the result of considerable observation of children in the act of learning in the classrooms of the nation. Teachers and children, in more than a thousand school systems over the globe, in all states of the Union and in eight other countries where this program is used, have been observed or have offered us their observations.

These observations have been analyzed and the findings have supported this revision, the Third Edition. We have received hundreds of communications from teachers and children which we have gladly built into the revision. In addition, we have conducted researches into the teaching-learning complex. These too are embodied in this revision.

A distillate of these observations, these analyses, these searches, is given in the following pages titled: "The Teaching of Science—and Its Methods of Intelligence." We are mindful of the great responsibility those of us who are privileged to build curricular and instructional modes have to our peers—the teachers of this globe. More so, we are mindful of our responsibility to the children we reach.

We are also mindful of our great debt to the teachers and children who have used these books. Just as scientists stand on the shoulders of the scientists who came before them, so we too stand on the shoulders of those who have taught children—as we have—and have put their experience into curriculum and accompanying instructional material such as *Concepts in Science* (CIS). More so, we owe a special debt of gratitude to those teachers and children who are represented in this program by picture and by deed, by letter and advice, by their trials of investigations and searches.

Teaching remains a personal invention ever enriched by those teachers who have taught and will teach. And as teachers, they advance the causes of civilization as they advance the causes of children!

The Teaching of Science—and Its Methods of Intelligence

All of us have observed children at work in the classroom. We have observed them at work using CIS in classrooms over the globe—singly, in groups, as a class. We have observed them in "graded" and "nongraded" situations, and off in corners absorbed in their own time, their own place, their own sequence, their own imaginations, their own inventiveness.

The photographs in *Concepts in Science*, Levels 1 through 6, illustrate some of the many situations in which we have observed children engaged in concept-seeking and in using methods of intelligence.

We will cite as examples nine types of observations we have made. These and many others are illustrated in the photographs on the covers and throughout the six textbooks from Levels 1 through 6. Many of these photographs were "taken on location." For example:

1. Children have been observed investigating on their own, using the Investigation pages in their textbooks as guides.

2. They have been observed in the field using information from their textbooks as a guide to the study of living things and the environment and following suggestions in the Experience books that accompany the textbooks for levels 3 through 6.

3. In certain schools, children have been able to make frequent use of the environment outside the classroom as the laboratory—searching, analyzing, synthesizing, and categorizing their observations.

4. Elsewhere, children have been seen observing a demonstration by their teacher and then working together on their own while the teacher came to each group as a consultant.

5. Children in some non-graded schools have proceeded to another concept-unit at their own pace.

6. From time to time children worked individually or in small groups on a variety of investigations and then pooled their findings through free discussion.

7. In some classes, children started with the CLASSROOM LABORATORIES, using them as guides to an Investigation and then proceeded to Searches on their own, using their textbook as a constant reference in concept-seeking.

8. Not infrequently, one child would demonstrate an investigation he had worked out himself while others observed intently and raised questions that were both numerous and searching.

9. Once in a while children were observed intently watching a bird or other part of their environment—perhaps in a moment's quiet on the playground—giving evidence that something in the complex act of learning was going on in their nervous systems.

The situations pictured, as well as other observations of children and reports from teachers and researchers, indicate clearly that from the time children are born, they watch, smell, feel, and listen: they are sentient to the objects and processes of the world. What they know largely derives from their senses, from their perceptions, and from the number and kinds of experiences they have had. They acquire meaning, whether true or false, from many kinds of experience, in the classroom, in backyard play, in the streets, in the kitchen, in solitary reflection. They ask questions in search of meaning and ask still more questions—and so probe further.

Because among individuals sensory perception varies and because human experiences vary in both kind and number, no two children begin school with the same knowledge, or with the same set of experiences. It cannot be presumed, therefore, that within the school framework they will move with equal speed or along precisely similar lines of growth. Some kind of provision has to be made to accommodate children of varying experiences and of varying ability, and that provision is not alone concerned with the broader questions of homogeneous grouping in schools or of an ungraded curriculum. It is also concerned with providing a scientifically sound structure of learning and teaching science that enables children to uncover the concepts of science in an orderly (though not overly prescriptive) way at a pace relative to their individual competency.

Toward a Definition of Science

A structure in the teaching of science is needed not only to accommodate the phenomenon of diversity in children, but also to manage the diversity of the content of science. Scientific research papers are currently published at the rate of more than 70,000 words a minute! That amounts to a body of information that would fill eleven sets of a thirty-volume encyclopedia every twenty-four hours. Obviously, unless an attempt is made to evaluate, to select, and to sort new information into some kind of structure for the classroom, students and teachers will fall further and further behind. There is, moreover, the necessity to recognize that scientific knowledge, while it proceeds from facts, is not in itself the mastery of facts. The facts of science are meaningful, and awareness of them productive, when they are perceived within the structure of basic concepts in science.

Probe into a Definition of Science

How shall we look at science? We may modify George Gaylord Simpson's definition as follows: *Science is the exploration of the material Universe for the purpose of seeking orderly explanations of objects and events, but these explanations must be testable.* The products of science, its orderly explanations (its concepts) and the technology that results from the application of them, are the results of certain processes. The processes comprise the observation and examination of data including experimentation, the formulation of explanations by inventing hypotheses and stating theories, and the testing of the explanations. But the product of all this, the orderly explanations (concepts), leads inevitably to other explorations and still other explanations. There are ends *in* science, but no end *to* science. In their activity, scientists engage in concept-seeking and in concept-forming and, as a matter of course, in concept-testing. This is clearly a function of scientific inquiry.

But what do children do when they are engaged in scientific activity? They explore the material Universe (observe a plant grow, observe an object move down an inclined plane, observe a balloon that has been untied shoot through the air) and they seek orderly explanations of the objects and events they observe. They also investigate and, where possible, they might even experiment (although in a school context it is most difficult for students to perform an experiment in the *pure* sense simply because all the variables are difficult to control). They verify the data obtained from observations and they seek to interpret the data. They seek to predict results on the basis of the knowledge they have gained. They attempt to uncover explanations that reliably relate seemingly disparate or "discrepant" objects and events, and that will make prediction of other events possible. They, too, are engaged in understanding concepts of science and in applying them to the world about them. They use the scientists' methods of intelligence.

A Schema of a Scientist's Methods of Intelligence

Investigations, and the experiments they may include, come out of knowledge and not, as is often implied, a total lack of knowledge. A scientist does not start with a problem; he starts by *knowing something.* So does a teacher. So does a child.

An investigator, whether adult or child, scientist or student, moves toward a concept which weds process and content. But before he begins his concept attainment, the investigator already has a concept, however faulty, however inadequate, however incomplete.

On the next page is a schema of the art of scientific investigation based on observation of the ways different scientists work. Essentially, the schema is rooted in James Bryant Conant's view in *On Understanding Science.** The schema represents the scientist's progression from the *old knowns* to the *unknown* in order to develop *new knowns.* The schema also represents the means by which children, as they move from level to level of *Concepts in Science,* acquire and expand their understanding of the fundamental scientific concepts. The schema comprises the scientist's methods of intelligence, his mode of investigation, or inquiry.

Toward a Modern Science Curriculum

An operational approach to the teaching of science is emphasized in this series. The operational approach is especially vital at the elementary levels, if only because children at age 6 may have lost their early propensity for what is often termed "discovery." It needs to be returned to them slowly, steadily. In the early 1900's, Dewey emphasized "learning by doing." Certainly, learning by and through experience has a long history in education. In present form, a valid concept is attained through a valid operation, in other words, an experience which may be validated. A simple illustration will suffice. When a ruler is used to measure *length,* the activity of measuring length defines the concept of length through a valid operation. If a ruler is used to measure weight, then the operation is not valid; use of a scale is the proper operation. Neither, for example, can a ruler be used to measure intelligence. Percy Bridgman, Nobel Prize winner in physics, proposed that "a concept is synonymous with the corresponding operation."

Thumb through this Teacher's Edition and note how again and again the child approaches concept attainment through a valid operation. This is not to say that the child irrevocably gains the concept at that point. It *is* to say that the concept is intuitively conceived through valid experience (valid operations). Thus, the operation is the base for further experience and further advancement in concept attainment.

Paul F. Brandwein, senior author of the series, has been repeating Jean Piaget's experiments with Surn's children's attainment of the concept of conservation of volume.** Clearly, children aged 4 to 9 have not attained this concept sufficiently to describe and transfer it to other situations. Piaget and his colleagues would ask a child to judge whether liquid poured from a wide container into a narrow container had gained or lost in volume, or remained the same. Most often the child indicated that there was "more" of the liquid in the narrow container. Our experiments confirm these findings. But, if the conditions of the Piaget "experiment" are changed to a *teaching situation,* we find a significant difference in the behavior of the children.

For instance, suppose a child (5 years of age) is given a glass-marking pencil and asked to mark the top of the liquid in the wide container. He is then asked to pour the liquid into the taller container and to mark the top of the liquid. The child is then asked to pour the liquid back into the wider container and discovers that the liquid goes up to the original mark. Now, when asked, "If you were to pour the liquid into the tall jar, would there be more, less, or the same?" children generally respond, "The same." They cite the observation that the liquid goes up to the mark they made. Thus, when given the opportunity to *analyze experience,* that is, to analyze their *valid action* (a valid observation) in response to a problem, they do develop a valid concept.

* *On Understanding Science: An Historical Approach,* Yale University Press, New Haven, Conn., 1947. James Bryant Conant, scientist and former President of Harvard University, developed *On Understanding Science* to explain the methods of the scientist.

** To be published when further confirmation is gained.

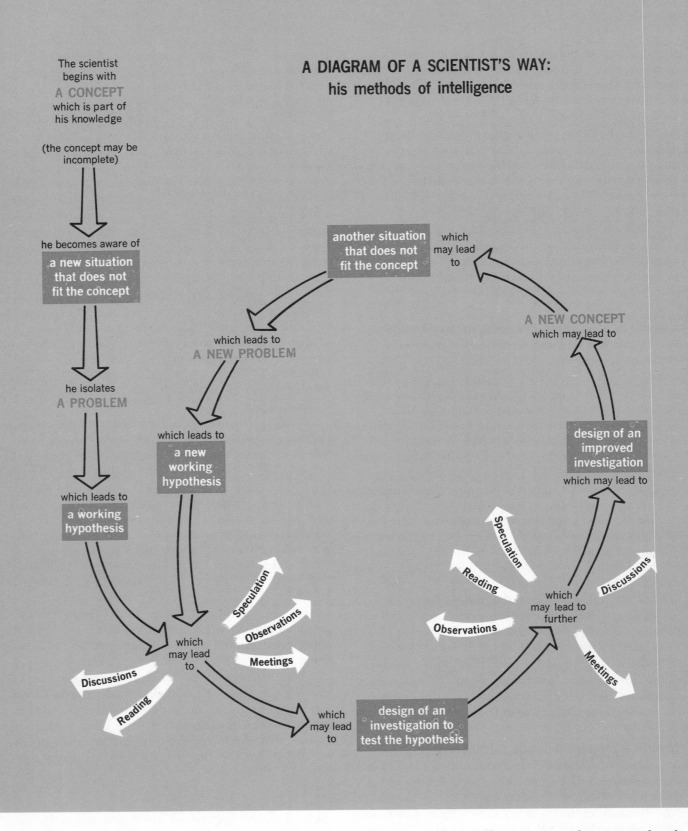

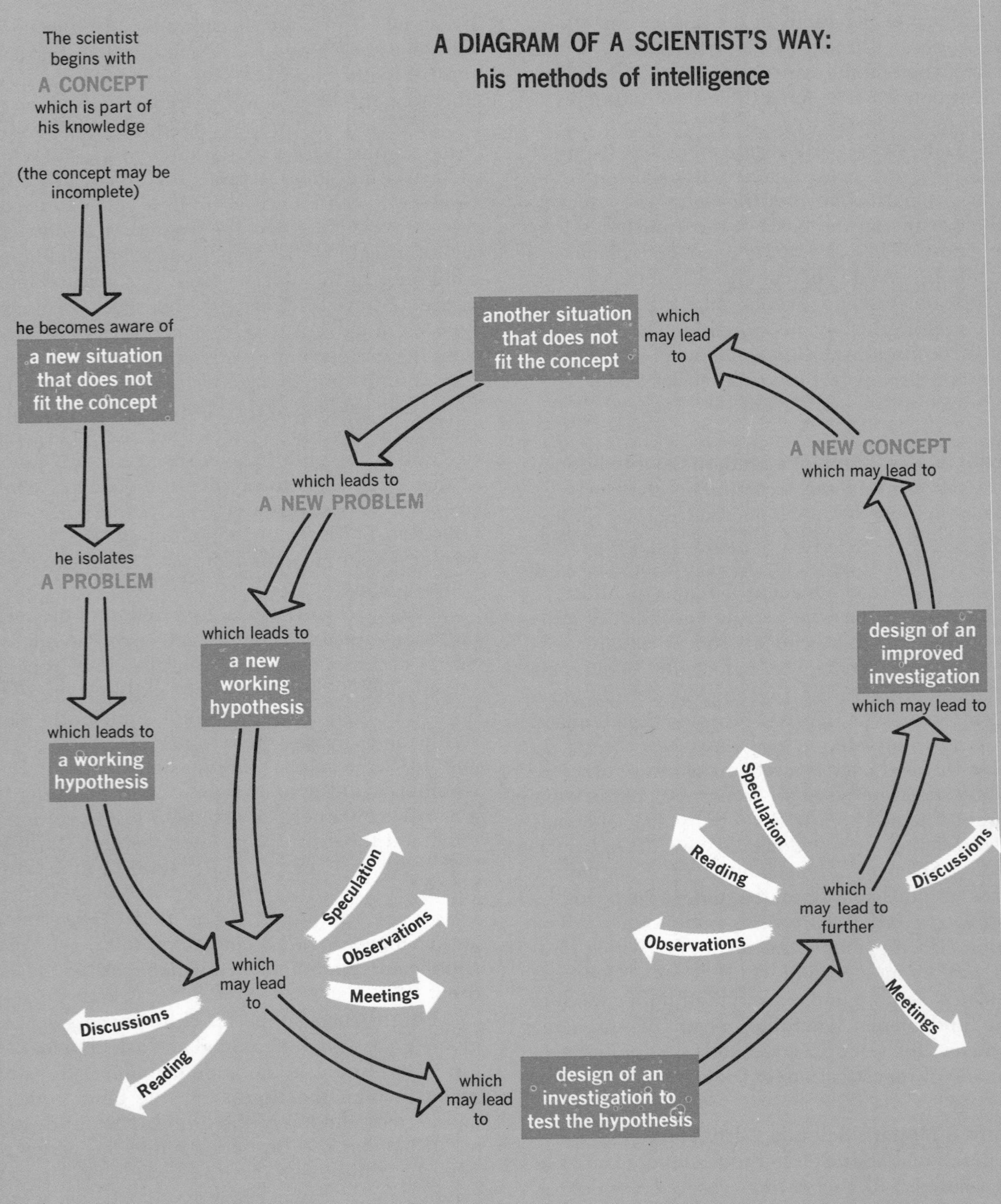
A DIAGRAM OF A SCIENTIST'S WAY:
his methods of intelligence
The scientist begins with
A CONCEPT
which is part of his knowledge
(the concept may be incomplete)
he becomes aware of
a new situation that does not fit the concept
he isolates
A PROBLEM
which leads to
a working hypothesis
which may lead to
Discussions
Reading
Speculation
Observations
Meetings
which may lead to
design of an investigation to test the hypothesis
which may lead to further
Observations
Reading
Speculation
Discussions
Meetings
which may lead to
design of an improved investigation
which may lead to
A NEW CONCEPT
which may lead to
another situation that does not fit the concept
which may lead to
which leads to
A NEW PROBLEM
which leads to
a new working hypothesis

In other words, the concept (conservation of volume) is associated with a valid operation (the child's activity in analyzing and synthesizing his specially designed non-random experience). In Bridgman's terms, the concept has become synonymous with the operation. Stated another way, if children are given opportunity to become apprentices in investigation, to gain experience in search of meaning, they will come up to the present level of the culture of science. They will gain the legacy of science, its cumulative knowledge, *as well as a way of gaining new knowledge.* For the unknown is sought best by those who have experience with the *known.*

It is sensible to predict that most jobs in the future, including that of teaching, will call for scientific orientation of one degree or another. Contemporary-minded teachers must teach science because society demands it. Helping children to undertake a progressively more sophisticated intellectual activity is a central function in teaching, and creating productive situations, that is, the learning environment, is the teacher's day-to-day responsibility. It is, in many respects, an awesome one. Which learning situations, which of all the countless ones that might be created, is the teacher to select? How is the teacher to cope with the incredible diversity of scientific information and, indeed, with the diversity of children themselves?

In our view, identifying the basic concepts of science is not the discrete task of the teacher. The teacher has the right to expect that he or she will be given help in identifying concepts and in forming a structure for the teaching of science, and this is a shared responsibility that the *Concepts in Science* authors and publisher, and the scientists, supervisors, and teachers who have advised them, have accepted. They recognize that school is time-binding, that work goes on in a certain time span—grades, terms, years—and that many teachers share in the development of each child. They know that a teacher must have a notion of what school experiences children have had before they come into the classroom, as well as what will follow once they leave it. The need for a curriculum in science which gives the teacher scope and flexibility is plain enough; what is sometimes not so plain is the need for a curriculum that has a scientifically and pedagogically sound structure. We have attempted to give structure to the teaching of science during the first ten years of schooling by informing the processes of science with an understanding of the concepts of science. We have, in short, sought to identify and define a structure that is not only verifiable scientifically but also viable, that is, practical and productive in teaching children.

A Framework of Science

Early in the twentieth century the school curriculum in the United States tended to be content-centered, or disciplinary. During the twenties and thirties this curricular approach gave way to a so-called child-centered approach; the emphasis was shifted, this is overstated for purposes of simplification, from the subject to the learner. Today, still another shift is occurring as content is being placed in a stronger and more relevant role in the curriculum. More and more the emphasis is placed on the interrelationship, more specifically the interaction, between the discipline and the pupil in the learning act. Again with some oversimplification, the contemporary curriculum can be said to be process-centered. Certainly this is apparent in science teaching, and the advance of this kind of curriculum has been most directly aided by the involvement of scientists in the elementary and secondary schools. They have been enormously helpful in proposing a teaching structure for the early school years of science study.

Within the various disciplines of science—biology, chemistry, physics, geology, etc.—data accumulate and change at a bewildering rate. Change is continual. Yet the concepts of science, which are a patterning of facts and a statement of the relationships between observable events and objects, are relatively stable. In a changing world, concepts offer, for this and other reasons, a reasonable foundation for the building of a science curriculum. They are, in a true sense, guides as well as aids to learning.

All of us have the task of sorting out events that come to our awareness in haphazard sequence. All of us have the task of discovering which of the objects and events we perceive are significant and which are not. To bring order out of our haphazard perceptions, we tend to seek a grouping of likenesses among a number of objects and events perceived; in short, we tend to seek concepts. To form a concept, we assort or group objects and events according to their attributes and properties, and we define categories. An example of what is meant by the "attributes" of an object or event will be useful.

A stone has shape, color, weight, and the like; these are some of the attributes of a stone. A bird also has shape, color, weight. Yet there are other attributes of the stone, for example, immobility and hardness, which we recognize as part and parcel of "stoneness." A bird, on the other hand, has mobility, it has feathers, it has egg-laying propensities, and it has a certain structure (from beak to tail), these and other attributes we recognize as essential to "birdness." In forming a concept, the brain selects those essential attributes (those which discriminate one object from another) which signal the whole configuration of the object or event. Thus the weight of an object is generally not an essential or discriminatory attribute; an attribute of a weight of one pound might apply to a one-pound chicken or a one-pound stone. But "feather" or "beak" is a signal, or cue, for categorizing or concept-forming. It is a signal of the whole concept of "birdness," and it enables us to fill in certain other essential attributes.

Now in learning, the *act of concept-forming* enables an individual to *infer;* from a few signals or cues he can *infer* a significant grouping, or category, of like attributes. These signals or cues can be related to *objects* (stones, birds, simple machines) or to *events,* such as the changing of one form of energy to another (for example, the friction of the hands resulting in heat), or the reproduction of organisms, or the splitting of an atom. A specific example in the teaching of a concept, in developing the ability in children to group the like attributes of an event, can be given here. Suppose we wished to create situations through which children would uncover the events that can be grouped within the concept: *Bodies in space are in continuous change.* This is precisely the objective of Unit Two in *Concepts in Science*, PURPLE. A series of seven lesson clusters is organized in a sequence in which situations are created whereby children come to *associate* an entire set of attributes of this event: *The matter and energy of Planet Earth are always changing.* Children engage in the analysis of many situations presented in the text and in selecting the essential attributes of each event. Such selection would enable them, in turn, to predict the event from one signal, say an erupting volcano. But the children's textbook suggests activity after activity to confirm the prediction—rocks are shaken with water, examples of erosion in the environment are observed, a model of sediment layers is made, the travel of waves is investigated, models of the Earth are built, rocks are examined, crystals are grown.

Perhaps you would care to examine Unit Two now for a fuller explanation of the way the textbook assists the teacher in creating situations through which children engage in concept-seeking and concept-formation. But, of course, the textbook is only part of a very rich program of science in which selection of processes (methods of intelligence) is central (see page F-15).

In brief definition, then, a *concept is a mental construct; it is a grouping of the common elements or attitudes shared by certain objects and events.* In other words, a concept isolates the *common attributes* of objects and events, and, if you will, behaviors. Once a concept is attained, economy in future learning is also attained. For, by engaging in the processes of concept-formation, the learner is active in selecting the essential attributes of the complete event, such as "the matter and energy of Planet Earth are always changing." And the learner is able to predict an entire sequence of events, or an entire set of characteristics or properties, from a small number of cues or signs. Thus an erupting volcano or a piece of petrified wood is a cue signalizing an entire event.

Defined in other words, a concept is a network of inferences stemming from observation of objects and events, resulting in the selection of common attributes among the objects and events under observation. Identifying and organizing the common attributes results in a significant category or grouping. That significant category is a concept. A concept is practical and useful because the perception of a small number of attributes, cues, or signals brings the whole object or event into satisfying recognition. To repeat, an eruption recalls the object (volcano) and the event (change in the Earth).

Because we are teaching children, it is well to *group* experiences in a way that will enable teachers to plan their work sequentially. Hence, we have ordered the concept structure of this curriculum. It provides for small blocks of experiences, dealing with objects and events with similar attributes which young children can handle. We have attempted, moreover, to develop a curricular structure which bears some correspondence to the school year, day, and class period. Further, for purposes of readier facility in planning the work of the first seven years of elementary school, we have grouped on pages F-16 and F-17 a given series of concept statements at ascending levels under a still larger category which we call a *conceptual scheme.*

Conceptual schemes provide, we believe, a framework within which the teacher can provide experiences that will lead students to participate in the processes of science—in observation and in interpretation—and emerge with the products of science, which are testable explanations of the workings of the material world. This seems to be a large order. It is. The authors and publishers spent eight years in the preparation of the curricular organization and materials in this program before publishing the first edition of *Concepts in Science.* Their belief that the conceptual approach is a feasible one that will produce excellent results has since been demonstrated in classrooms throughout the nation and abroad that have adopted the program in both its first and second editions. In an ultimate sense, their aim is to help the teacher produce an interaction between discipline and student, between the subject and the learner. For this reason, content is never skimped. For each level there is a core of content or subject matter essential for all children to participate in the processes of science, as well as ample extra material to challenge children capable of rapid progress.

What this program does, then, is to lay out a framework of conceptual schemes through the first ten years of schooling. The framework is capacious. It does not fix teacher or child into an inflexible curriculum. On the contrary, it gives the teacher freedom to plan a variety of experiences and the child freedom to plot his own experiences. In both instances, the experiences will be ones that are relevant to a search for meaning rather than the random acquisition of facts. Understanding is made simpler for children when they are able to conceptualize—to see patterns in their environment, to group objects and events on the basis of their common elements. A program that accomplishes this is essentially an economical one, economical in the time that is spent in learning. Because, as has been said earlier, concepts remain relatively stable, concepts provide an organization of information that is relatively stable. New observations, new data and variant experiences can all be fitted into the conceptual framework.*

At the time the first edition of *Concepts in Science* was published, teachers in St. Mary's County, Maryland, had been experimenting successfully with an elementary science curriculum based on conceptual schemes. Their course of study, initially developed by a curriculum committee, is now in its fifteenth year of development. Similar courses of study had also been developed by other schools, particularly the Nova School, Fort Lauderdale, Florida. At present, courses of study based on conceptual schemes have been instituted by countless schools and school systems.

If we interpret the psychology of learning (so far as it has advanced, which admittedly is not far enough!) with any degree of acuity, then we assume that it is important for children to learn in "wholes." In this sense, concepts are "wholes." Moreover, if we accept the definition that education results in a change of behavior in the student, then an understanding of concepts will provide him with intelligent means of deciding among alternatives. Conservation of natural resources, support of public health programs, questions of population growth, fallacies in ethnic discrimination—all are civic and social matters that confront a contemporary person. He is better able to judge what he perceives, and support what he believes, when he understands the basic scientific concepts. The teaching of science ought to help provide means by which one can comprehend what is today known although still not widely operative. Exploration of the Moon, for example, was a certainty even when it had not yet happened.

The *Concepts in Science* series is a curriculum for elementary, middle, and junior high school science which attempts to reflect commonly accepted and basic ideas of contemporary scientists, cognitive psychologists, and teachers. It is a systematic organization of instructional materials. It is also a laboratory-centered program. The framework of six conceptual schemes provides a learning sequence that is broadly outlined on the chart on pages F-16–F-17. The sequential development is represented on the chart as horizontal threads called *concept levels,* which increase in complexity as one advances from level to level toward a fuller grasp of the conceptual schemes.

The National Science Teachers Association Committee on curriculum development, in "Theory into Action,"** suggests seven conceptual schemes. The Committee agrees upon twelve statements. Seven of these statements discuss conceptual schemes, and five of them describe the processes of science as the base for science curriculum planning. In the *Concepts in Science* series, the concepts have been grouped under six conceptual schemes, but the differences between this organization and that of "Theory into Action" are not substantial or finally consequential. The authors suggest that the content of the science curriculum could be arranged in an orderly structure under six conceptual schemes in a way that effects economy in organization, time, and effort. Such a schema was originally suggested in the Burton Lecture, given at Harvard.***

A Developmental Structure

The major conceptual schemes can be stated in somewhat arbitrary terms; no doubt, different teachers will state them differently. Certainly they would be stated differently for the scientist-specialist than for the elementary-school teacher. Certainly the statements may be modified and restated under different conditions, with different pupils, and in different schools. Yet the authors have chosen to state the conceptual schemes in terms that can be used throughout the particular content and activities in the *Concepts in Science* series.

A Framework of Conceptual Schemes

The conceptual schemes and the general areas they subtend are:

A. *When energy changes from one form to another, the total amount of energy remains unchanged.* Energy transformation is a common phenomenon. If you rub your hands, mechanical energy is converted to heat energy. If you burn a candle, chemical energy is converted to heat energy and light energy; and in a dry cell, chemical energy can be converted to electrical energy. But whether one is concerned with burning oil in the home, gasoline in the automobile, glucose in the body, or whether the energy of moving water is

* See *A Study of Thinking* by Jerome S. Bruner, Jacqueline J. Goodnow, George A. Austin. John Wiley & Sons, Inc., New York, 1956.

** Published by the National Science Teachers Association, Washington, D. C., 1964.

*** The Burton Lecture: "Elements in a Strategy for Teaching Science in the Elementary School," by Paul F. Brandwein (in *The Teaching of Science* by Joseph Schwab and Paul F. Brandwein, Harvard University Press, 1962)

transferred into a flow of electrons in a conductor, the total amount of energy in any given system remains unchanged. This conceptual scheme is a primary concern in the discipline of physics.

B. *When matter changes from one form to another, the total amount of matter remains unchanged.* The world of matter consists of a world of things, from the very large bodies—stars, planets, moons—to the very small particles—atoms, molecules, subatomic particles. As matter in the Universe undergoes a physical change or a chemical change the total amount of matter undergoing chemical and physical change in a given system remains unchanged. This conceptual scheme lies within the discipline of chemistry.

C. *The Universe is in continuous change.* Every child seems to know that the solar system is changing. Certainly the Earth's atmosphere is continuously shifting. The Earth is in continuous motion, the Sun is in continuous eruption. We note the appearance of novas, of Cepheid variables. We interpret that the red shift in starlight indicates an expanding Universe. Change in the Universe comprises a conceptual scheme that is the primary concern of geology, astronomy, and meteorology.

D. *Living things are interdependent with one another and with their environment.* Around living things everywhere, there exists an environment of matter and energy; indeed, living things cannot be considered apart from their environment. Green plants capture energy from the Sun in the photosynthetic process; animals, in turn, transform the chemical energy of plants. And all plants and animals yield their matter and energy as they die and decay. The demands of living in a given environment result in a relationship between plants and animals in communities that display definite characteristics—deserts, forests, seas, etc. Understanding these interrelationships results in our ability to predict, within limits, the behavior and development of plants and animals. The conceptual scheme that describes them is a part of the study of biology, particularly ecology and conservation.

E. *A living thing is the product of its heredity and environment.* The organism is never the result purely of its heredity, but of the environment interacting with hereditary factors. For example: Beets in acid soil are stunted. Interaction of environment with heredity is true for any specific trait. It is important to comprehend that a human being's realization of his full physical development and vigorous health depends on hereditary traits interacting with environment. For example: An intelligent child (hereditary trait) needs an education; a child poorly fed and housed (environmental conditions) does not resist tuberculosis as well as one living in a healthful environment.

The concept that an organism lives in a kind of dynamic equilibrium encompassing the full range of the development of organisms, including the study of reproduction, heredity, growth, nutrition, behavior, and adaptation to the environment, is involved in this conceptual scheme of interaction of heredity and environment. This is the concern of several sciences—genetics, physiology, biochemistry, and of course, conservation, as part of ecology.

F. *Living things are in continuous change.* The Universe changes; the Earth changes; the single organism and the species change over the ages. Concepts of adaptation over the ages, divergence in form, convergence in geographical isolation, and organic change fall within this conceptual scheme, which involves genetics and ecology.

As the concepts in science are selected to fit the purposes of instruction in the elementary school, they seem to group themselves into a few broad groups or conceptual schemes. The rationale is: first, concepts should fall easily into a particular conceptual scheme; second, they should be ordered within the conceptual scheme from the simple to the complex. "Simple" is used here in the sense that the experiences provided should be easily recognizable. Young children do not deal with a complexity of cause and effect, that is, with *multiple variables.* Thus, it is fairly easy on the second level to present the concept: *Related living things reproduce in similar ways.* However the concept: *Man is the product of his heredity and environment* requires that more appropriate and complex experiences are brought to bear. This is on the higher sixth level. We do not imply that some children cannot deal on any level with concepts more complex than the norm expected for children at any lower level. A particular advantage of a conceptual structure is the provision that accelerated growth in individual children may progress without inhibition. The teacher can determine the level of understanding by asking appropriate questions at an appropriate level within the conceptual framework (pages F-16–F-17). If enough children are able to deal with a higher concept level, procedures may be modified.

The organization of a curriculum in terms of concept levels accommodates its own "multiple tracking." It is possible to have groups or individuals within the same class proceed at different rates up the concept "rungs" of the conceptual "ladder." By selecting various activities from the wide range of resources in the program, children can engage in experiences that are appropriate to their level of understanding and at the same time communicate with groups at other concept levels, for they are all on the same ladder, if on different rungs.

The conceptual structure for seven levels of *Concepts in Science* is charted on pages F-16–F-17. Concepts forming the rungs of the conceptual ladder can be stated in various ways, but the central purpose is to organize them in graduated order so that understanding of one (in a lower level) precedes the next for purposes of greater comprehension and utilization. There is some danger, we believe, in stating a conceptual scheme (or even a concept) by a single term (for example, *energy, matter, life*). However convenient this may seem, such easy rubrics may limit the effectiveness of this approach to science study.

Now, the structure for science in the primary and intermediate levels of the elementary school, here given as six conceptual schemes, with the concepts given at various levels (not necessarily grades), is purely for convenience and custom. The levels, until research proves this unwise, are in a rough order of precedence. Naturally, each concept has a number of subconcepts; the development of subconcepts depends on the judgment of the teacher.

Concept-Seeking Through Process

The essence of science is *investigation of the material Universe.* Its goals consist of a search for meaning; indeed, Albert Einstein once defined it as experience in search of meaning; it *seeks orderly explanations (conceptualizations) of phenomena, the objects and events about us.* Nevertheless, there is stubborn insistence by scientists that an orderly explanation *be testable.* If a concept is not testable, it is usually not acceptable. Science is, in short, the "art of investigation" (Beveridge's term). But one cannot investigate an object or event if the object or event is not first perceived. Each concept attained is "synonymous with the operation" used to seek it.

This book is literally a sourcebook of situations in which children participate and perceive objects and events. In each learning situation, children seek attributes of objects and events and their hidden likenesses. In *Concepts in Science* PURPLE, children engage in the processes of science according to their maturity level. For example: *they observe;* they *investigate* relationships; they *collect* relevant data; they *describe* and *discuss* their results; they confirm one another's results (through collaborating in an investigation); they *invent;* they *report* their results in a kind of colloquium. Note the processes—observation, investigation, collection of relevant data, description of results, discussion of findings, confirmation of findings, exercising inventiveness, reporting of work, and experimentation, among others. Children are engaged in valid operations leading to concept attainment.

Methods of Intelligence

The core of concept-seeking, the goal in the *Concepts in Science* (CIS) program, is investigation; and concept-seeking requires activity on the part of the children. Their investigations may be of many kinds, ranging through simple discussion, library research, field trips, collection and observation of specimens, and perhaps a laboratory investigation as culmination. During this central operation of investigating, children succeed only if they apply what Percy Bridgman called *methods of intelligence.* Two of these can be defined as *processes* and *behaviors.* Among processes often cited are observing, analyzing, measuring, and discussing. We might consider these as activities in search of evidence.

Behaviors might define the postures of the child as he organizes the evidence. Behaviors, in themselves, are difficult to evaluate. If, however, specific behaviors are isolated and clearly stated, the teacher has an *objective* means of evaluation; that is, of verifying progress. Observation and evaluation of behaviors are useful in giving insight into whether the child has used the correct process in obtaining evidence. Processes and behaviors, in the end, are indications that methods of intelligence are being applied by the child toward a larger goal of concept-seeking.

A teacher or observer can best determine behaviors in concept-seeking activity if the expected goal is stated as a behavioral objective;* we prefer the term performance objective. Since it is the teacher, and not the child, who states a performance objective for purposes of evaluation, it may be useful to describe a procedure that can be applied to the writing of statements of performance objectives. Most such statements indicate the operation to be performed and include either a specific or an implied reference to the processes that should be used. In stating the objectives, it is of course desirable to use verbs that are entirely free of any possible ambiguity. According to one estimate, the English language includes possibly ten thousand action verbs, many having synonyms with various shades of meaning. To use these synonyms interchangeably in stating performance objectives would only add confusion and ambiguity. For simplicity, nine definable action verbs have been defined for use in stating performance objectives:**

* Thus summary is adapted from *Behavioral Objectives in Concept-Seeking* by John R. Pancella, Harcourt Brace Jovanovich, 1970.

** "Action Words," pp. 23–33, in *Guide for Inservice Instruction; Science—A Process Approach; Response Sheets, American Association for the Advancement of Science,* 1967; and *Constructing Behavioral Objectives* by Henry H. Walbesser, Bureau of Educational Research and Field Services, University of Maryland, 1968.

A STRUCTURE FOR CONCEPTS IN SCIENCE

	CONCEPTUAL SCHEME A When energy changes from one form to another, the total amount of energy remains unchanged.	CONCEPTUAL SCHEME B When matter changes from one form to another, the total amount of matter remains unchanged.	CONCEPTUAL SCHEME C The Universe is in continuous change.
CONCEPT LEVEL VI Brown	The amount of energy gotten out of a machine does not exceed the energy put into it.	In nuclear reactions, matter is converted to energy, but the total amount of matter and energy remains unchanged.	Nuclear reactions produce the radiant energy of stars, and consequent change.
CONCEPT LEVEL V Purple	Energy must be applied to produce an unbalanced force, which results in a change in motion.	In chemical or physical changes, the total amount of matter remains unchanged.	Bodies in space are in continuous change.
CONCEPT LEVEL IV Orange	A loss or gain of energy affects molecular motion.	In chemical change, atoms react to produce change in the molecules.	The Earth's matter is in continuous change.
CONCEPT LEVEL III Green	The Sun is the Earth's chief source of radiant energy.	Matter consists of atoms and molecules.	There are seasonal and annual changes on Earth.
CONCEPT LEVEL II Red	Energy can change from one form to another.	A change in the state of matter is determined by molecular motion.	There are regular changes in positions of the Earth and Moon.
CONCEPT LEVEL I Blue	Force is required to set an object in motion.	Matter commonly exists as solids, liquids, and gases.	There are daily changes on Earth.
BEGINNING CONCEPT LEVEL Yellow	A force is needed to start, stop, or change the direction of motion.	Matter is characterized by certain properties by which it can be identified and classified.	Things change (implicit within the development of Conceptual Schemes A and B).

CONCEPTUAL SCHEME D Living things are interdependent with one another and with their environment.	CONCEPTUAL SCHEME E A living thing is the product of its heredity and environment.	CONCEPTUAL SCHEME F Living things are in continuous change.	
Living things depend basically on the capture of radiant energy by green plants.	Man is the product of his heredity and environment.	Changes in the genetic code result in changes in living things.	**CONCEPT LEVEL VI** Brown
Living things are adapted by structure and function to their environment.	The cell is the unit of structure and function in living things.	Over the ages, living things have changed in their adaptation to the changing environment.	**CONCEPT LEVEL V** Purple
Living things capture matter and energy from the environment and return them to the environment.	A living thing reproduces itself and develops in a given environment.	Living things are adapted to particular environments.	**CONCEPT LEVEL IV** Orange
The Earth's different environments have their own characteristic life.	Living things are related through possession of common structure.	Living things grow and develop in different environments.	**CONCEPT LEVEL III** Green
Living things depend on their environment for the conditions of life.	Related living things reproduce in similar ways.	Forms of living things have become extinct.	**CONCEPT LEVEL II** Red
Living things are affected by their environment.	Living things reproduce their own kind.	There are different forms of living things.	**CONCEPT LEVEL I** Blue
Environments differ (implicit within the development of Conceptual Scheme F).	Living things may differ in structure, but they have common needs and similar life activities.	Living things grow (implicit within the development of Conceptual Scheme E).	**BEGINNING CONCEPT LEVEL** Yellow

identify: select, by pointing to, touching, or picking up, a correct object of a class name.

distinguish: identify objects or events that are possibly confusing, or when two contrasting identifications are involved.

construct (or *build*): generate a construction (a model or drawing) that identifies a designated object or set of conditions.

name: supply the correct name, orally or in writing, for a class of objects or events.

order: arrange two or more objects or events in proper order according to a stated category. (The above two verbs include the acts of categorizing and classifying.)

describe: generate and name all of the necessary categories of objects, object properties, or event properties that are relevant to the description of a designated situation. (The description should be usable to identify the object or event.)

state a rule: make a verbal statement that conveys a rule or principle, including the names of proper classes of objects or events in their correct order.

apply a rule: use a learned principle or rule to derive an answer to a problem.

demonstrate: perform the necessary operations for the application of a rule or principle.

In any learning situation a child will exhibit many behaviors that an observer could identify and catalog and for which he could state performance objectives in unambiguous terms. The presence of such objectives should not negate more general objectives. For example, a general aim might be stated: "The child will observe and discover ideas about energy." It is not clear exactly what the child will do, but he will certainly do something to learn more about energy and not about some other topic. In pursuit of this general aim, in his concept-seeking activity, the child will certainly engage in several investigations for which performance objectives can be clearly stated. For example: "The child will *demonstrate* that bands of color are formed as sunlight passes through a glass prism."

On each level of the *Concepts in Science* program, behaviors expected are indicated in several ways in the Teacher's Edition. First, within the introduction to each unit, processes and behaviors are indicated in an outline grid under Methods of Intelligence (page T-7 for example). Second, they are included under methods of intelligence at the beginning of each lesson cluster (page T-10, for example). Behaviors are stated informally through the use of the behavioral action verbs, but the intent is clear in terms of performance expected. In addition, activities in the section on "Verifying Progress" are in many instances investigational in nature, and performance objectives easily could be written for them in unambiguous terms.

The experiences in *Concepts in Science* have been carefully designed to guide the child through a series of observations and investigations that build one upon another. In this way the child acquires information and evidence that lead him up the conceptual ladder to a conceptual scheme.

Resources for a Comprehensive Program

The structure of concepts and conceptual schemes yields knowledge and understanding in the ordering of objects and events. At no time, however, could such a structure exist without the materials of science and the methods of intelligence (processes and behaviors), that provide the base for investigation, whether by reading or by carrying out a sophisticated experiment. The materials for *Concepts in Science,* which extend from the pre-reading level through junior-high levels, supply the supporting facts and tools that are relevant to both the methods of intelligence and the conceptual framework of modern science.

Textbooks

Each book of the *Concepts in Science* series is designed to create an atmosphere of concept-seeking; to stimulate personal involvement; to maintain sharp curiosity; and to lay a firm base for intelligent, independent inquiry. Use of methods of intelligence (processes and behaviors), as well as the products of science, is emphasized.

Photographs, especially on the primary and intermediate levels, are abundantly used showing children in the act of investigating their environment. They are supplemented by drawings that illustrate concepts and principles.

Frequent investigations help develop the main concept of a lesson cluster. The investigations are self-contained and self-explanatory, except at the primary levels where it is necessary to have a fuller development in the Teacher's Edition. Photographs that illustrate one trial investigation guide the children's observations as they investigate for themselves. The investigations are truly *apprentice investigations.* All of them have been tested for effectiveness and safety.

Apprentice Investigation pages, in the intermediate levels, extend the investigations through additional activities in applying methods of intelligence. In many of the lesson clusters at the upper primary and intermediate levels, a Search On Your Own encourages the child to develop his own independent investigations to enlarge the concept of the lesson cluster. These searches are strictly open-ended, as are a number of other activities at the end of the lesson clusters. Thus the apprentice investigations teach the techniques which the child can apply on his own to independent searches or investigations. The Teacher's Editions at all levels suggest similar open-ended activities that the teacher may use for suggesting in-depth concept-seeking by interested children. These activities usually appear under Verifying Progress.

Each textbook features concept reviews and evaluations so that children may verify progress in their search for concepts, apply acquired knowledge to new situations, hypothesize solutions to problems, and recognize relationships among concepts.

The reading vocabulary has been carefully chosen for each learning level and appropriate attention has been given to key concept terms that are central to the understanding and verbalization of concepts.

Teacher's Editions

This Third Edition of the *Concepts in Science* program is especially designed to give the teacher and the curriculum builder the maximum aid, not only in presenting the content of science but in guiding children in processes and behaviors leading to concept-seeking. The conceptual structure of the curriculum is outlined on pages F-16–F-17 in such a way that the intellectual growth in understanding conceptual schemes from level to level is immediately apparent. Each unit is similarly prefaced by an analysis chart, making immediately evident how the supporting statements for the lesson clusters build toward the unit concept-statement within the framework of the conceptual schemes of the program. The operations and methods of intelligence (processes and behaviors) used in concept-seeking are also clearly designated in this chart.

The Teacher's Editions contain the background information that enables teachers to present a unit with confidence and enthusiasm, and to obtain a preview of where the children are expected to go within each lesson cluster. The reproduced pages of the child's text are surrounded by helpful suggestions, which are keyed with a black, numbered circle to specific points in the child's text. Additionally, each lesson cluster states the specific concept-seeking operations in which the children will engage, the methods of intelligence relevant to the operations, and appropriate materials that will be useful. From time to time activities for verifying progress in concept-seeking behaviors are provided. Beginning with the third level, performance objectives are stated for all investigation pages.

This detailed conceptual structure of the curriculum and the suggestions for reinforcing concept-seeking through the relevant operations and processes of the scientist provide a firm base for the child and his teacher to move ahead with confidence and success.

Individualized Program for the Inadequately Prepared Reader

On My Own, a boxed classroom supply of individual investigation leaflets, provides an opportunity for children with reading difficulties to investigate the concepts and processes of science identified in *Concepts in Science,* levels 3 through 6. *On My Own* was developed for children whose reading ability is below the textbook reading level. Vocabulary, with the exception of certain science terms, is limited to readability that is at least two years below the textbook level. The science terms appear in boldface when first introduced in the pupil leaflet and are followed by a rebus; and the definitions of these words are found in the individual children's dictionaries that are included in the boxed set. Each unit is also accompanied by an assessment sheet in duplicating master form.

On My Own establishes a classroom learning climate in which children with reading difficulties have the opportunity to use a multisensory approach to science investigation that has been individualized for them in terms of their particular capacities. Within this sequentially developed framework, the child with little reading skill is able to conceptualize and develop certain science skills at grade level.

A Teacher's Edition of *On My Own* accompanies each classroom supply of leaflets. The Teacher's Edition states the science concept for each investigation, lists material needed for the investigation, offers teaching suggestions, and provides possible responses to investigation questions.

Classroom Laboratory Sets

There is perhaps no aspect of science learning that is more important than the child's personal involvement in the art of investigation, which includes working with materials and processes, and using the methods of intelligence characteristic of scientists. The child has direct confrontation, so to speak, with tangible and intangible things within a framework of inquiry; thus his work is self-initiated and he sets his own objectives.

The seven CLASSROOM LABORATORY sets (one for each level), as an optional part of the *Concepts in Science* program, are designed to facilitate such self-initiating experiences by children. The sets, which are planned for convenient classroom management, provide a practical way of converting an ordinary classroom into a laboratory.

To provide opportunities for an entire class to experience concept-seeking, each set contains materials for use by up to six groups of children. The quantities are sufficient for performing investigations that parallel most of those in the *Concepts in Science* textbooks. In addition, materials are provided for other investigations and for open-ended searches. Pupil's manuals and Teacher's Editions are supplied in the three upper levels, and Teacher's Manuals in the lower levels. The teacher may adapt the sets flexibly for use within specific capacities of the children and with regard to facilities of the classroom, and the children are enabled to proceed as fast and as far as they can go.

Some schools may have most of the materials that are called for in the textbook investigations. Whether or not materials are readily available, the use of the CLASSROOM LABORATORY sets is optional. The sets do, however, make available, in orderly, indexed, and compact storage cases, the manuals and materials that can bring to the children those direct experiences that are part of the art of investigation in science and so important to the intellectual development of children.

With normal use, some depletion of components in each CLASSROOM LABORATORY set can be expected each year, and a small portion of the components are consumable. Replacements are available from the publisher.

In addition to the CLASSROOM LABORATORY sets for the earlier levels, another similar series of five Laboratory Experiences sets is available for students at the junior high or middle school level for use with the *Concepts in Science* textbooks at that level.

Experience Books and Searchbooks

These publications, significantly different from the conventional science workbook, are available for Levels 3 through 9. They give children additional opportunities to reinforce and extend their understanding of the concepts developed in the *Concepts in Science* textbooks. Activities in the Experience Books (Levels 3–6) and Searchbooks (Levels 7–9) have been selected to provide experiences in various situations—at home, in the classroom, on a field trip, in the library, or in the laboratory. In these experiences, children obtain practice in basic laboratory skills—recording observations, tabulating data, interpreting data, and drawing conclusions—as well as practice in using scientific apparatus. Self-testing reviews are included for additional evaluation by the children. Teacher's Editions, separately available, provide suggested answers and the background information for the Experience Books and Searchbooks.

Tests

Teaching Tests, prepared and screened by the Harcourt Brace Jovanovich Science Testing Board, are available for *Concepts in Science*, Levels 3 through 9. For Levels 3–6, answer keys are in the Teacher's Editions; for Levels 7–9, in the Teacher's Manuals.

These tests are used with individuals or with the entire class after each unit in the child's book. They go beyond the testing of the child's retention of information and help teachers evaluate the child's understanding of concepts as well.

Laboratory Cards

100 Invitations to Investigate, a cased set of 100 ungraded laboratory cards, provide independent investigations in the biological, physical, and chemical sciences. Progressive in difficulty, the higher-numbered being more sophisticated, the cards are designed for those children who pursue an area of science apart from their regular classroom work. The cards also stimulate independent investigation by specially interested children and may be used, as well, in an ungraded science program.

Sourcebooks for the Teacher

Harcourt Brace Jovanovich publishes a number of professional books which provide the "tactics and strategy" as well as the techniques for teaching elementary and high school science. These are listed on the first page of this Teacher's Edition.

PART TWO: CONCEPTS IN SCIENCE – Purple

Structure and Content

Concepts in Science PURPLE is one of a series of coordinated textbooks that form the structure and design of an elementary science curriculum. It is the fifth level of a sequential and fully articulated program in which each unit builds upon concepts, processes, and behaviors developed in preceding levels. In *Concepts in Science* PURPLE, each lesson cluster enlarges on the Unit Concept-Statement around which the pattern of the unit is developed. The unit, in turn, is part of a still larger pattern, a year of concept-seeking in science that encompasses the six conceptual schemes at the concept level indicated on pages F-16–F-17.

Even a casual perusal of the two books, the child's and the teacher's, reveals the developmental structure of the program. The first unit is more slowly paced than the units that follow it, as are the lesson clusters in a unit. The subsequent lesson clusters are served by those that have gone before, but they are so flexibly arranged that a program can be developed to meet local or individual needs. Each unit, in turn, builds on preceding units and helps to deepen understanding of concepts as children encounter them in new situations and new relationships.

Science concepts are interrelated. The broad conceptual understanding of continuous change in bodies in space (Units Two and Four) is related to changes in motion (Unit One). Chemical and physical changes in matter on the Earth (Unit Three) are related to changes in matter and energy in the stars (Unit Four). The structures and functions of man and other living things (Units Five and Six) are related to the changing adaptations of organisms to the changing environment through time (Unit Seven).

Children should conclude that change is all around them and that change is normal, expected, and predictable. Interrelationship of concepts becomes increasingly clear as the children investigate how scientists have used concepts to explore the Universe at many levels, from the world of microscopic organisms to the vast regions of outer space. Concepts of science are introduced, reintroduced, and reused in every unit; out of the diversity of the world about them, the children see unity among the concepts that enable man to understand more and more of the Earth and other bodies in space, and of the interdependence of all living things with their environment.

The Unit Concept-Statements in this Teacher's Edition support the Conceptual Schemes of the program. The lesson clusters give children experiences in probing into objects and events in the world around them and thus in building Supporting Statements that lead toward a Unit Concept-Statement. A concept developed in one unit is frequently recalled and reapplied in new contexts in later units.

Although each of the seven units in *Concepts in Science* PURPLE is primarily concerned with one conceptual scheme, in some units this conceptual scheme is related to one or more other conceptual schemes. The seven units deal with a variety of areas in science: force and the laws of motion and gravitation; the conservation of matter in chemical and physical changes; the origins and motions of the Sun, planets, Moon, and stars; the roles of weathering and erosion, earthquakes and volcanoes, and mountain building in changing the face of the Earth; the structure and function of living cells, organs, organ systems, and organisms; reproduction of single-celled and many-celled organisms; fossil evidence of ancient life forms—to cite but a partial list. To the scientist, however, these areas are concerned only with three large categories: matter, energy, and life. The authors have chosen to develop understanding of the categories by presenting concept-seeking activities under six conceptual schemes in an ascending order of sophistication from the Beginning Level to the level of *Concepts in Science* PURPLE (pages F-16–F-17). These six conceptual schemes are basic to a child's understanding of the material Universe. Life, matter, and energy will be explored in succeeding years at still higher levels of sophistication.

Concepts in Science PURPLE builds upon earlier levels. Conceptual schemes are not *taught* to the children; rather, they are stated in the Teacher's Edition as goals that the children, as learners, progress toward through related experiences providing the maximum individual involvement in the operations, processes, and behaviors of concept-seeking. Concept formation has been proceeding in this manner through all levels, and will continue within the growing capacities of the children.

Exploration of the environment, certainly a major aim of science, does not begin at any particular age. Most young children enter school with a fund of information (and misinformation) and a fairly well-developed pattern of behavior that has served their need to satisfy their natural curiosity.

By the level of this textbook, they have had many new experiences that have been planned in search of meaning. In school, they have been guided in their search by experiences selected and organized for conceptual understanding, a necessity if the search is to be successful.

At each level, teachers help children to organize and evaluate their information, and to use and improve their habits and skills of investigating. Their investigating, however, proceeds no longer in the random fashion of early childhood; rather, it proceeds through thoughtful selection from the methods of intelligence inherent in scientific investigation. Thus, their progress is toward a sequential, developmental pattern of experiences systematically organized as a science curriculum.

Let us examine the pattern in *Concepts in Science* PURPLE, first as it is developed in the child's textbook and then in Teacher's Edition.

The Structure of a Unit

The child's textbook

All the units have the same structure and the same component parts:

A two-page ***unit introduction***, opens each unit. It is usually a short investigation consisting of a full page photograph, one or two smaller photographs, and several paragraphs of text. The intent of the pictures and text is to stimulate interest and arouse curiosity.

Each unit consists of ***lesson clusters***, which may be four to eight or more pages in length, furthering children's understanding of the conceptual scheme central to the unit. Concepts are not verbalized in the child's textbook until the final lesson cluster of a unit. The series of lesson clusters provides a sequence of textual information and operations that are basic to concept-seeking—all guiding the child's search for the concept of the unit.

The heart of many lesson clusters is the investigation, always indicated on a yellow-tinted page as an ***Apprentice Investigation.*** These investigations give children experience in using methods of intelligence as they engage in operations related to concept-seeking. The child's textbook does not tell what the outcome of an investigation may be, but inspection of photographs of an actual investigation apprises the child of the results of *one* trial. The illustration must be inspected to see what has happened. Thus, the importance of seeing or observing, is stressed, even if, for some good reason, the investigation is not actually performed. If it is performed, children have a guide by which to test their own results.

Evidence of progress in concept-seeking rests on ability to select from the scientist's methods of intelligence those processes or behaviors that will lead to the solution of a question for which the answers or outcomes are not known. Each of the Apprentice Investigations concludes with one or two related questions for which the child constructs hypotheses, makes a prediction, and designs his own method of investigating the solution. Thus, he enlarges his ability in independent concept-seeking. The Apprentice Investigations teach the techniques which the child can apply, on his own, to independent investigation. In each unit, one or more ***Searches on Your Own*** are provided. They are truly open-ended; the child engaging in some of these independent searches may reach a satisfying conclusion in a few days while other searches may lead to enough new questions to engage the child's attention for a much longer period.

Each lesson cluster concludes with several types of activities. In general, these enable a child to ***verify progress*** by testing his conceptual understanding and his ability to use the methods of intelligence in analyzing situations. They encourage investigation on a less rigorous level than that of the Searches on Your Own.

The Teacher's Edition

In structure each unit in the Teacher's Edition parallels the corresponding unit in the child's textbook, plus numerous resources for organizing, introducing, developing, enriching, summarizing, and evaluating the unit. The teacher's art is facilitated by the wise use of resources that this Teacher's Edition provides. A brief analysis of the suggestions and resources on pages T-2–T-7 will serve to explain how they can make the year's teaching experience rich and rewarding.

Teaching background (T-2–T-7). Preceding each unit, six to eight pages provide the teacher with background resource material in concise form that goes considerably beyond the learning level of the textbook. It is intended that these resources will make it unnecessary for teachers, even those who may feel insecure about their own science background, to do additional research in order to teach the unit effectively and with enthusiasm. It is also intended to provide sufficient resources to satisfy the probing questions of the most advanced, sophisticated children.

Concept statements. Across the top of page T-2, in the blue banner, is the ***title of the unit***, accompanied by the statement of the ***Conceptual Scheme*** of the series which the unit supports. At the top of the facing page appears the ***Unit Concept-Statement*** for the level, in this instance Level V (pages F-16–F-17). Similarly, all units fit the same Concept Level under one or another of the six conceptual schemes. A T-page number (teaching page) always appears on the blue banner at the top of the page to distinguish it from the page number of the child's textbook.

Basic behaviors sought (T-2). This heading introduces a few paragraphs that outline the processes and behaviors that children will use in the seeking of concepts.

A view of the unit (T-2). These introductory paragraphs give a succinct overview of the science content basic to this unit. Teachers will find it useful to review this information before presenting the unit introduction in the children's textbook. The material in the View of the Unit will not necessarily be taught to the children, but it supplies a frame within which the teacher can proceed with confidence to the activities of the lesson clusters.

Lesson cluster background (T-2). The heading preceded by a number in a square (1) provides more extensive science information for the first lesson cluster than that in "A View of the Unit" but in concise form. Each lesson cluster, designated by its own numeral, has background material to supplement the children's textbook. Thus, it is unnecessary to read all the background for the unit when preparing for the day's class. The final lesson cluster of each unit in the child's textbook is titled "The Main Concept." Specific background material is seldom provided for this lesson cluster as it brings into relationship all the concepts and supporting statements in the unit.

Supplementary aids (T-6). Each unit provides a listing of films and filmstrips and of books for the science reading table. The films and filmstrips have been previewed and selected under the direction of Elmer Stoll, Coordinator of Instructional Materials, Monterey Peninsula Unified School District, Monterey, California, by the following teachers: Richard Bucich, Sandra Holbrook, Carlos Rios de Los, Judith Treece, and William White, of the Monterey Peninsula Unified School District; and Linda Lynford of the Santa Rita Union School District, Salinas, California.

The majority of the books suggested in the child's textbook and for the science reading table in the Teacher's Edition were reviewed and recommended by Mrs. Margaret H. Miller, Supervisor, Elementary Libraries, Los Angeles School Districts, Los Angeles, California. In the Teacher's Edition, these books are evaluated as easy, average, and advanced. Many of those of advanced rating have interesting and unusual photographs or sections quite comprehensible to children with special interests.

The CLASSROOM LABORATORY sets and other supplementary aids for a comprehensive program are described on pages F-19–F-20. They are referred to from time to time in the teaching notes.

An analysis of behaviors in concept-seeking (T-7). This chart, or concept grid, appears at the end of the teaching background for each unit. Teachers can see at a glance the *Supporting Statements* for each Unit Concept-Statement, the *operations basic to concept-seeking* for each lesson cluster, and the *methods of intelligence (processes and behaviors)* children will use in their search for concepts. The grid indicates how the concept sought is synonymous with the operations and supported by the stated methods of intelligence. Reference from this grid to the series outline grid on pages F-16–F-17 shows at a glance how a unit fits into the ascending ladder of conceptual understanding.

In any subject area, wise teachers keep the program flexible to serve the needs of children's interests, abilities, and backgrounds, to fit available local resources and requirements, and to adjust to timely events and to the minutes allowed in the daily schedule. All these factors necessarily dictate choices. Choices will vary from unit to unit, from one class to another, and in different years.

The aim of *Concepts in Science* is to give children guidance in the art of concept-seeking rather than in "covering" the text completely; or even a specific number of pages. The program is so structured that children can progress up the concept ladder without studying all the lesson clusters in each unit. A lesson cluster that is clearly essential in one class may, perhaps because of children's earlier experiences, be considered optional in another class.

In *Concepts in Science*, some lesson clusters are more essential than others. That is, they are rungs on the ladder without which progress in concept-seeking might be retarded. The authors, in their studies of the use of the first two editions and with the help of hundreds of teachers, have become able to distinguish with a good degree of clarity those lesson clusters within each unit that are essential to successful concept-seeking. The titles for these lesson clusters are printed in blue on the grids which conclude the background material for each unit (T-7). The other lesson clusters, whose titles are printed in black, may be used whenever time allows, or presented for enrichment and extension of concepts or for deepening conceptual understanding by children interested in or capable of individual work on their own. In some units all lesson clusters are considered essential.

Only the individual teacher can distinguish how many lesson clusters to include in a unit. In their wisdom, teachers will adapt to local needs and opportunities as teachers always have done. They will find a sound concept-seeking program is both possible and satisfying where time is limited, and also that a fuller, richer program is possible—for certain children at certain times, and for all children when adequate time is available.

A program, *On My Own,* designed for the inadequately prepared reader, is described on page F-19.

Teaching notes (T-8–T-57). The pages of unit background material are intended to brief the teacher on the route to be followed in working with the children; they do not zero in on specific aids. These aids are provided in the teaching notes that accompany each of the reproduced pages of the child's textbook.

In the blue banner at the top of page T-8 appears the Unit Title number and on page T-9 appears the ***Unit Concept-Statement*** for Level V under the appropriate Conceptual Scheme (pages F-16–F-17). In the banner on the right-hand page following the two-page unit introduction appears the Lesson Cluster number and the ***Supporting Statement*** for that lesson cluster (T-11). This is identical with the lesson cluster number and the Supporting Statement as they appear in the unit grid (T-7). Thus, the rungs of the conceptual ladder are always apparent to the teacher, although these should not be presented to the children as their goals for the lesson cluster. They are guidelines for the teacher, a map of the route to be traveled by the children in their search for concepts. Supplementing these banners are further route markings which appear in the upper column next to the reproduced child's pages (T-8 and T-10, for example). The teacher sees immediately where background information is available, which concepts are to be sought, what the operations are and which methods of intelligence are especially pertinent, and what materials may be needed.

Introducing the unit (T-8 and T-9). These teaching notes, together with the reproduced two-page unit introduction from the child's textbook, serve to stimulate curiosity. Usually this stimulation rests on a simple investigation that suggests, but does not telegraph, the concept-seeking goal of the unit. The notes for the introduction encourage the raising of questions or preliminary statements of hypotheses. Several specific procedures are suggested that have been found useful in starting the children on their search for concepts. These are developed in a sequential pattern in each lesson cluster.

The pattern of a lesson cluster

In each lesson cluster (pages T-8–T-17, for example), the child experiences objects or events that enable him to make progress toward understanding an important or useful concept. A lesson cluster may focus on only one important idea or it may deal with several related ideas. It may be completed in one day with some classes; in others, several days may be needed. A lesson cluster does not imply a fixed amount of time, but the gaining of an understanding of a concept, even though the child has never seen or heard the concept stated.

Like good lessons in other subjects than science, each lesson cluster has three main divisions:

Introducing the lesson cluster—in which a problem is raised and curiosity stimulated; that is, thought is linked to action.

Developing the lesson—in which the content (the main body of the lesson cluster) is organized for concept development and then summarized. The body of the lesson includes independent investigation.

Verifying progress—in which children give evidence of the application of methods of intelligence (processes and behaviors) in the analysis of situations or the solution of problems. Progress may be verified at the conclusion of a lesson cluster or at different stages within it; such opportunity is provided by suggestions in this Teacher's Edition.

In the lesson clusters the children become aware of new relationships as they discover similarities among objects and events that previously may not have appeared to them to be related. Gradually, as they recognize and understand more clearly some of the complicated patterns of relationships in the Universe, the children build in depth their conceptual schemes of science. These conceptual schemes take shape in the child's mind as, with each experience, he progresses toward more mature conceptual understandings.

The methods by which the teacher may introduce or develop a lesson cluster are varied. Basically, they should encourage involvement by the child in some form of activity that will enable him to see the beginning of an order in the objects and events of his environment and, eventually, to build a conceptual scheme for himself. Such a goal is possible of achievement with all children at all levels, however simple or complex the conceptual understanding may turn out to be.

Introducing the lesson cluster. In general, the first lesson cluster has been introduced by the introduction to the unit, and may build on it. Later lesson clusters may begin by suggesting an activity that raises questions or poses a problem. The activity may be a demonstration by the teacher, the construction of a model, a class discussion, or a simple investigation. Occasionally some objects are desirable for examination. The objects are listed as ***Useful materials*** in the column adjacent to the reproduced pages of the child's textbook.

In the teaching notes for introducing the lesson—and throughout the lesson—the teacher will find suggested questions to stimulate and guide the children's attention and curiosity. These questions are printed in bold-faced type and frequently suggest sample responses in parentheses. However, to work toward uncovering the data or evidence, the children turn naturally to their science textbooks and continue with the main part of the lesson.

Developing the lesson. Circled numbers on the pages of teaching notes are directly keyed to the reproduced child's pages. They may start children thinking, call attention to a pitfall in an investigation, or supply additional information that may be useful for children in their concept search.

In exercising the art of questioning, teachers will be guided by the outlines of concept-seeking behaviors, and also by the Unit Concept-Statement and the Supporting Statement for the lesson cluster. Children's behavior thus becomes oriented toward development of specific science concepts, resulting in economy in teaching and in learning.

It is useful to call attention to the role of photographs, drawings, and diagrams. These require skill in the interpretation of visually recorded evidence. Unfortunately, few of us can observe very many objects and events at first hand; in fact, we must often rely on indirect evidence for what we learn, and a photograph is a form of indirect evidence. Often such film-recorded evidence is difficult to read, because we tend to look at an illustration before we know what it is supposed to tell us, and then we do not come back to it for fuller study. To make reasonably certain that an illustration is "read" at the appropriate time, it is keyed into the text of the child's pages. If an illustration key is included in a section of the child's textbook to which a teaching note refers, the teacher should make certain to include in the teaching process the reading and interpretation of the photograph or diagram. This keying of illustrations gives improved control over the learning process in a given situation.

Many lesson clusters involve an Apprentice Investigation, always indicated in the child's textbook by the yellow-tinted background. In the margin next to the reproduced pages of all Apprentice Investigations appears a statement of ***Performance objectives*** (for fuller description, see pages F-15 and F-18). These involve certain specific behaviors. In addition, if materials similar to those listed for the investigation are available in the CLASSROOM LABORATORY sets (described on pages F-19–F-20), this fact is also indicated.

Variations in results are to be expected. The teaching notes, keyed by the circled numbers, give the teacher possible reasons for variations, or alert them to faulty techniques that may explain conflicting results. When such variances from the expected occur, children should be encouraged to make several trials to uncover reasons for any discrepancies between their results and those illustrated.

Suggested procedures for developing the investigations. The most effective way toward concept-seeking is through direct, individual experience. This is the heart of the Apprentice Investigations, which are designed for maximum participation. Most of the investigations are suitable for total class involvement, with children working together cooperatively in small groups.

Each child should have a specific responsibility. Let us say that children are working in groups of four. One child can be the Lab Technician who secures the materials needed and takes responsibility for returning them at the conclusion of the investigation. A second child can be designated as Reader. He should have the requisite skill to read the directions and make sure that they are being followed. The third child, who has manual dexterity, may be assigned as the Investigator. He sets up apparatus and follows directions as they are read and verified. The fourth child acts as Recorder. His responsibility will be to read or check temperatures, weights on scales, and other data and to make a table or record of observations and results. All children, with the Recorder's help, will be expected to report when the class resumes for group discussion. If a fifth child is in the group and has ability to record information and procedures graphically, so much the better!

At first, you may wish to assign the roles according to known or suspected capacities, but roles should be rotated so that each child has opportunity to assume responsibilities and to work in cooperation with others.

As an occasional variation on individual group work, for reasons of safety perhaps or to cue other groups into a more complicated investigation, you may wish to select a demonstration team of three or four children to carry through the investigation in front of their classmates. Such a demonstration should be pre-scheduled to permit the demonstrators to collect and arrange equipment, and to practice a dry run. A teacher who performs the demonstration for children or who relies too often on demonstration teams deprives the other children of discovering for themselves. The advantage of the demonstration team is that it provides children unaccustomed to working with science equipment a mental image to follow when they perform the investigation for themselves. It also allows the teacher as observer full opportunity to capitalize on reactions of both demonstrators and their classmates.

Children who are demonstrating for the entire class can secure better attention if those in the back can see too. A box on its side makes a fine demonstration table when placed in full view. It also allows the children to capitalize on the element of *surprise* by letting them keep equipment concealed inside until ready for use. If you have the CLASSROOM LABORATORY for your level, its fire-resistant top provides safety as well as utility as a demonstration table. Also, for the sake of back-row visibility, keep on hand a small household four-color food coloring pack for tinting solutions.

Any investigations involving heat should stress *science* and *safety*. They should be carried out on an asbestos sheet with kitchen tongs and pot holders handy. Prepare a small can of sand as depository for used matches. Except for Bunsen burners, table-top propane burners offer the best classroom source of intense heat. All heat sources should be turned off or extinguished as soon as the investigation has been completed as far as heating is concerned. An open flame, if used, should conform with school or local rules for fire safety.

An electric hotplate and Pyrex saucepan are basic for multiple use in science. If water is to be removed from a burner, set the saucepan on an asbestos pad, and have pot holders handy. Children should never carry boiling water in open vessels. They should never be permitted to point a test tube that is heating or has reacting chemical substances in it toward themselves or toward another person.

Give children "thinking" time. *Silence* is golden, for the learner learns more. If you too are judiciously silent, with qualifications, your example encourages your demonstrators to ask others or individual groups to ask themselves these questions: What is happening? Why? How is this investigation related to a concept—some object or event within their experience? This is what silence means—a time to ponder. Then fruitful questions are asked.

Science can, and should be linked to *surprise*, *safety*, and *silence*, as outlined above and, in terms of the apprentice investigations, to *simplicity* in equipment, procedure, and additional steps toward concept-seeking.

Verifying progress. There are many ways to verify progress in concept-seeking. Within the structure of each lesson cluster, performance objectives are stated for each Apprentice Investigation. The degree to which a child or a group of children succeeds in carrying out the described investigation is evidence of one type of progress. From time to time, in the upper right- or left-hand column adjacent to the reproduced child's pages, additional activities are suggested which the teacher may present to inquisitive children; these activities call for application of the methods of intelligence. They are entitled "Verifying Progress" or "Extending the Lesson."

The main aspects of verifying progress in concept-seeking and in using the methods of intelligence are to be found at the end of each lesson cluster in the child's textbook; the statement of the methods of intelligence likely to be applied are clearly stated in the Teacher's Editions.

A good science lesson may end here for most children; but there are always others who remain unsatisfied. One criterion for evaluating the effectiveness of the classroom procedures is the enthusiasm with which children continue to observe and investigate on their own. Many of the lesson clusters within a unit suggest open-ended Searches, on tinted pages, in which the children are largely left on their own to design investigations and to pursue them to a satisfying conclusion by using methods of intelligence characteristic of scientific investigation. All the activities in the child's textbook and the teaching notes in the Teacher's Edition serve to point the way and to give meaning to children's continuing observations and investigations in their daily lives.

Closing the unit. The last lesson cluster of each unit (see pages T-48–T-57), titled "The Main Concept," brings the Supporting Statements together in a summary that relates them to the Unit Concept-Statement within the overall Conceptual Scheme of the program. Here the textbook states the conceptual ideas toward which the children's study has been directed; the children have an opportunity to test their own progress. Furthermore, this final lesson cluster summarizes the conceptual development in a short section titled "Focus on the Concepts" and requires the application of methods of intelligence in a short section titled "Focus on the Scientist's Ways." The exact words of any conceptual statement, whether it appears in the child's textbook or the Teacher's Edition, is not important. What is important is that each child be able to voice a reasonable approximation of a statement of concept relationships.

A New View

A comparison of the six conceptual schemes of *Concepts in Science* (pages F-16–F-17) shows that all these schemes are interrelated. At Concept Level V children can begin to see these concept relationships and get a glimpse of the unity of the world in which they live. Hence, at two stages during their search for concepts, children take stock of conceptual relationships in separate sections appearing after Unit Four and Unit Seven. These "New View" sections, appearing on blue-tinted pages, are "A New View of Matter and Energy" and "A New View of Change." In each section, conceptual schemes are examined in their interrelationship to one another, as on pages T-218–T-223 following Unit Four.

These "New View" sections encourage children to note and appreciate their growth in science. This growth is, of course, individual. But all the children obtain an awareness of relationships among concepts. They can and do share an understanding of the world they have explored, each to his own capacity.

The ultimate goal

Each science lesson is designed to permit the child to engage in several kinds of concept-seeking behaviors.

1. to explore the material Universe (through a "mix" of activity);
2. to seek orderly explanations of the objects and events explored (the explanation is an assertion we have called a *concept*);
3. to test his explanations (through a variety of activities).

For all the children, the text, carefully ordered in activities and investigations, growing in complexity as each child grows in maturity, provides firm foundation stones on which all may be guided to firmer understanding of the higher ordering of concepts in *Concepts in Science* PURPLE.

The teacher's art is an individual one; the child's learning activity is an individual one. Nevertheless, the teacher's art is congruent to the scientist's when the child—in the teacher's hands—explores his world and, because of the teacher's great skill and understanding, is not crushed by the immensity of it.

Each lesson, in short, becomes an experience in search of meaning. A new concept of the way the world works becomes part of the child's equipment; it becomes part of his posture toward the world he lives in. He grows.

Useful Teacher References

Many books in science education offer splendid opportunities for additional study and investigations by children or for enrichment of teaching background. Harcourt Brace Jovanovich publishes a number of textbooks for higher levels as well as several sourcebooks. Since they are referred to in this Teacher's Edition from time to time, the titles are cited below. In addition, a few other sourcebooks useful for reference and also cited in this Teacher's Edition are listed. Any of these are sufficient in conceptual depth and in richness of content to provide broad avenues of exploration for the most exacting teacher or the most inquisitive, imaginative, or creative child. The names and addresses of all the publishers whose titles are suggested here and in suggestions for individual units are on pages F-28–F-29.

The Earth: Its Living Things by Paul F. Brandwein et al., Harcourt Brace Jovanovich, 1970. An introductory textbook for junior high school, stressing biological science from an ecological viewpoint.

The Earth: Its Changing Form by Paul F. Brandwein et al., Harcourt Brace Jovanovich, 1970. An introductory textbook for junior high school, stressing matter and energy relationships with attention to Earth, space, and related physical science.

Exploring the Sciences by Paul F. Brandwein et al., Harcourt Brace Jovanovich, 1964. A complete textbook for the average student in a general course in junior high school science.

The Physical World, Third Edition, by Richard Brinckerhoff et al., Harcourt Brace Jovanovich, 1968. A textbook in the physical sciences, including the nature of matter and energy, atomic theory, chemistry, heat, machines, astronomy, and technology. Low mathematical content.

A Sourcebook for Elementary Science, Second Edition, by Elizabeth B. Hone et al., Harcourt Brace Jovanovich, Inc., 1971. Descriptions of projects and experiments for children; techniques, field trips, demonstrations and suggestions for planning instruction in biological and physical science are presented.

A Sourcebook for the Biological Sciences, Second Edition, by Evelyn Morholt et al., Harcourt Brace Jovanovich, 1966. Similar in organization and planning to the elementary sourcebook cited above. Although designed for high school, it contains much useful material for the teacher and for children who develop special interests.

Matter by Ralph E. Lapp and the editors of *Life*. Time-Life, 1965. From the *Life* Nature Library. Deals with the mysteries of matter that have stimulated the great intellectual explorations of our time. Each of the eight sections is accompanied by a picture essay. The narrative and pictures together constitute a survey of scientific advances in the subject. Teachers will want to bring much of the material to the attention of children.

Teaching Science Through Discovery by Arthur Carin and Robert B. Sund, Merrill, 1964. An intensely practical volume which can help teachers understand and practice a science program for the elementary school in accordance with the revolutionary nature of science education. The four sections titles, "Shaping Science Education in the Elementary School," "Organizing and Planning for Teacher Science," "Enrichment Activities for Science Teaching-Learning," and "Discovery Lesson Plans and Other Activities for Teaching Science," barely suggest the rationale and framework for science instruction and learning which permeate all sections. Emphasis is on problem-solving and the "discovery approach," but specific, detailed, step-by-step teacher activities for organizing, planning, and teaching science are given. The appendix contains bibliographies of professional books, sources of science equipment and supplies and many other helpful lists.

A Sourcebook for the Physical Sciences by Alexander Joseph et al., Harcourt Brace Jovanovich, 1961. Similar to the biological sciences sourcebook cited above, but for the physical science field.

Animal Worlds by Marston Bates, Random House, 1963. An authoritative study of animal adaptation and the science of ecology. Those characteristics that make each animal "world" unique are described and analyzed. Contains 245 illustrations, including 100 in full color. The reading level is definitely adult but not technical. Teachers will wish to share much of the information and many pictures with the children.

Foundations of Modern Biology Series, Prentice-Hall, 1964. A series of short, illustrated books on modern biology. Hard-to-locate descriptions of recent research and discoveries may be found in these books. The titles and authors are: *Man in Nature* by Marston Bates; *The Plant Kingdom* by Harold C. Bold; *Heredity* by David Bonner; *Animal Behavior* by Vincent Dethier and Eliot Stellar; *The Life of the Green Plant* by Arthur W. Galston; *Animal Diversity* by Earl D. Hanson; *Cellular Physiology* by Knut Schmidt-Nielson; *Animal Growth and Development* by Maurice Sussman; *The Cell* by Carl P. Swanson; and *Adaptation* by Wallace Bruce and A. M. Srb.

Investigating the Earth by Earth Science Curriculum Project, Houghton Mifflin Company, 1968. An integrated up-to-date story of planet Earth and its environment in space.

Biological Science: An Inquiry into Life, Second Edition by Biological Sciences Curriculum Study, Harcourt Brace Jovanovich, 1968. An inquiry approach to biology stressing the similarities among living things.

Teaching of Science in the Elementary School by J. E. Lewis and I. C. Potter, Prentice-Hall, 1970. Part One of this sourcebook deals with general aspects of science and science teaching—its goals, program, and evaluation. Part Two presents subject area inquiries with specific questions, demonstrations, and experiences which can be used to present the science to elementary children.

Addresses of Publishers

Many books in science and science education offer splendid opportunities for additional study and investigation by children or for enrichment of teaching background. In each unit of the Teacher's Edition under "Supplementary Aids" occurs a listing of reference books, for children and teachers, under the heading "Science Reading Table." Any of these books is of sufficient conceptual depth and richness of content to provide broad avenues for exploration by the most exacting teacher of this grade or by the most inquisitive, imaginative, or creative child. The names and addresses of all the publishers whose titles are suggested are given below.

Abelard-Schuman	Abelard-Schuman, Ltd., 6 W. 57th St., New York, N.Y. 10019
Atheneum	Atheneum Publishers, 122 E. 42nd St., New York, N.Y. 10017
Benefic Press	Benefic Press, 10300 W. Roosevelt Rd., Westchester, Ill. 60153
Bobbs-Merrill	The Bobbs-Merrill Company, Inc., 4300 W. 62nd St., Indianapolis, Ind. 46206
Childrens Press	Childrens Press, Inc., 1224 W. Van Buren St., Chicago, Ill. 60607
Coward-McCann	Coward-McCann, Inc., 200 Madison Ave., New York, N.Y. 10016
Creative Educational Society	Creative Educational Society, Inc., Mankato, Minn. 56001
Crowell	Thomas Y. Crowell Co., 201 Park Ave. So., New York, N.Y. 10003
Dodd, Mead	Dodd, Mead & Co., 79 Madison Ave., New York, N.Y. 10016
Doubleday	Doubleday & Co., Inc., 277 Park Ave., New York, N.Y. 10017
Dutton	E. P. Dutton & Co., 201 Park Ave. So., New York, N.Y. 10003
F. A. Owen	See Owen
Follett	Follett Educational Corporation, 1110 W. Washington Blvd., Chicago, Ill. 60607
Four Winds Press	Scholastic Book Services, 50 W. 44th St., New York, N.Y. 10036
Franklin Watts	Franklin Watts, Inc., 845 Third Ave., New York, N.Y. 10022
Grosset	Grosset & Dunlap, Inc., 51 Madison Ave., New York, N.Y. 10010
Harcourt Brace Jovanovich	Harcourt Brace Jovanovich, Inc., 757 Third Ave., New York, N.Y. 10017
Harvey House	Harvey House, Inc., S. Bukhout, Irvington-on-Hudson, N.Y. 10533
Hastings House	Hastings House, Publishers, Inc., 10 E. 40th St., New York, N.Y. 10016
Houghton Mifflin	Houghton Mifflin Co., 2 Park St., Boston, Mass. 02107
Henry Z. Walck	Henry Z. Walck, Inc., 19 Union Square W., New York, N.Y. 10003
John Day	The John Day Co., Inc., 275 Park Ave., New York, N.Y. 10010

Lantern Press	Lantern Press Inc., 257 Park Ave. So., New York, N.Y. 10010
Lippincott	J. B. Lippincott Co., E. Washington Square, Philadelphia, Penna. 19105
Lothrop, Lee & Shepard	Lothrop, Lee & Shepard, Inc., 105 Madison Ave., New York, N.Y. 10016
McGraw-Hill	McGraw-Hill Book Co., Inc., 330 W. 42nd St., New York, N.Y. 10036
Melmont	Melmont Publishers, 1224 W. Van Buren St., Chicago, Ill. 60607
Messner	Julian Messner, Inc., 630 Fifth Ave., New York, N.Y. 10018
Morrow	William Morrow & Co., Inc., 105 Madison Ave., New York, N.Y. 10016
Owen	The Instructor Publications, Dansville, N.Y. 14437
Prentice-Hall	Prentice-Hall, Inc., Englewood Cliffs, N.J. 07621
Random House	Random House, Inc., 201 E. 50th St., New York, N.Y. 10022
Scribner	Charles Scribner's Sons, 597 Fifth Ave., New York, N.Y. 10017
Silver Burdett	Silver Burdett Co., Park Ave. and Columbia Rd., Morristown, N.J. 07960
Simon & Schuster	Simon & Schuster, Inc., 1 W. 39th St., New York, N.Y. 10018
Singer	Singer School Div., Random House, Inc., 201 E. 50th St., New York, N.Y. 10022
W. R. Scott	William R. Scott, Inc., 333 Avenue of the Americas, New York, N.Y. 10014
Ward Ritchie Press	Ward Ritchie Press, 3044 Riverside Drive, Los Angeles, California 90039
Warne	Frederick Warne & Co., 101 Fifth Ave., New York, N.Y. 10003
Whitman	Albert Whitman & Co., 560 W. Lake St., Chicago, Ill. 60606
World Publishing	World Publishing Co., 2231 W. 110th St., Cleveland, Ohio 44102

Addresses of Audio-Visual Suppliers

The teaching suggestions for each unit of this Teacher's Edition list a number of films and filmstrips for classroom showing. Orders or further requests for information should be addressed to the following distributors or suppliers whose names are given in abbreviated form at the left and in the textbook.

Aims	Aims Instructional Media Services, Inc., P. O. Box 1010, Hollywood, Calif. 90028
BFA	BFA Educational Media, 2211 Michigan Ave., Santa Monica, Calif. 90404
Cahill	See Aims
Cenco	Cenco Educational Films, 2600 S. Kostner Ave., Chicago, Ill. 60623
Churchill	Churchill Films, 662 N. Robertson Blvd., Los Angeles, Calif. 90069
Coronet	Coronet Films, 65 E. South Water St., Chicago, Ill. 60601
EBEC	Encyclopaedia Britannica Educational Corp., 425 N. Michigan Ave., Chicago, Ill. 60611
Eye Gate	Eye Gate House, Inc., 146-01 Archer Ave., Jamaica, N.Y. 11435
Fleetwood	Fleetwood Films, Inc., 34 MacQuesten Parkway, Mt. Vernon, N.Y. 10550
Jam Handy	Jam Handy Organization, 2843 E. Grand Blvd., Detroit, Mich. 48211
Journal Films	Journal Films, Inc., 909 W. Diversey Parkway, Chicago, Ill. 60614
McGraw-Hill	McGraw-Hill Films, 330 W. 42nd St., New York, N.Y. 10036
SVE	Society for Visual Education, Inc., 1345 Diversey Parkway, Chicago, Ill. 60614
Universal	Universal Education and Visual Arts, Div. of Universal City Studios, Inc., 221 Park Ave. S., New York, N.Y. 10003
Ward's	Ward's Natural Science Establishment, Inc., P. O. Box 1712, Rochester, N.Y. 14603

Answer KEY to TEACHING TESTS

UNIT ONE
1. b
2. b
3. a
4. a
5. a
6. c
7. b
8. c
9. a
10. d
11. gravitation
12. thrust
13. unbalanced force
14. inertia
15. balanced force
16. b
17. a
18. a
19. c
20. a

UNIT TWO
1. c
2. b
3. d
4. c
5. b
6. c
7. d
8. b
9. c
10. a
11. sedimentary rock
12. metamorphic rock
13. granite
14. limestone
15. slate
16. c
17. a
18. b
19. d
20. c

UNIT THREE
1. a
2. b
3. a
4. b
5. b
6. b
7. a
8. a
9. b
10. d
11. oxygen
12. silicon dioxide
13. nitrogen
14. iron
15. calcium carbonate
16. d
17. c
18. a
19. a
20. b

UNIT FOUR
1. a
2. a
3. b
4. b
5. f
6. d
7. b
8. a
9. a
10. c
11. prism
12. mirror
13. spectroscope
14. mirror
15. lightmeter
16. d
17. c
18. d
19. c
20. c

UNIT FIVE
1. cell membrane
2. nucleus
3. cytoplasm
4. chloroplast
5. cell wall
6. b
7. a
8. b
9. c
10. d
11. carbon
12. DNA
13. starch
14. glucose
15. ATP
16. d
17. b
18. a
19. d
20. c

UNIT SIX
1. a
2. b
3. h
4. d
5. c
6. a
7. b
8. d
9. a
10. c
11. arm
12. lungs
13. spinal cord
14. small intestine
15. backbone
16. b
17. d
18. c
19. a
20. b

UNIT SEVEN
1. dinosaur
2. platypus
3. mammoth
4. trilobite
5. ostracoderm
6. d
7. c
8. c
9. b
10. a
11. reptiles
12. fish
13. amphibians
14. reptiles
15. mammals
16. a
17. d
18. b
19. d
20. c

This answer key is correlated to *Teaching Tests Concepts in Science* PURPLE, available in a separate booklet.

CONCEPTS IN SCIENCE

PURPLE

TEXTBOOK PAGES with accompanying TEACHING NOTES

CONSULTING SPECIALISTS IN THE SCIENCES

HERMAN R. BRANSON, *Physics*
President, Lincoln University, Pennsylvania

LAWRENCE P. EBLIN, *Chemistry*
Professor, Ohio University, Athens, Ohio

GARRETT HARDIN, *Biology and Ecology*
Professor, University of California, Los Angeles

RICHARD C. LEWONTIN, *Biology and Genetics*
Professor, The University of Chicago

ALISTAIR McCRONE, *Geology and Earth Science*
Professor, University of the Pacific, Stockton, California

FRANKLIN MILLER, JR., *Physics*
Chairman of Department, Kenyon College, Gambier, Ohio

LLOYD MOTZ, *Astronomy and Space*
Professor, Columbia University, New York

THE AUTHORS

PAUL F. BRANDWEIN
President, Center for Study of Instruction
Adjunct Professor, University of Pittsburgh

ELIZABETH K. COOPER
formerly Director of Elementary Education
Santa Monica, California

PAUL E. BLACKWOOD
Chief, Southeast Program Operations Branch
U.S. Office of Education*

ELIZABETH B. HONE
Professor of Education
San Fernando State College, Northridge, California

THOMAS P. FRASER
Professor of Science Education
Morgan State College, Baltimore, Maryland

*The work of Paul Blackwood on the *Concepts in Science* Series was done in his private capacity, and no official endorsement by the U. S. Office of Education is intended or should be inferred.

■■■■■■■■ PURPLE

CONCEPTS IN SCIENCE

THIRD EDITION

PAUL F. BRANDWEIN

ELIZABETH K. COOPER

PAUL E. BLACKWOOD

ELIZABETH B. HONE

THOMAS P. FRASER

HBJ HARCOURT BRACE JOVANOVICH, INC.

NEW YORK CHICAGO SAN FRANCISCO ATLANTA DALLAS

ACKNOWLEDGMENTS: For permission to reprint copyrighted material, acknowledgment is made to California Institute of Technology and Carnegie Institute of Washington for photographs from Hale Observatories pp. 42, 44, 156 to 158, 175; to Carolina Biological Supply House for photographs on p. 240.

COVER PHOTOGRAPHS: Front, Harbrace; Back, Mortimer Abramowitz

ILLUSTRATORS: Howard Friedman; Judy Skorpil; Dick Morrill Inc., N.Y.; Craven, Evans & Stone Inc., N.Y. and Harbrace Art Staff.

PICTURE ACKNOWLEDGEMENTS

Key: (t) top; (b) bottom; (l) left; (r) right;

All photographs are by Harbrace Photo Studio except the following:

INTRODUCTION: Page 1, Dick Smith. *UNIT 1:* Page 15, General Dynamics; 23, NASA; 32, both, NASA; 33, Yerkes Observatory; 35—41, all NASA; 42, 44, all © California Institute of Technology & Carnegie Institute of Washington, photograph from Hale Observatories; 47, NASA; 48, Courtesy of Dr. Harold Urey; 50, Courtesy of Mrs. Esther C. Goddard. *UNIT 2:* Page 54, Karen Collidge; 55, Bruce Roberts from Rapho Guillumette; 56, Josef Muench; 57(t), G. R. Roberts, 57(b), Josef Muench; 58, Josef Muench; 59, both, Grant Heilman; 61, U.S. Navy; 65, AMNH; 67, Jersey Production Research Co.; 68, National Earthquake Information Center; 73, both, Fred Ward from Black Star; 74, Neil Douglas from Shostal; 76, William Keith; 84, William Keith; 87(t), David Muench, 87(b), Hanson Carroll; 92, Karen Collidge; 93(t), Grant Heilman; 95, 96, both, Josef Muench; 98, NASA; 101, Pictorial Parade; 102, E. R. Degginger. *UNIT 3:* Page 130, Chris Reeberg from DPI; 143, both, Grant Heilman. *UNIT 4:* Pages 156–158, all, © California Institute of Technology & Carnegie Institute of Washington, Photographs from Hale Observatories; 159, Williams College Observatory; 160, E. R. Degginger; 161, Yerkes Observatory; 175, © California Institute of Technology & Carnegie Institute of Washington, Photographs from Hale Observatories; 176, Indiana University News Service; 188, Paul Sprague; 190, J. R. Eyerman from Black Star; 191, NASA; 194, Karen Collidge; 195(b), Josef Muench; 199, George Resch, Harbrace. *UNIT 5:* Page 229, James Cunningham, 230(b), Eric Grave; 237, all, James Cunningham; 239, General Biological Supply House; 240, all, © Carolina Biological Supply House; 241, all, Grant Heilman; 243, all, Allan Roberts; 246, H. Dowse; 248, 249, all, George Resch from Harbrace; 250, both, Grant Heilman; 251, Bettman Archives; 252, Boston Museum of Science; 254(tl), Russ Kinne from Photo Researchers, 254(b), Darsel K. Millen of the Salk Institute. *UNIT 6:* Page 268, Philip Morris Co.; 294, 297, Allan Roberts; 299, Ivan Massar from Black Star, Scurlock photo from American Red Cross. *UNIT 7:* Page 304–307, all, AMNH; 314, G. R. Roberts; 316, David Muench; 318, Allan Roberts; 320, Edna Bennett from Photo Researchers; 330, 331, 332(t), AMNH, 332(b), Paul Nesbit from National Audubon Society; 334(t), Allan Roberts, 334(b), Graham Pizzely from Bruce Coleman; 335, Grant Heilman; 336, G. R. Roberts; 337, Allan Roberts; 339, John Mayer from National Audubon Society; 341(t), George W. Thompson from Shostal, 341(b), J. March Penny from Shostal; 344, John H. Gerard from National Audubon Society; 346(tl), AMNH; 347, Erich Hailman from Magnum; 351, AMNH; 352(t), General Biological Supply House, 352(b), John H. Gerard from National Audubon Society; 354, J. J. Crete from Shostal; 355(b), Dick Smith.

ISBN 0-15-366129-1 PRINTED IN THE UNITED STATES OF AMERICA

CONTENTS

About This Book

Suppose you were picked to be a member of the crew of a space ship. You'd be excited, wouldn't you?

But you are one!

Your space ship is Planet Earth, the planet you call home.

You live on an exciting planet, a planet full of exciting things. However, this planet needs your help. Planet Earth needs to be used more wisely.

We are finding out that we have to take better care of this space ship. We can't go on filling the planet's air with harmful particles and gases. We can't go on dumping wastes in our planet's rivers and oceans. We must take care of the land.

How can we use Planet Earth more wisely? This year's work is meant to help you probe this question. Begin by analyzing your space ship, Planet Earth. Begin with an investigation. Turn the page and start your probe.

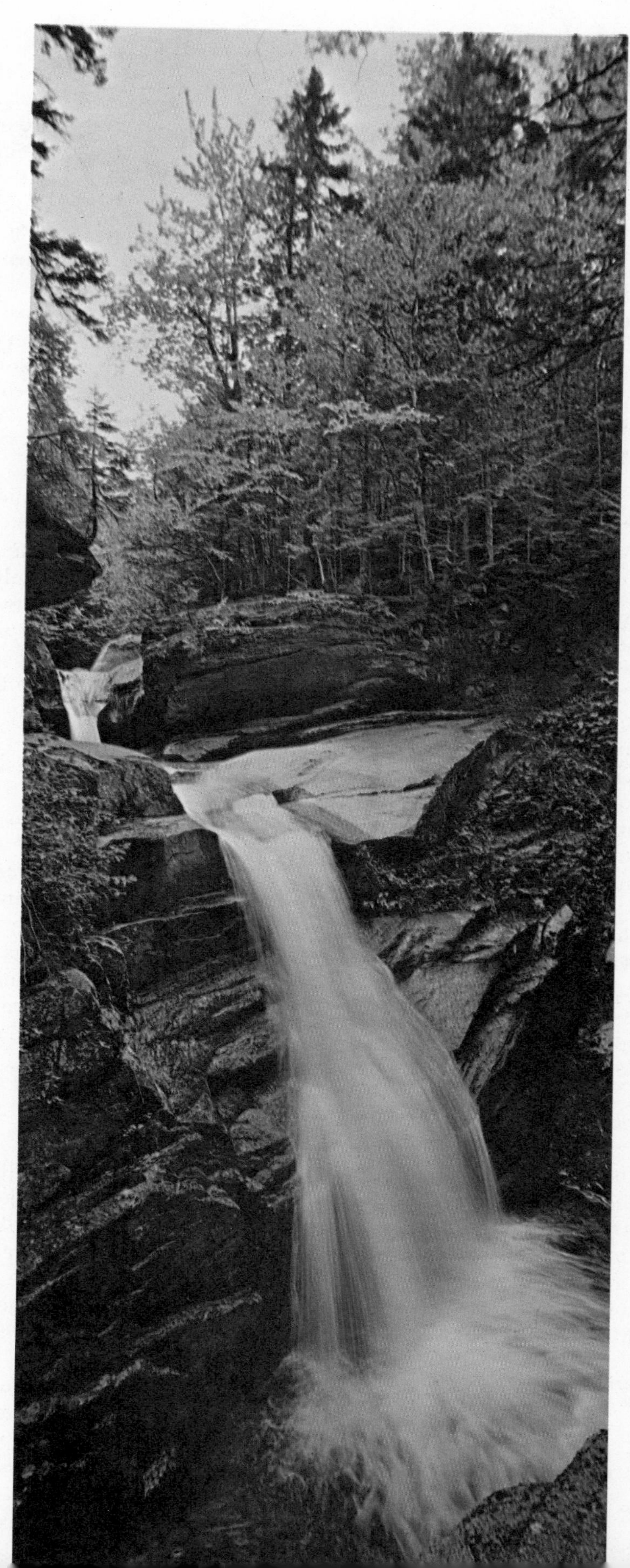

UNIT ONE

MAN AND EARTH—THEIR JOURNEYS IN SPACE

Basic behaviors sought: Children *observe* the weight of objects and *infer* that a force of gravitation exists. They *observe* the effects of unbalanced forces and *predict* the results when they change the forces. Children *observe* how the laws of gravitation and motion apply to the bodies of the Universe and to man-made satellites. They *analyze* and *explain* how the laws of gravitation and motion are applied to a Moon landing.

A VIEW OF THE UNIT

The workings of the laws of gravitation and motion are everyday experiences. The weight of an object is related to the force of gravitation between it and the Earth. We all know this force acts to pull all objects toward the center of the Earth. Another law of motion deals with the tendency of an object to remain at rest or remain in motion without change of speed or direction. This is termed its inertia. Force must be applied to overcome inertia. The forces are balanced on objects at rest or in motion at a constant speed. An unbalanced force must be supplied to change motion or direction of the object.

The laws of gravitation and motion apply throughout the Universe. They help us understand why planets and satellites orbit. From Newton's laws of motion and universal gravitation, scientists have developed theories of the origin of the solar system and described the orbits of all objects in space.

The Moon landings, then, would not have been possible without the proper application of these laws. The application of the concepts of gravitation, inertia, action, and reaction have resulted in the technology that has made it possible to launch astronauts in the spacecrafts, guide and land them on the Moon, and return them to the Earth. Because of these events we may someday collect enough information to enable us to explain the origin of the Moon and the Earth.

1 Force of gravitation

We can easily measure the weight of objects and observe that different objects have different weights. When we release the objects, we know each one will fall to the ground. Weight is a measure of the force of gravitation on an object. If a brick weighs 3 pounds, the Earth is pulling down on it with a force of 3 pounds. Everything on the Earth is pulled toward the center of the Earth by the force of gravitation. The more massive the object, the greater the pull of gravitation.

The force of gravitation is a property of mass. Mass is the amount of matter in an object. Since every object has mass, every object exerts a gravitational force on every other object. The more mass an object has, the greater the force it can exert.

When a boy stands at his desk, the desk pulls on him with a very minute force. If the boy stands near a large building, the pull on him is greater. A mountain will pull on him with a still larger force. Gravitational forces existed in these three cases. The forces, however, are so small that they are difficult to measure. But the force of gravitation between the boy and the Earth is measurable—it is his weight.

An astronaut may weigh 150 pounds on Earth. On the Moon, however, he weighs only 25 pounds. The force of gravitation between the astronaut and the Moon is $\frac{1}{6}$ that of Earth. The Moon is much smaller than the Earth and so it exerts a smaller pull on the astronaut walking across its surface. The mass of the astronaut hasn't changed. He still has the same amount of matter as he has on Earth. The force of gravitation on him has changed, and so his weight changes. If he were able to travel through the entire Universe, the same would be true. His mass, the amount of matter he is made of, stays the same. But the force of gravitation between him and whatever body he is on—or approaching—changes. We can, therefore, say his weight changes.

2 Action and reaction

If an object weighs 10 pounds, the Earth is pulling down on it with 10 pounds of force. If the object is hung from a support, a force equal to the pull of gravity keeps it suspended. The downward force of gravity is balanced by the upward force of the support. If the upward force is removed, the object is pulled downward with an unbalanced force of 10 pounds.

An unbalanced force occurs when an *external* force acting in one direction on an object is greater than an *external* force acting on the object in the opposite direction. A student rises from a chair by pushing down on the floor, on the chair, or some other object outside himself. The floor or the chair pushes back on him—it exerts an external force on him.

Force must be supplied to move any object, change its speed, or change its direction. In the model Dry Ice engine in the Investigation on page 13, carbon dioxide gas pours out of a hole in the side of the carton. The pressure is equal inside the carton except in the direction in which the CO_2 is streaming out. This creates an unbalanced force, and the carton rotates in a direction opposite to that of the streaming carbon dioxide. A rocket may weigh as much as 6 million pounds. To lift this rocket, a fuel (source of energy) must be used that will supply a tremendous amount of force. When the stream of burning gases is released, a large unbalanced force is produced. This force is greater than the pull of gravitation on the rocket. The inertia of the rocket is overcome and the rocket rises.

All the forces in the Universe come in pairs. The two forces of the pair are equal in force and opposite in direction. Thus, if a man steps forward from a rowboat onto the shore, the rowboat moves back, away from the shore. This exemplifies Newton's Law of Action and Reaction, which can be stated as follows:

> Every action is opposed by an exactly equal and opposite reaction.

However, in everyday activities, the two forces may not appear to be equal, because a third force, friction, is involved. Some of the original forces must be used to overcome friction. But outside the Earth's atmosphere there is no friction.

The action and reaction force do not work on the same object. If this were the case, an unbalanced force could not exist. The Law of Action and Reaction involves two forces and two objects, each exerting a force on the other. In the rocket example, the Earth and the rocket are the two objects. The burning exhaust gases and the pull of gravitation are the forces involved.

3 Inertia

In order to move a stationary object, we must supply an unbalanced force. We must also use force to stop, speed up, or change the direction of a moving object. When a baseball player hits a ball coming toward him, the force behind his bat sends the ball speeding off in a different direction. Another player may catch the ball and stop its flight. If no one catches the ball, it will continue moving in a straight line for a time until another force such as gravity changes its motion.

Inertia, the resistance of a body to a change in motion, is another property of mass. Objects at rest tend to stay at rest, and objects in motion tend to stay in motion. The more mass an object has, the more it resists a change in its state. That is, the greater the mass of the object, the greater its inertia.

Any moving object, a baseball or a man riding in a bus, tends to maintain its original direction of motion. The object remains in motion, in a straight line and at the same speed, unless acted upon by an unbalanced force. When a bus is traveling forward at a steady speed, a passenger travels at that same speed. The passenger has a certain inertia of motion. If the bus comes to a sudden stop, the passenger tends to maintain his forward motion. He feels himself moving to the front of the bus; he lurches forward. Again an unbalanced force has been applied.

When a Moon rocket is launched, it first takes a path that curves around the Earth. According to the Law of Inertia, however, the rocket should have maintained a straight-line path. The rocket must have been acted upon by an unbalanced force. The force that pulls the spacecraft into orbit around the Earth is the Earth's gravitation. The force of gravitation between the Earth and the rocket keeps the rocket in orbit. The Moon orbits the Earth for the same reason. The force of gravitation operates between the Earth and the Moon and keeps the Moon circling the Earth. This same law applies to all the bodies of the Universe.

The Law of Universal Gravitation explains why the planets in our solar system stay in orbit around the Sun. The Sun is a huge star. Because it is so massive, it exerts a pull on each planet. The gravitational pull between the Sun and another planet depends on the masses of each of these bodies and the distances between their centers. As the distance between these bodies increases, the gravitational force decreases. The relationship is that of the inverse square of the distance. Thus, if the distance between the bodies is doubled, the force of gravitation will only be one-quarter of the original.

The Earth is about 93 million miles from the Sun, and it is the third planet from the Sun. The gravitation between the Sun and Earth is strong enough to keep us in orbit, but not strong enough to pull us into the Sun. A satellite that orbits the Earth may be moving about 150 miles above the surface of the Earth. (Essentially, it is at the same distance from the Sun as from the Earth.) The force of gravitation between the Earth and the satellite is larger than the force between the satellite and the Sun because the Earth is closer. Thus, the satellite is not pulled into the Sun.

The other planets orbit at smaller or greater distances from the Sun. Pluto is the farthest planet from the Sun, about 3,670 million miles away. Yet the Sun exerts its gravitational force even over this tremendous distance. Gravitational force governs the motion of the nine planets. Many of the planets have their own satellites. For example, Jupiter has 12, and Saturn 9. The gravitational force between the planet and its satellites keeps them in orbit.

4 The solar system and the Universe

Scientists can predict the path of a spacecraft that they have launched. These man-made satellites continue in orbit, transmitting information back to Earth. Since there is no friction in space, a satellite will stay in orbit indefinitely. But if the orbit of the satellite falls inside the Earth's atmosphere, the friction of the atmosphere will cause the satellite to lose speed, and then the satellite falls closer to the Earth, where it encounters more friction. Eventually, the heat produced from friction may cause the satellite to burn up.

Scientists can also predict the position of a body orbiting in our solar system at any particular moment, because each planet and satellite moves at a predictable speed in its own distinct orbit. The Earth makes one revolution around the Sun in 365¼ days. The Earth also turns, or rotates, in a west to east direction. The Earth rotates on its axis, an imaginary line that runs through its center. It completes one rotation in 24 hours. As the Earth turns, the side that faces the Sun is in daylight and the side away from the Sun is in darkness. The Earth's axis is not perpendicular to the plane of the orbit. It is tilted about 23.5 degrees. The tilt remains at the same angle in relation to the plane of orbit, in the same direction, as the Earth moves around the Sun. The tilt is responsible for the changing lengths of day and night throughout the year. It also results in the change of season. The rays of the Sun strike the ground at different angles. If a beam of light reaches the surface at a right angle, it covers a small area, but all the energy from the light is concentrated in that area. This land area will be very warm. If the light beam hits the surface at a slant, the same amount of energy is spread over a larger area. The amount of energy the land area receives determines its climate. The angle at which the Sun's rays hit the Earth changes with the seasons, because the Earth's axis is tilted toward the Sun during one half of the orbit, and away from the Sun during the other half.

The other planets have their own periods of revolution and rotation. The lengths of days and years on each planet are, therefore, different. All the planets and their satellites orbit in approximately the same plane. Our solar system, consequently, has a flat, disk-like shape.

The reason why the solar system has this shape has been the subject of much speculation. There are many theories concerning the origin of our solar system. The nebular theory proposes that the solar system began as a cloud of gas, or nebula. The gases contracted and formed the Sun and the planets. Another theory, the collision theory, is based on the assumption that the Sun existed as a star before the other planets were formed. Our Sun could have collided with or passed very close to another star. This star pulled long streams of matter from the Sun. Later this matter formed the planets. These, however, are theories. No one theory completely satisfies all scientists.

The Sun is the largest body in our solar system, and the only one that emits its own light. The Sun, too, is revolving and rotating, as are all the other bodies that make up our solar system. The planets and the satellites do not move in perfect circles, but in ellipses. An ellipse is drawn using two points, or foci. The shape of an ellipse changes as the distance between the foci changes. The elliptical shape of the Earth's orbit explains why the Earth's distance from the Sun changes during the year.

The orbit of the Moon is an ellipse with the Earth at one focus. The Moon makes one revolution around the Earth in about 29 days. We always see the same side of the Moon, because the Moon makes one revolution around the Earth in the same time it takes to rotate once on its axis. As the Moon rotates, varying amounts of its illuminated side become visible. These portions are called phases.

The gravitational pull of the Moon and the Sun on the Earth causes tides. Even though the Moon is much smaller than the Sun, it is so much nearer the Earth that its effect on tides is more than twice that of the Sun. The highest tides occur when the Sun and Moon are in a line and their pull on the Earth is in the same direction.

Besides the planets and their satellites, there are other bodies that orbit in our solar system. Asteroids are tiny planets that orbit between Mars and Jupiter. Meteoroids are small pieces of stone and metal that travel through space. Comets appear to be collections of tiny particles. Radiation from the Sun forces the tail of the comet, which is made up of *very* tiny particles, to stream out in a direction pointing away from the Sun. A comet does not give off its own light. As it comes closer to the Sun, it reflects sunlight. Halley's Comet is one of the most famous. It is part of our solar system and has an orbit much like a planet. The orbit is a long, narrow ellipse with the Sun at one focus. Because the comet orbits in a regular fashion, scientists can predict when it will next appear. Halley's Comet will return about 1986.

Our Sun and the planets of our solar system are only a tiny part of a larger system. We are located within the Milky Way Galaxy, where our Sun is only a medium-sized star among 100 billion others. Although the exact number is not known, it is estimated that there are about 1 billion galaxies in space that are millions of light years apart! Stars visible with the naked eye are in our galaxy.

There are many kinds of galaxies, but our galaxy is shaped like a thick convex lens with a large bulge in the center. If you look along the plane of the galaxy, you see a great number of stars. When you look at right angles to the plane there are fewer stars to be seen. The Milky Way Galaxy is a spiral galaxy.

5 Man in orbit

A Saturn rocket, weighing 3,000 tons, is used to carry the Apollo missions toward the Moon. The rocket is launched toward the east, because the Earth rotates in that direction at about 1,000 mph. For this reason, before the rocket leaves the launch pad it has a speed of 1,000 mph.

The three sections, or stages, of Saturn are used to increase its speed. The first stage, the booster, creates a thrust of 7,500,000 pounds. In 2½ minutes its fuel supply is exhausted and this stage drops away. The engines of the second stage then fire, and the backward rush of gases produces an unbalanced force that pushes the rocket forward at an increased speed. The third stage first places the spacecraft in orbit around the Earth. When the craft is in the right position for a launch to the Moon, the third stage fires again. When this engine has used all its fuel, the Apollo has reached a speed of 7 miles per second. This is the speed (the escape velocity) needed to overcome the Earth's gravitational influence.

Apollo is made up of three sections: (1) the command module that carries the three astronauts; (2) the service module that contains the computers, research instruments, and fuel for in-course corrections and for the return trip; and (3) the LM, or lunar module. The LM is in the nose of the third stage. When the rocket has reached a speed of 7 miles per second, the LM is retracted from the rocket, and the third stage is released. As the Apollo nears the Moon, the Moon's gravity increases its speed. As Apollo comes quite close to the Moon, it fires its rockets toward the Moon. In this way it slows down enough to be able to orbit around the Moon. The command module remains in orbit while the LM makes a soft landing. The LM fires its engines downward to decrease its speed so it can touch down gently.

When the Moon walks are completed, the astronauts fire the engines that lift the Moon ascent stage of the LM off the surface to rejoin the command module. To leave the orbit of the Moon, the spacecraft needs a speed of 1½ miles per second (escape velocity). Since the Moon's gravitational force is smaller than the Earth's, less speed is needed to escape the gravitational attraction.

To return to Earth, the astronauts must fire their engines again to reduce speed as they enter the Earth's gravitational influence.

One of the manned space flights was Apollo 14 which landed on the Moon on February 5, 1971. This spacecraft, like all the Apollo missions, carried a three-man crew. Two of these men, Alan Shepard and Edgar Mitchell, were the fifth and sixth men to walk on the Moon. Stuart Roosa orbited the Moon in the command ship Kitty Hawk. Shepard and Mitchell collected samples of Moon rocks from the area around Cone Crater, and performed several experiments.

Examination of the Moon rocks may give us more information about the origin of the Earth and Moon. There have been many explanations of the origin of the Moon. Most of them are based on three general theories. The first theory assumes that the Moon originated separately from the Earth. It entered our solar system, was caught in the gravitational influence of the Earth, and remained in orbit. A second theory proposes that the Sun and all planets were formed at the same time from a cloud of gas. If the two bodies, the Earth and Moon, were close enough at the time of formation, the Moon could have been pulled into orbit. The third theory proposes that the gravitational pull of the Sun created a huge tidal bulge in the Earth's mantle. This material separated from the Earth and became an orbiting body.

SUPPLEMENTARY AIDS

All films and filmstrips are in color. All films are accompanied by sound; filmstrips are accompanied by sound only if so designated. Names and addresses of producers and distributors are on page F-29.

Filmstrips

Earth's Nearest Neighbor (45 frames), #427-14, SVE. Describes an imaginary exploration of the Moon; how to meet such environments.

Stations on the Moon (44 frames), #1311, Eye Gate. A review of the Apollo Program and its efforts in placing men on the Moon.

The Earth (52 frames), #71W2600a, Ward's. Several frames explain clearly the meaning of gravitation.

How Satellites Stay in Orbit (41 frames, sound), #S103, Coronet. Describes how a satellite is placed in orbit, and the scientific principles that keep it in orbit.

How Man Explores Space (60 frames, sound), #409-1, SVE. Photographs and drawings show how a speed of 25,000 mph counteracts gravitation; explains rockets; describes a space capsule.

The Sun and Its Family (46 frames), #427-15, SVE. Reviews concepts of planets, asteroids, comets, and other bodies of the solar system. Explains gravitation, solar energy, and the seasons.

Our Solar System (54 frames, sound), #409-2, SVE. Shows that solar system consists of nine planets, 31 moons, 50,000 asteroids, and meteor particles.

Films

The Moon—Adventure in Space (16 min.), 3rd ed., Cahill. Uses both live action and animation to illustrate the different features of the Moon. Appraises the current U.S. Moon programs. Appropriate for Intermediate or Junior High level.

Space Science: An Introduction ($13\frac{1}{2}$ min.), #1449, Coronet. Shows how a rocket overcomes the Earth's gravity when launching; describes forces at work during acceleration; explains satellites in orbit.

The Earth in Motion (12 min.) #58805, Cenco. Explains that the Earth moves in three different ways: it rotates on its own axis; it travels in a circular path around the Sun; and, as a part of the whole solar system, it moves around in our galaxy. Explains the periods day, night, year, and the different seasons.

Gravity: How It Affects Us (14 min.) #1786, EBEC. Shows how gravitation can be used to do work, how it affects man on Earth and in space.

Asteroids, Comets, and Meteorites (11 min.), BFA. Shows how astronomers have learned about these objects; what each group looks like; the place of each in the solar system. Also shows man-made satellites.

Mass and Weight (11 min.), Coronet, #1574. Explains the relationship between gravitational and inertial mass. Junior high level.

The Science Reading Table

Adventures with a Party Plate by Harry Milgrom, Dutton, 1968. Stimulating interest by the use of an ordinary paper plate with a rippled edge, the author demonstrates some of the basic principles of physics, such as forces that make machines work, and the force of gravity. (Average)

Around the World in Ninety Minutes by Rocco V. Feravolo, Lothrop, Lee and Shepard, 1968. The author follows the imaginary trip of two astronauts. A glossary of space terms is included, as well as illustrations of gravitation and related phenomena.

Gravity All Around by Tillie S. Pine, McGraw-Hill, 1963. An easy-to-understand account of the effects of gravity in our everyday life. Simple investigations. (Easy)

Isaac Newton: Pioneer of Space Mathematics by Beulah Tannenbaum, McGraw-Hill, 1959. A lively biography of Isaac Newton which gives a picture of his life and explains his theories about light, gravitation, and motion. (Advanced)

The Look-It-Up Book of Stars and Planets by Patricia Lauber, Random House, 1967. A clearly written reference book in dictionary form that helps explain such things as mass and weight, the constellations, asteroids, and so forth. Includes illustrations and other visual organization of the information. (Average)

Man in Space to the Moon by Franklyn Branley, Crowell, 1970. Using black and white illustrations, the author describes in detail the flight of Apollo 11 from the Earth to the Moon and back. (Average)

Mars by Isaac Asimov, Follett, 1967. The relation of Mars to the other planets in our solar system is presented and then compared to Earth as to its size, rotation, orbit, surface temperature, atmosphere, and force of gravity. (Average)

Push and Pull: The Story of Energy by Paul E. Blackwood, rev. ed., McGraw-Hill, 1966. Presents the sources of energy and the various uses of energy. Includes investigations that youngsters can perform on their own. (Average)

Satellites in Outer Space, rev. ed., by Isaac Asimov, Random House, 1964. Lucid description of facts needed for understanding of natural and artificial satellites. (Average)

Tasty Adventures in Science by Sally Fox, Lantern Press, 1963. Children may have their science and eat it, too, when they perform the investigations described. Simple materials and clearly stated directions for investigating a wide variety of science topics. Each investigation involves the use of something edible. (Average)

What Is a Solar System? by Theodore W. Munch, Benefic Press, 1961. Contains facts and figures about the planets, comets, meteors, meteorites, and moons of our solar system, for beginning study. Our solar system in relation to the Universe is touched upon. (Average)

An Analysis of Behaviors in Concept-Seeking*

Conceptual Scheme A: When energy changes from one form to another, the total amount of energy remains unchanged.

Unit Concept-Statement: Energy must be applied to produce an unbalanced force, which results in a change in motion.

Lesson Cluster titles in blue are essential to guide concept-seeking toward the Unit Concept-Statement and to enrich the Conceptual Scheme (*See page F-23*).

Lesson Cluster and Supporting Statement	*Operations Basic to Concept-Seeking**	*Methods of Intelligence (Processes and Behaviors)*
1. The Countdown—Starting 300 Years Ago The gravitational pull on an object is measured by its weight.	**Investigating** the pull on objects	**Observing** and **measuring** the weights of objects; **inferring** that it is the force of gravitation that gives an object its weight
2. Leaving the Earth For every action there is an equal and opposite reaction.	**Investigating** the concept of unbalanced force; **probing** Newton's Law of Action and Reaction	**Building a model** Dry Ice engine and **observing** forces of action and reaction; **predicting** the result of changing forces; **relating** the model to Newton's Law of Action and Reaction
3. Man in Orbit Inertia makes objects remain at rest or continue in motion.	**Probing** the behavior of objects at rest and objects in motion; **investigating** the effect of unbalanced forces on objects	**Identifying** kinds of motion; **seeking evidence** of the interrelationship between these motions and gravitation
4. Earth and Moon in Orbit The Laws of Inertia and Universal Gravitation explain the orbits of bodies in space.	**Investigating** the shape of the Earth's orbit; **probing** the motions of the Moon	**Constructing** an ellipse; **making a model** of a planetarium; **hypothesizing** on the nature of the solar system
5. Man on the Moon—and Beyond? Space exploration depends on the Laws of Universal Gravitation and the Laws of Motion.	**Applying** comprehension of the Laws of Motion and Gravitation to the exploration of the Moon	**Analyzing** a Moon landing; **explaining** the dependence of Moon exploration on the Laws of Gravitation, Inertia, and Action and Reaction
6. The Main Concept: Earth, Moon, and Man in Orbit Energy must be applied to produce an unbalanced force, which results in a change in motion.	Children **synthesize** the Laws of Gravitation and Motion to **explain** the structure of the Universe; **apply** these laws to **explain** that energy must be applied to produce an unbalanced force and that unbalanced forces change the motions of all objects in Earth and in space.	

* *A concept is synonymous with the corresponding operations. In turn, operations are served by relevant methods of intelligence.*

Conceptual Scheme A: When energy changes from one form to another, the total amount of energy remains unchanged.

UNIT ONE

MAN ON EARTH— THEIR JOURNEYS IN SPACE

Teaching background. "A View of the Unit" T-2

Concept-seeking. Children may begin their search into the Laws of Motion.

Operations. Children *investigate* action and reaction by making a model rocket from a balloon and launching it.

Methods of intelligence. Children *construct* a model rocket, *observe* its brief flight and *hypothesize* about why it does not keep going. They *reach tentative conclusions* as to how the model is like and unlike a real rocket.

Useful materials: Sausage-shaped balloons, paper, plastic straws, tape, scissors.

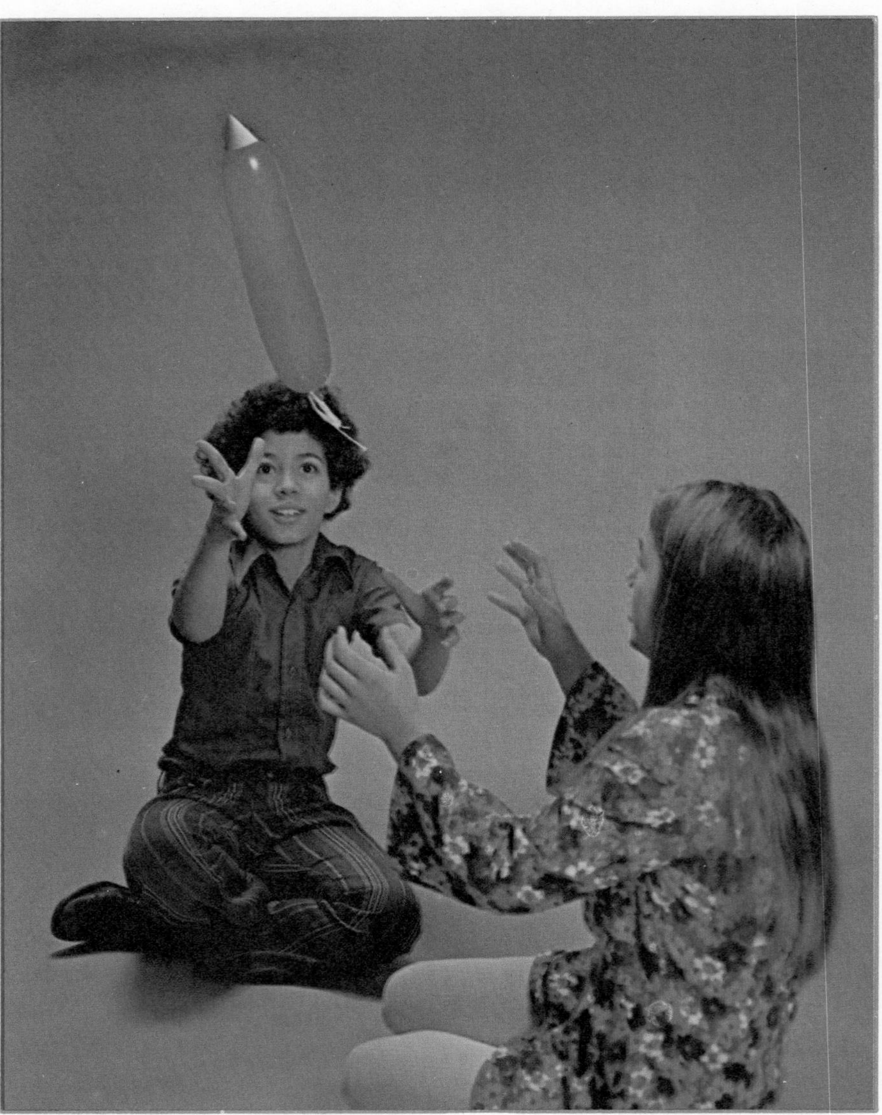

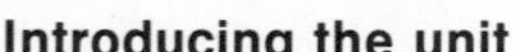

Introducing the unit

Try to have enough balloons, straws, and tape for half the number of your children for this first science class. Divide the class into pairs, and distribute a set of materials to each pair. Before the class begins, cut the strips of paper to be made into cones and distribute these with snipped-off pieces of straw and pre-cut pieces of tape.

Ask your children to open to pages 2 and 3, observe the pictures, and read the first paragraph (as far as the picture cue ■.) Then have them make their models—but not send them off.

Select a child to give the countdown and have all teams release their rockets at "zero". After a brief interval for a retrieval operation, ask the class to finish reading page 3 and discuss the questions. Encourage them to give all kinds of responses and, if you wish, have them write these in their notebooks so that they can check after they have finished the unit to see if their ideas have changed.

If you are unable to assemble enough materials for teams of two, at least plan to show the action of one rocket.

Choose three children to demonstrate it to the class, following the directions on the next page. One can act as Investigator, another as Reader, and the third as Reporter.

Unit Concept-Statement: Energy must be applied to produce an unbalanced force, which results in a change in motion.

UNIT ONE

Man and Earth– Their Journeys in Space

Tape the mouth of a sausage-shaped balloon ❶ around a short piece of a plastic soda straw. Blow up the balloon. Hold the air in the balloon by pinching the straw tightly. Ask a friend to tape a paper cone "spacecraft" on top. Now you have a model of a rocket. ■

Let go of the plastic straw nozzle. Air rushes out. "Liftoff!" The blast of air gives the rocket a push called **thrust.** The force of the thrust lifts the rocket model off its pad, and it is on the way. Alas, it soon falls back to Earth.

❷ Why didn't the model rocket go on?

Why didn't it go into space?

Why does a real rocket go into space?

How is a model rocket like a real rocket? How are they different? Write your responses in your notebook. After you have searched further, come back and analyze your responses.

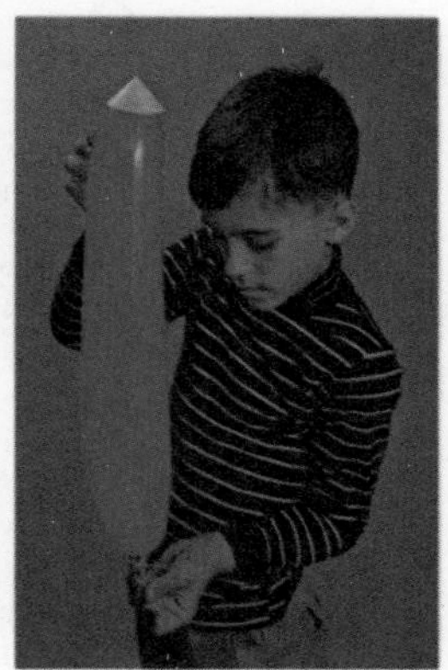

■

❶ The balloon rocket works best if the plastic straw is about 1 inch long, and the nose cone is no more than 1 inch in radius. The smaller your balloon, the more important it is to keep down the size, and hence the weight, of the attachments.

❷ Most children will infer that the rocket does not have enough power to go very far. Some may know that it is the force of gravity (or gravitation) that makes it fall back to Earth. However, if no one mentions gravitation, do not bring it up at this point. Instead, ask them to turn the page and start reading the first lesson.

Unit Concept-Statement: Energy must be applied to produce an unbalanced force, which results in a change in motion.

LESSON CLUSTER 1
THE COUNTDOWN—STARTING 300 YEARS AGO

Teaching background. 1 T-2.

Concept-seeking. Children seek to discover how a rocket lift-off and a falling apple are related to the concept of gravitation.

Operations. Children *investigate* the pull on objects by suspending them from a spring balance.

Methods of intelligence. Children *measure* the weights of various objects and *infer* that it is the force of gravitation that gives an object its weight.

1. The Countdown—Starting 300 Years Ago

Men make a rocket and a fuel that can carry the rocket into space. One day men enter the spacecraft on top of the rocket and fasten themselves in. They wait as the countdown goes on. Then the moment comes ". . . 4. . . 3. . . 2. . . 1. . . 0. . . Liftoff!" With a roar, rocket and men mount
1 into trackless space.

Suppose you are watching the liftoff. You know the countdown started days—even weeks—before. A countdown means that before the liftoff every part of the rocket and spacecraft is checked.

Finally, the scientists and engineers are as sure as they can be that every part works. We might say that the countdown really started at least 300 years ago, when man began to understand the way bodies move in space.

An Apple Falls to the Ground

About 300 years ago a young man named Isaac Newton noticed an apple fall to the ground. So the story goes. Of course, Newton had seen apples fall from trees before. But this apple made him think about something. Why do

4

Introducing Lesson Cluster 1

It is T minus 30 minutes and counting. What do you think this means? (It is 30 minutes to rocket launch.) Ten minutes have gone by. It is T minus 20 minutes and holding. What do you think this means? (Holding means a delay, so something must have gone wrong.) How does one say "everything is all right" in space language? (everything "go")

At T minus 3 minutes, the counting of seconds begins. What do you think happens after T zero is reached? Children may say that the counting now goes forward—as T plus 1, T plus 2, etc. They may also say that this is when the rocket is launched.

Developing the lesson

1 You may wish to discuss the word "trackless" with the class. Find out if they think that trackless means that there are no roads or highways in space. How can astronauts be so sure where they are going? Children may respond from their experience in watching TV. You may need to explain that a guidance system on the ground is in constant touch with the spacecraft by radio. In the spacecraft itself there is another guidance system. It obtains information from observations and from the ground crew and uses computers to put this information to use in checking position.

Supporting Statement: The gravitational pull on an object is measured by its weight.

❶ apples, sticks, leaves, stones—all things—behave the same way when they fall?

Newton's explanation now seems simple. You will see later, however, that it had an astonishing result. He said that there was a **force**, a push or pull, acting on the apples. It pulled the apple toward the center of the Earth. He called this force the force of **gravitation** (grav′ə·tā′shən).

The force of gravitation does not act on apples only. All objects are pulled to the Earth by the force of gravitation. ● This is why things are held to the Earth. This is why things fall. They are pulled to Earth.

You will hear people saying that it is the pull of **gravity** that holds things to the Earth. We often use the word gravity when we talk of the pull of gravitation on Earth. The force of gravitation is what prevents you from floating off the Earth into space. ▲ Clearly, it is an important force. How big is this force that holds you to the Earth? You can easily find out. Just step on a scale.

Whatever you happen to weigh is the amount of the ❷ force holding you to the Earth. If you weigh 100 pounds, you are being pulled to Earth by a gravitational force of 100 pounds. Weigh this book and you will find that the pull of gravitation attracting it to Earth is about $1\frac{1}{2}$ pounds. To lift this book from the Earth, then, you need to exert a force of a little over $1\frac{1}{2}$ pounds. A Moon rocket weighs about 6 million pounds. A force of more than 6 million pounds is needed to lift the rocket off the ground!

▲

●

❸

❶ Imagine that you are with Isaac Newton sitting in the garden. What do you think Isaac Newton thought when he saw the apple fall? What would you have thought? Have children hypothesize on the falling apple—from apple pie to the idea of gravity. Don't look for "right" answers. This merely develops the observation that different persons see different things. Isaac Newton possibly had many different thoughts about the apple before he wondered why it fell and started to develop the concept of gravitation.

❷ On which of you does the Earth pull the hardest? On which of you does the Earth pull the least? If children are uncertain of their weights, ask them to weigh themselves when they go home and compare their weights when they return to class.

If you have overweight children in the class who might be embarrassed, ask instead: On which animal does the Earth pull the hardest—a horse, a rabbit, or an elephant? On which animal does it pull the least?

❸ What do you think the red arrows in the drawing represent? Encourage children to use the key concept term ***force of gravitation*** in their responses. As they study the pictures, children will realize that even birds and airplanes are kept from flying off into space by the pull of gravitation of the Earth.

Unit Concept-Statement: Energy must be applied to produce an unbalanced force, which results in a change in motion.

The weight of different objects is different. Weight is a measure of the force of gravitation on an object. Instead of asking, "How much do you weigh?" you could say, "What's ❶ the force of gravitation on you?"

A scale could be called a force-of-gravitation meter. It shows how much force of gravitation is pulling on an object.

To understand more about weight and the force of gravitation, you can do as scientists do—investigate. As you may know, one type of investigation you can do is an ❷ Apprentice Investigation. An "apprentice" is a learner, and Apprentice Investigations—such as the one on the next page—are meant to help you learn the scientist's ways, the methods of intelligence. INVESTIGATE

A Probe into the Meaning of Fact and Inference

In finding the force of gravitation on the book and the carton, have you determined a *fact*, or have you made an *inference*?

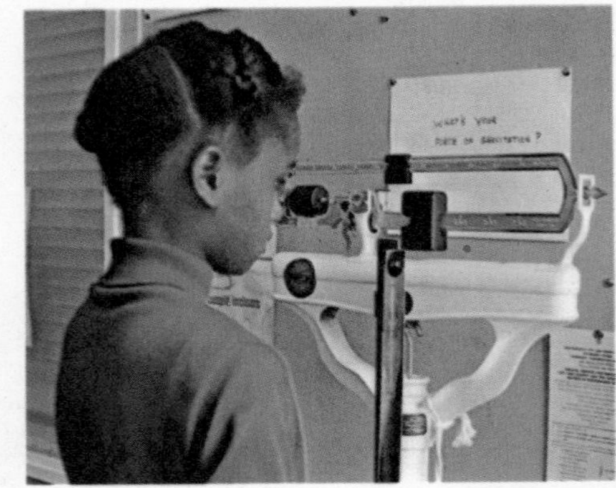

6

Continuing Lesson Cluster 1

❶ Have the children try to guess the weight of various objects. Use a spring balance or a bathroom scale. Use any suitable objects you find in the classroom or that the children may wish to bring. Pass each object around the class before you weigh it. What is the force of gravitation on the (______)? Have children write the number of pounds they think it weighs. (If you use a spring balance, they may guess in ounces.)

Two children can help you—one to weigh the objects, and the other to announce the weight after the class has had a chance to guess.

❷ Who knows where the word *apprentice* comes from? (If children do not volunteer the information, inform them that during the Middle Ages crafts like shoemaking, candlemaking, baking, and cloth-weaving were each formed into a giant organization called a guild. Anyone who wanted to become a shoemaker, for example, had to belong to the shoemakers' guild. And in order to belong to any guild, one had to work for that guild for seven years without pay while learning the trade. This seven-year learning period was called apprenticeship, and the learner was called an apprentice.)

Supporting Statement: The gravitational pull on an object is measured by its weight.

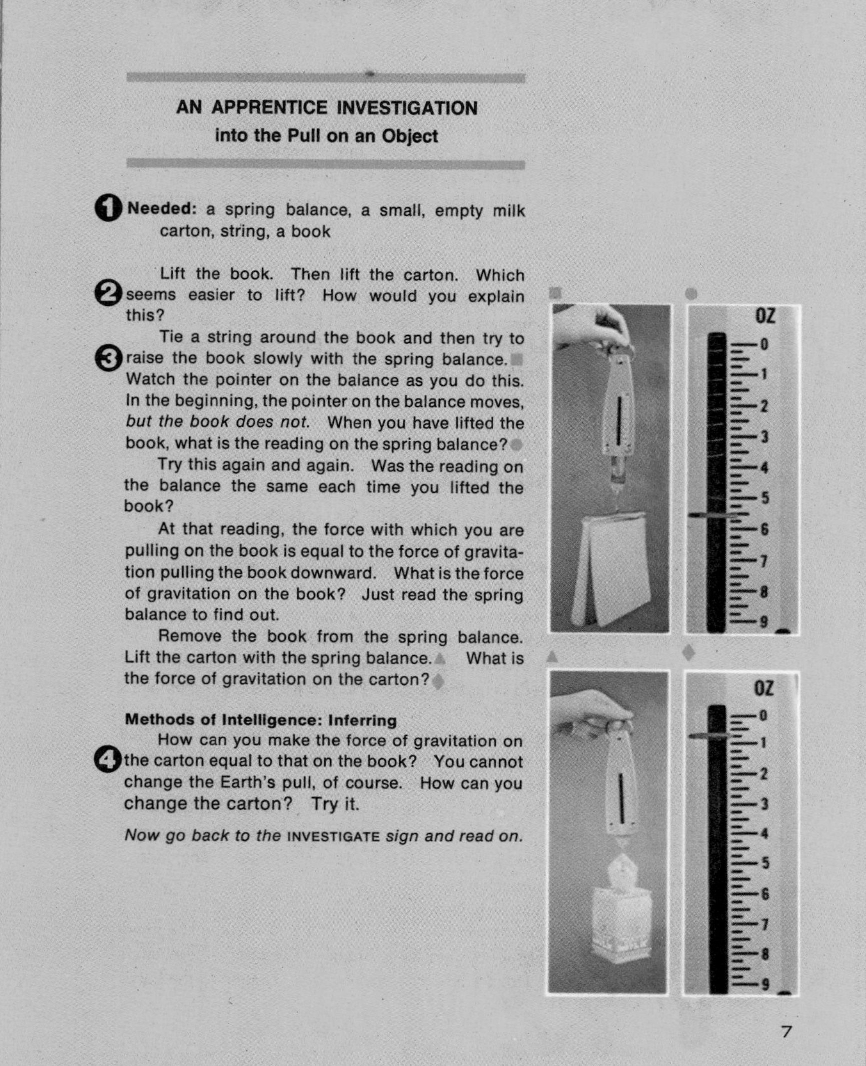

AN APPRENTICE INVESTIGATION
into the Pull on an Object

❶ **Needed:** a spring balance, a small, empty milk carton, string, a book

❷ Lift the book. Then lift the carton. Which seems easier to lift? How would you explain this?

❸ Tie a string around the book and then try to raise the book slowly with the spring balance.■ Watch the pointer on the balance as you do this. In the beginning, the pointer on the balance moves, *but the book does not.* When you have lifted the book, what is the reading on the spring balance?●

Try this again and again. Was the reading on the balance the same each time you lifted the book?

At that reading, the force with which you are pulling on the book is equal to the force of gravitation pulling the book downward. What is the force of gravitation on the book? Just read the spring balance to find out.

Remove the book from the spring balance. Lift the carton with the spring balance.▲ What is the force of gravitation on the carton?◆

Methods of Intelligence: Inferring

❹ How can you make the force of gravitation on the carton equal to that on the book? You cannot change the Earth's pull, of course. How can you change the carton? Try it.

Now go back to the INVESTIGATE *sign and read on.*

7

Performance objectives. Children *demonstrate* that different objects have different weights as shown by the readings on the spring balance.

Children *infer* that a force, that of gravitation, is pulling the different objects down toward the Earth with varying intensity, according to their different weights.

Children *observe* the reading for each object as they measure the Earth's pull on that object.

Useful materials: Some materials are available in CLASSROOM LABORATORY PURPLE.

❶ Divide the class into groups equal to the number of spring balances. If you only have one spring balance, let three children demonstrate to the class—two to weigh the objects and one to read the weight and write it on the board. You may ask the children to repeat each weighing several times, with small groups gathering around so that they can clearly observe the pointer record the weights.

❷ Children may say that the carton is easier to lift than the book because it weighs less, or because it is lighter.

❸ Be sure children doing the investigation place the book and carton on a table or desk-top and lift it from there, rather than suspend the book and carton from the hook in mid-air. Why do you think the pointer moves before the book does? (The force exerted is at first less than the weight of the book. The pointer moves until the force is great enough to move the book off the table. Children should note that the force stays the same once the book is lifted from the table.)

❹ Ask children for suggestions. (fill the carton with water, sand, pebbles, etc.)

When you lift an object with a spring balance, you **observe** the weight of the object. Each time you try the investigation, your observation is the same. Another boy or girl would also make the same observation. When many trained observers agree—and scientists are trained observers—the observation is confirmed. A confirmed observation is a **fact**.

On the other hand, to say that there is a force of gravitation pulling on an object is to make an **inference.** You were able to explain the fact that an object had a certain weight by saying that the force of gravitation was at work. ❶You did not observe the action of the force of gravitation, you **inferred** it. Your inference then led to your explanation of the object's weight.

The Pull of the Moon

Let's leave the Earth for a while. Let's see what happens to gravitation and weight on the Moon. Suppose that an astronaut weighs 150 pounds on Earth. How much will he weigh four days later when he steps on the Moon? If he could weigh himself on the Moon, the scale would show his weight to be only 25 pounds!

As you can see, an astronaut weighs six times as much on the Earth as on the Moon. Put another way, the astronaut's ❷weight on the Moon is $\frac{1}{6}$ of his weight on the Earth.

At first, going to the Moon may look like a good way to lose weight without dieting. What has really happened? Has the astronaut changed? Not at all. He hasn't shrunk.

The amount of matter that he is made of is called his **mass.** The astronaut's mass hasn't changed. The amount of ❸matter his pressure suit is made of is its mass. The mass in his pressure suit is the same on the Moon as on the Earth. What has happened, then?

The astronaut's weight has changed because the gravitational pull on him has changed. The force of gravitation on the Moon is less than the force of gravitation on the Earth.

Useful materials: Spring balance or other scale, Rice Crispies or similar cereal.

Continuing Lesson Cluster 1

❶ Children may say they did *observe* the force of gravitation because they saw the pointer go down. Did you see anything move the pointer? (no) What was it? (the weight of the book) What does this mean? (the force of gravitation) Did you see the force of gravitation? (no) Then how can you say that something called the force of gravitation moved the pointer? (an *inference*)

Give children an everyday example of an inference, such as, you hear the doorbell ring—you *infer* someone is at the door. What other examples can you give of an inference?

❷ Ask the children to calculate what they would weigh on the Moon. (All they need to do is divide their weight by 6.)

❸ Children may confuse *mass* with size. To make it clear that mass is independent of size show two small plastic bags filled with equal weights of a "puffed" type of cereal, such as Rice Crispies. You have, however, crushed the contents of one of the bags to bits. Does the smaller (crushed) bag have more or less mass than the larger (uncrushed) one? Children will probably say "yes", but some may ask for proof. Let one or two of the skeptics weigh the bags and report the results.

Supporting Statement: The gravitational pull on an object is measured by its weight.

■

Weight and Mass

Remember what weight is? Weight is the gravitational pull on an object. If, somehow, the pull of gravitation changes, then the weight of the object changes. The mass of the object, the amount of matter it is made of, does not change.

If a bag of sugar weighs 6 pounds on Earth, what will it weigh on the Moon? It will weigh 1 pound on the Moon; $\frac{1}{6}$ of its weight on the Earth. ■

Here on the Earth we usually talk as if weight and mass were the same thing. We use weight as a way of measuring mass. On the Earth this is very convenient. A mass of sugar that weighs 6 pounds in California will weigh about 6 pounds in Hawaii or Canada or Germany because the force of gravitation in each place is practically the same.

As long as we stay on Earth, using weight to measure mass works pretty well. Now, however, men have left the Earth. Suddenly we realize that weight and mass are not the same thing! Away from the Earth, the force of ❶ gravitation changes. As the pull of gravitation changes, weight changes, but the mass of an object stays the same anywhere in the Universe—whether it is on Earth, on the Moon, in a spaceship, or on Mars.

9

Useful materials: Clay, rock.

❶ If some children have difficulty with the idea of mass, mold a piece of modeling clay around a small rock or other small heavy object. Ask three or four children to feel its weight. Now carefully remove the rock from the center of the clay and put the clay back together again—leaving the space in the center hollow. (Be sure the children see what you are doing.) Ask the same children to feel its weight again, warning them to handle it lightly so as not to crush it.

Is the shape of the ball the same as it was the first time? (yes) Is the size of the ball the same as it was the first time? (yes) Is the *mass* of the ball the same as it was the first time? (no) Why? (The rock was removed, so the ball has less matter than it did before. What does the *mass* of an object mean? (The amount of matter in that object.) What happens when an object's *mass* becomes less? (The object weighs less than before, if still weighed at the same place.)

Now mold another piece of clay into a solid ball. Ask a few children to observe it. Ask a child to pound it into a long thin strip. Have him hold it up. Has the mass changed? (no) Why not? (No matter has been added or taken away.) Has the shape changed? (yes) Has its weight changed? (no) What will the object weigh on the Moon? (one sixth of its Earth weight) What will its mass be on the Moon? (same as on Earth) What happens to mass if we change its size or shape? (stays the same)

Unit Concept-Statement: Energy must be applied to produce an unbalanced force, which results in a change in motion.

VERIFYING PROGRESS

In concept-seeking

To help children determine progress in *distinguishing* weight and mass, have them *demonstrate* their responses. Give each group of children a paper cup of sand. Provide scales.

1. How can you determine the force of the Earth's gravitation on the cup? (Children *measure* the weight of the cup and then *state the rule* that the weight of an object is a measure of the force of gravitation on it.)
2. How can you change the mass of the cup? (Children remove some of the sand.)
3. How can you show that changing the mass of the cup changes its weight (at the Earth's surface)? (Children *measure* the weight of the cup and *observe* the change in weight.)
4. How could you change the weight of the cup without changing its mass? To change the weight noticeably one must take it to the top of a high mountain, or higher.)

❶ Have you wondered why the pull of gravitation on the Moon is only $\frac{1}{6}$ of the pull on the Earth? Here is a reason. When the mass of an object is greater, its gravitational pull is greater; when the mass is less, gravitation is less. ■ The Moon has less mass than the Earth. Since the Moon has much less mass than the Earth, it has much less gravitational force than the Earth.

■

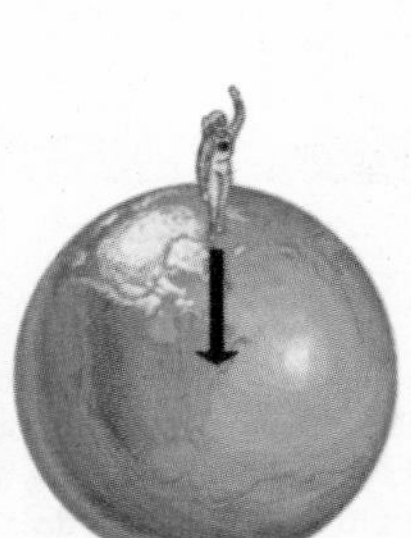

❷ BEFORE YOU GO ON

Check your understanding of the concepts of this section. Which ending would you choose for each statement below?

1. All objects on the Earth are pulled to the Earth by the force of
a. mass b. gravitation

2. An astronaut on the Moon finds that he has changed in
a. mass b. weight

3. An object's mass on the Moon, on Mars, and on the Earth would be
a. the same b. different

4. If a boy weighs 120 pounds on Earth, his weight on the Moon would be
a. 60 pounds b. 20 pounds

5. When you weigh an object with a balance, you are
a. making an observation
b. making an inference

6. The statement that fits the main concept of this section is
a. The weight of an object changes when the force of gravitation acting on it changes.
b. The weight of an object changes only when its mass changes.

10

Continuing Lesson Cluster 1

❶ A review of the key concept terms ***mass*** and ***weight*** may be useful in the discussion of this paragraph. What determines the *mass* of an object? (the amount of matter in that object) What is the *weight* of an object? (the pull of the Earth's gravitation when the object is at the Earth's surface) Why is the weight of that object less on the Moon? (The pull of the Moon's gravitation on the object is less) Why is this? (The mass of the Moon is less than the mass of the Earth) Another reason, which a few children may be aware of, is that the distance from the surface of the Moon to its center is much less than the distance of the surface of the Earth to the center. If the question should be raised, point out that this is to be expected since the Moon's mass is much less than the Earth's. Why do we so often measure mass of an object on Earth by its weight? (Almost all our calculations of mass and weight are at the surface of the Earth, or very near it, so that the relationship between mass and weight is about the same.)

VERIFYING PROGRESS

❷ **Before you go on.** Children *demonstrate* understanding of weight, mass, and the Earth's gravitation by selecting suitable responses to open-ended questions.

1. b	3. a	5. a
2. b	4. b	6. a

Supporting Statement: The gravitational pull on an object is measured by its weight.

❶ **USING WHAT YOU KNOW**

1. The astronauts of Apollo 11 brought back rocks that weighed 50 pounds on Earth. What would the rocks have weighed on the Moon?

❷ 2. An imaginary planet far off in space exerts about ten times the gravitational force of the Earth. On this far-off planet, what would be the weight of an astronaut who weighs 150 pounds on the Earth? Would the astronaut's mass have changed?

3. If you took a bowling ball to the Moon, what would happen to the ball's weight? to its mass?

INVESTIGATING FURTHER

1. Isaac Newton was 12 years old in 1654. What was his house like? his food? his clothing? What sort of boy was he? What was our own country like in those days? Where would you look for answers to these questions?

2. Perhaps you have heard that "oil ❸ is lighter than water." What does this mean? Does it mean that a cup of oil weighs less than a tablespoon of water? How would you change the saying to make it more correct? Write your correction, and then test it by weighing some water and some salad oil.

You may want to weigh some other liquids in your environment, as well: rubbing alcohol, milk, liquid detergent, maple syrup, and so on. What will you use as a container for your liquids?

What kind of balance will you use? You may use a platform balance, a spring balance, or a household scale.

Make a written record of the weight of the container with each liquid in it.

How will you determine the weight of each liquid without the container?

Look up the meaning of *density*. How can you find the densities of the liquids you have weighed?

A LOOK AHEAD

Toss a ball up a few feet, and down it comes. Throw the ball up as hard and as high as you can, but down it comes. "What goes up must come down," we used to say. Now, we are not so sure.

Put a spacecraft atop a huge rocket. With a terrific roar the rocket thrusts the spacecraft up—into space.

What goes up does *not* always come down. The old saying is out of date. We have begun to see why. The force of gravitation brings the ball back. But what of the rocket? What makes it keep going?

11

❶ **Using what you know.** Children *analyze* situations in which they must *distinguish* between and *apply* the concepts of ***weight*** and ***mass.***
1. $8\frac{1}{3}$ pounds
2. 1,500 pounds; no
3. The ball's weight would be one sixth of that on Earth. Its mass would not change.

❷ **Investigating further.** Children *consult authorities* for information about a famous scientist; they *investigate* and *infer* the relationship (density) of weight and volume, *design* procedures, *seek evidence* and *analyze* and *classify* it.
1. The encyclopedia is always a good source to begin with. Children who are especially interested should check the library catalog for biographies of Newton. One written especially for children is *Isaac Newton*, by Patrick Moore, Putnam, New York, 1958. A more advanced book, that some children will enjoy, is *Isaac Newton: Pioneer of Space Mathematics*, by Beulah Tannenbaum, McGraw-Hill, New York, 1959.

❸ 2. The investigation here is suitable for independent work at home. *Density* (mass per unit volume) is discussed in most high school science textbooks. Children who read well may consult *Matter: Its Forms and Changes*, second edition, by Brandwein et al., Harcourt Brace Jovanovich, Inc., 1972.

Unit Concept-Statement: Energy must be applied to produce an unbalanced force, which results in a change in motion.

LESSON CLUSTER 2
LEAVING THE EARTH

Teaching background. 2 T-2.

Concept-seeking. Children become aware that in jet action an imbalance of opposing forces results in a change of motion.

Operations. Children *investigate* the concept of unbalanced force in order to understand Newton's Law of Action and Reaction.

Methods of intelligence. Children *observe* the action and reaction of a model Dry Ice engine and *predict* what will happen when additional holes are punched in the sides of the "engine." They *relate* this to Newton's Law of Action and Reaction.

2. Leaving the Earth

A pair of twins are playing tug-of-war. They pull and pull but do not move.■ If another girl helps to pull on one side, however, then they all move.● A giant rocket roars into space. What has a rocket to do with girls playing tug-of-war? The moving rocket and the moving girls are alike in an important way.

Think of the twins pulling against each other. They do not move, because their forces balance. Then a friend begins to pull on one side. An *unbalanced* force has been added. The unbalanced force makes the rope begin to move—and, with it, the girls.

❶ An unbalanced force is what makes a rocket start to go, too.

Build the model on the next page. It will help you to see how a rocket engine works. MODEL

■

●

12

Introducing Lesson Cluster 2

Ask two children who weigh approximately the same and who seem about equally powerful to stage a gentle tug-of-war. Use a rope or a belt, and have a child tug at either end.

What are (*child's name*) and (*child's name*) doing? (pulling on each other) What word can we use to describe a pull? (a force) Is (*child's name*) or (*child's name*) using greater force? (Their forces are about equally balanced.) Now add another child to one side of the tug-of-war. Are the forces pulling on the rope still balanced? (no) What effect did this unbalanced force have on the rope? (It produced a greater force at one end, causing the child at the other to be pulled across the room.)

Developing the lesson

❶ What could an unbalanced force have to do with launching a rocket? (Children may speculate that the force of gravitation, that is, the weight of the rocket, keeps it down on Earth. An unbalanced force would be needed—unbalanced because it must be greater than the gravitational pull of the Earth on the rocket—if the rocket is to leave its pad.)

Supporting Statement: For every action there is an equal and opposite reaction.

MAKING A MODEL
A Dry Ice Jet Engine

Needed: an empty half pint carton, a length of string or thread, a toothpick, adhesive tape, ❶ Dry Ice, tongs, water, a paperclip, gloves

With the paperclip wire, make 2 small holes in the center of the carton top. Push the toothpick through the holes. Tie one end of the thread around the toothpick as shown. ■

Make a small hole with the paperclip near the left edge of the carton about 1½ inches from the bottom, as shown. Do the same near the left edge on the opposite side. Pour water into the carton to a depth of about an inch.

Wearing gloves, use the tongs to put two or three pieces of Dry Ice into the carton. ●

Caution: Do not hold Dry Ice with your fingers! It can cause painful blisters. Use ❷ adhesive tape to close the cap tightly. Suspend the carton so that it can turn on the thread. What does the carton do? Here is what happened in one trial. ▲ Why does the carton look blurred?

Dry Ice is solid carbon dioxide. The water in the carton gives enough heat to the solid to change it to carbon dioxide gas. Can you explain what the carton does as the gas escapes through the ❸ holes?

Methods of Intelligence: Predicting

What will happen if two more holes are made ❹ in the carton sides? There are several possible answers. For example: (1) The carton may move faster. (2) The carton may move more slowly. (3) The carton may not move at all.

What do you **predict**? Test your prediction.

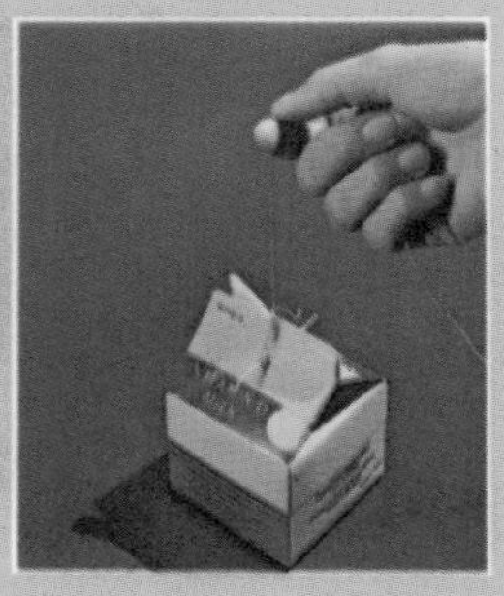
■

●

▲

13

Performance objectives. Children *construct* a model of a Dry Ice rocket engine, using a milk carton, thread, toothpick, modeling clay, water, and Dry Ice. They *demonstrate* how the engine works, causing it to revolve as Dry Ice comes in contact with water, producing carbon dioxide, which escapes through a hole in one direction, causing the carton to revolve in the other direction. They *describe* the above action as an example of Newton's Law of Action and Reaction.

Alternate procedure and materials: If Dry Ice is not available, a metal spice box may be substituted for the carton. Fill the box one quarter full of water and heat over a flame until water vapor escapes. Turn off the heat as soon as the jet action begins; it will continue to operate for a while.

Useful materials: Some similar materials are available in CLASSROOM LABORATORY: PURPLE.

❶ Dry Ice may be purchased at some food and ice-cream stores. If it is difficult to obtain, check with a refrigeration supply company in the Yellow Pages. It is advisable for you and the children to wear gloves when working with Dry Ice, as well as to use tongs or tweezers. The temperature of Dry Ice (−110°F) is so low that it can harm the skin. (See alternate procedure.)

❷ You may use clay instead of tape to seal the top of the carton, as shown in the picture. Children can make a stand by piling two equal-sized stacks of books on a desk top about a foot and a half apart. Place a yardstick or any long stick across the tops of the books and hang the carton from the center of this stick.

❸ A cloud of vapor pours from the holes. There must be a force to make the carton spin.

❹ What will happen depends on where the two new holes are made. If they are made on the sides that already have a hole but near the opposite corners, the carton will not spin around, though it may jiggle. If the new holes are made near those already made and on the same side, the carton may spin faster, or slower, depending on how vigorously the Dry Ice is fizzing. If the two new holes are made around the corners from the original holes, the carton will stop spinning and will jiggle. If the two new holes are made in the sides without holes, but near the opposite corners, the carton will spin faster.

UNIT ONE

Unit Concept-Statement: Energy must be applied to produce an unbalanced force, which results in a change in motion.

■

You Push It, It Pushes You

Observe the model rocket engine carefully. You will see that a jet of gas comes out of a hole in one direction. The carton moves in the opposite direction.

Remember that the jet of air from our balloon came out in one direction. But the balloon went off in the opposite ❶ direction. As hot gases squirt one way from the tail of a rocket, the rocket goes the opposite way.

Let's look at another example. Here is a photograph of an investigation. ■ The boy is on roller skates and is holding a heavy ball. He is going to throw the ball away. Predict what will happen to the ball and to the boy. Was your prediction correct? ● The ball goes away in one direction. The boy rolls away in the opposite direction. ❷ *As the boy pushes the ball away, the ball pushes the boy away.*

●

14

Continuing Lesson Cluster 2

❶ There are many examples in nature of a gas or liquid being shot out in one direction resulting in something else moving in the opposite direction. Do you know a kind of sea creature that, by squirting water in one way is able to move the other way? (squid, octopus)

❷ Encourage children to describe any experiences they have had of throwing a ball while on skates or in a wheeled toy such as a wagon. Why can it be dangerous to step ashore from a rowboat that has not been tied up? (action: stepping ashore; reaction: boat bobs away, possibly with one foot still on it, so that you might fall into the water)

Supporting Statement: For every action there is an equal and opposite reaction.

As our Dry Ice engine pushes gas away, the gas pushes the carton away.

❶ Almost 300 years ago, Isaac Newton stated the reason behind these events, although he never saw a giant rocket or a boy on roller skates throwing a ball. Newton stated that every **action** has an equal and opposite **reaction**. This is called the Law of Action and Reaction.

Let's apply this law. For example, the boy on roller skates throws the ball away in one direction. This is the ❷ *action.* The ball pushes the boy away in the opposite direction. This is the *reaction.* For each action there is an equal and opposite reaction.

Here is another example. A spinning lawn sprinkler throws a stream of water in one direction. This is the action. The sprinkler spins in the opposite direction. This is the reaction. The action gives rise to an equal and opposite reaction. As the sprinkler pushes the water away, the water pushes the sprinkler away.

Action: A rocket forces hot gases away in one direction.

❸ Reaction: The hot gases force the rocket to move away in the opposite direction. ▲ The action of the rush of hot gases makes an unbalanced force that is greater than the weight of the rocket. The unbalanced force makes the rocket move up—against the force of gravitation. Through action and reaction astronauts get off the Earth.

▲

❹ **BEFORE YOU GO ON**

Check your understanding of the concepts of this section. Which ending would you choose for each statement below?

1. To start something moving, you must

a. use a rope b. exert a force

2. The thrust that sends a rocket into space is

a. an unbalanced force

b. a balanced force

3. Every action has an equal reaction in the

a. same direction

b. opposite direction

15

❶ Children may be interested to know that Isaac Newton himself, who formulated the theory of gravitation, was at one time very much interested in a kind of horseless carriage, which moved by shooting hot steam from a big container through a small nozzle. How was this like your balloon investigation on page 3?

❷ What are some other examples of action and reaction from man's technology? (the kick of a gun when it shoots a bullet, or the recoil of a cannon firing a shell; a stationary hockey player sliding back on the ice when he shoots the puck hard) Why isn't a football player pushed back when he throws a long, hard forward pass? (The friction of his shoes against the ground is a force that balances the force of reaction from the action of throwing.)

❸ Modern physicists do not distinguish between action and reaction as forces, but say that if one force is considered the action, the opposing force is the reaction. Thus they may be considered interchangeable. However, for the purposes of study at this level, it it best to follow the convention developed in the textbook.

VERIFYING PROGRESS

❹ **Before you go on.** Children *demonstrate* understanding of unbalanced forces, action and reaction, by *analyzing* open-ended statements.

1. b 2. a 3. b

❶ **4.** In space, an astronaut sends a jet of gas to his right. He will move to

a. his right b. his left

5. The statement that fits the main concept of this section is

a. Action and reaction are always equal.

b. Action and reaction are always unbalanced.

❷ **USING WHAT YOU KNOW**

1. Scientists are planning a rocket's trip to the Moon. They estimate that the rocket will have to produce 9 million pounds of thrust to get its mass into a certain orbit. How much thrust would be needed to get the same mass off the Moon?

2. In 1865 Jules Verne wrote *From the Earth to the Moon*, one of the first science-fiction stories. Look for it in the library. Here is an artist's idea of Verne's Moon ship. What fuel was used to launch it? Could that fuel actually send a spacecraft to the Moon?

A LOOK AHEAD

Clearly some action is needed to move a spacecraft off the Earth. Some force that acts against the Earth's pull of gravitation must be made to work for there to be a liftoff. Why does the spacecraft go the way it does? Instead of landing on the Moon, why doesn't it go on, and on, and on?

16

VERIFYING PROGRESS (cont.)

❶ 4. b 5. a

❷ **Using what you know.** Children *analyze* two hypothetical problems in launching Moon rockets. In one instance they *compute* the thrust needed to get a rocket off the Moon, and in the other they *infer* that the rocket in a science-fiction story could not have reached the Moon.

1. A thrust equal to one-sixth of the weight of the rocket on Earth will be necessary to get the rocket off the Moon. Since the rocket weighs 9 million pounds on Earth, you will need a thrust of 1½ million pounds to get it off the Moon.

2. Verne's "rocket" was really just an engineless shell shot out of a big gun. The explosive used to fire the shell out of its huge gun was nitrocellulose, which, of course, could *not* have produced the force necessary to send the ship to the Moon.

Supporting Statement: Inertia of objects tends to make them either remain at rest or continue in motion in the same direction.

3. Man in Orbit

A spacecraft, with men aboard, is about to be launched. The huge rocket, perched on its launching pad, weighs 150 tons. The Earth's gravitational force holds it to the ground. Its fuel must give enough energy to move the rocket against that gravitational force and make the spacecraft reach a final ❶ speed of about 18,000 miles per hour. The blast of hot gases from the burning fuel is the action; the thrust is the reaction. The thrust is the force that pushes the rocket off its pad and gives it its final speed.

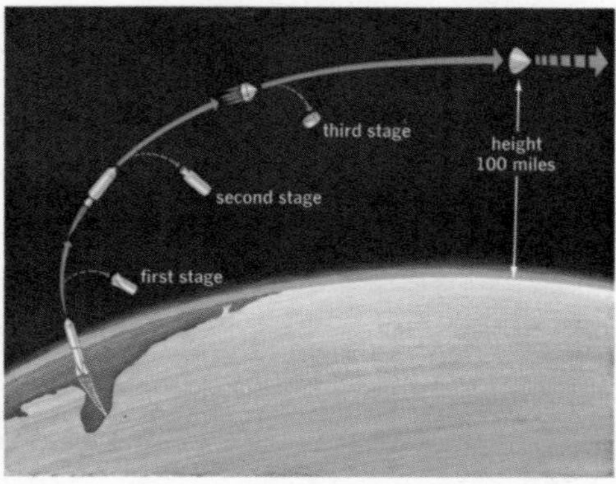

Path of a Spacecraft

At liftoff the rocket climbs into the sky with increasing speed. The rocket may be really three rockets, or stages, linked together. Each stage has its own rocket engines. As the fuel is used up in one stage, it drops away, and the engines of the next stage are fired. ● But the spacecraft itself does not stop. It keeps on going. When the last-stage rocket engines drop away, the spacecraft keeps on moving.

17

LESSON CLUSTER 3
MAN IN ORBIT

Teaching background. 3 T-3.

Concept-seeking. Children become more aware of the laws of motion and of how an unbalanced force acts against inertia of rest or motion.

Operations. Children *probe* into examples of objects at rest and objects in motion.

Methods of intelligence. Children *identify* kinds of motion and *seek evidence* of interrelationships between these motions and gravitation.

Introducing Lesson Cluster 3

Ask children to recall the balloon rockets they sent off when the unit was introduced. If you wish, send one off again. How is a balloon rocket like a real rocket? (They both take off because of the Law of Action and Reaction. The air rushing out of the balloon is like hot gases rushing out of the rocket.)

Developing the lesson

❶ Why do you think a space rocket has three stages? (Each stage provides additional force or thrust when needed to increase speed.) What is the advantage of using three engines rather than one big engine? (When the fuel in each engine is used up, the engine can drop off. This reduces the mass of the rocket and lets the remaining fuel give the rocket greater speed.) Why is it important to keep the mass of a rocket as small as possible? (The greater the mass, the greater is the force of gravitation acting on the rocket. This means a rocket with a large mass will need more fuel than one with a small mass.)

Unit Concept-Statement: Energy must be applied to produce an unbalanced force, which results in a change in motion.

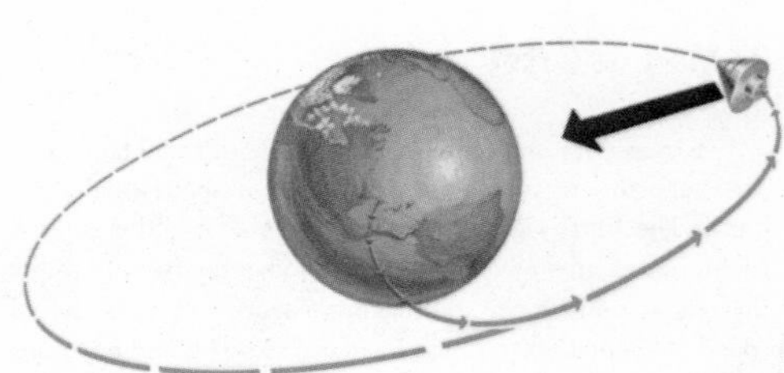

It takes a path that curves around the Earth. This curving ❶ path that a body takes in space around another body is called the **orbit**.

Inside the spacecraft the astronauts read their instruments. Below them on the Earth, the men in Ground Control read instruments, push buttons, and keep records. The spacecraft is on course and on time! It is following the planned orbit.

How is it possible to plan where a spacecraft will go?

Laws of Motion

As you read this, you are sitting down. You know from experience that if you remain at rest in your chair, you will ❷ stay there. To get you out of the chair, a force is necessary—one that you exert or that someone else applies to you. Things at rest tend to remain at rest. You know this from experience. In fact, men have known it for thousands of years.

Think now of an experience you might have in a moving ❸ car. The car stops suddenly. What happens to you? You keep on going, straight ahead, until brought to a sudden stop by a safety belt. In somewhat the same way, a bowling ball tends to keep going, until stopped at the end of the alley.

In other words, objects in motion tend to keep moving. This concept is not as easy to see at work as the concept that an object at rest tends to stay at rest. The great Italian scientist named Galileo (gal·ə·lē′ō) put the two ideas together.

18

Useful materials: Marbles, drinking glass, bowl.

Continuing Lesson Cluster 3

❶ Put a marble inside a large bowl. Let a child twirl the bowl slowly and evenly and observe how the marble inside moves into a great-circle orbit around the sides. How might you describe the motion of the marble around the center? (an orbit) How is this like a spacecraft whirling around the Earth? (also an orbit)

❷ What do you need to do to get out of your chairs? (stand up) What does it take to stand up? If children answer "legs," ask the following question. How do your legs make you stand up? (Children should begin to see that they use energy to stand up.) What does this energy do? (provides a *force*) If children say a force makes them stand, relate force and energy so that children clearly see that energy provides a force and that this force is applied to make things move.

❸ Put a marble in a drinking glass and lay the glass on its side on a table. Rapidly slide the glass mouth forward along the table for 20 inches or so. Then stop it very suddenly. What did the glass do? (stopped suddenly) What did the marble do? (kept on going fast, in a straight line) Where was the marble while the glass was moving fast? (pressed against the bottom of the glass) Why wasn't it in the middle of the glass? (When the glass was set in motion, it was moving faster than the marble. The marble moved to the end of the glass and then moved at the same speed as the glass.) What does this show? (An object, the marble, remains in motion unless something stops it.)

Supporting Statement: Inertia of objects tends to make them either remain at rest or continue in motion in the same direction.

Galileo said an object tends to remain at rest because of ❶ its **inertia** (in·ûr′shə). Once an object begins to move, it tends to remain in motion because of its inertia. Inertia, then, is a word that refers to the fact that objects tend to resist change.

Newton summed up how things behave, at rest or in motion, in one of his Laws of Motion: *An object at rest remains at rest, and an object in motion continues in motion in a straight line, unless acted on by an unbalanced force.*

This law is called the Law of Inertia. It merely means that an object tends to remain at rest or continue in motion because it has inertia.

As you can see, there are at least three parts to the Law of Inertia.

❷ First: An object at rest remains at rest. (A marble on the ground remains at rest on the ground. ●)

Second: Once in motion, an object in motion remains in motion, but in a straight line. (A moving marble keeps moving. ▲)

Third: The object continues to move in a straight line, unless acted on by an unbalanced force. (A marble in motion remains in motion until acted on by an unbalanced force—such as that applied by a boy's hand. ◆)

●

▲

◆

❶ Since *inertia* refers to objects both at rest and in motion, the term may offer difficulty. Can a rock move by itself? (no) We say that the rock has inertia. Can a sled coasting down a hill stop by itself? (no) What is needed to make the rock move and the sled stop? (a force) Explain that scientists say that anything that cannot move *by itself* or stop *by itself* has inertia. Which required the application of force: stopping the glass with the marble in it or letting the marble go on? (stopping the glass) Which then has inertia of motion, the glass or the marble? (the marble)

❷ Give the children marbles to investigate inertia. To demonstrate inertia of rest, a child should place a marble on a flat surface and observe that it rests there. Then have him put it on a sheet of paper and try to jerk away the paper without moving the marble. What kind of inertia is this? (inertia of rest)

To demonstrate inertia of motion, the child should push the marble and let it roll without stopping it. To demonstrate the action of an unbalanced force, he should push the marble but stop it with his hand before it stops rolling.

Children will probably point out that, in the second demonstration, the marble does not keep rolling and may swerve from a straight line.

Why does the marble stop or change its direction? (Children may observe that some object stopped it, or that rubbing of the rough floor changed its direction or slowed it down.) What kind of force caused these things to happen? (unbalanced force)

Unit Concept-Statement: Energy must be applied to produce an unbalanced force, which results in a change in motion.

A rocket at rest on its launching pad remains at rest
❶ because of its inertia. It remains at rest until an unbalanced force moves it. This force comes from the motion of the hot gases which squirt from the rocket's tail.

Out in space where there is no atmosphere, there is no drag of **friction.** Even with its engine stopped, the spacecraft in motion will continue in motion because of its inertia. Out in space, the spacecraft in motion should continue in motion, on and on and on. According to Newton's Law of Inertia, it should go in a straight line—unless it is acted on by an unbalanced force.

As you know, however, an orbiting spacecraft curves
❷ around the Earth. That is, it does not go in a straight line. Then, according to Newton's Law of Inertia, there must be an unbalanced force acting on that spacecraft. What force in space might pull a spacecraft from a straight path so that it circles around the Earth? What force holds a spacecraft in orbit? One of Newton's great discoveries gives us an explanation.

Gravitation Everywhere

An apple always falls to Earth. It doesn't fly off into space. The Moon, too, stays in its orbit. Why doesn't the Moon fly off into space? Isaac Newton asked himself this question.

Newton knew that objects close to Earth, such as a falling apple, were pulled by the Earth's force of gravitation. Then he had a tremendous idea! Perhaps, he thought, the force of gravitation reaches out beyond the Earth. Perhaps this force reaches out into space.

❸ There is a pull of gravitation between the Earth and an apple. Perhaps, Newton thought, there is a gravitational pull between the Earth and the Moon—and between the Sun and the Earth. ■ Perhaps there is a gravitational pull between the Sun and every planet. Perhaps every body in the Universe exerts a gravitational pull.

20

EXTENDING THE LESSON

Let children *analyze* these questions, *apply* the Laws of Inertia and Gravitation, and *state the laws* for each situation.

1. What shows that the Earth's gravitational pull on an orbiting spacecraft is an unbalanced force? (The spacecraft does not travel in a straight line.) What suggests that gravitation and the inertia of the spacecraft are in balance? (The orbit stays the same.)

If the craft comes a mile closer to the Earth on each orbit, what does this indicate? (Gravitation is the greater force and is an unbalanced force.)

2. The Moon orbits the Earth. What holds the Moon in orbit? (Earth's gravitation) Do you think the Moon's gravitation pulls on the Earth? Suggest that children look up the cause of tides to find a response. The Earth goes around the Sun. Why is this so? (The Sun has gravitation that pulls the Earth into orbit.)

Continuing Lesson Cluster 3

❶ This is a good time to review children's understanding of inertia and unbalanced forces. Why does the rocket remain at rest? (gravitation) How large must an unbalanced force be to start the rocket moving? (more than the pull of gravity, more than the rocket's weight) Recall the stopping of the marble by the floor. What force was this? (friction) Why is there no friction in space? (no matter, no air)

❷ Draw a circle on the board and label it "Earth." Ask a child to draw a path a spacecraft would take if it followed Newton's Law of Inertia of moving objects. The child should draw a straight line from the Earth as far as there is space on the board. Why did you draw a straight line? (An object in motion moves this way unless an unbalanced force acts on it.)

Now ask another child to draw the path of a spacecraft that goes into orbit. The child should draw a line outward from the Earth, and then curving around the Earth in a rough circle. What unbalanced force changes the direction of a spacecraft so that it circles the Earth? Let children hypothesize before going on.

❸ If a spacecraft could escape Earth's gravitation, would it travel in a straight line? (no) Why not? (It will come close enough to another body in space—Moon, Sun, another planet—to be pulled upon by its gravitation.)

Supporting Statement: Inertia of objects tends to make them remain at rest or continue in motion in the same direction.

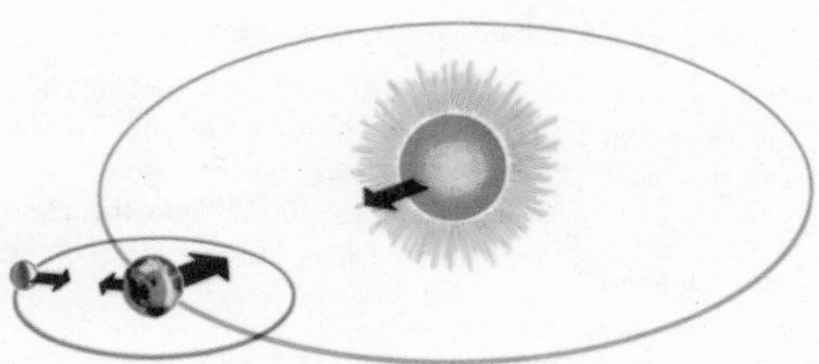

Perhaps, or so Newton thought, the force of gravitation holds the Universe together!

Newton showed, by mathematics, that the Moon, Sun, and planets do behave as if gravitation is pulling them. He showed that the Moon follows an orbit around the Earth. His explanation was: There is a force between the Earth and the Moon, the force of gravitation. Each planet curves around the Sun in an orbit, he said. This orbit is shaped by the pull of gravitation between that planet and the Sun. Newton believed that gravitation is everywhere—that is, it is universal.

Scientists call Newton's idea that gravitation reaches throughout the Universe the Law of Universal Gravitation. We can state it this way for the time being:

❶ *All bodies in space pull on one another with a force called gravitation.* This force of gravitation acts to keep orbiting bodies in their orbits.

What holds a spacecraft in an orbit around the Earth? Gravitation is the unbalanced force that pulls the spacecraft from a straight path, and makes it curve around the Earth. Newton's 300-year-old Law of Universal Gravitation helps us today to predict accurately the orbit of a spacecraft. It helps us to know where a spacecraft or a rocket will be at any moment.

❷ "No great discovery is ever made without a bold guess," Newton once said. Newton's bold guess about universal gravitation showed us how to find paths in space.

21

EXTENDING THE LESSON

Children interested in the life of Galileo should read in library references and report to the class. They will find that in many ways Galileo had a more eventful life than Newton. Ask them to be sure to find out what Galileo discovered in a church as a very young man. (He discovered that the period of a pendulum—the time for one complete round trip—has nothing to do with either the weight of its bob or the length of its swings.) Why was Galileo almost burned for heresy when he was an old man? How did he escape?

❶ What is meant here by a "body"? (anything made of matter, large or small) Have the children study the diagram. What do you think the arrows mean? (Sun and Earth pull on each other.) Which is larger, Earth or Moon? (Earth) Which do you think has the stronger pull? (Earth) Which has more gravitation, Sun or Earth? (Sun) Does the Law of Universal Gravitation mean that two bodies, no matter how small they may be or how far apart, are pulling on one another? (yes) What effect would the gravitation of a star billions of miles away have on our Earth? (Almost none, but the star does pull on the Earth and the Earth on the star. It is so far away, however, that the pull is too slight to be measurable in any ordinary way.)

❷ Newton said he had succeeded because he had stood on the shoulders of giants. What other great scientist's ideas helped Newton develop his Laws of Inertia and Gravitation? (Galileo's)

Unit Concept-Statement: Energy must be applied to produce an unbalanced force, which results in a change in motion.

EXTENDING THE LESSON

Children *identify* the differences between inertia of rest and inertia of motion in the following activity.

Have them copy the four following responses, with their code letters:

A. Inertia of rest

B. Inertia of rest—acted upon by an unbalanced force

C. Inertia of motion

D. Inertia of motion—acted upon by an unbalanced force.

Then write on the board these incidents in the careers of imaginary spacecraft. For each incident the children identify the appropriate condition by writing the code letter.

1. A spacecraft, its engines silent, is headed straight for its target on Mars. (C)
2. A spacecraft blasts off from the Moon. (B)
3. A Venus probe has landed on the surface of that planet and is taking photographs. (A)
4. A large chunk of matter deflects a probe from its course toward Mercury. (D)

---

❶ BEFORE YOU GO ON

Check your understanding of the concepts of this section. Which ending would you choose for each statement below?

1. The path of a body in space around another body is its
   a. reaction b. orbit

2. Inertia means that a body at rest
   a. tends to remain at rest
   b. moves without any outside force

3. Inertia means a body in motion
   a. will stop without any outside force
   b. tends to remain in motion

4. The statement that fits the main concept of this section is
   a. An object in motion in a straight line continues in motion in the same straight line, unless acted on by an unbalanced force.
   b. An object in motion in a straight line continues in motion in the same straight line, unless acted on by a balanced force.

❷ USING WHAT YOU KNOW

Place a card on top of a drinking glass. Place a coin on top of the card. If you remove the card quickly enough, you can make the coin fall into the glass, without touching the coin. Try it. How does this trick work?

❸ INVESTIGATING FURTHER

You know that the greater the mass of a body, the greater is the force of gravitation it exerts (at the same distance) on an object. The Sun has a greater force of gravitation than the Earth, because the Sun has a greater mass.

Why isn't a spacecraft pulled out of its orbit around the Earth and into the Sun? Here are a few facts: A spacecraft is 150 miles from the Earth. The Earth is about 93 million miles from the Sun. How far is the spacecraft from the Sun? What else must be important, besides ❹ the masses of the bodies? On the basis of your answer, predict whether a spacecraft could ever be pulled into the ❺ Sun or into orbit around the Sun.

A LOOK AHEAD

Man has learned how to hurl a spacecraft out into space and to bring it back again. The facts of putting a spacecraft into orbit are familiar now.

There are other familiar facts which you also need to understand, such as how *you* are in orbit—now. Right now you whirl about the Sun together with 3 billion other people. How did the Earth come to be in orbit around the Sun? That is the probe of the next section.

22

VERIFYING PROGRESS

❶ Before you go on. Children *demonstrate* understanding of gravitation and the Laws of Motion by selecting suitable responses to questions.

1. b 3. b
2. a 4. a

❷ Using what you know. Children *investigate* the inertia of a coin on a card, and *explain* their observations.

If a child flicks the card away with his fingers, the coin will fall into the glass. This happens because he pulls the card fast enough to make the friction between it and the coin less than the inertia of the coin. If he pulls the card slowly, the friction between it and the coin remains greater than the inertia of the coin, and the coin rides with the card.

❸ Investigating further. Children *analyze* the effect of various factors that determine the paths of spacecraft and *predict* the likelihood of a spacecraft's going into orbit around the Sun.

❹ How far apart the bodies are is important. The greater the distance between them, the less the pull of gravitation they exert on each other.

❺ The entry of a spacecraft into orbit around the Sun is the way some space probes end. The first spacecraft to enter solar orbit was the Russian Luna I, in January, 1959. It is still there, a small artificial planet between the orbits of Mars and Earth.

Supporting Statement: The Laws of Inertia and Universal Gravitation explain the orbits of bodies in space.

4. Earth and Moon in Orbit

You, too, are in orbit. Right now you are on a space station. It is in orbit around the Sun. It is moving at a ❶ speed of $18\frac{1}{2}$ miles a second along its orbit, and is spinning as it goes. Your station in space is planet Earth.

Space Station Earth

Your space station is well equipped for a trip through space. It has food and water, air, heat, and many other things that you need. You have plenty of company, too. There are about 3 billion people on this space station.

Scientists can predict the position of any spacecraft ❷ they have put into orbit. There are now many of these **satellites**, man-made moons that are in orbit around the Earth.■ They are laboratories that send information to us.

We know, too, what the path of space station Earth is. We can predict where the Earth will be at any time. We are about 93 million miles away from the Sun, in our orbit

■

23

LESSON CLUSTER 4
EARTH AND MOON IN ORBIT

Teaching background 4 T-4

Concept-seeking. Children seek to understand what determines the orbits of bodies in space.

Operations. Children *investigate* the shape of the orbits of the Earth and the Moon.

Methods of intelligence. Children *construct* an ellipse, *make a model* of a planetarium, and *hypothesize* from the model on the nature of the solar system.

Introducing Lesson Cluster 4

See that your children are all sitting still in their seats. Are you moving? Start a discussion on whether or not they are. Some children will realize that because the Earth is moving, they are, in a sense, moving too.

Developing the lesson

❶ Children may enjoy finding out how many miles per hour the average speed of Earth around its orbit is. To do this, have them multiply $18\frac{1}{2}$ by 60 for the average number of miles per minute (1,110) and then multiply this by 60 to get the speed in miles per hour (66,600).

❷ How many satellites do you think are orbiting the Earth right now? Children's responses may vary widely, depending on how aware they are of news reports of launchings. In recent years, an average of a hundred or more satellites and spacecraft have been launched each year by several different countries. Among the Earth-orbiting satellite series that children may have heard about are those for communications purposes, such as Intelsats; those for conducting experiments, such as OGO (Orbiting Geophysical Observatory), Explorer, and Cosmos (Russian); and those for weather-watching, such as Nimbus and ESSA. The satellite illustrated is one of those known as ESSA (Environmental Science Services Administration).

Unit Concept-Statement: Energy must be applied to produce an unbalanced force, which results in a change in motion.

around it. In spite of the Earth's tremendous speed, it takes us 365¼ days to make one **revolution** around the Sun.

Our space station is revolving around the Sun. At the same time, it is rotating or spinning like a top as well. The
❶ Earth makes a complete **rotation** in about 24 hours.

One revolution of the Earth around the Sun takes one year. One rotation takes one day. You may know that the revolution of the Earth around the Sun is one reason we have seasons. On the other hand the Earth's rotation
❷ results in day and night.

The Earth is in orbit around the Sun. The other planets in our solar system are also in orbit around the Sun. This is a map of the solar system, but there is not room
❸ enough on the page to make the map to scale. The information in this table will help you see why. ■

You can see that the solar system has a flat shape, like a plate. What explanation can there be for this? The flat shape of the solar system suggests a **theory** (thē′ərē) to **scientists.** A theory is one explanation of the facts discovered by investigation. The theory that may explain
❹ why the solar system has a flat shape is that the Sun and all the planets came from one huge cloud of gas.

A Cloud of Gas

Long ago, this theory goes, a huge cloud of gas whirled slowly in space, among other clouds of gas and stars. Slowly, some scientists think, the cloud of gas began to get smaller—

■ APPROXIMATE DIAMETERS OF BODIES IN SOLAR SYSTEM

Sun	864,000 miles	Jupiter	86,000 miles
Mercury	3,020 miles	Saturn	70,000 miles
Venus	7,600 miles	Uranus	30,000 miles
Earth	7,918 miles	Neptune	28,000 miles
Mars	4,180 miles	Pluto	8,000 miles

24

Useful materials: Classroom globe, lamp, tiny figure, tape.

Continuing Lesson Cluster 4

❶ Have the children demonstrate rotation and revolution with a classroom globe and a lamp with an uncovered light bulb.

What does a body in space do when it *revolves?* (It travels in a roughly circular path around a much larger body.) What does a body in space do when it *rotates?* (It turns around on its own axis, without going anywhere in space.) What is the axis of a rotating body? (an imaginary line from one pole through the center of the body to the other pole around which the rotating body spins) All bodies in space rotate, except perhaps the heads of some comets, about which little is known. What is the basic difference between rotating and revolving? (A body rotates around itself; it revolves around something else.)

❷ Have the children use a lamp and a classroom globe, with a tiny figure taped to it at the approximate spot for your city. As they rotate the globe counterclockwise, they can demonstrate sunrise and sunset.

Is it correct to say the Sun rises? (no) What really happens? (As the Earth rotates from west to east, the Sun seems to move from east to west.)

❸ Ask children to study the diagram of the solar system on the opposite page. Note that the table lists the planets in order of distance from the Sun, and may be used by children to refresh their memory of the planets' names and positions.

Supporting Statement: The Laws of Inertia and Universal Gravitation explain the orbits of bodies in space.

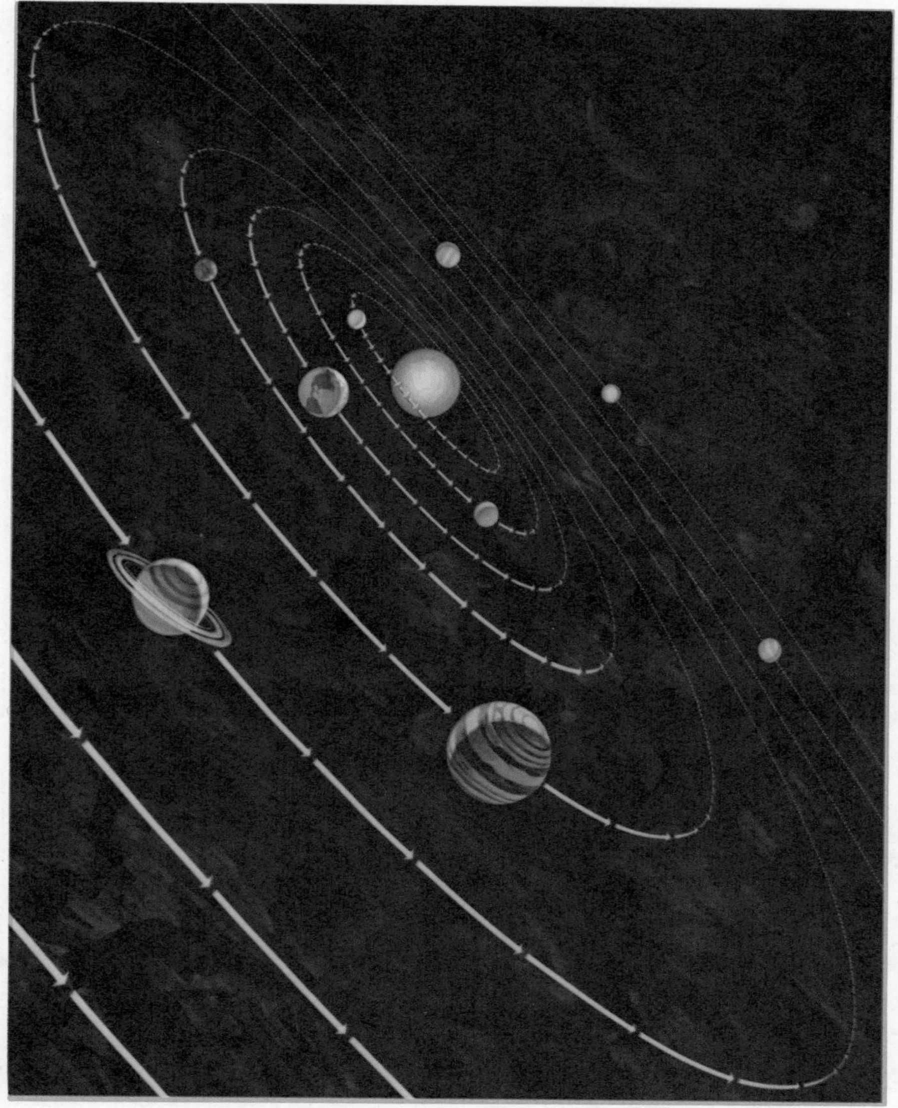

EXTENDING THE LESSON

1. Children may be interested to know about the Latin gods that the planets are named after. Have them look up the names of the planets in a dictionary of mythology.

If there is a planetarium near your school, try to arrange a visit for your class. Some planetariums have special shows for children as well as exhibits.

2. Which is the biggest planet? (Jupiter) Which is the smallest? (Mercury) Which is the warmest? (Mercury) Why? (It is closest to the Sun.) Which planet is the coldest? (Pluto) Why? (It is farthest from the Sun) Which two planets have orbits that are closest to Earth? (Venus inside our orbit; Mars outside)

Have children note that the orbit of Pluto seems to cross the orbit of Neptune. Explain that Pluto's orbit is longer and narrower than that of Neptune, and is actually nearer the Sun than Neptune about once every 140 years.

Why isn't it possible to draw the diagram to scale? For example, if the Sun were scaled at 1 inch in diameter, could you see Mercury on the diagram? Why not? (It would be a pinpoint—about $\frac{3}{100}$ inch in diameter.) If Mercury were drawn large enough to see, what would happen to the scale of the Sun? (It would be too large for the page.) Children may use data in the table to work out examples such as this one: If Mercury were drawn $\frac{1}{32}''$ across, the Sun would have to be $864 \div 3 \times \frac{1}{32}''$ across, which is about 9″ across.

❹ What makes the solar system have a flat appearance? (The planets all circle the Sun as if they were on a flat surface.) A flat surface like this is called a *plane*. If the planets all moved in different planes, what shape would the solar system have? (a three-dimensional shape, more like an oval ball)

Unit Concept-Statement: Energy must be applied to produce an unbalanced force, which results in a change in motion.

EXTENDING THE LESSON

The origin of the Universe has been a source of inspiration to artists, poets, and musicians. Give children a chance to express their talents in painting and poetry—ask them to depict their idea of the origin of the solar system. Or they may illustrate the theory of the text, using their favorite media. Then you can bring in some appropriate music (such as Gustav Holst's "The Planets") to play on a record player when the children describe and show their sequence.

and to spin faster. Some scientists imagine that the cloud
❶ may have looked like this. ■

As this cloud shrank, masses of the cloud began to come together. ● These masses were pulled toward one another by gravitational force. Over thousands and thousands of years the cloud shrank and formed the first planets. ▲ We call them **protoplanets** (prō′tə·plan′its). *Proto* means "first."

The protoplanets whirled around the mass of gas in the center. That mass of gas at the center later became the
❷ Sun. ◆ Each protoplanet got still smaller, and its heavier substances moved toward its center.

■

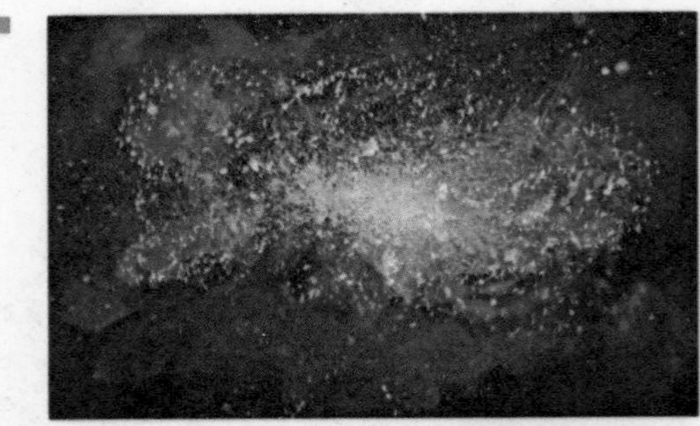

●

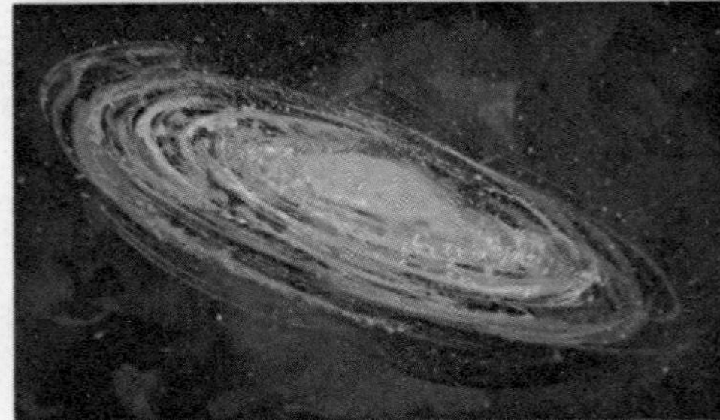

26

Continuing Lesson Cluster 4

❶ Call attention to drawings ■ and ●. What shape did the cloud turn into as a result of its spinning motion? (the flat shape of a disk) How does the cloud-of-gas theory account for the flat shape of the solar system? Children should be able to infer that the flat shape of the solar system could support the theory that it originally was a "cloud" of spinning gases.

❷ What else could we call the Sun? (a star) Point out that scientists think there may be countless other planetary systems in space revolving about other stars.

Supporting Statement: The Laws of Inertia and Universal Gravitation explain the orbits of bodies in space.

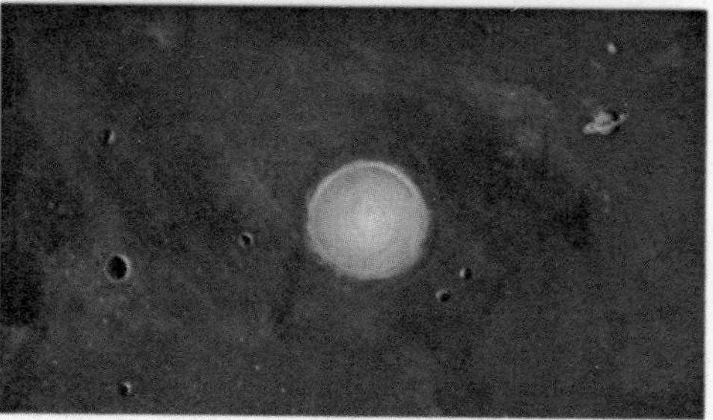

One of these protoplanets became the Earth. The Earth has a core of heavy material which scientists think is melted iron and nickel. The Earth has a lighter crust and a still lighter atmosphere. It is in orbit around the Sun because both the Earth and the Sun were formed out of the
1 same huge whirling cloud of hot gas. This is only one theory.

The amount of energy we get from the Sun is just right
2 because we are just the right distance away. If we were too close to the Sun, we'd burn to a crisp. If we were too far away, it would be too cold, and life as we know it would not be possible.

Ninety-three million miles away from the Sun, we get the right amount of energy. Our station in space is in a very satisfactory orbit! Let us see what kind of orbit it is.

27

VERIFYING PROGRESS

In methods of intelligence

Children may *design* an *investigation* to evaluate their progress in *constructing, demonstrating,* and *comparing.* The ratio of the diameters of the Earth and Sun is about the same as that of $\frac{1}{2}$ inch to $4\frac{1}{2}$ feet. Have children *construct* a circle that has a radius of $\frac{1}{2}$ inch. Then have them mark off $4\frac{1}{2}$ feet on a piece of string. Using the $\frac{1}{2}''$ circle and the $4\frac{1}{2}'$ string, children may *demonstrate* the ratio of the Earth's diameter to that of the Sun. The playground is a good place to do this. One sample plan might be to mark a circle with a $4\frac{1}{2}$ foot diameter around the $\frac{1}{2}$ inch circle. A *comparison* may be made by asking: **How many children can stand inside the "Earth" circle? the "Sun" circle?** Let children design other *comparisons.*

Useful materials: Compasses, rulers, string, yardstick.

1 For other theories of the origin of the solar system, see page T-4. Perhaps you have noticed how batter in a bowl is thrown out toward the edge when it is stirred by an egg beater. **How does this suggest another way in which planets might have formed?** (The planets might have been part of the Sun and somehow split off from it.)

Some children may want to look up the "capture" theory, by which a body may be moving through space and happen to come close enough to a larger body to get pulled into orbit by its gravitational attraction. Ask children if they have read of any man-made satellites that demonstrate the "capture" theory. Some satellites that fly by Mars or other planets go into orbit around the Sun at the conclusion of their missions.

2 "Just right" means just right for living things. Children may be interested to know that the extremes (in nature) of temperature on Earth are +132°F (at Wadi Halfa in the Sudan) and −72°F average mean temperature for Vostok, Antarctica). The extremes of hot and cold that living things on Earth can stand (experimentally produced) are: from −80°F for some plants and some seeds to −310°F; low and high for human beings, for short periods and suitably clothed: −40°F and 120°F.

Unit Concept-Statement: Energy must be applied to produce an unbalanced force, which results in a change in motion.

EXTENDING THE LESSON

Children *analyze* their knowledge of the solar system, *theorize* about what might have happened as the hot gases cooled and condensed, and *infer* that differences in the structure and temperature of the Sun and planets account for present conditions.

Is there any other member of the solar system in gaseous form besides the Sun? (no) Why did the planets cool to the solid stage, whereas the Sun is still gaseous? (The Sun is enormously bigger than any planet, and thus would take billions of years longer to cool to the solid state.)

Useful materials: String with small object tied to end.

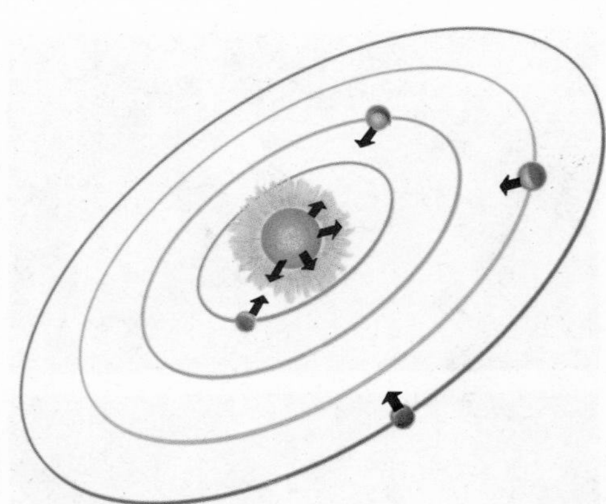

The Earth's Orbit

Of all the bodies in our solar system, the Sun has the largest mass. Therefore it exerts the greatest gravitational pull. Why, then, isn't Mercury, the planet nearest the Sun, pulled into the Sun? Why isn't the Earth pulled into the
❶ Sun? Why aren't the other planets pulled into the Sun?

As the protoplanets formed, they got energy from the great whirling cloud of gas, some scientists think. When the planets formed, they went on whirling around the shrinking gas cloud that became the Sun. The planets were in motion and they continued in motion, but *not* in a straight line. They moved in curved paths around the Sun. Why? The force of gravitation was the unbalanced force that held them in orbit around the Sun.■

Two laws of motion help explain the orbit of a planet. The Law of Inertia helps explain why a planet remains in motion. The Law of Universal Gravitation helps explain why a planet is in orbit around the Sun.

Have you wondered what the shape of the Earth's orbit
❷ is like? If it were a circle, the distance from the Earth to

28

Continuing Lesson Cluster 4

❶ Children can get some idea of the two laws, that keep the planets going around the Sun, by a simple demonstration. Have them tie a ball or a small weight securely to a length of string. Take them to the school yard or gymnasium and have them whirl the ball or object over their heads in a circle. (Be sure they stand far apart, or have only one or two children do this at a time.) What is exerting the force holding the ball in a circle? (the child) What does he represent in the solar system? (the Sun) What does the object at the end of the string represent? (the Earth or another planet) Why does the ball keep moving in a circle? (It has inertia of motion, but is acted on by the child's pull.) How is this a model of the motion of the Earth around the Sun? (Each has gravitation; the Sun has the greater force and therefore pulls the Earth into orbit.) What would happen if the child let go of the string? (The ball would fly off in a straight line.)

❷ Before going on, have the children consider the question of the Earth's orbit. What shape is it? Is it a circle or does it have some other shape? If it is not a circle, what would happen to the distance of the Earth from the Sun? Do not correct responses, but record any interesting variations.

Supporting Statement: The Laws of Inertia and Universal Gravitation explain the orbits of bodies in space.

the Sun would not change. Let's look at some information about the Earth's orbit:

❶ *Time of Year*	*Approximate Distance from Earth to Sun*
March	93 million miles
June	94 million miles
September	93 million miles
December	92 million miles

Does this information show us that the Earth's orbit is a circle? It does not, for the distance of the Earth from the Sun changes. Actually, the shape of the orbit is a slightly flattened circle called an **ellipse** (i·lips′). ● In fact, the orbit of every planet in our solar system is an ellipse. ❷ The orbit of a spacecraft around the Earth is an ellipse. ▲

The ellipse, then, is an important shape—especially for astronauts, space engineers, and astronomers. You can find out some interesting things about an ellipse by doing the investigation on the next page. INVESTIGATE

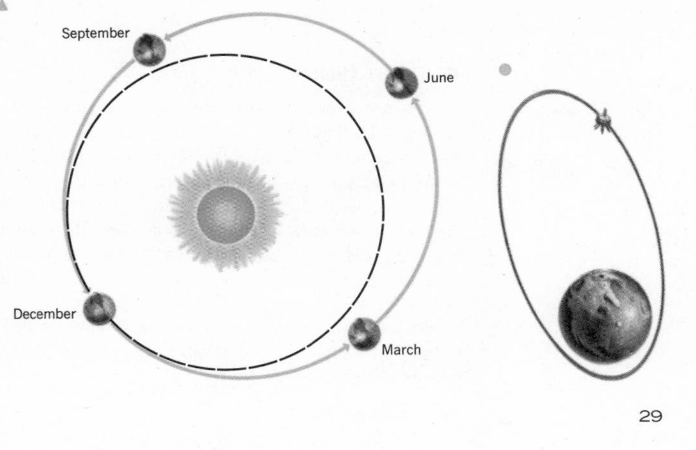

29

Useful materials: Yardstick.

❶ Have a circle about two feet in diameter ready which you can attach to the board with tape. Mark the exact center of the circle. How many more million miles from the Sun is the Earth in June than in December? (2 million) Have a volunteer place a yardstick through the center of the circle and draw a dot 2″ away from it at one side; this represents the Earth's position in June. Make another dot next to the other side of the circle; this represents the Earth's position in December. How does the number of miles in March and September compare with the number for June? (1 million less) Have the volunteer place the yardstick at right angles through the center of the circle and draw dots one inch from both opposite sides of the circle; these represent the Earth's position in September and June. Now ask the volunteer to draw a smooth curve connecting the four dots. What would that curve represent? (the path of the Earth in one year) Would this line be a circle? A comparison of the figure and the data used shows that it is not. Have the children compare their chalkboard model with the figure on the page.

❷ Where is the Sun in the ellipse of the Earth's orbit—in the center or nearer one end? (one end) Have children discuss the drawing of the man-made satellite in relation to these questions: When is the satellite farthest from the Earth? When is it nearest? Let them try to infer the points where the pull of gravitation will be greatest and least.

Unit Concept-Statement: Energy must be applied to produce an unbalanced force, which results in a change in motion.

Performance objectives. Children *construct* a diagram of the elliptical shape of the Earth's orbit, using paper, pencil, ruler, two thumb tacks, and string. They *construct* a hypothesis of what the ellipse will look like if the thumb tacks are moved closer together or farther apart, and they *demonstrate* that moving the thumb tacks farther apart causes a more elongated ellipse, while moving them together makes the ellipse more like a circle.

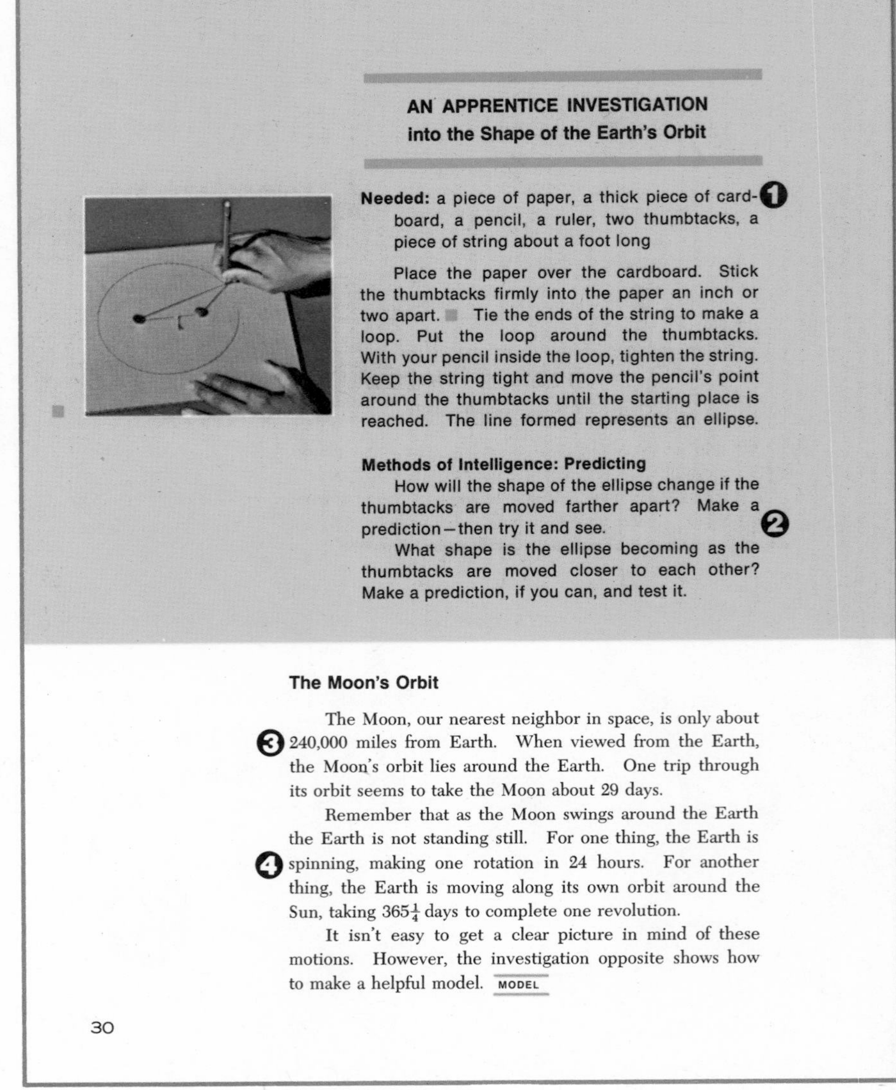

AN APPRENTICE INVESTIGATION into the Shape of the Earth's Orbit

Needed: a piece of paper, a thick piece of cardboard, a pencil, a ruler, two thumbtacks, a piece of string about a foot long ❶

Place the paper over the cardboard. Stick the thumbtacks firmly into the paper an inch or two apart. ■ Tie the ends of the string to make a loop. Put the loop around the thumbtacks. With your pencil inside the loop, tighten the string. Keep the string tight and move the pencil's point around the thumbtacks until the starting place is reached. The line formed represents an ellipse.

Methods of Intelligence: Predicting

How will the shape of the ellipse change if the thumbtacks are moved farther apart? Make a prediction—then try it and see. ❷

What shape is the ellipse becoming as the thumbtacks are moved closer to each other? Make a prediction, if you can, and test it.

The Moon's Orbit

❸ The Moon, our nearest neighbor in space, is only about 240,000 miles from Earth. When viewed from the Earth, the Moon's orbit lies around the Earth. One trip through its orbit seems to take the Moon about 29 days.

❹ Remember that as the Moon swings around the Earth the Earth is not standing still. For one thing, the Earth is spinning, making one rotation in 24 hours. For another thing, the Earth is moving along its own orbit around the Sun, taking $365\frac{1}{4}$ days to complete one revolution.

It isn't easy to get a clear picture in mind of these motions. However, the investigation opposite shows how to make a helpful model. MODEL

30

Continuing Lesson Cluster 4

❶ Try to assemble enough materials for everyone. If children can bring in a few cardboard cartons, these can be cut up to make many tack boards.

❷ Children should predict that the ellipse will get longer as the thumbtacks are moved apart; more and more circular as the tacks are moved closer.

❸ Compared to other distances in space, is 240,000 miles small or large? (small) Why do we say that the Moon's orbit takes about 28 days? (It takes this time for the Moon to appear again in the same position as seen from Earth.)

❹ Why do we say that Earth's rotation takes 24 hours? (The time of rotation is marked by the Sun's reappearance at one point in the sky.) At this point, the Sun is directly over a north-south line on the Earth. Why do we say the Earth takes $365\frac{1}{4}$ days for one revolution? (The return to one point in its orbit takes this time.) If children wonder why the days for an orbit do not come out even, explain that clocks measure only time of Earth's rotation and cannot measure other events, any more than a ruler can measure weight. What happens to the quarter of the day at the end of the Earth's orbit? (Every four years, one day is added to the calendar at the end of February. This is called leap year.)

Supporting Statement: The Laws of Inertia and Universal Gravitation explain the orbits of bodies in space.

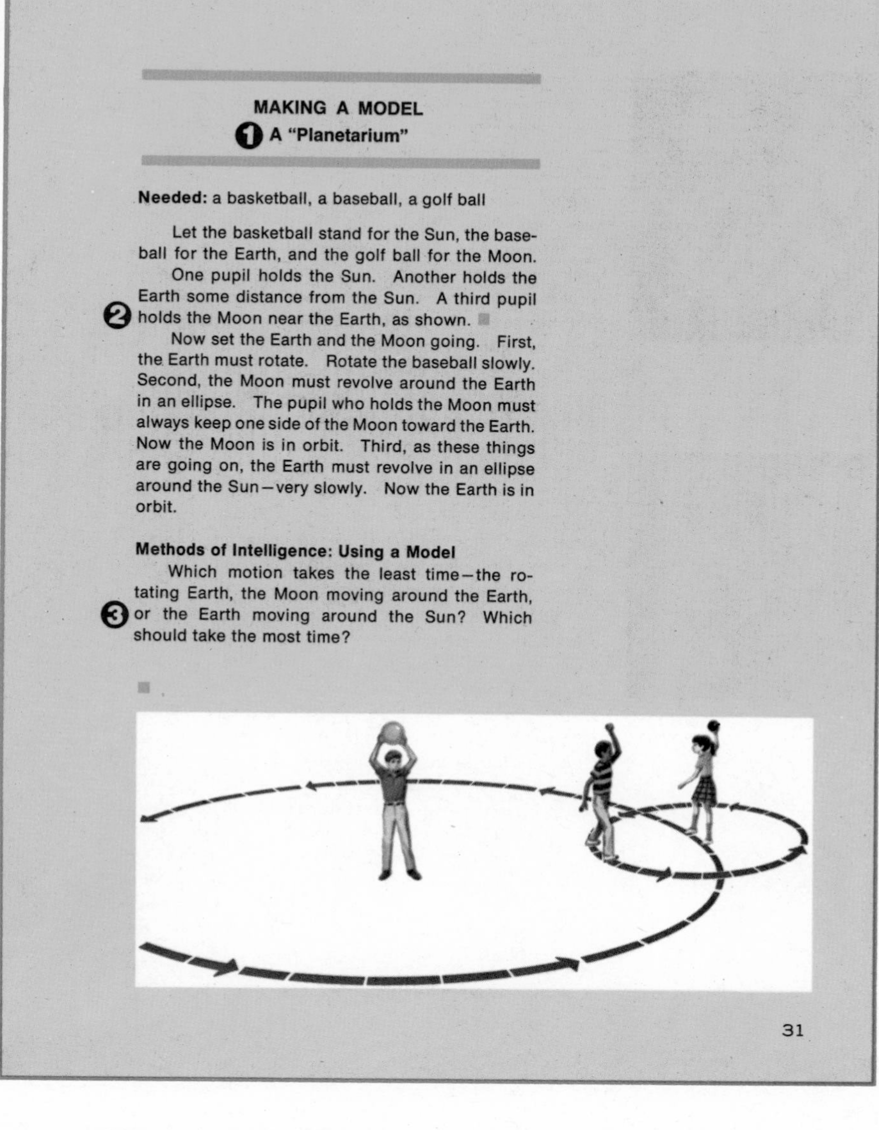

MAKING A MODEL
❶ A "Planetarium"

Needed: a basketball, a baseball, a golf ball

Let the basketball stand for the Sun, the baseball for the Earth, and the golf ball for the Moon.

One pupil holds the Sun. Another holds the Earth some distance from the Sun. A third pupil
❷ holds the Moon near the Earth, as shown. ■

Now set the Earth and the Moon going. First, the Earth must rotate. Rotate the baseball slowly. Second, the Moon must revolve around the Earth in an ellipse. The pupil who holds the Moon must always keep one side of the Moon toward the Earth. Now the Moon is in orbit. Third, as these things are going on, the Earth must revolve in an ellipse around the Sun—very slowly. Now the Earth is in orbit.

Methods of Intelligence: Using a Model

Which motion takes the least time—the rotating Earth, the Moon moving around the Earth,
❸ or the Earth moving around the Sun? Which should take the most time?

■

31

Performance objectives. Children *construct* a model of the Sun-Earth-Moon system. They *describe* that the time is least for the Earth to rotate, more for the Moon to revolve around the Earth, and greatest for the Earth to revolve around the Sun.

Useful materials: Alternative materials are available in CLASSROOM LABORATORY: PURPLE.

❶ What is a planetarium? Children may or may not know that a planetarium is a building where star shows are produced. This is done by projecting the motions of the stars and planets on a large domed ceiling. However, a planetarium also means any model of the planets. Be sure children learn both meanings. If it is possible, take your class to see a star show at a planetarium. If not, any children who have visited planetariums may tell about their experiences.

❷ You will find this easier for your children to do in a large open area such as the school yard or gymnasium. If you wish, you may let children mark the orbits in chalk before trying to walk them.

❸ The rotating Earth takes the least time to complete its motion, and the Earth moving around the Sun the most time. How long does it take the real Earth to make one rotation? (24 hours) How long does it take the Earth to make one revolution around the Sun? ($365\frac{1}{4}$ days) How long does it take the Moon to make one revolution around the Earth? (about 29 days) What is the difference between a rotation and a revolution? (A rotation describes the spinning of a body, and a revolution describes its travels around an orbit.)

Unit Concept-Statement: Energy must be applied to produce an unbalanced force, which results in a change in motion.

In the model on page 31, you have seen how the Moon moves around the Earth at the same time that the Earth moves around the Sun. ❶

The Sun is not standing still either! It, too, is rotating and revolving. The group of stars that includes the Sun is rotating. The group of stars that includes the Sun is revolving slowly, too.

If someone says, "Be absolutely still," you know that it's really impossible. You are on a rotating planet that is revolving around the Sun. The Sun itself is moving in space. You, the Moon, the planets, and the stars—including the Sun—are constantly in motion.

■ From your space station, you can get a fine view of the Moon, almost any evening. The Moon always keeps the same side of its surface toward the Earth. In this photograph, made through a telescope, you see the side of the Moon that faces the Earth. ■ ❷

We now know what men have wondered about for centuries—what the *other* side of the Moon looks like. Astronauts circling the Moon have seen its far side. On the right side of this photograph, taken from a spacecraft, you see parts of the Moon never seen from Earth. ●

● What is the shape of the Moon's orbit around the Earth? In the Apprentice Investigation on page 30, you found out that ellipses may vary in their shape. Some ellipses are long and narrow; others are nearly circular. The ellipse that is the Earth's orbit is nearly circular. Is this true for the Moon's orbit? You can see for yourself. Draw a picture of an ellipse, as shown on page 30. To get the right shape for the Moon's orbit, set the thumbtacks one inch apart and use a loop of string that is 18 inches long. ❸

To find out about another orbit, why not try the Search On Your Own on the next page? When you do a Search On Your Own, you *plan and design and carry out your own investigation.* You will, of course, check your plans and design with your teacher before you start work; but the Search will still be truly your own.

32

Useful materials: Large sheets of paper or cardboard, crayon or felt marker, string, thumbtacks.

Continuing Lesson Cluster 4

❶ The Moon is about 93,000,000 miles from the Sun. Is the Moon at the same distance from the Sun from month to month? (no) Why? (The Moon rotates around the Earth. When it is between the Earth and the Sun, it is 240,000 miles closer to the Sun than the Earth is. It gets to be 240,000 miles farther from the Sun than the Earth about fifteen days later.) Can we say the Moon revolves around the Sun? (Yes; it moves around with the Earth.)

❷ Does the Moon rotate? Children can act out the response by having one child circle another, always facing him. What evidence can you observe that the child acting the part of the Moon is rotating? (In one circling, the child has faced the four walls of the classroom.) How does this explain why we see only one side of the Moon?

❸ If children use the chalkboard, have two children each place a finger on the chalkboard an inch apart and within one end of the loop. A third child slips a piece of chalk into the other end of the loop and, keeping the loop taut, describes the ellipse. The loop will slip easily around the chalk.

If you have a cork bulletin board tack up a large (20 by 20 inch) sheet of paper or cardboard. Have children place two thumbtacks an inch apart in the center of the paper and draw the ellipse with a crayon or felt marker.

Supporting Statement: The Laws of Inertia and Universal Gravitation explain the orbits of bodies in space.

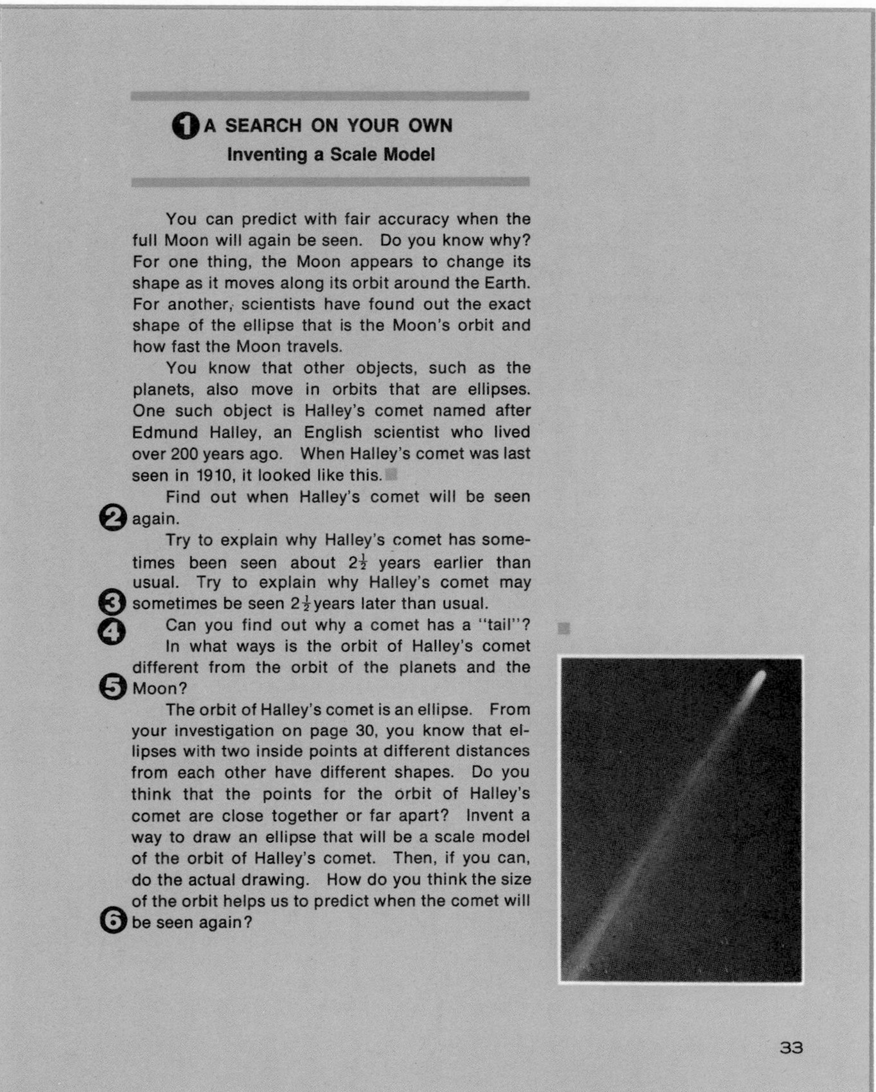

❶ **A SEARCH ON YOUR OWN**

Inventing a Scale Model

You can predict with fair accuracy when the full Moon will again be seen. Do you know why? For one thing, the Moon appears to change its shape as it moves along its orbit around the Earth. For another, scientists have found out the exact shape of the ellipse that is the Moon's orbit and how fast the Moon travels.

You know that other objects, such as the planets, also move in orbits that are ellipses. One such object is Halley's comet named after Edmund Halley, an English scientist who lived over 200 years ago. When Halley's comet was last seen in 1910, it looked like this.

Find out when Halley's comet will be seen ❷ again.

Try to explain why Halley's comet has sometimes been seen about $2\frac{1}{2}$ years earlier than usual. Try to explain why Halley's comet may ❸ sometimes be seen $2\frac{1}{2}$ years later than usual.

❹ Can you find out why a comet has a "tail"?

In what ways is the orbit of Halley's comet different from the orbit of the planets and the ❺ Moon?

The orbit of Halley's comet is an ellipse. From your investigation on page 30, you know that ellipses with two inside points at different distances from each other have different shapes. Do you think that the points for the orbit of Halley's comet are close together or far apart? Invent a way to draw an ellipse that will be a scale model of the orbit of Halley's comet. Then, if you can, do the actual drawing. How do you think the size of the orbit helps us to predict when the comet will ❻ be seen again?

33

VERIFYING PROGRESS

❶ **A search on your own.** Children *consult authorities* for information about the orbit of a comet, *invent a scale model* on the basis of this information, and *analyze* the relationship between the size of the orbit and the frequency of the appearances of the comet.

Not all children will elect to make a model of the orbit of Halley's comet but many will be interested in investigating the questions about the comet.

❷ Children should look for this information in encyclopedias. (Halley's comet returns approximately every 76 years. It is next expected in 1986.)

❸ The comet makes a very large orbit around the Sun, swinging out beyond Neptune's orbit and then coming back. If it passes near Jupiter—or another planet with a large mass—a great force of gravitation is exerted on the comet. The planet's gravitational pull may either speed the comet up or slow it down.

❹ There are several possible explanations for a comet's tail. One is that bits of dust and gas break away from the head of the comet and trail out behind it.

❺ The orbit of Halley's comet is very much more elliptical than the orbits of the Moon and the planets. Also, it is almost perpendicular to the orbits of the planets.

❻ Knowing the size of the orbit and how long it takes the comet to complete one orbit tells when the comet will be seen again.

VERIFYING PROGRESS

In methods of intelligence

To gauge children's ability to *describe* aspects of the solar system, encourage them to *build* and *explain* models. One child might assemble different sized clay balls to represent the different planets. Another child might show the distance of each planet from the Sun. (You may have to help children get the right scale.) Another child could model the Earth and its orbit, by passing a wire through a Styrofoam ball and curving the wire. Mobiles showing the Earth and the Moon, or the Sun and all the planets might be built.

Are these models good ones? Is there a better one? Have children *describe* and *invent* other *models*.

Useful materials: Clay, Styrofoam balls, wire, or other materials children may suggest.

❶ BEFORE YOU GO ON

A. Check your understanding of the concepts of this section. Which ending would you choose for each statement below?

1. One theory of how the sun and the planets came to be is that the solar system had its beginning in a cloud of
a. gas b. stars

2. One reason why the planets in our solar system form a group is that they began
a. together
b. at different times

3. Mars spins like a top. This kind of turning is called
a. revolution b. rotation

4. Jupiter travels in an orbit around the Sun. One complete trip around the orbit is known as one
a. revolution b. rotation

5. The side of the Moon we can see from Earth is
a. different each week
b. different each month
c. always the same

6. In its orbit around the Earth, the Moon seems to make one revolution in
a. 24 hours c. $365\frac{1}{4}$ days
b. 29 days

7. The statement that fits the main concept of this section is
a. The gravitational attraction between objects determines their rotations.
b. The gravitational attraction between objects determines their orbits.

B. Write a paragraph or two on: "Before the Protoplanets and After."

USING WHAT YOU KNOW ❷

1. Put the terms below in the order in which they appear in the theory of how the planets were formed.
protoplanets
planets
cloud of gas

2. Why is the Earth not pulled into the Sun?

3. If the Earth is rotating in space, why are we not thrown off its surface?

4. A satellite is launched to orbit the planet Venus. It misses Venus, however, and goes into orbit around the Sun. What is the shape of the orbit?

A LOOK AHEAD

Man's studies of the Moon go on. Scientists have learned much about the Moon. And there is much more to be learned. How did our first-hand investigations of the Moon get started? That story is a great event in history—a landmark—and it happened in your lifetime.

34

VERIFYING PROGRESS (cont.)

❶ Before you go on. Children *demonstrate* understanding of the motions of the Earth and Moon by selecting suitable responses to questions.

1. a	3. b	5. c	7. b
2. a	4. a	6. b	

❷ Using what you know. Children *identify* stages in a theory, *explain* how inertial motion balances the force of gravitation, and *infer* the shape of the orbit of a satellite.

1. Cloud of gas, protoplanets, planets.
2. According to one theory, the new-formed Earth (billions of years ago) was in motion in one direction in accordance with the Law of Inertia. The Earth was acted on by the pull of the Sun just enough to draw the Earth into a nearly circular orbit. The result was a balance between gravitational attraction and inertial motion.
3. We are moving at the same speed as the Earth's rotation; hence we have inertia of rest, and gravitational pull holds us to the Earth.
4. An ellipse.

Supporting Statement: Space exploration depends on applying the Law of Universal Gravitation and the Laws of Motion.

5. Man on the Moon—and Beyond?

It is July 16, 1969. At Cape Kennedy, Florida, three men enter "Columbia," the command module of the Apollo spacecraft. They are astronauts Neil A. Armstrong, Michael Collins, and Edwin E. Aldrin, Jr. ■ The spacecraft is to carry them 240,000 miles away—to the Moon. The
❶ astronauts are wearing pressure suits, which they will remove after lift-off.

The Apollo spacecraft is at the top of the giant Saturn rocket. Saturn 5 is made up of three separate rockets, or "stages." Each stage has its own group of rocket engines, which can throw a tremendous blast of gas backward. The
❷ reaction will be a tremendous force forward, called the thrust.

The total thrust of the three rocket stages is about 9
❸ million pounds. The energy comes from new fuels. The thrust is large enough to lift the huge rocket into space.

35

LESSON CLUSTER 5
MAN ON THE MOON—AND BEYOND?

Teaching background. 5 T-5

Concept-seeking. Children seek to recognize the concepts that make Moon landings possible.

Operations. Children *probe* the various theories of the origin of the Moon.

Methods of intelligence. Children *analyze* a Moon landing and *explain* how it depended on the Laws of Gravitation, Inertia, and Action and Reaction.

Introducing Lesson Cluster 5

Read the following dialogue and have children interpret what has happened.

Eagle: "Houston, Tranquility Base here. The Eagle has landed."

Houston: "Roger, Tranquility, we copy you on the ground. You got a bunch of guys about to turn blue. We're breathing again. Thanks a lot." (Eagle has just landed on the Moon. It is the first spacecraft to do so.)

Developing the lesson

❶ Astronauts wear space suits during lift-off as a safety measure. These suits supply pressure and oxygen, in case pressure in the cabin should drop during lift-off. They have devices that keep the ground crew aware of any body changes.

❷ Which of Newton's laws accounts for the thrust of a rocket? (action-reaction)

❸ Some of these newly developed fuels use liquid oxygen, called "lox", to support combustion. A child may be able to tell about "loxing" or putting liquid oxygen into a rocket. Have interested children find out how the fuels make the rocket go, and give a report.

EXTENDING THE LESSON

Children who are interested should look up other space flights and maneuvers, and present a report. Girls may enjoy finding out about the first woman to go into space. She was Valentina Tereshkova, a 26-year-old Russian, who made a flight in Vostok 6 in June 1963 and stayed in orbit for three days.

To the Moon

The astronauts are comfortable in the cone-shaped command module as they await the end of countdown. At ❶ lift-off, the rocket rises smoothly. ■ First and second stages of the Saturn rocket are fired, one by one. When ❷ their fuel is used up, their job is done and they fall away. The third rocket stage is then fired, taking the Apollo spacecraft into Earth orbit.

When the third rocket stage is fired the second time, the ❸ Apollo spacecraft reaches a speed of about 25,000 miles per hour—7 miles in a second or, as scientists say, 7 miles per second. At this speed, Apollo escapes from its orbit around the Earth.

From Earth, at the Manned Spacecraft Center in Houston, Texas, flight controllers guide every movement of the Apollo spacecraft and even speak with the astronauts.

Before the third and final stage of the Saturn rocket drops away, the astronauts prepare the Apollo spacecraft for the rest of the trip. At the top of the third stage is "Eagle," the Moon-landing craft (known to scientists as the lunar module, or LM). The astronauts turn their part of the spacecraft around to join it properly with the Moon-landing ❹ craft. It slows down on the way to the Moon.

❺ Other astronauts have already practiced "docking" in space, as this joining of ships is called, and found that it can be done. The manned spacecraft can be steered and turned in space. The men in the spacecraft can control its course and can even step out into space. The Law of Action and Reaction works in space as well as on the Earth—just as Newton predicted. A squirt of gas over to the left, for instance, will push the spacecraft to the right.

As the Apollo spacecraft approaches the Moon, it is attracted by the Moon's gravitational pull. It moves faster toward the Moon. Therefore, the astronauts now fire their rocket so that the blast of gas goes toward the Moon. The blast toward the Moon results in an equal and opposite thrust away from the Moon—against the Moon's gravitational pull.

36

Continuing Lesson Cluster 5

❶ What is the number that signals the end of countdown and the beginning of lift-off? (zero, or T minus zero)

❷ What are the stages of a rocket like? (Each stage is a complete rocket; it has its own engines and fueling system and supply; when it has used all its fuel, it is detached and dropped off.) What happens when a stage has dropped off? (The rocket has less mass; thus, the next stage can develop greater thrust, giving the spacecraft greater speed.)

❸ As children analyze the next paragraphs, be sure they note that the engines in the third stage can be turned on and off, that it goes into "parking" orbit for adjustments, and that it contains the Moon-landing craft with its own engines.

❹ Why does the craft slow down on its way to the Moon? Children should infer that the Earth's gravitation is acting.

❺ Have the children explain the steps in the approach to the Moon by the Law of Action and Reaction.

Supporting Statement: Space exploration depends on applying the Law of Universal Gravitation and the Laws of Motion.

1 This slows down the spacecraft enough for it to go into orbit around the Moon.

Now the Moon-landing craft, with astronauts Armstrong and Aldrin in it, separates from the rest of the spacecraft.

On July 20, 1969, astronauts Armstrong and Aldrin ride slowly down to the Moon's surface, becoming the first men to reach the Moon. In which direction do you think they
2 fired their rockets to make a soft landing? Why?

On the Moon

The two men have put on their spacesuits to leave the
3 craft. ● Each unit contains a heater, air conditioner, radio. Each suit supplies oxygen and is pressurized, for the Moon, has no atmosphere—no air and no water.

Daylight lasts for two weeks on the lighted side of the
4 Moon. During the day, the Sun beats unmercifully on the Moon's surface. The high temperature would kill any living thing not protected against it. The astronauts are well protected in their suits.

1 **Why does slowing down the spacecraft make it go into orbit around the Moon?** (The Moon's gravitation provides an unbalanced force acting against the craft's inertia of motion.) **Why must the craft be slowed just enough?** (If it is not slowed, inertia of motion might carry it beyond the Moon's gravitation and off into space. If it is slowed too much, the Moon's gravitation would be a force that would cause a crash landing.)

2 They fire their rockets toward the Moon to reduce the effect of the Moon's gravitational pull, and thus make a gentle landing. **Why are parachutes not used?** (The Moon has no air to provide an upward force on the chutes against the Moon's pull.)

3 The photograph shows Aldrin about to set foot on the Moon. **Why do lunar spacesuits contain both a heater and an airconditioner?** (At the time of landing, the lunar surface temperature was expected to be about 50°F in the Sun; air-conditioners are needed to maintain correct temperature and humidity, and to remove the wastes from breathing.) **Why do the astronauts carry a radio on the Moon?** (There is no air to carry sound, but radio waves can travel through space.)

4 **Why are the Moon's "day" and "night" each about two Earth weeks long?** (The Moon makes only one rotation in four weeks as it revolves around the Earth. Thus, it takes four weeks from one sunrise on the Moon until the next, or two weeks from one sunrise to sunset.)

Unit Concept-Statement: Energy must be applied to produce an unbalanced force, which results in a change in motion.

With back pack, each spacesuit weighs almost 200 pounds on Earth. How can a man move about and explore in such a suit? He can't, on the Earth. On the Moon, however, he
❶ can move with ease. Why? What does the suit weigh on the Moon? What does the astronaut himself weigh on the Moon?

The astronauts collect samples of the Moon's surface materials. They place instruments on the Moon to send
❷ scientific observations back to Earth. ■

Back to Earth

The astronauts then return to the Moon-landing craft to rest. Later, they blast off from the surface of the Moon,
❸ leaving the lower half of the landing craft behind.

This blast-off takes much less energy than the energy needed to leave the Earth. For one thing, the gravitational pull of the Moon is much less than the Earth's. For another, the craft leaving the Moon has much less mass than the huge Apollo-Saturn rocket that left the Earth. ●

Astronauts Aldrin and Armstrong rejoin astronaut
❹ Collins in the command module for the trip back to Earth. The Moon craft drops away.

■

38

Continuing Lesson Cluster 5

❶ The astronaut can move with ease on the Moon because he has the same muscles he had on Earth. He and his pack, however, weigh one-sixth of what they weighed on Earth. His 200-pound suit and pack weigh $33\frac{1}{3}$ pounds on the Moon.

❷ The instruments left on the Moon were the seismic sensor (center foreground in the picture) for recording moonquakes and other vibrations; special mirrors to reflect a laser beam from the Earth directly back to the Earth for the purpose of measuring the exact distance between the Earth and the Moon at any given moment; and some special aluminum foil to catch and record the impact of high speed particles from the Sun.

❸ **Why did the astronauts leave the lower half of the Moon-landing craft when they blasted off to link up with the command module in Moon orbit?** (It had served its purpose. The extra weight would reduce the thrust of the launching rockets.) At every stage, the amount of fuel in relation to mass must be closely calculated so that only essentials are carried.

❹ **What was the command module, with astronaut Collins, doing while Armstrong and Aldrin were on the Moon?** (orbiting the Moon — about once every two hours)

Supporting Statement: Space exploration depends on applying the Law of Universal Gravitation and the Laws of Motion.

After traveling through space for nearly three days, the spacecraft goes into orbit around the Earth. The last of its fuel is used to slow it down as it reenters the Earth's atmosphere. As soon as possible after the astronauts land, scientists begin work on the information and rock samples
❶ brought back.▲

This trip was one of the great "firsts" in history. It compares in importance with the discovery of America by Columbus nearly 500 years earlier. His three tiny ships were the first to open up discovery and settlement of a new world. Now great ships travel all the oceans.

The Apollo 11 astronauts also had a tiny spacecraft – one that could hold just three men. Theirs, too, was a voyage of discovery and travel in the larger world of space. It opened the way to other space voyages to the Moon, which have led to new discoveries in science. Who knows what the future of Moon travel holds for men on Earth? Who
❷ knows the future for travel beyond the Moon?

❸ Now that men are investigating the Moon's rocks many more facts are being discovered about the Moon. New theories on the origin of the Moon are being developed. Try a Search On Your Own, on the next page.

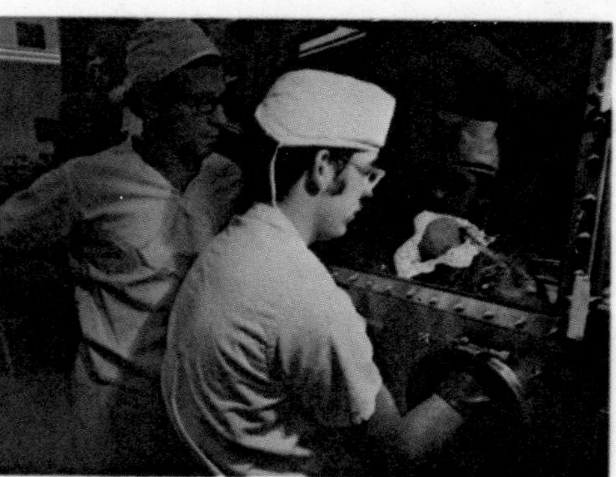

EXTENDING THE LESSON

If you or the school librarian have a current file on space exploration, encourage children to report on plans for later Apollo trips to the Moon and for an orbiting space laboratory, Skylab. They may also report on unmanned probes such as Mariner probes of Mars, Venus, and Mercury; the Pioneer probe of Jupiter; and two grand tours of the distant planets, each lasting ten years or more. The Soviet unmanned landings on the Moon in 1969 and 1970 should be included. Let children also locate information to solve these problems: Traveling at the same speed as Mariner 7 in 1969, how long would a manned flight to Mars and back take? (8 or 9 months) How long would a spacecraft take to reach Pluto, when Pluto is nearest the Earth? (28 years) And to reach the nearest star beyond the Sun? (256,000 years)

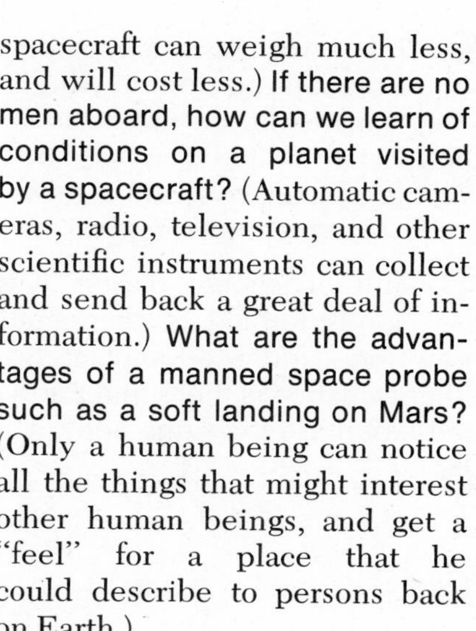

❶ The illustration shows scientists studying a sample of rock from the Moon. These samples were placed in a near-vacuum in the Lunar Receiving Laboratory at Houston to avoid contamination by the Earth's environment. They were studied by using remote-control instruments.

❷ Let the children have free rein to discuss and speculate about these questions. To guide them, you might ask: What are some advantages of an unmanned space trip over a manned trip? (The life-support equipment can be left out, so the spacecraft can weigh much less, and will cost less.) If there are no men aboard, how can we learn of conditions on a planet visited by a spacecraft? (Automatic cameras, radio, television, and other scientific instruments can collect and send back a great deal of information.) What are the advantages of a manned space probe such as a soft landing on Mars? (Only a human being can notice all the things that might interest other human beings, and get a "feel" for a place that he could describe to persons back on Earth.)

❸ If a Moon rock is on display in your area, encourage children to view it.

Unit Concept-Statement: Energy must be applied to produce an unbalanced force which results in a change in motion.

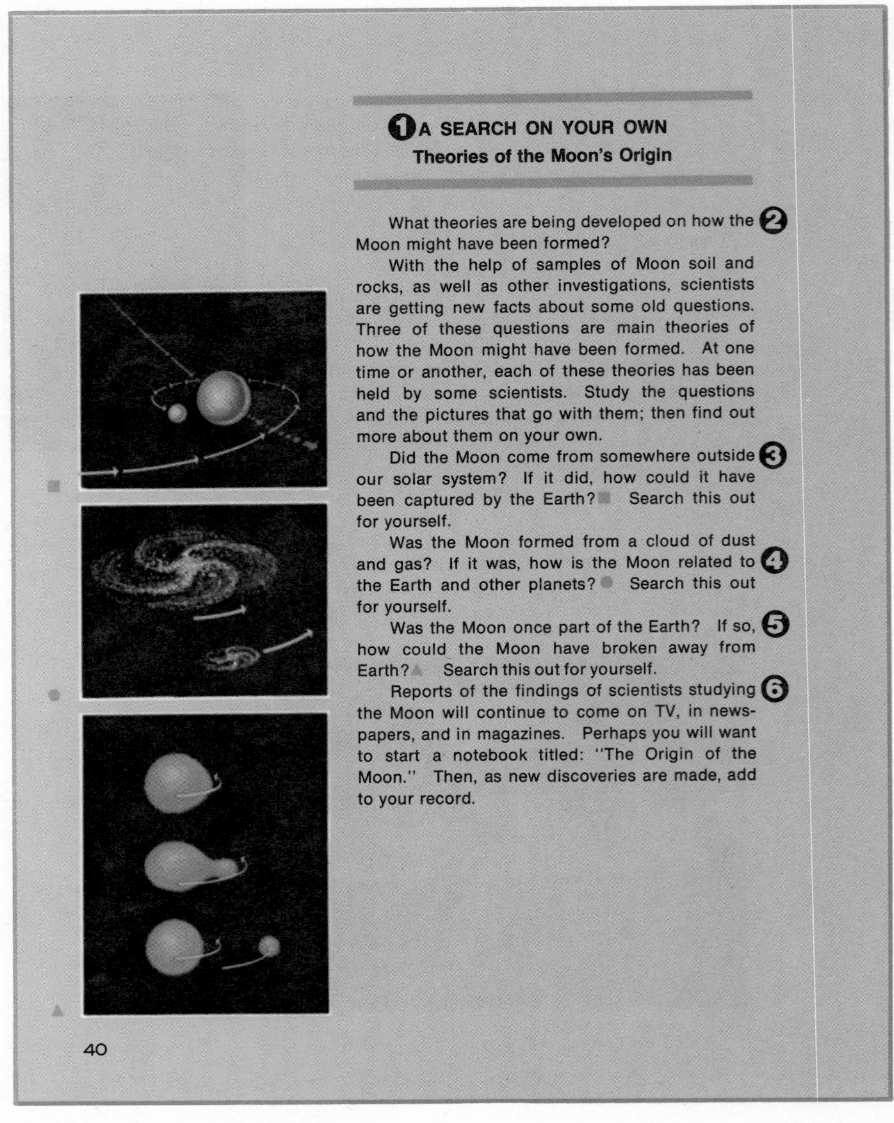

❶ **A SEARCH ON YOUR OWN**
Theories of the Moon's Origin

What theories are being developed on how the Moon might have been formed? ❷

With the help of samples of Moon soil and rocks, as well as other investigations, scientists are getting new facts about some old questions. Three of these questions are main theories of how the Moon might have been formed. At one time or another, each of these theories has been held by some scientists. Study the questions and the pictures that go with them; then find out more about them on your own.

Did the Moon come from somewhere outside our solar system? If it did, how could it have been captured by the Earth? ■ Search this out for yourself. ❸

Was the Moon formed from a cloud of dust and gas? If it was, how is the Moon related to the Earth and other planets? ● Search this out for yourself. ❹

Was the Moon once part of the Earth? If so, how could the Moon have broken away from Earth? ▲ Search this out for yourself. ❺

Reports of the findings of scientists studying the Moon will continue to come on TV, in newspapers, and in magazines. Perhaps you will want to start a notebook titled: "The Origin of the Moon." Then, as new discoveries are made, add to your record. ❻

40

VERIFYING PROGRESS

❶ **A search on your own.** Children *make hypotheses* about the Moon's origin, *seek evidence*, *consult* current sources of information, and *order* it in a reasoned report.

❷ Before any children begin their Search, have them recall that a theory is a reasonable explanation that fits the facts. Why can there be so many theories of the Moon's origin? (Not all the evidence is in, but some theories seem less likely than others.)

❸ Children can make a hypothesis on the basis of the drawings. They can reason on the basis of the inertial motion of a body becoming affected by Earth's gravitation. What is the evidence?

❹ Children should reason that the clouds formed at the same time and condensed separately. What evidence is there that Earth and Moon are the same age?

❺ Again, let children analyze the question. For example, a passing body may have pulled the Earth apart, or the Earth may have had a tremendous volcanic eruption. What evidence is there?

❻ Children should consult recent encyclopedias or search in articles in newspapers and magazines. Much information might be gained from reports of the study of rock samples brought back from the Moon. The age of the oldest Moon rock brought back by Apollo 12 has been estimated at 4.6 billion years. Has this estimate been changed by later samplings?

Supporting Statement: Space exploration depends on applying the Law of Universal Gravitation and the Laws of Motion.

① BEFORE YOU GO ON

Tell the story of the concepts of gravitation, inertia, and action and reaction under the title "Landing on the Moon." Include some or all of these:

The rocket on the Earth
The thrust at lift-off
The climb into space
Landing on the Moon
Walking on the Moon
The return to the Earth

② USING WHAT YOU KNOW

1. A spacecraft leaving the Earth for the Moon must reach a speed of about 25,000 miles per hour. Why? What are two things that might happen to the spacecraft if it does not reach this speed?

2. Why does it take less force for a spacecraft to leave the Moon than for it to leave the Earth?

INVESTIGATING FURTHER ③

1. Who becomes an astronaut? How? Design an approach to finding out the way a person can become an astronaut. Then, with the help of your classmates and the permission of your teacher, carry out your plan.

2. What have scientists found out about other planets in the solar system beyond the Moon? The Mariner spacecraft, for example, has been used to explore Mars. In the library, try to find out what discoveries were made by Mariner.

41

① Before you go on. Children *analyze* the first Moon landing and *identify* and *apply* the concepts to the main events of the journey.

② Using what you know. Children *analyze* a situation, and *apply* the laws of motion and gravitation to *predict* and *explain* events that might occur.

1. The speed is necessary to overcome the unbalanced force of gravitation and permit the craft to travel in a straight line in accordance with the Law of Inertia. If it does not reach a speed of nearly 25,000 m.p.h., it may go into orbit around the Earth. If its speed is not great enough to achieve orbit, about 17,500 m.p.h., it will fall back to Earth.
2. The gravitational pull of the Moon is only about one sixth of that of the Earth. Also, the mass of the craft leaving the Earth was far greater than that leaving the Moon.

③ Investigating further. Children *consult authorities;* they *organize* and *report* the information they find.

1. Children may consult recent encyclopedias or obtain information from NASA and other government sources.
2. Current magazines are especially useful sources.

LESSON CLUSTER 6

THE MAIN CONCEPT: EARTH, MOON, AND MAN IN ORBIT

Teaching background. T-2–T-5

Concept-seeking. Children become aware that the Laws of Gravitation and Motion apply throughout the Universe.

Methods of intelligence. Children *synthesize* the Laws of Gravitation and Motion to *explain* the structure of the Universe. They *apply* these laws to *explain* that energy must be applied to produce an unbalanced force and that unbalanced forces change the motion of all objects on Earth and in space.

Useful materials: Pepper or pulverized Styrofoam or instant oatmeal, shallow pans (such as pie tins), water.

6. The Main Concept Earth, Moon, and Man in Orbit

FOCUS ON THE CONCEPT

A model of the Earth's place in space is not hard to make.

Pour water into a pan. Sprinkle some pepper on the water. With your finger start the water circling in a kind of whirlpool. Some of the specks of pepper will sink a little below the surface. Take your finger out. You have a whirling cloud of circling specks of pepper. It is a rather flat, pancake-shaped, spinning cloud.

With a little imagination, you can change this pan of peppered water into a model of our part of the universe. *Imagine that each speck of pepper is a star.* The specks are now like a whirling cloud of stars, spinning around a center. Observe for a while how the specks move.

42

Introducing Lesson Cluster 6

Have a shallow pan or several pans of water in the classroom as well as a shaker of finely ground pepper so that individual children or groups of children can take turns making the pepper model of the galaxy. As an alternative to pepper, you may use instant oatmeal or pulverized Styrofoam, which is likely to float longer than pepper.

What does each speck of pepper stand for? (a star) What is a star? (Children may say that each star is a body like our Sun. Or they may know that each star is a mass of hot gas.)

Unit Concept-Statement: Energy must be applied to produce an unbalanced force, which results in a change in motion.

Here is a cloud of stars photographed through a powerful telescope. ■ This cloud of stars is spinning in space around a center, much as the specks of pepper were. We call this ❶ spinning group of stars a **galaxy** (gal'ək·se). The galaxy in this picture is many trillions of miles away.

We live in a galaxy much like the one you've just seen. Our star, the Sun, is just one of the stars in our galaxy. ❷ Astronomers have been able to figure out what our galaxy would look like from a distance. ● Notice that it is thicker in the middle than at the edges and that our Sun (yellow dot under *B*) is near one edge. How many stars are in this galaxy? Thousands of millions. And our Sun is just one of them.

Recall that around our Sun are nine planets. They are very small specks indeed in this spinning pancake of stars. One of these small specks is our Earth.

❸ Look again at the Sun's place in the galaxy. ● How should the galaxy look to us from the Earth? When we look ❹ in direction *A*, *into* the galaxy, there are many stars before our eyes. When we look in direction *B*, *out of* the galaxy, there are fewer stars to be seen.

Look up at the stars some clear night. In one part of the sky, the stars seem to form a path studded with stars. Perhaps you know the name of this path; it is the Milky Way.

43

Developing the lesson

❶ Our word *galaxy* comes from the Greek word *galaxaios*, which means "milky". What is our galaxy often called? (the Milky Way)

❷ Why can't astronomers use a telescope to observe what our galaxy looks like? (Earth is inside the galaxy; we can only see parts of it when we look out at it.) How can they figure out what our galaxy looks like? (Most other galaxies have a pancake shape.)

❸ Where will Earth be in the picture? (very near the Sun, represented by the letter B and far from the center of the galaxy) What does the fact that the galaxy is spinning mean? Children should infer that the solar system is revolving around the center of the galaxy. It is thought that the Sun has revolved around the center several times since the solar system originated.

❹ Study the picture of our galaxy again. What does it mean to say we are looking *into* it, or looking *out of* it? (It is as if you had a bug's-eye view from inside a blueberry pie, and very near one edge: if you could look through the center of the pie, across to the other side, you would see a lot of blueberries; if you could look out through the nearest edge, you would see many fewer blueberries.)

Why do the stars in the Milky Way seem to make a path across the sky? ■ When you look at the Milky Way, you are looking *into* the galaxy. But when you look away from the Milky Way, you are looking *out of* the galaxy and see fewer stars.

The milky appearance of many stars close together gives the galaxy we live in its name. It is called the Milky Way Galaxy.

The stars in the Milky Way Galaxy are very far apart from one another, even though they may look close together. ❶ Beyond the Milky Way Galaxy, great as the distances are, we can see through telescopes many other galaxies and many other stars.

Here, then, is our address in space. We live on one of nine planets, Earth. The nine planets revolve around one medium-sized star, the Sun. The Sun is only one star in a huge pancake of stars, the Milky Way Galaxy. The Milky Way Galaxy is only one of the many, many galaxies in space. And, like the Milky Way, each of those other galaxies has many, many stars.

■

Continuing Lesson Cluster 6

❶ Children may ask for information about distances. Although the light-year as a measure of distances in space is developed in Unit Four, you may want to explain the great distances in terms of light-years. Write "One Light-Year" on the board. Tell the children that light travels about 186,000 miles per second, and that it takes a little over 8 minutes for light to reach us from the Sun. **How do you think we could use light as a measure of distance?** (minutes, hours, years) When children suggest years, let them multiply 186,000 seconds by 60 and the result by 60 again. This comes to 669,600,000 miles per hour. Write on the board next to the term light-year, "about 6 trillion (6,000,000,000,000) miles." To go this distance, you would have to travel 236 million times around the Earth or about 25 million times the distance from the Earth to the Moon. **What do you suppose is the distance of the Milky Way Galaxy from one end to the other?** Children may speculate on this question, before you tell them it is about 80,000 light-years. Let skeptics look up the information in an encyclopedia.

Unit Concept-Statement: Energy must be applied to produce an unbalanced force, which results in a change in motion.

Gravitation

1 Stars are held together in a galaxy. Galaxies are held together in the Universe. The planets in our solar system are held so close together that they travel in orbits.

2 Planets, stars, galaxies—all are held together by the force of gravitation. Every body in the Universe attracts every other body. Sir Isaac Newton's Law of Universal Gravitation still satisfies us. It enables us to predict the path of a falling apple or the orbit of a planet, the Moon, or spacecraft. The law of Universal Gravitation even helps us to understand theories of the origin of the solar system.

Objects attract one another with the force of gravitation. The Earth attracts you, and so you can be weighed. The force of gravitation on the Moon is only $\frac{1}{6}$ of that on Earth. Your weight on the Moon, then, would be $\frac{1}{6}$ of your weight on Earth. Your mass would not change, however, on Earth or on the Moon, or anywhere in the Universe.

Rest and Motion

3 An object at rest tends to remain at rest. It has inertia. To move an object at rest means to overcome its inertia. This takes energy.

4 Suppose that energy is supplied to an object at rest, and the object moves. What happens to the energy? It provides a force. Your body supplies energy for the force to throw a ball, to pedal a bicycle, or to lift a book. The fuel in a rocket supplies energy for the force to lift the rocket into space. And once the rocket is in motion, it tends to keep moving in the same direction.

An object at rest tends to remain at rest, for it has inertia. An object in motion tends to keep moving for the same reason. It continues in motion because it has inertia. The Law of Inertia was stated for us by Newton:

An object at rest remains at rest; an object in motion continues in motion in a straight line, unless acted upon by
5 an unbalanced force.

45

1 Why don't stars, planets, and galaxies travel off in all directions through space? (The force of universal gravitation, the pull that each of these bodies exerts on every other body, balances their motion and keeps the Universe in order.)

2 How can we predict motions? (Each body exerts a gravitational force according to its mass.) Why is gravitational force on Earth different than on the Moon? (mass of Moon is less)

3 Place a large heavy object on your desk. What law does the (object) on my desk illustrate? (Law of Inertia of rest) What will it take to lift the (object)? (an unbalanced force) How much must this be? (more than the force of gravitation) How can we measure the force of gravitation holding the object to the desk? (weigh the object)

4 Ask a child to move the object across the desk. What has (child's name) applied to the object? (force) What did (child's name) use to produce the force? (energy) Where do we get our energy? (from food) How does a fuel supply energy? (burning, expanding gases)

5 What might an unbalanced force do to an object at rest? (move it) to an object in motion? (speed it up, slow it down, stop it, change its direction)

Unit Concept-Statement: Energy must be applied to produce an unbalanced force, which results in a change in motion.

Unbalanced Force

In space, the spurt of a jet of gas from a spacecraft sends the spacecraft forward. A spurt of gas from the left side of the spacecraft pushes it to the right. The action of the spurt of gases from the spacecraft has a reaction. This was stated by Newton in the Law of Action and Reaction: *Every action results in an equal and opposite reaction.* If the ❶ reaction is an unbalanced force, this force makes the spacecraft change direction.

A rocket is launched toward the Moon. Unbalanced ❷ forces drive it out into space. Men have set it on its course carefully and exactly. To do this, they have used concepts developed some 300 years ago—by Galileo and Newton.

The work of these men, and many other men and women, enables us to understand what is behind this concept of **energy**:

Energy must be applied to produce an unbalanced force. Unbalanced forces change the motions of objects.

FOCUS ON THE SCIENTIST'S WAYS

You may have wondered why Newton and Galileo, knowing what they did, did not shoot a rocket to the Moon. They may have imagined how it might be done. They may even have built such a rocket in their minds.

They could not have actually built a rocket, however, ❸ because they did not have the tools. They did not have the metals. They did not have the fuels. In other words, their *science* was ahead of their *technology*.

One thing a scientist does is to seek concepts. A ❹ concept brings together many things that are somehow alike. For example:

—an apple falls;
—a plane with its fuel gone must return to the Earth;
—you let an object go (a coin, a ball, a pencil), and it falls to the ground.

46

Continuing Lesson Cluster 6

❶ When a spacecraft uses a spurt of gas from a jet to turn to one side, why is the reaction an unbalanced force? (The spurt of gas produces an unbalanced force that acts to oppose the inertia of motion, thus causing the craft to turn or change direction.)

❷ What produces the unbalanced force that sends a rocket toward the Moon? (energy of fuel) What force does this oppose? (gravitation)

❸ Encourage children to speculate and find information on the work of scientists. What kinds of tools did Newton and Galileo not have? (machinery, precise instruments, electricity) Why didn't they have fuels? (Coal was too bulky, could never provide the thrust needed; no chemical fuels had yet been processed.) Other responses are possible.

❹ How are concepts useful? (They help us to recognize how things are alike or act alike.) How did Galileo and Newton use concepts without being able to make rockets? (They brought common experiences together and explained them. Without concepts, no mental image of how a rocket might work would be possible.)

There is a likeness about all objects on the Earth. If they are left alone, *they all fall to the Earth.* Newton related the behavior of all objects in one concept: gravitation.

1 As a scientist, Newton tried to explain why things happen. He tried to find likenesses in the objects and events around him. Concepts group likenesses together.

An engineer is a **technologist** (tek·nol′ə·jist). He applies science concepts. He designs, and builds, and plans.

An engineer has scientific training. Suppose, for example, he is a specialist in **aeronautics** (âr′ə·nô′tiks), the science of flight. The aeronautics engineer spends most of his time designing and building objects that fly: planes, or rockets, or command modules, or LM's. In other words, the engineer is mainly concerned with the way things work—he builds things that do work.

The engineer can, of course, do research, as scientists do. Engineers can develop concepts. Their main interest, however, is to design and build tools and machines.

On the other hand, scientists can and do design and build. They have a main interest, however, which is to uncover concepts that will help explain how the world works.

2 This is Wernher von Braun. ■ He has spent much of his life developing rockets. Once a German citizen, Dr. von Braun is now an American. He directed the Saturn

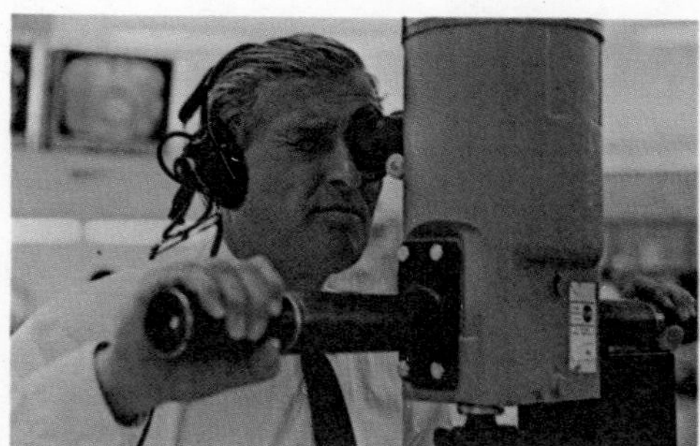

■

1 Discuss the difference between science and technology. What does a scientist do? What does a technologist do? Place children's responses under the headings SCIENTIST and TECHNOLOGIST on the chalk-board. Who works more with ideas? (scientist) Who works more with tools? (technologist) Does a scientist ever work with tools? How? Does he ever design tools? Does he usually make his tools? Does a technologist ever develop a new idea or a concept? Be sure all children give examples in their answers. It may be helpful to discuss the work of particular kinds of scientists (biologist, geologist, etc.) and technologists (engineer, architect, etc.)

Children interested in Newton and Galileo will enjoy *The Universe of Galileo and Newton*, by the editors of *Horizon Magazine* and William Bixby, published by Harper and Row, 1964.

2 Wernher von Braun is basically an engineer. But like every great engineer, though he does not do work in pure science himself, he is intensely interested in it. Encourage children interested in space science and space technology to look into his books, *Mars Project* and *History of Rocketry and Space Travel.*

Unit Concept-Statement: Energy must be applied to produce an unbalanced force, which results in a change in motion.

rocket program at the time of the historic first manned flight to the Moon. He now holds a high post with NASA—the National Aeronautics and Space Administration. What would you say his main interest is?

This is Harold Urey, a scientist who won the Nobel ❶ Prize in chemistry. ■ He is interested in the origin of the Moon. Did the Moon come from the Earth? Did it come from space? In your own words, state what you think is the difference between a scientist and an engineer.

Focusing on the Main Concepts

❷ **TESTING YOURSELF**

A. Test your understanding of important concepts in this unit by answering these questions.

1. If a girl weighs 78 pounds on the Earth, how much would she weigh on the Moon?

2. Would the girl's mass be more, less, or unchanged on the Moon?

3. If an astronaut could get completely away from gravitational force, what would he weigh?

4. A boy riding a bicycle to school had to stop suddenly. His lunch and books in a basket at the front of the bicycle were thrown out. Did they fall in front of him or behind? Why?

5. An astronaut in space steps out of his spacecraft. He does this so force-

48

Continuing Lesson Cluster 6

❶ From these pages, what do you think is the main difference between the way in which Dr. von Braun and Dr. Urey work? (Dr. Urey tries to explain objects and events; Dr. von Braun plans ways to get evidence.) Which is the technologist? the scientist?

VERIFYING PROGRESS

❷ **Testing yourself.** A. Children *apply* their knowledge of important concepts and key concept terms of the Unit by responding to questions.

1. and 2. The girl would weigh 13 pounds on the Moon, but her mass would be the same.
3. Nothing. But this is impossible because every body in the Universe, no matter how distant, attracts every other body.
4. In front, because their inertia of motion caused them to move in the direction the bicycle had been going.
5. He points the jet of his fire extinguisher in a direction away from his spacecraft.
6. The Moon always looks the same because the period of rotation and revolution presents the same side to the Earth.

Unit Concept-Statement: Energy must be applied to produce an unbalanced force, which results in a change in motion.

fully that he moves away from the spacecraft. He discovers that he has with him all the things he needs except, alas, the little jets that allow him to move around in space. But (for some reason) he has a fire extinguisher with him. How can he get back to his ship?

6. The Moon makes one complete revolution around the Earth in about one month. The Moon also makes one complete rotation on its axis in about one month. How do these motions help to explain the way the Moon looks from the Earth?

❶ **B.** Test your knowledge with this quick check.

1. Out in space an astronaut wants to turn to the left. He should spurt a jet

a. backward c. to the left
b. forward d. to the right

2. Earth is in orbit about 93 million miles away from the Sun. It is held in orbit mainly by the gravitational pull of

a. the Sun b. the Moon

3. A spacecraft is launched from the Earth to explore Saturn. It is packed full of instruments and has no astronaut aboard. On the way past Mars it veers and goes into orbit around Mars. This happens because

a. the spacecraft has too much energy
b. the spacecraft is caught by the gravitational pull of Mars
c. we'll never reach Saturn; it is too far away

4. The reason for developing bigger rocket engines is to

a. get more thrust
b. carry less weight
c. use less force
d. get less inertia

5. The statement that fits the main concept of this unit is

a. Energy must be applied to produce a balanced force, which results in a change of motion.
b. Energy must be applied to produce an unbalanced force, which results in a change of motion.

INVESTIGATING FURTHER ❷

1. In the Library

a. Life exists on Earth. On what other planet might life exist? Why do you think so?
b. Sir Isaac Newton stated the Law of Universal Gravitation, the Law of Inertia, and the Law of Action and Reaction. For what other work is he known?

2. Your Own Tracking Station

Space shots are taking place almost every day. Set up a bulletin board, at home or in the classroom, on which to track a space shot. Put up a map of the solar system. With colored pins, show the orbit of an Earth satellite or other spacecraft. Of course, you will have to follow the news of the space shot very carefully.

49

❶ B. Children *analyze* situations and *identify* the effects of applying an unbalanced force to an object at rest or in motion.

1. d 3. b 5. b
2. a 4. a

❷ **Investigating further.** Children *consult authorities, record data,* and *make inferences* about the possibility of life on other planets; *investigate* the work of Sir Isaac Newton, current space shots, and the history of rocketry; *interpret data* in a table and *calculate* the solutions to problems based on this data.

1. a. Be sure that the children distinguish between "life" and human life. No other planet in the solar system could support human life in its natural environment. Mars *might* have some very simple life forms. The reasons children give for this response may include the relative nearness of Mars to Earth, their surface temperatures, and their atmospheres.

b. Newton also did important original work in heat and light.

2. Children may reproduce in larger scale the map on page 25. If space probes only to the inner planets are involved, the map need go out only a little beyond the orbit of Mars.

If only Moon trips are involved, a scale diagram will fit on a standard piece of paper, using these measurements: distance from Earth's center to Moon's center $3\frac{3}{4}$ inches; diameter of Earth, $\frac{1}{8}$ inch; diameter of Moon, $\frac{1}{32}$ inch.

❶ **3.** To understand more about gravitation, try the investigations in *First Experiments with Gravity*, by Harry Milgrom, published by E.P. Dutton, New York, 1966.

4. In the days to come, newspapers and magazines will have exciting stories about space shots. Why don't you write your own book about these events? One student called his book *The Conquest of Space During My Early Years.* What will you call your book?

5. You might like to collect pictures or models of rockets. How might you show the development of the rocket? Begin in the 1920's as Dr. Robert Hutchings Goddard was developing his liquid-fuel models. ■

6. Reading a Table
Here is a table showing how far a dropped object may fall in a certain time, if it starts from rest. It also shows how fast the object is going.

FALL OF AN OBJECT

Time	*The distance the object has fallen is*	*The object's speed is*
at 0 seconds	0 feet	0 feet per second
in 1 second	16 feet	32 feet per second
in 2 seconds	64 feet	64 feet per second
in 3 seconds	144 feet	96 feet per second
in 4 seconds	256 feet	128 feet per second
in 5 seconds	400 feet	160 feet per second

50

VERIFYING PROGRESS (cont.)

❶ 3. and 4. One scheme could be to start a table of space shots made within the preceding two years, with names and launch dates, total weight at launching, distance from Earth attained, purpose and accomplishments of the space shot.

5. Collection of pictures and data can be arranged by (a) nonorbiting rockets; (b) Earth-orbiting rockets; (c) Moon probes; (d) planetary probes. Some interested students may extend their collection backward to the use of rockets by the Chinese, in the Napoleonic wars, and even into fiction (Jules Verne). Be sure to caution children not to gather pictures from any printed source unless they have permission of the owner.

6. Responses for the questions on page 51 are:

1. 256 feet
2. 5 seconds
3. a

Using this information, can you answer these questions?

1. How far will a baseball fall in the first 4 seconds?

2. If a baseball were dropped from a height of 400 feet, how long would it take to reach the ground?

3. Which of these is true?

a. The longer an object falls, the faster is its speed.

b. The longer an object falls, the slower is its speed.

FOR YOUR READING

1. *Galileo and the Magic Numbers,* by Sidney Rosen, published by Little, Brown, Boston, 1958. This is a short biography of the mathematician and scientist. It is an especially good account of the work of a scientist.

2. *Isaac Newton,* by Patrick Moore, published by Putnam, New York, 1958. A biography of Newton, with an account of his discoveries.

3. *Gift From the Sun,* by Margaret Cooper, published by Bradbury Press, New Jersey, 1969. In this book, the author shows you how all energy, except that which comes from splitting the atom, is received from the Sun. She also reminds us that we need to make some wiser decisions about how we use this energy than we have in the past.

4. *Space Travel (A First Book),* by Jeanne Bendick, published by Franklin Watts, New York, 1969. This book will answer such questions for you as: How big is space? What is space? Where does space begin?

5. *Footprints on the Moon,* by Associated Press Writers & Editors, published by Macmillan, New York, 1969. Many color photographs will help you to understand the events that led to the triumph of man's success in landing on the Moon.

6. *Push and Pull: The Story of Energy,* Rev. ed., by Paul Blackwood, published by McGraw-Hill, New York, 1966. By trying some of the investigations in this book you will learn of some of the sources of energy and how we can put this energy to work.

7. *The Giant Book of Things in Space,* by George Zaffo, published by Doubleday, New York, 1969. As you take an imaginary trip through space, you will visit and learn about a space station, the planets and the Moon.

8. *Satellites in Outer Space,* Rev. ed., by Isaac Asimov, published by Random House, New York, 1964. Learning about satellites will help you to understand how they are useful to scientists as they try to learn more about the universe.

UNIT TWO

WE PROBE BELOW THE SURFACE

Basic behaviors sought: Children *observe* the destructive forces that break down rock and carry away soil. They also *identify* forces that act to rebuild the land by sedimentation. Children apply this knowledge to explain the forces that are continually at work to change the environment.

Children learn that pressures within the Earth can cause earthquakes. They learn that the vibrations set up by earthquakes help scientists *construct models* to *explain* the interior of the Earth. Children *analyze* the production of heat inside the Earth by radioactive decay. They learn that this heat can melt rock, and that the molten material pushing through to the surface of the Earth creates volcanoes.

Children *distinguish* between volcanoes and other mountains. They *infer* that the pressure of molten material within the Earth can cause folding and faulting.

Children *observe* different rocks and *identify* them by the minerals they contain. The children *infer* that the way rocks are formed determines their composition. They learn that the study of rocks brought from the Moon enables scientists to *theorize* about the structure and origin of the Moon.

A VIEW OF THE UNIT

The forces of weathering and erosion are continually breaking down the Earth. Rock is worn away and soil is washed down into rivers and the seas. At the same time, material that deposited on the bottoms of lakes and oceans has been compressed and cemented into rock form once again. These processes constitute a geologic cycle which is constantly changing our physical environment.

The sedimentary rock that forms on the bottom of the seas contains fossilized remains. These records of plants and animals from earlier ages help paleontologists trace the development of life forms.

Sedimentary rock may not always remain undisturbed. The Earth's crust may bend or fold and even break or fault. This process of folding and faulting can help build mountain ranges, according to one theory. If portions of the crust next to a fault slide along each other, earthquakes can result. The vibrations that are sent out by an earthquake can tell scientists about the interior of the Earth.

Heat produced inside the Earth by the decay of radioactive isotopes may be sufficient to melt rocks of the crust. This molten material, or magma, lighter than the solid rock and subject to the pressure around it, can break through the surface in a violent eruption. The building up of the lava and volcanic ash that pour out from the fissure forms the cone-shaped volcano.

Sedimentary rock formed under water may be lifted high above sea level when mountain ranges form. Thus, the sedimentary rock along with the fossils it holds may be found in mountain ranges. If sedimentary rock is again exposed to pressure and heat, it undergoes a further change and becomes metamorphic rock.

Some kinds of igneous rock are formed within the Earth and other kinds by volcanic activity. Under certain conditions, igneous rocks can also be changed into metamorphic rock. The way in which rocks are formed determines their structure and composition. Different types of rocks contain different minerals. Minerals are elements and compounds of definite structure and composition that occur naturally.

Granite and basalt are igneous rock found on the Earth's surface. Granite is more common than basalt and is found in many forms. There are several theories on the formation of granite, but scientists are not sure how the process takes place.

Some rocks did not originate from sediment or lava, but from living things. Given the proper conditions, minerals can gradually replace the parts of an organism's body, until an exact duplicate, in mineral matter, of the organism is formed. In the Petrified Forest National Park, in Arizona, the trees have been mineralized in this way.

By understanding the forces that act upon the Earth, we can explain what took place in the past, and more important, we can predict what will happen in the future.

1 Weathering and erosion

Water and wind are constantly changing the face of the Earth. Large rock formations are broken down by wind and water in a process called weathering. The rocks tend to expand as they absorb heat from the Sun during the day, and to contract as they give off the heat at night. The alternate expansion and contraction causes layers of rock to crack and peel.

Water that seeps into shallow cracks may freeze there. As the water turns to ice, it expands. Thus the ice exerts a great deal of pressure on the surrounding rock. The crack widens and the rock may eventually break up into smaller pieces. Water running over the surface of a rock dissolves certain minerals and forms small crevices on the face of the rock. The roots of plants can take hold in these crevices and continue the rock-breaking, or weathering, process.

Lichens are plants that have a large role in the weathering process. A lichen is actually two plants, an alga and a fungus. The alga provides food through photosynthesis, and the fungus takes in water and gives the plant a definite shape and produces acids that help break up the rocks. When the lichen dies, it decays and, with the rock, helps form soil in which larger plants can take root and grow.

Once rocks are broken down, the smaller pieces can be carried away by wind and water. Erosion is the process where rock and soil are removed from their original location.

In dry areas, loose sand is picked up by the wind and acts as an abrasive to wear away the surfaces of rocks and hillsides. In cultivated areas, water running down the slope of a plowed field can cut a narrow channel in the field. Water collects in the channel and runs off faster, carrying soil and minerals with it. As the channel becomes deeper and wider, it forms a gully which enlarges very rapidly. Acres of farm land can become useless if the topsoil and minerals are washed away in this fashion. An inch of topsoil that has been formed over hundreds of years can be lost in a few days of rain.

The root systems of plants and trees can help to hold the soil and thus prevent erosion. If crops such as alfalfa and clover are planted between rows of corn, the soil is kept from washing away by the roots and the dense ground cover these crops provide. Contour farming is another method of controlling erosion. Furrows are plowed around a hill rather than up and down so that the water is caught in each furrow.

Although man has accelerated the process in some areas, there are many instances of natural erosion. By carrying away tons of material, the Colorado River has carved out the Grand Canyon. Another well-known example is Niagara Falls. Estimated to be about 25,000 years old, the falls recede upstream every year by eroding the lip of the falls. Before 1906, the falls moved back over one yard each year. The amount of erosion has decreased slightly since then, but the erosion process itself is still going on.

2 Sedimentary rock formation

Eroded material is carried away by streams and rivers. This material is eventually deposited on the bottom of rivers, lakes, and seas. Sediment is the term used for the sand, gravel, and mud that settles to the bottom of a body of water. Sedimentation occurs in a river or stream when the water slows down or stops flowing. It also occurs where a river meets a large body of water. The Mississippi River, for example, deposits 400 million tons of material into the Gulf of Mexico annually.

When the material begins to settle, the heaviest particles, pebbles or gravel, drop to the bottom first. If the water is quiet, sand follows, and finally particles of fine soil. Near the shore sedimentation will appear as a sort of underwater rainfall. As it settles, the sediment forms layers, the coarsest particles in the lowest level. Each succeeding layer, farther from the shore, is composed of finer and finer particles.

Throughout the years, the layers of sediment are covered over with new deposits. The lowest levels experience a great deal of pressure and they begin to harden. Also, minerals in the sediment, such as silica and calcium carbonate, cement the deposit together. The lower levels of sediment slowly become sedimentary rock. Thus the eroded material is converted back to rock form and serves to rebuild the Earth.

Sedimentary rock is also important because its layers may contain the fossilized bodies or impressions of plants and animals. These fossils are formed when a living thing or its dead parts become trapped in mud or the depositing sediment. Because the plant or animal parts are not exposed to the air, some or all of them may not decay. Instead, the minerals dissolved in the water penetrate the bones (of an animal) or cell walls (of a plant). The minerals harden in the form of the original plant or animal. Often, only the impression of the body remains. The formation of this kind of fossil is often called petrifaction, turning to stone. An imprint or impression is another kind of fossil. For example, animal tracks, leaf prints, or worm holes may originate in mud that later hardens into rock.

Fossils are important because they enable scientists to follow the changes that have taken place in the form of plants and animals. Scientists who study fossilized remains in order to describe the gradual development of life forms are called paleontologists. Scientists also use fossils to help determine the ages of rock layers.

3 Earthquakes and the interior of the Earth

Earthquakes provide much information about the interior of the Earth. An earthquake occurs when portions of the Earth's outer layer suddenly slide along each other. The violent movement sends out vibrations that travel through the Earth in all directions. During the earthquake in Los Angeles on February 9, 1971, tremors were felt as far away as Fresno, 200 miles to the north, and Las Vegas, 225 miles northeast. The vibrations are detected and recorded on seismographs. The magnitude of an earthquake is measured by the Richter scale. A value of 4.5 is considered potentially dangerous. The San Francisco earthquake of 1906 was measured at 8.5; the Los Angeles quake of 1971 at 6.5. The Peru quake of 1970 was measured at 7.75.

Several types of vibrations are set up by an earthquake. Pressure waves and shear waves provide most of the information concerning the interior of the Earth. Pressure waves travel through solid, liquid, and gas; much like sound waves, they are alternate bands of compressions and rarefactions. Shear waves move only through solids and glassy liquids. Although the direction of the shear wave is forward, the material the wave goes through moves back and forth at right angles to the direction of the wave. As the waves travel through the Earth, their velocities and directions are changed. Like sound, these waves travel faster through denser materials. Scientists can thus determine what type of material the waves are passing through.

Although they have no visible proof, scientists believe that they have devised an accurate model of the Earth's interior from the evidence provided by earthquakes. The Earth's outermost layer is called the crust. The crust is made up of basalt, a dark, fine-grained rock, with granite and sediment covering it.

The mantle lies under the crust. The material that composes the mantle is assumed to be very dense. Yet because of the high temperature and pressure of the mantle, scientists believe that the material may be able to flow very slowly. The crust and the mantle are separated by a definite boundary called the Mohorovičič Discontinuity or, simply, the Moho.

The other layers of the Earth are the inner and outer cores. The inner core is thought to be solid, and the outer core liquid. It is believed that both portions of the core are mostly iron with nickel and other materials.

4 Volcanoes

The Earth's expansion can produce large cracks, or fissures, through which magma can flow. Magma is molten material formed below the surface from rocks of the Earth's crust. The magma is heavily charged with gases and steam. It is lighter than solid rock and so tends to move toward the surface, pushed upward by pressure of the surrounding rock. If there is a break in the crust, the pressure on the gases in the magma is suddenly reduced. Thus the gases expand rapidly, creating a violent eruption. The magma loses its gases and steam to the rocks and atmosphere, and pours out onto the surface of the Earth as lava.

Other substances are ejected during a volcanic eruption. One of these materials is volcanic ash, formed by the hardening of the lava before eruption. Over many years, the lava and volcanic ash cool and harden into the familiar cone-shaped volcanoes, for example, Vesuvius or Lassen Peak. Volcanoes may form on the surface of the continents or on the sea floor. The areas of volcanic activity correspond to the regions of greatest earthquake activity.

The heat required to form magma is provided by the decay of radioactive isotopes. Atoms of all the elements (except hydrogen) are made up of protons and neutrons in a central nucleus, with the electrons orbiting the nucleus. Atoms of the same element have the same number of protons and electrons. However, atoms of the same element may have different numbers of neutrons. Two forms of the same element that differ only in weight are called isotopes. Isotopes of an element have the same chemical properties, but different weights. Some isotopes are stable; they do not break down. Others are radioactive. In radioactive decay, the nucleus of an atom breaks, gives off energy and smaller particles, and changes to a nucleus of a different element.

The most common radioactive isotopes in the Earth's crust are potassium-40, thorium-234, and uranium-238. The number that follows the name of the element is the mass number. It is the sum of the protons and neutrons in the nucleus. In the nucleus of uranium-238 there are 92 protons and 146 neutrons. When it decays, the nucleus gives off an alpha particle made up of 2 protons and 2 neutrons, what is left is a thorium nucleus with 90 protons and 144 neutrons.

Scientists can produce nuclear reaction by shooting particles such as neutrons at the nucleus of an atom. Two entirely different nuclei and energy are produced. This reaction is called fission. The radioactive decay within the Earth, however, spontaneously produces energy and a change in the nucleus. As each nucleus decays, the minute amount of energy that is released produces heat. This energy is absorbed by the surrounding rocks. Thus, the deep rocks may absorb enough energy to melt and become part of the magma in the mantle.

5 Making a mountain

Many of the high mountain ranges we can see today are composed of sedimentary rock. Because the layers of rock contain fossilized remains of sea organisms, geologists know that the sedimentary rock was formed in the sea.

According to one theory, a mountain range may have started to form when sediments piled up in a kind of trough, known as a geosyncline, in the shallow waters of a continental shelf. Pressure from both sides of the geosyncline on layers of sediment, may cause them to fold and fault. Layers of rock may be lifted by such folding and faulting, eventually resulting in a mountain range.

Volcanoes, we know, can be formed on land or beneath the sea. The magma pushes through the crust to the surface, and the cone-shaped mountain begins to form underwater. When the mountain rises above the surface of the water it forms a small island. In 1963, off the coast of Iceland, the islands of Surtsey and Syrtlinger were formed in this way. The islands of Hawaii were all created by cooling lava. Mauna Loa, the great volcano of Hawaii, is nearly 32,000 feet high, measured from its base in the sea. Mount Everest, by comparison, is 29,028 feet high.

According to another theory, radioactive decay and pressure of the crust on the magma of the mantle cause the magma to flow slowly. If there is no crack through which the magma can escape in volcanic eruption, the land may be slowly pushed upwards until the pressures are equalized. This upward pressure may form mountain ranges.

6 Minerals and rocks

Geologists distinguish the substances of the Earth according to the way these substances occur. Rocks are samples of compounds found in nature. They have no definite shape, and because their composition can vary, they have no fixed properties. Rocks can be identified by the minerals within them.

Minerals are composed of the same elements or compounds and so do have consistent properties. Gold, silver, salt, and quartz are examples of minerals.

Rocks are classified into three groups according to how they have been formed. These groups are igneous, sedimentary, and metamorphic rock. Igneous rock is formed from cooling lava. The molten magma beneath the Earth's crust may escape to the surface through a volcano. The magma, now called lava, cools to form various kinds of volcanic rocks. Obsidian is a dark, glassy material having no crystal structure at all. Granite, another form of igneous rock, is more common on the Earth's surface. There are several theories on the formation of granite, and scientists are not sure exactly how the process takes place.

Granite is made up of several minerals. And different types of granite contain varying amounts of these minerals. Quartz is a glossy, crystalline material that can often be found by itself. Feldspars are milky white or pink portions of granite that make up about 60 percent of the volume. Mica is a bright, brittle material that breaks off in sheets. Hornblende is a black, crystalline substance. The size of the mineral crystals depends on the rate at which they form. The more quickly the rock cooled, the smaller the crystals. Large crystals are formed if the material cools very slowly. Quartz, for example, can be found in aggregates of large crystals with six sides rectangular and two end faces. Impurities that are trapped as the quartz crystallizes give it the pale rose or purple color.

Sedimentary rock, as we know, was formed under water. There are several types of sedimentary rock: sandstone, limestone, chalk, and conglomerate. Layers of sand, cemented together by minerals, form sandstone. Limestone is mainly calcium carbonate. Chalk is a kind of limestone that has been formed from the shells of sea animals, such as clams, oysters, or coral. When the animals die, the empty shells fall to the bottom of the sea and get crushed into a fine powder. Shale is formed from layers of fine clay soil, compressed and cemented together.

Sedimentary rock that has been folded or buried under additional deposits is subjected to more pressure and heat. This sedimentary rock undergoes further change and is then called metamorphic rock. Given the correct conditions, igneous rocks, too, may change into metamorphic rock. Slate, marble, schist, and gneiss are metamorphic rocks.

Rocks have also been formed from living things. Trees buried for millions of years become mineralized; that is, petrified. Minerals dissolved in the water replace the wood and form an exact duplicate of the once-living tree.

The manned exploration of the Moon has provided scientists with samples of rock from the lunar surface. The form and composition of these rocks has shown that they were formed either by intense heat or by volcanic activity. Several theories have been proposed to support both positions.

Since the lunar rocks brought back by early Apollo missions appear to be of a composition similar to igneous rocks on Earth, it is possible that they have a volcanic origin. Also, volcanoes could explain the formation of the craters and mountains of the Moon. Whether these volcanoes are still active is a question that remains unanswered.

If the rocks are not volcanic in origin, they may have been formed by heat caused by the impact of a meteorite. Meteorites could also be the cause of the smaller craters.

SUPPLEMENTARY AIDS

All films and filmstrips are in color. All films are accompanied by sound; filmstrips are accompanied by sound only if so designated. Names and addresses of producers and distributors are on page F-29.

Filmstrips

The Ocean Basins (45 frames, sound), #503-2, SVE. Shows very clearly the topography of the ocean floor. Presents theories of how mountains and canyons are formed.

Our Changing Earth (40 frames), #143B, Eye Gate. Shows different kinds of mountains and how they were formed; illustrates changes caused by erosion, earthquakes, and temperature variations.

The Rocks (61 frames), #71w2000C, Ward's. Igneous, sedimentary, and metamorphic rocks are discussed, and many examples of each are pictured.

The Story of Mountains (58 frames), #7484, EBEC. Shows various ways mountains are formed.

Volcanoes and Earthquakes (40 frames), #431-5, SVE. Pictures a cross-section of a volcano and explains how lava may help in forming a mountain. Explains how earthquakes are caused. Discusses seismography.

Weathering and Erosion (68 frames), #71W2100, Ward's. Illustrates erosion by wind, running water, glaciers, gravity, and man's activities.

Films

Earthquakes and Volcanoes (14 min.), BFA. Presents the causes of both earthquakes and volcanoes and the relationship between them.

Rocks in Our Neighborhood (13 min.), #402068, McGraw-Hill. Tells the story of rocks—their formation, general characteristics, and uses.

What's Inside the Earth? (14 min.), BFA. Explores the interior of the Earth.

What's Under the Ocean? (14 min.), BFA. How scientists study the ocean in special craft, such as a bathyscaph and map the ocean floor.

Changing the Face of the Earth (41 frames), #431-11, SVE. Dramatizes the constant struggle between land-building and land-eroding forces.

Science Reading Table

About Caves by Terry Shannon, Melmont, 1962. Explains how caves are explored; the value of cave discoveries. (Easy)

All About the Planet Earth by Patricia Lauber, Random House, 1962. Planet Earth is described with interesting narrative pictures. (Average)

The Bottom of the Sea by Augusta R. Goldin, Crowell, 1966. In clear, simple language, the author describes the tools used by the scientists and the formation of the sea—its cliffs, mountains, canyons, and volcanoes. (Easy)

The Colorado: River of Mystery by Mary and Conrad Buff, Ward Ritchie Press, 1968. Through the use of beautiful illustrations and poetic prose, the authors tell the story of this magnificent river and the effect it has had on the Earth and the people who depend on it for water to irrigate the land. (Average)

Deep-Sea World: The Story of Oceanography by Charles Coombs, Morrow, 1966. A thought-provoking book about the formation of the oceans and deep-sea exploration. (Average)

Exploring the World of Oceanography by Dorothy Telfer, Childrens Press, 1968. Well-illustrated, detailed popularization of oceanographic exploration. (Advanced)

The Earth's Story by Gerald and Rose Wyler Ames, Creative Educational Society, 1962. An excellent reference. Interesting narrative and many photographs describe major changes which occur on and within the Earth. (Advanced)

Rocks All Around Us by Anne Terry White, Random House, 1959. The changes rocks undergo, and ancient formations of rocks in present use are described. (Easy)

The Rock Hounds by Donald Nasca and Glenn Sprague, F. A. Owen, 1964. A narrative story of the rockhound activities of two boys, interwoven with information about rocks. (Easy)

The Soil Story by Helen Heffernan and George Shaftel, Singer, 1965. A useful reference for such topics as conservation and the properties of soils. (Advanced)

Wonders of Rocks and Minerals by Richard M. Pearl, Dodd, Mead, 1961. Includes sections on rock formation and structure, minerals, crystals, precious stones, metals, and procedures for collecting. (Average)

An Analysis of Behaviors in Concept-Seeking*

Conceptual Scheme C: The Universe is in continuous change.
Unit Concept-Statement: Bodies in space are in continuous change.

Lesson Cluster titles in blue guide concept-seeking toward the Unit Concept-Statement. Other titles enrich the Conceptual Scheme (*see page F-23*).

Lesson Cluster and Supporting Statement	*Operations Basic to Concept-Seeking**	*Methods of Intelligence (Processes and Behaviors)*
1. Wearing Away a Mountain Weathering and erosion continually break down the land.	**Investigating** the effects of weathering and erosion on rocks	**Analyzing** the roles of weather, water and plants; **inferring** that these forces break down rocks; **observing** the forces that break down rocks; **hypothesizing** on forces that build up the land
2. A Visit to the Bottom of the Sea Sediment continually builds up the land.	**Probing** "rain under the sea" and fossilization; **investigating** sedimentation	**Inferring** that heaviest particles sort out first in sedimentation; **analyzing** the process of sedimentation; **theorizing** on how the process occurs; **hypothesizing** on how fossils are formed
3. A First Model of the Earth The Earth is always changing.	**Investigating** how sound waves travel; **probing** earthquake waves and the Earth's interior	**Distinguishing** between sound traveling in a solid and air; **theorizing** on a hole drilled through the Earth's crust
4. The Furnace in the Earth Heat and pressure cause continuous changes within the Earth.	**Probing** into the source of the Earth's heat, the structure of atoms and radioactive decay	**Identifying** volcanic activity; **distinguishing** volcanoes and other mountains; **analyzing** the structure of atoms and heat and pressure in the Earth; **distinguishing** the heat produced by radioactivity and heat from the Sun
5. Up Go the Mountains Heat and pressure are continually changing the Earth's crust.	**Probing** the formation of mountains by folding and faulting	**Identifying** that upward pressure of magma may cause folding and faulting
6. Treasure in the Earth and on the Moon The way in which rocks are formed determines their make-up.	**Investigating** the main kinds of rocks	**Observing** crystal structure; **identifying** minerals; **making inferences** from the variations in rocks
7. The Main Concept: The Changing Earth Bodies in space are in continuous change.	Children **synthesize** an understanding of the geologic cycle, **infer** that the Earth is in constant change, and **conclude** that man builds on the work of others.	

**A concept is synonymous with the corresponding operations. In turn, operations are served by relevant methods of intelligence.*

UNIT TWO
WE PROBE BELOW THE SURFACE

Teaching background. "A View of the Unit," T-58

Concept-seeking. Children begin to become aware of the forces of change at work in the Earth's crust.

Operations. Children *investigate* the wearing away of rocks by shaking them in a jar of water.

Methods of intelligence. Children *observe* that rocks become smaller and smoother when shaken in water, and that the water becomes muddy. They *explain their observations* by stating that shaking rocks in water causes the rocks to be worn away.

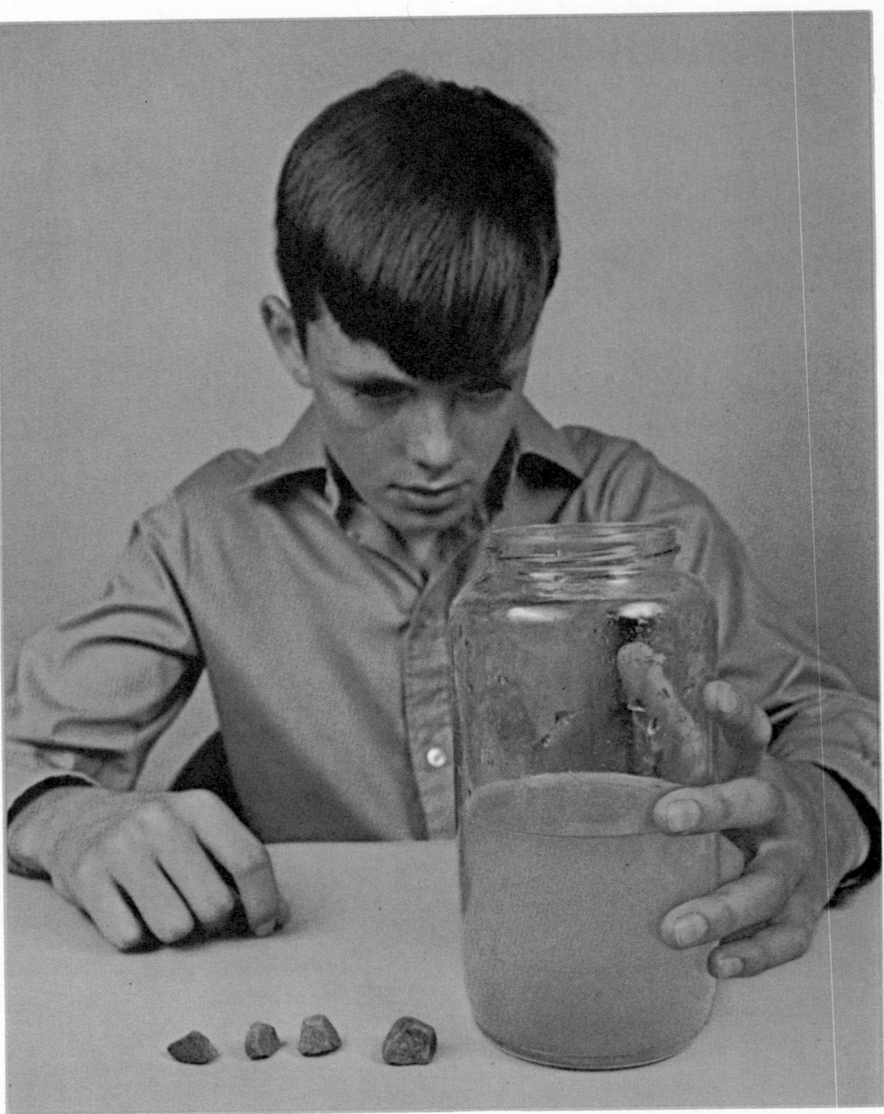

Useful materials: Limestone or sandstone, plastic bags, gallon jars with lids, water, fine sand, three covered containers (such as ice-cream cartons), paper.

Introducing the unit

Prepare in advance covered containers of fine sand, small pieces of broken rock, and one larger rock. Sandstone will do nicely.

Pour some of the sand on a piece of paper. **What do you think this came from?** Accept any responses without comment. (beach, store, rocks, and so on) Now empty the pieces of rock on another piece of paper. **What do you think these came from?** The responses may be more limited. Now show the large rock. **How could these three piles be related?** (all rock or parts of rocks)

You are now ready for the children to work in groups as directed on page 53.

UNIT TWO

We Probe Below the Surface

Obtain a hand-size piece of soft rock. Either limestone or sandstone will do fine. Place the ❶ rock in a plastic bag. Then use a hammer to break the rock into 3 or 4 pieces, each about an inch wide.■ Place the pieces in a large glass jar about half full of water.●

Close the jar tightly, and shake about 100 times. Then open the jar and remove one piece of the rock. Close the jar again, shake 100 times, and remove another piece of rock.

Repeat until you have removed all the pieces of rock. Arrange the rocks on a piece of paper in the order in which you removed them.

❷ What do you observe about the rocks? What is left in the jar of water?

How do you explain your observations?

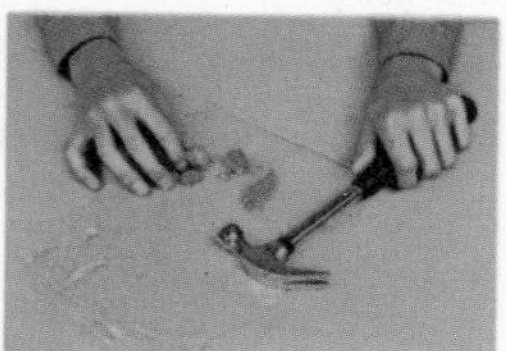
■

●

53

❶ To avoid injury from flying particles, be sure the children wrap the rocks in plastic bags, as directed, or in several layers of cloth or newspaper before they use the hammer. The work should be done on a surface that will not be marred, such as the floor.

❷ What happened to the rocks when you shook them with the water? (They were worn away.) Children should observe that the rock removed after 200 shakes is more worn (smaller and smoother) than the one removed after 100 shakes, and so on. They should also observe that bits of rock are left in the water after the rock pieces are taken out. How do all your observations suggest that water helps to break up rocks? To explain their observations, children may suggest that the collisions of the rocks with the jar and with each other, as well as their motion through the water, helped to wear away the rocks.

LESSON CLUSTER 1

WEARING AWAY A MOUNTAIN

Teaching background. 1 T-58

Concept-seeking. Children discover reasons for the constant wearing down of the Earth's surface.

Operations. Children *investigate* different kinds of rocks and their weathering and erosion in the environment around them.

Methods of intelligence. Children *analyze* the roles of weather, water, and plants, and *infer* that they produce forces that break down rock. Children *observe* and *identify* the forces at work in eroding rocks. They *hypothesize* what forces may act to build up the land again.

1. Wearing Away a Mountain

Suppose you could watch a mountain for a million years or so. How would the mountain change? After many years of study of the way mountains are formed, **geologists** (jē·ol′ə·jists), the scientists who study the Earth and its ❶ history, have come to know young from old mountains. When a mountain is young, its edges are rough and jagged. Its rocky peaks are pointed. ■ As a mountain ages, however, it wears down and its peaks become less sharp. Let's see how this happens.

Heating and Cooling Rock

❷ By day, the energy of the Sun acts on the bare rock of the young mountains. How does the Sun's energy heat the rock? Heat causes rock to expand. As you might expect, the outside of the rock is heated more than the inside.

By night, the rock cools and contracts—but the outside of the rock cools faster than the inside. Day and night the rock expands and contracts, expands and contracts, again and ❸ again. Cracks begin to show in the rock.

54

Introducing Lesson Cluster 1

Hold up your hands with finger tips together forming a cone shape. Then bend your fingers to form a rounded arch. Which of the two shapes is that of a young mountain? (the cone) of an older mountain? (the rounded arch) What led you to infer the rounded shape represented older mountains? (worn down) What forces could change jagged peaks into gently rounded hills? Children may mention water or other agents of weathering and erosion. Accept all responses without comment at this time.

Developing the lesson

❶ There's a mountain in North Carolina called Grandfather Mountain; its top is rounded. Would this mountain be younger or older than the Rockies? (older)

❷ Some children will know that we receive radiant energy from the Sun, but probably they will not be aware that the Sun's energy turns into heat only after being absorbed by some substance. What kind of energy does the Sun's energy become when it hits the rock? (heat energy)

❸ It is not always obvious why repeated heating and cooling, and the stresses this sets up, should make cracks. What happens when you pour ice water into a hot glass? (It cracks or breaks.) Glass and rock are brittle; what substances might not crack? (butter, etc.)

Supporting Statement: Weathering and erosion continually break down the land.

Water from rain and snow runs into the cracks. The water changes the rocks as they get hotter and cooler. Sometimes, when water freezes in a crack, the crack widens. If the crack widens enough, the rocks may split. In time, a rock may be worn down into a handful of sand.

The breaking down of rock by weather is called ❶ **weathering.** Watching a mountain for a million years or so, you would see the sharp edges and pointed peaks of the young mountain being worn by weathering. You would see the edges and peaks becoming round and smooth, as the forces of weathering worked on them.

Gentle Plants and Solid Rock

If you could watch a mountain over a million years or so, you would see how rocks can be changed by plants. Perhaps you might watch **lichens** (lī′kənz) at work. ● A lichen is really *two* plants; one a colorless plant called a **fungus,** the other a green plant called an **alga.** The two plants live together, with the threads of the fungus wrapped around the alga. The drawing in the circle shows how the fungus of one kind of lichen looks when magnified. The threads of the fungus soak in and hold water. The alga makes food. The two plants depend on each other.

❷ Lichens can stand great heat, great cold, and great dryness. Looking at lichens on the mountain, you would see them gripping the rock. You would see specks of wind-blown soil caught in the lichens and fastened to the rock. Most remarkable of all, you would find that lichens make and give off substances that help break down rock and form soil.

Some of this soil slides into a crack in the rock. Then seeds fall into the crack. As seeds soak up water, they expand. Soon they begin to sprout roots and to grow. Expanding seeds and growing plants can push with great force. Have you ever noticed a plant forcing its way through ❸ a crack in a sidewalk? Growing plants are powerful. They are so powerful that they can help break rock apart and wear down a mountain.

VERIFYING PROGRESS

In methods of intelligence

To determine children's ability to *identify* the parts of a lichen and *describe* their functions, they may *construct* labelled sketches of the lichen shown in the circled part of the illustration on this page. They should label one of the little green spheres ***alga,*** one of the colorless threads ***fungus,*** and write the title ***lichen*** above or below their sketch. Which part of the lichen makes food? (alga) Which part takes in water? (fungus)

Useful materials: Piece of rock with lichen on it, small plastic containers with lids, dried beans.

❶ *Weathering* generally refers to changes in the surfaces of things. Can wood be weathered? (yes) Can metal objects weather? (yes) Some children may have seen the green color on old metallic objects containing copper. Have children offer more examples: bricks, building stones, flagstones, mortar, steel and aluminum surfaces, etc. Children should see that weathering really means the changes that are brought about by the weather: changes in temperature; freezing and thawing.

❷ Who has seen *lichens* on rocks? If a child can bring in a sample of a lichen on a rock, let children examine it. How are lichens different from moss, grass, flat mushrooms? (Moss and grass grow taller and are usually greener than lichens; mushrooms and other fungus plants are not green at all.) Where does the alga get material for making food? (the air and water) Children may or may not be aware that the water contains dissolved substances plants can use in food-making.

❸ Who has seen rocks broken or house foundations or sidewalks split by growing plants? To show the force of expansion of seeds, let children fill some plastic containers with dried beans, then water to the brim, cap tightly, and leave overnight. As the beans soak up water, they may force the tops off the containers, or cause the sides to bulge or even break.

EXTENDING THE LESSON

What difference is there between weathering and erosion on the Earth and the breaking down and movement of rocks on the Moon? Children will recall (text page 37) that the Moon has no air and no water. Thus, it has no weather. Since there can be no movement of water and no atmosphere to create wind on the Moon, there is no erosion due to these forces. What other forces besides those of air and water are at work on the Moon? (temperature changes)

Useful materials: About a dozen each of smooth pebbles and angular flagstone fragments (from an aquarium store or builder's supply yard).

A "Saw" of Water

❶ Weather and plants are not the only forces that break down and wear away mountains. A visit to the Grand Canyon of the Colorado River will show you another force at work.

The sight of the Grand Canyon takes one's breath away. ■ The beauty of the colored bands in the light of the setting sun is hard to believe. Each band is a layer of rock.

Millions of years ago there was no canyon here. There was only the river, flowing across the plain. As the river flowed, however, it carried along rocks and pebbles. Rolling
❷ and bumping and scraping along the river bottom, the rocks and pebbles dug the channel deeper. Thus the river wore away the rock over which it was flowing. We call this
❸ wearing away of the Earth's surface **erosion** (i·rō′zhən).

■

56

Continuing Lesson Cluster 1

❶ What other forces could break up mountains and wear them away? Some children may mention such forces as earthquakes, meteorites, and volcanoes, but most are likely to agree on wind and water.

❷ Mix some smooth pebbles, and some angular flagstone fragments. Challenge children, with their eyes shut, to tell by touch alone which of the stones are waterworn. How can you tell which of these rocks may have been carried by water? (smooth ones are waterworn)

❸ Compare ***weathering*** and ***erosion:*** weathering brings about changes in the surfaces of objects and breaks them down; erosion wears away and removes them. Where did the rocks in the river come from? (They were broken by weathering, then carried into the river by water erosion or blown there by wind erosion.)

Supporting Statement: Weathering and erosion continually break down the land.

By erosion, the river cut its way down through the rock layers like a giant saw.

1 This gully was made by running water. ● At first, no one noticed the crack made by running rainwater. Every rain carried away more soil, however, making room for more water and more erosion. The result: Precious soil was lost.

2 There are other forces of erosion at work besides running water. Look at the strange forms of these rocks. ▲ When the wind blows here, it hurls sharp grains of sand against the rocks. Over the years, the rushing wind and biting sand have eroded the rocks, much as sandpaper wears down wood. Erosion is the sculptor of these forms.

57

EXTENDING THE LESSON

You will need these materials: soil, clay, gravel; fist-sized rocks, hose attached to outdoor faucet, small electric fan, shallow box of soil, white cheesecloth.

Demonstrate how the wind "airlifts" soil particles by directing a small electric fan at a shallow box of soil. A white cheesecloth tacked up behind the box will show the movement of soil. Who knows an example of man-made erosion used for a good purpose? (sandblasting of city buildings to clean them)

Useful materials. About two quarts of a mixture of soil, clay, and gravel; about a dozen fist-sized rocks; hose attached to outdoor faucet.

1 This is a good time for a short field trip. Have children look for gullies on slopes, sediment washing down onto a flat surface and fanning out, meandering streamlets after a rainfall. How do these miniature examples compare to real canyons, valleys, and deltas? Have children look along the borders of sidewalks for accumulations of fine soil carried down by sheet erosion. Feel for soil from splash erosion on the outside baseboard of frame buildings.

To illustrate erosion by water in the corner of the school yard: Pack a mixture of different kinds of soil, clay, and gravel around a dozen or so rocks as big as a fist. Turn a hose onto the model. Which particles wash away the easiest and quickest? (small ones) Which particles resist erosion the longest? (the heaviest) Does the water running off go in all directions or does it find and make a few set channels and stick to those?

2 What two things mainly cause erosion? (water and wind) Is it the water and wind themselves that cause the erosion, or the things they carry with them? (mostly the latter for the *wearing away* process; mostly the former for the *carrying away* process) Encourage the children to form their own hypotheses about these questions before the responses are discussed. List the hypotheses on the chalkboard.

Unit Concept-Statement: Bodies in space are in continuous change.

Thus weathering and erosion shape the land. Heating and cooling, water and plants, break rock down. Water and wind erode rock, and carry it away. In weathering, the
❶ rocks are broken down and loosened. In erosion, they are swept away.

The Changing Surface

During many millions of years, weathering and erosion break down rock and gradually wear down a mountain. The sharp peaks of the young mountain become the rounded
❷ peaks of an old mountain.

Where does all the weathered and eroded rock go? Some of it is spread on the land and becomes part of the soil. Some of it is carried by rains and rivers into the oceans.

❸ All around you the forces of erosion and weathering are carrying away soil, wearing away rock, and breaking down stone. Do you have to watch a mountain to see these forces at work? No, indeed. Wherever you live, in the country or in the city, you can see these forces at work—if you look. Why not search out the weathering and erosion around you?

58

Continuing Lesson Cluster 1

❶ It may be well here to review the difference between weathering and erosion. Various questions may help to bring out that weathering is a *changing* process; erosion is a *removing* process.

❷ What young mountains and old mountains have you seen? Where are they? Which are more likely to have trees growing right up to the top: old mountains or young mountains? (old) If the Rocky Mountains are young at 60 million years, how old do you think old mountains may be? (The Appalachians, for example, are estimated to be about 340 million years old.) About how many times younger are the Rockies? (nearly 6 times)

❸ What is it about water and wind that causes erosion? (They are in movement.) What happens to particles of soil being carried by a river when it reaches the sea? (They drop down and are deposited.) What happens to particles in the air when the wind stops blowing? (They drop down.) What are the places where a river can deposit its eroded soil? (where the river slows down: along its banks at a sand bar in the middle, and at its delta) Where can the wind deposit the soil it is carrying? (anywhere)

Supporting Statement: Weathering and erosion continually break down the land.

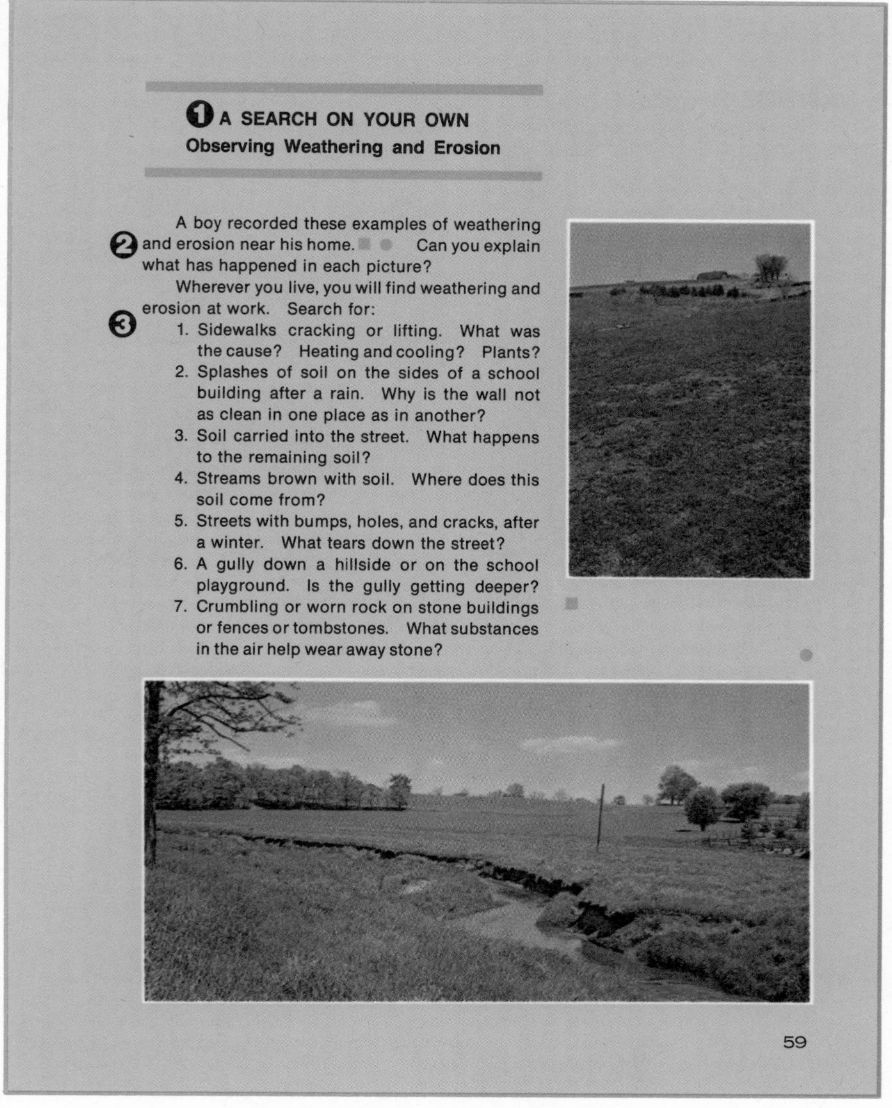

VERIFYING PROGRESS

❶ **A search on your own.** Children *observe* different types of weathering and erosion in their environment and *analyze* the causes of each kind of change.

❷ The pictures show sheet erosion (top) and stream bank erosion (bottom).

❸ 1. A string held tight will help determine if any slabs are out of line. Look for plant roots nearby, or for temperature changes.

2. Children might drive splash sticks into the ground at different locations and compare the height of splashed mud after a rain.

3. Rain tends to remove the fine topsoil and plant debris. Remaining soil may fissure, pack down, and dry out faster.

4. Check for two things: runoff and bank erosion.

5. Water freezes and heaves asphalt during extreme cold. In general, the more water at a given point, winter or spring, the more damage to the road at that point.

6. Which kind of channel seems to get deeper: a straight one or a crooked one? Are there tiny cliffs and caves in the side walls?

7. Can you find any rocks showing peeling of outer layers, due to heating and cooling? What is likely to be growing on old tombstones?

Unit Concept-Statement: Bodies in space are in continuous change.

VERIFYING PROGRESS

In methods of intelligence

Children may determine their progress as they *identify* the forces causing weathering and erosion, *distinguish* between these two processes and between wearing away and carrying away in erosion, and *demonstrate* these processes with their models.

In concept-seeking

Let each child *build* his own *model* to *demonstrate* one of the following:

(a) weathering through heating and cooling (a soft rock in a pan may be heated on the stove, then placed on ice cubes, several times);

(b) weathering through freezing (let a plastic container full of water, tightly capped, burst in freezer compartment overnight);

(c) erosion through wind-borne sand (blow sand through a straw at powder);

(d) erosion by wind or water (referring to previous pages, use loose soil and running water or air being blown).

❶ BEFORE YOU GO ON

A. Check your understanding of the concepts of this section. Which ending would you choose for each statement below?

1. When rocks are heated they
   a. expand b. contract
2. When rocks are cooled, they
   a. expand b. contract
3. When rocks are broken down by heat and cold, we call the process
   a. weathering b. erosion
4. When bits of rock and soil are worn away by wind or water, we call the process
   a. weathering b. erosion
5. The statement that fits the main concept of this section is
   a. Weathering and erosion build up the land.
   b. Weathering and erosion break down the land.

B. Write a paragraph or two on this topic: "How a Mountain Is Worn Down."

USING WHAT YOU KNOW ❷

1. A hillside may be plowed down or across the slope. Which way is better for saving water? Which way is better for saving soil? What are the reasons for your answers?

2. A farmer has a fast-running stream on his land. He is advised to build small dams (called check dams) across the stream. Of what use will check dams be?

3. How would you recognize an old mountain? How does an old mountain differ from a young one? If there are any mountains near your home, try to find out how old scientists think they are.

INVESTIGATING FURTHER ❸

As you have learned, lichens are one kind of plant that can grow on rocks. Once the lichens begin to break down a rock, however, other kinds of plants (such as mosses) can grow on the rock. Look for mosses growing on a rock. Describe what is happening to the rock.

A LOOK AHEAD

Slowly, slowly, over millions of years, mountains break down. Weathering turns mountains into tons of soil. Erosion carries the soil away. The land is worn down.

How, then, is the land built up? To find out, we must go, of all places, to the bottom of the sea! Can you think why? What is your hypothesis?

60

VERIFYING PROGRESS (cont.)

❶ Before you go on. Children *demonstrate* understanding of the role of weathering and erosion in breaking down the land by *identifying* suitable responses to questions.

A. 1. a 3. a 5. b
   2. b 4. b

B. An alternate activity is to let pairs of children make a series of labeled pictures and diagrams.

❷ Using what you know. Children *analyze* situations dealing with erosion; they *predict* and *describe* methods for correcting it.

1. Across, to save both soil and water. Furrows plowed straight down the hill would become gullies for the water to run down quickly. Furrows across the downward pitch of the hill tend to retain the water.

2. They will slow the stream and check the runoff of topsoil.

3. Young mountains are pointed, jagged, rocky, and often have little vegetation. Old mountains are smoother, flatter and more rounded, and may have more vegetation. For the estimated ages of mountain ranges that may be in your area, children should consult an encyclopedia.

❸ Investigating further. Children *observe, describe,* and *explain* the biological weathering of rock. Those interested in plants may *investigate* the difference between lichens and mosses. Could moss start growing on a bare rock before lichens were there? Why? (No; moss would need some soil in which to anchor itself, and lichens produce the soil by breaking down rock.)

2. A Visit to the Bottom of the Sea

❶ This man is an aquanaut. ■ His exciting work is to investigate the bottom of the sea. The vessel which you see in the picture takes him down to the part of the sea floor that is near the coast. The aquanauts who go down to the bottom observe many strange things. One thing they may see is a kind of slow rain, a rain of material falling through the water to the sea bottom near the shore. What is this rain under the sea?

Rain Under the Sea

❷ Tiny rocks, pebbles, grains of sand, specks of soil, and other material are raining to the bottom of the sea. Sometimes they can't be seen at all, but the rain goes on, year after year.

61

LESSON CLUSTER 2
A VISIT TO THE BOTTOM OF THE SEA

Teaching background. 2 T-59

Concept-seeking. Children become aware that weathering and erosion help to build land up through sedimentation.

Operations. Children *investigate* "rain under the sea," the process of sedimentation and how fossils form.

Methods of intelligence. Children *infer* that during sedimentation the heavier particles are sorted out first. They *analyze* and *describe* the process of sedimentation, and *theorize* as to how this process occurs as it does. They *hypothesize* as to how fossils are formed in sedimentary rock.

Introducing Lesson Cluster 2

When the children open to this page, ask them to suggest what the aquanaut in the picture might see underwater. Encourage them to speculate, and accept all their responses without comment. What kind of weather might an aquanaut encounter? (probably no responses other than "What do you mean?") What kind of rain might an aquanaut expect? After a pause add, Near the mouth of a river? The children are now primed to read the lesson.

Developing the lesson

❶ The vessel in the picture is the Buoyancy Transport Vehicle (BTV) built by the Naval Undersea Research and Development Center, Hawaii. Children interested in undersea research may want to find out more about the BTV, or other undersea vehicles, in the library.

❷ Why can't some of the particles raining down through the water be seen? (because they are so small, or so fine) Can a particle be too small to see yet heavy enough to fall through water? (Yes, a tiny particle of rock will fall.)

EXTENDING THE LESSON

Ask children to look again at the delta on the map. Why are there tongues of land sticking out into the sea? Children may be interested to know that the Mississippi, for example, lays down over a million tons of sediment every day. At such a rate, it is not surprising that enough sediment to make tongues of land into the sea would soon accumulate.

Children interested in maps may be able to read the contour lines on a physical map and tell which rivers flow fast, and which slowly.

Useful materials: Topographic maps, including one that shows delta of the Mississippi or another river.

Where does this rain come from? Think of the rivers flowing from the land down to the sea. Every river is doing its work of erosion and is carrying along particles of rock, soil, and other substances that it has picked up on its course. We call this material that it carries along **sediment** (sed′ə·mənt). The river dumps its load of sediment into the sea. All along ❶ the coast, sediment is poured into the sea by rivers. Year after year, these sediments rain down on the ocean floor.

You can make a model of layers of sediment piling up under water. See for yourself how this happens, as shown on the opposite page. MODEL ❷

Layers Under the Sea

Sometimes the rivers coming down to the sea are full almost to overloading. As they rush along, they bring a ❸ heavy load of coarse sediment, with many large pieces of rock. At other times, the rivers move slowly and do not have much force. Then the sediment they carry is made up of tiny particles. Because of these changes in rivers, something happens near the coastline at the bottom of the sea. Layers of sediment are laid down on the sea bottom. ■ ❹

Continuing Lesson Cluster 2

❶ Have the children look at physical maps of a coast, noticing the large and small rivers emptying into the sea, and the deltas formed by very large rivers. Which of these rivers are depositing the most sediment? the least? Why? Where did this sediment come from? (erosion of rock and soil upstream)

❷ Have the children read the page to this point in preparation for making a model of layers of sediment.

❸ What kind of river is most likely to be full to overloading with sediment? Why? (a fast river, because it exerts more force) What makes one river faster than another? (the steepness of the land it is coming down) Children may be interested to know that a half-foot drop per mile is slow, 40 feet per mile is fast. The upper 4 miles of the Uncompahgre River in Colorado drops 350 feet per mile. What kind of river is most likely to be carrying only fine sediment? (a slow, broad river) Why? (The heavier particles fall sooner to the bottom and thus don't get carried along very far.)

❹ Why does sediment carried in a river get deposited close to a shore? Show the children a topographic map. Ask them to observe the delta near a river mouth. How do some rivers, slowing down as they near the sea, deposit heavier particles at their mouths and even slightly upstream? Have children note in the drawing at the bottom of the page how the deposits sort out.

Supporting Statement: Sediment continually builds up land.

Year after year, hundreds after hundreds of years, the layers of sediment pile up. The top layers press down on the bottom ones. The bottom layers are squeezed harder and harder by the growing weight of layers above them. 1 *The bottom layers of sediment often turn into layers of rock.* These are **sedimentary rocks.**

Think how very important this forming of sedimentary rock is to us. First, the piling up of sediment helps to build up the land. While a river is eroding and carrying off land in one place, in another place it is laying down sediment and building up land. ●

2 Second, sedimentary rock is important because it is in sedimentary rock that **fossils** are found. A fossil is the preserved remains or the print of a living thing of long ago.

MAKING A MODEL
Layers of Sediment

3 **Needed:** about a pint of soil; about a pint of pebbles, gravel, and sand; a tall glass jar that will hold 2 quarts or more; water

Put the soil, pebbles, gravel, and sand in the jar. Add about the same amount of water.

4 Shake up the mixture, or stir it up thoroughly. Then let it stand. Observe how the sediment settles to the bottom.

Here is a photograph of one trial. ■ What do you observe?

Sedimentary layers on the ocean floor may be much like the layers in this model.

5 **Methods of Intelligence: Theorizing**

What sediment settles to the bottom first? Can you explain why? That is, can you develop a theory?

Performance objectives. Children *demonstrate* how layers of sediment are formed by mixing water, pebbles, gravel, and sand, and then allowing the mixture to settle, causing the heavier particles to accumulate nearer the bottom.

Children *describe* this activity as a model of how layers of sediment could form in the oceans.

Useful materials: Some alternate materials are available in CLASSROOM LABORATORY: PURPLE.

1 Have a child place his hand on the desk and have another child stack five books on it, then ten, then (if advisable) twenty. What do you feel? (weight, pressure) How is this a model of sedimentation? What would happen if something were squeezed a thousand or a million times harder? A child who has at some time squeezed damp flour or talcum powder so hard that it stayed together in one piece can report this as a model of the formation of rock from sediment.

2 Children will be interested to know that the term ***fossil*** comes from a Latin word meaning "dug up".

3 The soil samples should not include clay, as the particles are so fine that they may remain in suspension at all levels and blur the results after shaking.

4 For best results, the mixture should settle for 15 minutes or more after shaking.

5 In most such mixtures, the heaviest particles are also likely to be the biggest (the pebbles, but this is not always the case). For their theory, children may need to distinguish "biggest" from "heaviest." One way they may reason is this: The largest particles settle first, so they must be the heaviest ones. To test this assumption, children may suggest weighing some of the particles of different sizes.

EXTENDING THE LESSON

You will need a fresh shell from a clam, oyster, etc. and a fossil shell. Fossils are often preserved by mineral replacement. Let children handle the fresh and fossilized shells to see the difference between them. They will observe that the minerals in the fossil are harder than those in the fresh shell.

Are fossils the same thing as whole animals' bodies found in ice? Explain. How can soft parts of animals and plants be fossilized? Have children discuss how mineralization could replace a soft tissue with hard substances, just as a shell can. (Just as we keep foods from decaying by freezing them, sometimes the soft parts of animals in nature can be preserved in ice and in this way become fossils.)

The Making of a Fossil

❶ When a plant dies, it usually decays and disappears. It becomes part of the soil. When an animal dies, it too usually decays and disappears.

❷ On the other hand, sometimes a dead plant or a dead animal does not disappear completely.

Imagine that long, long ago, in an ancient sea or lake, a fish dies. It sinks slowly into the sediment at the bottom. Imagine it lying there. Now sediment rains on top of it. ■ Slowly, over thousands and thousands of years, layers of sediment build up over the remains of the fish. Slowly, the layers of sediment turn to rock. Within the rock, the ❸ remains of the fish are preserved. ●

■

●

The remains may have become rock themselves. Or they may have left their shape in the rock, as this ancient fish did. ▲ The remains have become a fossil, the preserved remains or the print of a living thing of long ago.

In this way, shells, plants, bones, even whole skeletons have become fossils in sedimentary rocks. It takes a long time, of course. Indeed, it may take millions of years for a fossil to form.

64

Continuing Lesson Cluster 2

❶ Be sure the children understand what "decay" means. What kinds of substances decay? What kinds do not? Do bones and shells decay as quickly as flesh or soft parts of plants? Do hair and wood decay as fast as flesh and fruits? In what other ways (besides decay) can the dead body of an animal, or a fish in the water, be broken up and disappear? (It can be eaten by other animals or fish.)

❷ What must happen to prevent decay, or another animal from eating or breaking up a dead fish or other animal? (It must be quickly covered with a layer of sediment.) What would happen where sedimentation is very slow? (decay)

❸ Point out in the pictures on pages 64 and 65 how a fossilized skeleton of a fish differs from the mere imprint of parts of the animal's body, where none of those parts actually remain. How can you tell a fossilized part from a fossil imprint? (A fossilized part, such as a bone, can be detached from the rock in which it is embedded.)

1 BEFORE YOU GO ON

Check your understanding of the concepts of this section. Which ending would you choose for each statement below?

1. Sediment carried by the rivers into the ocean is put down in
a. layers b. piles

2. The remains or print of an ancient animal or plant in sedimentary rock is a
a. skeleton b. fossil

3. Old sedimentary rocks may have in them a record of the Earth's
a. present life b. past life

4. The statement that fits the main concept of this section is
a. Sedimentary rock builds up the land.
b. Sedimentary rock breaks down the land.

USING WHAT YOU KNOW 2

There are four layers of sedimentary rock. Layer A is on the bottom, layer B is on top of A, C is on top of B, and D is the topmost layer. If the rock layers have not been disturbed, which layer is the oldest? Which is youngest?

INVESTIGATING FURTHER 3

You might want to try making a model of a fossil. Add plaster of Paris to water in a shoe box, until there is a layer of paste about an inch thick on the bottom of the box. While the paste of plaster is soft, place on it a clam shell covered with a very thin coat of Vaseline. Add a leaf also smeared lightly with Vaseline. Cover them with another inch of plaster and let it harden. How can you get at the "fossils" in the model?

65

VERIFYING PROGRESS

In methods of intelligence

To determine children's ability to (1) *demonstrate* sedimentation or (2) *make a model* of a fossil, let them carry out one of the following or *invent* ways of their own.

(1) Put an inch layer of dry gravel at the bottom of a glass jar; then, an inch of fine sand on top of it. Fill with water cautiously so as not to disturb the two layers. Cap, shake vigorously, and *predict* what will happen when settling has occurred.

(2) (a) Bury a plastic or clay animal or fish in wet cement; let it dry; crack the dry block open to find the "fossil".

(b) Press a leaf or evergreen branch into soft clay (inside a deep screw-top jar cover is good) to make a negative impression; then use plaster of Paris to obtain a positive mold.

Children should be able to *analyze* their *models* and relate them to the "real" event.

VERIFYING PROGRESS

1 Before you go on. Children *demonstrate* understanding of the formation of sedimentary rock by selecting suitable responses to questions. Ask the children to *explain* their reasons for responding as they do.

1. a 3. b
2. b 4. a

2 Using what you know. Children *describe* and *explain* a model of sedimentary rock layers. To be sure that the children have a clear picture of what is described here, have them draw a diagram and label it in accordance with the text. Have them describe their model.

3 Investigating further. Children *construct a model* of a fossil. They will need these materials: plaster of Paris, Vaseline, shoebox, clam shell (or other shell or bone). The method described here will yield negative molds of the objects used, after the dry block of plaster of Paris has been carefully cracked open.

To obtain positive molds, coat the hollow cavity of the negative mold (from which the original object has been carefully removed) with a small amount of Vaseline and fill with fresh plaster of Paris. When this has properly hardened it will be the positive mold and should come away easily from the hollow, negative mold.

Negative molds may also be made without embedding an object entirely in fresh plaster and cracking it out of the dry plaster later. A finger, an animal's paw, or some other interesting specimen may be pressed into a flat layer of fresh plaster, then removed when the plaster hardens.

LESSON CLUSTER 3
A FIRST MODEL OF THE EARTH

Teaching background. 3 T-60

Concept-seeking. Children learn that the crust of the Earth is constantly moving, and that the waves set up by this movement can be detected and studied.

Operations. Children *investigate* sound waves traveling through solids; they *probe* the Earth's interior.

Methods of intelligence. Children *distinguish* between sound waves traveling in a solid and those in air. They *theorize* as to what scientists would find if they could drill a hole all the way through the Earth's crust.

Useful materials: Globe, orange or grapefruit.

A LOOK AHEAD

Now the soil eroded from the mountains has found a place. Under the sea, the sediment turns into rock which builds the land. In forming rock, the sediment also preserves plants and animals that lived long ago.

You have seen what happens to soil on the surface of the Earth. What is the Earth like below the surface?

3. A First Model of the Earth

❶ Scientists often make models. They have a good reason. Models help a scientist to think and to understand. They are especially useful when he is dealing with something too large to handle, like the Earth, or too small to see, like an atom. Ask a scientist to explain something, and he may reach for some models to show you. Ask a scientist what the inside of the Earth is like, and he might reach for an orange.

An orange can be one model of the Earth. An orange is a ball; so is the Earth. An orange has a rather rough, thin, hard skin; so has the Earth. The soft inside of the orange can stand for the inside of the Earth.

❷ How can scientists know what the inside of the Earth is like, far beneath the layers of rock on the surface? The deepest hole drilled has gone down only a few miles—only into the orange skin, that is. How is it possible, then, for scientists to get an idea of the inside of the Earth, thousands of miles below your feet?

Studying Earthquake Waves

Men have invented instruments to explore areas where they cannot go themselves. To discover what the depths of the Earth are like, men use an instrument called the ❸ **seismograph** (sīz′mə·graf). ■ A seismograph is used to observe **earthquake waves.** When the waves caused by an earthquake reach a seismograph, its pen swings across the

66

Introducing Lesson Cluster 3

Hold up a globe and then an orange or a grapefruit. Which of these is a better model of the whole Earth? Children are likely to plump for the globe until you add: A model for the Earth inside and out? Encourage children to give reasons for their choices. Explain that they may confirm or correct their hypotheses as they study this lesson cluster.

Developing the lesson

❶ This is a good place to make sure that the children have a good understanding of the concept of a model. Why is a model a good way to show what some objects and events are like? (One reason is that a model represents something larger or smaller than it actually is.) Does a model usually show all the features and details in the original? (no, e.g.: toy cars, trains, planes) Which details are generally lacking in such models? (those inside) What is another kind of model that, on the other hand, does show the inside details? (a model of the inside of an animal)

❷ How do doctors learn what is going on inside a person's body without cutting it open? How do mechanics know what is wrong in a car motor without taking it apart completely? (often, by listening; by studying signals coming from the body or the motor)

❸ Inform the children that the word ***seismograph*** comes from a Greek root meaning "to shake violently".

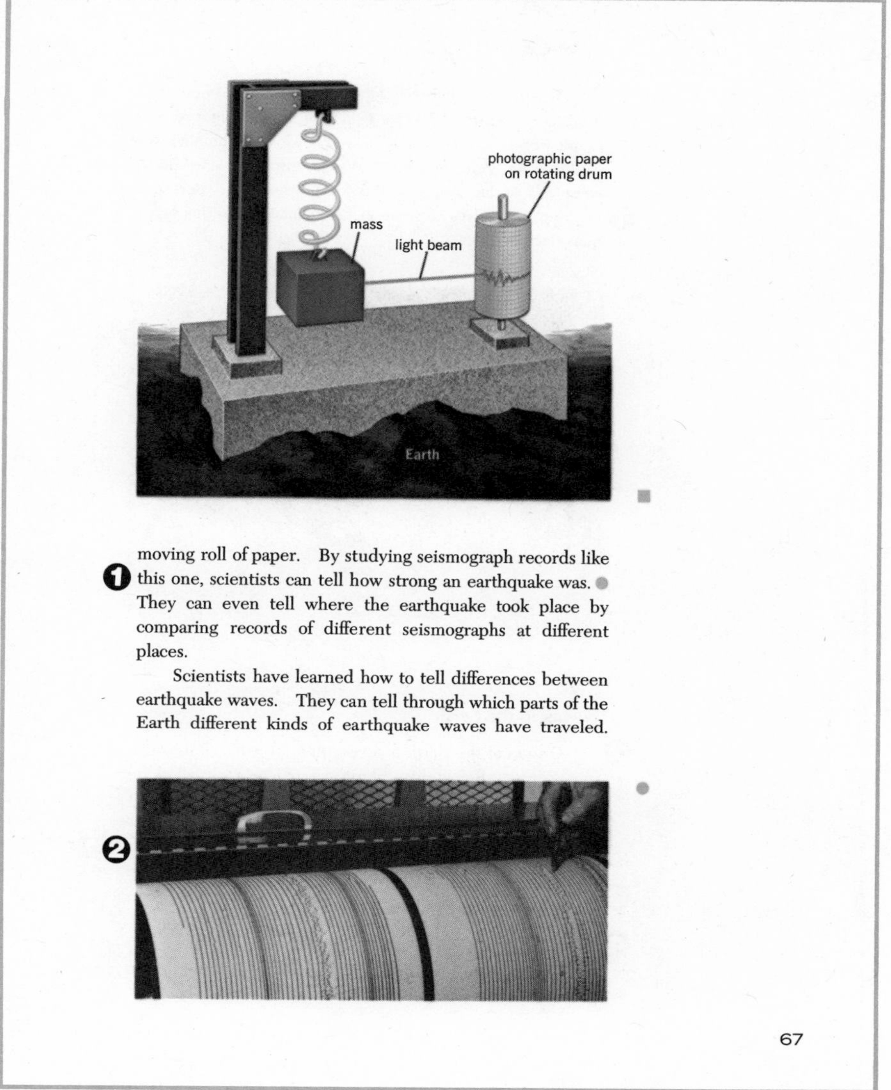

moving roll of paper. By studying seismograph records like ❶ this one, scientists can tell how strong an earthquake was. They can even tell where the earthquake took place by comparing records of different seismographs at different places.

Scientists have learned how to tell differences between earthquake waves. They can tell through which parts of the Earth different kinds of earthquake waves have traveled.

❷

67

Useful materials: Sewing elastic (about 25 feet).

❶ Children can demonstrate a model of ***earthquake waves*** as follows. Have a child hold in one hand the ends of a five-foot and a twenty-foot length of elastic, such as is used in home sewing. (This kind of elastic is sold in most dime stores.) Have two other children hold the other ends, standing just far enough away so that each ribbon is slightly tensed. Have a fourth child tap the child's hand holding both ends together. The two children at the receiving ends should each call out "Hit!" when they feel the impulse. Why did it take longer for the same impulse to reach the two different receiving ends? (The distances travelled were different.)

If we knew the speed of the waves along the ribbons, how could we tell how much farther away the impulse was from one receiving end than from the other? (by multiplying the speed of the waves by the time interval between the two "hits")

❷ In the picture here, did the scientist make the wavy lines with his pen? (no) Call attention to the diagram of the ***seismograph.*** How are the wavy lines produced? (by a light-beam that acts as a pen on light-sensitive paper)

VERIFYING PROGRESS

In concept-seeking

Children may *demonstrate* earthquake waves, and from their demonstration you can determine their progress in *setting up* and *interpreting models.* They will need a clothesline or other rope. They may do (1), (2), or both: (1) *Push-pull waves:* Stand in a row near one another, push forward, and then pull back. *Shake waves:* Move a rope up and down. *Observe* that both types of waves can be felt or seen at the end line of children, or the rope, as well as at the beginning.
(2) *Push-pull waves:* Hold up your hands, palms vertical, in the gesture you might use to warn someone away from danger, by pushing the air. *Shake waves:* Point up with your hands forward while shaking the index finger back and forth in the gesture of saying "no" emphatically.

Are these models good ones? Is there a better model? Have children *describe* or *invent* other models.

At the National Earthquake Information Center in Maryland, scientist Waverly J. Person is studying a seismograph record of an earthquake. ■ This earthquake was centered in Peru in 1970. Waves from the earthquake were felt as far away as Maryland, where Mr. Person is ❶ working. (Pictures of some of the damage from this earthquake are on page 73.)

■

Waves in the Earth

❷ On top of the Earth is a very thin layer of soil in which plants grow. Below this soil is a skin of hard rock called the **crust.** We usually think of the Earth's crust as firm and unmoving. "Firm as a rock," we say.

However, rock layers of the crust can move. Sometimes a part of the crust shifts to a new position. Sometimes the ❸ shift is very slow and takes hundreds of years. But sometimes the crust shifts suddenly. When that happens, ❹ there is an earthquake. The earthquake need not be one that destroys buildings and buries towns. It may be so gentle that it can be detected only by a seismograph.

68

Continuing Lesson Cluster 3

❶ Give the children maps of North and South America, or let them refer to wall maps. See if they can figure (using the map scale) about how far away the earthquake in Peru must have been felt, since it was recorded in Maryland.

❷ If it is feasible to take a field trip to see road cuts or excavations for foundations, children can see layers of topsoil and subsoil. Point out the thin topsoil with vegetation growing in it; the thicker subsoil; and the bedrock, where the true ***crust*** of the Earth begins.

❸ A good way to demonstrate shifting of the crust rock is to have one child put his hands in front of him, palms together. Another child can press at right angles to the back of the palms to try to keep the first child's hands from moving backward or forward. When the child with his hands on the outside presses against the hands on the inside, he is illustrating the pressure between rock masses in the crust, the main cause of earthquakes.

❹ Ask the children if any of them have ever been in an earthquake, even a very mild one. If no one has, perhaps a relative or friend of a child has been. Discuss what it was like.

Whenever there is an earthquake, however, earthquake waves are started. The waves travel out from that place
1 through the Earth in all directions.

Can a wave travel through anything as solid as the Earth? You can easily see—or, rather, hear—for yourself.

Put your ear to the top of a desk or table, at one end.
2 Have someone tap the other end. ● Listen to the sound. Then raise your ear and listen to the same sound as it reaches you through the air. What difference do you find between the sound traveling through the solid desk and the one traveling through air?

Put your ear to other parts of the desk and you will find that the sound of the tapping is traveling out from its starting point in all directions. Notice what happens to the sound as you come closer to the point where the tapping is
3 taking place. Is the sound louder or softer?

The tapping makes waves, waves that travel through the solid desk to your ear. Waves *can* travel through a

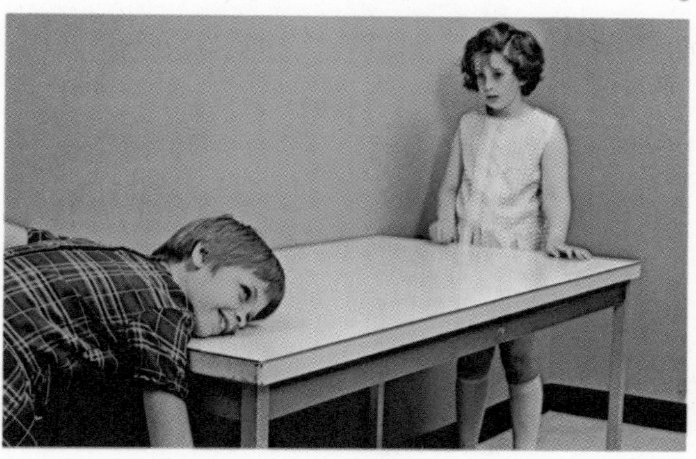

Useful materials: Dominoes, Ping-Pong or other small balls, marbles.

1 Children may use one or more of the following models to show the transfer of energy through a solid by vibration at some point.
(1) Set 3 dominoes on end atop one another. Jiggle the bottom one.
(2) Lay in a row two, three, or four balls just touching. Tap the ball at one end.

What event is represented in each of these models? [(1) earthquake; (2) transfer of energy]

2 Have children demonstrate as text suggests. To make the tapping sound of the same quality, a marble or a Ping-Pong ball might be dropped always from a certain height above the desk. The desk-top or table-top should be cleared of other objects, and the listener will shut out other sounds if he stops his open ear with a finger.

Who has read an adventure story in which a scout or Indian put his ear to the ground? What was he listening for? (the sound of the enemy, on foot or on horseback) Why could he hear better that way? (The Earth transmits sound better than the air.) Could he hear the sound of voices a long way off by listening to the ground? Why not? (Voices go through the air; air waves are not strong enough to set up audible waves in the ground.)

3 The sound gets louder as you come closer to the point of origin.

How can you tap so that you can't hear the tap through the air, but can through the desk? (Children demonstrate their responses.)

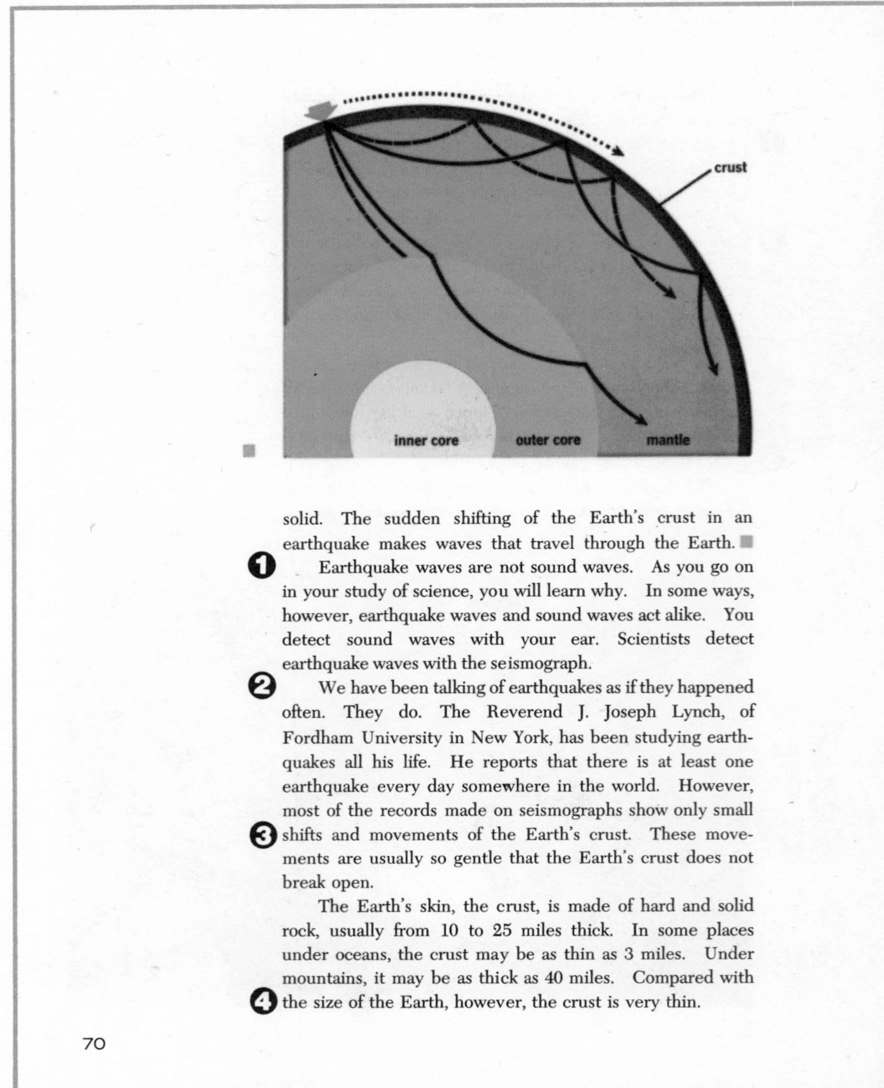

solid. The sudden shifting of the Earth's crust in an earthquake makes waves that travel through the Earth. ■

❶ Earthquake waves are not sound waves. As you go on in your study of science, you will learn why. In some ways, however, earthquake waves and sound waves act alike. You detect sound waves with your ear. Scientists detect earthquake waves with the seismograph.

❷ We have been talking of earthquakes as if they happened often. They do. The Reverend J. Joseph Lynch, of Fordham University in New York, has been studying earthquakes all his life. He reports that there is at least one earthquake every day somewhere in the world. However, most of the records made on seismographs show only small ❸ shifts and movements of the Earth's crust. These movements are usually so gentle that the Earth's crust does not break open.

The Earth's skin, the crust, is made of hard and solid rock, usually from 10 to 25 miles thick. In some places under oceans, the crust may be as thin as 3 miles. Under mountains, it may be as thick as 40 miles. Compared with ❹ the size of the Earth, however, the crust is very thin.

70

Useful materials: Cardboard, toy houses, cars, persons.

Continuing Lesson Cluster 3

❶ The long, surface waves of an earthquake may cause the most damage. Have the children illustrate this by placing small toy houses, cars, and persons on a sheet of cardboard. When they jerk the cardboard back and forth the figures tumble down.

❷ If earthquakes are happening every day, why don't we hear more about them? Why aren't they happening where we are? (We don't hear about them because they are mostly so slight; some may be happening where we are, but they're too slight to notice.)

❸ What would the world be like if major shifts in the Earth's crust were going on all the time? (chaos) If children do not respond readily, prompt them with a further question: Could mankind's cities and civilization ever have been what they are today? (no)

❹ After children have read through this point in the text, point out that the crust of the Earth is not merely the upper layers of loose topsoil and subsoil. The crust is solid rock, and the soil is like a blanket on the crust.

What do you think the Earth is like 50 miles down under the crust? What is your hypothesis?

This diagram shows how scientists think the Earth is made up. ● Under the crust is a layer of rock called the ❶ **mantle.** In the mantle are many of the different substances of which the Earth is made. The mantle surrounds the **core,** which seems to be made of iron and nickel. The mantle may be hot and melted near the core.

The Earth is about 8,000 miles thick. How thin is the crust you walk on, compared to the size of the Earth! Geologists would like to drill a hole through the thinnest part of the crust, which lies under the ocean. What do you think they would find if they were able to do so? You can follow the discoveries of geologists in newspapers and on television.

❷ The orange is not a good enough model to show what scientists may find. Let us try another model, the one on the next page. MODEL

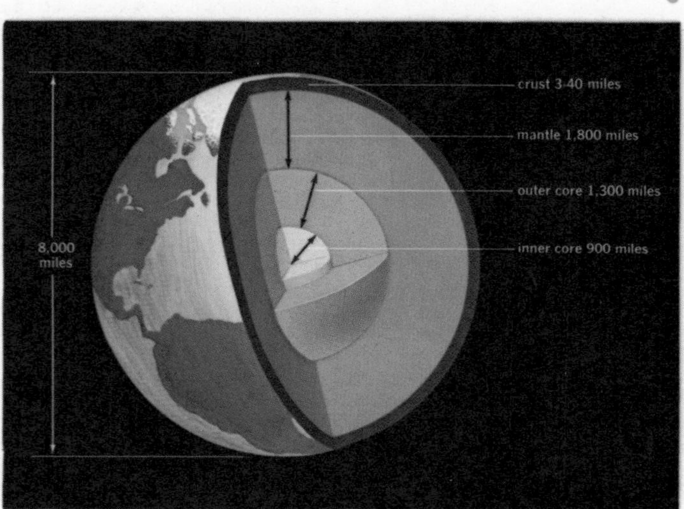

❶ Children can make a diagram of the Earth's interior from circles of construction paper. Using a scale of 1″ = 1000 miles, they can cut out circles of different diameters from 3 colors of paper: 8″ (the ***mantle***); $2\frac{10}{16}$″ (the ***outer core***); and $1\frac{13}{16}$″ (the ***inner core***).

When the smaller circles are laid on the larger circle and a thumbtack inserted through the center to hold them in place, a circle of a fourth color may be drawn around the edge of the mantle, to represent the ***crust.***

❷ Why isn't the orange a good enough model? What are some things inside an orange that do not represent anything in the Earth? (rind too thick to represent crust; no central core) Actually, although it is usually not spherical, an avocado makes a much better model.

Performance objectives. Children *construct* a model of the Earth by filling a balloon with toothpaste, then forming clay around the balloon. They *identify* those parts of the model that represent the Earth's mantle and the Earth's core, and *evaluate* different kinds of models of the Earth.

Useful materials: Some materials are available in CLASSROOM LABORATORY: PURPLE.

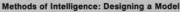

MAKING A MODEL
A Model of the Earth

Needed: a tube of toothpaste, a small round balloon, modeling clay, string ❶

Tie the balloon tightly to the toothpaste tube, as shown. Then squeeze all the toothpaste out of the tube and into the balloon. ■

Now tie another string around the neck of the balloon, so that the toothpaste cannot escape. ●

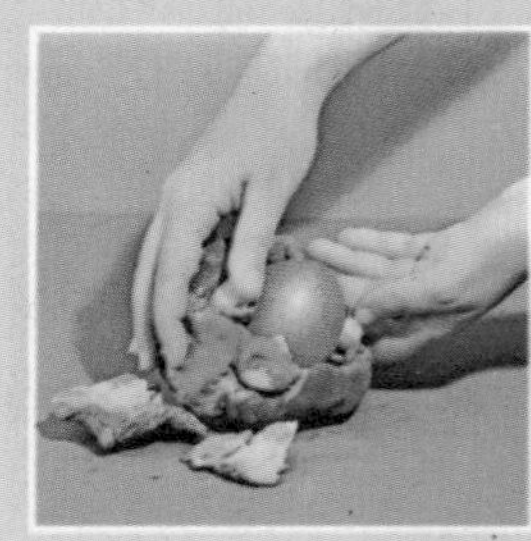

Untie the first string and remove the balloon from the tube.

Mold the modeling clay around the balloon, about an inch deep. ▲ Now you have another model of the Earth.

One layer of the Earth has been left out. It is the layer upon which we walk. What is this layer? ❷

Methods of Intelligence: Designing a Model

Invent your own model of the Earth. Show it ❸ to your classmates. Ask them how you might improve it. How is the model helpful?

One boy brought in a baseball as a model of the Earth. The leather cover was the Earth's crust, he said. The layer of cord beneath it was the Earth's mantle. The rubber ball inside the cord binding was the core of the Earth. Was this a good model? Explain whether it helps you to understand the structure of the Earth.

72

Continuing Lesson Cluster 3

❶ Paste or soft clay or any other substance of the right consistency may be used instead of toothpaste.

Wire ties, such as those used to close plastic bags of produce in supermarkets, may be used instead of string.

❷ Encourage children to invent a way to show the Earth's crust. Some ways are: coating with paint; coating with a thin layer of glue that can dry; coating with a thick paste of detergent powder and water. This "crust" may even be deliberately made a little thicker in some places and a little thinner in others.

❸ Encourage children to be inventive. Other kinds of fruit besides an orange may be thought of. The fairly round stone of a peach can represent the Earth's core, and its skin (thinner than an orange's) is a good approximation of the crust. (Its fuzz might even suggest the atmosphere.)

Others might like to wrap a core of foil with string, or cut apart a tennis ball and fill it with plasticine or soft clay in different colors.

Inside the Earth

Toothpaste is a thick fluid; it flows slowly. Scientists believe that the core of the Earth may be somewhat fluid. It flows much more slowly than toothpaste. Around the fluid core is a thick layer of rock, the mantle. The solid outside surface of the Earth is the crust.

Our model helps us understand that the Earth is not all solid. The rocks of the crust are not smooth and even. Scientists believe they are in broken sections and slabs that move on the fluid rock of the mantle.

❶ Sometimes there is a sudden shift of rock layers. The Earth's crust heaves and trembles, cracks, yawns open. ■ Buildings fall. ● Whole cities may be destroyed. The city of Manila, capital of the Philippines, was struck by an earthquake in August 1968. The damage to buildings added up to millions of dollars. In a devastating earthquake in ❷ Peru in 1970, at least 70,000 people were killed, and over 500,000 were left homeless.

You might well think that there is nothing men can do about earthquakes. It turns out, however, as scientists investigate, that something can be done. Scientists have made maps showing where earthquakes happen. The areas

■

●

73

VERIFYING PROGRESS

In concept-seeking

To evaluate progress in *constructing models*, children may *investigate* shifting crustal layers and earthquakes as follows. They will need a rectangular pan; strips of plastic or cloth, each half as wide and a few inches longer than the pan; damp soil; toy cars, houses, or other small light objects.

Lay two separate strips of cloth or plastic next to each other on the bottom of the pan. Let the excess length of one strip hang out at one end of the pan, the other at the other end. Cover the strips with damp soil up to the edge of the pan and pack it down firmly. Place toys on the soil to represent houses, cars, bridges, etc. Now pull the protruding strip at one end and the other at the other end, simultaneously.

Children *describe* what happens; they *predict* what might happen if similar events were to occur on Earth.

❶ You may mention that deep layers of rock in the Earth shift only an inch or two, even in a violent earthquake. Point out the cracks in the Earth in the picture at the right. By examining the cracks, children may be able to see that the slippage of rock is up and down, rather than sideways.

❷ The Peru earthquake of 1970 was the most devastating one ever known. Some of your children may recall the Los Angeles earthquake of February 9, 1971—the worst one to hit California in 38 years—in which 60 people were killed. In discussing earthquakes, encourage children to use the terms ***crust*** and ***mantle.*** Which part of the Earth must break during a sudden shift or movement such as happens during a quake? (the crust) Why the crust and not the mantle? (The crust is solid and brittle, but the mantle is fluid.)

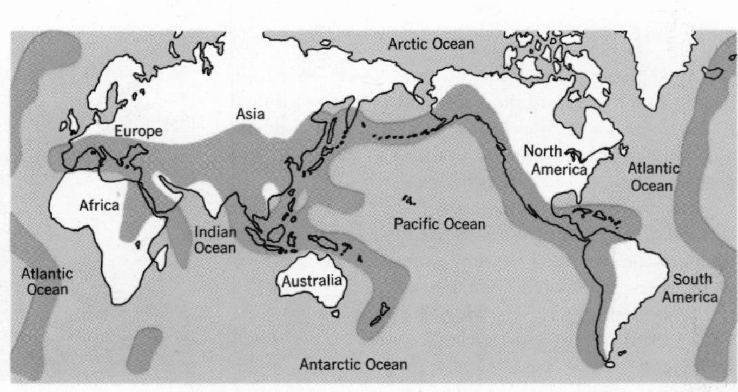

■ ❶ colored orange on this map are called earthquake belts. ■ Notice that earthquake belts are along some seacoasts. Some belts are along chains of islands. These belts show where earthquakes are likely to happen. A building put up in an earthquake belt can be built to resist earthquake shocks.

In time, too, scientists may be able to predict when earthquakes are likely to take place, as well as where. Then people can protect themselves, and many lives may be saved. Scientists are working on the problem now.

❷ **BEFORE YOU GO ON**

Check your understanding of the concepts of this section. Which ending would you choose for each statement below?

1. The layer of the Earth beneath the crust is called the
a. core b. mantle

2. The inside of the Earth is believed to be
a. cold b. hot

3. Both earthquake waves and sound waves can travel through
a. the air
b. a solid

4. Scientists believe that the Earth's mantle is a
a. thick fluid b. thin gas

5. The statement that fits the main concept of this section is
a. The Earth is a solid at the core.
b. The Earth is always changing.

74

Continuing Lesson Cluster 3

❶ Have children study the map. Do you live in or near an earthquake belt? What kind of buildings are there to protect against earthquakes? What would you do to protect yourself in an earthquake? (turn off the gas, get out into the open away from buildings, etc.)

VERIFYING PROGRESS

❷ **Before you go on.** Children *demonstrate* understanding of the Earth's structure by selecting suitable responses to questions.
1. b 3. b
2. b 4. b

Supporting Statement: Heat and pressure cause continuous changes within the Earth.

A LOOK AHEAD

You have begun to see that the Earth is always changing. Sometimes the changes happen slowly and quietly—as when the land is worn down or when sedimentary rocks are built up. Sometimes the changes are sudden and noisy—as when there is a strong earthquake. Another kind of change in the Earth that can be sudden and noisy happens when a volcano comes to life. How does this happen?

4. The Furnace in the Earth

It happened in a quiet Mexican town called Paricutín ❶ (pä′rē·kōō·tēn′). A farmer saw smoke coming from his cornfield. He hurried over. There was an opening in the ❷ ground! Steam and other hot gases, ashes, and molten rock poured from the opening, building a mound that grew higher and higher. There was nothing he could do. The Paricutín volcano had been born.

LESSON CLUSTER 4
THE FURNACE IN THE EARTH

Teaching background. 4 T-60

Concept-seeking. Children become aware that great heat within the mantle below the Earth's crust can cause pressure that forces molten rock to escape to the surface through volcanoes. They learn that this heat results from radioactive decay of substances such as uranium within the Earth.

Operations. Children *probe* into the source of the Earth's heat, into the structure of atoms, and into the release of energy when certain atoms decay.

Methods of intelligence. Children *identify* volcanic activity and *distinguish* between volcanoes and other mountains. They *analyze*, from a model, the structure of atoms, and of heat and pressure within the Earth resulting in volcanoes. They *distinguish* heat produced by radioactivity from heat produced by the Sun's energy.

Useful materials: Hotplate, paraffin, pan, balloon.

Introducing Lesson Cluster 4

Heat some paraffin until it softens. (*Caution:* For safety, heat paraffin indirectly over hot water as in a double boiler.) When the paraffin has cooled enough to hold, but is still soft, give each of two or three volunteers about a cubic inch. Have them hold the paraffin tightly in one hand and squeeze hard (helping with the other hand, if necessary). Most children should be able to squeeze hard enough to force some paraffin between their fingers.

Could you have squeezed paraffin out between your fingers when it was cool and hard? What two *conditions* were needed to squeeze it out? (heat and pressure)

Developing the lesson

❶ What happens when there is a crack in a tube of toothpaste? (Pressure pushes the toothpaste out through the crack.) Something like this happened in the farmer's field in Mexico, and molten rock poured out. But what caused the pressure? Let the children offer hypotheses. If they don't suggest heat as a cause of pressure, let one child demonstrate the following: Hold an air-filled balloon over a hotplate or radiator. Let children watch the balloon expand, and, perhaps, even burst. Why does the balloon burst? (because of the pressure of the heated air inside)

❷ Volcanic ash should not be confused with the ashes that are left when an organic substance such as wood or coal is burned. Volcanic ash is formed by the solidification of some of the molten rock *before* it erupts from the volcano into the air.

VERIFYING PROGRESS

In concept-seeking

To evaluate their progress in *building models*, children may represent volcanoes in one of these ways. They will need: puffed rice or other dry cereal, blender or other instrument for mashing cereal, plastic bags, funnel, flour, balloon, water.
(1) Pulverize the cereal by mashing it or running it through a blender. Place the powdered cereal in a plastic bag. Squeeze the bag through the spout of an inverted funnel. The cereal bits are ejected in spurts.
(2) Fill a balloon with a fairly thin paste of flour and water. Attach the neck of the balloon to the spout of a funnel. Squeeze the balloon to make the "lava" come up into the funnel. If the "lava" is repeatedly squeezed up and layers of paste flows allowed to dry, a volcanic cone may be simulated.

■

Whenever a volcano forms, some rock in the Earth's ❶ crust has become molten. Great heat within the crust has melted the rock. Mixed with the melted rock are large amounts of hot gases. These gases have great pressure.

Pressure causes hot gases and melted rock to burst through the Earth's hard crust. A river of molten rock flows along the ground, destroying whatever lies in its way. ■ This molten rock from within the Earth is called **lava** (lä′və).

Lava may cover the land for many miles around a volcano. Over the years, lava and ashes may pour out of a volcano again and again, adding layer upon layer, cooling and hardening into a cone-shaped mountain. Notice the **crater,** or opening, at the volcano's top. ●

❷ Lassen Peak in California was formed in this way by a volcano. Now and then it seems as if Lassen Peak might become quite active again and pour out more lava from its crater. But so far Lassen Peak has just made rumbling sounds from time to time.

❸ Ixtaccihuatl (es′tä·sē′wat·l), is a volcano in Mexico. Ixtaccihuatl is no longer the fierce volcano it used to be. ▲ Alaska has a number of volcanoes, too. Some are active; some just rumble now and then. None seem dangerous at ❹ the present time.

76

Continuing Lesson Cluster 4

❶ You can explain the connection between the gases, heat, and pressure within the Earth, as follows: Heat melts the rock, some of which changes to gases, which have great pressure. The more pressure there is, the more heat, and vice versa, in an enclosed space. Thus, both heat and pressure tend to increase until the pressure is great enough to break the solid rock of the crust.

❷ What could cause Lassen Peak to become active again? What makes it rumble? (There may be shifting of molten rock and gases within.)

❸ Some children may know that a long inactive volcano is called *extinct*. Ixtaccihuatl, for instance, is considered extinct, since it has not erupted since 1868.

❹ Encourage children to use the key concept terms ***lava*** and ***crater*** as they discuss this page. Is a rumble an active volcano? (not necessarily) Can it become active? What could cause it? (enough heat and pressure to force molten rock or ***lava*** from the volcano's ***crater***)

Supporting Statement: Heat and pressure cause continuous changes within the Earth.

Only a short time ago, however, several volcanoes burst ❶ into life in Chile. Many people were killed and many homes destroyed. Have you read about the fierce volcano Vesuvius in Italy? In one eruption 2,000 years ago, it buried three cities.

❷ What causes a volcano to erupt? Hot rock bursts through the Earth's crust, pushed by pressure that is caused by heat. What produces this heat?

Useful materials: Pictures of destruction by volcanoes in Chile, Peru, Pompeii, etc., and of the volcanoes themselves; thermometers.

❶ If you can get pictures of destruction by volcanoes in Chile, Peru, or Pompeii, and of the volcanoes themselves, let children prepare an exhibit of these. What makes a volcano destructive? Why are people killed? (heat and mechanical force of lava, suffocating smoke and ashes, etc.) What is the smoke rising from an inactive volcano? (steam) How is a crater a safety valve? (It allows a ready-made "escape route" for ***lava.***)

❷ What usually happens to a substance when it is heated? (It expands.) When something expands, does it need more space or less? (more) When a liquid expands, which way does it go to get more space? (in the direction of least opposing pressure; or, whichever way is easiest) What is a good example of this? (a thermometer) If thermometers are available have children make the mercury or fluid rise by placing the bulbs of the thermometers in warm water.

Heat in the Earth

You may know that to start anything moving, you must use energy. To start a baseball moving, you use the energy of your body. To start an automobile moving, the energy of burning gasoline is used. When a volcano starts up, energy in the form of heat is being used. Heat, as you know, causes matter to expand.

❶ Energy has to come from somewhere. Where does the energy of a volcano come from? It comes from within the Earth, we know. Still, this leads to another question. Where does the Earth get its heat?

For a long time scientists puzzled over this question. At last they have found a useful explanation. To understand this explanation, we must take a look inside the **atom,** the tiny particle of which substances are made.

Inside an Atom

Imagine a balloon blown up a bit and filled full of ❷ popcorn. It is a model of the center of an atom, a **nucleus** (no͞o′klē·əs). An atom is very tiny, of course. The nucleus of an atom is smaller still. Yet, inside the nucleus there are even smaller parts, or particles, somewhat like the popcorn inside the balloon. The main kinds of particles in the nucleus are **protons** (prō′tons) and **neutrons** (no͞o′trons).

No one has ever seen the nucleus of an atom, not to mention the protons and neutrons inside it. Even so, scientists have managed to find out a great deal about the nucleus. They have *imagined* what a nucleus might be like, according to what they know about it, and have made ❸ models of it. Here is a picture of one model of an atom. ■ This is a model of an atom of oxygen. The nucleus is in the center.

❹ What are other atoms like? Every atom has a nucleus. The nucleus of the hydrogen atom is the simplest. It is made up of only one proton. The nucleus of every other atom has both protons and neutrons. There are protons

78

Useful materials: Plastic bags, popcorn and caramelized popcorn, or marbles of two different colors.

Continuing Lesson Cluster 4

❶ Let children continue to hypothesize. Can the heat in the Earth all be from the Sun? Where else could heat come from? Children's responses may vary widely, but do not at this time indicate whether their answers are "correct."

❷ Children may make a simple model of an atomic nucleus by filling a plastic bag with marbles or popcorn, or they may stick pieces of popcorn together with glue. To represent the two kinds of particles, protons and neutrons, they can use plain and caramelized popcorn, or marbles of two different colors.

❸ Count the number of protons (orange spheres) and neutrons (green spheres) in the model of the oxygen atom. What do you see? (the same number of each) Point out that there are also 8 *electrons* around the nucleus, but that these particles aren't central to the concept of energy from the atomic nucleus. Thus, they have been omitted altogether in the diagrams on the opposite page.

❹ Have children compare the nuclei of various atoms in the models on the opposite page. Are all atoms alike? (no) What is one way in which they differ? (different numbers of protons and neutrons)

Supporting Statement: Heat and pressure cause continuous changes within the Earth.

❶ and neutrons in the nucleus of an atom of helium, oxygen, or uranium, as you can see in these models. ●

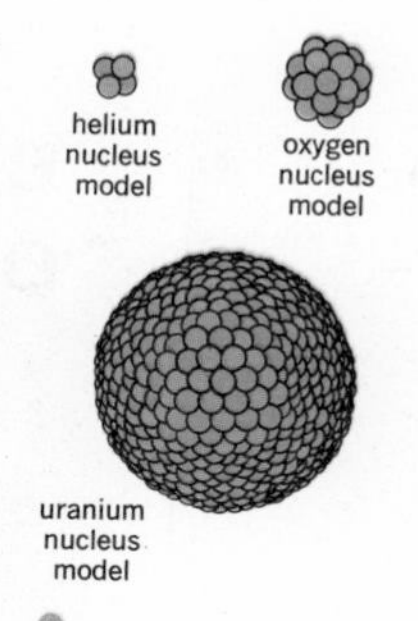

●

The protons and neutrons in a nucleus are held together very tightly indeed. Even so, scientists have managed to pry them apart and to split the nucleus. When scientists say they have split an atom, they mean they have split its nucleus. Splitting a nucleus is called **fission** (fish′ən).

To split the nucleus takes tremendous energy, because the protons and neutrons are so tightly bound together. To do this isn't easy. Yet down in the Earth, beneath your feet, the nuclei of certain atoms are breaking up *naturally*. Particles are breaking out of certain atoms now, beneath your feet, in the Earth's crust and mantle. As each nucleus breaks up, it releases a burst of energy. Much of that energy ❷ causes heat. This is where a great deal of the heat in and below the crust of the Earth comes from.

The Earth's "Fuel"

The element uranium is a metal. We get it by mining, ❸ so we know there is uranium in the Earth's crust. It is probably scattered not only through the crust but through the mantle as well.

The important thing about uranium in the Earth is this. Uranium atoms give up particles and **radiation** (rā′dē·ā′shən) from their **nuclei** (no͞o′klē·ī). (The singular of *nuclei* is *nucleus*.) As uranium nuclei break up, heat is given off. ▲

▲

❹

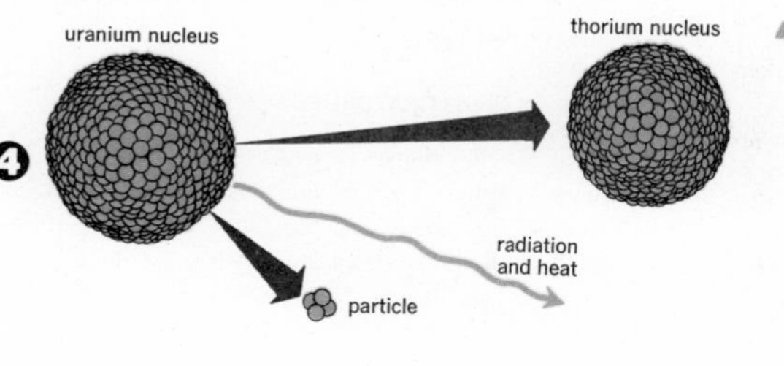

79

Useful materials: Marbles, glue, plastic bags, bag ties, scissors.

❶ To make a good permanent model of the nucleus of an oxygen atom, have the children mix eight white marbles with eight blue marbles (or any other two colors) in a plastic bag. Twist the marbles into a tight round mass. Tie the neck of the bag and cut off excess plastic. What do the white and blue marbles stand for? (***protons*** and ***neutrons***) How is this a good model of tightly-held protons and neutrons in the nucleus of an oxygen atom? (hard to pull apart)

❷ Invite children to think of different ways in which energy of motion is transformed into heat. Rub sandpaper over wood, and the wood gets hot. Put your hand on a tire after driving 10 miles and the tire feels warm. Use energy to pull a nail out of wood and the nail feels quite hot. What is often produced when energy is used? (heat) What happens when heat affects matter? (Matter expands.)

❸ Since uranium is a metal, what does it consist of? (atoms) Let's suppose uranium is an element that decays—what happens? (nucleus changes, gives off energy) What kind of energy is this likely to be changed into? (heat)

❹ Point out that *thorium* is an element somewhat like uranium, but a little lighter. How is this indicated in the diagram? (Uranium loses particle to become thorium.)

Unit Concept-Statement: Bodies in space are in continuous change.

These uranium atoms inside the Earth's crust and mantle do not break up quickly. They break up very slowly, over millions of years. Slow as it is, this natural breaking up of
❶ uranium atoms produces heat in the Earth.

The natural breaking up of the nucleus of an atom is
❷ called **radioactivity.**

How important is radioactivity? If our Earth's crust did not have the heat energy that comes from radioactivity, it would soon cool down.

The heat produced by radioactivity, within the Earth, gets to the surface of the Earth. Then the heat usually escapes into the air. Sometimes, however, it cannot escape. The heat in one place may be trapped under a blanket of rock. The trapped heat may melt the rock. The melted rock may be pushed up through a crack and spurt out at the surface as a volcano, such as Paricutín.

❸ **BEFORE YOU GO ON**

A. Check your understanding of the concepts of this section. Which ending would you choose for each statement below?

1. The breakup of atoms accounts for some of the Earth's
a. ice and snow b. heat

2. When an atom of uranium breaks up, particles fly out of its
a. neutrons b. nucleus

3. The natural breaking up of an atom is known as
a. radioactivity b. erosion

4. The statement that fits the main concept of this section is
a. Changes in the Earth are caused by heat and pressure.
b. Changes in the Earth are caused by weathering.

B. Write a paragraph or two on this topic: "The Earth's Heat."

USING WHAT YOU KNOW ❹

Lava is rich in substances upon which plants can grow. Knowing something of weathering and erosion, try to predict what may happen, in time, to the substances in lava in a valley at the foot of a volcano.

INVESTIGATING FURTHER ❺

Is there a volcano in your state? Where can you find out about this? in the dictionary? in an encyclopedia? Would you ask your teacher's help or your librarian's help?

80

Continuing Lesson Cluster 4

❶ Why aren't we all cooked to death by the heat given off by uranium? (given off too slowly) Uranium takes many billions of years to decay to a stable form of lead. But what happens as radiation produces heat, even though slowly? Let children hypothesize.

❷ It is important to distinguish between ***fission*** and ***radioactivity.*** Point out that fission is an artificial process that results in at least two different elements almost instantaneously, with a burst of energy. Radioactivity is a natural process of decay during which energy and nuclear particles are released at a constant rate, relatively slowly.

VERIFYING PROGRESS

❸ **Before you go on.** Children *demonstrate* conceptual understanding by completing open-ended questions and *analyzing* the source of the Earth's heat.
A. 1. b 2. b 3. a 4. a
B. Children should *distinguish* between the heat provided internally by radioactivity and externally by the Sun's energy.

❹ **Using what you know.** Children *apply* concepts of weathering and erosion in *predicting* that lava breaks down into soil rich in minerals for the growth of plants.

❺ **Investigating further.** Children *seek evidence* of volcanic activity and their effects through *consulting* references and other authorities.

Supporting Statement: Heat and pressure are continually changing the Earth's crust.

A LOOK AHEAD

It seems that the source of the Earth's heat is not only the Sun. There is a kind of furnace below the Earth's surface. Heat gathering under the Earth's surface may cause volcanoes to become active. When volcanoes grow, they change the Earth's surface.

Heat given off by radioactive atoms helps change the Earth's surface in other ways, too. Scientists believe that heat from within the Earth can even help to raise mountains. How can this be?

5. Up Go the Mountains

Do you recall how sedimentary rock is formed? It forms in layers, like a blanket of rock laid on the sea bottom.

What is happening underneath this blanket? Deep in ❶ the Earth's crust and mantle, heat is being produced. Usually this heat passes out through the Earth's surface. However, sometimes a blanket of many layers of rock holds the heat in. Then the heat collects in that place.

As the heat collects, it melts the rock nearby. This ❷ melted rock is called **magma** (mag'mə). Think of magma as a very thick paste of molten rock. Sometimes, as you have read, melted rock finds its way to the surface. Then it may escape through a volcano, and we call it lava instead of magma. Most magma, however, remains deep in the Earth.

As magma is heated, it expands. As it expands, it pushes against the rock. This is one way in which pressure can build up in the Earth. Pressures in the Earth, scientists think, are part of the reason sedimentary rock layers become parts of mountains. Let's see how.

The Lifting of the Rock Layers

❸ One theory of how a mountain range is formed starts with the piling up of sediments at the bottom of the sea. Slowly, slowly the sediments turn into rock.

81

LESSON CLUSTER 5
UP GO THE MOUNTAINS

Teaching background. 5 T-61

Concept-seeking. Children learn that magma, under deep rock, causes mountains to form by upward pressure, and that sidewise pressure causes upward folds to occur and form mountains.

Operations. Children probe mountain formation by producing upward folds resulting from sidewise pressures; they *investigate* faulting caused by the breaking of rock layers.

Methods of intelligence. Children recognize that upward pressure of magma may cause folding and faulting resulting in mountain formation or volcanoes.

Useful materials: Modeling clay; paper cut into strips about $2\frac{1}{2}'' \times 8\frac{1}{2}''$, shallow pans, water, stacks of ruled paper, colored construction paper, or towels.

Introducing Lesson Cluster 5

Children can demonstrate mountain uplift as follows: Make a sandwich of three layers of modeling clay between four strips of paper. The strips should be about $2\frac{1}{2}''$ by $8\frac{1}{2}''$. The layers of clay should be made as thin as possible. (Different colors of clay are effective.) When the sandwich is ready, immerse it in shallow water. Press slowly and firmly at both ends to raise the central part of the sandwich above the water. What do the layers in the sandwich stand for? (sediments) the water? (the sea) the raised part? (mountains)

Developing the lesson

❶ What causes this heat deep within the Earth? (energy from the decay of radioactive substances)

❷ Children may be interested to know that the word ***magma*** is Greek for "thick dough". To clarify the difference between ***magma*** and ***lava,*** explain that lava is magma that has lost most of its gases and ash before it flows out of a crater. Where do the gases and ash go? (out through the crater, during first stage of a volcanic eruption)

❸ While we can see changes due to sedimentation over thousands of years, it takes millions of years to pile up enough sedimentary rock to form the basis for a mountain range.

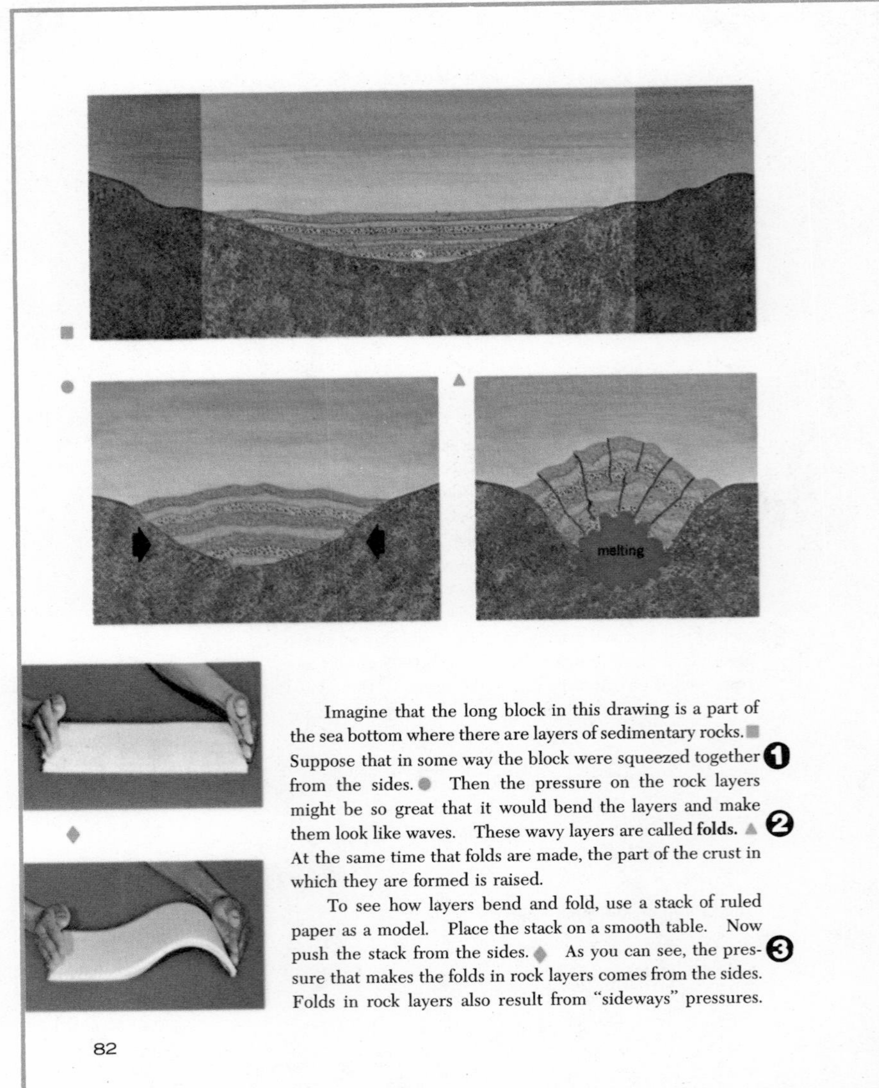

Imagine that the long block in this drawing is a part of the sea bottom where there are layers of sedimentary rocks. ■ Suppose that in some way the block were squeezed together ❶ from the sides. ● Then the pressure on the rock layers might be so great that it would bend the layers and make them look like waves. These wavy layers are called **folds.** ▲ ❷ At the same time that folds are made, the part of the crust in which they are formed is raised.

To see how layers bend and fold, use a stack of ruled paper as a model. Place the stack on a smooth table. Now push the stack from the sides. ◆ As you can see, the pres- ❸ sure that makes the folds in rock layers comes from the sides. Folds in rock layers also result from "sideways" pressures.

82

Useful materials: Flour, sausage-shaped balloon.

Continuing Lesson Cluster 5

❶ In what way might the block be squeezed together? Fill a sausage balloon with a thick flour-water paste. Tie securely. What will happen if I make a dent in the balloon? Let children predict, and then try it.

❷ Call attention to the diagram of the formation of folds. Pointing out the region of melted rocks (labeled *melting*) at the base of the folds, explain that the sedimentary rock layers have sunk so deep into the mantle that the heat within the Earth is melting them.

❸ To demonstrate how lateral pressure causes folding, children can use ruled paper, as illustrated, or colored construction paper, or a stack of small towels.

It might be well at this point to determine whether any children have a common misconception about hills and mountains: that they are just big piles of dirt. If you were to dig deep into the side of a mountain, would you be digging through earth all the way, or would you come to solid rock? Who has seen mountains that were just bare rock sticking up into the sky? Who has seen mountains where softer layers of rock have been worn away with harder rock underneath showing?

Supporting Statement: Heat and pressure are continually changing the Earth's crust.

In layers of rock, the pressure is sometimes so great that ❶ the layers fold and break. This break is called a **fault.** Therefore, there may be both folds and faults, as in this picture. ★ Can you invent your own model of a fault?

Fossils on Land

❷ Why are fossils found on dry land? Now we can answer this question. Pressure within the Earth may raise the layers of sedimentary rock out of the sea. Thus, rock layers that were at the bottom of a sea can become dry land. They may even become mountains. Sedimentary layers, often containing fossils, have been lifted up above the surface of ❸ the water. So it is that we find fossils of sea creatures on dry land.

Sometimes the forces acting on rock layers have been so strong that layers have been tilted up on end and the edges laid open by erosion. We can sometimes walk over the open end of such layers and collect the fossils and rocks in it.

When Mountains Make Islands

Imagine a break in the Earth's crust deep under the ocean. Melted rock bursts through and begins to form a volcanic mountain *under the sea.* The lava builds the

❶ What seems to have happened where the fault occurred in this picture? (A break in the folds occurred and one side was pushed up higher than the other.)

If there is a good example of a fold or a fault in the neighborhood of the school, a field-trip to study it is a possibility. Encourage children to use clay, wood, or "silly putty" to build a model of a fault.

❷ A fossil-hunt is an excellent reason for a field trip. If there are any fossil-bearing formations near the school, the class should try to take advantage of them.

❸ Imbedded in stone above the fireplace in a lodge near Laramie, Wyoming, is a large fossil fish. An ocean type, it was found nearby. How is this possible?

This may be a good time to review how fossils are formed. See if the children can give a good explanation without turning back to the pages where this is discussed.

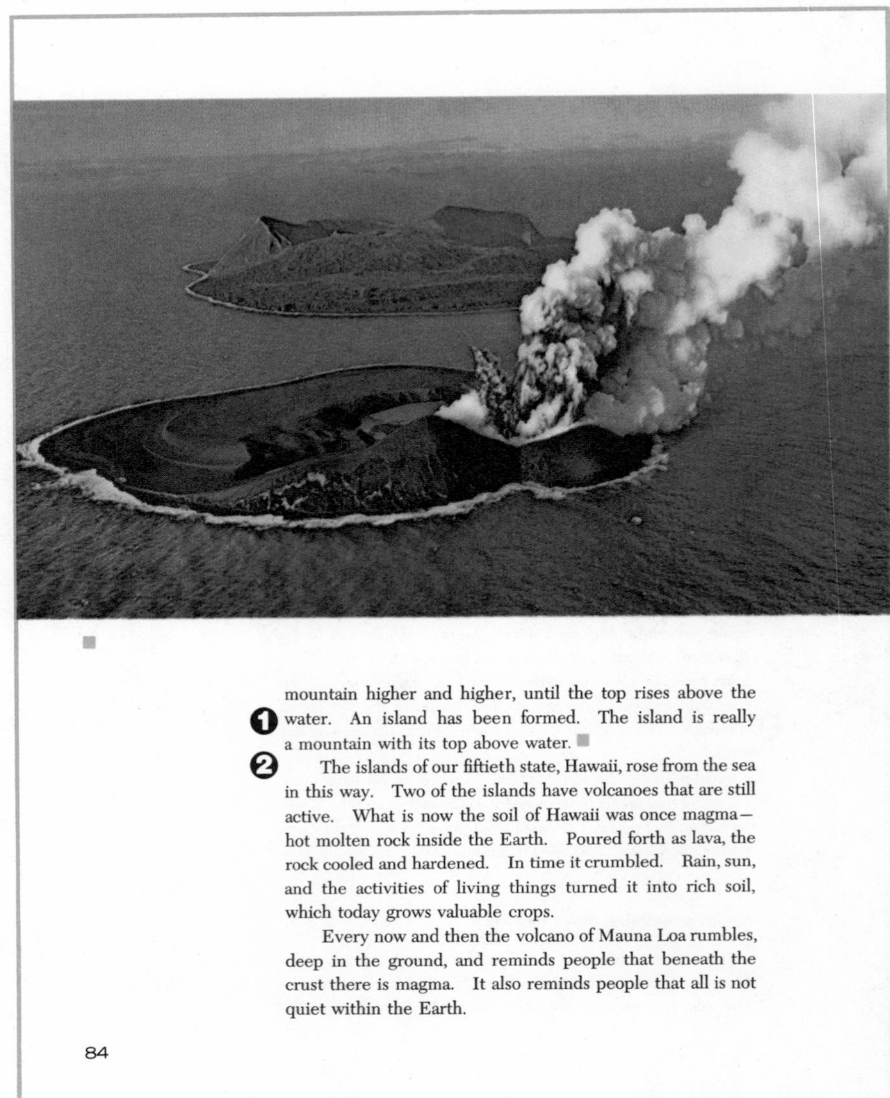

mountain higher and higher, until the top rises above the
❶ water. An island has been formed. The island is really a mountain with its top above water. ■

❷ The islands of our fiftieth state, Hawaii, rose from the sea in this way. Two of the islands have volcanoes that are still active. What is now the soil of Hawaii was once magma—hot molten rock inside the Earth. Poured forth as lava, the rock cooled and hardened. In time it crumbled. Rain, sun, and the activities of living things turned it into rich soil, which today grows valuable crops.

Every now and then the volcano of Mauna Loa rumbles, deep in the ground, and reminds people that beneath the crust there is magma. It also reminds people that all is not quiet within the Earth.

84

Continuing Lesson Cluster 5

❶ In November, 1963, fishermen noticed clouds and smoke issuing from the water not far from the Iceland coast. They were witnessing the birth of the volcanic island of Surtsey.

Three years later, a second island, Syrtlinger, pushed its way through the sea nearby. In the picture here, Surtsey is seen in the background and Syrtlinger, in the foreground.

For a graphic account of mountains rising from the sea, you may wish to read aloud from the opening chapters of James Michener's novel, *Hawaii.* Here, as in the Pacific Northwest, volcanic soil contains many important substances (minerals) for crops. Geologists studying Hawaii's live volcanoes are studying ways of using sensitive instruments to predict eruptions.

❷ The islands of the Hawaiian group all consist of volcanoes rising from the floor of the sea, and the island of Hawaii itself was built up by five different volcanoes merging their cones together as they rose. The rock that forms the island of Hawaii is made up entirely of cooled magma.

Supporting Statement: Heat and pressure are continually changing the Earth's crust.

❶ BEFORE YOU GO ON

Check your understanding of the concepts of this section. Which ending would you choose for each statement below?

1. Mountains are worn down by weathering and
a. erosion
b. folding

2. The Earth's heat can be trapped by
a. sedimentary layers
b. weathering

3. Pressure on rock layers may be produced by
a. heated magma
b. the expanding core

4. The statement that fits the main concept of this section is
a. The mountains are pushed up by the Earth's atmosphere.
b. The mountains are pushed up by the Earth's heat.

USING WHAT YOU KNOW ❷

You may have heard that radioactivity due to atomic bombs is dangerous. It is. You know that radioactivity can also be natural, and very important. Write about one hundred words on the importance of radioactivity in the Earth. If your teacher wishes, share your report with your class.

INVESTIGATING FURTHER ❸

Get a piece of pumice stone (a drugstore may have it). Place it in a pan of water. What happens? Can you find out why this happens?

A LOOK AHEAD

There seems to be a kind of cycle. Mountains are weathered and eroded. Sediment is laid down and, in time, layers of sedimentary rock form. Pressures under and inside the Earth's crust can push the rock up once again, and new mountains are raised up. Then they are eroded, and so on again and again. Scientists call this the *geologic cycle*, which helps us to understand how the same materials of the Earth's crust are used over and over again to make mountains and sedimentary rocks.

Are there rocks near your home that may have once been at the bottom of a sea? Are there rocks made from materials that once came forth from a volcano? How would you know?

VERIFYING PROGRESS

❶ Before you go on. Children *demonstrate* understanding of mountain-forming forces by completing open-ended questions.
1. a 2. a 3. a 4. b

❷ Using what you know. Children *analyze* their knowledge of radioactivity within the Earth, *order* the sequence in which events relative to radioactivity take place within the Earth, and *explain* and *describe* the uplift of the crust.

❸ Investigating further. Children *investigate* the floating of pumice in water, *observe* the porosity of pumice, and *infer* that the pores contain enough air to make the mass less dense than water. They *seek evidence* of the formation of pumice and *infer* that gases are trapped during the cooling process of lava containing a high percentage of gases. Children *explain* the process.

Encourage children to *compare* heavy whipped cream, Swiss cheese, or other porous materials with pumice formations.

LESSON CLUSTER 6
TREASURE IN THE EARTH AND ON THE MOON

Teaching background. 6 T-61

Concept-seeking. Children become aware that the Earth's rocks have formed in different ways.

Operations. Children *investigate* the three basic kinds of rock, the differences in their composition, and the ways they are formed.

Methods of intelligence. Children *observe* differences in crystalline structure in different minerals, *identify* specimens, and *make inferences* about variations in rocks.

6. Treasure In the Earth and on the Moon

Robert Louis Stevenson wrote a famous story, *Treasure Island.* In it a boy, Jim Hawkins, and a pirate, Long John Silver, search for treasure on an island. When at last they find it, there are bars of gold and heaps of coins.

However, there is treasure all around us that many people don't know about. In truth, all the Earth's crust is treasure. In the crust are not only gold and silver but copper and aluminum, iron for making steel, and many, many other materials. In the crust are the substances that make up soil, on which plants and animals live. There are coal, oil, and natural gas in the Earth's crust, too.

❶ In the Earth's crust are many of the substances we need for living. What greater treasure could there be?

Some of the substances in this treasure are called ❷ **minerals.** Minerals are elements and compounds that are part of the Earth's crust. Gold is a mineral, for example, and so is salt. ■ ● Both are found in the crust of the Earth. Rocks have many minerals in them. In fact, rocks can be identified by the minerals in them, as you shall see.

■ 

● 

86

Introducing Lesson Cluster 6

Pass around a collection of materials; some of them need not be familiar to the children. (See **Useful materials** on page T-99 for suggestions.) Which of these are minerals or mixtures of minerals? Why do you think so? Children will probably be unable to sort all the materials accurately. Allow them to try to explain, but hold off definitive sorting until later.

Developing the lesson

❶ Why do you think all the Earth's crust is a treasure? How is soil, for example, a treasure? (Without soil we could not grow food.) What if there were no iron or copper or aluminum in the Earth's crust? (We could have nothing made of those metals.) What are some of the things we could not have? (automobiles, railroads, airplanes, cooking vessels, tall buildings, etc.)

❷ What are some elements you know? Children may know that metals such as iron, gold, silver, copper, aluminum, and tin are elements. All these may be considered to be *minerals* but some are found in the earth as elements (gold, silver, some copper, some iron) and others as compounds (aluminum, tin, most copper, most iron).

Supporting Statement: The way in which rocks are formed determines their make-up.

The Look of Fire-Formed Rocks

When magma flows out of a volcano, it is called lava. One kind of lava rock has the Hawaiian name pahoehoe (pə·hōē′hōē). ▲ Of course, most magma does not become lava but stays below the surface. There, the magma cools and hardens and forms rock. This rock is one kind of granite that may have formed from magma below the surface. ◆

❶ Any rock formed by the cooling and hardening of fire-hot magma is called an **igneous** (ig′nē·əs) rock. Igneous means "formed by fire." Thus, pahoehoe is an igneous rock that cooled and hardened above the surface. Granite is an igneous rock that cooled and hardened below the surface. Both kinds of rock were formed from hot magma.

❷ You might think that scientists would agree that igneous rocks such as granites came from magma. Not all geologists do agree, however, on this theory about granites. Some geologists hold the theory that igneous rocks like granites

▲

◆

87

Useful materials: For use throughout this lesson cluster, it is desirable to have on hand rocks and minerals such as different varieties of granite, pahoehoe, scoria, obsidian, basalt, mica, pumice, coal, marble, talc, fluorite, iron ore, galena, limestone, conglomerate, gneiss, sandstone, slate, sulfur, etc.; lumps or blocks of nonmineral substances such as wood, paraffin, crude rubber, and lucite (or other plastic); magnifying glasses.

❶ What other words besides igneous begin with "igni-"? (ignite, ignition) What do all these words refer to? (fire) What was pahoehoe before it hardened? (magma that became lava) What is the difference between how pahoehoe and granite were formed? (Granite was magma that cooled and hardened below the surface.)

❷ Why don't scientists always agree on the explanation of facts? (Some facts support one theory, some another; there may be not enough facts yet to establish or overthrow either theory.) Why don't scientists agree about the origin of granite? (It forms where direct observations are not possible: below the surface of the Earth, over a long time, and at high temperatures.)

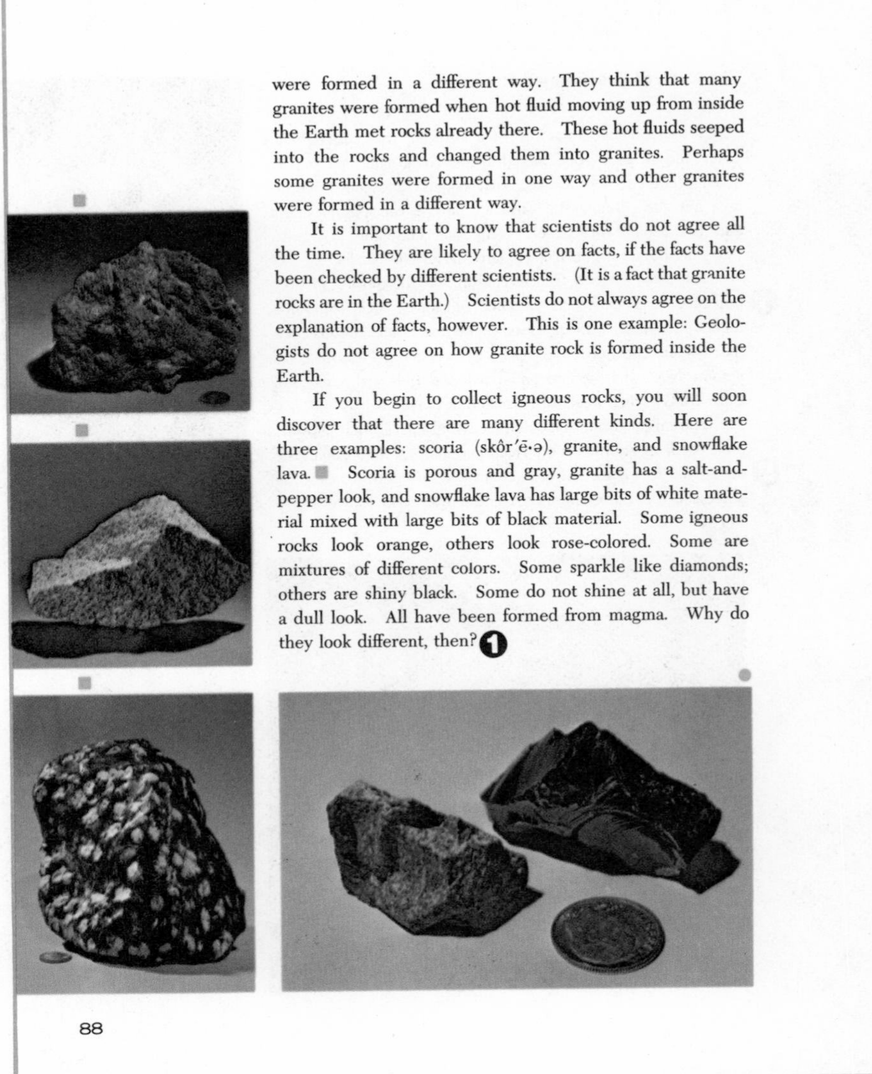

were formed in a different way. They think that many granites were formed when hot fluid moving up from inside the Earth met rocks already there. These hot fluids seeped into the rocks and changed them into granites. Perhaps some granites were formed in one way and other granites were formed in a different way.

It is important to know that scientists do not agree all the time. They are likely to agree on facts, if the facts have been checked by different scientists. (It is a fact that granite rocks are in the Earth.) Scientists do not always agree on the explanation of facts, however. This is one example: Geologists do not agree on how granite rock is formed inside the Earth.

If you begin to collect igneous rocks, you will soon discover that there are many different kinds. Here are three examples: scoria (skôr′ē·ə), granite, and snowflake lava. Scoria is porous and gray, granite has a salt-and-pepper look, and snowflake lava has large bits of white material mixed with large bits of black material. Some igneous rocks look orange, others look rose-colored. Some are mixtures of different colors. Some sparkle like diamonds; others are shiny black. Some do not shine at all, but have a dull look. All have been formed from magma. Why do they look different, then? ❶

Continuing Lesson Cluster 6

❶ Display several different igneous rocks, or point out those illustrated in the text. **Why do igneous rocks look different from other rocks?** Encourage children to hypothesize before beginning the next section, "Why Rocks Look Different."

Supporting Statement: The way in which rocks are formed determines their make-up.

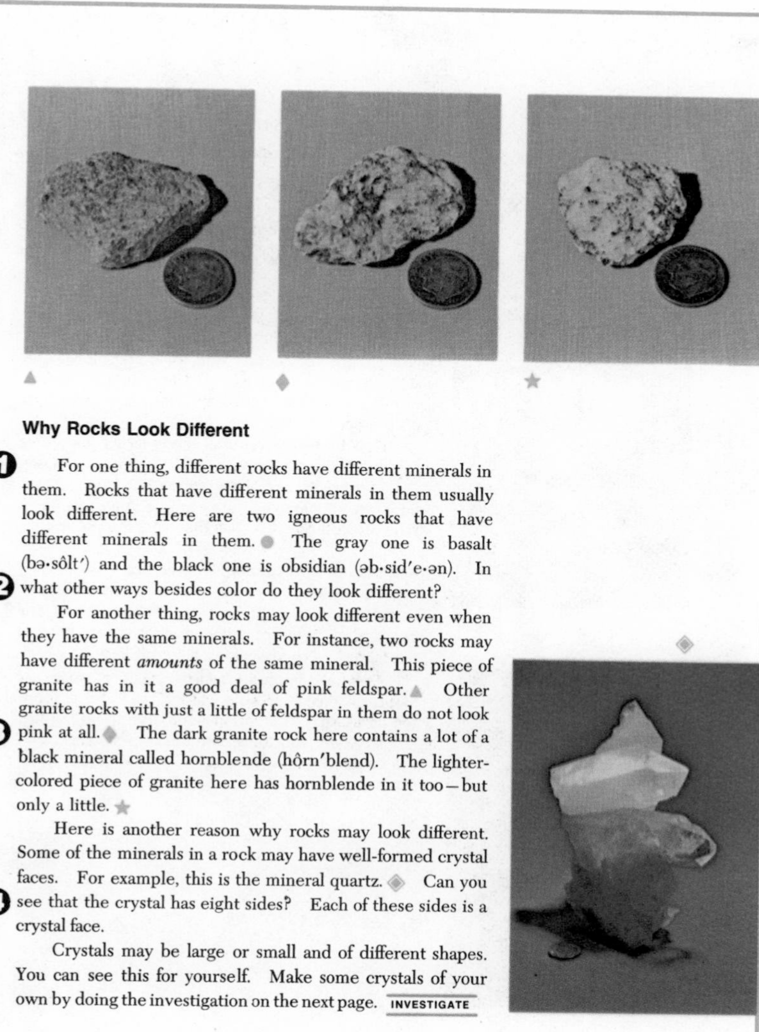

▲ ◆ ★

Why Rocks Look Different

❶ For one thing, different rocks have different minerals in them. Rocks that have different minerals in them usually look different. Here are two igneous rocks that have different minerals in them. ● The gray one is basalt (bə·sôlt′) and the black one is obsidian (əb·sid′e·ən). In
❷ what other ways besides color do they look different?

For another thing, rocks may look different even when they have the same minerals. For instance, two rocks may have different *amounts* of the same mineral. This piece of granite has in it a good deal of pink feldspar. ▲ Other granite rocks with just a little of feldspar in them do not look
❸ pink at all. ◆ The dark granite rock here contains a lot of a black mineral called hornblende (hôrn′blend). The lighter-colored piece of granite here has hornblende in it too—but only a little. ★

Here is another reason why rocks may look different. Some of the minerals in a rock may have well-formed crystal faces. For example, this is the mineral quartz. ◈ Can you
❹ see that the crystal has eight sides? Each of these sides is a crystal face.

Crystals may be large or small and of different shapes. You can see this for yourself. Make some crystals of your own by doing the investigation on the next page. INVESTIGATE

89

❶ There are about 2,000 different minerals, of which about 30 are quite common. If you were to mix 30 common minerals in different proportions, how many kinds of rocks would you be likely to have? (a great many) Explain that the number of kinds of rocks that actually exists is not as great as the number of mixing possibilities, since chemical elements can only combine in certain ways.

❷ Let children examine basalt and obsidian, with a magnifying glass if possible. What differences do you see? (Basalt is rough, gray, dull; obsidian is usually glassy, black, shiny.) What might make the difference? (different mineral composition) All granites contain four minerals: quartz, feldspar, mica, and some hornblende, but the proportions vary.

❸ Let children examine samples, if you have them. Have the children try to identify by the amount of hornblende and feldspar visible on a broken surface. Some will have quartz and mica which may result in discussion which you may need to resolve.

❹ Quartz has six rectangular faces and two hexagonal faces, or eight sides altogether. Not all of these are actually visible in the picture, but children should be able to infer the faces they do not see.

Performance objectives. Children *demonstrate* the formation of sugar crystals in a cooling saturated solution in water. They *observe* and *describe* their results, and *compare* them with those pictured and with those obtained by their classmates. They *develop a hypothesis* as to why crystals of different substances are different in appearance.

Useful materials: Alternative materials are available in CLASSROOM LABORATORY: PURPLE.

AN APPRENTICE INVESTIGATION
into Making Crystals

❶ **Needed:** a Pyrex beaker, a teaspoon, a pencil, a piece of string, a bolt or large nail, a hot plate, water, $\frac{3}{4}$ cupful of sugar

Put $\frac{1}{2}$ cupful of water in the Pyrex beaker and heat it on the hot plate. When the water is boiling, add $\frac{3}{4}$ cupful of sugar. Add the sugar slowly and stir constantly until all the sugar has dissolved. Remove the beaker from the hot plate; then turn off the heat.

Now tie the bolt or nail to the string and hang it in the beaker as shown. ❷

Let the beaker of sugar solution cool. What ❸ do you observe? Here are some results. What do you notice? Are these results like yours?

Methods of Intelligence: Comparing

Try making crystals of salt by evaporation. Compare them with sugar crystals. Why are ❹ crystals of different substances different in appearance? Try to develop a hypothesis.

At what temperature do crystals of sugar or salt grow best? in cold water? in water at room temperature? Plan an investigation to find out.

How will you tell where the crystals are growing best? by their number? by their size? or is there another way?

90

Continuing Lesson Cluster 6

❶ If Pyrex beakers are not available, saucepans may be used for heating the mixture of water and sugar. Then, when the mixture is slightly cooled, pour into a wide-mouth jar such as a peanut butter jar. To be sure of obtaining good crystals, heat the syrup until a few drops of the syrup added to cold water make a soft ball (or to a temperature of 234° to 238° F on a candy thermometer).

❷ The bolt or nail should be sanded or cleaned thoroughly before using.

❸ While cooling takes place, you may wish to have children set up the investigation to obtain salt crystals by evaporation. Let children have freedom to observe the formation of crystals of sugar. Where did the first crystals form: on the bolt, the string, or at the bottom of the beaker? Did crystals continue to form where there were crystals to attach themselves to, or did they form in new places?

❹ Have the children describe the difference between salt crystals and sugar crystals (if any) and observe whether the crystals formed in the same way. Could you get sugar crystals to form by evaporation? (yes) Could you grow salt crystals inside a cooling solution? (yes) Crystals form in different ways, depending on arrangement of the atoms making up the compound that crystallizes.

Supporting Statement: The way in which rocks are formed determines their make-up.

■

A Problem in Cooling

Some rocks have large crystals in them. Some have small crystals. Some rocks have crystals so small that the rocks look almost glassy.

❶ Here are three such rocks.■ They are all igneous rocks formed from magma. Each rock cooled at a different speed. One cooled underground, very slowly. One cooled near the surface, not as slowly as the one underground. One cooled on the surface, quickly. Examine the picture carefully. Which rock do you think cooled most slowly? Which cooled
❷ a little faster? Which cooled the fastest? (Answers are on page 93.)

Igneous rocks can indeed have different colors and shapes. Even rocks that look alike at first may turn out to be different when examined closely. This is one reason why some people like to collect rocks; there are surprises. At the end of this unit there is a long-term Search On Your
❸ Own. It is designed to help you probe the Earth. Why not look at it now?

If you were to collect fire-formed rocks only, you would still be able to have a large collection. However, there are also two other general kinds of rocks. As you will see, it is
❹ possible to tell which is which.

91

❶ If possible, pass around samples like the three pictured, so that the children can examine them (with a magnifying glass, if available). Their opinions as to the relative rates of cooling will be better informed if they can do this. They can make good hypotheses just from the picture, however. You may hint that A and C are granites, and that B is obsidian. You may want to point out that crystals formed in rocks cannot always assume their typical shapes.

❷ Ask the children to give their hypotheses. If they seem perplexed, suggest that they try to rate the three rocks in terms of coarseness and fineness. What connection might there be between how coarse- or fine-grained a rock is, and how fast it cooled?

❸ Children can prepare for the Long-Term Search On Your Own by taking field trips to bring in rocks, by bringing in collections from home for later study, by obtaining or borrowing equipment, and by looking at rock collections in a museum.

❹ If you have a mixture of samples of igneous, sedimentary, and metamorphic rocks, ask children to sort out the igneous rocks. How did you sort the rocks? (familiar and unfamiliar) The other rocks can make two groups. Try to sort these, too. Set these aside and look at them again after children have studied sedimentary and metamorphic rocks. At that time, children may want to regroup some of the rocks.

The Look of Sedimentary Rocks

Sedimentary rocks have their own beauty and meaning. As you know, they form in layers, and they are the main fossil-carriers. Most of them are formed from sediment carried by streams and rivers and oceans. Think for a moment how many different sorts of sediment there must be. It won't surprise you, then, that there are many different sorts of ❶ sedimentary rocks. Sedimentary rocks form nearly three quarters of the Earth's exposed rock surface. Let's look at a few of them.

Sand, for instance, can be pressed into a sedimentary rock called sandstone. As you can see, sandstone forms in many layers. ■

❷ Perhaps you have seen old brownstone houses made of brown sandstone. Most sandstone is not very hard and is easily weathered by substances in city air. Yes, the stone of ❸ a building may be broken down by weathering, like the stone of a mountain. Perhaps you have observed this.

Shale is formed from pressed mud or clay squeezed into sedimentary rock. Shale can be gray-blue or reddish-❹ brown, or other colors. Wet a piece of shale and smell it for a clue as to what it comes from. It will smell like clay or mud!

■

Continuing Lesson Cluster 6

❶ Where does sediment come from? What happens to mountains when sediment is carried away? Where does the sediment go? Children should be able to recall the role of weathering and erosion in wearing away mountains and forming sediments that move down to lower levels of the land and into the seas. What does the amount of sedimentary rock suggest about the time that changes in the Earth have been taking place? (that the time has been tremendous, more than our imaginations can grasp)

❷ If there are no brownstone or other sandstone buildings near the school, it may be possible to get samples of sedimentary rocks from suppliers of flagstone and other building supplies. If you can also get some samples of igneous rocks, have the children try rubbing together two pieces of sandstone and then two pieces of igneous rock. Note how easily some sandstones break and crumble, while igneous rocks do not. Why are sedimentary rocks seldom used for tombstones and curbstones? (because they wear away too quickly)

❸ Who has seen old sandstone buildings in the city? What are some of the signs of weathering of these buildings? (the stone is pitted, crumbling, cracked, worn down)

❹ What causes differences in the colors of sedimentary rocks? (different minerals in them)

Supporting Statement: The way in which rocks are formed determines their make-up.

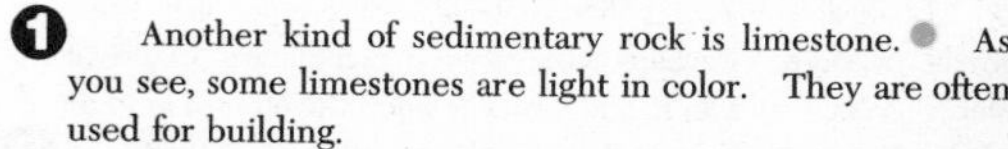

1 Another kind of sedimentary rock is limestone. ● As you see, some limestones are light in color. They are often used for building.

2 If you can get some bits of limestone, try this. Place the limestone in some vinegar. Notice the bubbles. ▲ The reason the limestone will bubble if placed in vinegar is that limestone is made up of a calcium carbonate.

The rock called chalk is also made of calcium carbonate. This is not, however, the chalk you usually find in the
3 classroom. The chalk you use at the chalkboard is not made up of shells. The sedimentary rock, chalk, is commonly made up of the shells of tiny animals. ◆ The chalk cliffs of Dover, in England, contain billions of tiny shells.

The animals that once lived in these tiny shells lived in
4 the sea. When these animals died and sank to the bottom, their shells piled up in sediment any layers that later were pressed into chalk.

Answers to a problem in cooling on page 91.

Cooled most slowly: Rock (*A*), coarse-grained granite.
Cooled a little faster: Rock (*C*), fine-grained granite.
Cooled the fastest: Rock (*B*), glassy-black obsidian.

93

Useful materials: Marble chips, vinegar or lemon juice, beaker or dish.

1 What do you think limestone is formed from? Why do we call it sedimentary rock? Accept all responses for the moment.

2 As suggested by the photograph, have children chip off small bits of limestone and place them in white vinegar, for best results. Some stones will react well with fresh lemon juice. Others, however, may be too hard to respond to either vinegar or lemon juice. For such hard limestone, you can try drugstore acetic acid, if available. The bubbles formed are carbon dioxide, but it may be best to postpone discussion of this fact until Unit Three, where the reaction will be studied in more detail.

3 Schoolroom chalk may be made from a type of talc. Natural chalk consists of the skeletons of billions of microscopic sea animals (foraminifera).

4 Since limestone is a sedimentary rock, what interesting things can be found in it? (fossils of marine animals: these may sometimes be seen in the foundations of houses) If anyone knows of such fossils in the stone of a building near the school, it might make a suitable field trip to go and study them.

Unit Concept-Statement: Bodies in space are in continuous change.

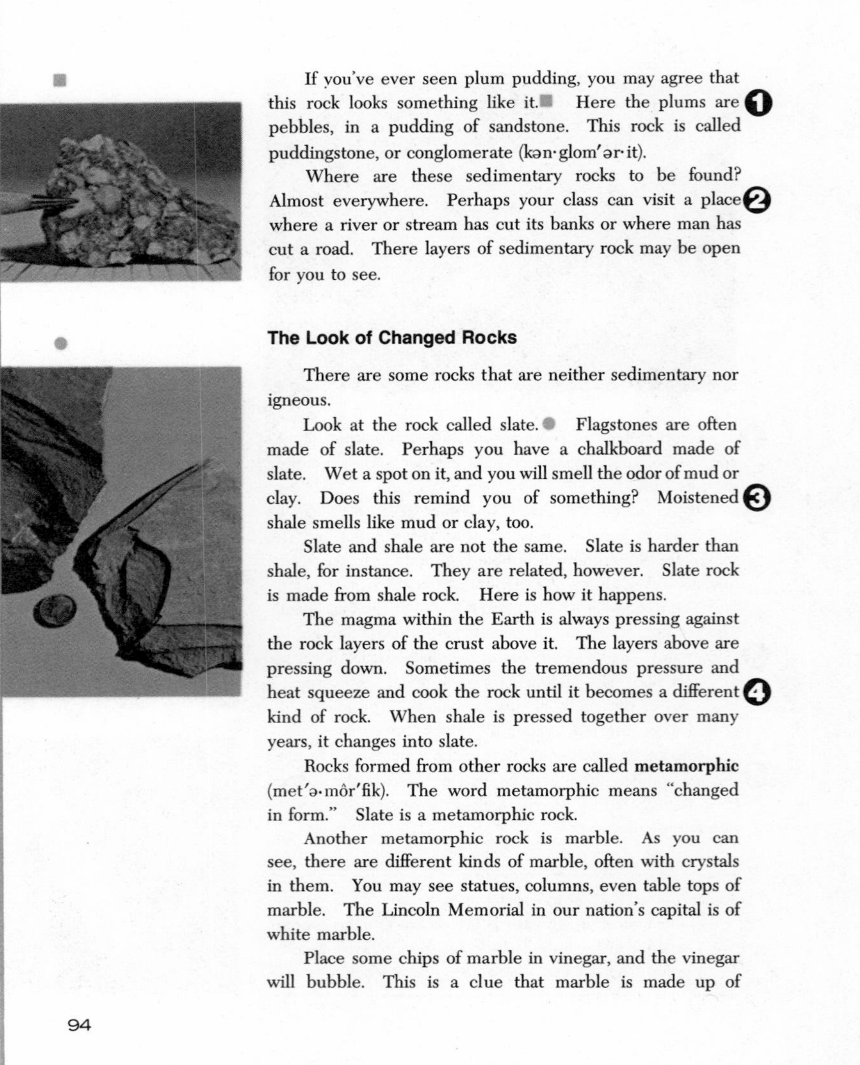

If you've ever seen plum pudding, you may agree that this rock looks something like it.■ Here the plums are ❶ pebbles, in a pudding of sandstone. This rock is called puddingstone, or conglomerate (kən·glom′ər·it).

Where are these sedimentary rocks to be found? Almost everywhere. Perhaps your class can visit a place ❷ where a river or stream has cut its banks or where man has cut a road. There layers of sedimentary rock may be open for you to see.

The Look of Changed Rocks

There are some rocks that are neither sedimentary nor igneous.

Look at the rock called slate.● Flagstones are often made of slate. Perhaps you have a chalkboard made of slate. Wet a spot on it, and you will smell the odor of mud or clay. Does this remind you of something? Moistened ❸ shale smells like mud or clay, too.

Slate and shale are not the same. Slate is harder than shale, for instance. They are related, however. Slate rock is made from shale rock. Here is how it happens.

The magma within the Earth is always pressing against the rock layers of the crust above it. The layers above are pressing down. Sometimes the tremendous pressure and heat squeeze and cook the rock until it becomes a different ❹ kind of rock. When shale is pressed together over many years, it changes into slate.

Rocks formed from other rocks are called **metamorphic** (met′ə·môr′fik). The word metamorphic means "changed in form." Slate is a metamorphic rock.

Another metamorphic rock is marble. As you can see, there are different kinds of marble, often with crystals in them. You may see statues, columns, even table tops of marble. The Lincoln Memorial in our nation's capital is of white marble.

Place some chips of marble in vinegar, and the vinegar will bubble. This is a clue that marble is made up of

94

❶ If you have samples of conglomerate, let children examine them. Point out that many puddingstones they may see have "plums" that are less colorful than those in the picture.

❷ If there is a really good place, not far from the school, to study sedimentary rock layers, the trip can be considered very worthwhile. Geology and mineralogy are typically field studies, and the pupils will gain a much clearer idea from fieldwork how scientists in these areas gather data than can be done only in the classroom.

❸ Have some of the children test some slate or shale by smell before they read this page. You may even have them close their eyes. Then wet a clean rag, rub it on some slate, and let the test children smell it. If they say "Clay" or "Mud" without prompting, it can be a very convincing demonstration for the whole class.

❹ The word "cook" is important here. Point out that metamorphic rock is not produced merely by squeezing sedimentary rock still harder. Chemical changes due to heat are also involved. Rearrangement of crystal structure takes place, too.

Supporting-Statement: The way in which rocks are formed determines their make-up.

calcium carbonate. Do you recall meeting calcium carbonate
❶ before? On page 93 this same test showed that limestone is made of calcium carbonate. Can you guess now which sedimentary rock is changed to the metamorphic rock marble? It is limestone. Pressure and heat may change limestone
❷ to marble.

Metamorphic rocks, then, are simply rocks that have been changed. All kinds of rock can be changed—igneous,
❸ sedimentary, even the metamorphic rocks themselves.

The Look of Living Things Changed to Rock

Strangely enough, there are rocks that did not begin by being igneous or sedimentary. Some rocks began with living things.

In the Petrified Forest National Park in Arizona, the trees are made of stone.▲ (*Petrified* means "changed to stone.") Once, a long time ago, these trees were alive.

▲

Continuing Lesson Cluster 6

❶ Try to demonstrate the reaction between marble chips and vinegar. What sedimentary rock acts as marble does? (limestone) What do you infer from this fact? (that marble may contain the same mineral as limestone) As children read the text, they will discover that marble and limestone do both contain the same mineral—calcium carbonate. If you have samples of marble and limestone, let children examine them.

❷ Would you expect many fossils in marble? (no) Why not? (Pressure would crush, and heat would change fossils that had been in the limestone from which marble is formed.)

❸ How is an igneous rock such as granite formed? (by cooling of magma) What could happen to granite that is strongly heated again, after cooling? (It could change again.) The kind of rock called "gneiss" may be an example of metamorphosed granite. (See the picture of gneiss on page 112 of the text.) If you have samples of granite and gneiss, let children examine them.

UNIT TWO

Unit Concept-Statement: Bodies in space are in continuous change.

❶ Usually, when a tree falls, tiny living things go to work on it. The tree decays. Insects and worms change it into powdery material that makes soil rich. The trees in the Petrified Forest National Park, however, fell where water flowed over them, and there they were buried millions of years ago. In fact, the minerals in the water took the place of the wood in the trees. Bit by bit the trees of wood became trees made of minerals—trees of stone. The minerals colored the petrified wood in different ways.

You can tell that this stone was once a tree. You can see the rings of growth—one ring for each year.

Rocks and the Moon's Make-up

The rocks that men have brought back from the Moon are, in a way, the world's most valuable rocks.

Why would scientists want rocks from the Moon? ❷ For one thing, rocks from the Moon provide us with evidence for a theory of the way the Moon was built, that is, its structure.

Remember that scientists build theories to explain the facts. For example, scientists have a theory that the inside of the Earth is hot. You could call this the "hot Earth" theory. This theory is supported by facts such as these:

1. Whenever a volcano erupts, lava flows out through the break in the Earth's crust. You know that lava is hot, melted rock.

2. The make-up of some kinds of rocks show that they were formed at high heat, deep within the Earth. That is, they are fire-formed, igneous, rocks.

Was the Moon, like the Earth, ever hot on the inside? You can find at least two theories in the writings of scientists. One is the theory of the "hot Moon." Another theory, the "cold Moon" theory, says that the Moon was never hot on the inside. ❸ What is the evidence for the "hot Moon" theory?

A volcano, as you know, has an opening called a crater at its top. There are craters on the Moon, too. Some of

96

Continuing Lesson Cluster 6

❶ When living tissue (typically that of trees) is "petrified", the soft parts are replaced by mineral deposits while the harder parts, such as cell walls, remain just long enough for the soft parts to be replaced. It is as if liquid Jell-O were poured into a mold made of ice. After the Jell-O has taken the shape of the mold and hardened, the ice itself may melt, but the Jell-O will still be there, maintaining the original shape of the ice.

❷ How can rocks from the Moon provide evidence as to how the Moon was formed? (The kinds of rock found on the Moon would offer evidence.) What kinds of rock do we know? (igneous, sedimentary, metamorphic) If all the rocks found were igneous, what would this suggest? (The Moon was once in a hot, molten or plastic state.) If many sedimentary rocks were found, what would this indicate? (Once there was water and probably air and wind on the Moon.) If metamorphic rocks are found, what would this suggest? (heating of cooled rock and recooling) Children might infer that this would mean the Moon has a hot interior, as does the Earth. You should suggest that heat might be supplied by impact of a large meteoroid.

❸ Why would the few rocks brought back from the Moon not give us all the evidence we need? (Some might have landed on the Moon from space; other areas of the Moon might have other kinds of rock.) Be sure that children understand that the answers will not be certain for a long time.

Supporting Statement: The way in which rocks are formed determines their make-up.

❶ these craters may be the remains of old volcanoes, like some of the craters on the Earth. More evidence is needed before scientists can be sure.

There is another kind of crater on the Earth that scientists believe is not formed by volcanoes. How do these craters form, then? If you have ever seen "shooting stars," what you have seen are not stars at all, but showers of **meteors** (mē′tē·ərs). A meteor is a bit of matter from space that may enter the Earth's atmosphere. If the meteor burns up as it does so, it makes a streak of light—a "shooting star." Sometimes, however, a meteor does not burn up, but hits the ❷ Earth. Then it is called a **meteorite** (mē′tē·ə·rīt′). When a meteorite hits the Earth, it may make a crater. Scientists believe that meteorites caused many of the craters on the surface of the Moon, too.

If the evidence shows that the Moon has had volcanoes on it, which theory will be supported—the "hot Moon" or the "cold Moon"? If scientists find that all the craters on ❸ the Moon were formed by meteorites, which theory will be supported?

Fire-formed Rocks From the Moon

Scientists have identified some Moon rocks as anorthosite (an·ôr′thə·sīt). Layers of anorthosite found on the Earth in North America, India, Siberia, and Scandinavia are known to have formed from molten rock. Recall that rocks such as this are igneous, which means "fire-formed." Anorthosite, then, is an igneous rock. Does this mean that the "hot Moon" theory is true? Scientists aren't sure.

The anorthosite brought back from the Moon was found in one of the Moon's lowlands, the Sea of Tranquility. In future flights to the Moon, astronauts will explore the highlands. Suppose they find thick layers of anorthosite in the Moon's highlands. Which of the two theories would this ❹ discovery support?

❶ Have children look on page 32 of their text for a picture that shows craters on the far side of the Moon.

Where are craters of volcanoes found on Earth? (usually mountain tops) Refer children to the pictures on pages 76 and 77. How do these craters seem different from the crater of a volcano on Earth? (very wide across, very low, and close to the surface)

❷ Children may have seen a *meteorite* in a museum or a picture of one and the kind of crater it makes—such as the one in Arizona. Why would a meteorite have been larger before it struck the Earth? (part burned up in atmosphere) What effect would the Moon's lack of atmosphere have on the size of craters? (larger) Would more craters be likely on the Moon? (yes) Why? (none of the meteors would have burned up)

❸ Volcanoes would support the "hot Moon" theory. Finding of only meteorite craters would tend to support the "cold Moon" theory. Will meteorite craters alone prove the cold Moon theory? Let children speculate on this question and then present evidence thus far reported as well as theories not yet tested.

❹ Anorthosite in quantity would tend to support the "hot Moon" theory. Why? (On Earth, anorthosite is igneous in origin.) Why would finding large layers of this rock not prove the theory? (They may not have come from inside the Moon; they may have always been there if the Moon cooled without volcanoes forming.)

1

Rock 13 and the Moon's Age

Like all the rocks from the Moon, this rock, known as Rock 13, is very valuable, but for a special reason. The rock is called "Rock 13" because it was the 13th one taken out of a box of rocks brought back by the Apollo 12 astronauts. Rock 13 is about as big as a lemon, and looks like ordinary granite. But Rock 13 is far from ordinary—it is very special. What makes it special is that it is the oldest rock yet to be found on the Moon. It is, in fact, 4.6 billion
2 years old—older than any other Moon rock brought back to Earth so far. The oldest rocks known to be part of the make-up of the Earth are only 4.5 billion years old, so Rock 13 is older than any known rock on Earth.

Perhaps you are wondering how scientists can tell the age of rocks. They can do this if the rock contains certain radioactive substances, like uranium, that break down slowly over millions and millions of years. By measuring the radioactivity of rocks, scientists can tell how old the rock is. In a way, radioactive rocks have their own built in "clocks." Scientists can use these "clocks" as one way of "telling time" on Earth. In this way they have used radioactive rocks to measure the age of the Earth. Now that rocks from the Moon can be studied, scientists can measure the age of the

98

Continuing Lesson Cluster 6

❶ In this photograph the rule is in centimeters, in the metric scale. Have children calculate the width of the rock:

$$10.0 - 5.3 = 4.7 \text{ cm.}$$

This is $1\frac{13}{16}$ inches, a very small sample of the Moon.

❷ What reasons can you think of that no rocks older than 4.5 billion years have been found on Earth, yet an astronaut picked up a Moon rock that was 4.6 billion years old? Children should be able to infer (from recall of weathering and erosion) that Earth's rocks at the surface are continually being worn away and covered by sediments. Sedimentary and metamorphic rocks are relatively "new" rocks, therefore, and the oldest rocks may be buried deep in the Earth or may have been changed by the heat within the Earth.

Is there any weathering on the Moon? If children respond negatively, ask: How were the craters made? They should now infer that meteorites could break up rocks on the Moon and that heat of impact could change them. They should also infer that the great differences in temperature between day and night can break up rocks, but probably not change them. How does this help explain the age of Rock 13? (Rocks on the Moon can break up mechanically but not change chemically.)

Supporting Statement: The way in which rocks are formed determines their make-up.

❶ Moon, too. One rock, however, is not enough. To say definitely how old the Moon is, scientists would need many rocks. Therefore, the conclusion that the Moon is at least 4.6 billion years old is not final, but *tentative* (ten′tə·tiv). ❷ A tentative conclusion is one that may be changed later, when new facts are available. (Why are tentative conclusions part of the scientist's methods of intelligence?)

❸ **BEFORE YOU GO ON**

Check your understanding of the concepts of this section. Which ending would you choose for each statement below?

1. Granite is a kind of rock classed as
   a. igneous b. sedimentary
2. Limestone is a kind of rock classed as
   a. metamorphic b. sedimentary
3. The rocks we see in the ground are in the Earth's
   a. mantle b. crust
4. According to the "hot Moon" theory, the Moon may be hot
   a. on its dark side
   b. at the center
   c. above its surface
5. The statement that fits the main concept of this section is
   a. The makeup of rocks is determined by the way in which they are formed.
   b. The makeup of rocks is determined by the way in which they are broken down.

❹ **USING WHAT YOU KNOW**

1. Below, on the left, is a list of common rocks. On the right are the three groups into which common rocks are classified. Try to classify each rock correctly by naming its group.

Rock	*Group*
slate	igneous
marble	sedimentary
limestone	metamorphic
puddingstone	
shale	
chalk	
granite	
sandstone	
obsidian	

2. You are given two highly polished stones. One of them is said to have come from a tree. The other is said to be an igneous rock. How might you tell one from the other?

3. Some scientists have reached the tentative conclusion that the Moon is 4.6 billion years old. Does this tell us how old the Earth may be? Explain your answer. (*Hint:* Read the Search on the Moon on page 40.)

99

VERIFYING PROGRESS

In concept-seeking

Children may *investigate* different rocks and *describe* their composition and appearance. They will need freshly broken samples of granite, basalt, slate, marble, sandstone, and limestone.

1. Have children *classify* the rocks. (igneous: granite, basalt; sedimentary: sandstone, limestone; metamorphic: marble, slate)
2. Have children *observe* the crystals in the two igneous rocks.
3. Let children moisten the remaining four samples with water. Which sample smells like mud? (slate) What does this tell about its origin? (sedimentary changed to metamorphic)
4. Have children place vinegar on these four samples. Which give off bubbles? (limestone, marble) What does this indicate? (Both contain the same mineral—calcium carbonate.)

❶ Children may wonder how scientists estimate the age of this Moon rock. See T-340 for a discussion of this.

❷ How are tentative conclusions like hypotheses? (Both are subject to later testing.) A tentative conclusion results when limited evidence supports a hypothesis. In this instance, only one rock met the test. But that might have come from space and not even be a "real" part of the Moon at all. If enough other Moon rocks test 4.6 billion years or older, the conclusion can be more final. The purpose of your teaching in the lesson cluster should be to encourage an open mind.

VERIFYING PROGRESS

❸ **Before you go on.** Children *demonstrate* understanding of the makeup and formation of rocks by selecting suitable responses to questions.

1. a 2. b 3. b 4. b 5. a

❹ **Using what you know.** Children *classify* rocks, *infer* the origin of rocks, and try to *explain* a tentative conclusion.

1. *igneous:* granite, obsidian; *sedimentary:* puddingstone, limestone, shale, chalk, sandstone; *metamorphic:* slate, marble.
2. The rock that was once part of a tree will show the evidence of replacement of its parts by minerals.
3. Not necessarily. The Moon could have been older or younger. Weathering and erosion by air and water have changed the Earth, but not the Moon. The oldest rocks on Earth may have been changed by its hot interior. If the Moon had a hot interior, it may no longer have one. We need more evidence.

LESSON CLUSTER 7
THE MAIN CONCEPT: THE CHANGING EARTH

Teaching background. T-58–T-61

Concept-seeking. Children become aware of the concept that the Earth and other bodies in the solar system are in continuous change.

Methods of intelligence. Children *synthesize* their understanding of weathering, erosion, sedimentation, and mountain formation, and *infer* that the Earth is in continuous change. They examine the ways of the scientist and *conclude* that he builds on the work of others.

Useful materials: Pebbles, garden loam or sand, box, photographs of erosion, weathering, and mountains; samples of different kinds of rocks or mineral crystals.

❶ **7. The Main Concept**
The Changing Earth

FOCUS ON THE CONCEPT

Billions of years ago, our Earth and Sun were formed out of a cloud of hot gas, some scientists think. The Earth became a hot ball revolving around the Sun.

Over billions of years the Earth formed and cooled. The ocean of air that now surrounds the Earth began to form. As this **atmosphere** (at′məs·fir) cooled, water vapor in the air changed to water. From this water came the first seas.

The crust cooled slowly. The rocks began to weather as ❷ the Earth cooled. Rains carried stones, pebbles, and bits of rock into the valleys. There the first thick soil was formed. Some of the weathered rock was carried into the seas and eventually formed the first sedimentary rocks.

Even as the sedimentary layers were being laid down, ❸ new mountains were rising up. The process still goes on. The Earth's mountains have been built up and worn down many times. They will be worn down many times more.

Understanding the concepts of science, we can look back to the past and explain what happened. We can do more. ❹ We can look forward and predict the future. We can predict, for instance, what will happen to rock that is exposed to heat, cold, and rain. Today, the Rocky Mountains are pointed.

Our concept of *change* is becoming ever clearer:

The Earth is in continuous change.

Introducing Lesson Cluster 7

It would be useful to have an enlarged map of the solar system; photographs of erosion, weathering, and mountains; and samples of different kinds of rocks or mineral crystals to which children may refer as you synthesize the evidence in this unit with them.

Developing the lesson

❶ Place on the chalkboard the main concept that appears in boldface type at the bottom of the page. What does this statement mean? Have children cite evidence, either by describing it or by illustrating it with photographs and materials on display.

❷ When could weathering have begun? erosion? Why did soil form in the valleys? What other kind of weathering took place once plants could grow on land?

❸ How do we know that the Earth is still changing? (Weathering, erosion, sedimentation, earthquakes, volcanoes, etc.) How do we know that mountains have risen? (fossils of marine life found high above sea level)

❹ Fill a box with some pebbles mixed with garden loam or sand like a gardening plot. Tilt the box by placing a support under it. Present a watering can filled with water. What will happen if we pour the water at the top of the box? (erosion) How were you able to predict this? (understood concepts)

Unit Concept-Statement: Bodies in space are in continuous change.

1 **FOCUS ON THE SCIENTIST'S WAYS**

To geologists, the International Geophysical Year, called IGY for short, had special meaning. Actually, IGY was a "year" of 18 months—from July 1, 1957 to December 31, 1958. What does this historic "year" tell us about the ways of the scientist?

The 18-Month Year

2 During the IGY, there was cooperation among
—66 nations
—30,000 scientists and technicians (including weather observers, forest rangers, geologists, oceanographers, and space scientists)
3 —several thousand laboratories and observing stations all over the Earth and even in space.

One station was at McMurdo Sound in the Antarctic, where this ship pounds the ice. ● Other stations included some of the first man-made satellites to orbit the Earth.

IGY included a carefully planned study of the solid, liquid, and atmospheric (at′mas·fir′ik) regions of the Earth.

What was studied? For example:
4 —oceans and their currents or "ocean rivers"
—the Earth and its earthquakes
—the Sun and its sunspots
—weather and climate
—the Arctic and the Antarctic
—glaciers and icebergs
—Earth's magnetic field and radiation in space.

There were scientists in all fields: biology, chemistry, physics, geology, astronomy, and a great number in the various branches of these fields, such as ecology and radioastron-
5 omy.

Perhaps you will want to find out more about IGY.
6 Where will you search as a beginning? (By the way, many of the findings of IGY are described in this book and others on earlier or later levels of study.)

101

1 The purpose of this section is to focus the child's attention on the methods by which scientists obtain and share information.

2 How can cooperation speed up scientific discoveries? (many persons and nations work on similar problems and share results)

3 Why are laboratories important? (have the tools for investigating and putting information together) Tell the children that the first satellites were put into orbit in 1957 and 1958 by the United States and the Soviet Union. Why were these important? (gave new knowledge of conditions beyond the atmosphere; led to Moon and space probes by testing procedures)

4 Let the children try to classify the studies that gave knowledge of (a) Earth's surface (b) the Sun (c) space. Have them review what they have studied in this unit and hypothesize as to how the studies might have been made.

5 Why should so many kinds of scientists have worked for I.G.Y.? Responses will vary, but the important point to bring out is that the biologist learns from the chemist, the astronomer from the physicist, and so on.

6 The search should begin in the library. It can also include sharing of information by children's parents who have scientific interests or backgrounds.

Unit Concept-Statement: Bodies in space are in continuous change.

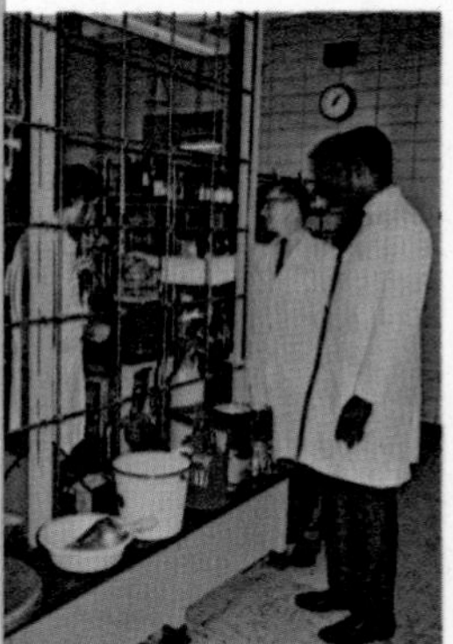

A Major Method of Intelligence

Scientists do not work alone. They depend on one another. Discoveries in science are open to all. In a real way, the different parts of the world of science, as in the world of living things, are interdependent. One scientist's discoveries are used by others in the field. And scientists in different fields also depend on one another's findings. ❶

Here are some scientists at work. ■ What does the picture tell you of one of the major reasons why scientists are very often successful in solving their scientific problems? ❷ Why do scientists publish their findings in scientific journals (special magazines for scientists)? ❸

Scholars who study the way of the scientist conclude that science is *cumulative* (kyo͞om'ye·lə'tiv). This means that one scientist may build on the findings of many others.

■

Focusing on the Main Concepts

❹ **TESTING YOURSELF**

A. Test your understanding of important concepts in this unit by answering these questions.

1. A fossil of a fish is found on high land. How did it get there?

2. A sidewalk has cracks in it. A huge slab of igneous rock showing through soil is cracked. What force might have cracked both the sidewalk and the rock?

3. A sedimentary layer has good-sized pebbles in it. Was the river that carried the pebbles flowing quickly or slowly when it dropped its pebbles? What is your reasoning?

4. Why is there a good chance for sedimentary rock to build up in the shallow water along the seacoast?

5. We sometimes find that a river lengthens where it empties into the sea. The Mississippi River, for instance, has added to its length near New Orleans. How do you explain this?

B. Test your knowledge with this quick check.

1. The action of heat and ice on rock is
a. erosion
b. weathering
c. radioactivity
d. fission

102

Continuing Lesson Cluster 7

❶ What is meant by the statement that the different worlds of science are interdependent? (Each field can learn from the others.) What does this tell us of the scientists' ways of work? (They learn from the findings of all the others.)

❷ The photograph shows that scientists do not work alone, but discuss problems and results with others.

❸ Children may have various ideas about why scientists publish—from making money to gaining a reputation and a better job. Bring out through discussion with judicious questioning that the main purpose is to share information and encourage others to check the results. One key question to ask is: Why are several investigations better than one?

VERIFYING PROGRESS

❹ **Testing yourself.** Children *analyze* situations and *apply* conceptual understanding.

A. 1. It was buried in sediment below the sea level, changed, and was uplifted during mountain formation.
2. The force of an earthquake.
3. Quickly. A fast-moving river can move larger masses, like pebbles; these are deposited before smaller particles, as water slows down.
4. Slow-moving water cannot hold soil particles. In the absence of seacoast currents, sediments will build up.
5. Sediment is deposited at the river's mouth, builds up land, and extends the land the river flows through, and hence its length.

2. Water and wind wear away bits of rock and soil. When this happens, which one of these is going on?

a. erosion
b. weathering
c. radioactivity
d. mountain building

3. The results of radioactivity are all but one of these:

a. particles are given off from nuclei
b. magma cools off
c. heat energy is produced
d. rays are given off from nuclei

4. You would most likely expect to find a fossil in

a. igneous roc!·
b. sedimentary rock
c. metamorphic rock

5. We can be certain that 100 years from now

a. the Earth will not be the same
b. the Rocky Mountains will have been completely eroded
c. no sedimentary rock will be forming

6. The statement that fits the main concept of this unit is

a. The Earth is the same now as it was a million years ago.
b. The Earth is in continuous change.

❶ INVESTIGATING FURTHER

1. Begin your rock collection now, if you haven't already done so. First read pages 104–113 of this book, which will help you.

2. Find out how the different rocks that you have collected are used. Read about the rocks. Examine buildings to find out which rocks they are made of. Observe workmen building things from rocks. What makes each kind of rock useful for its particular purpose?

3. There is a theory that mountains actually float on the rock below them. What can you find out about this?

FOR YOUR READING

1. *Wonders of Stones,* by Christie McFall, published by Dodd, Mead, New York, 1970. This is a very interesting book which tells you, for instance, how gravel, crushed rock, and building stones are different; and what effect bacteria, mosses, weather, and pollutants in the air have on stones.

2. *Why the Earth Quakes,* by Julian May, published by Holiday House, New York, 1969. Unusual drawings on every page will help you to understand the formation of rocks, earthquakes and volcanoes, and the continental drift.

3. *Rocks and Rills,* by A. Harris Stone and Dale Ingmanson, published by Prentice-Hall, Englewood Cliffs, New Jersey, 1968. This book will give you many ideas for investigations.

4. *The Shape of the Earth,* by Jeanne Bendick, published by Rand McNally, Skokie, Illinois, 1965.

103

VERIFYING PROGRESS

In methods of intelligence

To determine progress, children *synthesize* evidence of changes on Earth and *apply* it in *constructing hypotheses.* Each child may *analyze* these hypothetical situations and *apply* what they have learned to suggest solutions.

1. Scientists have concluded that erosion of mountains occurs at an approximate rate of a certain number of feet per thousand years. How can they make this calculation? (by studies of rainfall and temperature, sedimentation rates in plains and river deltas, and analyses of rock composition in the laboratory)

2. Radioactivity was discovered about 80 years ago. How could volcanoes have been explained before then? (Pressure builds up heat that would melt rock. Heat could expand the mantle, and the pressure from the expanding mantle would break the crust. Molten rock could be pushed up through the break. Children may be able to infer this from what they know, or they may need to read about early theories in library references.)

B. 1. b	3. b	5. a
2. a	4. b	6. b

❶ **Investigating further.** Children collect kinds of rocks and *classify* them, *investigate* and *describe* uses of rocks, and *analyze* the theory that mountains float on the rocks below them.

1. As children collect rocks, they classify them as igneous, metamorphic, or sedimentary.

2. Examination of buildings suggests individual or group field trips. Children should try to *identify* rocks used for exterior construction and *compare* them with facing stones and those used for interior decoration. They might *analyze* the resistance of rocks to weathering, to pollution from acid-forming substances in the air, or to their ability to take and retain a high polish.

3. This is known as the theory of isostasy. Refer children to encyclopedias, earth science textbooks, or to magazines such as *Science News*, and to the *Reader's Guide to Periodical Literature.*

Unit Concept-Statement: Bodies in space are in continuous change.

A LONG TERM SEARCH
THE ROCKS IN YOUR ENVIRONMENT

Teaching background. T-58–T-61 and handbooks listed on page 113.

Concept-seeking. Children increase awareness of changes in the past environment of the Earth from studying the composition of its rocks.

Operations. Children *investigate* rocks by collecting local specimens on field trips.

Methods of intelligence. Children *observe* rock types, *analyze* their composition and crystal structure, *consult authorities* for identification, *name* and *classify* the rocks they collect, and *infer* changes in the environment.

Useful materials: Rock collecting equipment listed on pages 106–07 and accompanying teaching notes.

A LONG-TERM SEARCH ON YOUR OWN
The Rocks in Your Environment

Some Searches you have done may have taken a short time—perhaps a few days or a week. Scientists generally plan their studies for longer periods. Most of their investigations take months, or years.

You may now be ready to take on a long-term Search into your own environment. You may want to seek out the rocks around you, for rocks and rock materials are important parts of the environment in which you live. Finding out about rocks is part of the science of **geology**—the study of the Earth, what it is made of, how it behaves, and its history. When you know the common rocks in your environment, you will begin to know the geology of your planet.

All Around You

There are rocks and minerals all around you. Look for them where land has been eroded, leaving rock layers exposed. Look where new roads are being made, where ditches are being dug, where foundations are being excavated. Wherever the ground is broken open, dug up, cut into, or washed away, you are likely to see freshly exposed pieces or layers of rock.

Wherever you go for rocks, however, take care to ask permission. The owner of a property may be glad to have you look around, but he will want to know what you are doing before he gives permission. So will your parents, and your teacher.

104

Introducing the Search

The success of this Search will depend on the interest you can generate. You might display a collection of local rocks, or, if a child in the class is a "rock hound," let him talk about his collection and how he got interested in rock collecting.

How would you like to go on a field trip to see what kind of rocks we can find? The mere suggestion of an excursion will be met with enthusiasm.

Developing the Search

The first trip needs careful planning; there's no point in random exploration. You should make a dry-run of the area in advance, noting possible sites for collecting and the time needed for a profitable trip. Metallurgical and petrochemical operations, if there are any in the area, may allow access to rubble brought from within the Earth, and the county or state geologists may be able to provide maps.

You will, of course, need to arrange for permission to leave the school property, especially if a large block of time is to be used. For trips of more than ten children, it is advisable to enlist the aid of adults. Scout leaders and parents with outdoor interests will be glad to assist, if the trip does not interfere with normal working hours.

After the children have had one supervised field trip and know what they are looking for, they can be trusted to collect on their own from areas you know are safe. Just the same, urge that no one goes into the field to collect on his own without another person along.

Concept Relationships: Physical and chemical changes in the rocks are an index of the Earth's changing environment.

Some Field Trips

If you live near a beach or a stream, or can get to one easily, perhaps your teacher or another adult can arrange a trip for collecting. On the banks of a ❶ stream such as this one, you can find many interesting specimens.

Another place you may find many rock specimens is where the ground is being prepared for a new building or road. Here you may find some rocks that are smooth and some that are jagged. How do ❷ you account for both kinds?

If you live in a city, perhaps you can go for a trip to study the rocks in a park near your school or home. On a trip of this kind you can sometimes classify large rocks as igneous, sedimentary, or ❸ metamorphic just by looking at them carefully.

❶ A stream will show effects of erosion, especially if it has cut through sedimentary layers to expose older underlying rock on the stream bed or in the banks. A stream gorge reveals a great deal of Earth history. If the area was once glaciated, children may find boulders scored by debris-carrying ice.

❷ The jagged rocks were probably recently broken and will show crystal structure. Smooth rocks may indicate the action of erosion and sedimentation. When these events occurred can be roughly estimated from the depth of the soils in which the rocks are embedded.

❸ In a large city, buildings may be faced with marble, granite, gabbro, or other building stone; or they may be constructed of sandstone, limestone, granite, or coquina (in Florida, especially). Even the school building, interior and exterior, can be a source of rock identification. Laboratory table tops, for instance, will probably be made of soapstone, which is resistant to acids.

Headstones in a cemetery offer a variety of rocks for examination, and the older ones will show evidence of weathering and chemical erosion. Of course collecting will not be possible, but identification will reveal the possible uses of many kinds of rocks.

Look for the different kinds of rocks that are used in the construction and decoration of city buildings, walls, and pavements.

Wherever you go to search, take along a handbook that illustrates common granites, sandstones, limestone, and so on, to help you recognize rocks. (Some useful books are listed on page 113.)

Some Useful Equipment

❶ What will you need for collecting rocks? Here are some items you may find useful.

1. A knapsack to carry rock specimens and equipment.
2. A geologist's hammer to make small specimens out of big ones, and to expose fresh surfaces of rocks that have been worn smooth.

❷ 3. Goggles or plastic glasses to protect your eyes when you chip rocks; or a piece of tough cloth (such as gunny sack).

❸ 4. A notebook and pencil to make a record of the specimens.

5. A hand lens to examine details too small to see with the naked eye.

Continuing the Search

❶ Children should be urged to put on suitable clothes for the field. They should wear heavy shoes and long trousers, especially if they are to cross rock-strewn areas or pass through fields in which there may be brambles or poison ivy. At least one adult on the field trip should have a small first aid kit with squares of bandages and adhesive tape, Band-Aids, and an antiseptic. On even the best organized trip, an emergency such as a cut or scrape can arise.

❷ Anyone not far enough away from the hammer to be out of danger from flying chips should also have his eyes protected or turn his back. Plastic sunglasses can be used instead of goggles.

❸ To each sample they pick up, children should tape a number to correspond to the notebook record. A good plan is to place each specimen, with a label or recorded data, in a small plastic bag. You might suggest several days in advance of the trip that children bring in plastic bread-wrappers or other similar containers, so that there will be enough on hand for collecting in the field.

Concept Relationships: Physical and chemical changes in the rocks are an index of the Earth's changing environment.

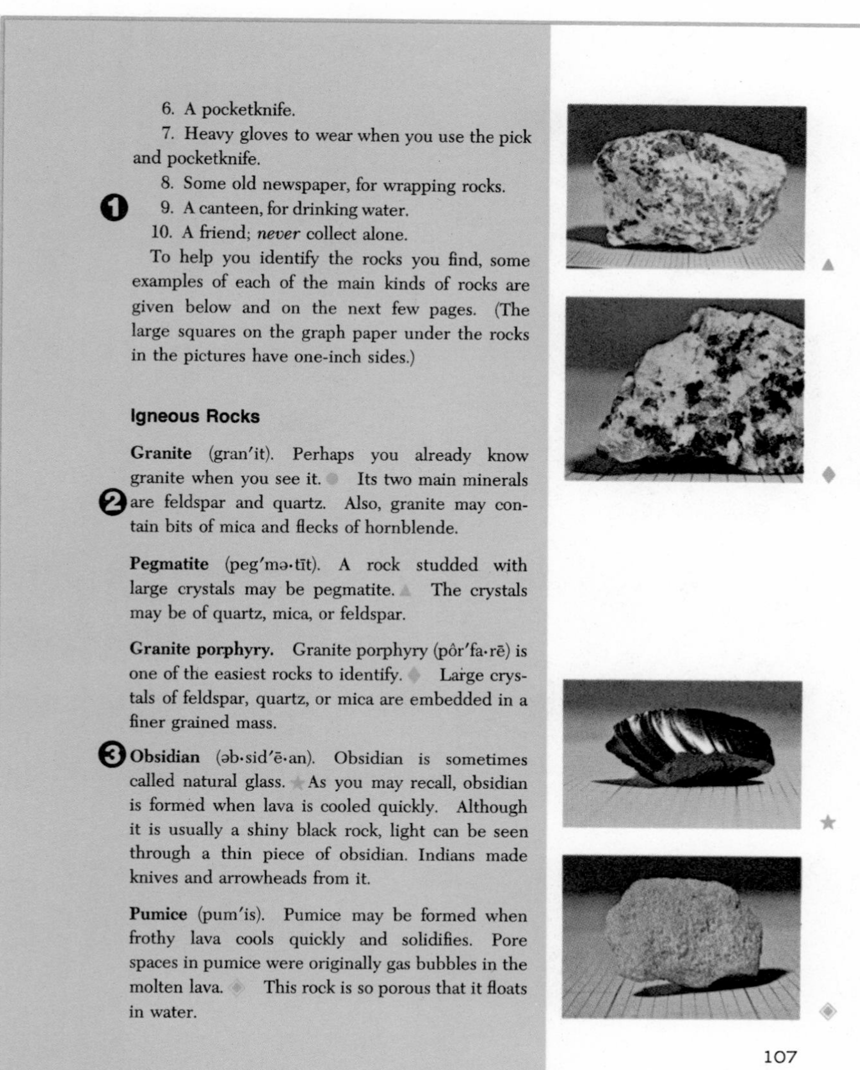

6. A pocketknife.
7. Heavy gloves to wear when you use the pick and pocketknife.
8. Some old newspaper, for wrapping rocks.

❶ 9. A canteen, for drinking water.

10. A friend; *never* collect alone.

To help you identify the rocks you find, some examples of each of the main kinds of rocks are given below and on the next few pages. (The large squares on the graph paper under the rocks in the pictures have one-inch sides.)

Igneous Rocks

Granite (gran′it). Perhaps you already know granite when you see it. ● Its two main minerals ❷ are feldspar and quartz. Also, granite may contain bits of mica and flecks of hornblende.

Pegmatite (peg′mə·tīt). A rock studded with large crystals may be pegmatite. ▲ The crystals may be of quartz, mica, or feldspar.

Granite porphyry. Granite porphyry (pôr′fa·rē) is one of the easiest rocks to identify. ◆ Large crystals of feldspar, quartz, or mica are embedded in a finer grained mass.

❸ **Obsidian** (əb·sid′ē·an). Obsidian is sometimes called natural glass. ★ As you may recall, obsidian is formed when lava is cooled quickly. Although it is usually a shiny black rock, light can be seen through a thin piece of obsidian. Indians made knives and arrowheads from it.

Pumice (pum′is). Pumice may be formed when frothy lava cools quickly and solidifies. Pore spaces in pumice were originally gas bubbles in the molten lava. ◈ This rock is so porous that it floats in water.

▲

◆

★

◈

107

❶ No canteen should ever be filled from a pond or stream in the field. Explain the dangers of drinking water that may be polluted with microscopic germs even though it looks clean and clear.

❷ Feldspar can be recognized in freshly broken granite by the crystals that reflect light like a mirror. Feldspar occurs in different colors which give granite different hues and tints. Mica also has shiny flat surfaces, but these can be peeled off in flakes. Quartz, when broken, looks like bits of glass. Pegmatite is a form of granite, distinguishable by its crystal structure and composition.

❸ Obsidian and pumice will not be found on a field trip unless the area was once one of volcanic activity.

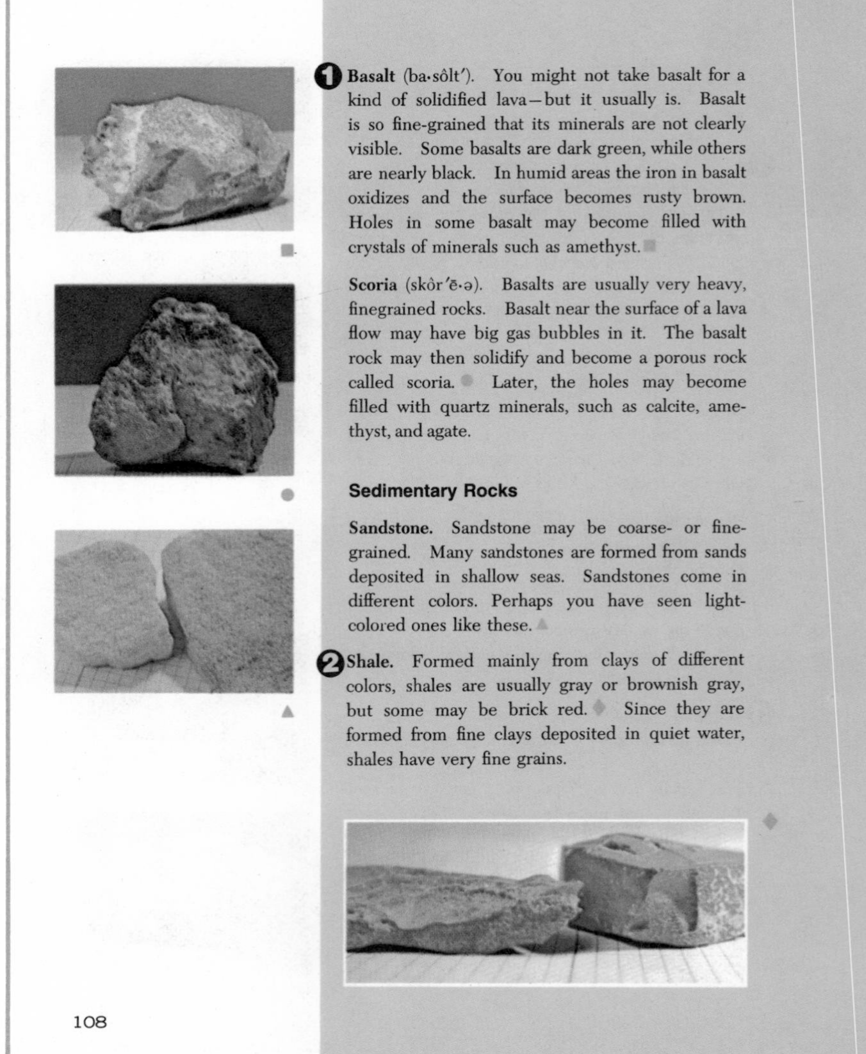

❶ Basalt (ba·sôlt′). You might not take basalt for a kind of solidified lava—but it usually is. Basalt is so fine-grained that its minerals are not clearly visible. Some basalts are dark green, while others are nearly black. In humid areas the iron in basalt oxidizes and the surface becomes rusty brown. Holes in some basalt may become filled with crystals of minerals such as amethyst.

Scoria (skôr′ē·ə). Basalts are usually very heavy, finegrained rocks. Basalt near the surface of a lava flow may have big gas bubbles in it. The basalt rock may then solidify and become a porous rock called scoria. Later, the holes may become filled with quartz minerals, such as calcite, amethyst, and agate.

Sedimentary Rocks

Sandstone. Sandstone may be coarse- or fine-grained. Many sandstones are formed from sands deposited in shallow seas. Sandstones come in different colors. Perhaps you have seen light-colored ones like these.

❷ Shale. Formed mainly from clays of different colors, shales are usually gray or brownish gray, but some may be brick red. Since they are formed from fine clays deposited in quiet water, shales have very fine grains.

108

Continuing the Search

❶ Unless you are in a region of former volcanic activity, you are unlikely to find basalt except at or near the bottom of deep cuts in the Earth, on well eroded mountain tops, or in excavated rubble. Mining or petrochemical engineers may prove helpful in suggesting sources of basalt.

❷ Have children recall the test for shale on page 92. Sandstone and shale result from the deposition of eroded materials by water that loses its energy when it fans out from a stream mouth into a shallow sea—or in flood areas, when a stream overflows.

See if children can hypothesize that the heavier materials will be deposited first and the lightest materials last. They can observe this by shaking up a jar of garden soil and water and letting it settle.

Concept Relationships: Physical and chemical changes in the rocks are an index of the Earth's changing environment.

Sometimes shale will be formed in pairs of light
1 and dark layers, each pair of layers taking one year to form. The time during which this shale was formed may be determined by counting the pairs of layers.

2 **Limestone.** There are many kinds of limestones. They come in a great many different colors (because of different impurities they may contain) and different textures. Limestones are made of the mineral calcite (calcium carbonate). They are formed under many different conditions. A geologist may be able to tell the origin of a limestone from the rock texture. ★

Limestone is formed from the remains of both plants and animals. Coral reefs are limestones made by colonies of tiny coral animals below the surface of the warm sea water. ◆

Fossils. Recall that fossils, the remains, prints, or traces of ancient plants and animals, are found most often in sedimentary rock. To find fossils, a limestone or shale quarry is a good place to go. (*Caution:* Never go into a quarry without permission, and don't explore a quarry alone.) Why are lime-

★

◆

1 The layers may also be of different thicknesses. **What would this suggest about the amount of rainfall and erosion?** (Heavier when deposition is greater, i.e. a greater amount of runoff will have greater energy to carry soil.)

2 If you are in a region of limestone caves, a guided trip would be instructive—under adequate safety supervision, of course. Limestone has been dissolved by carbonic acid in rainwater—just as vinegar dissolves limestone. The weird formations from ceiling and floor of such caves are formed when the water evaporates slowly from the dripping solution. **What would a limestone cave tell you about the past environment of the area?** (It was once under water where the shells of sea animals could be deposited and compressed into a sedimentary layer.)

stone and shale good for hunting fossils? How ❶ should the rock be split to find fossils? Why? The best-preserved fossils are hard parts of the animals, such as a bone or a shell. These are fossil ❷ shells.

A leaf may decay, however, and yet leave a ❸ print. Or part of a plant may be replaced cell by cell by rock-forming minerals, thus producing petrified wood in which the wood structure can be seen. (Look again at the pictures on pages 95 and 96 of petrified wood from the Petrified Forest National Park in Arizona.)

Coquina (kō·kē′na) is limestone made almost entirely of shells that are naturally cemented together.

Crystalline limestone is formed when calcium carbonate crystallizes. It looks somewhat like marble, which is also made of calcium carbonate, but marble is formed in a different way.

Coal. Coal is considered to be a kind of sedimentary rock. When ancient trees fell, they were ❹ sometimes covered by mud and other sediment. Over thousands of years, pressure of the sediment, and some heat, changed the trees into coal.

110

Continuing the Search

❶ If children have been able to visualize that sediment is laid down in layers, they should infer that the layers should be split apart horizontally and not broken across.

❷ The fossil on the left is a brachiopod, a relative of the scallop. Brachiopods first appeared in the seas about 500 million years ago. The one on the right is in the family of ammonites, coiled shells that first appeared in the seas about 300 million years ago. Ammonites became extinct about 80 million years ago.

❸ Children should recognize this as a fossil fern leaf.

❹ Fossilized leaves of ancient tree ferns and other plant life can often be found in coal. Of course, a number of chunks can be split without finding any fossils, because long ago the plant matter was changed to carbon by heat and pressure under deep loads of sediment.

Concept Relationships: Physical and chemical changes in the rocks are an index of the Earth's changing environment.

Metamorphic Rocks

❶ **Slate.** Slate is a metamorphic rock formed from shale. Shale, you may recall, is a sedimentary rock formed from clay. Like shale, slate can be split into sheets of rock. Have you ever seen a slate roof? The slate shingles are weather-proof and will last a long time, if they are properly fixed in place. They are cut from sheets of slate.

Some slate is red, like this. ★ But some is black, like the slate in some school blackboards.

❷ **Schists** (shists). These are metamorphic rocks that have a layered appearance. In some schists, bits of minerals can be seen clearly. Mica schist contains flakes of mica, a silvery mineral that sparkles as it reflects light. ◎

Marble. Marble is limestone that has metamorphosed (changed). ◈ It can be made to have a very smooth and highly polished surface. Marble is used by sculptors as well as by builders, as you may know. It is often tinted by the presence of other substances, such as iron oxide, among the calcite crystals that make up most of the rock. Thus, you may see marble in many colors, including white, red, pink, and black. The Lincoln Memorial in Washington, D.C. is made of white marble.

◈

◆

★

◎

❶ Slate and marble can easily be distinguished from shale and limestone by their hardness. Slate and marble are harder to scratch with a knife blade. One reason is that heating of the sedimentary rocks under pressure realigned the crystals of the minerals so that they are much more tightly packed and present a surface that is flat, with few if any pore spaces.

❷ Some schists are sources of mica used for insulation against fire. Because of the layers, apparent in the photograph, how do you think the rock will split? (with the layers, not across them)

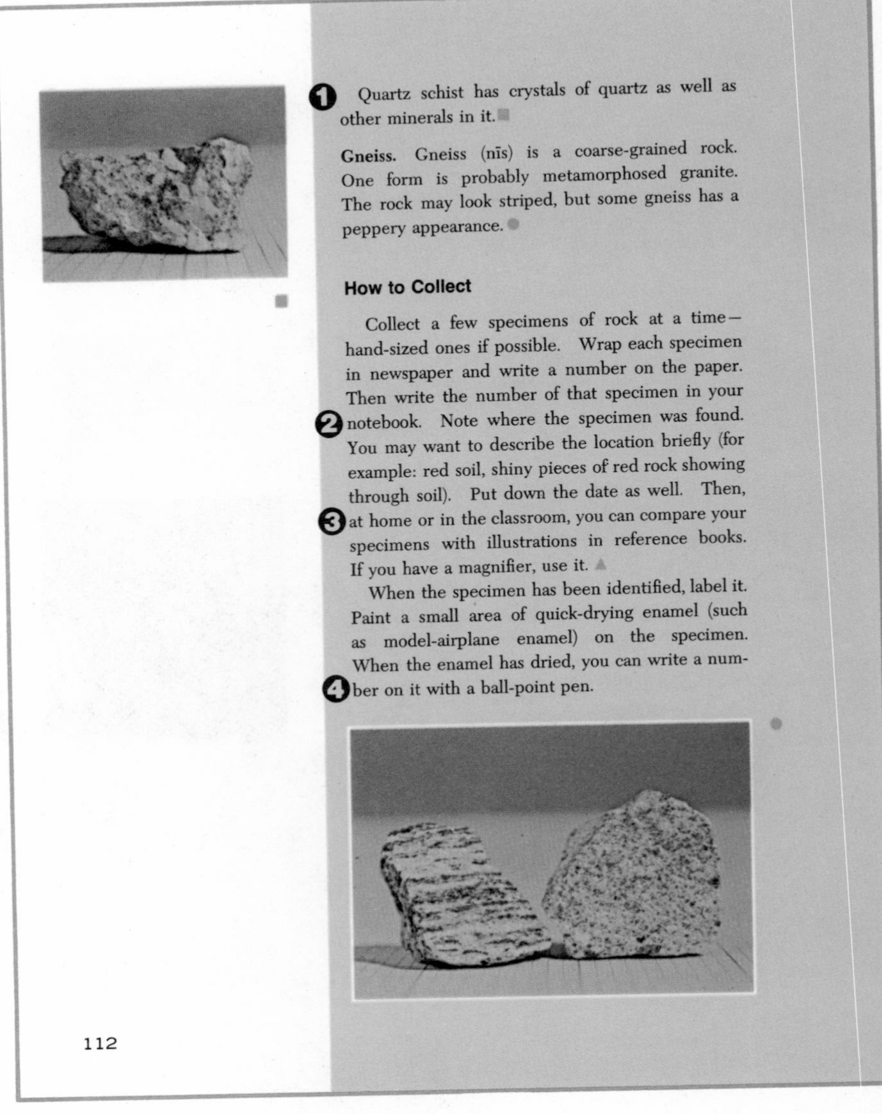

❶ Quartz schist has crystals of quartz as well as other minerals in it.

Gneiss. Gneiss (nīs) is a coarse-grained rock. One form is probably metamorphosed granite. The rock may look striped, but some gneiss has a peppery appearance.

How to Collect

Collect a few specimens of rock at a time—hand-sized ones if possible. Wrap each specimen in newspaper and write a number on the paper. Then write the number of that specimen in your ❷ notebook. Note where the specimen was found. You may want to describe the location briefly (for example: red soil, shiny pieces of red rock showing through soil). Put down the date as well. Then, ❸ at home or in the classroom, you can compare your specimens with illustrations in reference books. If you have a magnifier, use it.

When the specimen has been identified, label it. Paint a small area of quick-drying enamel (such as model-airplane enamel) on the specimen. When the enamel has dried, you can write a num❹ber on it with a ball-point pen.

112

Continuing the Search

❶ Some quartz schists make attractive building stones.

❷ Where one collects a rock is important, because the place it is found tells something important about the geology of the region. For example, the rock may record a history of erosion and deposition, or volcanic activity, or of mountain building (finding fossil shells on top of a mountain, for instance).

❸ Doubtful specimens can also be tested. Two tests are the moisten-and-smell test for shale and slate and the vinegar test for limestone and marble. Have children look up the Mohs scale of hardness in an earth science textbook or field guide. They will find it useful as a tool for classification.

❹ Once the collected rocks have been identified and classified, and notes recorded and analyzed, children should attempt to house their collections. Egg cartons make ideal trays for holding small specimens. The compartments can be numbered and descriptions taped to the inside cover.

Children who continue their search beyond the field trip that starts their interest should be encouraged to bring in new discoveries. Let them explain or display their finds from time to time. One ingredient that makes any hobby fun is sharing it with others.

Concept Relationships: Physical and chemical changes in the rocks are an index of the Earth's changing environment.

Some Useful Books

The books below will help you to identify many kinds of rocks and to make simple rock tests at home. Most are in paperback.

1. *The Story of Rocks,* by Dorothy Shuttlesworth, published by Doubleday, New York, 1966. Color illustrations will help you to identify the rocks you have collected. You can learn much about rocks, minerals, gems, and fossils from this book.

2. *Let's Find Out About Rocks and Minerals,* by David Knight, published by Franklin Watts, New York, 1969. This book includes the names of various types of rocks, how they are formed, and where they may be found.

3. *The Junior Science Book of Rock Collecting,* by Phoebe Crosby, published by Garrard, Champaign, Illinois, 1962. This book explains how to make a rock collection, and how various kinds of rocks are formed.

4. *Rocks and Minerals,* by Herbert S. Zim and Paul R. Shaffer, published by Golden Press, New York, 1960. This is a very useful little book to carry on trips. It contains many pictures to help you identify the rocks that you collect.

5. *Collecting Rocks, Minerals, Gems, and Fossils,* by Russell P. MacFall, published by Popular Mechanics Press, New York, 1963. This is another well-illustrated book.

6. *The True Book of Rocks and Minerals,* by Illa Podendorf, published by Childrens Press, Chicago, 1958. This little book is an introduction to the field of geology.

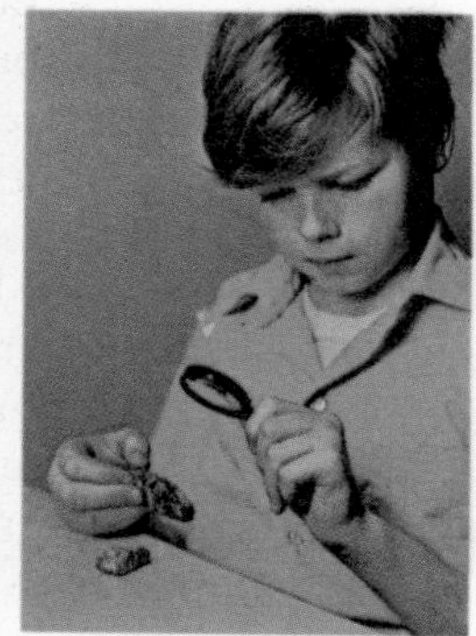

113

VERIFYING PROGRESS

Let children relate their own experiences of rock collecting with the collecting of rocks on the Moon. In doing so they *infer* the necessity for careful identification of exact location for *analysis* of the age of the Moon's rocks and soils and for *theorizing* on the origin of the Moon.

Astronauts Alan Shepard and Edgar Mitchell landed on the Moon February 5, 1971. They spent nearly nine hours in scientific experiments and collected about 98 pounds of rocks and soil from the surface and from below the surface. Analysis of these rocks will go on for many years.

Encourage children to consult NASA reports on the rocks brought back by the Apollo 11, 12, and 14 missions and news reports or NASA information about later collecting trips. What do the rocks show us about the Moon's composition? about its formation? about its age? about volcanic activity? about erosion from meteorites or the solar wind?

UNIT THREE

WE SEARCH FOR HIDDEN LIKENESSES

Basic behaviors sought: Children *demonstrate* that water is held inside an inverted, cardboard-covered glass and *hypothesize* that air is made up of molecules that exert force and keep the water in place.

Children *analyze* the nature of molecules and their chemical properties. They *infer* that these properties are related to the molecular structure of a substance. They *demonstrate* that substances can be broken down into elements, and that elements can be combined to form a compound with different properties.

Children *distinguish* between certain groups of compounds by means of chemical tests. They *observe* a chemical reaction that releases carbon dioxide and tests for its presence. They *identify* some common elements, their properties, and their compounds.

Children *hypothesize* that when rusting occurs in a closed system the weight remains the same. They *demonstrate* and *observe* that there is no change in the total weight in a chemical change. Children *compare* physical and chemical changes and *theorize* that all matter is made up of atoms and molecules, and that no atoms are lost or gained in a physical or chemical change.

A VIEW OF THE UNIT

The nature of matter was always a subject for speculation. As early as the fifth century B.C., two Greek philosophers, Leucippus and Democritus, had proposed an atomic theory. The Greeks reasoned that if you could continually subdivide a material, you eventually reach a point where you can divide no further. This smallest particle of matter was called an atom, from the Greek word meaning indivisible. In their view, atoms were separated by empty space, and atoms differed according to each substance. Atoms existed in unlimited variety and could combine in an infinite number of ways. The details of this atomic theory were vague, and so it was generally not accepted.

Other civilizations approached the science of chemistry from a practical rather than a theoretical point of view. Although they didn't understand what took place, the Egyptians had developed an advanced technique for making glass by 1350 B.C. Different colored glass was produced by adding various metals. The Egyptians had also produced permanent dyes for cloth by combining certain substances.

Certainly, the Egyptians and the later alchemists of the Middle Ages hadn't formulated any chemical theory. But because they performed many experiments and often recorded their results, they left a wealth of information for the scientists that came after them. In the third century A.D., alchemists were obsessed with the notion that metals could be transformed into gold. Their procedures and results were usually involved with magic and superstition, and they depended on color to determine what had taken place—chemically testing the nature of the substance was never even considered. They did know, however, that heat could separate the components of a substance, and this method was widely used for the following 1,500 years.

In the early 1800's John Dalton re-examined the atomic theory. At that time, Dalton was experimenting with gases. His observations showed that elements always combined in the same ratio to form a certain compound. To explain this phenomenon, Dalton returned to the atom as the basic unit of matter. His conclusions held true for all substances. He determined that atoms of different elements had different weights.

Chemists were now provided with definite rules which governed chemical reactions. When they realized that the existence of atoms explained their observations, they accepted Dalton's theory. Dalton's work became the basis on which modern atomic theory was built.

1 Molecules

Properties are characteristics that distinguish one substance from another. They can be divided into two categories, physical and chemical. Physical properties can be observed without transforming the substance. They include color, odor, taste, density, solubility, and others. Chemical properties, the way substances react with one another, include the ability to support combustion and the ability to burn. When a glowing splint is inserted in a test tube of oxygen, it will burst into flame. Oxygen supports combustion. A burning splint in a test tube of hydrogen can ignite the hydrogen which burns with a blue flame. Physical and chemical properties are useful tools for identifying substances.

The size of the sample of a substance has no

effect on its properties. As you subdivide a substance, each smaller part exhibits the same properties. If you could continue to subdivide the substance, you would eventually reach the basic unit, the molecule. Molecules are the smallest units of a substance that still have the properties of that substance.

The molecules of an element are composed of one type of atom. All the molecules of oxygen gas are made up of oxygen atoms, and all of the molecules of hydrogen gas are made up of hydrogen atoms. Thus oxygen and hydrogen are elements. They cannot be broken down into simpler substances.

Molecules of the elements may contain one or more atoms. Diatomic molecules are made up of two atoms, Oxygen and hydrogen are examples. The symbols O_2 and H_2 are used for these elements; the subscript 2 is added to show that there are two atoms in each molecule. The atoms in these diatomic molecules are held together by chemical bonds. Bonds are formed when atoms share electrons or transfer them to another atom. Bonds can be formed between like or unlike atoms. Monatomic molecules are made up of one atom; helium and neon are examples. The symbols for these elements are written without subscripts: He for helium and Ne for neon.

Compounds are made up of two or more kinds of atoms. They can be decomposed into their elements by electrolysis, heat, or reaction with other substances. Water, for example, can be decomposed by electrolysis. The water molecule is represented by H_2O. In the water molecule, one atom of oxygen is bonded to two atoms of hydrogen. If an electric current is passed through water, hydrogen gas can be collected at one electrode and oxygen gas at the other. This result is evidence that water is a compound formed from two different elements.

When water is decomposed, the reaction can be represented by a word equation which shows what has taken place:

$$\text{water} \rightarrow \text{hydrogen} + \text{oxygen}$$

If symbols are used in place of words, the equation becomes quantitative:

$$2\ H_2O \rightarrow 2\ H_2 + O_2$$

The number of atoms of each element on the left side of the equation must equal the number on the right. Thus we need two molecules of water to form two molecules of hydrogen and one molecule of oxygen.

2 Forming a compound

When two or more elements combine chemically, they form a compound. The substance that we recognize as table salt is a compound of the elements sodium and chlorine. Sodium is a soft, silvery-white metal; chlorine is a poisonous, greenish-yellow gas with a strong, irritating odor. Merely mixing these two elements does not change the identity of either element. When a chemical change occurs, however, a new substance is formed. Heating the mixture of iron and sulfur enables the chemical change to occur. Iron sulfide, the compound which is formed, has properties unlike those of the two elements.

3 Acids and bases

Initially, acids and bases were classified by the properties of their water solutions. Acids have a sour taste, and react with certain metals to produce hydrogen gas. Bases have a bitter taste and have a soapy feel. This is only one of the ways acids and bases can be classified; other methods depend on composition rather than properties.

Acids and bases can be identified by their effects on litmus paper—a common laboratory indicator made of paper treated with a mixture of dyes. When a solution of the acid or base is touched to the paper, the dyes change color through complex chemical reactions. Acids turn litmus pink; bases turn litmus blue.

There are many other indicators which can be used to detect the presence and measure the strength of an acid or base. In addition to litmus, which comes from certain lichens, the coloring material from red cabbage and some ripe fruits are natural indicators. Phenolpthalein is a common synthetic indicator which turns red in the presence of a base and remains colorless in the presence of an acid.

In one classification system, the acids are the hydrogen compounds of nonmetals and nonmetal groups. Hydrochloric acid (HCl) and nitric acid (HNO_3) are examples. According to this definition, bases are compounds of metals or nonmetals and a hydroxide group (OH). Sodium hydroxide ($NaOH$) and ammonium hydroxide (NH_4OH) are examples.

4 Chemical tests

Chemical analysis is concerned with testing substances. The physical properties of a substance and any information concerning the preparation or history of the substance are first noted. Then chemical tests can be carried out to classify the compound in a general group. The use of litmus and other acid-base indicators is one kind of chemical test. Further tests can narrow down the possibilities until the specific compound is identified.

A test with limewater, for example, can give specific information about the compound carbon dioxide. Limewater is made by dissolving calcium hydroxide in water. When carbon dioxide gas is bubbled through the limewater, a milky white substance is formed. Since this substance, which is calcium carbonate, is not soluble in water, it forms a cloudy precipitate. We can write an equation for the reaction as follows:

$$\underset{\text{calcium hydroxide}}{Ca(OH)_2} + \underset{\text{carbon dioxide}}{CO_2} \longrightarrow \underset{\text{calcium carbonate}}{CaCO_3} + \underset{\text{water}}{H_2O}$$

5 The elements

The Greeks believed that all matter was composed of four elements—earth, air, fire, and water. The differences in substances lay in the varying proportions of these elements. Aristotle added a fifth "essence" which he located beyond the Moon to explain the apparent immutability of that region of the heavens. The theory of four basic elements was accepted for centuries—in fact, it was still held by most people during the Middle Ages.

Today, we recognize 90 naturally occurring elements and 15 that have been man-made. The elements differ according to their atomic structure. Hydrogen is the simplest element. An atom of hydrogen consists of one proton in the nucleus and one orbiting electron. An atom of helium has 2 protons and 2 neutrons in the nucleus and 2 orbiting electrons. The number of protons in an atomic nucleus is called the atomic number. The build-up of the elements continues in this way, each successive element having a larger atomic number. When all the elements are arranged in this way, they form a Periodic Table. Similar properties can be attributed to elements in the vertical columns of the table.

Elements can be classified as metals or nonmetals. Metals fall on the left side of the Periodic Table, nonmetals on the right. The black ziz-zag line that starts at the left of boron (atomic number 5) in the table opposite separates the metals from the nonmetals.

Atomic structure determines the ease with which elements form compounds. Oxygen reacts very readily, and for this reason it is found in compounds with other elements on the Earth. Of the 90 naturally occurring elements, about 30 can be found in the free, or uncombined, state. Two of these are silver and gold. Silver is sometimes found in the Earth in shiny, twisting branches. It is also mined in an ore called argentite. Gold can be found free in certain rocks.

The elements beyond uranium in the Periodic Table are called the transuranic elements. These elements, from atomic number 93 to 105, have been produced artificially. This has been accomplished by bombarding certain atoms with high-energy particles. The transuranic elements have been prepared in very minute quantities and are too unstable to exist in nature. All are radioactive. Also, the elements between 82 and 90 are radioactive in varying degrees.

6 Conservation of matter

In the electrolysis of water, the compound is broken down into its component parts, hydrogen and oxygen. Weighing the system before and after the reaction would show that there is no change in weight. If the original weight of the water is 10 grams, the weight of the remaining water plus the weight of the hydrogen and the oxygen will be 10 grams. The atoms have rearranged themselves to form the elemental gases—no atoms have been lost or created. The concept of Conservation of Matter applies to all chemical reactions:

> During a chemical change, matter is neither created nor destroyed; it is changed from one form to another.

The concept of conservation of matter also applies to physical changes. Physical changes do not involve changes in composition, but do alter the state or form of matter. Matter exists in three states: solid, liquid, and gas. Freezing water, melting ice, and boiling water are examples of changes of state. If 10 grams of ice are melted, 10 grams of water are formed. Boil the 10 grams of water, and 10 grams of steam are formed. The steam occupies a much larger volume than the water, but its weight and the weight of the water are equal. Matter is conserved as substances are changed from one state to another. Physical and chemical changes are alike in that the concept of conservation holds for both types of changes.

PERIODIC TABLE

	IA	IIA	IIIB	IVB	VB	VIB	VIIB	VIII			IB	IIB	IIIA	IVA	VA	VIA	VIIA	O
1	1 H Hydrogen 1.00797																	2 He Helium 4.0026
2	3 Li Lithium 6.939	4 Be Beryllium 9.0122											5 B Boron 10.811	6 C Carbon 12.01115	7 N Nitrogen 14.0067	8 O Oxygen 15.9994	9 F Fluorine 18.9984	10 Ne Neon 20.183
3	11 Na Sodium 22.9898	12 Mg Magnesium 24.312											13 Al Aluminum 26.9815	14 Si Silicon 28.086	15 P Phosphorus 30.9738	16 S Sulfur 32.064	17 Cl Chlorine 35.453	18 Ar Argon 39.948
4	19 K Potassium 39.102	20 Ca Calcium 40.08	21 Sc Scandium 44.956	22 Ti Titanium 47.90	23 V Vanadium 50.942	24 Cr Chromium 51.996	25 Mn Manganese 54.9380	26 Fe Iron 55.847	27 Co Cobalt 58.9332	28 Ni Nickel 58.71	29 Cu Copper 63.54	30 Zn Zinc 65.37	31 Ga Gallium 69.72	32 Ge Germanium 72.59	33 As Arsenic 74.9216	34 Se Selenium 78.96	35 Br Bromine 79.909	36 Kr Krypton 83.80
5	37 Rb Rubidium 85.47	38 Sr Strontium 87.62	39 Y Yttrium 88.905	40 Zr Zirconium 91.22	41 Nb Niobium 92.906	42 Mo Molybdenum 95.94	43 Tc Technetium [99]	44 Ru Ruthenium 101.07	45 Rh Rhodium 102.905	46 Pd Palladium 106.4	47 Ag Silver 107.870	48 Cd Cadmium 112.40	49 In Indium 114.82	50 Sn Tin 118.69	51 Sb Antimony 121.75	52 Te Tellurium 127.60	53 I Iodine 126.9044	54 Xe Xenon 131.30
6	55 Cs Cesium 132.905	56 Ba Barium 137.34	57 La Lanthanum 138.91	72 Hf Hafnium 178.49	73 Ta Tantalum 180.948	74 W Tungsten 183.85	75 Re Rhenium 186.2	76 Os Osmium 190.2	77 Ir Iridium 192.2	78 Pt Platinum 195.09	79 Au Gold 196.967	80 Hg Mercury 200.59	81 Tl Thallium 204.37	82 Pb Lead 207.19	83 Bi Bismuth 208.980	84 Po Polonium [210]	85 At Astatine [210]	86 Rn Radon [222]
7	87 Fr Francium [223]	88 Ra Radium [226]	89 Ac Actinium [227]	104 — [257]	105 — [260]													

LANTHANIDE SERIES	58 Ce Cerium 140.12	59 Pr Praseodymium 140.907	60 Nd Neodymium 144.24	61 Pm Promethium [147]	62 Sm Samarium 150.35	63 Eu Europium 151.96	64 Gd Gadolinium 157.25	65 Tb Terbium 158.924	66 Dy Dysprosium 162.50	67 Ho Holmium 164.930	68 Er Erbium 167.26	69 Tm Thulium 168.934	70 Yb Ytterbium 173.04	71 Lu Lutetium 174.97
ACTINIDE SERIES	90 Th Thorium 232.038	91 Pa Protactinium [231]	92 U Uranium 238.03	93 Np Neptunium [237]	94 Pu Plutonium [242]	95 Am Americium [243]	96 Cm Curium [247]	97 Bk Berkelium [247]	98 Cf Californium [249]	99 Es Einsteinium [254]	100 Fm Fermium [253]	101 Md Mendelevium [256]	102 No Nobelium [253]	103 Lw Lawrencium [257]

SUPPLEMENTARY AIDS

All films and filmstrips listed are in color. All films are accompanied by sound; filmstrips are accompanied by sound only if so designated. Names and addresses of producers and distributors are on page F-29.

Filmstrips

Changes All Around Us (50 frames), #151156, McGraw-Hill. Presents the concept of chemical change; simple experiments and safety rules in the laboratory; oxygen's role in burning; the limewater test.

Chemical Changes (44 frames), #427-21, SVE. Demonstrates differences between chemical and physical change; shows the expression of chemical changes in formulas; discusses how to produce and prevent certain chemical change.

Understanding Chemical Change (46 frames), #400303, McGraw-Hill. Uses many common substances to develop the concept of chemical change.

What Things Are Made Of (44 frames). #427-20, SVE. Illustrates the properties of elements, and explains what compounds are. Simple experiments show the building of compounds from elements, and the forming of mixtures.

Films

Chemical Change (12 min.), #401982, McGraw-Hill. Explains that a chemical change produces one or more substances that are different from those present before the change. Illustrates that, through chemical change, two or more elements may produce a compound or the compound may be broken down to produce the elements.

Evidence for Molecules and Atoms (19 min.), #1886, EBEC. Demonstrates that, although unseen, molecules and atoms in solids, liquids, and gases can be proven to exist; that atoms are building blocks of molecules; and that modern science is based on the existence of atoms and molecules.

Explaining Matter: Atoms and Molecules (14 min.), #1673, EBEC. Shows atoms as the building blocks of matter that form molecules; explains elements, compounds, and mixtures.

Explaining Matter: Chemical Change (11 min.), #1746, EBEC. Explains that a chemical change takes place when atoms from the molecules of two or more substances join and form molecules of entirely different substances; reveals that important changes take place in everyday situations such as burning, digestion, and photosynthesis.

Materials of Our World ($13\frac{1}{2}$ min.), Universal. Points out similarities and differences between materials of our world; introduces children to a simple study of chemistry.

Science Reading Table

Building Blocks of the Universe by Isaac Asimov, Abelard-Schuman, 1961. An introduction to the elements. Describes the properties of the different elements and the various uses to which man has put them. (Advanced)

Chemistry by Experiment by Paul Boberson, John Day. 1965. Using materials and equipment which are easy to obtain, the student is encouraged to do some explorations. (Average)

Chemistry: First S-T-E-P-S by Keith Gorden Irwin, Franklin Watts, 1963. Introductory survey of chemistry in familiar living and nonliving things. Included are a few simple investigations. (Average)

Drop by Drop: A Look at Water by A. Harris Stone, Prentice-Hall, 1969. The physical and chemical properties of water are discussed. The importance of water in the weathering process, the crystallization of minerals, and in our life processes are told in an interesting and stimulating manner. (Average)

Humphrey Davy and Chemical Discovery by Elba Carrier, Franklin Watts, 1965. This biography tells the life-story of Humphrey Davy, who did much to establish the science of electrochemistry. He did research on gases, identified chlorine as an element and diamond as carbon, and found sodium and potassium. (Advanced)

The True Book of Chemistry: What Things Are Made Of by Philip B. Carona, Childrens Press, 1962. Elements and compounds, atoms and molecules, chemical symbols and formulas, and the difference between chemical and physical change are described. (Easy)

Physics: Its Marvels and Mysteries by Daniel Q. Posin, Whitman, 1961. Simple and witty explanations of difficult science topics, including flight, magnetism, behavior of liquids and gases, heat, sound, light, electricity, and the atom. Easy experiments and questions are directed to the curiosity of children. (Average)

Science Experiments with Air by Sam Rosenfeld, Harvey House, 1969. By carrying out the thought-provoking investigations described in this book, children will gain greater understanding not only of concepts of matter but of methods of inquiry as well. (Advanced)

The Story of Chemistry by Mae and Ira Freeman, Random House, 1962. Molecules and atoms are described with simple examples. Facts about elements, compounds, and chemical change are included. Reference to commonplace items and experiences help to clarify difficult concepts. (Easy)

What Is Chemistry? by Daniel Q. Posin, Benefic Press, 1961. A miniature encyclopedia on atoms, molecules, elements, chemical change, and recent discoveries and uses. Many facts are presented and a few simple experiments are described. (Average)

An Analysis of Behaviors in Concept-Seeking*

Conceptual Scheme B: When matter changes from one form to another, the total amount of matter remains unchanged.

Unit Concept-Statement: In chemical or physical changes, the total amount of matter remains unchanged.

Lesson Cluster titles in blue guide concept-seeking toward the Unit Concept-Statement. Other titles enrich the Conceptual Scheme (*see page F-23*).

Lesson Cluster and Supporting Statement	*Operations Basic to Concept-Seeking**	*Methods of Intelligence (Processes and Behaviors)*
1. The Things We Can't See A molecule is the smallest particle of a substance that still has the properties of that substance.	**Investigating** the properties of a substance and the composition of a compound.	**Inferring** that the properties of a substance are related to its molecular structure; **hypothesizing** that compounds can be broken down; **testing** this hypothesis; **inferring** that a molecule is the smallest particle of a substance
2. Building Up a Compound Elements can be combined to build up compounds.	**Investigating** the formation of iron oxide	**Observing** the formation of rust; **inferring** that oxygen combines with iron to form a compound; **identifying** as oxides a group of compounds containing oxygen
3. Two Common Groups of Compounds Compounds are grouped by chemical properties.	**Investigating** a chemical test for acids and bases	**Observing** the action of substances on litmus paper; **inferring** that acids turn litmus pink and bases turn litmus blue
4. An Important Test The presence of some substances can be determined by chemical tests.	**Investigating** a test for **identifying** carbon dioxide	**Observing** chemical reactions involving the release of carbon dioxide; **testing** for the presence of carbon dioxide; **comparing** chemical reactions of carbon compounds; **inferring** the identity of certain substances
5. A Chemist's View of the Earth The Earth's matter is built up of atoms combined in many ways.	**Probing** the chemist's view of the Earth's matter	**Analyzing** information in a table; **identifying** common elements and properties
6. More Weight or Less In ordinary chemical reactions, matter is neither gained nor lost.	**Probing** the weights involved in a chemical change	**Hypothesizing** whether a change in weight takes place when iron oxide is formed from iron and oxygen; **observing** that the jar and the weights remain in balance; **inferring** that there is no change in total weight
7. The Main Concept: Likenesses Within the Earth In chemical or physical changes, the total amount of matter remains unchanged.	Children **compare** physical and chemical change; they **conclude** that all matter is made up of atoms and molecules and that no atoms are lost or gained in physical or chemical changes.	

** A concept is synonymous with the corresponding operations. In turn, operations are served by relevant methods of intelligence.*

UNIT THREE
WE SEARCH FOR HIDDEN LIKENESSES

Teaching background. "A View of the Unit" T-126

Concept-seeking. Children become aware that, even though invisible, air has visible effects.

Operations. Children *investigate* the ability of air to hold water inside an inverted, cardboard-covered glass.

Methods of intelligence. Children *observe* that water is held inside an inverted, cardboard-covered glass, and *infer* air consists of molecules that exert a force that keeps the water in place.

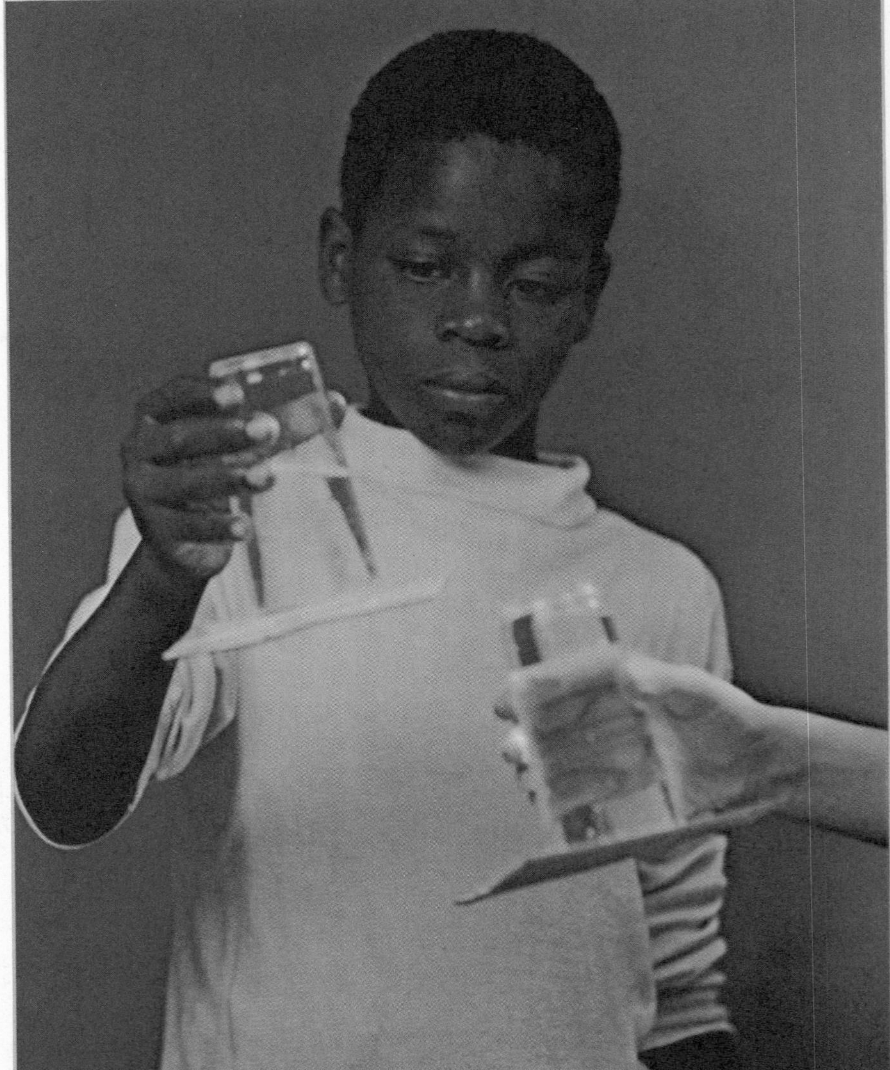

Useful materials: Drinking glass, water, cardboard large enough to cover mouth of glass, large basin or pot.

Introducing the unit

Stretch your fingers wide apart! What is between your fingers? (Accept all kinds of responses, such as: air, nothing, molecules, atoms, space.) Do you feel anything between your fingers? Do you see or hear anything there? (no) Then how do you know what (if anything) is between your fingers? (You have to assume; or reason that something is there.) What do we call it when we reason something out in science? (making an inference or ***inferring***)

Unit Concept-Statement: In chemical or physical change the total amount of matter remains unchanged.

UNIT THREE

We Search for Hidden Likenesses

Stretch your arm out as far as you can. Spread your fingers. What is between your wide-apart fingers?

This question was asked of 24 boys and girls in 13 different states. Everyone of them said "air." Some of them said "atoms." Others said "molecules." What would you say?

If you say "atoms" or "molecules," you are making an inference. What evidence do you ❶ have for your inference?

To begin to collect evidence, you can do this: ❷ Pour water into a glass.■ Place cardboard over the mouth of the glass.● Turn the glass upside down. Why doesn't the cardboard fall? Why ❸ doesn't the water run out?

■

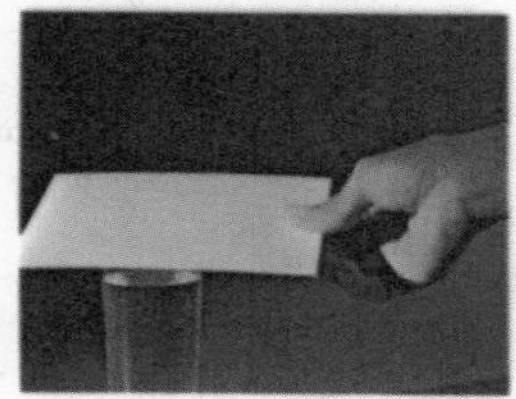

●

❶ When children have read this far on the page, let them tell about any evidence for the existence of molecules in the air from their earlier experiences.

❷ How can we use a glass of water and a piece of cardboard to get evidence for our inference that something is between our fingers? Let a volunteer fill the glass to the brim with water, hold the cardboard over the top of the glass and turn the glass upside down. Then he should let go of the cardboard.

Why doesn't the cardboard fall? Why doesn't the water run out? (Air is pushing the cardboard to the glass and holding the water in the glass.)

Warning: The water *will* run out if the cardboard is not held firmly when reversing the glass, or if the cardboard becomes soaked. Therefore be sure the child demonstrates • over the basin or pot.

❸ If the water runs out, ask: Why do you think the cardboard fell off? Why did the water run out? (Children may mention the force of gravitation, or the weight of the water.)

Have the child try again, using a dry piece of cardboard and pressing it firmly to the glass until he lets it go. What is holding the cardboard to the glass? (air or molecules pushing up against the cardboard)

Unit Concept-Statement: In chemical or physical change the total amount of matter remains unchanged.

LESSON CLUSTER 1
THE THINGS WE CAN'T SEE

Teaching background. 1 T-126

Concept-seeking. Children become aware of properties of substances and their relationship to molecules, elements, and compounds.

Operations. Children *investigate* the properties of a substance (perfume) and the composition of a compound (water).

Methods of intelligence. Children *infer* that the properties of a substance are related to its molecular structure, *hypothesize* that compounds can be broken down into simpler substances, *test* this hypothesis by breaking down water into two substances having different properties, and *infer* that a molecule is the smallest particle of a substance having properties of that substance.

Useful materials: Pocket mirror, saucer, waxed paper, mirror, foil pan or coffee can, hotplate or burner.

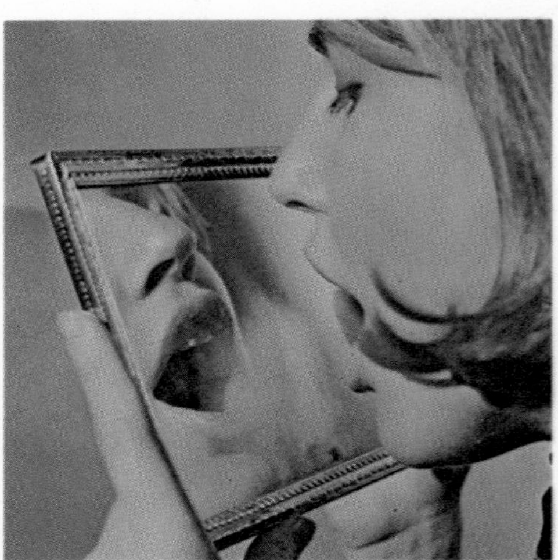

1. The Things We Can't See

Blow into the air. Can you see your breath? Blow against a mirror. A thin film forms on the mirror—a film of water. ■ Clearly, you blow water from your lungs. Why can't you see the water as it comes out of your mouth?

❶ You cannot see it because the very tiny particles that you blow out are so small. These tiny particles are droplets, and must contain many molecules of water. However, the mirror catches enough molecules to make small visible drops. Each drop has billions of molecules in it.

How can we believe in something we can't see? Why do we believe in molecules? What makes scientists think that there are molecules all around us? Why do they think that we ourselves are made up of molecules?

116

Introducing Lesson Cluster 1

Put on the chalkboard the tiniest dot that you can make with a piece of chalk. Have I made a dot on the board, or have I only pretended to make a dot? (Children in the front of the room may or may not be able to see the dot, but in any case, have the entire class discuss whether or not there really is a dot on the board. Then let several children examine the board closely and report what they see. If we do not see something, does this always mean that it is not there? (no)

Developing the lesson

❶ Ask everyone to breathe out. Can you see your breath? (no)

Ask a child to breathe on a pocket mirror. What do you see on the mirror? (a mist of water)

Why didn't you see this water when you breathed out without the mirror? (The droplets of water are too small to be seen when they spread out into the air. The mirror catches these droplets so that they come together as large visible drops.)

Supporting Statement: A molecule is the smallest particle of a substance that still has the properties of that substance.

Scientists have gathered evidence for many years about molecules, and have reasoned from the evidence. Let's look at some of this evidence, and some of the reasoning of scientists who have studied these tiny particles.

Molecules

1 What is a molecule?

Wet a finger and put it in a sugar bowl. Then put the finger in your mouth. ● You expect a certain taste, don't you? Why? Sugar has a certain taste. Scientists say that this taste, which you say is the taste of sugar, is a **property** of sugar. Salt, too, has a certain taste, which is a property of salt.

Taste is one kind of property. There are other kinds, too—odor, for example. Ammonia has a certain odor. That odor is a property of ammonia.

Water is colorless. In other words, a property of water is that it has no color. (It has other properties as well, of course.)

Have you ever used salt when you meant to use sugar? You knew at once which was salt and which was sugar! Sugar and salt have different properties. Different substances, like salt and sugar, like water and ammonia, have
2 different properties.

We recognize a substance by its properties, don't we? The properties of a substance help to tell us what the
3 substance is. The properties of salt tell us that it is not sugar.

The idea that substances have properties may help scientists answer the question, "What is a molecule?" Scientists have studied the properties of many substances. On the basis of a great deal of evidence, they say: A **molecule** is the smallest part of a substance that still has the properties of that substance.

Collect some evidence yourself that the properties of a substance go with these tiny particles. Try the investigation on the next page. INVESTIGATE

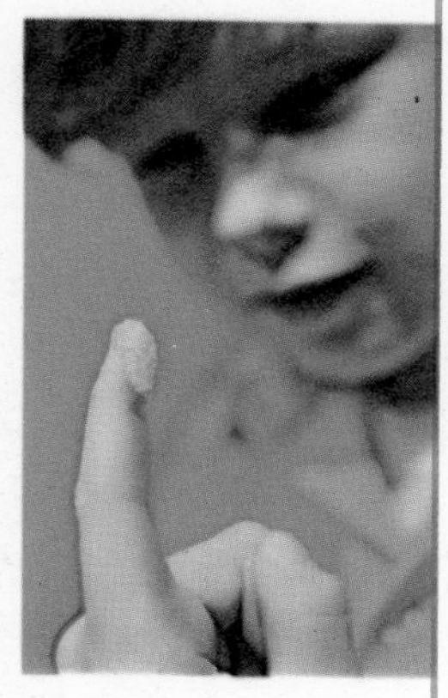

●

117

VERIFYING PROGRESS

In methods of intelligence

Fill a tank or large pan with water. Have a child hold an empty glass upside down and perpendicular to the surface of the water. **What will happen if you push the glass into the water?** Children *predict* that the air in the glass will prevent water from going into the glass. Children may then *test* their *predictions* by carrying out the investigation, and *explain* their *observations*. Water does not go into the glass, because air is in the glass and two things cannot occupy the same space at the same time)

Useful materials: Salt, sugar, aluminum foil.

1 Before class begins, prepare tiny packets of salt and sugar in squares of aluminum foil. Make enough packets for each child—half with salt and half with sugar. Mix the packets together and distribute. **What do you think is in the packet?** Let children feel and smell the substance, but not taste it. They may not realize that there are different substances in the packets, but they will probably be able to guess that the substance is either salt or sugar. (Warn children that they must never taste an unknown substance. Then confirm their guess that the substance they have is either salt or sugar.)

How can we tell what the substance is for sure? (taste it) Have them wet a finger and pick up a few grains to taste. **What is in the packet?** (Half the class will say salt and half sugar.) **How can we distinguish between the two?** (by taste)

2 Have the children read the first five paragraphs, if they have not already done so.

What can we call the color, size, or taste of a substance? (the ***properties*** of the substance)

3 **How many properties can you name that may help you recognize a substance?** (color, smell, size, shape, texture, hardness, taste, the sound it makes, etc.)

Why is it useful to know the properties of a substance? (We can know what to use it for, when, how, and perhaps where to use it.)

UNIT THREE

Unit Concept-Statement: In chemical or physical change the total amount of matter remains unchanged.

Performance objectives. Children *demonstrate* that molecules of perfume are small enough to pass through a rubber balloon, by placing a few drops inside a balloon, inflating the balloon, sealing it, and pushing it into a clean jar for fifteen minutes, causing the odor of the perfume to seep into the jar.

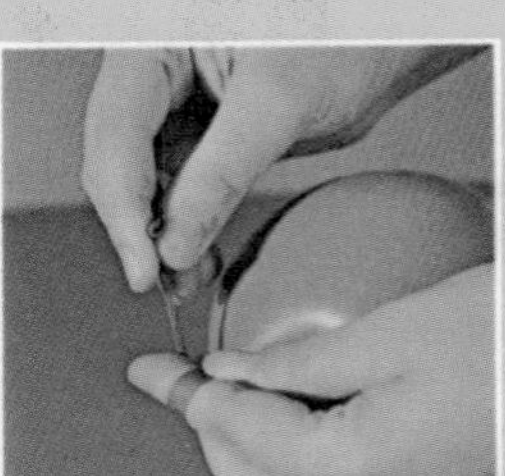

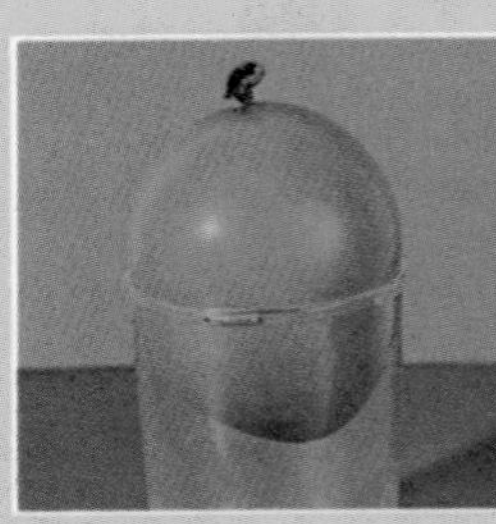

AN APPRENTICE INVESTIGATION into the Properties of One Kind of Molecule

Needed: a balloon, a jar with a wide mouth, a funnel, perfume

First, smell the air in the jar to be sure that there is no perfume in it. Now, using the funnel, place a few drops of perfume in the balloon. ■

Blow up the balloon and tie a knot firmly in its neck so that no air can escape. ● Fit the balloon tightly into the mouth of the jar. ▲

Let the balloon stay in the jar for 15 or 20 minutes. Then carefully take the balloon out of the jar. Smell the air in the jar. What do you smell? ❶

Methods of Intelligence: Evaluating Evidence

How could perfume get from the inside of the balloon to the air in the jar? What is your inference? Let's look at the evidence.

At first, the air in the balloon has perfume in it—is this an observation or an inference? ❷

Also at first, the air in the jar has no perfume in it—is this an observation or an inference? ❸

Later, there is perfume in the jar—is this an observation or an inference? ❹

The perfume must have passed through the rubber of the balloon. How could this happen? Is this an observation or an inference? ❺

118

Useful materials: A medicine dropper may be substituted for the funnel and scented toilet water for the perfume. Half-pint to one pint jars are suitable. Some materials are available in CLASSROOM LABORATORY: PURPLE.

Continuing Lesson Cluster 1

❶ The air in the jar now smells of perfume.

❷ This is an observation because children saw the perfume put into the balloon.

❸ This is an observation because children smelled the air in the jar before the balloon was put in.

❹ This is an observation because children smelled the perfume in the jar after the balloon was taken out.

❺ The perfume must have been in such small bits that it could travel through the walls of the balloon into the jar. Perhaps these bits were molecules. This is an inference.

Supporting Statement: A molecule is the smallest particle of a substance that still has the properties of that substance.

An Explanation and a Question

❶ How can perfume pass through the rubber of a balloon? The particles of perfume are so tiny that they can pass through the rubber. Indeed, these tiny particles are molecules, and they carry with them the properties of perfume. Thus, you were able to smell perfume in the air of the jar.

❷ The smallest part of a substance that is still that substance is a molecule. The smallest part of perfume that is still perfume is a molecule of perfume. The smallest part of sugar that still has the properties of sugar is a molecule of sugar. The smallest part of ammonia that still has
❸ the properties of ammonia is a molecule. The smallest part of water that still has the properties of water is a molecule.

Next, let's explore these questions: What are molecules made of? What happens if you break down a molecule?

Breaking Down a Molecule

Let's break down a molecule. Of course, you can't handle just one molecule. You can, however, handle a bunch of molecules of one substance.

Let's break down a molecule of ordinary water. This molecule is made up of two different kinds of atoms and can be broken down right in the classroom. Atoms, as you may remember, are bits of matter that are even smaller than molecules. What kinds of atoms are in water?

Water is made up of atoms of hydrogen and oxygen. These are two invisible gases, not at all like liquid water. At room temperature, water is usually a colorless liquid. Atoms of oxygen, however, form a colorless, invisible gas. So do atoms of hydrogen.

Can two invisible gases combine to make water? Suppose that you break down molecules of water. Suppose that you then get hydrogen and oxygen. Does this help answer the question as to which substances formed water? Turn the page. INVESTIGATE

Useful materials: Perfumed room deodorizer in aerosol spray can, balloon, gauze or nylon stocking, jar, water.

❶ Give a quick spray from a can of perfumed room deodorizer in front of the room. How soon does a child smell it at the back? This gas seems to mix with the air in the room. Did the air go through the balloon along with the perfume? Blow up a balloon, tightly fasten it and observe the next day. The balloon should be smaller. Why? (Air must be able to go through a balloon.)

❷ Let a child try to divide a small drop of water. It is almost impossible because water likes to stick together. But we can break up water into very small drops by using several thicknesses of gauze or nylon stocking over the mouth of a jar. Depending on the cloth, water placed on it will seep through in a few moments. Let children suggest that this is a model showing how perfume might have squeezed through rubber.

Are the drops molecules? (no) Why not? Let the children draw an inference from their breathing on a mirror (page 116). (couldn't see breath, but could see drops later)

❸ If hydrogen and oxygen are colorless and odorless, as water is, how would we know they are not just water in the form of a gas? (Children should predict properties would be different.) How would you know? (make some kind of test)

Unit Concept-Statement: In chemical or physical change the total amount of matter remains unchanged.

Performance objectives. Children *demonstrate* that the passage of electric current breaks down the compound water into the gaseous elements hydrogen and oxygen, which are collected in separate test tubes by the displacement of water. Children *identify* the oxygen gas by glowing splint test, and the hydrogen gas by lighted splint or "pop" test.

Useful materials: In addition to the materials listed, a small amount of waterproof paint or fingernail polish is desirable. Any widemouthed food jar may be substituted for a beaker. Alternate materials are available in CLASSROOM LABORATORY: PURPLE.

❶ **AN APPRENTICE INVESTIGATION into Breaking Down Molecules**

❷ **Needed:** glass jar or beaker, 2 test tubes, 2 corks to fit the test tubes, 2 pieces of covered wire, 2 carbon electrodes, water, sodium sulfate, 2 wooden splints, 3 rubber bands, a 6-volt battery, tongue depressor

Break the tongue depressor in half to make 2 narrow strips of wood. Fasten these strips to the tubes with 3 rubber bands, as shown. ■

Your teacher will give you some water to which sodium sulfate has been added. Pour this water into the beaker until it is about ⅔ full. Lower the test tubes into the water and let them fill up. Then turn them upside down, as shown. ■

❸ Attach one end of a wire to each of the electrodes. Then slip each electrode into a test tube,

120

Continuing Lesson Cluster 1

❶ Unless you can use a laboratory electrolysis apparatus (such as the Hoffman apparatus) that you do not set up yourself, plan to start this investigation one day and complete it the following day.

❷ Unless you have carbon electrodes from a scientific supply house, you may use a carbon rod, broken in half, from an old dry cell. Instead of wooden splints, children may devise other ways in which to support the test tubes. Two holes to fit the diameter of the test tubes can be cut in the top of the plastic lid of a food container. The lid should be at least as wide as the top of the beaker or jar.

❸ After the bare ends of the wires are attached to the electrodes, coat the ends lightly with waterproof paint or clear fingernail polish. Let the paint dry overnight. This procedure prevents the solution from reacting with the copper of the wire.

Supporting Statement: A molecule is the smallest particle of a substance that still has the properties of that substance.

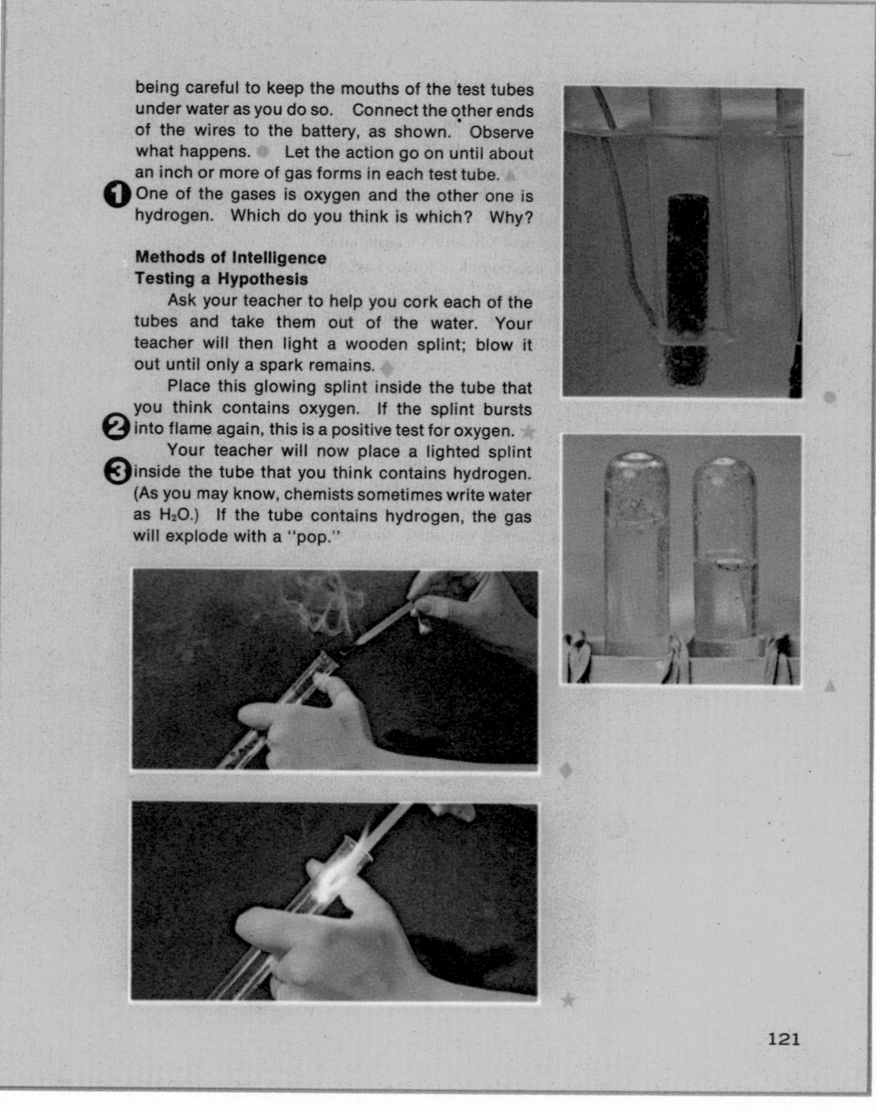

being careful to keep the mouths of the test tubes under water as you do so. Connect the other ends of the wires to the battery, as shown. Observe what happens. Let the action go on until about an inch or more of gas forms in each test tube.

❶ One of the gases is oxygen and the other one is hydrogen. Which do you think is which? Why?

Methods of Intelligence
Testing a Hypothesis

Ask your teacher to help you cork each of the tubes and take them out of the water. Your teacher will then light a wooden splint; blow it out until only a spark remains.

Place this glowing splint inside the tube that you think contains oxygen. If the splint bursts ❷ into flame again, this is a positive test for oxygen.

Your teacher will now place a lighted splint ❸ inside the tube that you think contains hydrogen. (As you may know, chemists sometimes write water as H_2O.) If the tube contains hydrogen, the gas will explode with a "pop."

121

❶ One tube will contain about twice as much gas as the other tube. Feed clues to support childrens' hypothesis that the tube with twice the amount of gas contains hydrogen, for example, recalling the formula for water, H_2O.

❷ Why is this a positive test for oxygen? (Oxygen in air makes things burn; nearly pure oxygen should make them burn faster and more rapidly.) What if the splint does not burst into flame? (tube does not contain pure oxygen) Which tube probably contained oxygen? (the other) How will we find out? (test again for oxygen)

❸ If the first tube did not give a positive test for oxygen and the second tube had to be tested, use another set of tubes from another investigation.

Unit Concept-Statement: In chemical or physical change the total amount of matter remains unchanged.

Getting the Elements

Hydrogen is an **element.** Molecules of hydrogen are ❶ made up only of atoms of hydrogen. Oxygen is an element. Molecules of oxygen are made up only of atoms of oxygen. The elements hydrogen and oxygen can combine to form a new substance—water—as this model shows.■ Chemists call this new substance a **compound.**

A compound is formed when two (or more) elements are combined. Water is a compound of the elements hydrogen and oxygen. No other atoms are part of this compound.

Let's think of this compound in a slightly different way. Water is made up of molecules. Each molecule of water is made up of two different kinds of atoms—atoms of hydrogen and atoms of oxygen. Passing an electric current through water makes the molecules break apart. The water molecules break apart into molecules of hydrogen and molecules of oxygen, as these models show. ●

A chemist can write about the breaking down of water in this way:

water ⟶ hydrogen + oxygen

■ ❷

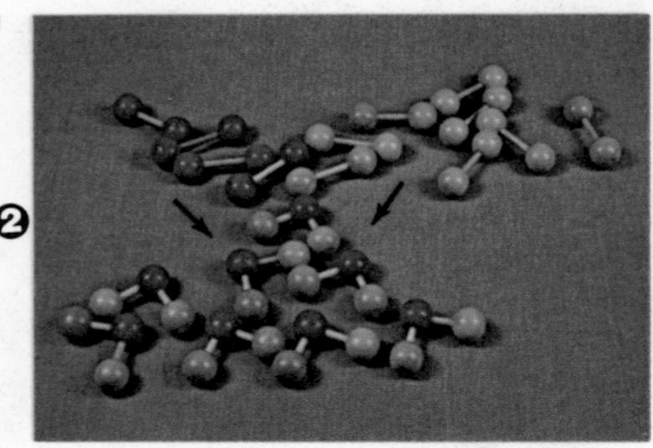

122

Continuing Lesson Cluster 1

❶ Do you think water is an element? (no) Why not? (Water molecules are made up of two different kinds of atoms.)

How many kinds of elements can you name? Children may name any of the following (or others): aluminum, argon, carbon, copper, gold, uranium, hydrogen, iron, mercury, neon, nitrogen, oxygen, zinc, platinum, radium, silver, sulfur, tin. They need not learn these names. What is alike in the elements you named? (one kind of atom)

❷ In the photograph of the models of molecules, oxygen atoms are red and hydrogen atoms yellow. What do you observe about molecules of hydrogen (2 atoms) oxygen? (2 atoms) water? (3 atoms; 2 hydrogen and one oxygen). Scientists believe from many investigations that atoms in the water molecule are joined together at an angle. However, the molecules of some other compounds may have other ways in which atoms are joined.

Supporting Statement: A molecule is the smallest particle of a substance that still has the properties of that substance.

❶

❷ This is called a **word equation**. Chemists use the arrow to mean "becomes" or "yields." You would say, "Water becomes hydrogen and oxygen."

Clearly, you can't tell what elements are in a compound by looking at it. You must separate a compound into its elements to find out what it is built of. Elements are the building blocks of compounds. The molecule of water, for instance, is made up of atoms of the elements hydrogen and oxygen. Thus, water is a compound.

What about a substance like oxygen? Oxygen is made up of only *one* kind of atom. For this reason, oxygen is called an element. An element is made up of only one kind of atom. Oxygen atoms, linked together, travel in pairs. It takes *two* oxygen atoms to have the properties of oxygen. *Two* oxygen atoms, then, make up a molecule of oxygen. ▲ The molecule of oxygen is the smallest part that has the properties of oxygen. The molecule of hydrogen is the smallest part that has the properties of hydrogen.

All molecules are made up of one or more atoms. Molecules may be made up of different kinds of atoms or of one kind of atom.

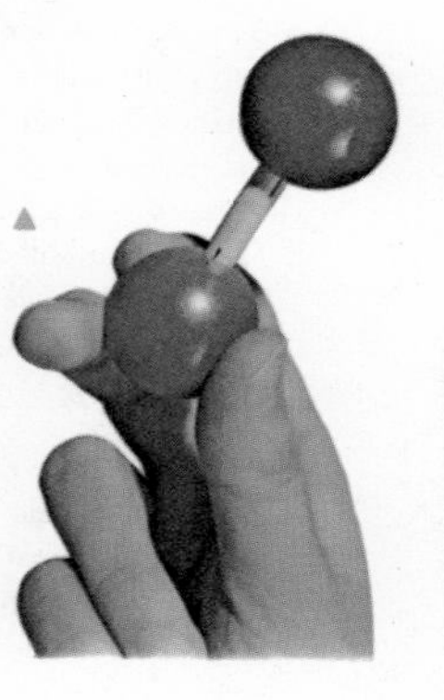

123

VERIFYING PROGRESS

In methods of intelligence

Let children *demonstrate* their ability to *make a model.* Have available a supply of different colored beads, Styrofoam balls, or Tinkertoy or similar sets. Children can build a model of a water molecule, using balls of any two different colors.

Tell children the formulas for ammonia (NH_3) and carbon dioxide (CO_2), and let them make models of how atoms of the elements could combine to make models of these substances.

Useful materials: Assorted colored beads, wooden or Styrofoam molecular model kit.

❶ What happens to the atoms in the water molecule when it is broken apart? (Oxygen atoms combine to form oxygen molecules; hydrogen atoms combine to form hydrogen molecules. Are any atoms lost or gained? Children may count the atoms.

In discussing these photographs, you may wish to make certain children regard the pictures as models and not as real pictures of atoms. Scientists make models to help explain behavior of things, and there are many different ways in which such models can be made.

❷ Why is a word equation useful? (With one glance, everyone understands the result of a chemical change.)
Place on the chalkboard:

hydrogen + oxygen → water

What does this equation say? (Hydrogen atoms combine with oxygen atoms to yield water molecules.) If children investigated the composition of sugar, suggest they write on the chalkboard a word equation for what they observed.

(sugar → water + carbon)

Extending the lesson

Recall the number of atoms in a molecule of hydrogen, in a molecule of oxygen, and in a molecule of water. So that no atoms are left over, how many hydrogen molecules must combine with how many oxygen molecules? Children may infer that: 2 hydrogen molecules combine with 1 oxygen molecule to make 2 water molecules. With children's help, place on the board

hydrogen + oxygen → water

$$2H_2 + O_2 \rightarrow 2H_2O$$

Unit Concept-Statement: In chemical or physical change the total amount of matter remains unchanged.

❶ BEFORE YOU GO ON

Check your understanding of the concepts of this section. Which ending would you choose for each statement below?

1. Substances, such as sugar and salt, may be told apart by properties that are
a. the same b. different

2. Perfume can pass through rubber of a balloon. This is an
a. observation b. inference

3. Water is
a. an element b. a compound

4. In pure oxygen, a spark on a wood splint will
a. go out b. burn brighter

5. Compounds are made up of different
a. elements b. properties

6. The statement that fits the main concept of this section is
a. The smallest particle of a substance that still has the properties of that substance is an atom.
b. The smallest particle of a substance that still has the properties of that substance is a molecule.

❷ USING WHAT YOU KNOW

1. These substances are elements: nitrogen, hydrogen
These substances are not elements: sugar, starch
a. Which of these substances are made up of only one kind of atom?
b. Which of these substances are made up of different kinds of atoms?

2. Sugar is made up of the elements carbon, hydrogen, and oxygen. How many kinds of atoms are there in sugar? How do you know?

❸ INVESTIGATING FURTHER

1. An element is made up of only one kind of atom. Which of these is made up of just one kind of atom: a bar of pure silver? a drop of pure water? a lump of pure sugar? a ring of pure gold? a wire of pure copper?

2. As a mercury thermometer gets warmer, the mercury expands. What happens when mercury expands? Mercury is an element. Do more molecules of mercury appear? Or do the same number of molecules just spread out more?

A LOOK AHEAD

From a little evidence, you have inferred that matter is made up of molecules. From a great deal of evidence, scientists have come to this great theory: Matter is built up of particles. As you go on in your work, you will come upon more and more evidence to support this theory.

124

VERIFYING PROGRESS

❶ Before you go on. Children *demonstrate* understanding of atoms and molecules by *identifying* suitable responses to questions.

1. b 3. b 5. a
2. b 4. b 6. b

❷ Using what you know. Children *distinguish* elements from substances that are not elements.
1. a. Elements, such as nitrogen and hydrogen, are made up of only one kind of atom. b. Substances that are not elements, such as sugar and starch, are made up of different kinds of atoms.
2. Three kinds of atoms, since each element is made up of a different kind of atom.

❸ Investigating further. Children *distinguish* substances made up of one kind of atom from substances made up of more than one kind; they *infer* that the number of molecules remains constant when a substance is heated.
1. Pure silver, gold, and copper are elements, and therefore made up of one kind of atom. Water and sugar are made up of more than one kind of element.
2. When mercury gets warmer, no more molecules appear; they move faster and spread farther and farther, and the mercury rises in the thermometer. Thus, the mercury column in a thermometer rises as the temperature goes up.

Supporting Statement: Elements can be combined to build up compounds.

2. Building Up a Compound

You have seen how a compound can be broken down. You have seen how the compound water can be broken down into the elements hydrogen and oxygen. Next, you can see how a compound can be built up from elements. The compound you can build up is called iron oxide. Perhaps you know iron oxide as rust, as it forms on some iron objects like this. ■

To build up the compound iron oxide, you need two common elements—iron and oxygen.

For iron, you can use steel wool and a nail. ● A nail ❶ isn't pure iron—it is made of steel, like steel wool. However, steel is made up mainly of iron. The iron in the steel wool and the nail will do for your purpose.

You will also need oxygen. Of course, you could use the oxygen in the air. Air is only about $\frac{1}{5}$ oxygen, though. You can get more oxygen than that to act on the iron. You can use a compound that gives off oxygen. This compound is ❷ hydrogen peroxide (pə·rok sīd). See for yourself that hydrogen peroxide gives off oxygen. Try the investigation on the next two pages. INVESTIGATE

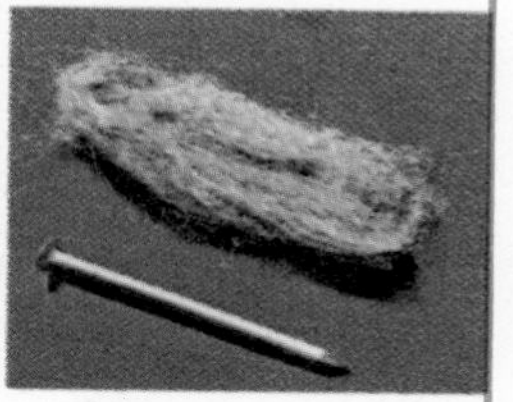

125

LESSON CLUSTER 2
BUILDING UP A COMPOUND

Teaching background. 2 T-127

Concept-seeking. Children seek to understand how elements can combine to form compounds.

Operations. Children *investigate* the formation of iron oxide by placing steel wool in fairly pure oxygen.

Methods of intelligence. Children *observe* the formation of rust, *infer* that oxygen combines with iron to form a compound with different properties, and *sort* compounds of oxygen and other elements into a group called oxides.

Useful materials: A piece of steel wool or an iron nail. Bottle of hydrogen peroxide.

Introducing Lesson Cluster 2

Hold up a piece of steel wool or an iron nail. What do you think would happen if we left these out in the rain? (They'd rust.) What elements have recombined? Does iron combine with water or with something in water?

❶ Steel is made from iron, but has other elements added to it to give it different properties. Iron is fairly soft, but some steels can cut through metals like butter; others are stainless; others are flexible as in a steel spring; and others are strong and won't break under heavy duty.

Explain that steel wool and the iron nail you show are mainly iron that has very little of another element mixed with it.

❷ Since you have presented H_2O as the formula for water, have children find the formula for hydrogen peroxide (H_2O_2) on the bottle label. What does the formula tell us? (more oxygen combined with hydrogen than for water)

Unit Concept-Statement: In chemical or physical change the total amount of matter remains unchanged.

Performance objectives. Children *construct* an oxygen gas generator, using plastic or rubber tubing, a flask, modeling clay, hydrogen peroxide, and yeast.

Children *demonstrate* the use of the apparatus to collect oxygen by displacement of water from an inverted test tube.

Children *demonstrate* the formation of rust, by placing an iron nail in one test tube of oxygen and steel wool in a second, and allowing the tubes to remain until rust forms.

Children *describe* the rust that forms as a chemical compound, iron oxide.

AN APPRENTICE INVESTIGATION into Making Rust

Needed: a bottle of 3 percent hydrogen peroxide ❶ (obtainable in a drugstore), a package of powdered yeast, about 1½ feet of plastic or rubber tubing, 2 test tubes with corks to fit, a pan, a small flask, a piece of modeling clay, an iron nail, steel wool, a friend

Mold a ball of clay around the tubing, about an inch from one end, big enough to plug the neck of the flask. Don't plug the flask yet.

Fill the pan ½ full of water. Fill a test tube to the top with water. Put your thumb over the mouth of the test tube, turn the test tube upside down, and stand it in the pan. Do the same with the other test tube. Ask a friend to hold the test tubes in place.

Pour 3 percent hydrogen peroxide into the ❷ flask until it is about ½ full. Pour in the yeast powder. Quickly plug the flask tightly by putting ❸

Useful materials: Be sure that the nail is iron. Many nails sold in hardware stores are now galvanized (coated with tin or zinc) to prevent rusting. Similar materials are available in CLASSROOM LABORATORY: PURPLE.

Continuing Lesson Cluster 2

❶ Be sure that you use recently dated packages of yeast powder and recently purchased or unopened bottles of hydrogen peroxide. Once opened, or with age, both lose effectiveness. Avoid steel wool cleaning pads that contain soap or detergent. Plain steel wool pads are best.

❷ Try to pour the peroxide down the side of the flask so that agitation will not cause oxygen to fizz off.

❸ Why should you quickly plug the flask? Once children place the yeast in the hydrogen peroxide, they will see intense bubbling of gas being given off. This is the gas they want to collect.

Supporting Statement: Elements can be combined to build up compounds.

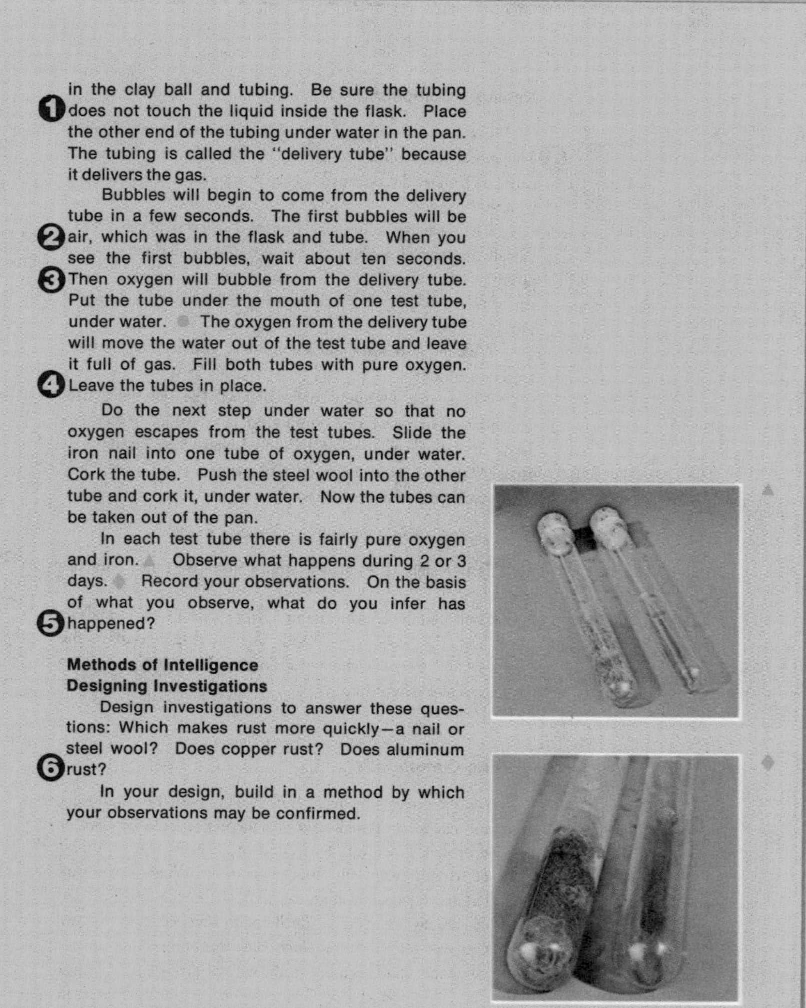

in the clay ball and tubing. Be sure the tubing ❶ does not touch the liquid inside the flask. Place the other end of the tubing under water in the pan. The tubing is called the "delivery tube" because it delivers the gas.

Bubbles will begin to come from the delivery tube in a few seconds. The first bubbles will be ❷ air, which was in the flask and tube. When you see the first bubbles, wait about ten seconds. ❸ Then oxygen will bubble from the delivery tube. Put the tube under the mouth of one test tube, under water. ● The oxygen from the delivery tube will move the water out of the test tube and leave it full of gas. Fill both tubes with pure oxygen. ❹ Leave the tubes in place.

Do the next step under water so that no oxygen escapes from the test tubes. Slide the iron nail into one tube of oxygen, under water. Cork the tube. Push the steel wool into the other tube and cork it, under water. Now the tubes can be taken out of the pan.

In each test tube there is fairly pure oxygen and iron. ▲ Observe what happens during 2 or 3 days. ◆ Record your observations. On the basis of what you observe, what do you infer has ❺ happened?

Methods of Intelligence
Designing Investigations

Design investigations to answer these questions: Which makes rust more quickly—a nail or steel wool? Does copper rust? Does aluminum ❻ rust?

In your design, build in a method by which your observations may be confirmed.

▲

◆

127

❶ If the tubing touches the liquid, the liquid will rise through the tube and ruin the collection of the gas.

❷ Why will air come from the tube first? Children should infer air was in the top of the flask and in the tube and has to be cleared out.

❸ Where does the oxygen come from? (Yeast is a plant that causes hydrogen peroxide to give off oxygen and change to water.)

❹ The delivery tube can be left under water, letting oxygen bubble harmlessly through the water until the reaction is completed. Removing the clay plug might cause spraying of the yeast and peroxide mixture.

❺ Children may infer that iron molecules have combined with oxygen molecules to form the rust. What evidence do you have? (Only oxygen from hydrogen peroxide and iron are in the tube.)

❻ Children may suggest leaving steel wool and a nail in moist open surroundings to see which becomes crumbly rust first. (In the corked tubes all oxygen will soon combine and no further action occurs.) The same set-up may be used for a strip of copper or a strip of shiny aluminum. The copper will turn greenish and the aluminum grayish. These reactions exemplify oxidation of these metals, although the copper oxide and aluminum oxide properties differ from those of iron oxide.

Unit Concept-Statement: In chemical or physical change the total amount of matter remains unchanged.

VERIFYING PROGRESS

In concept-seeking

Is sugar an element or a compound? How can you test your hypothesis? (try to break sugar apart) If we succeed in doing this, how will we know? (The properties will change.) Heat a teaspoonful of sugar in a disposable foil pan or a coffee can. Let a child hold a mirror above the pan. Is what you see forming on the mirror melted sugar? How can you find out? (taste it) Let a child put a drop of the liquid on his tongue. Is it sweet? (no) What does this show about sugar? (Sugar must contain water.)

Keep heating the sugar until it turns black. What do you think the black substance is? (carbon) Is sugar an element or a compound? (compound) Why? (Each of its parts, carbon and water, has properties different from sugar.)

Making a Compound

In a few days oxygen acts on a moist nail or steel wool. ❶ The metal takes on a red-brown coating of rust. Chemists call rust iron oxide, because it is a compound of the elements iron and oxygen.

What are the elements iron and oxygen made up of? Recall that the molecules of an element are made up only of atoms of that element. Thus, the element oxygen is made up of atoms of oxygen, and the element iron is made up of atoms of iron.

What happens when the element oxygen and the element iron combine?

When the element oxygen and the element iron combine, they form the compound iron oxide. Chemists have discovered that what happens when they combine is this: Atoms of iron and atoms of oxygen combine. They often write the change this way:

❷ iron + oxygen ⟶ iron oxide

Remember that the arrow stands for "becomes" in the equation.

Look again at the name "iron oxide" and analyze it. First, the word "iron" tells us that iron is part of the compound. Second, the word "oxide" tells us that oxygen is part of the compound.

Sorting Compounds

You have seen how iron oxide can be made by combining iron and oxygen. Recall that you have also seen how water can be broken down into hydrogen and oxygen. It would be correct to call water "hydrogen oxide." What is the one element in these combinations that is the same? You are right if you say "oxygen." Both compounds contain oxygen.

You can tell from its name that the compound copper oxide is made up of copper combined with oxygen. Copper oxide is a compound that forms when copper is heated in

128

Continuing Lesson Cluster 2

❶ Children can get evidence that iron atoms combine with oxygen atoms in another way. Dampen a wad of steel wool and place it in a test tube, jar, or glass. Invert the container in a pan containing an inch or two of water. Place a rubber band around the container at the water level. After several days, place another rubber band at the level of water inside the container.

Children will observe that the water rises inside the container. Why does the water rise? (Something is being taken from the air inside the container, and water rises to take its place.)

What do you think has happened? Children may hypothesize that oxygen in the air has been used. How can you test? Let them recall flame test for oxygen. Then they should be able to predict that if oxygen is used the test won't work.

Cover the container under water and remove it. Quickly uncover and insert a glowing splint. The glow will go out quickly and will not burst into flame. Children may infer that no oxygen was in the air in the container. As a further test of oxygen, light a candle in a closed container of ordinary air. The candle soon goes out. Why? (Burning and rusting both use oxygen; when all or most of the oxygen is used, chemical combination stops.)

❷ If you have developed the idea that hydrogen plus oxygen yields water, ask: What kind of an oxide is water? (hydrogen oxide)

Supporting Statement: Elements can be combined to build up compounds.

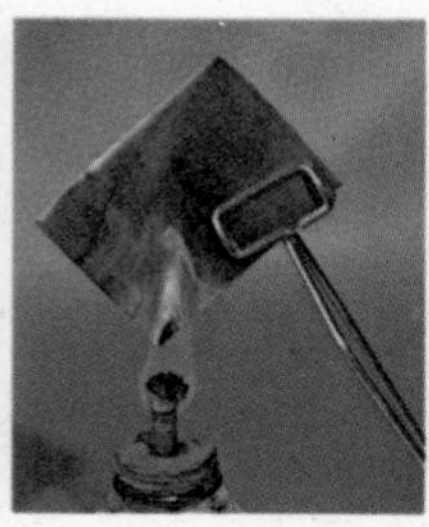

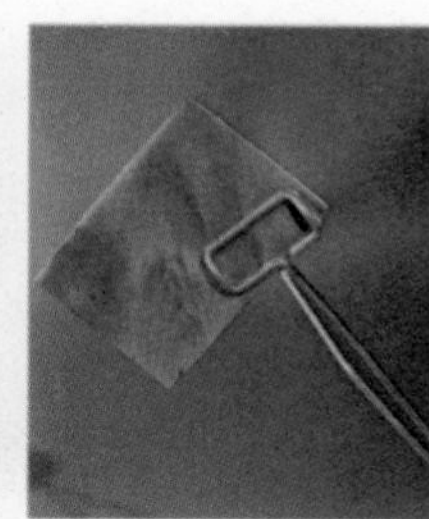

a flame. ■ There are many kinds of oxides. In fact, there is a whole group of compounds of oxygen called **oxides.**

One important task of scientists is to group or classify things. They classify matter into solids, liquids, and gases, ❶ for example. They classify matter into elements and compounds, too. One group of compounds is made up of oxides.

See how classifying can give us useful information. From now on, when you hear the word "oxide," you will ❷ know it has to be a compound of oxygen and another element.

The Importance of Iron Oxide

❸ Think again about iron oxide. Why is this compound of iron and oxygen important?

A bridge can be weakened by rusting, as the iron in steel combines with the oxygen in the air. It is easy to see why the steel of a bridge is painted. Paint can help keep oxygen atoms in the air from reaching iron atoms in the bridge and forming iron oxide. The coat of paint on an automobile also helps stop rusting. If the coat of paint is broken, however, oxygen can combine with iron to form iron oxide, and perhaps even make a hole in the steel body of the car. Iron combines easily with oxygen.

Think now about this question: When iron rusts, can it be used again? Try the Search on Your Own on the next page.

❶ Why do scientists classify substances? (It gives them a key to the properties, whether the substances combine with others, or whether they can be broken down into simple substances.)

❷ What would you infer from any substance with oxide as part of its name? (contains oxygen) If you broke an oxide down, what substance could you be sure of getting? (oxygen) List these terms on the chalkboard: carbon dioxide, carbon monoxide, carbon disulfide, carbohydrate, sodium bicarbonate. What element can you be sure all the substances contain? (carbon)

❸ What difference does rusting (combination of iron and oxygen) make to people? If you leave metal tools and equipment out in the rain, what happens? (Saws and chisels get dull, wheelbarrows rust through, bicycles and lawnmowers don't work as well because of rusted parts.) What is the best way to keep your bicycle from rusting? (Wax it, to keep it dry and keep oxygen from the metal parts.)

UNIT THREE

Unit Concept-Statement: In chemical or physical change the total amount of matter remains unchanged.

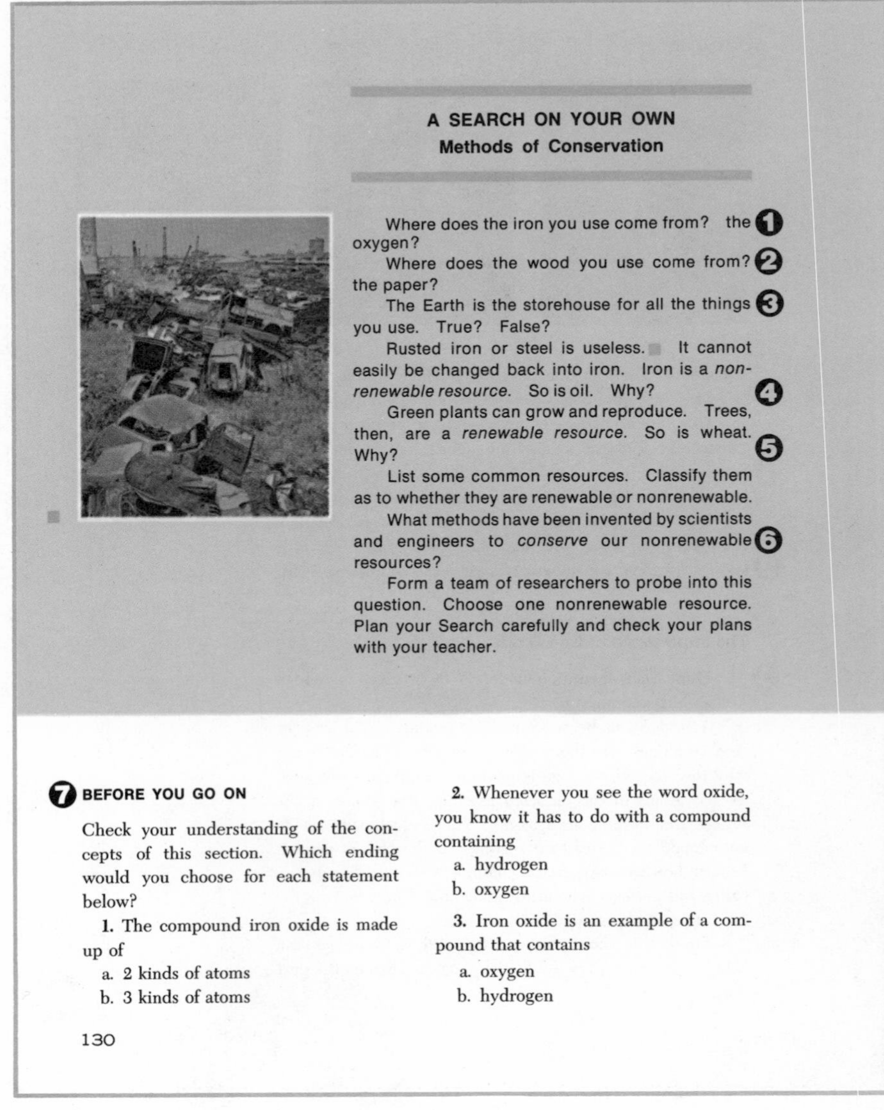

A SEARCH ON YOUR OWN
Methods of Conservation

Where does the iron you use come from? the oxygen? ❶

Where does the wood you use come from? the paper? ❷

The Earth is the storehouse for all the things you use. True? False? ❸

Rusted iron or steel is useless. It cannot easily be changed back into iron. Iron is a *nonrenewable resource*. So is oil. Why? ❹

Green plants can grow and reproduce. Trees, then, are a *renewable resource*. So is wheat. Why? ❺

List some common resources. Classify them as to whether they are renewable or nonrenewable.

What methods have been invented by scientists and engineers to *conserve* our nonrenewable resources? ❻

Form a team of researchers to probe into this question. Choose one nonrenewable resource. Plan your Search carefully and check your plans with your teacher.

❼ **BEFORE YOU GO ON**

Check your understanding of the concepts of this section. Which ending would you choose for each statement below?

1. The compound iron oxide is made up of
a. 2 kinds of atoms
b. 3 kinds of atoms

2. Whenever you see the word oxide, you know it has to do with a compound containing
a. hydrogen
b. oxygen

3. Iron oxide is an example of a compound that contains
a. oxygen
b. hydrogen

130

VERIFYING PROGRESS

❶ **A search on your own.** Children will need to read in the school or public library. They should find that iron comes from iron ore from which iron is separated by smelting processes. Oxygen comes from air and is continually renewed by food-making processes of plants.

❷ Wood and paper come from the food-making process of green plants, mostly trees.

❸ If a child says "false", ask: What do you get that is not on this Earth? If he responds that we get energy from the Sun, ask: Where is the Sun's energy stored? (in green plants)

❹ The obvious response is that once iron ore and oil resources are used, there are no more of them for our needs. Changes in the Earth may be forming iron ore, and plant and animal decay may be forming oil reserves somewhere, but the time when they might be available is far distant—millions of years, perhaps.

❺ Green plants reproduce new plants from seeds or in other ways. Will they continue to do so if the environment changes too much?

❻ Children who do this search should report on the wise use of land, laws against pollution, dams for water conservation, regulation of the atmosphere, protection of wild life, etc.

❼ **Before you go on.** Children *demonstrate* understanding of elements and compounds by *identifying* suitable responses to open-ended statements.
1. a 2. b 3. a 4. 2

Supporting Statement: Elements can be combined to build up compounds.

4. The statement that fits the main concept of this section is
   a. Elements can be combined to build up compounds.
   b. Molecules can be combined to build up atoms.

❶ USING WHAT YOU KNOW

1. Hydrogen peroxide is a compound of the elements hydrogen and oxygen. Next time you put peroxide on a cut, watch for the bubbles. What is happening to the liquid peroxide compound?

2. Carbon is an element. Oxygen is an element. When carbon is burned in oxygen, they combine to form the compound called carbon dioxide. If the compound carbon dioxide is broken down, what elements must it yield?

3. Which of these does not contain atoms of oxygen?
magnesium oxide   sodium chloride
potassium hydroxide

Explain your answer.

❷ INVESTIGATING FURTHER

1. Why are steel cans coated with tin?

2. What does galvanized mean? Why are some objects galvanized?

3. Why doesn't stainless steel get rusty?

4. Of what metal are the water pipes in your school or home made? Is the water that comes from these pipes ever rusty? If so, how do you explain this?

5. Rusting means that iron combines with oxygen. Does rusting take place only when there is moisture? In the investigation on pages 126–7, the nail and steel wool were moistened. Plan an investigation to show whether dryness helps or stops rusting. Show your plan to your teacher. Then try it.

6. Iron is often found in nature as iron oxide. Find out how iron oxide is treated to separate the iron from the oxygen.

A LOOK AHEAD

Elements combine. When elements combine, they form compounds.

Objects can be classified into solids, gases, and liquids. Compounds can also be classified.

As you go on in your study of science, you will find yourself classifying the things around you. As you classify, you will group things with common likenesses. In what one way, at least, will you find that different kinds of matter—wherever they are found—are alike?

131

❶ **Using what you know.** Children *analyze* situations and *infer* that compounds can be broken down into the elements of which they consist; they also *distinguish* compounds that contain oxygen from those that do not.
1. Hydrogen peroxide breaks down into water and oxygen. (Oxygen kills certain types of bacteria.)
2. The elements carbon and oxygen, because the compound was built up from these elements.
3. Sodium chloride. "Oxide" is always a clue that oxygen is in the compound.

❷ **Investigating further.** Children *consult authorities, analyze situations,* and *plan investigations* into inhibiting rusting, and *seek evidence* of how iron is separated from its ore.
1. Tin keeps oxygen atoms from reaching the iron atoms and combining to form rust.
2. When metals are galvanized, they are coated with zinc by an electrical process. The zinc coating keeps oxygen atoms from coming in contact with iron atoms.
3. Stainless steel is a mixture of chromium, zinc and iron which together resists rust. This combination of metals is called an alloy.
4. Many water pipes are made of rust-resistant copper and brass. Some pipes are made from iron coated with zinc (galvanized). Water may contain mild acids that slowly eat away even the galvanized coating of an iron pipe.
5. Children should design an investigation using dry metal and wet metal and compare results.
6. Basically, the oxygen in the iron ore is made to combine with carbon, setting free the iron.

Unit Concept-Statement: In chemical or physical change the total amount of matter remains unchanged.

LESSON CLUSTER 3
TWO COMMON GROUPS OF COMPOUNDS

Teaching background. 3 T-127

Concept-seeking. Children become aware of how some compounds are grouped as acids, others as bases.

Operations. Children *investigate* a chemical test for acids and bases.

Methods of intelligence. Children *observe* the action of substances on litmus paper, and *infer* acids turn blue litmus paper pink and bases turn pink litmus paper blue.

Useful materials: Vinegar, ammonia, two vials, jars, or bottles with tightly-fitted tops; pink and blue litmus paper, orange or grapefruit (or juice).

3. Two Common Groups of Compounds

You have looked at a few compounds belonging to the group called oxides. You have seen how the group name of a compound helps us to know at once what makes it up. Thus, the word *oxide* tells us that the compound has oxygen in it.

Let's look at some other groups of compounds. Two groups of compounds are very common and easy to identify. A **chemical test** is used to find out whether a compound belongs to one of these two groups. This chemical test is (1) made with **litmus paper**.

There are two colors of litmus paper. One is pink, the other is blue. How is each used in a chemical test? Find out for yourself. Try the investigation on the opposite page. INVESTIGATE

+ acid ↓

Testing with Litmus Paper

When blue litmus paper is touched with a drop or two of vinegar, the blue color changes to pink. What makes this change happen? Vinegar has in it a compound called acetic acid. Acetic acid is one of a whole group of compounds (2) called **acids.** Acids turn blue litmus to pink. If acid is touched to pink litmus paper, there is no change in color—the paper stays pink.

However, when pink litmus paper is touched with a drop of household ammonia, the pink paper turns blue. Household ammonia is a compound called ammonium (3) hydroxide. Ammonium hydroxide is one of a group called **bases.** Bases turn pink litmus paper blue.

+ base ↓

Litmus paper is used to test two groups of compounds—acids and bases. Acids turn blue litmus pink. ■ Bases turn pink litmus blue. ●

Litmus paper is used as a chemical test for acids and bases. Put this chemical test to work on some common substances. Try the Search on Your Own on page 134.

132

Introducing Lesson Cluster 3

Before class, pour into separate small, tightly stoppered vials or small jars some clear white vinegar and ammonia. As the lesson begins, place the vials on your desk and tell the children that one bottle contains vinegar and the other ammonia. What is in this bottle? Some children may guess; others may say they don't know.

How could we find out without smelling the substances? Explain that smelling—like tasting—unknown substances is unwise and not a sure test of every substance. Some children may suggest that they can use ***chemical tests*** for unknown substances.

(1) Litmus paper is a paper treated by a dye made from one kind of lichen (page 55).

(2) Can you think of something from the acid group you may have had for breakfast? (oranges, grapefruit or their juices) What do you think would happen if you placed a drop of juice on pink and blue litmus paper? (no change in pink, blue would turn pink) If possible, allow several children to try this out.

(3) What does the hydroxide part of the name tell you about the compound? Children should infer it contains hydrogen and oxygen from what they know about oxides and water. When you made rust, what did you combine with iron? (oxygen) What was the compound called? (iron oxide) A substance resulting from this kind of combination is always an oxide. Bases, however, are not made this way. If children want to know more about the composition of bases—and of acids, as well—see T-127.

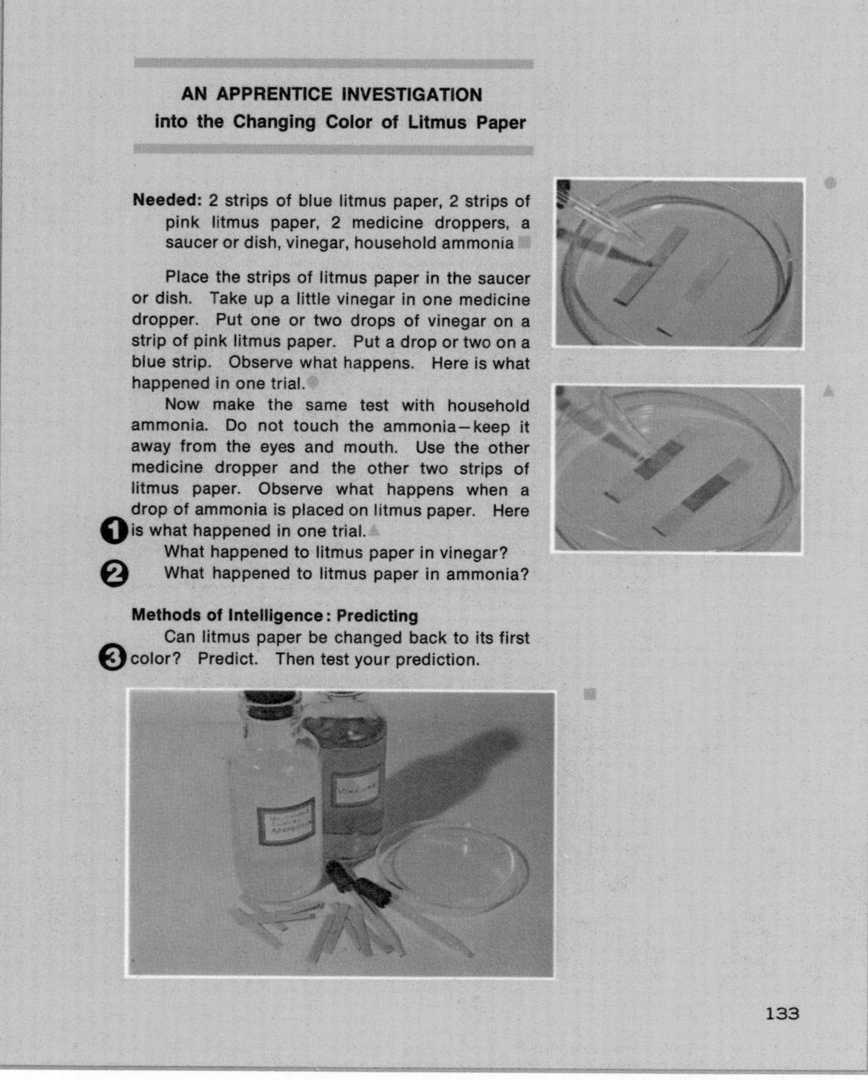

AN APPRENTICE INVESTIGATION into the Changing Color of Litmus Paper

Needed: 2 strips of blue litmus paper, 2 strips of pink litmus paper, 2 medicine droppers, a saucer or dish, vinegar, household ammonia

Place the strips of litmus paper in the saucer or dish. Take up a little vinegar in one medicine dropper. Put one or two drops of vinegar on a strip of pink litmus paper. Put a drop or two on a blue strip. Observe what happens. Here is what happened in one trial.

Now make the same test with household ammonia. Do not touch the ammonia—keep it away from the eyes and mouth. Use the other medicine dropper and the other two strips of litmus paper. Observe what happens when a drop of ammonia is placed on litmus paper. Here
❶ is what happened in one trial.

What happened to litmus paper in vinegar?
❷ What happened to litmus paper in ammonia?

Methods of Intelligence: Predicting

Can litmus paper be changed back to its first
❸ color? Predict. Then test your prediction.

133

Performance objectives. Children *demonstrate* the changing color of litmus paper by placing vinegar on pink and blue litmus, causing the blue to turn pink; and by placing ammonia on pink and blue litmus, causing the pink to turn blue.

Useful materials: Litmus paper is usually available from drugstores. From scientific supply houses it may be listed under indicators. Alternate materials are available in CLASSROOM LABORATORY: PURPLE.

❶ Children should observe that vinegar turns the blue litmus paper pink and the ammonia turns the pink litmus paper blue. **How do you account for these changes?** Let children hypothesize before continuing from the middle of page 132.

❷ Now let several children apply the test to identify the contents of the vials used at the beginning. Use tape or a marking pencil to identify the vials with a number.

❸ Children should predict that colors will be restored. They may suggest testing by putting a drop of vinegar on the blue spot made by the ammonia on the pink litmus paper. They may also wish to place a drop of ammonia on the pink spot made by the vinegar on the blue litmus paper. When children test their predictions, they may find that it takes more than one drop of vinegar or ammonia to cause the expected color change. The strength of acetic acid in the vinegar may not be equal to the strength of the base in the ammonia. Be sure to use only one drop at a time, especially of ammonia because of its irritating fumes.

Unit Concept-Statement: In chemical or physical change the total amount of matter remains unchanged.

VERIFYING PROGRESS

In methods of intelligence

Ask children to *analyze* the following situation, *apply evidence* from their study of tests and *infer* results.

Mary dropped a bottle of vinegar. Some splashed onto her bright blue skirt. What may happen if she does not immediately wash her skirt? (The acid vinegar may cause the blue dye in the skirt to discolor, perhaps to turn pink.)

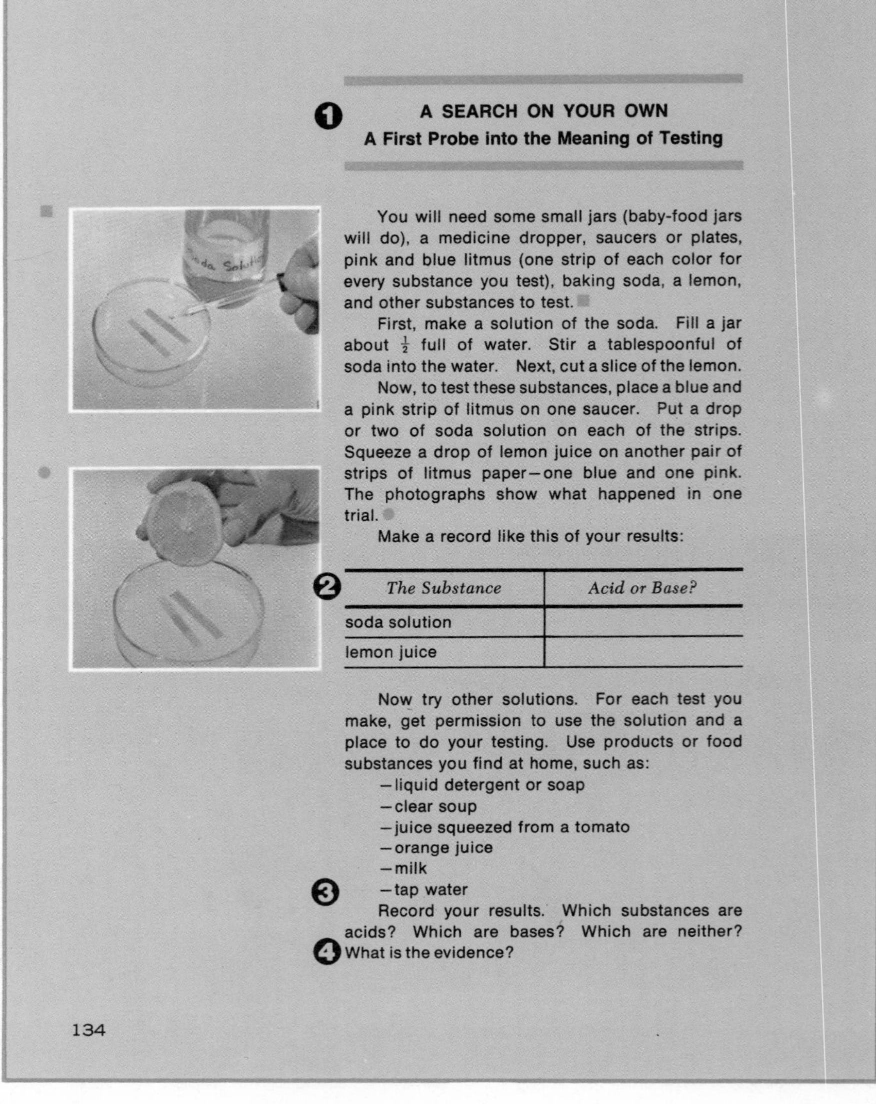

❶ **A SEARCH ON YOUR OWN**
A First Probe into the Meaning of Testing

You will need some small jars (baby-food jars will do), a medicine dropper, saucers or plates, pink and blue litmus (one strip of each color for every substance you test), baking soda, a lemon, and other substances to test.

First, make a solution of the soda. Fill a jar about $\frac{1}{2}$ full of water. Stir a tablespoonful of soda into the water. Next, cut a slice of the lemon.

Now, to test these substances, place a blue and a pink strip of litmus on one saucer. Put a drop or two of soda solution on each of the strips. Squeeze a drop of lemon juice on another pair of strips of litmus paper—one blue and one pink. The photographs show what happened in one trial.

Make a record like this of your results:

❷

The Substance	*Acid or Base?*
soda solution	
lemon juice	

Now try other solutions. For each test you make, get permission to use the solution and a place to do your testing. Use products or food substances you find at home, such as:

—liquid detergent or soap
—clear soup
—juice squeezed from a tomato
—orange juice
—milk
❸ —tap water

Record your results. Which substances are acids? Which are bases? Which are neither?
❹ What is the evidence?

134

VERIFYING PROGRESS

❶ **A search on your own.** Children should collect and assemble the materials needed on their own, bringing them to the class if the search is to be done at school. You can provide litmus paper. (Be sure they get their parents' permission, if they carry out the search at home.)

❷ Anything that changes blue litmus to pink will be listed as an ***acid,*** pink to blue as a ***base.*** If no change takes place, the substance should be listed as neutral.

❸ Tap water may test slightly acid, slightly basic, or neither, depending on where you live. (Basic water is often called hard water. Water treated with chlorine to purify it is likely to prove acid.)

❹ The evidence is that an acid will turn blue litmus paper pink while a base will turn pink litmus paper blue. If neither pink or blue litmus paper changes color, the substance is neutral.

Supporting Statement: The presence of some substances can be determined by chemical tests.

1 BEFORE YOU GO ON

Check your understanding of the concepts of this section. Which ending would you choose for each statement below?

1. Litmus paper is used to make
   a. acids and bases
   b. a chemical test
2. Ammonium hydroxide is
   a. an acid
   b. a base
3. In ammonium hydroxide, pink litmus paper will
   a. turn blue b. remain pink
4. In vinegar, pink litmus paper will
   a. remain pink b. turn blue
5. The statement that fits the main concept of this section is
   a. Some compounds may be grouped as acids and bases.
   b. Some compounds may be grouped as pink litmus and blue litmus.

A LOOK AHEAD

Oxides are one group into which you can classify some compounds. Acids and bases are two more groups of compounds. A chemical test helps you classify acids and bases. Other chemical tests are useful to identify other substances. In an earlier section, you learned the tests for oxygen and hydrogen. In the next section, you will find out about an important test for another common—but invisible—gas. What gas do you suppose it may be?

4. An Important Test

A compound you will meet again and again is carbon dioxide gas. How can you recognize it, when it has no color and no odor? As it happens, there is a simple chemical test for carbon dioxide. The test makes use of a liquid called 2 limewater.

Limewater is a clear and colorless liquid. When carbon dioxide gas combines with it, however, limewater turns a cloudy, milky color. Whenever limewater turns milky, you will know at once that carbon dioxide is present. To see for yourself how this happens, try the investigation on the next page. INVESTIGATE

135

LESSON CLUSTER 4
AN IMPORTANT TEST

Teaching background. 4 T-127

Concept-seeking. Children discover that another chemical test will detect the presence of carbon dioxide and can be used to identify substances containing calcium carbonate.

Operations. Children *investigate* a means of testing for the presence of carbon dioxide and for identifying compounds containing carbon and oxygen.

Methods of intelligence. Children *observe* chemical reactions involving the release of carbon dioxide and use limewater to *test* the presence of carbon dioxide; they *compare* chemical reactions of certain carbon compounds and *infer* the identity of the substances tested.

1 Before you go on. Children *demonstrate* understanding of a chemical test for acids and bases by *identifying* suitable responses to questions.
1. b 3. a 5. a
2. b 4. a

Introducing Lesson Cluster 4

Have the following materials handy for a quick demonstration: A length of flexible tubing around which you have molded modeling clay to serve as a cork, a bottle of limewater and a small jar, and a bottle of club soda. Open the bottle of soda. What do you think the bubbles are? Let children hypothesize. Some may do so correctly, but others may say air rather than carbon dioxide. Plug the bottle with the clay cork and tubing so that the tubing is above the liquid in the bottle. Pour some limewater into the jar and let the gas bubble into the limewater until it turns cloudy. Then remove the tubing. What gas was this? How do we know?

2 Limewater is available from a chemical supply house or drug store. To prepare limewater yourself, put one teaspoonful of calcium hydroxide in a clean jar and add a cupful of water. Cap tightly and shake vigorously to dissolve as much of the calcium hydroxide as possible. Let stand overnight to allow the undissolved powder to settle. Then pour the clear liquid through a filter into a clean jar and cap tightly. Discard the residue.

UNIT THREE

Unit Concept-Statement: In chemical or physical change the total amount of matter remains unchanged.

Performance objectives. Children *construct* a carbon dioxide generator, by using marble chips in vinegar in a flask and collecting gas bubbles by water displacement.

Children *demonstrate* a test for carbon dioxide, by adding limewater to the gas they have collected, and mixing, causing the limewater to turn milky.

Useful materials: For marble chips, you may substitute bits of eggshells, seashell fragments, or small pieces of limestone. Similar materials are available in CLASSROOM LABORATORY: PURPLE.

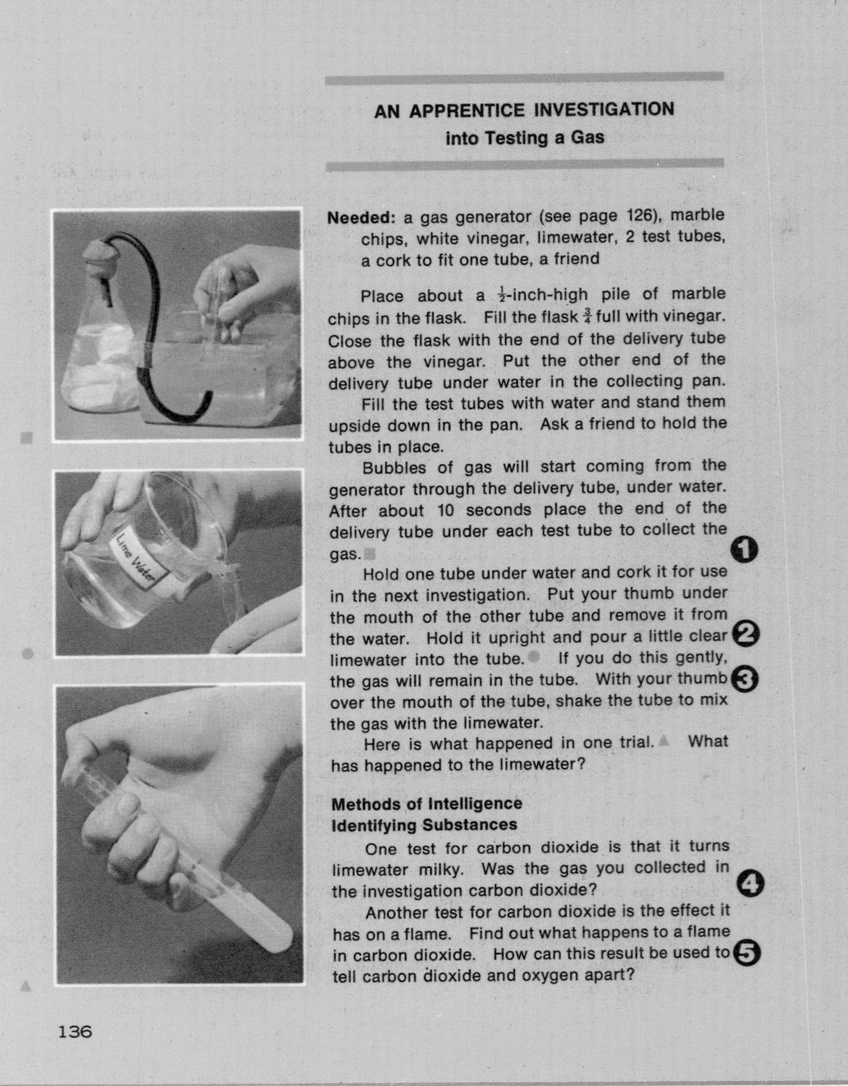

AN APPRENTICE INVESTIGATION
into Testing a Gas

Needed: a gas generator (see page 126), marble chips, white vinegar, limewater, 2 test tubes, a cork to fit one tube, a friend

Place about a ½-inch-high pile of marble chips in the flask. Fill the flask ¾ full with vinegar. Close the flask with the end of the delivery tube above the vinegar. Put the other end of the delivery tube under water in the collecting pan.

Fill the test tubes with water and stand them upside down in the pan. Ask a friend to hold the tubes in place.

Bubbles of gas will start coming from the generator through the delivery tube, under water. After about 10 seconds place the end of the delivery tube under each test tube to collect the gas. ■ ❶

Hold one tube under water and cork it for use in the next investigation. Put your thumb under the mouth of the other tube and remove it from the water. Hold it upright and pour a little clear ❷ limewater into the tube. ● If you do this gently, the gas will remain in the tube. With your thumb ❸ over the mouth of the tube, shake the tube to mix the gas with the limewater.

Here is what happened in one trial. ▲ What has happened to the limewater?

Methods of Intelligence
Identifying Substances

One test for carbon dioxide is that it turns limewater milky. Was the gas you collected in the investigation carbon dioxide? ❹

Another test for carbon dioxide is the effect it has on a flame. Find out what happens to a flame in carbon dioxide. How can this result be used to ❺ tell carbon dioxide and oxygen apart?

136

Continuing Lesson Cluster 4

❶ This will permit any air in the generator and tube to be expelled.

❷ Before they remove the test tube, children should wait until the carbon dioxide gas displaces all the water in the test tube.

❸ To add the limewater gently, use a medicine dropper to drop it into the test tube. At least an amount that would fill the dropper should be used.

❹ Since the gas collected by the children turned limewater milky, they may infer that the gas was carbon dioxide. Save the test tubes containing the milky mixture for use in the following section, "What Is the White Solid?", on page 137.

❺ Children may collect another tube of carbon dioxide gas and quickly insert a long lighted match or splint into the tube. They should also insert a lighted match or splint into a tube of air (which is about one fifth oxygen gas) and, if possible, into a tube of pure oxygen. (See pages 126 and 127 for how to collect it.) The match or splint will go out in both carbon dioxide and ordinary air, but will burn brighter and faster in the pure oxygen.

Supporting Statement: The presence of some substances can be determined by chemical tests.

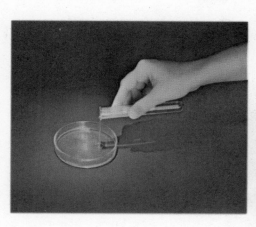

What Is the White Solid?

Limewater turns milky when combined with carbon dioxide. It turns milky because a new substance is formed that is made up of tiny white specks. Suppose you pour the mixture of the liquid and the white substance into a flat ❶ plastic dish. ■ Then let the liquid evaporate. The white substance is left in the dish. ●

What is this white solid that comes from putting together carbon dioxide and limewater? Let's reason from the evidence. Can this white substance be carbon dioxide? No, for carbon dioxide is a gas. Can the white substance be limewater? No, limewater is a liquid. This white substance is a solid.

The white substance is not limewater. Limewater is calcium hydroxide dissolved in water. The white substance is not calcium hydroxide then. Calcium hydroxide dissolves in water. The white substance does not. And chemists have found that it is not an acid or a base. What is this ❷ substance? The investigation on the next page will help you discover for yourself what it is. INVESTIGATE

137

Useful materials: A funnel, limewater, paper toweling, scissors, flat dish, hotplate.

❶ Children will be able to separate the white substance from the liquid almost immediately if they use a filter rather than the evaporation method shown in the text.

Children can make a filter by using a funnel and paper toweling. Cut a circle with a radius approximately the height of the funnel out of the paper toweling. Fold the circle in half and then in half again, so that a cone is formed. Place the cone inside the funnel and the funnel over a jar. Pour the milky limewater gently into the filter. Remove the filter when all the liquid has seeped through. If it is difficult to free the white substance from the damp filter, hold the filter over some gentle heat until the paper is dry.

❷ Encourage hypotheses. What must the substance have formed from? (carbon dioxide and calcium hydroxide—the chemical name for limewater—which are the only substances in the tube) Could the substance be carbon? (no) Why not? (Carbon is black.) Is the substance a compound or an element? (Encourage children to speculate, or feel free to say they don't know.)

Unit Concept-Statement: In chemical or physical change the total amount of matter remains unchanged.

Performance objectives. Children *demonstrate* the similarity of the white substance from milky limewater to marble, by comparing the bubbling action of vinegar on marble with a similar action on the white substance.

Children *describe* the bubbles of gas given off as carbon dioxide.

Children *describe* that marble and the white substance are calcium carbonate.

Useful materials: Use marble chips, eggshells, seashells, or limestone chips, as you did on page 136. Similar materials are available in CLASSROOM LABORATORY: PURPLE.

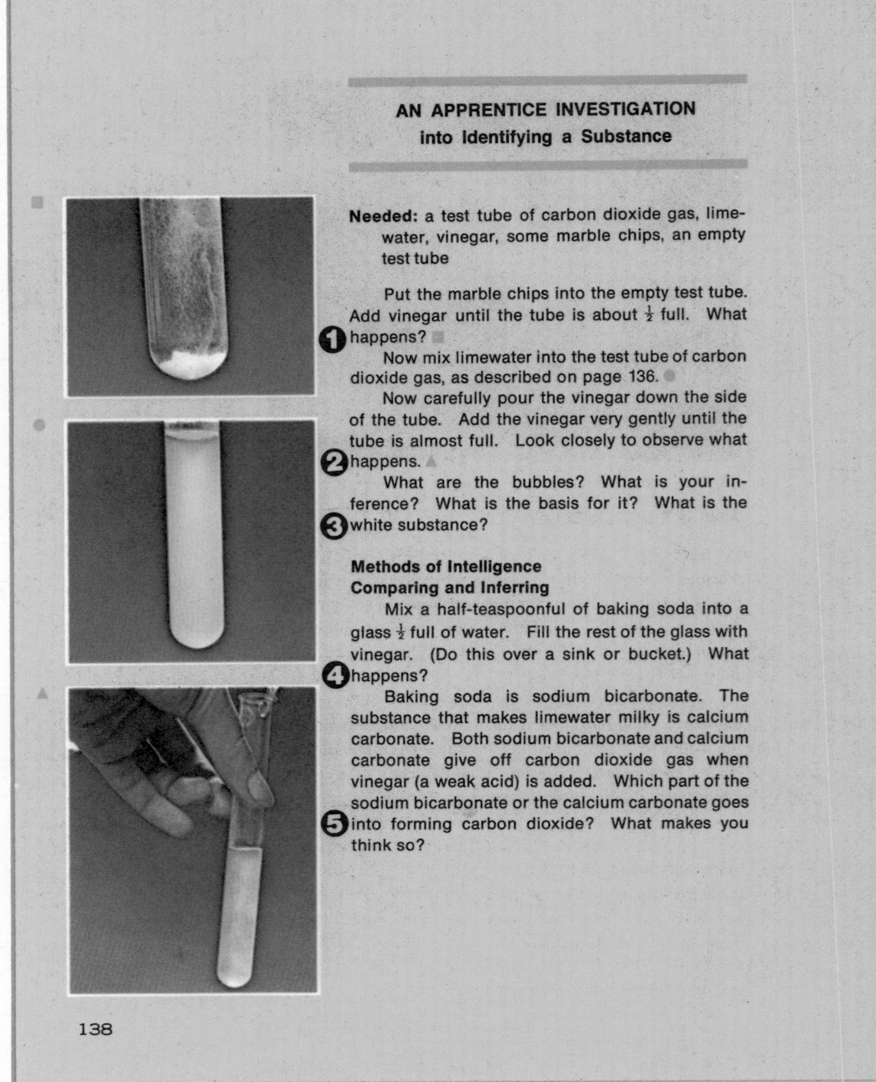

AN APPRENTICE INVESTIGATION into Identifying a Substance

Needed: a test tube of carbon dioxide gas, limewater, vinegar, some marble chips, an empty test tube

Put the marble chips into the empty test tube. Add vinegar until the tube is about $\frac{1}{2}$ full. What ❶ happens?

Now mix limewater into the test tube of carbon dioxide gas, as described on page 136.

Now carefully pour the vinegar down the side of the tube. Add the vinegar very gently until the tube is almost full. Look closely to observe what ❷ happens.

What are the bubbles? What is your inference? What is the basis for it? What is the ❸ white substance?

Methods of Intelligence
Comparing and Inferring

Mix a half-teaspoonful of baking soda into a glass $\frac{1}{2}$ full of water. Fill the rest of the glass with vinegar. (Do this over a sink or bucket.) What ❹ happens?

Baking soda is sodium bicarbonate. The substance that makes limewater milky is calcium carbonate. Both sodium bicarbonate and calcium carbonate give off carbon dioxide gas when vinegar (a weak acid) is added. Which part of the sodium bicarbonate or the calcium carbonate goes ❺ into forming carbon dioxide? What makes you think so?

138

Continuing Lesson Cluster 4

❶ As tested in the investigation on page 135 the acid in the vinegar reacts with the marble chips, causing bubbles of carbon dioxide gas to be formed.

❷ As vinegar is added, the cloudiness of the mixture begins to clear, since the acid dissolves the white substance. Bubbles of carbon dioxide also result from this reaction.

❸ On the basis of their last investigation, children may infer that the bubbles are carbon dioxide gas. They may begin to wonder if the white substance formed in the limewater could be of the same composition as the marble chips.

❹ The liquid in the glass foams up.

❺ Children may infer that the carbon atoms from sodium carbonate and calcium carbonate go into forming carbon dioxide. They infer this is so because they can see that carbon is an element present in all three compounds. They can see this from the *names* of the compounds. And since the "-ate" in the endings of "sodium carbonate" and "calcium carbonate" indicates oxygen, children may infer that some of the oxygen atoms that help make up carbon dioxide came from these carbonates.

Supporting Statement: The presence of some substances can be determined by chemical tests.

Why the Test Works

The solid white substance that forms in limewater when carbon dioxide is present is calcium carbonate. This ❶ is the same substance that marble, limestone, egg-shells, and some other kinds of shells are made of.

Let's see how this calcium carbonate is formed in limewater. It is produced when carbon dioxide reacts with limewater. Limewater is dissolved calcium hydroxide. To show what happens when carbon dioxide reacts with limewater, we can write this equation. ■

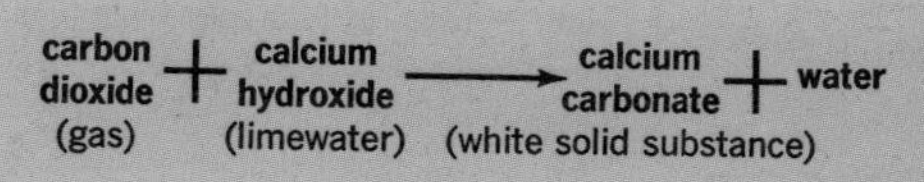

This equation stands for a **chemical reaction**, for the atoms have changed places to form new substances. This chemical reaction is a test for carbon dioxide. You will make use of this chemical test again and again. Whenever limewater turns milky, this chemical reaction is taking place. Whenever this chemical reaction takes place, the substances shown in the equation are present.

Scientists can depend on chemical tests. Scientists can tell from the substances produced what substances must have been there to begin with. Wherever you find calcium carbonate, you can be sure that certain elements are present. These elements are calcium, carbon, and oxygen. These elements are the building blocks of calcium carbonate. Whenever limewater turns milky, you know that carbon dioxide must have combined with the calcium hydroxide of the limewater.

❷ For example, suppose you blow through a straw into a test tube containing limewater. ● If you can, try this and see how the limewater turns milky. ▲ After a short time, a white solid substance will settle to the bottom of the tube. ❸ What does this tell you about your breath? Examine the equation above. ■

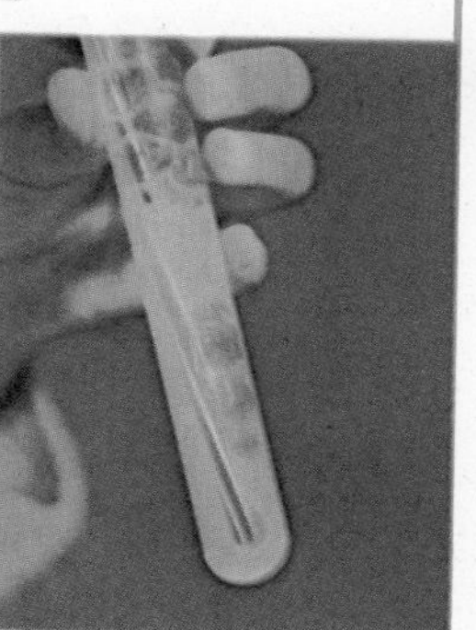

139

VERIFYING PROGRESS

In methods of intelligence

Children can *design an investigation* to *demonstrate* that green plants give off carbon dioxide gas during the night or when no light is present. (They should suggest placing a small, actively growing green plant into a sealed jar and leaving it in a dark room overnight. Then the plant should be removed and the contents of the air in the jar tested immediately by pouring limewater into the jar, covering the jar, and shaking it to mix the limewater with the air. If the limewater turns slightly milky, it will show that the plant gave off carbon dioxide in the dark.)

Useful materials: Vinegar, glass or jar, rock samples, seashells, test tubes, straws, limewater.

❶ Children may want to pour vinegar over various rock samples and bits of seashells to see if carbon dioxide gas is produced. (Be sure they do this in a glass or jar.)

Why do you think seashells and certain rocks are made of the same substance—calcium carbonate? (These rocks were formed in layers under the sea and are partially or wholly made up of seashells.)

❷ Let children try blowing into limewater, as illustrated. To prevent spills, use only a small amount of limewater—to a depth of about $\frac{1}{2}$ inch in a large test tube.

❸ When the limewater you breathe into turns milky, it tells you that the breath you exhale must contain carbon dioxide gas.

Unit Concept-Statement: In chemical or physical change the total amount of matter remains unchanged.

VERIFYING PROGRESS

In concept-seeking

Testing Dry Ice in water. Let children test the mixture of Dry Ice and water with red and blue litmus paper. What happens? (Blue litmus turns pink and pink litmus stays pink.) What do you conclude from this observation? (The solution of carbon dioxide and water is an acid and not a base.)

1 BEFORE YOU GO ON

A. Check your understanding of the concepts of this section. Which ending would you choose for each statement below?

1. A common compound of carbon that is a gas and is found in air is
a. carbon dioxide
b. calcium carbonate

2. When carbon dioxide is bubbled through limewater, the limewater
a. turns milky b. remains clear

3. Carbon dioxide + calcium hydroxide ⟶
a. calcium carbonate + water
b. limewater

4. The statement that fits the main concept of this section is
a. The presence of a substance can be determined by adding calcium carbonate.
b. The presence of a substance can be determined by a chemical test.

B. Write a short paragraph or two on this topic: "A Test for Carbon Dioxide."

2 USING WHAT YOU KNOW

Soda water (such as is put in soft drinks and ice cream sodas) has a gas dissolved in it. When soda water is poured into a glass, bubbles of the gas appear.

One boy took a little plain soda water and added it to limewater. A milky white substance formed. What compound must have been present? How do you know?

3 INVESTIGATING FURTHER

With your teacher's help and a pair of tongs, put a small piece of Dry Ice in a glass of water. *Do not touch the Dry Ice with your hands. It can freeze the tips of your fingers.*

What happens?

Test the gas with (1) litmus paper and (2) limewater.

A LOOK AHEAD

The limewater test is not your first experience with testing a compound. You did several tests to find out whether compounds were acids or bases. Chemical tests are very important because they help the scientist be accurate.

You have been studying a few of the Earth's numerous elements and compounds. Let's look next at the Earth as a chemist might see it. What are the main elements and compounds the chemist finds in and on the Earth?

140

VERIFYING PROGRESS

1 Before you go on. Children *demonstrate* understanding of chemical testing for carbon dioxide gas by identifying suitable responses to questions.
1. a 2. a 3. a 4. b

2 Using what you know. Children *analyze* a situation and *infer* the identity of a substance (carbon dioxide).

3 Investigating further. Children *observe* the results of placing Dry Ice in water and *perform chemical tests* to *identify* substances that form. A gas (carbon dioxide) bubbles through the water. To collect the gas for testing, children may place another piece of Dry Ice in water in a gas generator (page 126 of child's text). (1) Moist blue litmus turns pink, indicating the presence of carbonic acid, which forms when carbon dioxide reacts with water. (2) Limewater turns milky.

Supporting Statement: The Earth's matter is built up of atoms combined in many ways.

❶ 5. A Chemist's View of the Earth

By careful testing, the chemist has found out what elements and compounds are in the Earth's crust. He knows what elements and compounds are in the waters of lakes, rivers, and oceans. He knows the elements and compounds in the atmosphere. ■ His knowledge has come from the hard work of many scientists, from many years of work, and from many careful tests.

See if you can answer these questions, using the information in the table below.

❷ Which element is most common in the Earth's crust? in the waters? in the air?

❸ Which element is more common in the crust, aluminum or iron?

Oxygen is a gas. What element that is *not* a gas makes ❹ up more than 25 pounds of 100 pounds of the Earth's crust?

About how many quarts of air must you inhale and exhale to get 1 quart of oxygen and about how many to get ❺ 1 quart of nitrogen?

■

COMMON ELEMENTS IN LAND, WATER, AND AIR

Elements in 100 pounds of the Earth's crust		Elements in 100 pounds of the Earth's waters		Elements in 100 quarts of the Earth's air	
oxygen	46.7 pounds	oxygen	85.0 pounds	nitrogen	78 quarts
silicon	27.7 pounds	hydrogen	10.7 pounds	oxygen	21 quarts
aluminum	8.1 pounds	chlorine	2.1 pounds	argon	0.94 quart
iron	5.0 pounds	sodium	1.2 pounds	neon	0.02 quart
calcium	3.7 pounds	magnesium	0.14 pound	other gases	0.04 quart
sodium	2.7 pounds	sulfur	0.09 pound		100.00 quarts
potassium	2.6 pounds	calcium	0.05 pound		
other elements	3.5 pounds	potassium	0.04 pound		
	100.0 pounds	other elements	0.68 pound		
			100.00 pounds		

These figures are averages.

141

LESSON CLUSTER 5
A CHEMIST'S VIEW OF THE EARTH

Teaching background. 5 T-128

Concept-seeking. Children become aware of the most common of Earth's elements and how atoms of elements combine to form compounds.

Operations. Children *probe* into the chemist's view of the Earth's matter.

Methods of intelligence. Children *analyze* and *interpret* information in a table; they *identify* common elements and some of their properties and their compounds.

Useful materials: Objects made of or containing aluminum, carbon, chlorine (salt), copper, hydrogen (water), iron, nitrogen (ammonia), oxygen (water), sulfur, zinc.

Introducing Lesson Cluster 5

❶ What are the things of which this classroom is built? (wood, brick, plaster, stone, steel—depending on your room)

What would a chemist name as the building blocks of the things in this classroom? Children may mention oxygen in the air, and various metals in the classroom. (You might have objects on display that are mentioned among "useful materials.") The chemist's building blocks are atoms or molecules of elements, the parts of substances that can be taken apart or put together to make compounds. Substances like wood or soil are not building blocks because they are mixtures of elements and compounds.

Developing the lesson

❷ One of the important skills of the scientist is the interpretation of data in a table. As you read this page with children, pause continually and aid them in extracting the data. For example, the commonest element in the Earth's crust and in the water is oxygen; the element most common in the air is nitrogen. You may wish to observe that nearly all of the oxygen in the Earth's crust is combined with other substances to form many compounds.

❸ Aluminum is more common than iron in the Earth's crust.

❹ Silicon makes up over 25 of 100 pounds of the Earth's crust. (Most rock, sand, and soil contain some silicon.)

❺ You must inhale approximately 5 quarts of air to get 1 quart of oxygen; you must inhale approximately 1 and $\frac{1}{5}$ quarts of air to get 1 quart of nitrogen.

❶ Substances in the Earth

Nearly half of the Earth's crust is oxygen. Oxygen is a gas. Yet the Earth's crust is a solid. How can we explain this large amount of oxygen in the Earth's crust?

Recall that oxygen combines readily with other elements to form oxides. For instance, iron and oxygen combine to form iron oxide, or rust, which is a solid. Aluminum and oxygen combine to form aluminum oxide, another solid. There is a great deal of silicon dioxide in the crust. In fact, you may have dug shovelfuls of it, for sand is silicon dioxide. ■

Oxygen, you see, is a very *active* substance. That is, it combines readily with other substances. Oxygen is mainly found with other elements, in compounds. You won't find lumps of pure iron or pure aluminum in the crust of the Earth. You will find iron and aluminum compounds, for  most elements have combined with other elements, especially with oxygen.

Substances in the Waters and the Air

Chemists have studied the elements and compounds in the waters of the Earth—the rivers, lakes, and oceans. Here, too, the most common element is oxygen, as the table shows. Indeed, there is almost 6 times as much oxygen as all the other elements in the waters combined.

How is oxygen held in the waters of the oceans and lakes? Most of the oxygen is combined with hydrogen. It makes an oxide of hydrogen—hydrogen oxide. Of course, this compound is better known as water. ❸

Most of the sodium in the oceans is combined with the element chlorine. This makes a compound, sodium chloride, which we have on our dining tables. It is the salt we use to season food.

There are elements and compounds in the air, too. Two elements make up almost all of the air, as the table shows. These elements are nitrogen and oxygen. Most of the nitrogen in the air around us has not combined with any other

142

Continuing Lesson Cluster 5

❶ What are the three forms a substance may take? (solid, liquid, or gas) What are substances composed of? (atoms, or different combinations of atoms) If children say "molecules," ask: What are molecules composed of? (atoms) What is the smallest unit of a substance that has all the properties of a substance? (a molecule) What molecules have different kinds of atoms in them? (water molecule: hydrogen and oxygen; sugar molecule: carbon, hydrogen, and oxygen; carbon dioxide molecule: carbon and oxygen)

What is meant by an element? (An element is a substance whose molecules are made up of only one kind of atom.)

❷ How could you get pure aluminum or pure iron? (by mining and processing aluminum and iron compounds)

❸ What is the chemical formula for water? (H_2O) What does this formula tell us? (Each molecule of water contains two atoms of hydrogen and one of oxygen.)

Direct children to look at the chart on page 141 and continue interpretation of it. How much more oxygen is there than hydrogen in one hundred pounds of water? (about 8 times more oxygen than hydrogen)

Since there are *two* atoms of hydrogen and *one* atom of oxygen in every water molecule, what can you infer about the weight of oxygen? (Oxygen must be much heavier than hydrogen.)

element. Nitrogen is a fairly *inactive* gas; that is, it does not combine easily. There is plenty of oxygen in the air that has not combined with other elements. However, as you
❶ know, oxygen does combine easily. Oxygen is an *active* gas.

We breathe air. Inside our bodies, the oxygen from the air we breathe combines with substances in our food. It is this combination of oxygen and food, taking place in our
❷ bodies, that yields us energy.

Many living things besides ourselves take in oxygen and use it for energy. Water insects, for example, get oxygen from air that has mixed with the water in which they live. One water insect that does this is the water scavenger beetle. ● Another is the nymph (nimf) of the dragonfly. ▲ (A nymph is a young insect just before it becomes an adult.) How is it, then, that all the oxygen in the air was not used
❸ up long ago? Luckily, through the work of green plants, oxygen goes back into the air all the time, as you may know.

●

▲

Our Store of Elements

We have the elements of the Earth all around us. We combine atoms of these elements to make different molecules. We break up molecules to get different elements. Elements are most important, then. What is our store of elements?

There are 90 elements found naturally in the Earth. Scientists have now made 15 new elements in addition to the 90 elements that exist around us. Scientists have found 15 new building blocks to go with the 90 building blocks we have, and they expect to find still more.

Some of the elements are much more common than others. In fact, a very large part of the Earth's crust is made
❹ up of only 7 elements, as the table on page 141 shows: oxygen, silicon, aluminum, iron, calcium, sodium, potassium. And nearly all of the air is made up of only two elements: nitrogen and oxygen.

On the next two pages are listed some of our most important elements, some of their properties, and some uses we make of them.

143

VERIFYING PROGRESS

In methods of intelligence

Encourage children who exhibit interest in the 90 natural elements to *collect, organize* and *report* information from an encyclopedia or high school chemistry textbook. How are these 90 elements grouped? (in families) What do the families have in common? (certain properties) Which are the man-made elements? (neptunium, plutonium, americium, curium, etc.) Which are the radioactive elements? (all the man-made elements, plus uranium, thorium, radium, polonium, etc.) For what practical reason did man start making elements? (partly for new sources of radioactivity) What are some uses for radioactive elements? (medicine, electric power, atomic-powered submarines, etc.)

❶ What examples can we see around us showing that oxygen combines with other elements? (rusting of metals and burning wood, coal, gas, etc.)

❷ How do we know combining oxygen with another substance gives energy? (heat and light from burning) How can we infer that oxygen gives us energy when it combines with foods? (We feel warm; oxygen combines with carbon and hydrogen inside us and we give off carbon dioxide and water.)

❸ Children who have previously learned that plants use up carbon dioxide and give off oxygen during the process in which they make food (photosynthesis) may need to have their memories refreshed. For example, ask: Who knows the process during which plants return oxygen to the air?

❹ What are the 7 main elements found in the Earth's waters? the two main elements found in the Earth's air? (See table on page 141.)

A Dozen Important Elements

❶ 1. *Aluminum* is a silvery-colored metal and very light. Like most metals, it is shiny and can be bent and worked. Aluminum is not found free in the ground. It must be obtained from its compound, aluminum oxide. What do you have at home that is made of aluminum?

2. *Carbon*, like hydrogen, is present in all living things. Carbon is usually black. Soot is mainly carbon. So is coal. A diamond is pure carbon. Do you have any objects made of carbon in your home?

3. *Chlorine* is a green gas. It is poisonous. Yet you eat a compound containing the element chlorine every day. Salt is sodium chloride, a compound made up of the elements sodium and chlorine. When atoms of different elements combine, the compound is often useful. The sea is salty mainly because of sodium chloride.

4. *Copper* is a metal that has a reddish luster. It was one of the first metals that man learned to use. As you know, it can be worked into pots and pans and wire, among other things. ■ Brass contains copper.

5. *Helium* is a colorless and odorless gas. It is lighter than air, like hydrogen gas, but it doesn't burn, as hydrogen does. The same amount of helium weighs twice as much as the same amount of hydrogen. It is the changing of hydrogen into helium that produces energy in the Sun. ●

Continuing Lesson Cluster 5

❶ Encourage children to assemble a display of objects, (or pictures, as from advertisements) made of the elements mentioned on this page. Often, an object will be made mainly from one element but combined with other elements in order to make the objects stronger, more durable, rust resistant, etc.—alloys of metals, for example.

Some objects the children might bring in to represent elements discussed on this page are: an aluminum utensil, a sheet of aluminum foil; a piece of coal, or charcoal, a piece of burned toast (carbon); salt, a box or bottle of household chlorine bleach; copper wire, a copper pot or pan; a helium balloon or picture of the Sun.

❶ 6. *Hydrogen* is another colorless and odorless gas. Hydrogen atoms are an important part of many fuels we use. ▲ Of course, hydrogen is an important part of that very useful compound, water.

7. *Iron* is the most frequently used metal. Iron combined with carbon forms steel. Steel combined with other metals forms substances of useful qualities, such as stainless steel. What things made of iron or steel do you have in your home?

8. *Nitrogen* is a colorless and odorless gas. It makes up about $\frac{4}{5}$ of the air you are breathing. Nitrogen is an important part of the meat, cheese, and fish that we eat. You and all other living things are made up mainly of these 4 elements: carbon, hydrogen, oxygen, and nitrogen.

9. *Oxygen* is still another colorless and odorless gas. Every breath you take is important because you breathe in oxygen. It is perhaps the most important gas for all living things and makes up about $\frac{1}{5}$ of the air. Without oxygen, fuels like gasoline and oil and coal would not burn.

Pure oxygen is often stored in tanks, like this. ◆ Tanks of oxygen have many uses. One of these is in hospitals, where sick people are sometimes placed in an oxygen tent to help them breathe better.

10. *Sulfur*, found as crystals, is not a metal. However, it can combine with many different metals. For example, sulfur can combine with zinc. It forms white zinc sulfide, which is very useful in paints. Sulfur combines so easily with metals that it tarnishes many of them. Silver, for instance, blackens as it combines with gases having sulfur in them. ★

11. *Uranium* is one of the heaviest metals, more than twice as heavy as iron. It is used for producing nuclear energy. You may remember that uranium is radioactive: its atoms break up.

12. *Zinc* is a silver-gray metal. When iron is coated with zinc, the iron is protected against rusting and is called galvanized iron. Zinc is an important part of many dry cells and batteries, in which electricity is produced.

▲

◆

★

❶ Objects for an actual or pictorial display of elements discussed on this page might be: water, hydrogen peroxide, or a picture of a container of hydrogen gas; a roller skate, an iron pot, an *unopened* package of razor blades (steel), pictures of food high in nitrogen content, such as fish, meat, and cheese; some powdered sulfur or a picture of sulfur, an egg (contains sulfur); pictures of uranium samples or of a uranium mine; a piece of zinc galvanized pipe, some zinc paint, etc.

If you live in an area where any of these elements are mined in open pits, see if it is possible to arrange a field trip to the mine.

UNIT THREE

Unit Concept-Statement: In chemical or physical change the total amount of matter remains unchanged.

VERIFYING PROGRESS

In methods of intelligence

Tarnishing of metals. Pass around a piece of tarnished silver. What do you infer has happened from looking at this ______________? (Oxygen has combined with atoms of the metal and formed a new substance which is the discolor or tarnish.)

Models of atoms. Children may look up the structures of some of the elements studied in this section and *make models* representing the structure of their atoms. Materials are fairly firm but flexible wire, modeling clay or Styrofoam balls which may be colored with water paints.

❶ BEFORE YOU GO ON

Check your understanding of the concepts of this section. Which ending would you choose for each statement below?

1. Which of these elements is more common in the Earth's crust?
a. oxygen
b. aluminum

2. Which of these compounds is the more common in the Earth's crust?
a. silicon dioxide
b. calcium oxide

3. Which of these compounds is the more common in the waters?
a. hydrogen oxide
b. carbon dioxide

4. How many elements are there?
a. about 50
b. about 100

5. Which of these elements is needed to make fuels burn?
a. nitrogen
b. oxygen

6. The statement that fits the main concept of this section is
a. The Earth's matter is built up of atoms combined in only a few ways.
b. The Earth's matter is built up of atoms combined in many ways.

❷ USING WHAT YOU KNOW

1. Which of these gases in the air is inactive, oxygen or nitrogen?

2. Is aluminum oxide or sodium chloride more common in sea water?

3. Why are there so many oxides in the Earth's crust?

4. What 7 elements are the most common in the Earth?

❸ INVESTIGATING FURTHER

If you live near the sea, put a pint of sea water in an open dish and let it evaporate. Let a pint of water from the faucet evaporate as well, in another pan.

How much more solid material is there in sea water than in tap water? How can you find out the answer to this question?

A LOOK AHEAD

You have come upon one of the important concepts with which the scientist works. All substances are built up of a few kinds of atoms, combined in many ways. Can you find any object on Earth—a rock, a pillow, a clam shell, a corn plant—that is not? You need not come to a final conclusion. Perhaps there is evidence you have not yet found. In the next section you can find more evidence.

146

VERIFYING PROGRESS

❶ Before you go on. Children *demonstrate* understanding of the makeup of the Earth's matter by *identifying* suitable responses to questions.

1. a 3. a 5. b
2. a 4. b

❷ Using what you know. Children *describe* nitrogen as an inactive gas and sodium chloride as a common compound of sea water; they *explain* the presence of many oxides in the Earth; they *identify* the seven most common elements.

1. Nitrogen gas is inactive in air.
2. Sodium chloride is more common in sea water—this is one of the main salts of the sea. Aluminum oxide is a solid.
3. Oxygen combines readily with many other elements.
4. Oxygen, silicon, aluminum, iron, calcium, sodium, and potassium.

❸ Investigating further. Children *plan an investigation* in which they *measure* and *compare* the amounts of dissolved matter in sea water and tap water.

If children carry out the investigation, be sure they weigh each dish before and after evaporation. Then, by subtraction, they will obtain the weights of the solids left after evaporation.

Supporting Statement: In ordinary chemical reactions, matter is neither gained nor lost.

6. More Weight or Less

❶ Put some steel wool in a quart jar. The jar already has air in it, of course, and air contains oxygen. Two elements, iron and oxygen, begin a chemical reaction in the jar.

Add a few drops of water to help the reaction go faster. Cap the jar tightly. Rust—iron oxide—is forming. You have seen this reaction before.

However, there is something here that you may not have noticed. There is an interesting problem. As iron and oxygen combine, does the weight inside the jar change? What is your hypothesis?

Does the Weight Change?

Of course, you may make an inference from what you already know. After all, a hypothesis is based on what we know. In the end, however, we use an investigation to test the hypothesis and any inference.

❷ A good balance can give us some evidence. ■ On one side is the closed jar of steel wool and moist air. On the other side are weights that balance the weight of the jar.

147

LESSON CLUSTER 6
MORE WEIGHT OR LESS

Teaching background. 6 T-128

Concept-seeking. Children become aware that when oxygen and iron combine to form iron oxide there is no change in the total weight of the combining substances.

Operations. Children *probe* into whether matter changes in total weight when a given amount of one substance combines with a given amount of another substance.

Methods of intelligence. Children *hypothesize* whether a jar in which iron and oxygen are sealed will change in weight when the oxygen and iron combine to form rust; they *observe* that rusting has no effect when the jar is balanced with a set of weights on an equal arm balance, and *infer* that there is no change in total weight.

Useful materials: Construction paper, postage or food scale, platform balance, weights, steel wool, jar with screw top, water.

Introducing Lesson Cluster 6

In a physical change is matter either lost or gained? Encourage hypothesis. Then hold up a large piece of tagboard or construction paper. Let a child place it on a postage or food scale, and record the weight of the paper on the chalk board. Now ask another child to "physically change the paper". (He should tear the paper into pieces.) What do you think the paper will now weigh—more, less, the same? Encourage predictions, and let the predictions be tested. What do you observe?

How could you make the piece of paper undergo a chemical change? (burn it) If you could weigh *all* the substances that took part in the burning, do you think the total weight of these substances would be more, less, or the same? Accept hypotheses without comment.

Developing the lesson

❶ Since we can't capture all the gases of burning, let's combine oxygen with iron again. Present the steel wool and the jar. If we place the wool inside the jar and cap it, what will be in the jar? (air and steel wool) Can anything get in or out? (no)

If the steel wool rusts, how can we test your hypothesis about change of weight when oxygen combines with something else? Let the children study the photograph before responding.

❷ Now let several volunteers set up the test. Any equal arm or postal balance can be used and any size of jar with a screw top. After the jar is balanced, leave it undisturbed for two or three days, or until rust formation is visible.

Unit Concept-Statement: In chemical or physical change the total amount of matter remains unchanged.

VERIFYING PROGRESS

In methods of intelligence

Children can evaluate progress by *analyzing* and *explaining* an everyday situation. How is it that a grown man may have to carry in the log for a fireplace, but a child can carry out the ashes? Has matter been lost? (No; oxygen from the air has combined with hydrogen and carbon in the log to form water vapor and carbon dioxide.)

❶ What will happen if the jar gets heavier? The leveled balance will tilt, as the jar pulls it down, of course.

If the jar gets lighter, the balance will tilt the other way as the jar moves up.

The jar is left standing on this balance for several days. Rust forms. Does the balance tilt? ■

You can see that the balance shows no change of weight. Chemists have found, by many experiments with the best balances, that the weight does not change. Chemists have found that when the elements iron and oxygen combine,

the weight of the iron + the weight of the oxygen
= the weight of the iron oxide

The iron and the oxygen do form a new substance, the ❷ compound iron oxide. But the oxide has exactly the same weight as the iron and oxygen that combined. ■

No matter is added, no matter is lost, as iron and oxygen become iron oxide. The same thing is true for all the ordinary chemical reactions that go on around us every day. *In a chemical reaction, matter is neither gained* ❸ *nor lost.* The atoms change places.

■

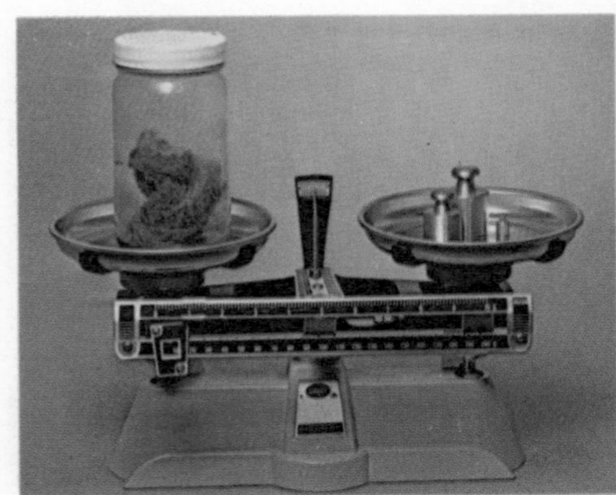

148

Continuing Lesson Cluster 6

❶ Since several days must elapse, let the children reason from the text and later verify their reasoning. Have each child record his hypothesis as to which way the balance will tilt.

❷ Has the steel wool in the jar lost or gained weight? (gained) Explain. (Atoms of oxygen from the air have been added to atoms of iron in the steel wool.) Has the air in the jar lost or gained weight? (lost) Explain. (The air has given up atoms of oxygen to the steel wool.) Why do we say then that no weight was lost or gained? (Since nothing could get in or out, oxygen must have lost the weight that iron gained. The weight of all the atoms in the jar has not changed.)

If we had left the steel wool to rust in an open dish, what result would we have obtained? (Steel wool would gain weight.) What would we not have been able to measure? (the weight of oxygen lost by the air around the steel wool)

❸ Chemists have found that the products of chemical changes always weigh the same as the substances taking part in the reaction. Candles, wood, and many other things that burn contain the elements carbon and hydrogen. Write on the board:

hydrogen + oxygen → water

carbon + oxygen → carbon dioxide

When a candle burns, is matter lost? (no) What happens to it? (Oxygen in the air combines with hydrogen and carbon in the candle to form water vapor and carbon dioxide.)

Unit Concept-Statement: In chemical or physical change the total amount of matter remains unchanged.

❶ **BEFORE YOU GO ON**

The main concept of this section is in the answer to this question: In ordinary chemical reactions, is matter gained or lost? Explain your answer.

❷ **USING WHAT YOU KNOW**

1. The elements iron and sulfur can combine to form a compound, iron sulfide. Suppose that 56 pounds of iron and 32 pounds of sulfur are used. How much iron sulfide is formed?

2. You know this reaction:

iron + oxygen ⟶ iron oxide

Suppose that 72 pounds of iron oxide were made and 16 pounds of oxygen were used to make it. Then

iron + oxygen ⟶ iron oxide
? + 16 pounds ⟶ 72 pounds

How much iron was used?

3. water ⟶ hydrogen + oxygen
Suppose 72 pounds of water are broken down. How many pounds of oxygen are formed?

7. The Main Concept Likenesses Within the Earth

FOCUS ON THE CONCEPT

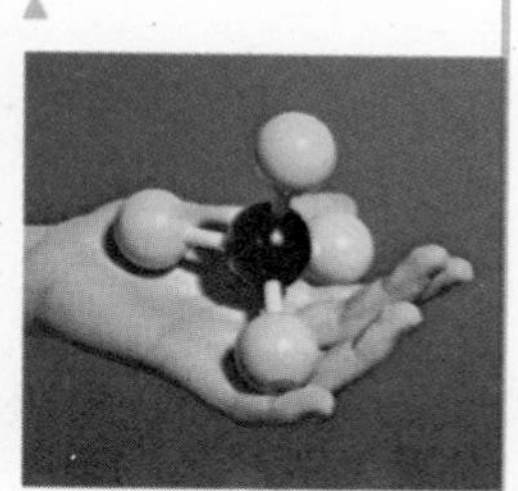

Different scientists look at the world in different ways. A geologist, for instance, looks at the Earth as a planet. ● The geologist's world is big. He can climb and walk over the things he studies.

The chemist has another way of looking at the world. The chemist studies things so small that they can't be seen. ❸ He works with atoms and molecules. ▲

He combines elements into compounds and breaks down compounds into elements. A compound is made up of at least two different elements. By breaking down compounds and building them up, the chemist tries to find out what the world is made of.

A chemical reaction means that substances have changed. The kind of change which takes place in a chemical reaction is called a **chemical change**. For example, iron combining with oxygen to form iron oxide is a chemical change. Iron oxide is a new substance, with different properties from the iron and the oxygen from which it is formed.

149

LESSON CLUSTER 7
THE MAIN CONCEPT: LIKENESSES WITHIN THE EARTH

Teaching background. 7 T-126–T-129

Concept-seeking. Children increase awareness that in physical and chemical changes matter is neither gained nor lost.

Methods of intelligence. Children *compare* physical and chemical change; they *conclude* that all matter is made up of atoms and molecules, and that no atoms are either gained or lost in physical and chemical changes.

VERIFYING PROGRESS

❶ **Before you go on.** Children *demonstrate* understanding of the concept of the conservation of matter by *explaining* a statement of it.

Matter is neither gained nor lost, because the number of atoms that take part in the reaction is the same as the number in the product. A loss in one substance may result in a gain in another, but the total remains unchanged.

❷ **Using what you know.** Children *analyze* problems based on chemical reactions and *compute* solutions to the problems by *applying* the concept of conservation of matter.

1. 88 pounds 2. 56 pounds

3. Unless children are given the information that 8 pounds of hydrogen are formed, they cannot compute the amount of oxygen formed (which will be 64 pounds).

Introducing Lesson Cluster 7

Call attention to the two photographs. What does each represent? (Earth, molecule) How are both alike? (made up of atoms) How are they different? (size) What are the kinds of substances in the Earth called that are made up of atoms? (elements and compounds) Which of these does the Earth mainly consist of? (compounds)

Developing the lesson

❸ Is the picture at the bottom a model of an atom or a molecule? (molecule) Why? (two kinds of atoms)

The yellow ball represents a hydrogen atom and the black ball a carbon atom. The model represents a molecule of methane gas having the formula CH_4.

❶ In a **physical change**, only the form of the substance changes. For example, ice changing to water is a physical change. Only the form of the water has changed—from solid to liquid. Tear up a piece of paper and you have made a physical change in the paper. Burn the paper, on the other hand, and new chemical compounds form; a chemical change is taking place.

Whatever the chemical change may be, one theory seems to explain what happens in many places and at many times, all over the Earth. The theory explains one of the hidden likenesses in all things on the Earth. Elements combine. Compounds break down. Whatever happens, the amount of matter put into a chemical reaction is the ❷ amount that comes out. We come, then, to a clearer understanding of this concept of **matter:**

Whenever there is chemical change, matter is neither gained nor lost.

FOCUS ON THE SCIENTIST'S WAYS

❸ What do you do when something new interests you? Suppose, for instance, you want to find out about a strange bird you have seen, or some unusual object in the sky. Perhaps you are interested in some object suggested by one of the investigations or searches in this book.

If you want to investigate the way a scientist would, you will begin with what you know and what others know. You will look into what is known by reading, and, if you can, by asking questions from experts in the field. You may find what you are searching for. But you may not. You may be trying to find out something that is unknown. What then?

On the next page is a model of one way scientists search into the unknown. Perhaps you can use the model, or parts of it, as the basis for some of your own searches. The model is built after one that was first prepared by James Bryant Conant, a scientist whose special field is chemistry. In his book *On Understanding Science,* Dr. Conant wrote about the way in which scientists do their work.

150

Continuing Lesson Cluster 7

❶ Have a child sharpen a pencil and empty the shavings into an aluminum pie tin. What kind of change has taken place? (*physical change*) Light a match to the shavings. What change? (*chemical change*). How did the changes differ? (Pencil sharpener merely changed the wood and pencil lead to smaller pieces. Burning changed wood to new substances—ashes and gases.)

How are the changes alike? (The amount of matter has stayed the same.) Explain. (The pencil shavings would weigh the same as the original wood and pencil lead. The ashes of the burned shavings, plus the oxygen with which they combined and the gases given off, would weigh the same as the unburned shavings plus the oxygen in the air.)

❷ Suppose a bridge gains 8 pounds of rust. How much would the bridge gain in weight and how much would the oxygen from the air around the bridge lose in weight? (8 pounds) Is this a physical change or a chemical change? (chemical) Explain. (A new substance, rust, is formed.)

❸ Imagine you have found a rock with a gold color. How would you find out if it contains gold, or "fool's gold", or neither? (Children may mention investigating, consulting a book, talking to an expert, comparing the rock with a display in a museum, etc.) Children are now primed for reading the remainder of this page and examining the diagram on page 151.

Unit Concept-Statement: In chemical or physical change the total amount of matter remains unchanged.

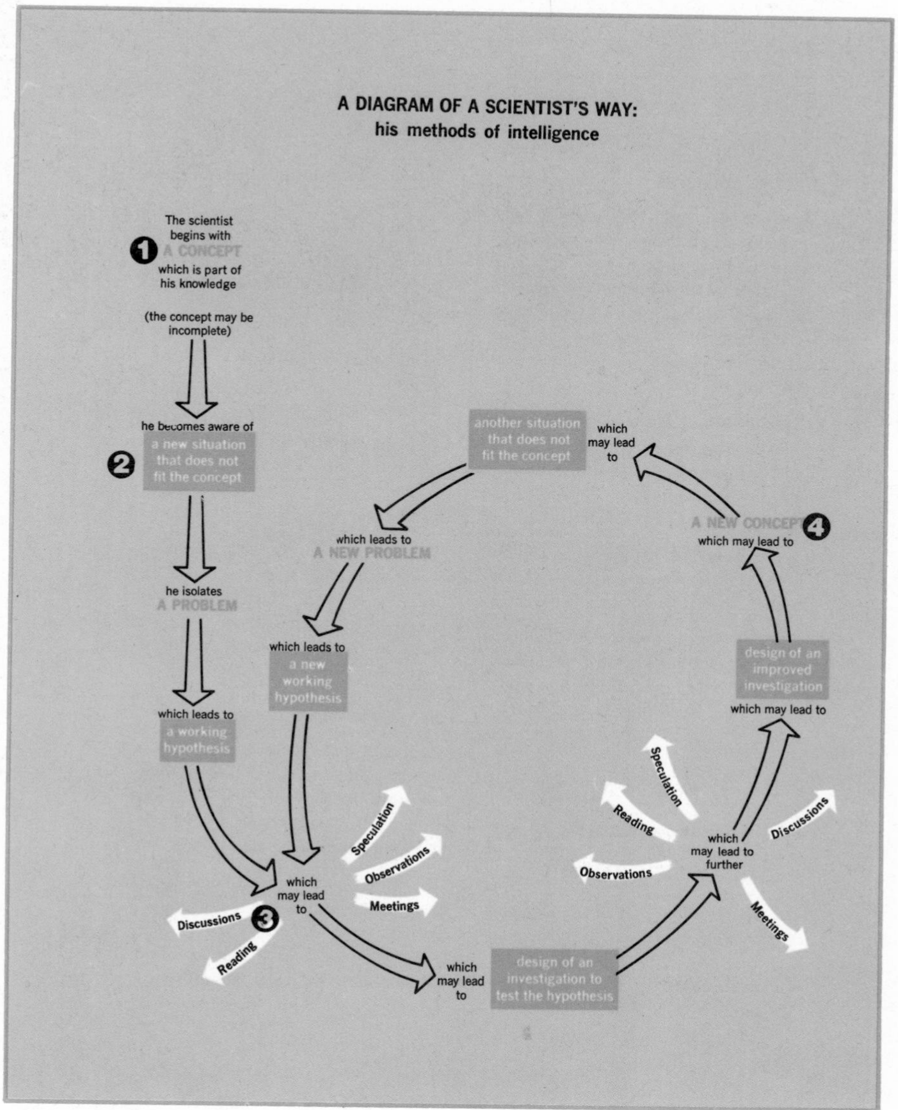
A DIAGRAM OF A SCIENTIST'S WAY:
his methods of intelligence
The scientist begins with
1
A CONCEPT
which is part of his knowledge
(the concept may be incomplete)
he becomes aware of
2
a new situation that does not fit the concept
he isolates
A PROBLEM
which leads to
a working hypothesis
which may lead to
3
Discussions
Reading
Speculation
Observations
Meetings
which may lead to
design of an investigation to test the hypothesis
which may lead to further
Speculation
Reading
Observations
Discussions
Meetings
design of an improved investigation
which may lead to
A NEW CONCEPT
4
which may lead to
another situation that does not fit the concept
which may lead to
which leads to
A NEW PROBLEM
which leads to
a new working hypothesis

❶ To help children read the diagram, you might ask them to give examples from the unit just studied. **What is an example of a concept with which a scientist might begin?** (Whenever there is a chemical change, matter is neither gained nor lost.)

❷ Encourage children to think of possible situations that do not seem to fit the concept of the conservation of matter. One might be that the weight of a rusted iron nail might be more than that of the unrusted nail. Explain that at one time this could have been a real problem, which scientists solved—by learning how to account for the extra weight as that of oxygen from the air—in ways indicated in the diagram.

❸ **Why are discussions, readings, and meetings necessary?** (Children may mention pooling of knowledge by experts in the field and comparing knowledge with experts in different fields, to make sure the solution to the problem is not already known or partially known.) **Why are observations and speculations necessary?** (to help get ideas for the designing and carrying out investigations)

❹ **Does a scientist's work ever seem to end once he has started?** (no) Children should see that the step in the diagram marked "A New Concept" starts the process all over again.

UNIT THREE

Unit Concept-Statement: In chemical or physical change the total amount of matter remains unchanged.

Focusing on the Main Concepts

1 TESTING YOURSELF

A. Test your understanding of important concepts in this unit by answering these questions.

1. Ammonia is a compound made up of the elements nitrogen and hydrogen. Is the molecule of ammonia larger or smaller than either of the atoms that make it up?

2. Substance X is tested with pink and blue litmus. The pink litmus remains pink. However, blue litmus is turned pink by the substance. To what class of substances does X belong?

3. One pound of water is broken down into hydrogen and oxygen. What must the two elements together weigh?

4. The element iron can be combined with oxygen. Suppose that one pound of iron is used. Would the iron oxide weigh more or less than one pound? Why?

B. Test your knowledge with this quick check.

1. On this planet Earth, the number of elements is about

a. 25 b. 50 c. 75 d. 100

2. The smallest part of a compound that has the properties of the compound is

a. an element c. a molecule
b. an atom d. a substance

3. Scientists classify a solution that turns pink litmus blue as

a. acid c. oxide
b. base d. solid

4. In an ordinary chemical reaction, matter is

a. lost
b. almost all destroyed
c. gained
d. neither gained nor lost

5. In the Earth's crust, the compounds found in the greatest amount are

a. acids c. oxides
b. bases d. gases

6. The statement that fits the main concept of this unit is

a. In a chemical change, matter is either gained or lost.
b. In a chemical change, matter is neither gained nor lost.

FOR YOUR READING

1. *Atoms and Molecules,* by Irving and Ruth Adler, published by John Day, New York, 1966. From this book, you will find out more about what scientists think atoms and their parts are like.

2. *The Chemistry of a Lemon,* by A. Harris Stone, published by Prentice-Hall, Englewood Cliffs, New Jersey, 1966. With the help of this book, you will be able to do many interesting investigations on your own. You will

152

VERIFYING PROGRESS

1 Testing yourself. A. Children *analyze* situations and *apply* the concept of the conservation of matter and *explain* the result of a chemical test.
1. larger
2. acids
3. one pound
4. more, because the weight of the oxygen is added to the weight of the iron

B. Children *demonstrate* their understanding of concepts of the unit by *identifying* correct endings to statements.
1. d 3. b 5. c
2. c 4. d 6. b

discover how important it is to repeat your investigations, to keep good records, and to carry out many of the other methods of scientists.

3. *Let's Meet the Chemist,* by Carla Greene, published by Harvey House, Irvington-on-Hudson, New York, 1966. This book explains how an understanding of atoms and molecules helps us get better health, food, and clothing, and helps us in many other ways.

4. *Crystals From the Sea: A Look At Salt,* by A. Harris Stone, published by Prentice-Hall, Englewood Cliffs, New Jersey, 1969. There are many investigations using salt in this book.

5. *Ask Me a Question About the Atom,* by Sam Rosenfeld, published by Harvey House, New York, 1969. The author answers many questions you might ask about molecules, atoms, atomic weights, and chemical elements.

❶ INVESTIGATING FURTHER

1. Keep a notebook titled "New Work in Science." Scientists are at work adding to knowledge. Their work is often reported in newspapers, in magazines, and on television. Watch for new developments and discoveries. Record them in your notebook. For instance, has element 106 been discovered? If so, who discovered it, and what properties does it have?

A notebook of this kind can be very useful for keeping you up-to-date in science. You may want to share your notebook with your classmates.

2. As soon as you open a bottle of soda pop, the soda pop bubbles. Do these bubbles remind you of any of the results in the investigations in this unit? Can you think of a way of testing whether these bubbles are carbon dioxide gas?

Some other substances used in the household also give off bubbles. For instance, sodium bicarbonate gives off bubbles when you add vinegar to it. Some of the tablets used for headaches give off bubbles when mixed with water.

In each case above, are the bubbles being given off carbon dioxide gas or some other gas? What do you think? Why do you think so? How can you find out if you are right?

153

VERIFYING PROGRESS

In methods of intelligence

Give children a box of colored beads (or a molecular model kit, if you have one) and ask them to *demonstrate* their ability to *construct models* of elements and compounds. Let one bead stand for an atom. Ask children to pick from the box materials to assemble a molecule of oxygen, O_2. (Children should pick out two beads of the same color and shape.) Is oxygen an element or a compound? (element) How does your model illustrate your response? (consists of two atoms that are alike)

Next ask children to assemble a water molecule, H_2O. (They should use one bead from the oxygen model, and add two new matching ones for the two hydrogen atoms.) Is water an element or a compound? (compound) What is the difference between an element and a compound? (In an element the atoms are all the same kind. In a compound there are atoms of more than one kind.)

❶ **Investigating further.** Children *analyze, record,* and *report* information on current work in science; they *design an investigation* into the production of carbon dioxide from common substances, and *explain* their observations and inferences.

1. Children may look in recent editions of encyclopedias, world almanacs, and higher level science textbooks.

2. When vinegar was poured over substances containing calcium carbonate, bubbles were given off. When tested with limewater, the bubbles proved to be carbon dioxide gas. To test the bubbles in soda pop children should mix soda pop with limewater. When the mixture turns milky, they may conclude that the bubbles in soda pop are carbon dioxide gas. They can use limewater test on other substances, as well.

UNIT FOUR

THE EARTH AND THE STARS—HIDDEN LIKENESSES

Basic behaviors sought: Children become aware of how a telescope operates and how it increases our knowledge of bodies in space. They *observe* that light from space can be recorded on camera film.

Children *investigate* the reflection of light by mirrors and *infer* that light travels in a straight path. They *demonstrate* that a prism separates white light into a spectrum of colors and *hypothesize* that invisible radiations exist at each end of the spectrum.

Children *analyze* the characteristics of light waves and explain certain phenomena as due to wave motion. They *distinguish* between wavelengths of waves vibrating at different rates. They *apply* the wave theory to *explain* the formation of the spectrum.

Children *compare* properties of light and *construct a theory* that light behaves sometimes as waves and sometimes as particles. They *investigate* the spectra of some substances and *infer* that the composition of a star can be learned from its spectrum.

Children *analyze* how distances can be measured in light-years. Finally, they *synthesize* the knowledge they have acquired about light and *infer an order* in the Universe.

A VIEW OF THE UNIT

Objects around us are visible when they reflect light. Light travels out from a source at a constant speed in straight lines. The direction of travel can be changed by lenses and prisms which refract light and by surfaces that reflect light.

White light is composed of radiations of many wavelengths all traveling at the same constant speed. A beam of light travels at approximately 186,000 miles per second. As light passes at an angle from one medium to another, the different wavelengths are bent, or deflected, by different amounts so that a beam of white light spreads out into a spectrum of different colors, each color characteristic for the wavelength. The spectrum also includes infrared and ultraviolet radiations, which are invisible to the human eye. In any medium, the speed of light remains constant throughout the medium.

Several explanations or models of the behavior of light have been proposed. The wave model helps to explain how a prism can form a continuous spectrum. The fact that light can be polarized, as in certain types of sunglasses, supports the wave model.

Since the speed of light is constant, light rays having different wavelengths will have different frequencies. The frequency of a light wave is the number of wavelengths per second that pass any point. The photoelectric effect is observed when certain metals are exposed to certain frequencies of light. This characteristic is utilized in the photographer's light meter and in the automatic opening of doors in supermarkets and other places. The emission of electrons by atoms of these metals can be explained only by a particle model of light. Each model explains one of two aspects of the behavior of light. The particle model indicates that light consists of tiny bundles of energy, called photons, and explains certain phenomena. The wave model indicates that light travels in a wavelike manner and explains other phenomena. The quantity of energy a photon has depends on the wavelength of the light.

An element in the gaseous state that has been made incandescent in the laboratory produces a bright-line, or emission spectrum, consisting of colored lines. The lines in an emission spectrum correspond to the wavelengths of light emitted by the incandescent element. The Sun and the stars yield a dark-line, or absorption spectrum, which shows dark lines against a continuous spectrum. When dark-line spectra of elements are produced by laboratory analysis, the positions of some lines are found to be identical with the dark line spectra from stars, and this leads to identification of the elements in bodies in space.

The distances between bodies in space are so great that many scientists use a special unit, the light-year, which is derived from units of speed and time. The units are the speed of light, 186,000 miles per second, and the time unit of one year. A light-year is the distance light travels in one year.

1 Telescopes and light

Lenses change the direction of light by refraction. Refraction occurs whenever light passes from one medium into another. As an example, light from the Sun at sunrise or sunset is bent, or refracted, as it passes from space into the atmosphere, and we see the Sun higher than it really is.

Similarly if you stand on the bank of a stream, you will see a fish not where it actually is, but higher in the water.

Telescopes collect light from distant objects, and allow scientists to study the light. The collecting lens may be a convex lens, that is, thicker at the center than it is toward the edges, and thus all the rays converge at one point, the focus. The lens refracts or bends the light rays.

A refracting telescope has an objective lens that gathers light. This lens refracts the light and concentrates it as a small, inverted image at the focal point. An inverted image is upside down and reversed from side to side. An eyepiece lens in the telescope magnifies the image.

The direction of light can also be changed by reflection. We see ourselves in a mirror because light from us is reflected from its shiny surface to our eyes. Reflection depends on the characteristics of the surface. If a ray of light hits a highly polished flat surface at an angle to the left of an imaginary line drawn perpendicular to the surface, the ray will be reflected to the right of the perpendicular at an equal angle. All the rays that strike the surface at this angle will be reflected in the same direction. If rays of light strike a rough surface, each ray will be reflected at a different angle. This difference in the way smooth and rough surfaces reflect light accounts for the way these surfaces appear when we look at them.

The Hale telescope at Mt. Palomar is a reflecting telescope. Light from a distant object is collected by a curved mirror that focuses the light to form an image of the object. This image is reflected by a small flat mirror to the eyepiece which magnifies the image. A camera can be attached to the eyepiece and the image recorded on film.

Light that reaches the eye passes through the lens of the eye and is focused as a small, inverted image on the retina. The brain interprets the image as right side up. When objects at different distances from the eye are viewed, muscles change the shape of the lens to focus the objects clearly. Irregularities in the eye may cause the lens to focus the image behind the retina, causing farsightedness, or in front of the retina, causing nearsightedness. Eyeglasses refract light so that the lens forms the image at the retina.

2 The spectrum

Light moves out in straight lines and in all directions from a source: the Sun, a burning candle, and a light bulb are light sources. We see the objects around us and some objects in space because they reflect the light emanating from a source. Moonlight is actually light from the Sun that is reflected by the Moon. The Moon emits no light of its own.

Because light travels in straight lines, we can see only what is in a direct line with our eyes. We can't see a man walking toward us around the corner of a building, even though we can hear him walking. But because objects reflect light, we can place a mirror that reflects light so that we can see around a corner. A periscope is a special device that changes the path of light by reflecting it twice. The light from an object first hits a mirror tilted at a 45° angle. Then that mirror reflects the light to a second mirror which is also at a 45° angle. The beam of light that is seen is parallel to the beam from the light source but displaced by the distance between the two mirrors.

If light from the Sun, called white light, is passed through a prism, it is seen as a band of colors. This continuous spectrum ranges from red to violet in a certain order: red, orange, yellow, green, blue, violet. White light is made up of radiations of different wavelengths that give rise to the colors of the visible spectrum. It also consists of radiations of other wavelengths that fall outside the visible range. Light that has a short wavelength has high frequency; that is, more waves pass a point in one second than if the waves were longer. Light that has a long wavelength has a lower frequency. The next section will discuss wavelength in more detail. Infrared radiation appears beyond red at one end of the spectrum, and ultraviolet appears beyond violet at the other end. The human eye cannot see either of these radiations.

The light from a glowing tungsten wire in an electric light bulb yields a continuous spectrum. This spectrum also includes visible and invisible radiations.

A spectrum is formed by the refraction of light. As white light enters a prism, it is slowed down. The speed of light is less in a material medium than in space, and differs in different mediums. The speed of light in air is approximately 186,000 miles per second and its speed in water at room temperature is 140,000 miles per second. However, the speed in each medium remains constant for the medium. Light is unchanged, except for its speed; if it passes from one medium to another at an angle, the rays of light are deflected and spread out, and may form a spectrum.

Violet light has a higher frequency than any other color with the result that it is bent more than light of other wavelengths. The reverse is true for red, at the other end of the spectrum. It has a lower frequency than light of other wavelengths and thus it is bent the least. The higher the frequency, the greater the bending of light rays.

3 Light as waves

A study of light will reveal several properties. Light travels in straight lines at a constant speed (approximately 186,000 miles/second). Light is a form of energy. As a form of energy, it can be transformed into other forms of energy, such as chemical energy and heat. Yet the exact nature of light is still not completely understood. Several theories have been proposed to explain light phenomena. About 300 years ago, Christian Huygens described light as a wave motion. Energy can be transmitted along a wave; waves set up in the sea can rock boats at great distances from the source of the disturbance. The wave model would explain how light is broken up by a prism into a spectrum. The colors of the spectrum represent different wavelengths of light. Wavelength is the distance from one point on one wave to a corresponding point on another, usually measured from crest to crest. The wavelengths of radiation in the visible spectrum range from 1/30,000 of an inch for red to 1/65,000 of an inch for violet. A beam of white light travels through air at a constant speed of about 186,000 miles/second. The frequency of each color in the spectrum differs, however. For example, if in a given period of time, 30,000 waves of red light pass a certain point, in the same period of time, 65,000 waves of violet light will pass the point. The relationship, which holds true also for sound waves, is as follows:

$$\text{speed} = \text{wavelength} \times \text{frequency}$$

The shorter the wavelength the higher the frequency; the longer the wavelength the lower the frequency.

Polarized light, a phenomenon that supports the wave theory, can be illustrated as follows. A rope is tied to a support at one end and waves are sent along the rope. The waves must pass through narrow slits in two boxes. If the slits are positioned identically, the waves pass through them. When one box is turned on its side, the wave is stopped. A similar effect can be seen with light. Several types of crystals have atoms so arranged that they act like slits. If transparent film is treated with these crystals, a polarizer or polarizing film is produced. Light will pass through one polarizer, but if a second polarizer is rotated through 90 degrees, the light waves cannot go through. Polaroid glasses take advantage of this effect to reduce the glare on a sunny day.

The color of a transparent object is the color of the wavelength of light that it transmits. A green glass, for example, allows the wavelength of green light through, but absorbs the others. The color of an opaque object is the wavelength or combination of wavelengths of the light it reflects; all the other wavelengths are absorbed. A green dress, for example, absorbs all colors except green, which it reflects.

Color blindness occurs when certain cells on the retina of the eye do not function properly. People who are color-blind have difficulty distinguishing between certain colors, for example between red and green or between blue and green.

4 Light as particles

Isaac Newton proposed that light is a stream of very tiny particles moving in all directions at great speeds. Particles of different sizes produce different colors. These moving particles would have energy of motion much as the droplets in a stream of water. Some aspects of the behavior of light support the particle theory. When light strikes certain metals, electrons are given off. The flow of current in response to light is called the photoelectric effect. Like the electrons in any electric current, these electrons can be made to do work. The door of a supermarket may be operated by an "electric eye." A beam of light shines across the door, onto a tube which contains the light-sensitive metal. The tube is connected to an electric circuit. While the light is on, electrons are given off by the metal, and an electric current flows through the circuit. When a person stands in front of the light, the flow of electrons is stopped, and the circuit is broken. This activates a mechanical device which opens the door.

The wave model of light doesn't explain how the photoelectric effect takes place. The energy of a wave is spread out over a large area. Coming into contact with an atom, it wouldn't have enough energy at the point of contact to cause the removal of an electron. If light were composed of a stream of particles, a single particle would have the necessary energy.

Since both the wave explanation and the particle explanation are needed to describe the different ways in which light behaves, scientists have accepted them both. At present, they believe that light exists in small, indivisible "packages" of energy called photons. Photons have different amounts of energy depending on the wavelength of the light. Photons in light of long wavelength (red) have less energy than photons in light of short wavelength (violet).

The visible spectrum comprises only a very small part of the entire electromagnetic spectrum. Beyond ultraviolet, there are several forms of radiation with extremely short wavelengths. Cosmic radiation consists of proton showers from space. This type of radiation has the shortest wavelength. Gamma radiation, with wavelengths of about 10^{-11} cm, is given off by radioactive atoms during decay. X rays have a wavelength of about 10^{-8} cm. They are produced in the laboratory by heating a filament with an electric current; the electrons that are given off hit a metal target which gives off energy in the form of X rays. This radiation is familiar as a diagnostic tool. X rays pass easily through flesh and show bones and metal as white, unexposed areas on film.

At the other end of the spectrum, radio waves have wavelengths longer than infrared. The shortest radio waves are used in radar devices. Television programs are transmitted from the broadcasting studio to individual antennas by longer waves, and the longest waves carry radio broadcasts. Some radio waves have wavelengths of several miles.

5 Spectra from the stars

Some elements produce characteristic colors in a flame when their compounds are heated. A spectroscope is used to identify elements more accurately. The spectroscope is essentially a slit and a prism with two lens. Rays of light that pass through the slit are gathered by the first lens, and then pass through the prism. The second lens focuses the light of each wavelength so that a slit image of each color in the source can be seen. Incandescent gases produce bright-line or emission spectra. These are seen as bright lines of color. The positions of the lines correspond to certain wavelengths of light being emitted by the element. Each element has a characteristic spectrum; thus spectra can be used as a means of identifying the elements in a substance.

The light from the Sun and the stars when analyzed by a spectroscope forms a dark-line or absorption spectrum. It consists of the continuous spectrum with dark slit images at certain wavelengths. In the solar spectrum, the dark lines appear at the same wavelengths as the bright lines of the hydrogen gas emission spectrum. The Sun is surrounded by a relatively cool layer of hydrogen gas. When light from the Sun passes through the hydrogen blanket, the hydrogen atoms absorb the wavelengths of light that they would normally emit if they were hot enough.

When the spectra from the stars are examined, information about their composition can be obtained. If dark lines corresponding to elemental hydrogen are visible in the spectrum, scientists can infer that the gas is present in the outer layers of the star.

Niels Bohr proposed a theory to explain the formation of spectra. The electrons that surround the nucleus of atoms travel in orbits or energy levels. When atoms are supplied with a great deal of energy (excited), an electron jumps from its own orbit to an orbit of higher energy, farther from the nucleus. When the electron falls back into an orbit closer to the nucleus, it releases the energy it had absorbed. This energy is emitted in definite quantities, as photons. The electron may fall back to its original orbit in one step or in many, like a ball falling down a flight of stairs. Each fall is accompanied by the release of a certain amount of light energy.

Analysis of spectra from the Sun and most bright stars show these bodies to be mainly composed of hydrogen and helium. The formation of helium from hydrogen by a nuclear fusion reaction is the source of most of the Sun's energy. In essense, 4 protons (hydrogen nuclei) are converted to 1 helium nucleus (2 neutrons and 2 protons) whose mass is slightly less than the sum of the masses of the four original protons. In the fusion reaction, a minute amount of matter is converted to energy according to Einstein's equation, $E = mc^2$. Energy results from the complete destruction of matter. The amount of energy released is equal to the amount of matter destroyed, m, multiplied by the square of the speed of light, c. In the Sun, the destruction of the small amounts of matter involved in the fusion reaction releases tremendous amounts of energy.

6 Light-years

The light-year is a unit of measurement of astronomical distances. It is the distance traveled by light in the course of one year, approximately 6×10^{12} miles. The light-year unit is seldom used technically; astronomers use the *parsec*, which is equivalent to 3.26 light years. The light from the Moon takes 1.3 seconds to reach the Earth, light from the Sun, about 8 minutes.

The laser is a remarkable device that has been developed in recent years. The name is derived from *L*ight *A*mplification by *S*timulated *E*mission of *R*adiation. The laser can cut, weld, and drill holes in hard materials; it can even repair detached retinas in the human eye.

The laser amplifies the light that is emitted by the excited atoms of certain substances. These substances include ruby, or other crystals, gases, and certain types of glass.

Laser light is an intense, narrow beam of monochromatic (one wavelength), coherent (waves are "in step") light. Experiments now being conducted demonstrate that laser beams can carry radio, television, telephone, and telegraph messages.

SUPPLEMENTARY AIDS

All films and filmstrips listed are in color. All films are accompanied by sound; filmstrips are accompanied by sound only if so designated. Names and addresses of producers and distributors are on page F-29.

Filmstrips

Light (37 frames), #400083, McGraw-Hill. Explains that all light comes from a source; illustrates reflected light, how light travels, and refraction.

Light and Color (42 frames), #400351, McGraw-Hill. Illustrates the properties of light; why objects have different colors.

Light and Color (38 frames), #1205, Jam Handy. Explains the spectrum, and that different light waves are seen as different colors.

Light and How It Travels (40 frames), #1204, Jam Handy. Shows that the Sun is the most important source of light; explains transparence, translucence, shadows, reflection and refraction.

Man Becomes an Astonomer (49 frames), #8861, EBEC. Cartoon drawings show many early superstitions about the Moon that might be used for comparison with the "scientific approach."

Films

How to Bend Light (11 min.), #1878, EBEC. Proves that light travels in a straight path; explains reflection and refraction; shows how lenses magnify objects.

How We Explore Space (16½ min.), BFA. Introduces the instruments astronomers use and the methods by which they obtain information about objects in space.

Light and Color (14 min.), #1876, EBEC. Experiments illustrate that light and color seem to be connected, that color depends on the ability of an object to absorb certain colors and to reflect other colors back to our eyes; that every element, when heated, has a characteristic set of colors—"color fingerprints."

Science Reading Table

Andy's Wonderful Telescope by G. Warren Schloat, Jr., Scribner, 1958. The principles of reflecting and refracting telescopes are pictorially explained. Describes the solar system and constellations. (Average)

Exploring Light and Color by Charles D. Neal, Childrens Press, 1964. The properties of light are discussed, particularly as they relate to the study of optics. Directions for constructing a kaleidoscope, a microscope, and a telescope. (Advanced)

Exploring the Universe, rev. ed., by Roy A. Gallant, Doubleday, 1968. Following introductory material on the development of astronomy from early times to the present, the topics of stars, novae, meteors, comets, and the expanding universe are explored. (Average)

The First Book of Light by George Russell Harrison, Franklin Watts, 1962. Describes the relation of light waves to the radio-wave spectrum. (Advanced)

Fun and Experiments with Light by Mae and Ira Freeman, Random House, 1963. Thirty-three investigations to help children study the properties and characteristics of light are described with explicit directions and photographs. Most of the materials needed for the investigations can be found at home or at school. (Average)

Galaxies by Isaac Asimov, Follett Publishing, 1968. An introduction to astronomical concepts accompanied by excellent illustrations and a section of Things to Do. Children who enjoy this book should investigate a similar one, *Stars,* by the same author. (Easy)

Light and Color by Frederick Healey, John Day, 1962. Describes the basic properties of visible light. Experiments and illustrations develop understanding of reflection, refraction, color blending, and other light phenomena. The importance of the Sun as man's source of energy is emphasized. (Average)

Light You Cannot See by Bernice Kohn, Prentice-Hall, 1965. Discusses infrared rays, ultraviolet light, radio waves, microwaves, X rays, cosmic rays, gamma rays, lasers, and lensless cameras. (Advanced)

The Stars by Colin A. Ronan, McGraw-Hill, 1966. Introduces the Sun, Moon, familiar stars, and other features of the night sky. (Average)

Telescopes and Observations by Patrick Moore, John Day, 1962. Descriptions of the smallest hand telescopes to the largest observatory instruments are included. Optical principles are explained with narrative supplemented by diagrams. Instructions for the reader to make his own telescope are given in simple terms. (Average)

An Analysis of Behaviors in Concept-Seeking*

Conceptual Scheme C: The Universe is in continuous change.

Unit Concept-Statement: Bodies in space are in continuous change.

Lesson Cluster titles in blue are essential to guide concept-seeking toward the Unit Concept-Statement and to enrich the Conceptual Scheme (*see page F-23*).

Lesson Cluster and Supporting Statement	*Operations Basic to Concept-Seeking**	*Methods of Intelligence (Processes and Behaviors)*
1. The Big Eye Component bodies of the Universe are in continual motion.	**Investigating** how light from space can be recorded on camera film	**Observing** the effect of a mirror; **analyzing** recorded light of stars on film; **inferring** that a telescope must synchronize with the Earth's rotation
2. The Light We See Light traveling in a straight path can be made to change direction.	**Investigating** the reflection of light in a mirror; **investigating** the spectrum of visible light	**Inferring** that light travels in a straight path; **observing** that a prism separates light into the spectrum; **identifying** and **ordering** the colors in sequence; **hypothesizing** invisible radiations
3. Light as Waves The behavior of light energy can be explained as waves traveling through space.	**Probing** the characteristics of water waves and light waves	**Inferring** that wave length measures wave vibration; **theorizing** wavelengths; **applying** this theory to explain the spectrum; **inferring** that vision depends on sensing different wavelengths
4. Light as Particles Light energy sometimes behaves as waves and sometimes as particles.	**Probing** deeper into the nature of light; **investigating** the conversion of light energy to electric energy in a light meter	**Comparing** some behaviors of light; **inferring** that light behaves as waves and particles; **synthesizing** an explanation that includes both behaviors
5. What Light from the Stars Shows The composition of the stars is determined by analysis of their radiant energy.	**Investigating** the specta of compounds; **probing** the use of a spectoscope to analyze the elements in stars	**Analyzing** burning substances; **distinguishing** their characteristic colors and position in a spectrum; **inferring** a star's composition from the spectrum and **inferring** that great heat makes elements incandescent
6. A Ruler to the Stars Distance can be measured in units of time.	**Investigating** the use of time to measure distance	**Analyzing** measurement of distance in space; **inferring** that time can be a unit of measurement; **applying** light to calculate distances
7. The Main Concept: Hidden Likenesses in Planets and Stars Bodies in space are in continuous change.	Children **synthesize** their acquired knowledge by **analyzing** the light from bodies in space; they **infer** an order in the Universe that is based on the concept that matter and energy in space are always changing.	

** A concept is synonymous with the corresponding operations. In turn, operations are served by relevant methods of intelligence.*

UNIT FOUR

THE EARTH AND THE STARS — HIDDEN LIKENESSES

Teaching background. "A View of the Unit" T-172.

Concept-seeking. Children begin their search into the likenesses between the Earth and the stars.

Operations. Children *investigate* the appearance of a few stars by building and using a starfinder.

Methods of intelligence. Children hypothesize about the likenesses of the Earth and the stars; they *construct* a starfinder and use it to *identify* a few stars; they *observe* that the position of stars seems to change from hour to hour and night to night.

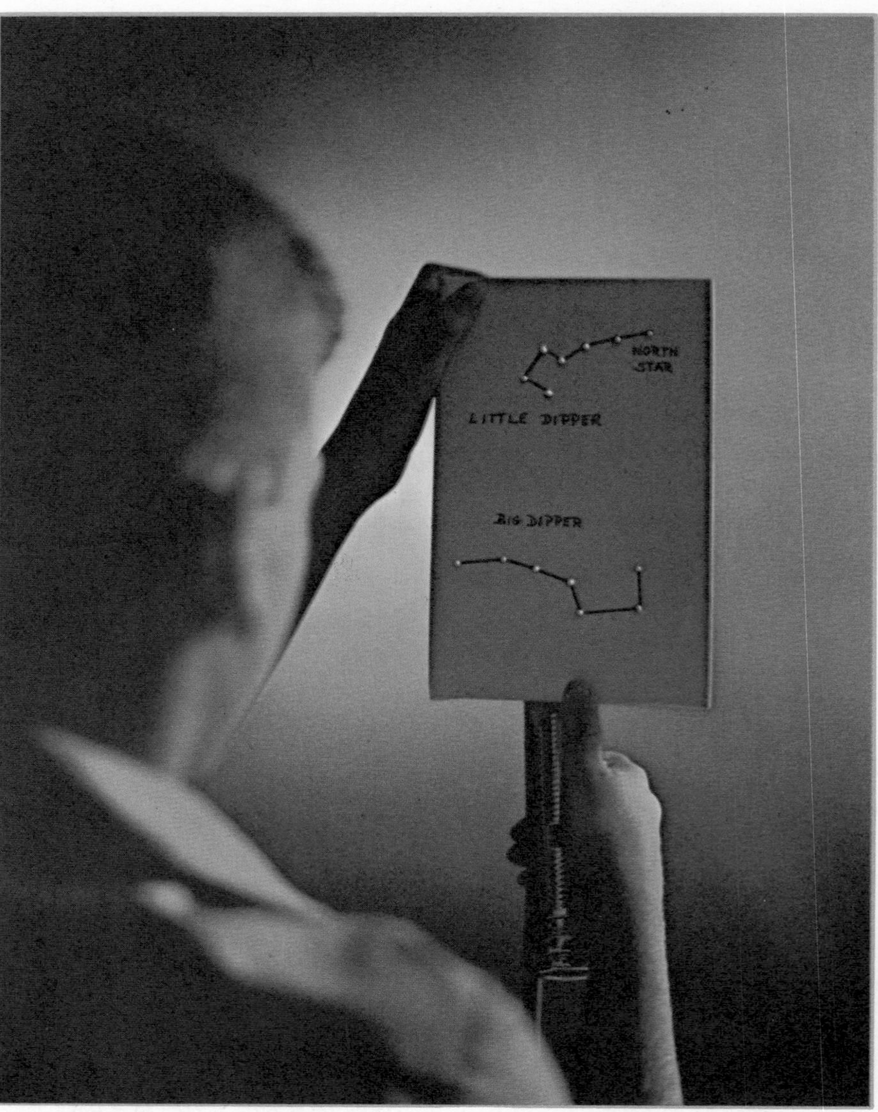

Useful materials: Shoeboxes, flashlights, reference books containing star maps.

Introducing the unit

Have on hand enough materials for several groups of children to make starfinders as illustrated. If flashlights are in short supply, children can take turns using those that are available. Instead of shoeboxes, a piece of opaque cardboard can serve. (For an alternative using milk cartons, see *A Sourcebook for Elementary Science*, 2nd edition, by Hone, et al., Harcourt Brace Jovanovich, Inc., 1971.)

Start the class by asking children to relate any experiences they have had in looking at the stars — perhaps in a summer camp. Who has identified any stars or groups of stars? Do you know any of their names? (Children may know that groups of stars or *constellations* are often used as aids to navigation and in locating individual stars. They may name the Big Dipper, Little Dipper, Orion, or other constellations. If they mention the "morning star" or the "evening star", explain that these are not stars, but planets. Let a volunteer look up and report their identities.

Unit Concept-Statement: Bodies in space are in continuous change.

UNIT FOUR

The Earth and the Stars
Hidden Likenesses

Are all bodies in space different or are they ❶ alike? If so, how are they alike? Begin your probe into these questions by making a simple starfinder. To make one, start with a star map, ❷ such as this one.■ Draw the map on a sheet of white paper and paste the paper on the bottom of a shoebox. Use a nail to punch a hole for each star. Then cut a hole in the end of the box. The hole in the side should be just large enough for you to place the lighted end of a flashlight inside. Turn on the light and hold up the box. How do the two stars marked "pointers" help you to find the North Star?

❸ If you can, take your starfinder outdoors at night. Turn on the light and hold the box up to the sky, facing north. Look for the Big Dipper or the Little Dipper. Try the starfinder at different times of night. Do the "dippers" change position? ❹ Why? Turn the page.

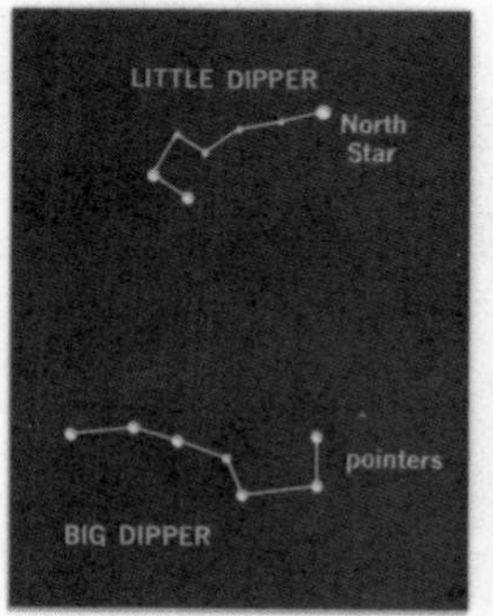

■

155

❶ Let children respond to the questions without comment, at this time, on the correctness of their hypotheses.

❷ If you live in the southern hemisphere, substitute a map of a part of the sky that is familiar.

❸ In many localities, the stars are unfortunately not visible, due to smog, even if children are able to get away from city lights.

❹ The dippers change position from hour to hour as the Earth rotates on its axis and from month to month as the Earth revolves around the Sun. The position of the dippers shown in the map here is approximately what it would be in October at 8:00 p.m. standard time. If the time is earlier than 8:00 p.m., rotate the map clockwise by 15 degrees per hour. If the time is later, rotate the map counterclockwise by 15 degrees per hour. If the month is September, or earlier, rotate the map counterclockwise by 30 degrees per month. If the month is November, or later, rotate the map clockwise by 30 degrees per month.

LESSON CLUSTER 1
THE BIG EYE

Teaching background. 1 T-172

Concept-seeking. Children become aware of how a telescope acts as a tool to increase our knowledge of bodies in space.

Operations. Children *investigate* how light from space can be recorded on camera film.

Methods of intelligence. Children *observe* the light-gathering effect of a mirror and the magnification of an image by a lens; they *analyze* the problem of recording the light of stars on camera film and *infer* that a telescope with camera attached must be moved to synchronize with Earth's rotation.

Useful materials: Mailing tubes.

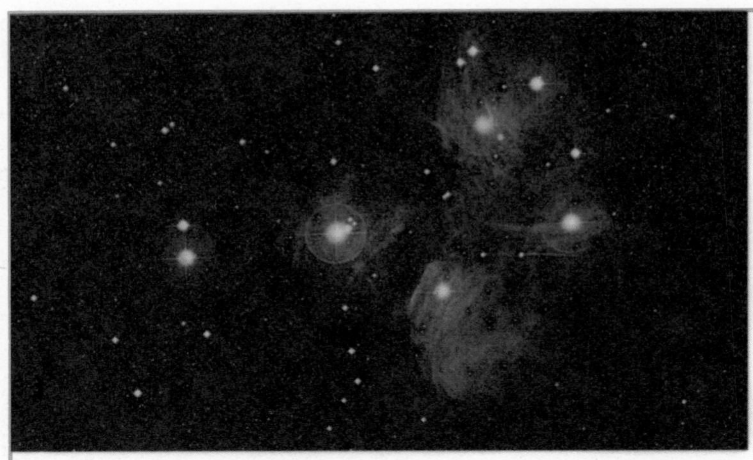

1. The Big Eye

High on top of Mount Palomar in California is the Big Eye—the Hale telescope. It is the world's largest telescope of its type. Let's visit it on a cold winter night.

The astronomer, dressed in an electrically heated suit, ❶ greets us. The giant telescope towers above us. To reach the cage where the observer sits, we enter a little elevator. It rises slowly and stops 75 feet above the floor. Carefully we step into the observer's cage.

In the Observer's Cage

We are near the top of the telescope and inside it. We notice that the elevator seems to be moving away. No, it is we who are moving, as the telescope swings smoothly into position. The astronomer turns some dials, then puts his eye to an eyepiece. He beckons us to look in. We see the night sky, crowded with stars we have never seen ❷ before. How does this happen?

156

Introducing Lesson Cluster 1

You will need hollow cardboard mailing tubes at least one inch in diameter and 15 inches long. Have a small child with a tube sit in a chair, put one end of the tube to his eye, and sight a small distant object. Now have two or more larger children slowly rotate the chair he is sitting in through a quarter-circle. Ask the seated child: What did you have to do to keep sighting on the object? (swing the tube) Did you swing the tube in the same direction as you were being turned, or in the opposite direction? (the opposite direction) How fast did you have to swing the tube in comparison with the speed at which you were turned? (same speed) When you sit outdoors at night, and look up at a star, is your chair staying still, or is it being rotated? (It is being rotated.) Why? (In reference to the star, the Earth is rotating and taking the chair with it.)

Developing the lesson

❶ Why do you think the astronomer wears an electrically heated suit? You will need to give a clue by asking: What happens when objects are heated? (They expand.) Children may be able to infer that a big difference in temperature between the inside and outside would distort the view of the stars and might cause uneven expansion of parts of the telescope and its delicate equipment.

❷ Allow time for children to speculate or contribute information for verification on the next page.

Supporting Statement: Component bodies of the Universe are in continual motion.

In the Hale telescope, light from the stars is collected 1 by a huge mirror almost 17 feet across. Such a mirror can collect far more light from a distant star than your eye can. The Hale telescope can "see" the fainter stars that your eye cannot. The Big Eye can see farther out into the universe than any human eye.

The giant mirror is curved like a saucer.▲ The curved mirror brings the light from a star to a point. This point is 2 called the **focus**, as the diagram shows.◆ Suppose you were to hold a piece of paper at the focus. You would see an **image** of the star on the paper. However, the image would be very small indeed. The eyepiece inside the observer's 3 cage magnifies the image of the star. And the eyepiece magnifies each spot of light.

When we look into the eyepiece, we see many stars we could not see before. Why? The huge mirror collects much more light than the eye.

Strangely enough, the astronomer does not spend much time looking through an eyepiece. He has a better way of 4 studying the stars. He takes photographs of them.

The Big Eye is really a collector of light for a camera. The camera film is a better recorder of light than the astronomer's eye in many ways. How? For one thing, the

▲

◆

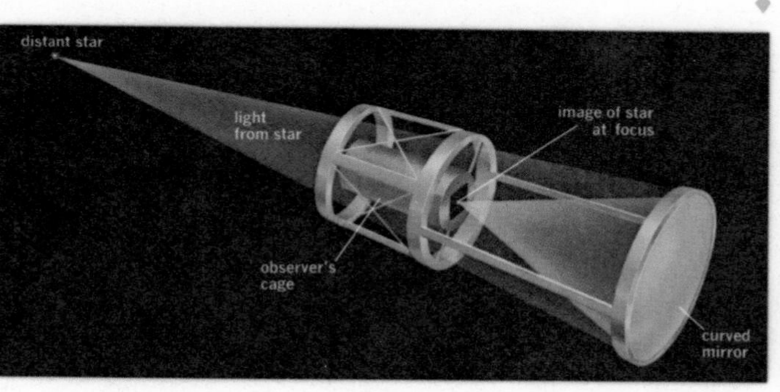

Useful materials: Waxed paper, magnifying glass.

1 To give an idea of the size of this mirror, have about thirteen or fourteen children hold hands and stretch out to make the biggest circle they can. It will have a diameter of roughly 17 feet.

2 Have the children analyze the source of light in the drawing and observe how the rays come to a focus at a small point. If all the light collected by the curved mirror comes to a point, why will it be brighter? (concentrated) This is difficult to show by demonstration, but you can use a magnifying glass to focus on waxed paper a bright object such as a shiny marble in sunlight. Let children see the small image on the waxed paper. Now let them use another magnifying glass to view the image from the back of the waxed paper. The object, image, and "eyepiece" will be in line. Compare this second glass to the eye-piece. Explain, however, that the Hale telescope is much more complex than the simple light collecting (focusing) lens and the magnifying lens you have demonstrated.

3 Children should realize that the mirror focuses only a very small area of the sky, usually a single star or a very small cluster of stars. Therefore the eyepiece magnifies only an extremely small area. Children also should realize that the eyepiece is just a stronger magnifying lens than they use in science classes.

4 Why is photographic film better than personal observation? (It gives a record for later study and does not depend on the observer.)

EXTENDING THE LESSON

A child interested in mathematics can *calculate* that in one hour the eye of the telescope must move at constant speed through $\frac{1}{24}$ of 360° opposite the direction of the Earth's rotation, or 15 degrees. The speed of rotation of the base of the telescope is the same as that of the Earth. This can be figured by dividing 25,000 miles (the Earth's circumference) by 24 hours or approximately 1040 miles per hour. The Earth's revolution around the Sun has little effect on blurring of star photographs.

film can be studied for as long as the astronomer wishes. The astronomer doesn't study the stars directly; he studies photographs of them. When he, or his assistant, is in the observer's cage, he is taking photographs of the stars most ❶ of the time.

Taking photographs of stars isn't easy. The astronomer asks to have the Big Eye pointed at a certain bit of the sky. The stars he wants to study are in that bit of sky. To photograph those stars, the telescope must stay pointed at ❷ them – sometimes for several hours. Meanwhile, the Earth is moving. It is turning on its **axis,** the imaginary line around which the Earth spins. To stay pointed at those stars, the telescope must also keep moving. (At what speed must the ❸ telescope keep moving? Figure this out for yourself.) The engineer controls the machinery that keeps the Big Eye, all 500 tons of it, pointed at the stars.

❹ What would happen if the telescope did not move? See for yourself. Try the investigation on the opposite page.

INVESTIGATE

The Big Eye at Work

If the Earth were standing still, a camera pointed at the night sky would record a point of light for each star. The Earth does not stand still, however. It turns on its axis. Since its axis is pointed at the North Star, the other stars appear to circle around the North Star – when the camera is ❺ fixed to the Earth. On Mount Palomar, the machinery of the Big Eye keeps the telescope and its camera moving and pointing at the star being studied.

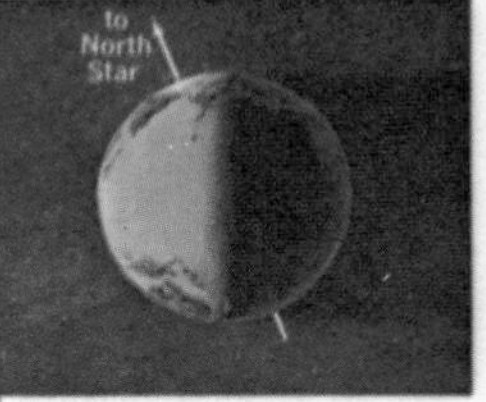

The Big Eye collects light for a camera. At times color film is used, but for much of the work black-and-white film does the job. When the light from a star is very faint, the film may be exposed for hours. The longer the film is exposed, the more light it collects. Thus, the telescope with a camera attached can "see" much more than the telescope alone.

158

Continuing Lesson Cluster 1

❶ Why does an astronomer continually photograph stars during a period of observation? (So that he has a record over a time span; he can then compare photographs and observe any changes.)

❷ Why must the telescope somtimes need to stay pointed at a star for several hours? (The light may be so faint that a long film exposure is needed.)

❸ The telescope must keep moving in step with the Earth's rotation, moving in a direction opposite to rotation. Only in this way can a clear, unblurred record of the star's light be recorded.

❹ Have children make hypotheses before doing the investigation. Will pointing the telescope at different parts of the sky make a difference?

❺ Have the children realize that this effect is evident only when the camera is in line with the Earth's axis – pointing to the North Pole of the heavens. Why will the stars appear to circle? (The Earth rotates; stars are relatively fixed.)

Supporting Statement: Component bodies of the Universe are in continual motion.

AN APPRENTICE INVESTIGATION into Why a Telescope Must Move

Needed: a clear, moonless night; a camera with a time exposure; black-and-white film

Set up the camera on a solid support so that ❶ the camera is pointed at the North Star. (If you are not sure which is the North Star, see page 155.) Use the smallest opening for the lens that ❷ your camera has. This will keep down starry sky light. Set the shutter for a time exposure. Open the shutter and leave it open for 3 or 4 hours. Then close the shutter and remove the camera.

When the film is developed, you may see a photograph like this. Can you locate the North Star in the photograph? What causes the lines ❸ that seem to be parts of circles?

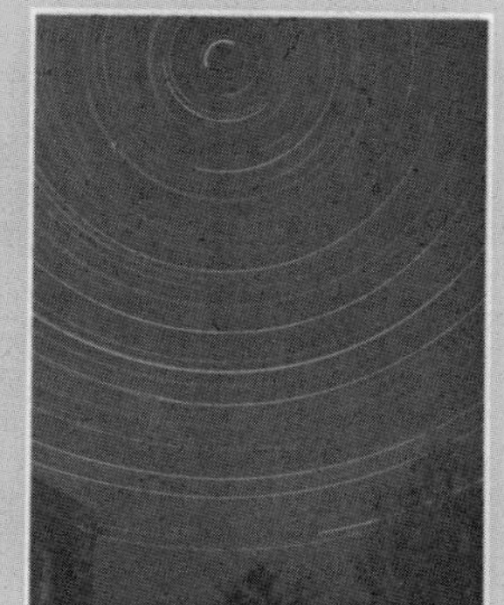

Methods of Intelligence
Designing an Investigation

How should the camera be moved to get an ❹ unstreaked picture of the stars? Design an investigation to find out.

When the film is developed, the astronomer's real work begins. He studies the photographs. Through them, the astronomer reaches into the great distances beyond the Earth. He reaches beyond our solar system, and even beyond our galaxy. He discovers many other ❺ galaxies besides our own.

You have begun to see how a telescope can add greatly to our knowledge of the stars. Would you like to make a telescope of your own? Try the Search On Your Own on the next page.

159

Performance objectives. Children *demonstrate* that a telescope must move to stay pointed at the same star, by using a camera to simulate a telescope. The camera remains motionless, pointing at the North Star, with the shutter open for three or four hours, causing curved tracks on the developed film.

Children *describe* the camera rotating as the Earth turns with it, causing light of the stars to be recorded as long curved streaks. They may *identify* the star trails from a photograph if they have been unable to photograph star trails.

Useful preparations: Be sure that the night chosen is clear and that the weather forecast predicts no change. If possible, select a place far from city and other light. Check camera and film before starting out.

❶ A star finder can be something as simple as a mailing tube. Find the North Star in the center of it and line up the camera so that it is parallel to the tube. Then find the North Star in the center of the exposure window. A tripod or other support must be used, and it must be placed firmly so that it will not be jarred out of position.

❷ Cameras, except those with a fixed exposure, usually have an *f* 11 or *f* 16 opening as the small one; the larger the *f* number, the smaller the opening. The purpose of the smallest opening is to avoid blurring.

❸ Help children to cite evidence (e.g. day and night) that the Earth has rotated.

❹ The Earth rotates from west to east. Every 15 minutes, slowly move the camera from east to west to bring the North Star into the center of the finder. There will be some blurring, but the concept will be clear that the camera must move counter to the Earth's rotation.

❺ How is the astronomer able to discover new stars or galaxies? (Light is captured on film in a camera attached to a telescope that is kept pointed in one position.)

Unit Concept-Statement: Bodies in space are in continuous change.

Building a Simple Telescope. Children may make a very simple telescope with two cardboard tubes of about equal length, so that one just fits inside the other, and two magnifying convex lenses. Fasten one lens inside the end of the larger tube. Fit the other lens inside one end of the smaller tube. (The lens in the larger tube gathers and focuses light as an image. The lens in the smaller tube enlarges the image.) Fit the empty end of the smaller tube into the empty end of the larger one. Look at a distant object through the lens in the smaller tube and slide this tube back and forth until you find the focus.

A SEARCH ON YOUR OWN ❶
Building a Telescope

The boy in the picture is doing what many boys and girls are doing these days—studying the skies. But he has gone farther than most. He made his own telescope. Perhaps you would like to make one of your own. Perhaps your class would. You may want to begin by studying *How to Make and Use a Telescope*, by H. P. Wilkins and Patrick Moore, published by W. W. Norton, New York, 1956.

How many stars in a small piece of the sky ❷ can you count without the telescope? How many stars can you count with the telescope?

Look at the Moon with the telescope. Compare what you see with a map of the Moon. What ❸ parts of the Moon can you identify? *(Caution: Do not aim a telescope or any other instrument at the Sun, and do not look directly at the Sun even without a telescope. Serious damage to the eyes can result.)*

Find out when the planet Saturn will be in ❹ view. Can you observe the rings of this planet with the telescope?

There are many other objects in the sky you can examine with a small telescope, or even without a telescope. Some of these are constellations, ❺ such as the Big and Little Dippers (see page 155), Orion the Hunter, Cassiopeia the Queen, and Gemini the Twins. Others are individual stars, such as the North Star (Polaris), Deneb, and Antares. You will need a book with star maps in it to help you search the sky. Try one of these:

Stars: A Guide to the Constellations, Sun, Moon, Planets, and Other Features of the Heavens, by Herbert S. Zim and Robert H. Baker, Simon and Schuster, 1956.

Experiments in Sky Watching, by Franklyn M. Branley, Crowell-Collier, 1959.

160

VERIFYING PROGRESS

❶ **A search on your own.** Children *construct* a simple telescope and use it to *observe* the Moon and some stars and planets. They *compare* the number of stars they can see with and without the telescope, and their view of the Moon with a map of the Moon.

❷ Determine the area of the sky by looking through the telescope and locating several stars as a visual reference. Count the stars in this area with and without using the homemade telescope.

❸ Many lunar maps are inverted and will correspond to the image seen in the telescope; that is, the homemade telescope will give an inverted image. Some maps show the north and south of the Moon as they would appear without a telescope; the view through the homemade telescope will be inverted in relation to these maps.

❹ Some newspapers will give this information. *Sky and Telescope*, published by Harvard University Press, and *Science News* will also give this information. Whether the rings of Saturn can be seen will depend on the lenses used. Children will need to learn from their references where to find Saturn in the sky.

❺ Children may need to be given the information that constellations are groups of stars forming a pattern and that individual stars, such as those cited, are the brighter stars in a constellation and help to locate it.

❶ BEFORE YOU GO ON

Check your understanding of the concepts of this section by answering these questions.

1. You can see many more stars with the Hale telescope than without it. Why?

2. Would the Hale telescope work without a mirror? Explain your answer.

3. The statement that fits the main concept of this section is

a. The stars are fixed in space.

b. The stars are always moving.

❷ INVESTIGATING FURTHER

1. Get a magnifying lens. Look at a small object, such as a penny, through the lens, keeping your eye close to the lens. Hold the lens close to the penny, then move the lens farther away. Does the lens magnify the penny more or less as it is moved away?

Can the lens magnify the penny as much as you please? Or is there a limit to its magnifying power?

The eyepiece of a telescope magnifies in the same way.

2. The star trails in the investigation on page 159 are circular in shape. It is possible, however, to make a photograph of star trails that are straight lines. Can you figure out how you would have to set up your camera to get a photograph of star trails like these?

3. The Hale telescope on Mount Palomar is known as a 200-inch telescope. In nearby Pasadena, California, there is a 100-inch telescope on Mount Wilson. Find out why the sizes of telescopes are given in inches.

A LOOK AHEAD

The Hale telescope collects light. This is one way a telescope helps us build a map of space.

However, the light tells us more than the fact that a star is there.

Do you know what light is? Do you know what it is made of?

161

VERIFYING PROGRESS

In methods of intelligence

Children may *analyze* the evidence given and *infer* outcomes.

1. Astronomers using a 100-inch telescope suspect that there is a star in a certain place in the sky, but camera film does not reveal it on a 12-hour night exposure. How can they obtain a further check? (Use a telescope with a larger light-collecting mirror.)

2. An astronomer takes a time exposure of the stars around the North Star. When he develops his film, he not only sees the bright curved star trails that he expected, but also long bright trails of light crossing them at a different angle. How might he explain this? (meteor, comet, man-made satellite)

❶ **Before you go on.** Children *apply* the principles of the telescope and *describe* and *explain* how we obtain knowledge of bodies in space.

1. It collects more light from a small area of the sky than the human eye can, focuses the light as a sharp image, and magnifies the image for better viewing.

2. No. The mirror collects and focuses the light as a small image; the eyepiece alone could not both collect light and magnify its image.

3. b. (The stars always appear to be fixed at a given time of the year, but in our galaxy they are moving around the center of the galaxy.)

❷ **Investigating further.** Children *apply* what they have learned about lenses and telescopes to *explain* what happens as light passes through the lens to the eye.

1. There is a limit to how much a lens will magnify because light passing through the lens focuses at only one point and forms a clear image there. It will be blurred if not focused.

2. The camera would have to be set up to point at right angles (90°) to the North Star. This would be the angle of the Earth's rotation.

3. In the 200-inch telescope the mirror measures 200 inches across; in the 100-inch telescope, the mirror measures 100 inches across.

LESSON CLUSTER 2
THE LIGHT WE SEE

Teaching background. 2 T-173

Concept-seeking. Children become aware of the composition of light beams and how light travels.

Operations. Children *investigate* reflection of light by mirrors; they *probe*, by using a prism, the separation of visible light into a spectrum and the effects of radiation above and below this spectrum.

Methods of intelligence. Children *infer* that light travels in a straight path, and *observe* that light passing through a prism is separated into colors; they *identify* the colors and *order* them in a sequence; from given evidence, they *hypothesize* that there are invisible radiations at each end of the visible spectrum.

Useful materials: Pocket mirrors, larger mirror (about 6″ × 8″), flashlight.

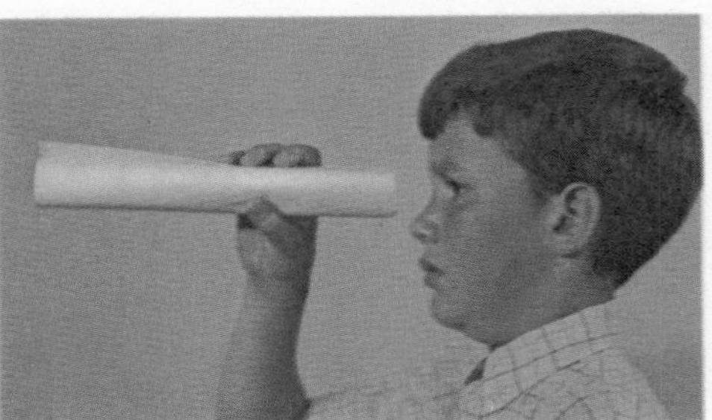

2. The Light We See

❶ Suppose that you make a long tube out of newspaper. You will be able to look through it as long as the tube is straight.■ Bend the tube a bit, however, and you will no longer be able to see through it.● Why? Can light turn a corner?

The Way Light Travels

Light doesn't travel around corners, does it? There is a way, however, of seeing around a corner by using a mirror.▲ ❷ Perhaps you have already tried this. How does the mirror

162

Introducing Lesson Cluster 2

❶ Can you see someone coming down the hall from where you sit? If a child is alert enough to suggest a mirror, ask: Could you see around a corner without a mirror? Why not? This sets the stage for the question implied in this paragraph: How does light travel? What is your evidence? Encourage children who have travelled through a tunnel with a bend in it to report their experience with light in the tunnel.

Developing the lesson

❷ If a child anticipated that a mirror could be used to see around a corner, let him offer his experiences without comment at this point. Have a mirror and a flashlight handy. To a child who thinks light can travel around a corner, suggest the following: Have a friend hold the mirror in front of his eyes while you shine the flashlight on the mirror. The mirror should be large enough so that the child holding it cannot see the flashlight. Ask this child: Did you see the light? Who did? Where did you see it? Why?

Supporting Statement: Light traveling in a straight path can be made to change direction.

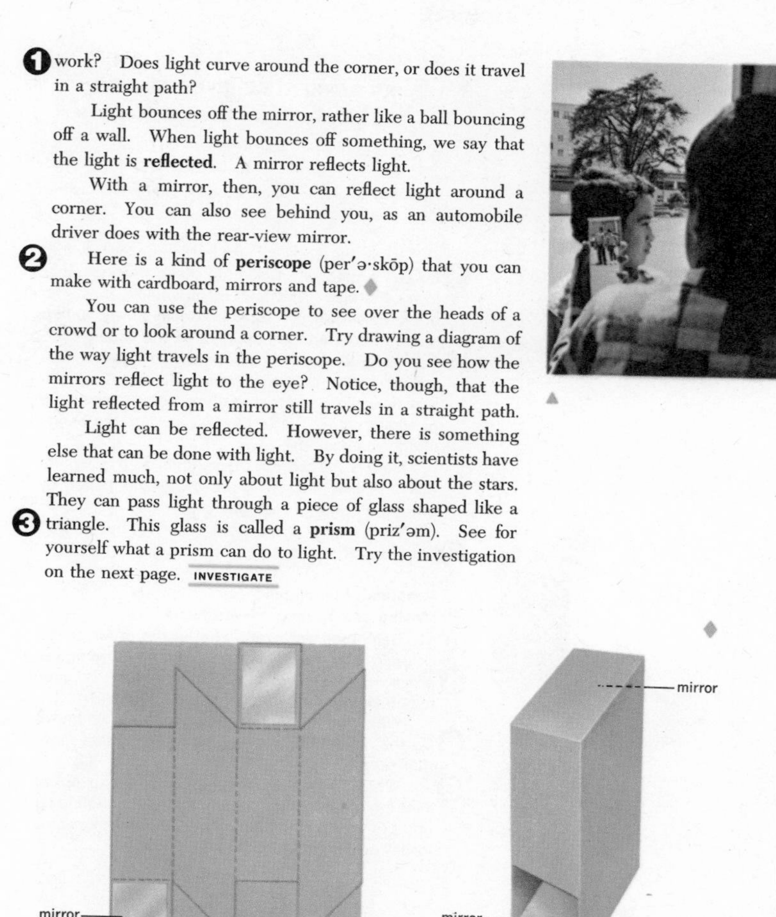

❶ work? Does light curve around the corner, or does it travel in a straight path?

Light bounces off the mirror, rather like a ball bouncing off a wall. When light bounces off something, we say that the light is **reflected**. A mirror reflects light.

With a mirror, then, you can reflect light around a corner. You can also see behind you, as an automobile driver does with the rear-view mirror.

❷ Here is a kind of **periscope** (per′ə·skōp) that you can make with cardboard, mirrors and tape. ♦

You can use the periscope to see over the heads of a crowd or to look around a corner. Try drawing a diagram of the way light travels in the periscope. Do you see how the mirrors reflect light to the eye? Notice, though, that the light reflected from a mirror still travels in a straight path. ▲

Light can be reflected. However, there is something else that can be done with light. By doing it, scientists have learned much, not only about light but also about the stars. They can pass light through a piece of glass shaped like a ❸ triangle. This glass is called a **prism** (priz′əm). See for yourself what a prism can do to light. Try the investigation on the next page. INVESTIGATE

163

Useful materials: Cardboard, pocket mirrors, cellophane tape, scissors, prism. A crude prism can be made by taping together three microscope slides to form a triangle.

❶ What else could you use to reflect light? Children's hypotheses should be placed on the chalkboard and kept there, if possible, throughout the remainder of the unit. Hypotheses might include: Light bounces from shiny surfaces such as windows, water, metals, diamonds and other crystals; from walls of a room; from faces and clothing; from the Moon, etc. Could we see very much if light could not be reflected?

❷ Children will enjoy making a periscope as shown in the construction diagram. They should cut on the solid lines and fold on the dotted lines. Mirrors can be attached with cellophane tape. Children should realize that the mirror at the top of the diagram at the right is recessed at just the same angle as the one shown at the bottom. Draw two diagonal lines on the chalkboard some distance apart and parallel to each other. Draw a line to represent a light beam striking one diagonal line. Have children show how this beam would be twice reflected if the diagonal lines were mirrors.

❸ Show a prism. What do you think this "piece of glass" would do if it were placed in a beam of light? Let the children offer hypotheses. Perhaps this will end the day's lesson. Leave the children with the anticipation of possibly discovering something new.

Performance objectives. Children *demonstrate* that bands of colored light are formed as sunlight passes through a glass prism; they *order* the sequence of the colors and *name* the regular band of colors as a spectrum.

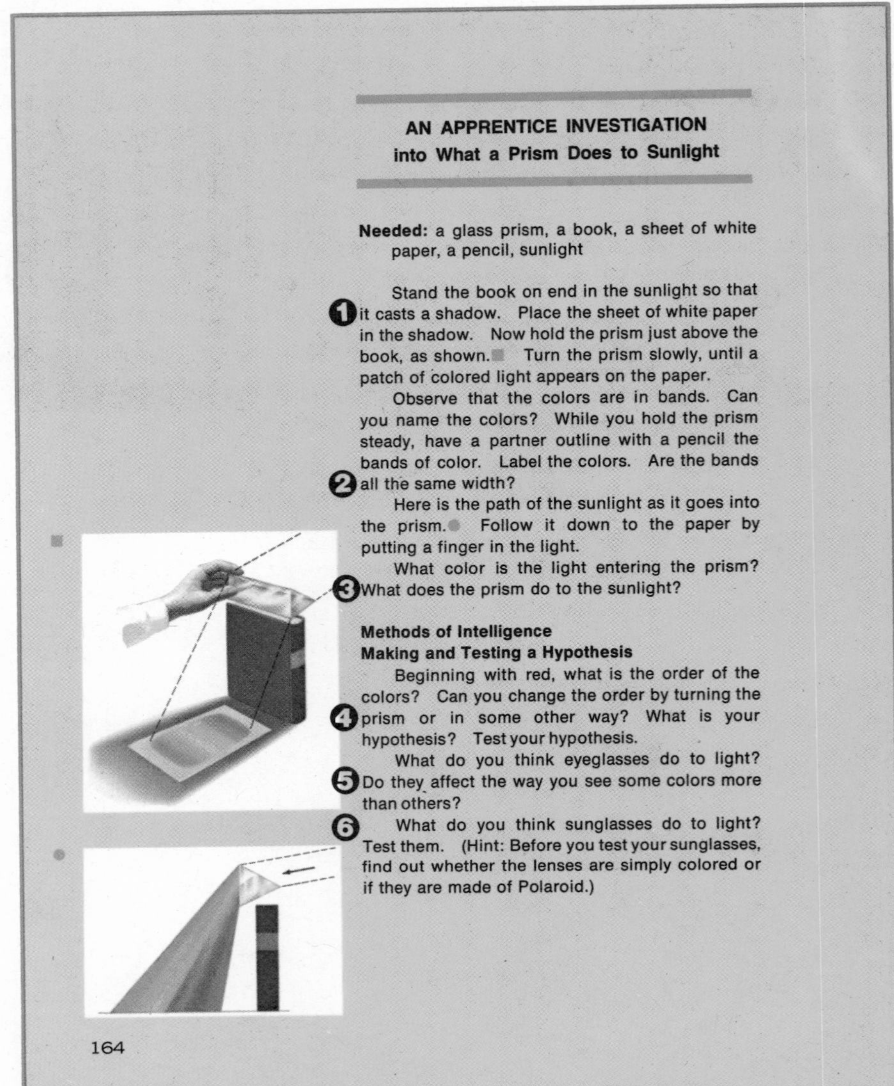

AN APPRENTICE INVESTIGATION into What a Prism Does to Sunlight

Needed: a glass prism, a book, a sheet of white paper, a pencil, sunlight

❶ Stand the book on end in the sunlight so that it casts a shadow. Place the sheet of white paper in the shadow. Now hold the prism just above the book, as shown.■ Turn the prism slowly, until a patch of colored light appears on the paper.

❷ Observe that the colors are in bands. Can you name the colors? While you hold the prism steady, have a partner outline with a pencil the bands of color. Label the colors. Are the bands all the same width?

Here is the path of the sunlight as it goes into the prism.● Follow it down to the paper by putting a finger in the light.

❸ What color is the light entering the prism? What does the prism do to the sunlight?

Methods of Intelligence
Making and Testing a Hypothesis

❹ Beginning with red, what is the order of the colors? Can you change the order by turning the prism or in some other way? What is your hypothesis? Test your hypothesis.

❺ What do you think eyeglasses do to light? Do they affect the way you see some colors more than others?

❻ What do you think sunglasses do to light? Test them. (Hint: Before you test your sunglasses, find out whether the lenses are simply colored or if they are made of Polaroid.)

164

Useful materials: A prism is available in CLASSROOM LABORATORY: PURPLE.

Continuing Lesson Cluster 2

❶ If possible, arrange for the light passing through the prism to pass first through a slit. The window shades may be lowered, or an opaque card with a slit cut in it may be placed between the sunlight source and the prism.

❷ Children may not be able to distinguish indigo from blue and violet, and it is not necessary that they do so at this level. If they can name red, orange, yellow, green, blue, and violet in order from apex to base of the prism, this is sufficient. The bands will seem to be of about equal width.

❸ White light is separated into colors by the prism. A good response could be "The light was mixed and the prism unmixed it."

❹ Some children may answer affirmatively if the prism is inverted from its original position.

❺ Eyeglasses bend some light rays more than others, so that the glasses and the lens of the eye together focus the light inside the eye for better vision. Clear glasses do not affect colors.

❻ Sunglasses let some colors through and hold back others. Polaroid glass and colored glass have different effects, but you need not go into polarization unless the question is raised by the child (T-174).

Supporting Statement: Light traveling in a straight line can be made to change direction.

The Spectrum

White light from the Sun enters a glass prism. When it comes out, the light is no longer white. It is light of different colors. It forms a band of colors in this order: red, orange, yellow, green, blue, violet.

The colored band formed when light passes through a prism is called a **spectrum** (spek′trəm). Of course, you have seen a spectrum before. When you see a rainbow, you see a spectrum. Drops of water can act like a prism when sunlight is reflected from inside the drops.

What does this spectrum mean? It means that the white light of the Sun is not a simple thing. White light is made up of many different colors of light. The prism sorts
1 white light into these different colors.

The prism sorts out something else as well. It sorts out some light we cannot see. There is an interesting story about the discovery of this unseen light.

Light We Cannot See

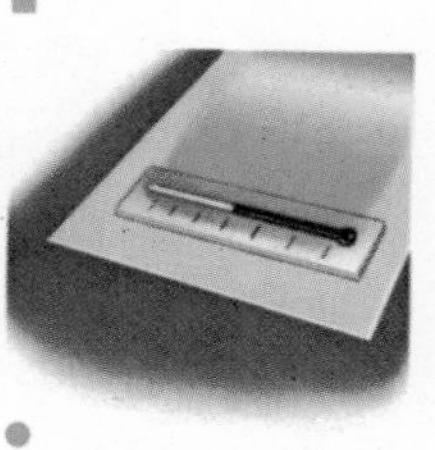

In the year 1800 a scientist named William Herschel looked at the colored bands in a spectrum of sunlight, and wondered. He wondered which of these bands of color
2 were hottest. Herschel designed an experiment. He placed the bulb of a thermometer in each band of color for a while and observed its temperature. He found that the red band had the highest temperature. ■

He found something else besides—something he had not expected to find at all. He held the thermometer bulb just outside the red end of the spectrum. There was no light to be seen there. Yet the temperature rose even higher than it did in the red band! ●

William Herschel reasoned that there must be a kind of
3 light there that the eye could not see. He reasoned that this invisible light raised the temperature of the thermometer. More experiments showed that he was right.

165

VERIFYING PROGRESS
In concept-seeking

1. Provide two prisms. Let one child hold a prism in a beam of light and a second child *hypothesize* what will occur when a second prism is brought a few inches from the first and held in the colored beams. The children *investigate* different positions of the second prism and *demonstrate* that inverting the prism results in a beam of white light from the second prism. From this they *infer* that the colors of the spectrum can be mixed to produce white light.
2. If you have a thermometer, have children duplicate Herschel's investigation and *demonstrate* the noticeable heating effect toward the red end of the spectrum and just beyond it.

1 When a prism casts a spectrum on white paper, do we see direct light or reflected light? (reflected) Do you think white paint is a mixture of different colors of paint? Some children might try mixing the colors in the spectrum using water paint. The result will be a dirty, dark brownish color. Let them conclude that mixing light is not the same as mixing colors. We see colors around us because light is reflected. We see a spectrum when white light is separated.

2 Children will be aware that light is a form of energy. What did Herschel find out? (Light energy can be changed to heat energy.) How would you arrange the differences in heat energy in relation to the colors in the spectrum? (same order from cool to hot from violet end of spectrum)

3 Why did Herschel think that his discovery was a kind of light we cannot see? (All the light came from the Sun and was spread out by a prism. It could not have come from anywhere else.) Children may recall that energy from the Sun is called radiant energy. This term includes both visible light and Herschel's invisible form.

How do we know invisible light has energy? (thermometer) What happens in the thermometer? (The liquid expands, showing a change of light energy to heat.)

We call this kind of invisible light **infrared light**. *Infra* ❶ means "below." This light is below the red band of the spectrum. Our eyes cannot see this light, but a special type of camera film can. Because of this, photographs may be taken in the dark by infrared light.

At the other end of the spectrum is the violet band. Beyond the violet band is another kind of invisible light. It is called **ultraviolet light**. *Ultra* means "beyond." Probably you know of ultraviolet lamps, which can produce a suntan. ❷ Usually such lamps give off some visible light. We know that some insects can see ultraviolet light.

The prism sorts out the colors that make up white light. It sorts out some invisible light as well. Certainly light is no simple thing!

❸ BEFORE YOU GO ON

A. Check your understanding of the concepts of this section. Which ending would you choose for each statement below?

1. Light is reflected in
a. a curved path
b. a straight path

2. Our eyes cannot see
a. infrared light
b. red light

3. Our eyes can see
a. violet light
b. ultraviolet light

4. The statement that fits the main concept of this section is
a. Light can be spread out into a spectrum of colors as it passes through a prism.
b. Light can be spread out into a spectrum of colors as it passes through a mirror.

B. Write a paragraph or two on this topic: "Light That Is Invisible."

❹ USING WHAT YOU KNOW

1. It was a dark night. The thieves coming out of the building thought they were safe. They saw no lights and heard no sounds. However, a special camera had taken pictures of the thieves in the dark. Later they were caught.
How was this possible?

2. Two boys watching fish in an aquarium suddenly saw a rainbow of colors (a spectrum) on the floor nearby, as the Sun shone through the tank.
How was this possible?

166

Useful materials: Colored chalk.

Continuing Lesson Cluster 2

❶ The terms ***infrared*** and ***ultraviolet*** may offer memory difficulties because children cannot see the relationship of *below* and *beyond* to the pictured spectrums. You might let children draw a colored or labeled spectrum on the board with violet at the top and red at the bottom (see page 164). Children can visualize position in this way. It will then be useful in the next lesson cluster when you explain wavelength.

❷ Children who have had a sunburn may know that the ultraviolet rays of the Sun caused the burn. Why is it dangerous to use a sunlamp for more than a short time? (You may get a burn.)

VERIFYING PROGRESS

❸ **Before you go on.** A. Children *apply* their knowledge of light energy to analyze and respond to questions.
1. b 2. a 3. a 4. a

B. Children should *demonstrate* or *describe* effects and practical uses of infrared and ultraviolet light.

❹ **Using what you know.** Children *analyze* problems and *apply* their understanding of some behaviors of light to *explain* the solutions.
1. The camera was loaded with infrared film that could take pictures in the dark. The thieves were thus identified.
2. The light struck the tank in such a way that the water between two adjacent sides formed a prism.

Supporting Statement: The behavior of light energy can be explained as waves traveling through space.

A LOOK AHEAD

Light can be reflected. Light travels in a straight path. White light is made up of colored light. Some light is invisible. These are facts. How do scientists explain these facts? Do scientists have a theory to explain the way light behaves? Indeed, they do. The theory allows two ❶ explanations. Sometimes one explanation works, sometimes the other.

3. Light as Waves

❷ Drop a pebble into still water. Watch the wave it makes. The wave spreads across the surface of the water in all directions at once, in a growing circle. The wave travels at a certain speed, until it fades away. Somehow, energy is being carried across the surface of the water.

Take a stick and slowly dip its end in and out of the water. ❸ It makes a parade of waves. One wave follows another across the water, all at the same speed. Suppose you were to dip the stick in and out with a steady rhythm. Do you find the waves follow one another at the same distance? (Try it, if you can.)

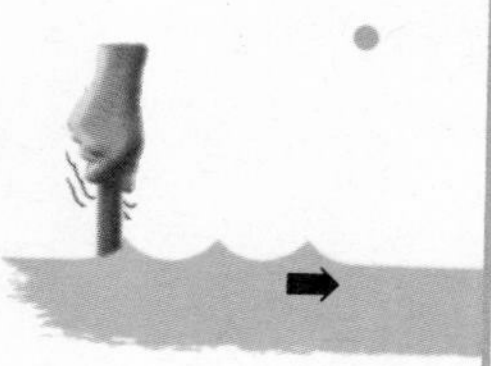

167

LESSON CLUSTER 3
LIGHT AS WAVES

Teaching background. 3 T-174

Concept-seeking. Children are introduced to behaviors of light that can best be explained by wave motion.

Operations. Children *probe* into the characteristics of water waves and light waves.

Methods of intelligence. Children *infer* wavelength from the behavior of water waves made to vibrate at different rates; they *theorize* that the faster the vibration the shorter the wavelength; they apply this theory to *explain* the separation of light into a spectrum, and *infer* that our vision depends on sensing different wavelengths of reflected light as colors.

Useful materials: Wide-mouthed white bowls or cooking pots; pencils or slender twigs as "dippers"; vegetable dye (optional).

Introducing Lesson Cluster 3

❶ Before beginning the lesson cluster, encourage the children to *hypothesize* what the two explanations might be.

❷ Have you ever been on the bank of a quiet pond and thrown a pebble in it? Or seen a fish surface to catch an insect? Let children with such an experience describe it. If there was a leaf or a bit of wood, what happened to it? (bobbed up and down)

Developing the lesson

❸ It would be desirable to have children investigate waves in small groups. If possible, provide a bowl or container about 10–12 inches across, for each group. Or you may have an Investigator, Reader, Recorder team to demonstrate. A white bowl or cooking pot is better for viewing, and the water in it might be colored with food coloring. Have them follow directions in the text. The twig or pencil should be dipped up and down, not sloshed back and forth.

❶ Notice that there is a top part, or **crest**, to each wave. The distance from one crest to the next crest in a wave is called the **wavelength**. Suppose you dip the stick in and out with a steady rhythm. Then the waves all have the same wavelength. ■

Suppose you dip the stick in and out quickly. Do the ❷ wavelengths move across the water more quickly? No, they move at the same speed as before. However, there is a difference. The waves are closer together. ● In other words, now the wavelength is shorter. Waves can have different wavelengths. You can see this for yourself in a bathtub. Try it—if you haven't already done so.

The Wave Nature of Light

One explanation of how light behaves is that light is made up of waves. Suppose you turn on a lamp. Then, according to this explanation, waves of light go out in all directions, somewhat like the waves on a pond. We're not saying that light waves look just like water waves. However, light waves do have crests of a kind. In fact, ❸ scientists have measured the wavelengths of light waves. Recall that a wavelength is the distance from one crest to the next.

The wavelength of a light wave is very short indeed. ❹ The light we see as red, for instance, has about 30,000 waves in an inch! Put another way, one wavelength of red light is only about $\frac{1}{30,000}$ of an inch long.

Red light is at one end of the spectrum, you remember. What about the color we see at the other end of the spectrum—violet? Violet light has a different wavelength from red light. It has about 65,000 waves in an inch. In other words, the wavelength of violet light is about $\frac{1}{65,000}$ of an inch long.

Scientists have measured the wavelengths of the other ❺ colors in the spectrum, too. These are the colors between violet and red. They have also measured the wavelengths of the invisible light beyond each end of the spectrum.

Here are the approximate number of waves to the inch to be found in each color of the spectrum.

168

Useful materials: Small bits, such as Styrofoam granules, that will float.

Continuing Lesson Cluster 3

❶ Now have each group (or the team of three demonstrators) scatter bits of a floating material on the water. Styrofoam will do nicely. This will help them visualize crests as the material bobs up and down. Unless a dishpan or a sink can be used, the dipping must be very slow.

❷ Let the children note from the drawings that the distance traveled is the same but that the wavelengths differ.

❸ Children may wonder how wavelengths of light could be measured. Explain that scientists have developed special measuring instruments based on the effects of light or on its behavior.

❹ **How many pen-marks can you make in one inch and still see the marks?** Let children try it. Then have them divide the result into 30,000. This tells them the number of times smaller a wavelength of red light is than the marks they can make in a one-inch length.

❺ Refer children to the table on page 169 and the second drawing on page 164. **What inference can you make?** (The more waves in an inch, the more light will bend in passing through a prism.) **How does this explain the spectrum?** (The light separates out according to wavelength.) If children do not make the inference readily, prompt them by asking: **How is the number of waves in an inch related to the amount that the light bends as it goes through a prism?**

Supporting Statement: The behavior of light energy can be explained as waves traveling through space.

❶

Waves in an inch	*Color*	
70,000	ultraviolet	(invisible)
65,000	violet	
55,000	blue	
48,000	green	
44,000	yellow	
36,000	orange	
30,000	red	
25,000	infrared	(invisible)

Our eyes sense the colors in the spectrum from red to violet. Now we can say this in another way. Our eyes sense light that has between 30,000 and 65,000 waves in an inch. Human eyes usually do not sense waves longer than the red waves. Because infrared light is invisible, you may not know you have been photographed. Why? Pictures can be taken in the dark with special film that reacts to infrared waves. Human eyes also do not sense waves shorter than the violet waves in the spectrum. However, there are some insects, such as bees, that can sense ultraviolet waves.

Did you know that some persons cannot see all the colors in the spectrum? Some persons are *color-blind*; that is, their eyes do not sense certain colors. For instance, a person with one kind of color blindness cannot sense any difference
❷ between red and green. Such a person is usually able to see other colors, however.

Color itself is an interesting thing to investigate. Why
❸ is blue cellophane blue? Why is a green sweater green? If you wish, try the Search On Your Own on the next page.

169

VERIFYING PROGRESS

In concept-seeking

Children *design investigations* to test how different colors reflect light; they *describe* and *interpret* what they *observe* by *applying* their knowledge of wavelengths of different colors. They should have several large sheets of construction paper of different colors as well as two small pieces of yellow and black cut to different shapes.

Have the children attach the small pieces to the large sheets, and set these up about 12 feet away in the darkest part of the room. Children can then shine a flashlight on the sheets and observe how clearly the white or the black shape appears. Let them try different combinations. Children should also *infer* that black absorbs all light and white reflects all light.

❶ According to the table, which has the larger number of waves in an inch, violet light or blue light? (violet) Which, then, has the smaller wavelength, violet or blue? (violet) If children do not easily answer such questions, ask them to pretend there are only four violet waves and two blue waves in an inch. Then have them draw two one-inch lines, and divide one into four equal parts. They can then visualize that the larger the number of waves in an inch, the smaller each individual wave.

❷ If a person is colorblind to red and green, do you think that his lens is poor or that he has no cells for sensing these colors? (the latter) What wavelengths can he not see? (those above green) Why would he be a poor person to hire to pick raspberries? (He couldn't see colors, only shapes—and thus couldn't tell which were ripe.) Some persons are totally colorblind and see only shades of light and dark. They live in a world of gray colors.

❸ Let children speculate, state a hypothesis, and then try the Search on page 170.

A SEARCH ON YOUR OWN
The Colors of Objects

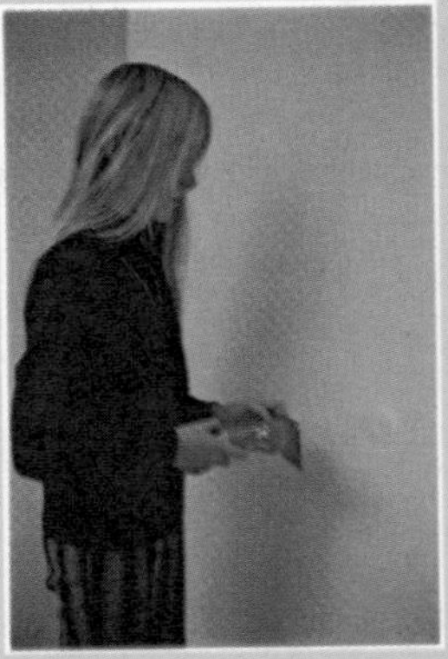

Direct the beam of a flashlight through a piece of colored cellophane or transparent plastic. (You may use red, as shown, or any other color that you wish.) What do you observe? ■ How do you explain why the white light of the flashlight comes out another color? What theory could you build to explain this event? ❶

Next, direct the beam onto a colored wall or sheet of colored construction paper. What do you observe? Does your theory explain what happens here? ❷

To test your theory further, try some of these or invent your own tests.

– What happens if you shine a yellow light through a piece of red cellophane? ❸
– What happens if you shine a red light onto a blue surface?

❹ **BEFORE YOU GO ON**

A. Check your understanding of the concepts of this section. Which ending would you choose for each statement below?

1. The top of a wave is called the
a. crest b. valley

2. The wavelength is shortest for
a. infrared light
b. ultraviolet light

3. One kind of light that is invisible is
a. red light b. infrared light

4. A theory
a. is always true
b. can be changed if the evidence changes

5. The statement that fits the main concept of this section is:
a. One explanation of the behavior of light is that it is made up of waves.
b. One explanation of the behavior of light is that it is made up of molecules.

B. Write a paragraph or two on this topic: "The Wave Nature of Light."

170

Continuing Lesson Cluster 3

❶ Children may think that the red plastic or cellophane *added* more color. What colors make up white light? (all colors)

❷ Children should conclude from observation that a colored object tends to reflect wavelengths of its own color and to absorb other wavelengths.

❸ The red filter will absorb all wavelengths, since yellow light has no red wavelength in it. If a yellow light is shone on a green surface, the surface appears black; similarly, a blue surface appears black in red light. That is, no light is reflected unless the source of light includes the wavelength of the color of the reflecting surface. Actually, some color may be visible since few light sources or reflecting surfaces are "pure" for color.

VERIFYING PROGRESS

❹ **Before you go on.** Children *apply* the concept of the wave nature of light to *analyze* questions.

A. 1. a 3. b 5. a
2. b 4. b

B. Children should *demonstrate* understanding by *describing* effects produced by waves and *applying* the wave nature of light to *explain* the behavior of light passing through a prism.

Supporting Statement: Light energy sometimes behaves as waves and sometimes as particles.

❶ **USING WHAT YOU KNOW**

1. List the following colors in an order that you can explain by their wavelengths: green, yellow, blue, red. What is your explanation?

2. Do both waves in the diagram move at the same speed? ■ Why?

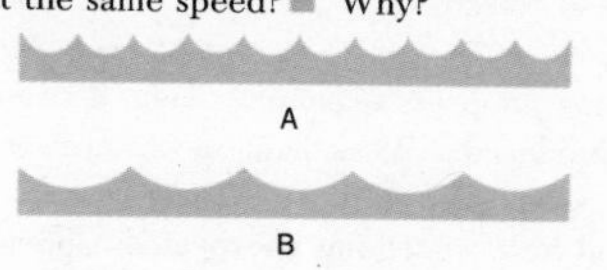

❷ **INVESTIGATING FURTHER**

1. Tie a long rope to one end of a table leg. Move the rope from side to side to make waves. Get a friend to measure the wavelength of your waves. How can you make the wavelength larger or smaller?

2. Light is not the only form of energy that behaves as though it were made of waves. Find out about the wavelengths of cosmic rays, radio waves, X rays, and gamma radiation.

A LOOK AHEAD

Light must surely be made of waves. In fact, there is a good deal more evidence than you have just studied in favor of the wave nature of light.

However, there is also evidence that points to a different explanation of what light is!

How could there be two explanations of the behavior of light?

4. Light as Particles

As you know, photographers often use a light meter when taking pictures to measure the strength of the light. ❸ Perhaps you have used one yourself if you take pictures as a hobby.

Here is a light meter. ● As you can see, the photographer is about to take a picture of an unusual starfish he has found. How does the light meter work? Light produces an electric current in the meter. Strong light produces a

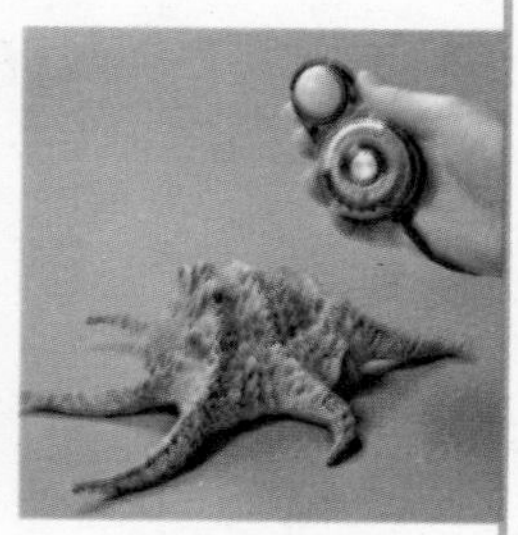

171

LESSON CLUSTER 4
LIGHT AS PARTICLES

Teaching background. 4 T-174

Concept-seeking. Children are made aware that certain behaviors of light can best be explained by considering light as particles, as well as waves.

Operations. Children *probe* deeper into the nature of light by *investigating* the conversion of light energy into electrical energy in a light meter.

Methods of intelligence. Children *compare* some behaviors of light, *infer* that light may sometimes behave as waves and sometimes as particles, and *synthesize* a possible explanation that can embrace both behaviors.

❶ **Using what you know.** Children *apply* the wave nature of light in *classifying* colors in a spectrum and in *explaining* differences in wavelengths.
1. The order should be blue, green, yellow, red, or the reverse. Colors may be ordered according to their wavelengths, from shortest to longest, or vice versa.
2. Yes. Waves in the same medium travel at the same speed; only the wavelength can vary.

❷ **Investigating further.** Children *seek evidence* through *investigating a model* and *consulting authorities.*
1. By shaking the rope more slowly (for longer waves); or more quickly (for shorter waves).
2. Children will need to consult a junior high or high school science text.

Introducing Lesson Cluster 4

❸ If you have or can borrow a light meter, show the children how a bright light and a dim light are indicated. What kind of light will the photographer use to get a picture of the starfish? (reflected) What energy change explains the operation of the meter? (light to electrical)

strong current. Weak light produces a weak current. By measuring the strength of the current, the strength of the light is measured.

How does light produce an electric current in the meter? On the meter there is a plate of a kind of metal called selenium (si·lē′·nē·əm). Selenium is an element. Suppose a light shines on the selenium. It will give off tiny bits of matter called **electrons** (i·lek′trons). Streaming
❶ electrons are what make up an electric current. Strong light makes many electrons jump off selenium. Then a strong electric current is produced. Weak light means that few electrons leave the selenium. A weak electric current is then produced. And here something unexpected happens.

The Particle Nature of Light

When light strikes selenium, electrons jump off. The weaker the light is, the fewer the electrons that leave. In fact, it is possible to make the light so weak that just *one* electron jumps off. This shouldn't happen, however, if light is a wave.

A wave of very weak light cannot make just one electron jump off. A wave of light hasn't energy enough. Why? The energy in a wave is too spread out. Only a *particle,* a speck, can make a single electron jump off. A particle has
❷ its energy bunched, or concentrated, like a tiny bullet.

If light has its energy concentrated, then light seems to
❸ behave as if it were made up of particles. Particles are separated from one another. Waves, you remember, go on, and on, and on. To explain why an electron jumps off selenium, another explanation of light is needed. The wave explanation just doesn't work. Thinking of light as waves doesn't explain the way selenium acts when light shines on it. Light does not always behave as waves.

Thinking of light as particles would mean that light is made up of very tiny specks, or particles, of energy. According to this explanation, what happens when you turn on a lamp?

172

Useful materials: Light meter, 18-inch-long container, water, small wood block, tongue depressor.

Developing Lesson Cluster 4

❶ **What happens when a bright light strikes the light meter?** (A needle or device moves to indicate a high number.) **What does this show?** (Light makes something move.) Now focus the light meter on a less bright object, continue the same kind of questioning, and have the children read this paragraph.

❷ Children may not at first agree that a particle "bunches up" energy more than a wave does. If you have a container about 18 inches long that you can fill with enough water to float a small wood block, you can demonstrate the difference. Place the block near one end and agitate the water vigorously between the end of the container and the block, using a tongue depressor. The block moves slowly. Now give a very slight push with the end of the depressor. Or have some children try this at home in the bathtub and report. **Where is the energy concentrated?** (in the depressor)

❸ If a child remarks that an ocean has a lot of energy and can knock a house down, get him to infer that the water (many particles of matter) did that. This prepares for the wave *plus* particle explanation.

Supporting Statement: Light energy sometimes behaves as waves and sometimes as particles.

❶ Tiny particles of light fly out from the lamp in all directions and in great numbers.

According to the explanation that light is made of particles, what happens when you point a flashlight at someone and turn it on? You squirt a stream of particles at that person—not waves.

There is more evidence in favor of the particle nature of light, which we cannot go into here. As you go on in science, you will go further into a study of light. What all the evidence comes to is this: *At times light behaves as if it were made up of waves. At times light behaves as if it were made up of particles.* There are two explanations in the theory about light, the wave explanation and the particle explanation. ■ ●

Which explanation is better? Oddly enough, scientists believe that *both* explanations are correct. Part of the trouble is this: The particles we can see around us do not seem to behave like waves. The waves we see around us do not seem to behave like particles. We find it very hard to
❷ imagine, then, that light can be *both* particles and waves. This may be so, however. Particles of light are very, very tiny. The world of such tiny things is not like the world of things we know.

■ 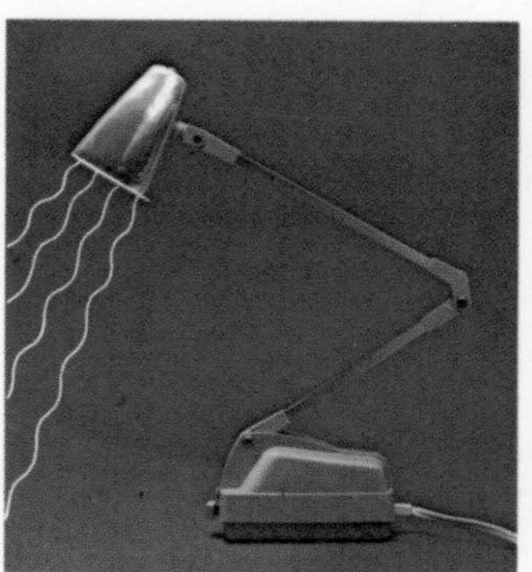

● 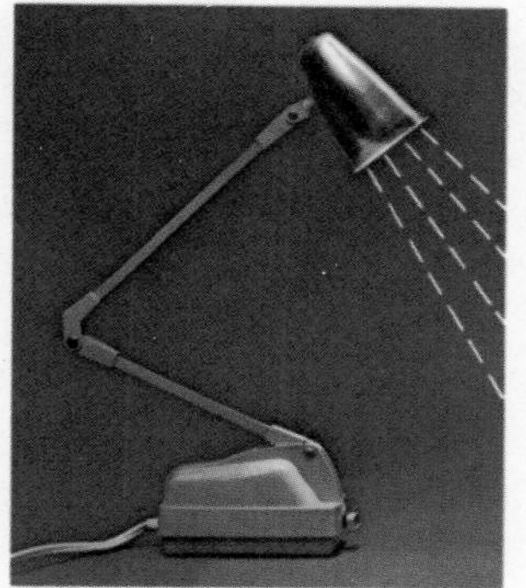

Useful materials: Corrugated cardboard, BB shots or small ball bearings.

❶ Be sure that children understand that light does not move out in a circle like water waves, but in all directions.

❷ If you drop a marble and a feather, which reaches the floor first? Why? Children may say that the marble is heavier, or that air holds the feather up. Recall the law of gravitation. At one time, before Galileo experimented, no one realized that the behavior of the feather could be explained by the upward pressure of air on its surface. It was believed that some things naturally moved upward, while other things naturally fell to Earth. Now we accept only one law of gravitation.

There may be one explanation for several behaviors of light. Why can't we know yet? (Light travels too fast, particles are too small if they exist.) Why do scientists build theories? (to explain what things are and how they behave)

VERIFYING PROGRESS

In methods of intelligence

Children may *analyze* a situation in which an "electric eye" (photoelectric cell) is at work. Tell the story of the housewife who saw the garage door, equipped with electric eyes, opening and closing as swallows flew in and out. Why did this happen? (When a light beam on an electric eye is interrupted, the electric current goes off, and a spring or other mechanical means operates the door.)

❶ BEFORE YOU GO ON

A. Check your understanding of the concepts of this section. Which ending would you choose for each statement below?

1. When light strikes the metal selenium, the selenium gives off
- a. electrons
- b. protons

2. When light makes electrons jump off selenium, light acts like
- a. waves
- b. particles

3. To understand why light behaves as it does, scientists use
- a. one explanation
- b. two explanations

4. The statement that fits the main concept of this section is
- a. Light sometimes behaves as if it were made up of molecules.
- b. Light sometimes behaves as if it were made up of particles.

B. Write a paragraph or two on this topic: "The Particle Nature of Light."

❷ USING WHAT YOU KNOW

Here are two pieces of evidence:

a. Light can be broken up by a prism into a spectrum.

b. Light can knock an electron out of a metal such as selenium.

Which piece of evidence is best explained by the wave nature of light? Which is best explained by the particle nature of light?

A LOOK AHEAD

Scientists have two explanations of the behavior of light—as particles and as waves. The particle nature of light explains certain ways in which light behaves. The wave nature of light explains other ways in which light behaves.

Recall, for instance, that the different colors of light have different wavelengths. We use the wave explanation, then, to help explain how white light can break down into a spectrum of colors.

Scientists can use the spectrum of light from a star in a remarkable way—to learn what the star is made of. How can they do this? In the next section, you can begin to find out.

174

VERIFYING PROGRESS

❶ Before you go on. Children *demonstrate* understanding of concept and key concept terms by selecting suitable responses to questions.

1. a 2. b 3. b 4. b

❷ Using what you know. Children *identify* two behaviors of light by matching evidence with possible explanations. The wave theory best explains a; the particle theory best explains b.

Supporting Statement: The composition of the stars is determined by analysis of their radiant energy.

5. What Light from the Stars Shows

To find out what a cake is made of, you take a bit of it and test it—usually by putting it in your mouth. To find out what the Earth is made of, we take bits of its rocks and minerals and test them in various ways.

With the aid of spacecraft, we have been able to get bits of the Moon to test. However, even without the aid of spacecraft, we have managed to find out what the Sun and ❶ other stars are made of. How? By studying the light that comes to Earth from the Sun and from the other stars. The beautiful Crab Nebula, for example, is so far away that it takes 4,000 years for its light to reach us. ■ Even so, scientists can tell from that light what the Crab Nebula is ❷ made of!

175

LESSON CLUSTER 5
WHAT LIGHT FROM THE STARS SHOWS

Teaching background. 5 T-175

Concept-seeking. Children seek to understand the composition of the stars from a study of their light energy.

Operations. Children *investigate* the spectra of compounds by using a flame test and *probe* into how astronomers use a spectroscope to analyze the elements in stars.

Methods of intelligence. Children *analyze* flames of burning substances, *distinguish* their characteristic colors and their position in a spectrum, and *infer* a star's composition from characteristic lines in a spectrum. They further *infer* that great heat is needed to make these elements incandescent.

Introducing Lesson Cluster 5

How many can tell what a traffic light shows? What do red, green, and yellow mean? (stop, go, caution) What can you tell about traffic at an intersection from the color of the lights? (which way it is moving, or whether it is moving at all) If you were colorblind, how could you tell which light was on, red or green? Observant children may note that red is above the green, with amber in between. What do the colors in a Fourth of July rocket or the special color-sticks used in fireplaces tell us? (Different chemical substances show different colors when burned.)

Developing the lesson

❶ How does light from the Sun and other stars differ from light from our Moon and the planets? (The Sun and stars make their own light; the planets and Moon only reflect the light of the Sun—they do not make their own light.)

❷ Let children hypothesize how light from the stars can tell us what they are made of. What, for example, do we already know about sunlight? (It forms a spectrum when passed through a prism.) Place variant responses on the chalkboard and encourage the let's-find-out attitude.

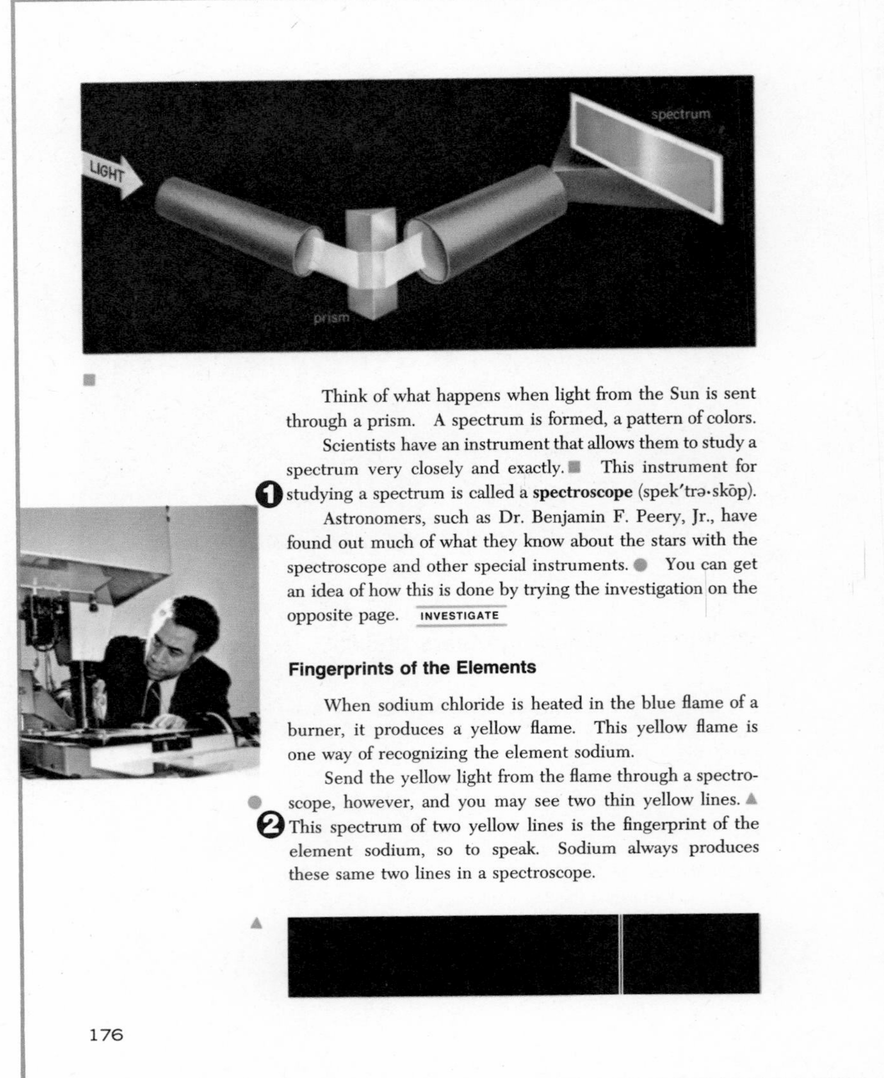

■

Think of what happens when light from the Sun is sent through a prism. A spectrum is formed, a pattern of colors.

Scientists have an instrument that allows them to study a spectrum very closely and exactly. ■ This instrument for ❶ studying a spectrum is called a **spectroscope** (spek′trə·skōp).

Astronomers, such as Dr. Benjamin F. Peery, Jr., have found out much of what they know about the stars with the spectroscope and other special instruments. ● You can get an idea of how this is done by trying the investigation on the opposite page. INVESTIGATE

Fingerprints of the Elements

When sodium chloride is heated in the blue flame of a burner, it produces a yellow flame. This yellow flame is one way of recognizing the element sodium.

●

Send the yellow light from the flame through a spectroscope, however, and you may see two thin yellow lines. ▲ ❷ This spectrum of two yellow lines is the fingerprint of the element sodium, so to speak. Sodium always produces these same two lines in a spectroscope.

▲

176

Continuing Lesson Cluster 5

❶ Call attention to the formation of a spectrum through a prism. What does this show about sunlight? (It can be separated into a band of colors.)

❷ Why do you think sodium always has the same yellow lines in a spectrum? (Sodium always has the same atoms.) When does a solid produce light? (when it burns) What is needed for it to burn? (must change to a gas) Is it likely you would get a spectrum if you shone a flashlight on a large crystal of sodium chloride and directed the reflected light through a prism? (No; it's the flashlight, not the crystal, that produces the light.)

Supporting Statement: The composition of the stars is determined by analysis of their radiant energy.

AN APPRENTICE INVESTIGATION into a Flame Test

1 **Needed:** sodium chloride, lithium chloride, and potassium chloride powders; burner; stainless steel teaspoons; metal tray

Sodium chloride is common table salt. The other substances can be obtained by your teacher.

2 The burner should be placed on the metal tray, or another fireproof surface. Your teacher will light the burner and will remain nearby as you work with the flame.

Wet the tip of a clean teaspoon with water so that the powder will stick to it. Dip the tip of the teaspoon into the sodium chloride. Then hold in the flame the tip of the spoon with the sodium chloride sticking to it. Here is what happened on 3 one trial. ■ What color is the flame?

This is called a *flame test.* When a compound has sodium in it, the flame is yellow. Clean 4 the spoon. Try the flame test with potassium chloride. ● Clean the spoon. Do the flame test 5 with lithium chloride. ▲ Use a clean spoon each time. Why? What flame colors do lithium and potassium show?

Methods of Intelligence
Identifying a Substance

With your teacher's help, try the flame test with boric acid and baking soda. Use a clean spoon each time and do not touch the powder with your hands. Which substance has sodium in it? How do you know?

■

●

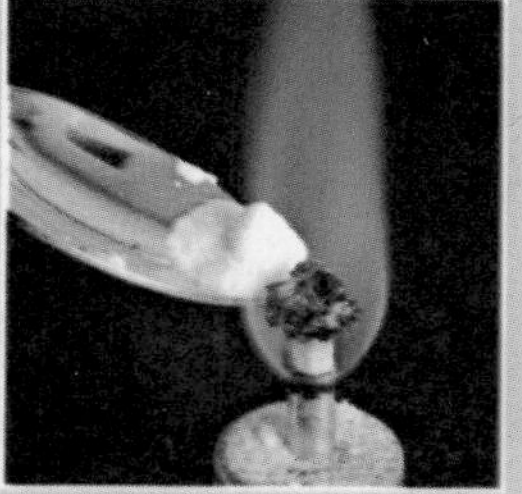
▲

177

Performance objectives. Children *demonstrate* the flame test for identifying chemical substances by holding different metallic salts in an open flame, causing different colors to be formed as they burn.

Useful materials: Some equivalent materials are available in CLASSROOM LABORATORY: PURPLE.

1 Be sure to have an asbestos sheet or a container of water at hand. As you work with the children, point out the safety precautions you take. A stirring rod or a wire loop may take the place of the stainless steel spoon.

2 It is well to limit the number of groups doing this investigation to the closeness of supervision you can give. You may prefer to make this a demonstration for reasons of safety.

3 Children may note both that the salt is glowing yellow and that the flame is a characteristic yellow.

4 Why should you make sure the spoon is clean? (Some substances may stay on it and burn with the new substance. The mixture may affect the flame test.)

5 Some child may note that these are all chlorides (salts of chlorine and a metal). You may need to explain that it is the metal that provides the flame color and not the chlorine.

The substance that has a yellow flame will have sodium in it. This will be baking soda.

Most substances can be turned into gases by heating them. If the gas is heated enough, the substance gives off light. Examine that light through a spectroscope and you will find something astonishing. *Each element has its own* ❶ *spectrum.* Here are the spectrums of the elements neon and mercury, for example. ■ These are the fingerprints of mercury and neon. The color of the lines in each spectrum, and where the lines are, is a property of that substance, and only that substance.

■

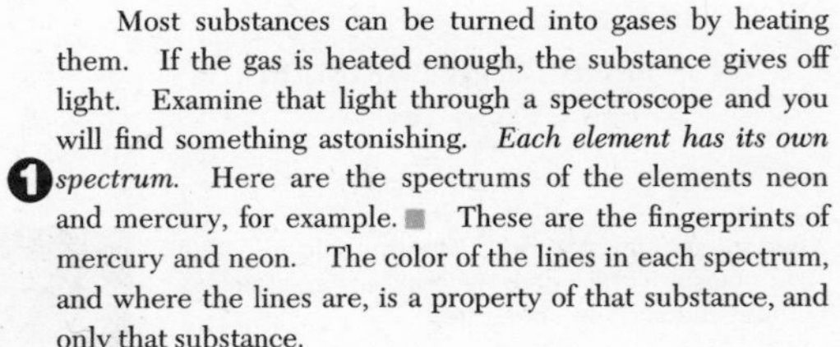

What has this to do with the stars? Well, let's take our Sun, for example. The Sun is so hot that all the substances in it are hot, glowing gases. Aim a spectroscope at the Sun. ❷ Take a photograph of its spectrum. Many different lines appear, in many different places. Among these lines, the astronomer can recognize the spectrums of substances we know. In this spectrum of the Sun, the dark lines match the colored lines that are seen in the spectrums of elements in the Sun. ●

With the spectroscope, astronomers have found at least ❸ 62 elements in the Sun. Hydrogen, helium, aluminum, tin, lead, and iron are among them. Each substance has been identified by its fingerprint, its spectrum. By our study of the Sun's spectrum, then, we know what the Sun is made of.

●

178

Continuing Lesson Cluster 5

❶ Call attention to the spectra of neon and mercury. **How are they different?** Have children note the number of lines and their position against the sunlight spectrum. Have them also compare with the spectrum for sodium (page 176). Suppose light is emitted from a star and shows the lines for these two elements. **What inference can you make?** (The star has mercury and neon in it.)

❷ The Sun's spectrum when analyzed with a spectroscope shows many dark lines against the spectrum that is formed by a prism. By matching these lines against the spectrum lines of a known element, astronomers can tell the elements in the Sun's gases. **Where would the sodium lines be formed?** (in the yellow wavelength band) **neon?** (in the red, orange, yellow, green, blue, and violet bands) **mercury?** (in the red, yellow, green, and violet wavelengths)

❸ **Why are there so many lines in the Sun's spectrum?** (must be many elements in the Sun) If children ask if there are compounds—salt, for example—in the Sun, explain that heating to very high temperatures breaks compounds into their separate atoms (or parts of atoms) which exist as gases.

Supporting Statement: The composition of the stars is determined by analysis of their radiant energy.

The Spectroscope Searches the Stars

The astronomer turns his telescope toward the star he wants to study. He does this on a dark night when the sky is clear. His spectroscope is attached to the eyepiece of the telescope. The spectroscope is attached to a camera, which records the spectrum on film.

Carefully, the telescope is aimed at the star, and the telescope machinery keeps the spectroscope aimed. The shutter of the camera is opened.

❶ When the astronomer has the record of the star's light on the film, he can study the star's spectrum. He then identifies the sets of lines. In this way, he can identify the substances in that star. Many observations with spectroscopes have shown scientists that most bright stars are made
❷ up mainly of hydrogen and helium. Here are the spectrums of these two elements. ▲ The Sun and other stars do contain many substances that are found on the Earth. However, these substances are present in very small amounts. Our Sun and many other stars are mainly hydrogen and helium gas. Scientists believe that the hydrogen is turning into helium, deep inside the Sun.

The Energy of the Stars

Hydrogen becomes helium. This means that atoms of one kind become atoms of another kind. Do you recall that we came across a change like this before? Radioactive

▲

179

❶ What are the tools an astronomer needs, and what does each do? Have the children arrange them in order. (a device to gather and focus light, a lens to magnify the image, machinery to keep his telescope focused on the star in time with Earth's rotation, a spectroscope to analyze the light from a star, and a camera to record details on film for later study)

❷ Why might hydrogen and helium be the most common elements in the Sun and other stars? (simplest structure) Have children recall that hydrogen has only one proton in its nucleus and helium two protons and two nutrons. Lead them to the inference that simple atoms would somehow have to combine to form more complex atoms.

uranium atoms became lead atoms, changing from one kind
❶ of atom to another. As this happened, energy was given off.

When hydrogen turns into helium, energy is given off. In fact, this is the energy that makes our Sun, and other stars, give off heat and light. The energy made as hydrogen
❷ turns into helium is the energy that keeps us alive.

How does hydrogen turn into helium and give off energy? Four nuclei of hydrogen join together to form one nucleus of helium. In the drawing, each single circle stands for the nucleus of a hydrogen atom; the four circles in the center stand for the nucleus of a helium atom. ■ We say that the
❸ nuclei of hydrogen *fuse* to form a helium nucleus. This **fusion** happens only at a tremendously high temperature, such as exists on the Sun. When four hydrogen nuclei fuse
❹ to form one helium nucleus, a little of their matter disappears. This matter that disappears is turned into energy.

You may be wondering now, how long can this go on? Won't the Sun in time run out of hydrogen to fuse into helium? It will, so far as we know. However, astronomers have calculated that it may take a long, long time, a few billion years, perhaps.

❺ BEFORE YOU GO ON

A. Check your understanding of the concepts of this section. Which ending would you choose for each statement below?

1. An instrument for studying the spectrum is the
a. spectroscope
b. microscope

2. By using the spectroscope, scientists have discovered on the Sun many substances
a. like those on Earth
b. unlike those on Earth

3. Most of the mass of the Sun is made up of the gases
a. hydrogen and helium
b. hydrogen and oxygen

4. The Sun gets its energy from the fusion of hydrogen into
a. helium
b. oxygen

5. The statement that fits the main concept of this section is
a. We can discover what the stars are made of by studying their prisms.
b. We can discover what the stars are made of by studying their spectrums.

Continuing Lesson Cluster 5

❶ What happens to the atom of a radioactive element when it breaks down? (gives off energy, loses particles in nucleus)

❷ How does the Sun's energy keep us alive? (enables plants to make food, gives Earth the right temperature for life, etc.)

❸ How does radioactive breakdown differ from fusion? (In the former, atoms split, become simpler; in the latter, they combine.) What happens in both processes? (Energy is given off; some matter changes to energy.)

❹ This can be diagrammed: $H + H + H + H \rightarrow 1\ He + energy$
The process is not this simple, but the end result is the same. Also have children note the illustration.

VERIFYING PROGRESS

❺ **Before you go on.** Children *demonstrate* understanding of the dual nature of light by completing open-ended statements.
A. 1. a 3. a 5. b
2. a 4. a

Supporting Statement: The composition of the stars is determined by analysis of their radiant energy.

B. Write a paragraph or two on one of these topics: "The Sun, Our First Source of Energy" or "The Importance of Hydrogen."

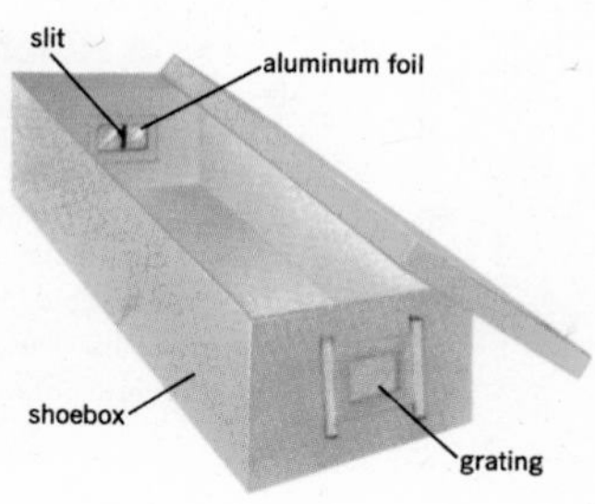

❶ USING WHAT YOU KNOW

When hydrogen turns into helium, a small amount of its matter is destroyed. What happens to this matter that disappears?

❷ INVESTIGATING FURTHER

1. Suppose that more than 9/10 of a body in space is made up of heavy metals such as iron, lead, copper, and other substances such as sulfur, oxygen, and nitrogen. There is about 1 percent of hydrogen on the body. Is this body more likely to be a star like our Sun or a planet?

2. Make a model to show how hydrogen atoms come together to form helium atoms and energy. Ping-Pong balls make good atom models, for example. They are easily glued and painted.

3. One way, as you know, to separate light into a spectrum is with a prism. Another way is with a *diffraction* (di·frak′shən) grating. If your teacher, or a teacher in a high school in your area, has a diffraction grating, borrow it. Find out how to use the grating to see a spectrum—or even use the grating to make a spectroscope such as the one in the picture. ● (***Caution:*** *Do not aim the grating, or a spectroscope, at the Sun. Serious damage to the eyes can result.*) Use the grating or spectroscope to look at flames or reflected sunlight.

A LOOK AHEAD

Light has great uses—other than helping us to see our environment. Light helps us analyze the stars. Through analyzing their light, we have learned much. We have come to know that there are likenesses in the Earth and the stars. Both are made up of *particles*—atoms and their parts. There are also differences. What are some of these?

Light has still other uses. What are some of these?

VERIFYING PROGRESS

In concept-seeking

To determine children's progress in *interpreting data,* have them *observe* the following *model* of the relationship between color and temperature in the stars.

Explain that astronomers recognize that some stars are hotter than others from their colors. Then heat filaments of copper, steel, carbon, tungsten, or other wires in a hot flame. Have children *observe* the changes in color from cool to hot. (red, orange, yellow, white, blue-white) Have children *order* these colors from cool to hot and *construct* a theory that explains how color can be used to indicate temperature.

❶ Using what you know. Children *analyze* a problem, *apply* a concept, and *describe* the solution.

It is turned into energy: that is, the matter is not lost; it merely is changed so that the total amount of matter and energy is unchanged.

❷ Investigating further. Children *analyze* a situation, *design* a model, and construct a homemade spectroscope to *investigate* spectra.

1. It is probably a planet, made up of solid elements like our own, since stars are made up primarily of the elements in gaseous form with hydrogen the most plentiful.
2. Styrofoam balls permit the use of toothpicks. Good models can be hung in the classroom as mobiles.
3. Diffraction gratings may be obtained from Edmund Scientific Company, Barrington, New Jersey, 08007. Make certain to stress the importance of never using either optical instruments or the naked eye for direct viewing of the Sun or any strong source of light (such as a welder's torch).

LESSON CLUSTER 6
A RULER TO THE STARS

Teaching background. 6 T-175

Concept-seeking. Children become aware of the great distances between bodies in space and seek a means to describe these distances in units that can be comprehended.

Operations. Children *investigate* the ways in which the passage of time can be fixed as a measurement in units.

Methods of intelligence. Children *analyze* ways in which distances can be measured in units and *infer* that the passage of time can be used as a unit of measurement. They further *infer* that electromagnetic waves, because of their constant rate of travel, are an accurate means of calculating distances between bodies in space. They *apply the rule* that light waves travel at a constant rate to the calculation of distances to bodies in the solar system.

6. A Ruler to the Stars

If you wanted to measure the distance from the top of this page to the bottom, you'd probably reach for a ruler. Using a ruler, as you know, is a way of measuring distance. It is marked off in units, such as inches or centimeters. You must have used one often. Have you ever thought what different rulers you make use of?

Rulers on Earth

You use different kinds of rulers for measuring distance. Sometimes you measure distance in units of *length*, such as inches, feet, and miles. Sometimes you measure distance in units of *time*, such as minutes, days, and years.

For example, you may say that a certain town is 30 miles away. Another time, you may say that the same town is an hour away. When you say that the town is an hour away, of course, you mean that a bus (or car) would reach it in about an hour. When you speak of distance in this way, you are ❶ using a ruler that measures distance in units of time.

People often make use of this "time" ruler. "How far do you live from school?" asks one student. "Oh, about 5 minutes' walk," says the other. In other words, the distance from school to home is about 5 walking-minutes. In the same way, you can say that the distance to that certain town is about 1 bus-hour – the distance a bus can travel in an hour. The distance from New York to London is about 3,500 miles, or 6½ jet-hours – the distance that a jet plane can travel in ❷ 6½ hours. ■

We often measure distance in units of time. Notice that when we do so, we are careful about two things. First, we make clear what is doing the traveling – a car, a bus, a plane, or whatever it may be. Second, the distance covered in each unit of time is always the same. It should not be 2 miles in one minute and 4 miles in the next minute. The distance covered in each minute must be the same.

182

Introducing Lesson Cluster 6

Suppose you had no rulers, yardsticks, or tapemeasures. How would you invent a way to measure lengths and distances? the thickness of your textbook, for example? (perhaps first joint of thumb or second joint of index finger) the length of the room? (foot or pace) the distance to your home? (pace, or walking time) Would any of these measurements be useful in measuring the distance to the Moon, Sun, another planet, or a distant star? (no) What might you use instead? Let children speculate, then begin reading the text page.

Developing the lesson

❶ How accurate are these units of time? (not very) Why? (A bus may travel at different rates, perhaps traffic will affect time, etc.) The time is accurate if the timepiece used is accurate, but the rate of motion of the object to which time is compared varies.

❷ If someone told you that the football stadium was about five minutes away, what else would you need to know? (whether it was by bus, walking, running, etc.) If someone told you he could walk three miles in an hour, what else would you need to know? (condition of the terrain – rough, smooth, wooded, uphill or downhill)

Supporting Statement: Distance can be measured in units of time.

Rulers in the Solar System

We often use the ruler of units of length when we speak ❶ of the distance to the Sun. The distance to the Sun is 93 million miles. However, the distance to the Sun could also be measured with the ruler of units of time. Suppose that you can walk a mile in 15 minutes. Then it would take about 23 million hours to walk the distance to the Sun! This is about 1 million days. Thus, it would be correct to say that the distance to the Sun, from where you are on the Earth, is ❷ about 1 million walking-days.

A walking-day is not a very good unit to use, is it? Distances in space are very great. The nearest star, for instance, not counting the Sun, is about 25,000,000,000,000 miles away. (This is 25 trillion miles.) Astronomers would want a ruler for measuring distances in space that would give smaller numbers, if possible. In fact, astronomers have actually made such a ruler. You will see shortly what this ruler is. First, let's get an idea of how distance can be measured in our solar system.

Take a flashlight and try to find a mirror in a dark room. How would you find it? You know light will be reflected from the mirror. Turn your flashlight until you see the flash of light in the mirror. The light is bouncing back at you. This is one idea behind measuring distances between planets. Light energy is not used, however; a form of energy with the ❸ speed of light, a radio wave, is used.

❶ Why is it incorrect to say that the Sun is exactly 93 million miles away? (Earth's orbit is a slightly egg-shaped ellipse, and is therefore sometimes closer to the Sun than at other times. The figure is an average distance.)

❷ How long is 1 million days? (1,000,000 ÷ 365 = 2,739 years plus 365 days, or 2,740 years—not counting leap years) To give children some idea of how long this span of time really is, you might first ask: How many days do you think there have been since the year A.D. 1? (Example: 1,971 × 365 = 719,415 days)

❸ What do you need to know about a radio wave to use it to measure distance? (its rate of travel) Why would a radio wave bounced from the Moon be like light bounced from a mirror? (Both are reflected at same speed.) If you sent a radio wave to the Moon and back, how far would it travel? (twice the distance)

Unit Concept-Statement: Bodies in space are in continuous change.

VERIFYING PROGRESS

In methods of intelligence

To determine children's progress in *consulting authorities*, let them *investigate* the following questions by reading and *reporting* on authoritative articles in encyclopedias.

1. Why is there nothing we know of that travels at a rate of no time at all?
2. How long does it take the sensation of a pinprick to travel from finger to brain?
3. Do scientists suspect that there may be things that go faster than light?
4. How is a laser beam produced, and what are some of its uses on Earth?

❶ Scientists have taken great pains to measure the speed of radio waves. It may surprise you to learn that radio waves take any time at all to go from one place to another. However, scientists have discovered that radio waves have a speed of 186,000 miles a second. If you thought that radio waves took no time at all to get from one place to another, it is no wonder!

Radio waves can be sent out into space and bounced off the Moon, then caught when they come back to the Earth. ❷ This is what radar equipment does. ■ We know that a radio wave can go to the Moon, bounce, and return to the Earth in 2.6 seconds. The trip to the Moon takes 1.3 seconds, the trip back to Earth takes another 1.3 seconds.

❸ Can you calculate the distance to the Moon?

■

184

Continuing Lesson Cluster 6

❶ Have children look at the photograph on page 38 (in Unit One) showing the laser reflector set up on the Moon by the Apollo 11 astronauts. If a laser beam is sent to this equipment, the signal is returned to Earth. How will this help measure the distance to the Moon? (If we know the speed of the laser beam and can determine the time it takes for a round trip to the Moon, we can calculate the distance by the formula rate × time = distance.) How can this help us plot the orbit of the Moon? Measurements thus far appear to give us an accurate measure of distance within inches for each beaming of the laser.

❷ *Radar* is an acronym for "radio detection and ranging". The waves are shorter than radio waves but they travel at the same speed, that of light, 186,000 miles per second. (The speed of light is actually a little greater than this, but it is rounded off here to the nearest thousand miles.)

❸ Multiply the number of seconds by the speed of radio waves: $1.3 \times 186{,}000 = 241{,}800$ miles.

Supporting Statement: Distances can be measured in units of time.

A Ruler Made of Light

For many centuries men believed that the speed of light could not be measured. Later, scientists experimented and ❶ found that they could measure the speed at which light travels. Like radio waves, light has a definite speed—about 186,000 miles per second.

❷ In 1 second light can travel a distance of more than 7 times around the Earth. In the time it takes you to blink an eye—about $\frac{1}{10}$ of a second—light travels over 18,600 miles.

The nearest star to the Earth, our Sun, is 93 million ❸ miles away. It takes about 8 minutes for light to travel that distance, traveling at 186,000 miles per second. We can say, then, that the Sun is 8 light-minutes away from the Earth.

The next nearest star, some 25 trillion miles away, is ❹ Alpha Centauri (al′fə sen·tôr′ē). Alpha Centauri is about 27,000 times as far away from us as the Sun. The distance from the Earth to Alpha Centauri is about 2,200,000 light-minutes. This is the distance that light travels in 2,200,000 minutes, at a speed of 186,000 miles per second.

Now we are getting into larger numbers again! We can get around this, though, by using a larger unit of time. What is a larger unit of time than the minute? Astronomers have decided to use a *year* as the unit of time. As a ruler for measuring great distances in space, astronomers use the **light-year.** A light-year is the distance light travels in one ❺ year. (Can you calculate how many miles this is?)

❶ How would you use an echo to measure the speed of sound? (Time the seconds from the production of a sound until the echo is heard. If the distance is known, the speed of sound can be calculated.) To determine the speed of light, special instruments were devised to measure the time of reflection of a light beam over a measured distance.

❷ Children should not infer that light can travel in a circle. This comparison is with distance only.

❸ What distance is covered in one light-minute? (60 seconds × 186,000 miles = 11,160,000 miles)

❹ Children may be interested to know how this star is named. Centaurus is a constellation. Alpha is the first letter in the Greek alphabet. The brightest stars in a constellation were designated by Greek letters in their alphabetical order. Why are light-minutes still difficult to use for distances? (distances too vast to be measured in minutes of travel)

❺ How many seconds in an hour? (60 × 60 = 3600) How many seconds in a day? (3600 × 24 = 86,400) How many seconds in a year? (86,400 × 365 = 31,536,000) So how far does light travel in a year? (31,536,000 × 186,000 = 5,865,696,000,000 or about 6 trillion miles)

VERIFYING PROGRESS

In concept-seeking

To determine children's progress in seeking concepts, have them *demonstrate* one or both of the following.

1. Bounce a rubber ball against a near wall, and then against a far wall. (The gymnasium is a good place for this.) Without measuring the distance, how could you tell which wall was farther away? (The one requiring the longer bounce, or the longer time for the ball to return.)
2. Watch a scene in the playground or school cafeteria. Note what you see. Take a second look 8 minutes later. Better yet, take pictures. What changes do you notice? If it takes 8 minutes for light to travel 93,000,000 miles, why is the Sun we see 8 minutes younger than it really is? (As on the playground or in the cafeteria, changes take place during the lapse of time.)

What is the distance to Alpha Centauri in light-years? Alpha Centauri is $4\frac{1}{3}$ light-years from the Earth. That is, it takes $4\frac{1}{3}$ years to travel the distance from Alpha Centauri to Earth, at the speed of 186,000 miles every second of that time.

Alpha Centauri is $4\frac{1}{3}$ light-years distant from our Earth. This is an easier number to work with than 25 trillion miles, certainly. Perhaps it is easier to imagine, too. If you could ❶ travel in a spaceship at the speed of light, it would take you about 4 years and 4 months to reach Alpha Centauri. Traveling at the speed of light, it would take you 80,000 years to ❷ cross our Milky Way Galaxy from end to end. In other words, the distance across the Milky Way Galaxy is 80,000 light years. ■ Our solar system, the Sun and its planets, is about 30,000 light-years distant from the center of the galaxy and about 16,000 light-years from the outer fringe of the galaxy.

How far away are some of the farther stars? With the help of the Big Eye on Mount Palomar, we have recorded ❸ on film light from a group of stars 2 billion light-years away!

Look up at the stars tonight. Look at the North Star, in the Little Dipper. ● Its light takes about 400 years to reach you. Light from most of the other stars you see takes many more years to reach you.

You see the universe as it was, not as it is.

186

Continuing Lesson Cluster 6

❶ Children will probably recall that the astronauts on their way to the Moon reached a speed of about 24,250 miles per hour. How many miles per second is this? (nearly 7 miles per second) How much faster would a space ship have to travel to reach the speed of light? (nearly 27,000 times faster)

❷ What chance is there of a space ship reaching Proxima Centauri in your lifetime? Some of your children may enjoy making up their own problems to find out how much time it would take to reach any of the bodies in space mentioned on this page. In any event, let the children have time for an awareness of these distances to sink in.

❸ When did the light you see on Earth as Alpha Centauri start to your eye? ($4\frac{1}{3}$ years ago)

Supporting Statement: Distances can be measured in units of time.

❶ **BEFORE YOU GO ON**

A. Check your understanding of the concepts of this section. Which ending would you choose for each statement below?

1. A unit of length is the
a. minute b. inch

2. A unit of time is the
a. year b. mile

3. Light travels from the Sun, 93 million miles away, to the Earth in about
a. 8 minutes b. 16 minutes

4. The light-year is a unit for measuring
a. distance b. time

5. The statement that fits the main concept of this section is
a. A good unit of measurement for great distances in space is the light-mile.
b. A good unit of measurement for great distances in space is the light-year.

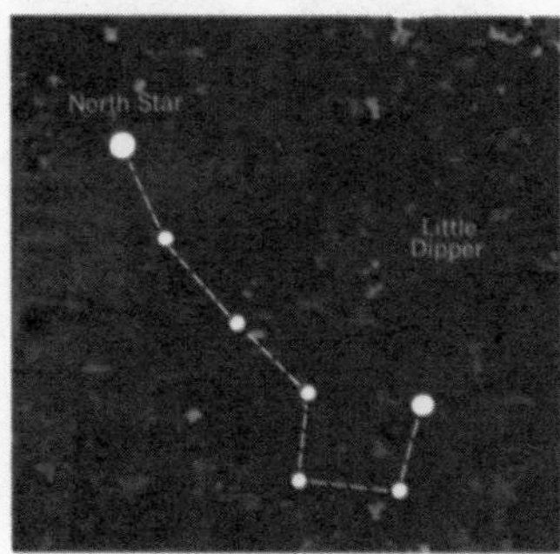

B. Write a paragraph or two on this topic: "A Ruler for the Universe."

❷ **USING WHAT YOU KNOW**

Suppose that a spaceship could travel at the speed of light. (It's impossible, we know, but suppose it could.) How long would the spaceship take to reach
a. Alpha Centauri?
b. a star 400 light-years away?
c. the Sun?

❸ **INVESTIGATING FURTHER**

1. Find out the distances, in light-years, to these stars:
a. Sirius (the Dog Star)
b. a star in the constellation Orion (the Hunter)
c. a star in the Big Dipper

2. Invent a model of how radar works by using water waves or sound waves. Explain your model to your classmates. What do they learn about radar from your model?

3. You have seen that radar equipment can bounce radio waves off the Moon. An instrument that receives radio waves from the stars is the radio telescope. At the Jodrell Bank Experimental Station in England, there is a radio telescope called the Big Dish. To find out how the Big Dish works and what we learn from it, you might want to read *The Big Dish,* by Roger Piper, Harcourt Brace Jovanovich, Inc., 1963. This book has many good pictures.

187

VERIFYING PROGRESS

❶ **Before you go on.** Children *complete* open-ended statements to *demonstrate* the usefulness of units relating to time and distance.

1. b 3. a 5. b
2. a 4. a

❷ **Using what you know.** Children *demonstrate* understanding of the light-year as an astronomical unit for measuring distance.

a. 4 years and 4 months (4.3 yrs.)
b. 400 years c. 8 minutes

❸ **Investigating further.** Children *consult authorities* to *seek evidence;* they *invent* and *explain* a *model* of reflection by using water waves or sound waves.

1. a. 8.7
b. Orion has seven bright stars. The two brightest are Betelgeuse (300 light-years) and Rigel (100 light-years).
c. The two bright stars in the Big Dipper are the pointers, Dubhe (105 light-years) and Merak (76 light-years).

2. A child might start a water wave moving vigorously toward the flat end of a container about 2 feet long. A slit barrier placed between the agitation and the end will produce better results. Once the wave is started, watch it progress to the end of the container and return. To use sound waves an echo is needed. The reflecting surface should be a cliff at least a quarter mile away. A large auditorium or empty room without furniture, drapes, or sound-absorbing materials on floor or ceiling will give an echo. Both demonstrations are a model of how radar reflects a signal.

Unit Concept-Statement: Bodies in space are in continuous change.

LESSON CLUSTER 7
THE MAIN CONCEPT: HIDDEN LIKENESSES IN PLANETS AND STARS

Teaching background. T-172–176

Concept-seeking. Children become aware of the concept that the stars and other bodies in space are in continuous change.

Methods of intelligence. Children *synthesize* the knowledge they have acquired by *analyzing* the light from bodies in space; they *infer* an *order* in the Universe that is based on the concept that matter and energy in space are always changing.

7. The Main Concept Hidden Likenesses in Planets and Stars

FOCUS ON THE CONCEPT

You have studied the Earth—its place in space and its building blocks. Now you have reached out in space to ❶ study the stars. Since we can't scoop out bits of stars to examine, we study the light that the stars give off. The star in this photograph is our Sun, as seen through a special in- ❷ strument during the total eclipse of March 7, 1970. ■

❸ The light of a star shows where the star is. We use the time light takes to travel the distance from the star to Earth to tell how far away a star is. We call this unit of distance a light-year.

The light of a star also tells its makeup in matter. White light can be broken up into a spectrum, for it is made up of

■

188

Introducing Lesson Cluster 7

Call attention to the title of the lesson cluster. What do you think are some hidden likenesses in planets and stars? (consist of matter, have many of same elements in some form, are far away in space) What are some differences between planets and stars? (many more stars; stars are masses of hot, glowing matter that give off energy; planets are cold bodies of matter; stars give direct light energy; planets reflect light)

❶ Why can't we scoop out bits of stars? (too far away, too hot for any spacecraft from Earth) Where have we scooped up matter? (Moon)

❷ What does the photograph show? (The Sun is a glowing ball that sends energy in all directions; we see it as light, feel it as heat.)

❸ Actually we see only the light from the star as it reaches the Earth. Why is it useful to study light that started from stars many light-years ago? (We can draw inferences about stars from any changes we can observe.) The study of light from the stars over many years shows patterns of change so consistent that we can make accurate predictions.

light of different colors—red, orange, yellow, green, blue, violet. When a substance is heated until it glows, it gives off light. That light has its own spectrum. Thus each ❶ substance can be identified by its spectrum. The spectrum of a substance may identify the substance as a fingerprint identifies a person.

❷ A telescope collects light from a star. A spectroscope attached to the telescope shows the spectrum of the star. By studying that spectrum, the substances of which the star is made can be identified. Thus, by studying the light from a ❸ star, we discover the building blocks of the star.

Building Blocks of the Stars

❹ The building blocks of the stars are atoms and parts of atoms, as on Earth. The study of light from the stars reveals that elsewhere in this Universe there are particles of matter like those found on Earth. Elements such as iron, oxygen, copper, aluminum, lead, and zinc have been identified in the stars.

The stars, however, are made up almost entirely of atoms of hydrogen and helium. More than $\frac{99}{100}$ of all the Sun's mass is made up of hydrogen and helium. Only a very small part of the Earth is hydrogen and helium gas.

In the Sun, nuclei of hydrogen atoms fuse to produce nuclei of helium atoms. As they do so, part of the mass of ❺ the hydrogen atoms is changed into energy. On Earth, we depend on the Sun's energy.

For ages, people thought of the stars as unchanging. Now we know that some of the matter of the stars—including our Sun—is being changed into energy. We know, too, that the matter of the Sun and the other members of our solar system, including the Earth, the Moon, and the other planets, is made up of similar particles. In your study, you more and more come to understand this concept of **change:**

❻ **Bodies in space, as well as their matter and energy, are always changing.**

189

❶ How does a scientist distinguish more than one element in glowing matter he is studying with a spectroscope? (Each element has its own characteristic lines that occur always in the same relative places in the continuous spectrum.)

❷ How does a telescope gather light from a star? (A lens or mirror focuses light to a point where the image of a star can be enlarged by a magnifying lens.)

❸ What does a scientist mean by the "building blocks" of a star? (the particles of which that star consists)

❹ How does a scientist know a star has these building blocks? (Elements always have the same structure as revealed by the spectroscope.)

❺ How is the amount of hydrogen and helium in the Sun important to us? (Their fusion gives energy for plants to make food on Earth; also light and heat.)

❻ Have the children debate this concept-statement, offering evidence as to changes of matter on Earth and the Moon and changes of matter in the stars. Evidence of change in state, change in composition, and change in atomic nuclei should be cited with evidence of how we determine the changes.

Unit Concept-Statement: Bodies in space are in continuous change.

FOCUS ON THE SCIENTIST'S WAYS

On any clear night you can look out into space and see the stars. At certain times of the year, you can look out into space and observe certain planets. For example, you ❶ can observe Jupiter. So too did the great Italian scientist Galileo in 1609.

Up to this time, Jupiter had been observed by astronomers, but only with the unaided eye. But Galileo saw something more than a planet reflecting the Sun's light. What he saw, he recorded in his notes like this. ■ These ❷ were his symbols for the moons of Jupiter. No one had ever seen them before.

How could he see something no one had seen before? Galileo, of course, observed with his *eyes*—but he also had ❸ an aid to his eyes. He had invented a telescope, a way to observe much more. He had made it possible to observe more than anyone else up to this time.

The Meaning of Observation

Why is modern man able to make more useful observations than did ancient man? Modern scientists build on the ❹ inventions of scientists who have gone before them.

190

Continuing Lesson Cluster 7

❶ Why is it possible to see Jupiter on a clear night, and not Uranus, or Pluto? (Jupiter is a large planet and is much closer to Earth.)

❷ While Galileo was observing Jupiter, he sometimes saw black spots moving across the brighter surface. These were shadows cast by the moons as they came between the Sun and Jupiter's surface. Why had no one ever seen them before? (no tools yet invented to aid the eye)

❸ Galileo had made a very simple telescope. Refer children to the activity suggested on T-181 where they focused an image on a piece of waxed paper and magnified the image. What change in the activity would make this a telescope? (putting the lenses in tubes, one of which could be moved to focus the image)

❹ What tools can you name that have given us more knowledge of the stars than was possible in Galileo's day? (mirror telescopes; moving telescopes—to offset blurring from Earth's rotation; radar; radio telescopes; space probes; recording instruments—camera, spectroscope, tape, and others)

▲

Modern scientists have improved upon the work of the ancients. Technology applies science concepts to the in- ❶ vention of tools and machines. With the help of technology, scientists extend their eyes. For example, with instruments like the telescope they can see farther than with the naked eye. They extend their observations with the radio telescope, the "Big Dish." ● This one receives radio waves from space which can be changed to signals we can read.

Clearly, Galileo (and others) did more than observe. To *observe* does not only mean to use one's senses. To observe means not only to look, listen, smell, touch, taste, ❷ feel. To observe means to extend our senses with tools and instruments. Scientists do not merely observe—they put observations together into concepts as Newton did. They ❸ try to develop tools as instruments, as Galileo did, to extend the senses.

Galileo used a simple telescope to extend his sense of sight. "Ground Control" in Houston, Texas does much the same thing. Here, men observe astronauts in space, record their experiences, and give the astronauts instructions. ▲ Without radio and TV to extend men's observations, flights to the Moon would not be possible.

191

❶ How is the big dish on page 190 a better tool than Galileo's telescope? (collects more light, sees farther, is built on a different concept) On what concept was Galileo's telescope developed? (magnifying an image focused by a lens) the big dish? (reflecting light to a point by a mirror and magnifying the image)

❷ Would you say that Newton was more a scientist or a technologist? (scientist) Why? (He made observations, put them together, and built concepts.) Could scientists observe without the help of technology? (no) Why not? (New tools extend the ability to observe.) Could technology advance without the scientist? (Up to a point, but each new concept may suggest a new invention to the technologist.)

❸ Let the children discuss the role of science and technology that led to the development of the tools for travel into space. (Concepts of environment, laws of gravitation, laws of motion, energy of waves led to sealed capsules for astronauts, new fuels and materials for rockets, computers to calculate changes of motion, recording and monitoring instruments to maintain communication.) Not all these may be mentioned, but the relationship of science and technology can be brought out.

Unit Concept-Statement: Bodies in space are in continuous change.

Focusing on the Main Concepts

1 TESTING YOURSELF

A. Test your understanding of important concepts in this unit by answering these questions.

1. We are all unable to see some wavelengths of light. In other words, we cannot see some parts of the spectrum of white light.

Which parts of the spectrum can we not see? Which parts can we see? Which part of visible light has the longest wavelength? the shortest?

2. An engineer built a special kind of lock for a door. When he wanted to lock the door, he flashed light on a plate of selenium metal. In this way, a current of electricity was started. The electricity was used to lock the door.

An explanation of light which helps explain this lock is that light is made of

a. waves b. particles

3. Examine your text carefully on this point. How does studying the light from a star help scientists find out what the star is made of?

B. Test your knowledge with this quick check.

1. Which one of these colors has the longest wavelength?

a. violet c. blue
b. orange d. red

2. In the Hale telescope, light is collected first by a

a. camera c. mirror
b. cage d. telescope

3. On the Sun, energy is produced when

a. oxygen is burned
b. hydrogen is burned
c. hydrogen is turned into helium
d. oxygen is turned into helium

4. A rainbow is an example of

a. a light-year c. fusion
b. a flame test d. a spectrum

5. To stay pointed at one star, a telescope must

a. break up light c. collect light
b. be turned d. stay fixed

6. A light-year is used to measure

a. weight c. distance
b. force d. time

7. The statement that fits the main concept of this unit is

a. Bodies in space are made of particles entirely unlike those on Earth.
b. Bodies in space are always changing.

2 INVESTIGATING FURTHER

1. Sir William Herschel did more than investigate the spectrum. Find out more about Herschel, a great scientist. You may be surprised to find who his great friend among scientists was.

192

VERIFYING PROGRESS

1 Testing yourself. Children *analyze* situations, *explain* them on the basis of evidence they have acquired, and *demonstrate* understanding of some characteristics of light as energy from space.

A. 1. Violet light has about 65,000 waves to the inch, and therefore the shortest visible wavelength. Red light has about 30,000 waves to the inch, and the longest visible wavelength.

2. b

3. By studying a star's spectrum, we can find the lines characteristic of each different element and infer the presence of these elements in the star.

B. 1. d 3. c 5. b 7. d
2. c 4. d 6. c

2 Investigating further. Children *consult authorities* to seek evidence, and they *investigate* some effects of light.

1. A German by birth, Herschel was first a musician and then an astronomer. His first work was on variable stars and the mountains of the Moon. He discovered the planet Uranus and some of the moons of Saturn and was appointed private astronomer to King George III of England. He also studied double stars, the rotation of the planets, and inferred the motions in space of the Sun and planets which eventually led to the concept of the rotation of our galaxy. Some think his greatest achievement was building a reflecting telescope with a 48″ mirror, the largest in the world in its day.

❶ 2. New experiments with light are going on now. Some that are often written about in newspapers and magazines deal with *lasers.* Take for a project "A Report on the Laser."

Share the report with your class.

3. In a radiometer, one side of the square pieces of metal (called vanes) is shiny, the other side black. The square pieces of thin metal turn in light. The brighter the light, the faster they turn. Is the explanation of light as particles or as waves needed to explain the turning of the vanes? ■

4. Set up an aquarium tank in sunlight, and fill it with clear water. Move the tank into a position that makes a spectrum appear on the wall. If your wall is not white and smooth, place a sheet of white paper or cardboard against it. Make a diagram that shows the path of sunlight through the tank to the spectrum.

Now stir the water with your finger. What happens to the spectrum? Why?

■

FOR YOUR READING

1. *All About Light and Radiation,* by Ira Freeman, published by Random House, New York, 1965. Concepts of light energy are explained with the use of many illustrations.

2. *The Art and Science of Color,* by Harold Hellman, published by McGraw-Hill, New York, 1967. You will learn of some interesting effects of light around you.

3. *The Stars for Sam,* by W. Maxwell Reed, published by Harcourt Brace Jovanovich, Inc., New York, 1960. Here is a useful book which will take you further toward an understanding of the stars. There are chapters on light from the stars and the uses of the spectroscope.

4. *Stars and the Universe,* by David Dietz, published by Random House, New York, 1968. In this book, you can read about some new astronomical advances, how astronomical research is carried out, and how we have learned what we know about the universe.

5. *The World of Candle and Color,* by Earl Ubell, published by Atheneum, New York, 1969. This book suggests some very interesting investigations which can help you learn such things about light as why it moves in a straight line, why it bounces back from objects, and how it is able to let us see.

❶ 2. The laser is a beam of very short wavelengths concentrated through a ruby crystal, so that its energy is not dispersed as is that of ordinary beams. Children should at least include the laser package set upon the Moon by the Apollo 11 mission and the laser's application in surgery.

3. Neither theory of light is really needed to explain the turning of a radiometer, since heat alone, without light, will cause it to turn. Light striking the vanes is converted into heat, which causes them to turn.

A NEW VIEW

Concept Relationships: Matter can change into energy; but the sum of matter and energy in the Universe is constant.

A NEW VIEW OF MATTER AND ENERGY

Teaching background. T-2–T-175 (Background for Units One through Four).

Concept-seeking. Children examine concepts of matter and energy that they have studied in Units One through Four.

Methods of intelligence. Children *order* the forms of matter and *infer* that all matter is made up of particles. They *synthesize* concepts of physical, chemical, and nuclear change, and *conclude* that matter in the Universe is in continuous change.

A NEW VIEW OF MATTER AND ENERGY

We are rained on, snowed on, hailed on. We swim in streams, ponds, lakes, oceans. We walk on roads and meadows, we climb hills and mountains, we ride about in all kinds of vehicles. We see, hear, feel, taste, smell thousands of different things. We study the Earth and its neighboring planets, the Sun and other stars, solid rock, and open space—thousands of different things. They are all in some important ways alike. Let's look again at these likenesses—the likenesses you found in your study of matter and energy.

A View of the World of Matter

You see, for instance, that the substances you know have likenesses. Thus, substances can be classified ❶ into three groups: solids or liquids or gases, according to their likenesses.

194

Introducing the New View

How do you think likenesses of different things can help us know more about them? In what ways do you think all things are alike? Let children hypothesize. Record different hypotheses for later discussion and investigation. Perhaps a few children will mention that all things are made of invisible particles, but do not be surprised and do not comment if none do.

Developing the New View

❶ What are some examples of solids? (rocks, wood, glass, plastic, paper, dirt, sugar, butter, ice) What are some examples of liquids? (water, syrup, honey, uncooked eggs, milk, mercury, gasoline, alcohol, ink) What are some examples of gases? (air, bubbles in soda water, cooking gas, oxygen, steam, helium inside big balloons, neon in signs, the Sun or any other star)

Concept Relationships: Matter can change into energy; but the sum of matter and energy in the Universe is constant.

Rocks can be classified as igneous, sedimentary, or metamorphic. Mountains, too, can be grouped—as young mountains or old mountains.

Classifying things around us is one way you can put them in order. *Things can be grouped or classified by their make-up or structure.* ❶

As you examine things closely, you find another important **concept.**

All matter is made up of particles.

❷ There are at least one hundred and five elements known (so far). Each element is made up of one kind ❸ of atom. *All elements are made up of atoms.*

We do not stop here. Atoms are made up of ❹ still smaller particles: of electrons, protons, and neutrons. Whether an atom is one of iron or sulfur or carbon or uranium, it is made up of these particles—electrons, protons, and neutrons.

❺ *All matter is made up of particles.* Particles make up different kinds of molecules. For example, the element carbon can combine with other elements to form ❻ many different compounds. The carbon atom can combine with many different atoms to form many different molecules.

195

❶ Have each child mention one thing around him, as you list their selections on the board. How can you classify them by make-up or structure? (nonliving–living; male–female; rough–smooth; solid–liquid, etc.) Now, can you think why we can say all these are made up of particles?

❷ How can we classify elements? (by the weights of the atoms, or by their structure)

❸ How does the structure of atoms of different elements differ? (by the number of electrons, protons, and neutrons)

❹ What is the difference between an element and a compound? (An element is made up of one kind of atom; a compound, of two or more kinds of atoms.)

❺ What is a molecule? (the smallest particle of a substance that has the properties of the substance)

In the light of responses, suggest that children discuss the usefulness of the concept that all matter is made up of particles. For example, what would life be like if atoms did not combine? if substances did not change state? if nuclei did not combine in the stars?

❻ In the models, each black ball stands for a carbon atom, each red one for an oxygen atom, and each yellow one for a hydrogen atom. The lower left model, then, is carbon dioxide (CO_2); the lower right, methane (CH_4); and top, glucose ($C_6H_{12}O_6$). Children should be familiar with the names of carbon dioxide and glucose. Tell them that methane is a gas often used for cooking.

A NEW VIEW

Concept Relationships: Matter can change into energy; but the sum of matter and energy in the Universe is constant.

Atoms combine into molecules. But molecules also can break apart into atoms. As this happens, ❶ the number of atoms does not change. When carbon and oxygen atoms combine to form carbon dioxide, no atoms are lost or gained. When water is broken down into hydrogen and oxygen, no atoms are lost and no atoms are gained. In other words, no matter is lost and no matter is gained in these reactions. The number of atoms remains the same. You come upon this concept:

❷ **In a chemical change, matter is not destroyed: it is only changed from one form to another.**

Indeed, men used to believe that matter could never be destroyed. You have learned otherwise.

Atoms of uranium, for instance, *can* break apart. ❸ We call the process radioactivity. When radioactive atoms break up, they are no longer the same atoms. They change into other atoms, and into some energy as well. As this energy appears, a little matter disappears. We now understand that *matter can be changed into energy.*

In the Sun, for example, matter is always being changed into energy. In the Sun, hydrogen atoms are

196

Continuing the New View

❶ We often hear someone say that a substance (such as sugar, ink, oxygen, wood) is all used up. How true is this statement? (Not at all, if by "substance" we mean the particles it is made of—molecules break up, their atoms recombine, new substances form.)

❷ What do we mean by a chemical change? (The decomposition of a substance or the combination of substances to form new ones.)

❸ What is the process of radioactivity? (A slow breakdown of a radioactive element. It gives off energy and particles from its atoms and becomes substances with other properties.) How long would it take for uranium to lose its radioactivity? (billions of years)

Concept Relationships: Matter can change into energy; but the sum of matter and energy in the Universe is constant.

changed into helium atoms. As hydrogen is changed
❶ into helium, some matter is changed into energy.

Matter can be changed into energy. Nothing is lost. Thus scientists now state the **concept** this way:

❷ **Matter can be changed into energy, but the total amount of matter and energy in the universe remains the same.**

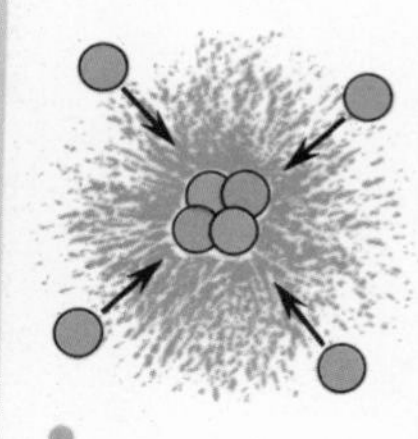

Energy and Motion

This Earth, this collection of atoms and molecules, is a planet. It is one of nine planets in our solar system. Like all matter, the Earth doesn't remain unchanged. As you have learned, for instance, the Earth is in motion around its star, the Sun.

How is it that the Earth moves around the Sun?
❸ How is it that the Moon moves around the Earth? Isaac Newton must have asked himself these questions almost 300 years ago. His answers give us two very important concepts.

One of these concepts helps us to understand how it is that the Earth continues in motion. The Earth
❹ and the Sun were formed from the same vast whirling cloud of gas in space. As the cloud whirled, the early planets began to form. These proto-planets, coming from the whirling cloud, were in motion too. And they continued in motion. As Newton's Law of Inertia states, *an object at rest remains at rest, and an object in motion continues in motion in a straight line, unless acted on by an unbalanced force.*

However, the Earth's motion is *not* in a straight line. The Earth moves in an orbit around the Sun. The Moon's motion is not in a straight line. The Moon is in orbit around the Earth. What unbalanced force pulls the Earth out of a straight line around the
❺ Sun and the Moon out of a straight line around the Earth? We know it is the force of gravitation. The force of gravitation between the Sun and the Earth

❶ How fast is hydrogen changed into helium? (at once) How is this process different from radioactivity on Earth? (Radioactivity is a breakdown with release of energy; hydrogen combines with release of energy.) What part of the atom is changed during both processes? (the nucleus)

❷ Children may ask whether matter will sometimes disappear if it changes to energy; and at the same time wonder whether energy also changes into matter. This is a good time to review the point that scientists do not know, that they are constantly seeking evidence that energy can be changed to matter.

❸ Have children try to recall Newton's two concepts. (Laws of Motion, Law of Gravitation)

❹ Why doesn't the Law of Inertia alone explain the formation of protoplanets from a whirling cloud of gas? (The cloud should not have been whirling if the Law of Inertia was the only force; all the matter should have been moving in a straight line.)

❺ Have children explain how gravitation and inertia working together could have formed the solar system. (Center would have the greatest mass and therefore the greatest gravitational attraction. Straight-line motion would have been pulled into circular motion. Matter accumulated at different places, and its mass set up own gravitational fields. Thus, the bodies in space might have been formed.)

A NEW VIEW

Concept Relationships: Matter can change into energy; but the sum of matter and energy in the Universe is constant.

VERIFYING PROGRESS

In concept-seeking

To determine children's progress in concept-seeking, have them *construct*, with pencil or chalk, their responses to the following.

Have ready string or compasses for use when children ask for them. **What is the shape of the Earth's orbit?** Children should draw an ellipse that is nearly circular. **Since the Moon is going around the Earth, but at the same time is following the Earth as it goes around the Sun, what kind of path does the Moon make around the Sun?** Children should draw a wavy or scalloped path that coincides with the orbit of the Earth.

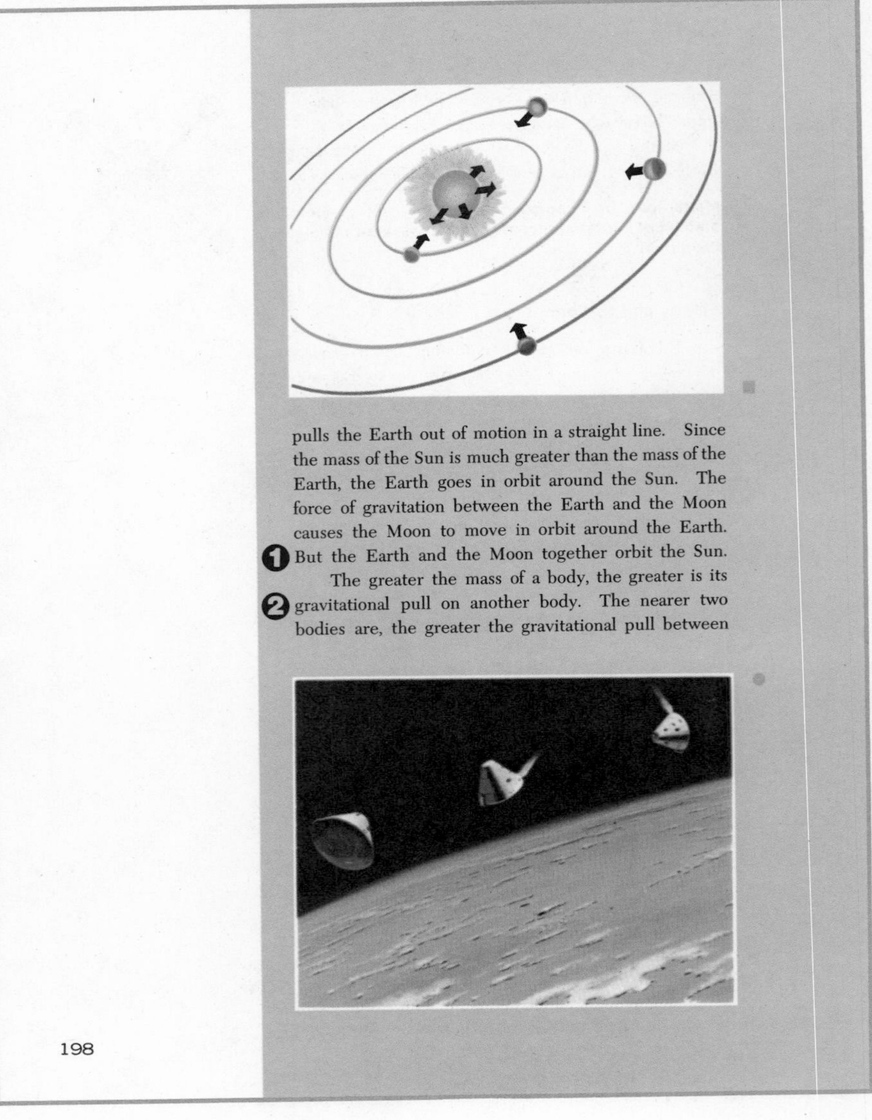

pulls the Earth out of motion in a straight line. Since the mass of the Sun is much greater than the mass of the Earth, the Earth goes in orbit around the Sun. The force of gravitation between the Earth and the Moon causes the Moon to move in orbit around the Earth.
1 But the Earth and the Moon together orbit the Sun.

The greater the mass of a body, the greater is its
2 gravitational pull on another body. The nearer two bodies are, the greater the gravitational pull between

198

Continuing the New View

1 Be sure the children see that the force of gravitation pulls the Moon into orbit around the Earth, and that the Sun pulls on both as if the Earth and Moon were a single mass. **How would you explain the moons around Mars and Jupiter or the rings around Saturn? Why don't they fly off into space?** (force of gravitation of the planets) **Why, then, aren't they pulled into the planets?** (Law of Inertia)

2 Children may wonder why the pull of gravitation of the Sun is greater than that of the Earth, or the Earth's is greater than that of the Moon. **Where does gravitation seem to act?** Children should infer that it acts from the center of a mass. **If the Moon were to fall to the Earth, how would Earth's mass be affected?** (greater) **its gravitation?** Children should infer that the greater mass would increase Earth's gravitation.

Concept Relationships: Matter can change into energy; but the sum of matter and energy in the Universe is constant.

them. Newton's Law of Gravitation made these things clear by stating that *all objects are attracted to one*
1 *another by the force of gravitation.*

The two laws, that of universal gravitation and that of inertia, help us to understand many things that we observe on Earth.

2 Once an object is in motion, its direction can be changed with an unbalanced force. The force may be gravitation, for instance. If a spacecraft goes too near the Moon, it may be pulled into the Moon with increasing speed by the Moon's force of gravitation.

An astronaut in space can make use of another of Newton's Laws, that *every action has an equal and opposite reaction.* This is another great concept in science. An astronaut sends a jet of gas in one direc-
3 tion from his spacecraft. The spacecraft moves in the opposite direction. It does so because the action of the jet has a reaction, which causes the movement of the capsule.

In our study of the Earth, we have come upon important **concepts.**

Matter is made up of particles.

Matter can be changed from one form to another.

Energy exists in different forms.

Energy can be changed from one form to another.

We have also come upon a new understanding, a new **concept,** arising from our search into the way the world works. This is

Matter can be changed into energy.

This concept needs further building. It will be built up, by you, as you go further in science.

4 As you begin to understand these great concepts, you begin to understand how the world works.

1 Children should be made aware that the force of gravitation acts *between* objects. Each exerts a force on the other, the one with the larger mass exerting the greater force.

2 Children should also be made aware that the force decreases with distance. The evidence of increase in speed of a spacecraft approaching the Moon or on re-entry to Earth should be cited.

3 How does the use of a jet in a spacecraft set up an unbalanced force? (can oppose gravity, reduce speed, or add to gravity or speed of motion) What would have to happen for the Earth to be pulled out of its orbit? Children should be able to infer that another body of large mass would have to come near enough for an increase of gravitation to set up an unbalanced force.

4 You may find it useful to have children cite and defend examples of each of the five concept-statements on this page. Conclude by asking: How is the boy using a microscope to understand how the world works? Most children will associate the microscope with study of cells and living things. Be sure they realize that crystal structure and other nonliving particles can also be studied with a microscope.

UNIT FIVE

THE EARTH'S LIVING THINGS—HIDDEN LIKENESSES

Basic behaviors sought: Children *investigate* oxidation in yeast cells and *probe* and *explain* the cell's energy process. They *observe* cell structures and *model* the action of the cell membrane. They *analyze* differences among the structures of cells and *infer* differences in their functions.

Children *probe* cell division and *infer* its relation to reproduction, growth, and repair. They *investigate* single-celled organisms and *infer* that these organisms carry on all life functions. They *investigate* the development of eggs and *infer* that cell differentiation occurs.

Children *investigate* the composition of cells, *observe* the results of testing substances, and *distinguish* among nutrients.

A VIEW OF THE UNIT

The basic functional unit of a living thing is the cell, whether it is a complete organism in itself or one of millions of cells in a highly complex plant or animal. There are striking similarities among all cells, whether they belong to a yeast, an ameba, a frog, a tree, or a man. The microscope reveals that the cells of these diverse organisms generally have three basic parts: the nucleus, the cytoplasm, and the cell membrane.

The nucleus is the cell's control center and figures prominently in the cell's reproduction. The cytoplasm is the site of the cell's special functions. The cell membrane defines the cell's boundary and regulates exchange of substances with the environment.

Other similarities among cells of all kinds include the essential functions of the cell's energy process, in which ATP plays a key role; the diffusion of substances across the cell membrane; and the self-duplication of material in the nucleus when the cell divides into two, in which DNA plays a key role.

Cells of all kinds are alike in another fundamental way: their chemical make-up. Six main classes of nutrients—carbohydrates, fats, proteins, vitamins, minerals, and water—are common to the cells of all living things.

The differences among cells of different organisms are as remarkable as the likenesses. For instance, single-celled animals such as ameba, paramecium, and vorticella, each have distinctive characteristics that make them easy to identify under a microscope. The examination of cells from various tissues of the same multicellular organisms reveals distinctive differences, too.

Just how cell differentiation takes place, during the development of a complex organism from a single fertilized egg cell, is not yet well understood. Two main factors, however, are recognized: the hereditary code that lies hidden within the cell and the environment in which the cell lives. In other words, every living thing is a product of its heredity, in interaction with the environment.

1 Oxidation and reproduction in yeast

Yeast is a member of the large group of simple nongreen plants known as the fungi. Because they lack chlorophyll, the green substance that enables most plants to make their own food, yeast and other fungi must take in food in order to oxidize it for energy. When placed in a mixture containing sucrose (table sugar), yeast sends out enzymes that digest the sucrose into simpler sugars, such as glucose, that can diffuse through the yeast cell membrane.

When there is enough oxygen present, yeast oxidizes glucose. Water and carbon dioxide are formed, and energy is released. This energy is bound up in molecules of ATP, which make it available for the life activities of the yeast cells, as needed. (See the next section for a discussion of the role of ATP.)

The oxidation of glucose ($C_6H_{12}O_6$) can be represented as follows:

$$C_6H_{12}O_6 + 6O_2 \rightarrow 6CO_2 + 6H_2O + \text{energy}$$

When oxygen is in short supply, yeast can obtain energy by fermentation, a process that yields carbon dioxide and alcohol. Beer, wine, and other alcoholic beverages—as well as alcohol for industrial and medicinal uses—are made by fermentation.

When yeast is placed in a favorable environment—warm, with plenty of food for growth—the cells grow. When a yeast cell reaches optimum size, it reproduces by budding. In budding, a small swelling that later becomes the bud forms on the surface of the parent cell. The cell nucleus doubles itself and then divides in half. One half remains in the parent cell, and the other half becomes the nucleus of the bud or daughter cell. The daughter cell may separate from the parent cell, but it usually stays attached, grows larger, starts forming buds of its own. By continued budding, a many-celled chain of yeast cells develops. This form of reproduction in yeast is asexual (without sex) since there is no fusion of cells but only division of cells.

2 The release of energy in the cell

Burning and rusting are two everyday examples of oxidation, the combining of oxygen with another substance. In both these examples, energy in the form of heat is released. But in the case of rusting, the reaction is so slow that the heat energy released is ordinarily not noticeable, although chemists can measure it by special methods.

The combining of oxygen with glucose in the cells of all living things is oxidation, too. As in the oxidation reactions that occur in nonliving things, oxidation in cells releases energy; but the energy is not used directly by the cell. Instead, the energy from the oxidation of glucose in cells goes into the cell's energy process. This process can be compared to a machine, such as an electric motor. Energy must be put into the motor before energy to do any work can be taken out. Electrical energy may be brought to the motor from a generator that converts the energy in steam, for example, into electrical energy.

In somewhat the same way, energy must be put into the cell's "energy machine" before energy to do the cell's work can be taken out. In the input phase of the cell's energy process ATP molecules are built up. Another way to represent ATP is APPP, each P representing one of the three phosphate parts in the molecule. These three phosphate parts are said to be tied together by two high energy bonds. A large amount of energy is needed to form a high energy bond, and a large amount of energy is released when the bond is broken. When a high energy bond is written as a short wavy line, ATP (or APPP) is written as A—P~P~P. There are, then, two high energy bonds in ATP. It is in these bonds that the energy produced by oxidation of glucose in the cell is somehow stored during the input phase of the cell's "energy machine." Whenever one of these high energy bonds is broken, the energy stored in it is released and made available for the cell's work. As a result, one P part is split off from ATP, and ADP, adenosine diphosphate, is formed. What happens can be written like this:

ATP (A—P~P~P) → ADP(A—P~P) + P + energy

If all the ATP in a cell were broken down and used up in this way, the supply of energy for the cell's work would soon run out. As long as the cell is oxidizing glucose, however, energy from that oxidation is stored into new high energy bonds formed by the combining of ADP with P, thus renewing the supply of ATP:

ADP(A—P~P) + P + energy → ATP (A—P~P~P)

Combining both reactions, the breaking down of ATP (output phase of the cell "energy machine") and the building up of ATP (input phase of the cell "energy machine"), we can think of the entire cell energy process as a cycle, as diagrammed on page T-240.

3 Cells in animal and human tissues

The basic parts of an animal or a human cell are the nucleus, cytoplasm, and the cell membrane. These parts can be recognized in cells from a variety of human tissues.

For example, epithelial (skin) cells from inside the cheek, muscle cells from the arm, cartilage cells from the ear, red and white cells in the blood, and nerve cells from the brain are all different in appearance. Yet they all have a nucleus, cytoplasm, and cell membrane—with the exception of mature red blood cells, which lack nuclei. (When red blood cells are first formed, in the marrow of certain bones, they do have nuclei. But shortly before they leave the bone marrow and enter the blood stream, these cells lose their nuclei.)

The cytoplasm of a cell consists of all the living material outside the nucleus and inside the cell membrane. The structure and function of the cytoplasm varies according to the kind of cell. It is the nucleus, however, that controls the activity of the cytoplasm, by producing substances that move out into the cytoplasm and cause it to do its special work. For example, the special work of nerve cell cytoplasm is to produce and carry the nerve message; and the special work of muscle cell cytoplasm is to contract.

The cell membrane is living and has important functions. It not only serves to hold together liquid cell contents, but acts like a control gate, permitting some—but not all—substances to enter and leave the cell. In short, the cell membrane is selective.

One explanation of the cell membrane's selectivity is that large molecules or undissolved particles cannot diffuse through the membrane, whereas smaller, dissolved particles can. Thus, for example, starch cannot cross a cell membrane in the small intestine, while glucose can. Starch consists of large molecules that do not dissolve in water, while glucose consists of small molecules that do dissolve. The glucose is said to enter the cell by diffusion—a process that is best explained by considering first how it can take place where no cell membrane is involved.

Suppose a spoonful of sugar, or any other soluble substance, is placed in a glass of water. In time, even without stirring, the sugar spreads out, or diffuses, evenly through the water. How does this happen?

The molecules of all substances are in continual motion. When sugar is placed in water, the molecules of both the water and the sugar move about. After a time, the sugar and the water are completely mixed.

Just as sugar and water will mix by diffusion in a glass, substances can diffuse across cell menbranes. One model that illustrates the process of diffusion through a membrane is made by placing a starch-gelatin mixture in a plastic bag and suspending the bag in iodine solution. Iodine diffuses through the bag, causing the starch to turn blue-black.

4 Plant cell structure

Like animal and human cells, plant cells have three main parts: nucleus, cytoplasm, and cell membrane. In addition, plant cells have a cell wall made up of cellulose, a nonliving substance. The cell wall lies just outside the cell membrane, and is thicker and more rigid than the cell membrane.

Three of the main parts of a flowering plant such as the bean are the roots, stem, and leaves. Each of these parts has specialized kinds of cells.

Cells in the outer layer of a root, for example, have root hairs. These are tiny projections of cytoplasm, covered by the cell membrane, that are surrounded by the soil in which the plant grows. Water and dissolved minerals diffuse into the plant through the root hairs.

Some of the cells in the stem of the bean plant are specialized for conducting water and dissolved minerals from the roots to the leaves. Others conduct dissolved food from the leaves to the roots. These conducting cells have especially thick cellulose walls, and occur in bundles that branch throughout the whole plant. In a leaf, these bundles are the veins. Because of the extra thickness of their cell walls, the veins form a kind of "skeleton" for the leaf. But if the conducting cells in the veins do not contain enough water, the leaves will wilt. Thus, water as well as cellulose is needed to hold leaves upright.

Many of the cells in a leaf are specialized for making food by photosynthesis. In these cells, the green bodies known as chloroplasts are prominent. Chloroplasts contain chlorophyll, a substance that must be present for photosynthesis to take place.

The parts that plant and animal cell have in common, and the differences between them, can be seen in the drawing.

5 A whole skin

The outermost layer of the human skin consists of cells that are no longer alive. These cells are constantly being removed by friction, and the cells that take their place are formed by cell division under the surface. This process of growing new skin cells temporarily speeds up when there is a break in the skin that has to be repaired.

New cells in the skin are produced by cell division in the living layer under the surface. The role of the nucleus in a dividing cell is of central importance. All the nuclear material first duplicates itself and then divides into half, so that each of the two daughter cells has a nucleus that is identical to that of the parent cell. As the doubled nucleus is separating into two equal parts, the cell elongates and the cell membrane and cytoplasm begin to pinch in the middle. The nucleus continues to divide, and the cell membrane and cytoplasm to pinch in the center, until two new cells are formed.

Like the outermost cells in human skin, the cells on the surface in the bark of a tree are no longer alive. As a tree grows in girth, new bark cells are produced by the cambium, a living layer of cells underneath the surface. When a cambium cell divides, the material in its nucleus duplicates itself and then separates into two new nuclei, just as when a human skin cell divides. The cell membrane and cytoplasm also pinch in two. Finally, a new cell wall forms between the two daughter cells.

6 Pond water, protozoans, and protists

In the microscopic examination of pond water, one can often see a surprising number and variety of organisms. Among these are one-celled animals such as paramecia, amebas, euglenas, and stentors.

Unit Concept-Statement: The cell is the unit of structure and function in living things.

Pond water usually contains some very tiny multicellular animals, too. These include rotifers, which are a kind of worm, and water fleas, which are relatives of shrimp. Very simple green plants, such as spirogyra, and nongreen plants, such as water molds, are often present in pond water.

A protozoan is a one-celled animal that is a complete organism in itself. Thus, it is able to perform all the basic life functions: (1) it is sensitive and responds to stimuli, (2) it moves around, (3) it gets and uses food for energy, growth, and repair, (4) it gets rid of wastes and excess water, (5) it reproduces.

The paramecium is a protozoan that has a number of specialized parts known as organelles ("little organs") for carrying out its life functions. Among these are the cilia, tiny hair-like projections all over the paramecium's body that enable the animal to swim and to propel food into its mouth. Another protozoan that has cilia is the stentor.

The flagellum, a whiplike projection on the body of the euglena, is another example of an organelle.

According to one scheme of classification, all living things can be grouped into the Plant Kingdom and the Animal Kingdom. This works well for many-celled organisms, but it is not always easy to determine whether one-celled organisms are more animal-like or plantlike.

The euglena, for example, has some animal-like characteristics, or traits, so that it is claimed by zoologists and classed among the protozoans in the group known as the Protozoa. At the same time, the euglena has some plantlike traits, so that it is claimed by botanists and classed among the algae.

Partially in order to classify borderline organisms, biologists have another scheme of classification that includes the Kingdom Protista. Organisms assigned to this kingdom are referred to as protists, which means, essentially, the "very first" forms of living things. Protists include protozoans, bacteria, algae, and others. All are alike in being simple, one-celled forms of life.

7 Fission, chromosomes, and DNA

Fission is the asexual reproduction of one-celled animals by simple cell division. An ameba in the process of fission looks quite different from a budding yeast, which is also undergoing asexual reproduction. But in both cases, what happens is essentially the same: all the material in the nucleus duplicates itself and then divides in such a way that each of the two new cells receives a nucleus identical to that of the original cell. The same thing—basically—happens in cells dividing to heal a break in human skin or the bark of a tree, and in countless other examples of repair or growth in nearly all organisms.

Biologists refer to simple cell division as *mitosis,* a term that comes from a Greek word for "thread." In a dividing cell, the thread-like bodies that can be seen with a good microscope are the chromosomes. In a cell about to undergo mitosis, the chromosomes duplicate themselves. A human body cell, for example, has 46 chromosomes. If the cell is about to divide by mitosis, each of the 46 chromosomes duplicates itself, forming a total of 92 chromosomes—46 pairs of "identical twins," so to speak. As the cell divides, each "twin" separates from its partner. Thus, each new cell receives a complete set of 46 chromosomes identical to those of the original cell.

Scientists have long understood the basic importance of the chromosomes, and their self-duplication. Chromosomes are the means by which the hereditary traits of the parent cell are passed along to the offspring, as you will see shortly. This is the central notion of the chromosome theory of heredity. In an effort to gain more detailed understanding of heredity, scientists such as Hermann Muller in 1927 and George Beadle in the 1940's, collected evidence that each chromosome contains thousands of determiners, or *genes.* According to the theory, the genes are responsible for the inherited traits of all living things. In human beings, these traits include the color of hair and eyes, height, blood type, and numerous other characteristics both physical and mental. Actually, a gene is only one factor in the development of any trait, for genes act as predicted only in a certain environment.

In 1953, the scientists James Watson and Francis Crick developed evidence that the genes are parts of molecules of DNA (*d*eoxyribo*n*ucleic *a*cid). DNA, then, makes up the bulk of the chromosomes. As might be expected from the behavior of chromosomes in cell division, it was found that DNA molecules can make other molecules like themselves. It seems that the basis of the self-duplication of chromosomes is the self-duplication of molecules of DNA. When cells divide by mitosis, each new cell receives the same amount and kind of DNA that the original cell had.

Recent studies have shown that DNA molecules carry within themselves a kind of chemical code that somehow determines what each cell inherits. We know that DNA acts inside a cell to make it become a certain kind of cell. And we know that in interaction with the environment, DNA determines an individual's hereditary traits. (When exceptions to this general rule occur, it is due to *mutation*, an important source of change in living things that will be discussed in Unit Seven.) But scientists have not yet broken the code—they do not yet know *how* DNA does its work.

As part of the reproductive process in many-celled organisms of all kinds—plants, animals, and human beings—a special form of cell division takes place. This is *reduction division.* In reduction division, no duplication of chromosomes takes place before the cell divides and produces egg cells or sperm cells. As a result, each egg or sperm contains only *half* the number of chromosomes—and only half of the DNA—that is in the body cells of each parent.

For example, a human egg or sperm cell has only 23 chromosomes. But when a sperm fertilizes an egg, the contents of their nuclei combine, and the full number of 46 chromosomes is present in the body cells of the offspring. At the same time, the fertilized egg gets DNA in equal amounts from both parents. The ultimate effect, then, of reduction division, is the production of an individual that is *not* identical to its parents, but has some traits of both, while it still contains the normal number of chromosomes for the kind of organism it is.

8 The development of a frog and a chicken

The egg of a frog is a single cell. But because of the large supply of food in its cytoplasm, the cell is enormous in size, as cells go; about $\frac{1}{16}$ inch in diameter and thus visible without magnification. The frog lays a mass of 2,000 to 3,000 eggs. Each egg is surrounded by jelly. During the 10 to 12 day period between fertilization and the hatching of the tadpole, the embryo is nourished by the food supply stored in the original egg.

The fertilized egg divides first into two cells, then four, then eight, and so on, until a ball of cells forms. As the cells in the ball continue to divide, the embryo begins to elongate. In time, the elongated mass of cells becomes a tadpole. During all these cell divisions, something remarkable has taken place—*cell differentiation.* That is, the two new cells formed in cell division are not identical to, but different from, the original cell. And yet the cell divisions that have taken place are all mitosis, the kind of division in which the chromosomes received by the new cells are the same as those of the original cell. Put another way, what has happened is that cells have been formed with all the same DNA content in their nuclei as the original egg cell had, and yet they are different kinds of cells. A tadpole has muscle cells, blood cells, cartilage cells, nerve cells, and so on, and none of these looks or acts like a fertilized egg cell. It is clear *that* cell differentiation takes place, but scientists have not yet learned *how* it happens.

When the frog embryo becomes a tadpole, its first food is the jelly with which it has been surrounded since the egg was laid. After that, the tadpole begins to feed upon vegetation in the pond. At this stage the tadpole is somewhat like a tiny fish; it has a streamlined shape, gills, and a tail. It is just entering the stage of its development known as *metamorphosis*, which means "changing form."

During the period of metamorphosis, which lasts between 75 and 90 days for most kinds of frogs, the gills and tail are lost and legs and lungs appear. The hind legs develop first, while the tail is still quite long. Later, the forelegs develop; at this stage the tail has shortened somewhat. The tail continues to shorten, and by the time it is completely resorbed, the gills have been replaced by lungs. The frog is now an adult, ready to hop out upon the land. It is a land animal, and yet it can swim and stay submerged for long periods. Other amphibians, such as toads and salamanders, undergo stages of development similar to those of the frog.

When talking about the development of a chick from a hen's egg, it is important to distinguish the *egg cell* from the whole egg, that is, the eggshell and its entire contents. The egg cell is microscopic in size, and is located within a small white disk on the surface of the yolk. Both the yolk and the white (*albumen*) of the egg serve as food for the developing embryo. As soon as fertilization occurs, the egg cell starts to divide. Meanwhile, the shell is formed and the whole egg is laid. In a freshly laid, fertile egg, then, the white disk contains a group of cells—the beginning of a chick embryo.

When the egg is incubated, the cells start to divide again. Within 50 hours, it has grown enough so that the heart is beating. Blood vessels spread over the yolk, conducting food to the embryo and wastes from the embryo to the *allantois*, a special sac that collects and stores wastes. Respiration occurs through the shell, which is porous enough to allow oxygen to diffuse through it into the embryo's blood and carbon dioxide to diffuse out into the air.

After 21 days, the chick is fully formed and is ready to peck its way out of the shell. As in the frog, cell differentiation has produced many different kinds of cells.

Most cold-blooded aquatic or amphibious animals, such as fishes and frogs, lay their eggs in the water where they develop without parental protection. As a result, many of the eggs are eaten by other animals, and only a small percentage of them survive long enough to grow to adulthood. The fact that these animals commonly lay thousands of eggs at a time is an adaptation that helps insure continuation of their kind.

Birds are warm-blooded, and their eggs require warmth in order to develop. As the parent bird sits on the eggs keeping them warm, the eggs are also being protected from possible predators. Thus, a relatively high percentage of the eggs of birds are likely to survive, so that only a few eggs are needed to perpetuate their kind. In mammals, too, only a few (and often only one) offspring develops at a time. The growth of the embryo inside the mother's body affords a high degree of protection. And parental care of the young after birth continues. As a rule, the less mature the young at birth, the longer the period of parental care.

9 The composition of living cells

Living cells of all kinds are made up of the food substances, or nutrients, that they take in, or build, from other materials in the environment. Nutrients can be grouped into six main classes: carbohydrates, fats, proteins, minerals, vitamins, and water.

The main "food factories" among living things are green plants. All living things depend directly or indirectly upon the process of photosynthesis, in which carbon dioxide and water are built into simple sugars. Only green plants can carry on photosynthesis. From simple sugars, complex sugars, starches, and cellulose are built. All these substances together are the carbohydrates. Carbohydrates contain only the elements carbon, hydrogen, and oxygen.

Fats, too, are made up of only the elements carbon, hydrogen, and oxygen. But in fats the proportions of these elements are different than in carbohydrates. Both plant and animal cells can build molecules of fats, but among the starting materials there must be glucose, or some substance derived from glucose.

Proteins can be built by both plant and animal cells. A protein molecule consists of thousands of atoms, mainly carbon, hydrogen, oxygen, and nitrogen. The molecule may also contain other elements, such as phosphorus, sulfur, magnesium, or iron.

Carbohydrates, fats, and proteins are the main nutrients that supply energy for the cell, build up the cell's "living stuff," and repair it when damaged or worn out. Carbohydrates, fats, proteins, and water make up the bulk of man's foods. Vitamins and minerals are also present, in much smaller amounts than the other nutrients, but they play essential roles in the functioning of cells. Together, the six nutrients supply energy for the cell, build up the cell's "living stuff," and repair it when damaged or worn out.

SUPPLEMENTARY AIDS

All films and filmstrips are in color. All films are accompanied by sound; filmstrips are accompanied by sound only if so designated. Names and addresses of producers and distributors of filmstrips are on page F-29.

Filmstrips

Introduction to the Microscope (44 frames), #448-1, SVE. Explains the functions of each part of the microscope, how to get the microscope ready for use, and how to examine specimens.

Introduction to Protozoa (32 frames), #448-3, SVE. Tells how to prepare a culture of protozoa, and how to make a satisfactory examination of it. (Microscopes are necessary.)

One-celled Animals (51 frames), #10751, EBEC. Pictures and discusses the ameba, paramecium, and other single-celled animals as seen through the microscope. Instructions for the preparation of a microscope slide and for the use of the microscope are given.

Films

The Incubator: Classroom Science (12 min.), BFA. Shows the development of the chick; the construction of an incubator, and the techniques that will result in success.

Life Story of the Paramecium (11 min.), #2081, EBEC. Presents a unique photographic study of the one-celled paramecium—physical characteristics, life functions, adaptation to environment, and means of reproduction.

Microbes and Their Control (13 min.), BFA. Demonstrates that microbes are living things too small to be seen with the eyes alone; that in order to grow, they need food, moisture, and warmth, and that we can control their growth.

Science Reading Table

A World in a Drop of Water by Alvin and Virginia Silverstein, Atheneum, 1969. An introduction to microscopy that is particularly useful if a simple microscope is available so that children may see for themselves what is pictured here in photographs and labeled drawings. (Average)

The First Book of Microbes by Lucia Z. Lewis, Franklin Watts, 1955. Introduces the cell as the basic unit of life. Describes types of animal and plant microbes including amebas, paramecia, algae, molds, yeasts, and bacteria. (Average)

Hatch and Grow by Ivah Green and George A. Smith, Abelard-Schuman, 1968. Stages in the life cycles of some 30 or so insects are shown in photographic sequences of lifelike quality. (Average)

Microbes Are Something Else by Harris A. Stone, Prentice-Hall, 1969. An inquiry-oriented presentation which shows that microbes are living organisms capable of causing changes which can be observed in familiar substances through their physical and chemical activities. (Average)

Pioneer Germ Fighters by Navin Sullivan, Atheneum, 1962. Biographies of scientists important in bacteriological study and the continuing fight against disease. The interdependence of scientists is seen. (Average)

Puddles and Ponds: Living Things in Watery Places by Phyllis S. Busch, World Pub., 1969. Pictures and text help the young reader understand the ecology of living things which inhabit a pond and to make discoveries on his own. (Easy)

Understanding Food: The Chemistry of Nutrition by Beulah Tannenbaum, and Myra Stillman, McGraw-Hill, 1962. The major portion of this book deals with the chemical components of food, the needs of the body for particular elements, vitamins, and what happens to the body if it is deficient in vitamins. (Advanced)

What Is a Cell? by Fred M. King and George R. Otto, Benefic Press, 1961. Simple definition and description of cell structure, grouping, specialization, and reproduction. (Average)

Why You Look Like You, Whereas I Tend to Look More Like Me by Charlotta Pomerantz, W. R. Scott, 1969. In entertaining verse, the author humorously points out to the young reader Gregor Mendel's theory. (Easy)

Wonders Under a Microscope by Margaret Cosgrove, Dodd, Mead, 1959. An introductory book on the use of the microscope as a tool for exploration. Concentration is on the viewing of larger specimens to help the child develop dexterity in use of the instrument. (Average)

Your Skin and Mine by Paul Showers, Thomas Y. Crowell, 1965. Text and illustrations combine to explain to the reader the many functions of the skin. (Easy)

An Analysis of Behaviors in Concept-Seeking*

Conceptual Scheme E: A living thing is the product of its heredity and environment.

Unit Concept-Statement: The cell is the unit of structure and function in living things.

Lesson Cluster titles in blue guide concept-seeking toward the Unit Concept-Statement. Other titles enrich the Conceptual Scheme (*see page F-23*).

Lesson Cluster and Supporting Statement	*Operations Basic to Concept-Seeking**	*Methods of Intelligence (Processes and Behaviors)*
1. A Cell at Work Cells interchange matter and energy with the environment.	**Investigating** the action of yeast in a solution of sugar	**Observing** production of carbon dioxide gas by yeast; **inferring** that yeast uses sugar for food
2. The Cell's Energy Process The cell is the unit within which energy from the environment is changed into energy for the work of cells.	**Probing** oxidation and the ATP-ADP cycle	**Analyzing** the input of energy into cells through oxidation and output as the work cells do; **synthesizing** evidence and **constructing** a theory that helps explain energy change within a cell

Unit Concept-Statement: The cell is the unit of structure and function in living things.

3. Getting Inside a Cell Plant and animal cells have basically similar structures.	**Investigating** the structure of the cell and the action of the cell membrane	**Observing** and **analyzing** cell structure; **demonstrating** a function of the cell membrane by **making a model** of a cell and its membrane
4. Cells in a Plant Cells are specialized for different functions.	**Probing** plant cell structures and the skeleton of a leaf	**Analyzing** observations of different plant cells and **inferring** that they have different functions
5. A Whole Skin Cells reproduce themselves.	**Probing** cell division in body cells	**Analyzing** the relation of cell division to growth and repair
6. Just One Cell A single cell may function as a complete organism or have specialized functions in many-celled organisms.	**Investigating** single-celled organisms in pond water	**Observing** single-celled organisms; **inferring** that a single cell can carry on all the life activities of a complete organism
7. Like Begets Like The pattern of a living thing is passed along to its young by duplications of DNA and chromosomes.	**Probing** the reproduction and multiplication of similar cells by fission	**Analyzing** structures in dividing cells; **inferring** that the structures duplicate themselves; **constructing** a theory of inheritance
8. From One Cell When a many-celled organism develops, the egg cell grows into many more cells of many different kinds.	**Investigating** the development of a frog's egg; probing the development of a chicken's egg	**Observing** the development of fertilized egg cells; **inferring** cell differentiation from their development; **applying** knowledge; **synthesizing** cell growth and development and **explaining** how traits of parents determine those of offspring
9. From Earth Into Cell The living stuff of a cell contains elements that are found in the Earth's crust.	**Investigating** cells to determine the compounds of which they are made	**Observing** the results of testing substances derived from cells; **distinguishing** among various nutrients; **inferring** that all living cells consist of elements combined into compounds
10. The Main Concept: Likenesses in Living Things The cell is the unit of structure and function in living things.	Children **analyze** evidence of cell structure and function and **synthesize** it into a broad unifying concept that the cell is the unit of structure and function in living things.	

** A concept is synonymous with the corresponding operations. In turn, operations are served by relevant methods of intelligence.*

UNIT FIVE

THE EARTH'S LIVING THINGS—HIDDEN LIKENESSES

Teaching background. "A View of the Unit" T-224

Concept-seeking. Children become aware that a living thing and a candle, a non-living thing, can both give off the same substance.

Operations. Children *investigate* the gas given off by a burning candle and by germinating beans.

Methods of intelligence. Children *identify* carbon dioxide as a product of a burning candle, *predict* that germinating beans will also produce carbon dioxide, and *test* their prediction.

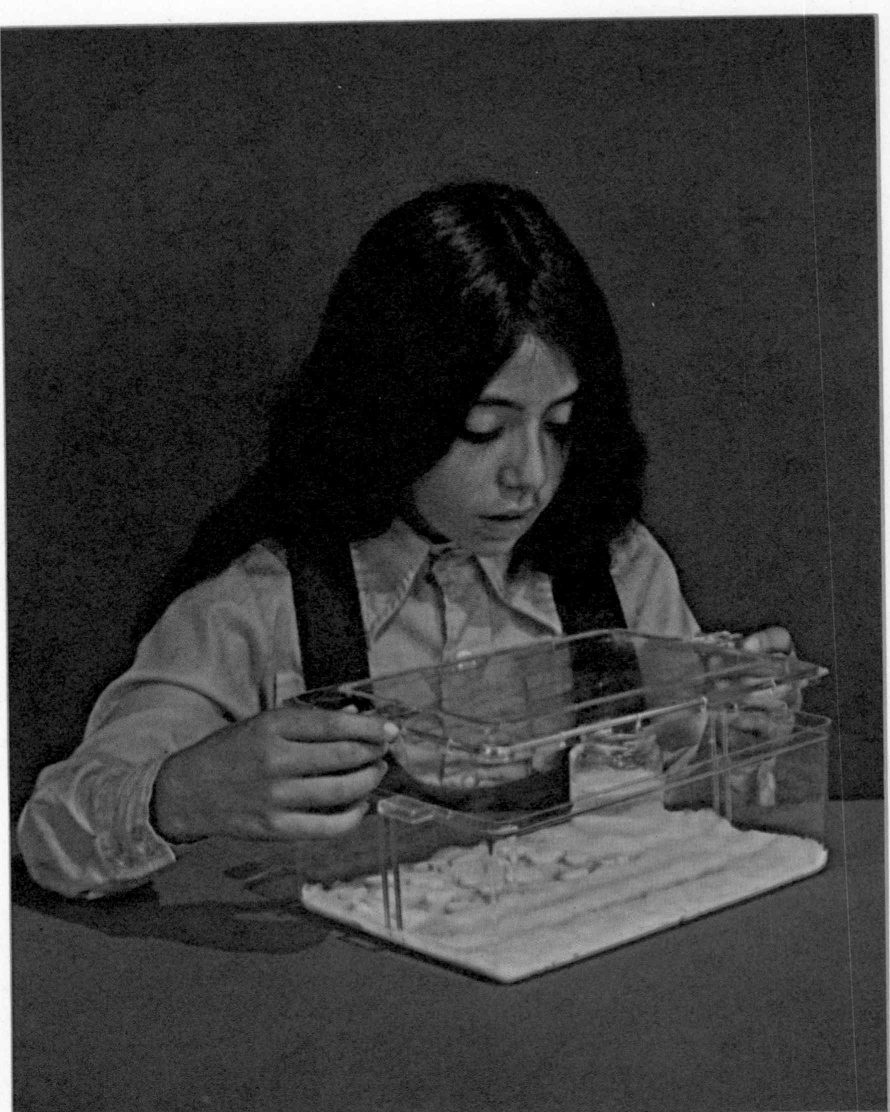

Useful materials: Plastic box or glass container, candle, baby-food jar, limewater, bean seeds, aluminum foil, cotton.

Advance preparation. Soak the lima beans for three hours (or overnight) before class.

Introducing the unit

How is a candle like a lima bean? How are they not alike? Encourage children to hypothesize, but do not comment on the correctness of their ideas. Present the materials, and let several children volunteer to carry out the directions on page 201 as another volunteer reads them.

If a plastic box is used, heat from the candle may melt the plastic. To prevent this, line the top with aluminum foil, or use a sheet of foil in place of the plastic top. Children may use a large glass container, such as a fish tank, in place of the plastic box.

Be sure the lima bean seeds have not been processed to prevent germination.

Unit Concept-Statement: The cell is the unit of structure and function in living things.

UNIT FIVE

The Earth's Living Things— Hidden Likenesses

Stand a candle inside a large, clear plastic box.
❶ Place a small jar of limewater beside the candle. ■
Light the candle, and then cover the box. ●
❷ Predict what will happen to the limewater.
Soak 20 lima beans in water for about 3 hours. Place them on soaked cotton inside another plastic box. Place a small jar of limewater in the box as before. Now cover the box. Predict
❸ what may happen.
What is the hypothesis on which you based your predictions? (Hint: What substance is
❹ given off by both the bean and the candle?)
There are other questions: Is the candle
❺ alive? Is the bean alive?
Think awhile; then turn the page.

■

●

201

❶ For directions for making limewater, see teaching notes for page 137.

❷ Children may predict that the limewater will turn milky on the basis of their knowledge that carbon dioxide is a product of burning and that carbon dioxide turns limewater milky.

❸ Children may predict that the limewater may turn milky solely because they know that *if* carbon dioxide gas is given off the limewater will turn milky.

❹ The limewater in the box with the beans *does* turn milky. Thus, the beans as well as the candle give off carbon dioxide.

❺ Children may disagree about whether or not a substance needs to be alive in order to give off carbon dioxide. They know from blowing into a tube of limewater (page 139) that *they* give off carbon dioxide and may conclude that the bean is alive because it gives off carbon dioxide.

How do you know a candle is not alive? (doesn't grow; can't reproduce itself) In Unit Three, what did you find that all matter—living or nonliving—was made of? (atoms) What two kinds of atoms must be in the bean and the candle to produce carbon dioxide? (carbon and oxygen)

UNIT FIVE

Unit Concept-Statement: The cell is the unit of structure and function in living things.

LESSON CLUSTER 1
A CELL AT WORK

Teaching background. 1 T-224

Concept-seeking. Children become aware of the yeast plant's source of energy.

Operations. Children *investigate* the action of yeast in a solution of sugar and warm water.

Methods of intelligence. Children *observe* that yeast in a solution of sugar and warm water produces carbon dioxide gas; they *infer* that the yeast is using the sugar as food.

Useful materials: Granulated yeast, microscope, slides, cover slips.

❶ 1. A Cell at Work

Look at your finger. A silly request, perhaps. But the question that might come out of your observation is not silly.

Suppose you had some ice cream. How would the energy in the ice cream get to your finger?

It is clear that food substances are used by all animals—by elephants and eels, cats and canaries, whales and mice. Food substances are used by all plants—maples and mosses, oats and orchids, geraniums and wheat, molds and all the plants of the sea. Food substances are used by your body.

Just where in a living thing are food substances used? Let's investigate a simple living thing, about as simple a one as we can get. We shall need a very simple living thing that is easily obtained and kept alive. That living thing is the yeast plant.

The Yeast Plant

❷ Yeast is made up of millions of tiny yeast plants. Observe yeast under a microscope and you will see many tiny balloonlike bodies. ■ They have no green color, even though they are plants. Each of the "balloons" is a yeast **cell.** Each yeast cell is a living thing.

To live, the yeast cell uses food substances, especially sugar. The yeast cell can live on sugar and grow on it.

As the cell grows, something astonishing happens. It produces another yeast cell. That is, the yeast cell **reproduces** itself.

How long does it take a yeast cell to do this astonishing trick? It takes only a few hours when the cell has enough sugar and oxygen and when the temperature is right.

It takes energy to live and grow, of course. Where does a yeast cell get energy? The yeast cell gets energy for growth from sugar. See for yourself what yeast plants do to sugar. Do the investigation opposite. INVESTIGATE

■

202

Introducing Lesson Cluster 1

❶ If children carried out the investigation (blowing into limewater) pictured on page 139, have them recall their results—or do the investigation now. What change do you observe? (Limewater turns milky.) What do you infer from this? (The body gives off carbon dioxide.) Children now have evidence that at least two kinds of living things, beans and human beings, produce carbon dioxide. Where did the carbon dioxide come from? Let children speculate. What elements make up carbon dioxide? (carbon and oxygen) Where does the oxygen come from? (air) the carbon? (food) Where in your body does oxygen combine with food? Encourage hypotheses. This is a key question that will be investigated throughout this unit.

Developing the lesson

❷ Spread some of the contents of a packet of granulated yeast on a sheet of paper, and let the class have a chance to examine the yeast grains. How many one-celled yeast plants are in one yeast grain? Encourage speculation. How might we be able to see a one-celled yeast plant? (Examine under the microscope.) Mount some yeast grains in a drop of water on a slide, add a cover slip, focus the microscope, and let children observe them. (See page 212 for instructions on the use of the microscope.)

Supporting Statement: Cells interchange matter and energy with the environment.

AN APPRENTICE INVESTIGATION into the Uses of Sugar by Yeast

❶ **Needed:** a packet of yeast, sugar, warm water, limewater, a glass flask, a delivery tube, modeling clay

Dissolve two teaspoonfuls of sugar in half a ❷ glass of warm water. Take about half the powdered yeast out of the packet and put it into the water also. Pour this mixture into the flask. Close the flask. Insert the delivery tube and quickly seal the flask with clay. Place the other end of the delivery tube in the limewater. ■

In one trial here is what happened several minutes later. ●

What happens inside the flask when yeast ❸ and sugar and warm water are mixed? Recall your investigation on page 201. How is yeast like the bean? the candle?

Methods of Intelligence: Using a Control

Put the other half of the yeast in half a glass of warm water with *no* sugar in it. This is a **control.** A control is the part of the investigation that has all the conditions the same *except* the one ❹ being investigated. Predict what will happen. How do you explain the result?

Performance objectives. Children *demonstrate* that the action of yeast on sugar produces carbon dioxide, by placing powdered yeast, sugar, and warm water in a gas generator and letting it stand until gas bubbles turn limewater a milky color.

Useful materials: Some similar materials are available in CLASSROOM LABORATORY: PURPLE.

❶ Granulated yeast can be purchased in most supermarkets.

❷ The water should feel comfortably warm on your wrist. Water that is too hot will kill yeast. Cold water will inhibit active growth.

❸ The limewater turns milky. The candle and the bean turned limewater milky. Therefore, the yeast is like the candle and the bean. It gives off carbon dioxide.

How can all three—the yeast, the germinating bean plant, and the candle—produce carbon dioxide? (They are all using fuel or food. Some children may say immediately that they are all using energy.) What is the bean plant's food? (The bean plant's food is part of the bean seed.) What is the candle's fuel? (paraffin or wax) What is the yeast plant's food? (sugar)

What does food or fuel make available to the bean, the candle, and the yeast? (energy) If children respond "carbon dioxide gas," ask: What must all three use to produce this gas? (energy)

❹ Children should predict that nothing will happen. In other words, the yeast needs food—which is the sugar—in order to produce carbon dioxide gas. Children should test their prediction.

UNIT FIVE

Unit Concept-Statement: The cell is the unit of structure and function in living things.

VERIFYING PROGRESS

In methods of intelligence

Children can *build models* to *demonstrate* the budding of yeast. They will need to obtain some of the materials mentioned. The budding of yeast can be visualized by modeling clay, by balloons and tape, by different sizes of Styrofoam balls and toothpicks, or by the plastic material that comes in a tube and is blown and pinched into various shapes. Encourage children to *invent* other *models* of their own.

Useful materials: Flour, yeast, water, sugar.

How does a yeast cell reproduce? As a yeast cell grows, it forms a bud.■ The bud grows and becomes a new yeast cell. Then that cell buds, and so on. Yeast cells reproduce by budding.

It is not hard to make a model of a yeast cell reproducing. Take a piece of modeling clay and make a ball. Then, from another piece of clay, make a smaller ball and stick it to the larger one. You now have a model of a yeast cell with a new cell coming from it.

■

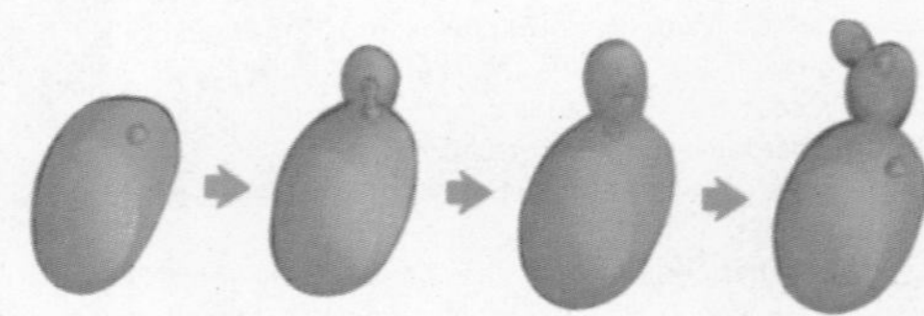

Breaking Down Molecules

When yeast cells are put into a sugar solution, they make ❶ carbon dioxide gas. (You know this, because in the investigation the bubbles that came off caused the limewater to turn milky.)

You already know something about carbon dioxide. You know that it is a combination of carbon and oxygen. To make carbon dioxide, the yeast cells must get atoms of carbon and atoms of oxygen from somewhere.

Where do the yeast cells get carbon atoms from? Sugar is made up of atoms of carbon and hydrogen and oxygen. In the yeast cells, sugar and oxygen combine to form carbon dioxide and water. We can write an equation about this.

$$\text{sugar} + \text{oxygen} \longrightarrow \text{carbon dioxide} + \text{water}$$

The yeast cell, a tiny living thing, can break down sugar ❷ molecules.

204

Continuing Lesson Cluster 1

❶ What are the elements in water? (hydrogen and oxygen) Why can't yeast cells make carbon dioxide from water? (no carbon) What also besides water was in our investigation? (sugar) Since sugar was the only other substance in the jar with the yeast, what element must be in sugar? (carbon) Where must the energy come from? (sugar) What two substances contain oxygen? (water and sugar) Children may infer that the yeast *must* be using the sugar to get the carbon atom and *may* be using either the water or the sugar to get the oxygen atoms. What must yeast cells do to the sugar molecule to produce carbon dioxide? (break it down)

❷ When bread is made, yeast is used to make the bread light and spongy. Add enough flour to a solution of sugar and yeast to form a heavy dough. What do you think will happen to the dough if it stands for several hours in a warm place? Encourage hypotheses. After observation, ask: What is happening in the dough? (Yeast is producing bubbles of carbon dioxide as it uses sugar in the dough. The carbon dioxide remains trapped in the dough and causes it to rise.)

Supporting Statement: Cells interchange matter and energy with the environment.

1 BEFORE YOU GO ON

Check your understanding of the concepts of this section. Which ending would you choose for each statement below?

1. A yeast plant is a living thing made up of
   a. one cell
   b. many cells

2. When a yeast cell buds, it
   a. reproduces
   b. only grows

3. When a yeast cell uses sugar, the cell gives off
   a. oxygen gas
   b. carbon dioxide gas

4. The statement that fits the main concept of this section is
   a. The yeast plant gets its energy from the food it uses.
   b. The yeast plant get its energy from reproduction.

2 USING WHAT YOU KNOW

Yeast can be used, like baking powder, to make bread rise. What does yeast do that raises bread?

3 INVESTIGATING FURTHER

1. Find out why yeast is classified as a plant. Why isn't yeast classified as an animal?

2. If you have the use of a microscope, study some yeast cells. First, make a mixture of yeast, sugar, and water as in the investigation on page 203. Let the mixture stand overnight in a warm, dark place.

Next, make a slide of your yeast mixture, and study it under the microscope. (See pages 212–13 for directions for making a slide and for using the microscope.)

Look for yeasts that are reproducing by budding. Will yeasts reproduce at very hot or very cold temperatures? Design an investigation to find out.

A LOOK AHEAD

Yeast is a living thing. What are the first clues that tell us when an object is alive? First, it uses a fuel (food). Second, it produces carbon dioxide. Third, it reproduces itself.

In a way, the paraffin of a candle is a fuel. A candle also makes carbon dioxide. But does a candle reproduce itself? What is the difference in the way a cell uses food?

Another difference between the candle and the cell is in the way the cell uses its fuel—the cell's energy process. Let's see what that process is.

205

VERIFYING PROGRESS

1 Before you go on. Children *demonstrate* understanding of some of the life functions of yeast cells by *identifying* suitable responses to open-ended questions.

1. a   2. a   3. b   4. a

2 Children *analyze* the action of yeast in bread dough and *infer* that yeast uses sugar and gives off carbon dioxide, causing bread dough to rise because of the trapped bubbles.

3 Investigating further. Children *consult authorities* to determine why yeast is classified as a plant; they *observe* yeast cells with a microscope and *design an investigation* into conditions for the asexual reproduction of yeast.

1. Children will need to read ahead (through page 223) to find out that classification is determined by the cell structure. Plant cells have a cell wall and animal cells do not.

2. Children should try making slides of yeast cells placed in very hot and very cold solutions of sugar and water.

Unit Concept-Statement: The cell is the unit of structure and function in living things.

LESSON CLUSTER 2
THE CELL'S ENERGY PROCESS

Teaching background. 2 T-225

Concept-seeking. Children become aware of how cells obtain energy from food substances.

Operations. Children *probe* into oxidation and the ATP–ADP cycle.

Methods of intelligence. Children *analyze* the input of energy into cells through oxidation of food and the output of energy as the work cells do; they *synthesize* evidence and *construct a theory* that helps to *explain* the energy changes that take place within a cell.

Useful materials: Rusted and non-rusted objects such as steel wool pads or nails.

2. The Cell's Energy Process

Gasoline supplies the energy to make a car go. Oil is burned in a diesel locomotive so that it can do work. Kerosene supplies energy for jet engines. If work is to come out of a machine, energy must be put in, as you know. The same thing is true of a yeast cell. Energy must be put into a cell, if the cell is to do its work.

In the yeast cell, food substances are the fuel. Food substances supply energy for the cell's work. How does the cell change food into energy? Does the cell burn the food as a candle or a jet engine burns its fuel, to get energy?

Changing Food into Energy

What is "burning," anyway? What is happening when a thing burns?

When a candle burns, its paraffin fuel combines with oxygen taken from the air. This combining with oxygen is called **oxidation,** as you may remember having learned in Unit Three.

In oxidation, compounds called oxides are formed. One oxide you know is carbon dioxide. The burning candle forms carbon dioxide gas by combining carbon and oxygen.

Oxidation can happen *without* a flame, as well. When ❶ iron rusts, for instance, it is combining with oxygen taken from the air. This is oxidation, too. Iron oxide is formed. Rusting, then, is a combining with oxygen without flame. Oxidation can happen with a flame, or without a flame.

In your body, right now, food substances are combining ❷ with oxygen. Oxidation is happening in your body. Food substances are oxidized in your body. This oxidation takes place at a much lower temperature than the oxidation that takes place in burning.

The sugar in a food substance can combine with oxygen in your body. Oxidation takes place. At the same time, energy is being released.

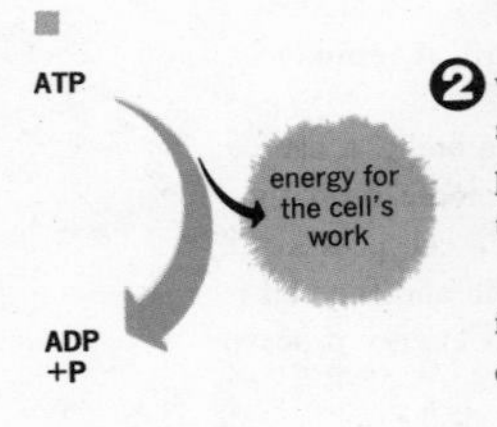

206

Introducing Lesson Cluster 2

Light a candle. What is the food for the flame? (the candle wax) Hold up a cube of sugar and a yeast package. What fed the yeast? (sugar) How are the candle and the sugar alike? (sources of energy) How were they alike when they were used for energy? (Both produced carbon dioxide.)

You use sugar on your cereal, in iced lemonade, and in candy. What does sugar give you? (energy) Why couldn't you eat the candle for energy? What is the difference between the way we get energy from a fuel and the way we get it from food?

Developing the lesson

❶ Help children recall the word equation describing the chemical changes in a burning candle. With the children's help, write the equation on the chalkboard:

candle + oxygen →
carbon dioxide + water + energy

Rapid oxidation producing a flame is known as *combustion.*

❷ Slow oxidation (without a flame) is also accompanied by release of heat energy. Feel the skin on your wrist or neck. What is the evidence that oxidation is going on in your body? (Body temperature is 98.6°.) Where does oxidation take place in you? Children may respond: "All over". Try to get them to localize the process more specifically by asking: Where did the yeast oxidize sugar? What is the yeast plant? (single cell)

Supporting Statement: The cell is the unit within which energy from the environment is changed into energy for the work of cells.

We can write an equation about this.

sugar + oxygen ⟶ carbon dioxide + water + energy

This is how you get energy. In your body cells, *now*, oxidation is going on. Oxidation of food substances supplies you with energy.

There is a hitch, though. This energy must be changed into another form before a cell can use it. However, your cells manage to do this too. ❶

The Cell's Energy Machine

When you turn on an electric fan, you are really turning on a machine for changing energy. The fan changes energy from one form to another. After all, the electrical energy in the wall outlet isn't of much use to you just as it is. So you turn on a machine that can change that energy into a useful form. The electric fan changes the energy of electricity into the energy of moving air.

A cell has a kind of machine for changing the energy it gets into the sort of energy it can use. There is a huge molecule that does the job.

❷ This molecule is called an **ATP** molecule. ATP stands for adenosine triphosphate (ad′ə·nō′sēn trī·fos′fāt). But scientists say ATP; so, why don't you?

Let's imagine how a cell's energy machine works. To begin with, the cell has inside it a good supply of ATP molecules. These ATP molecules begin to break down inside the cell. *As the ATP breaks down, energy is given up.* This is the sort of energy that the cell can use for its work.

As ATP is broken down by the cell to yield energy, the ATP breaks into smaller pieces. Scientists call these smaller pieces **ADP + P**, for short. Here is one way of showing this. ■

❸ If all the ATP the cell had was broken down into ADP + P, the cell would have no ATP and no more energy for its work. However, the cell gets more ATP. The cell's energy machine can change the ADP + P back to ATP. ●

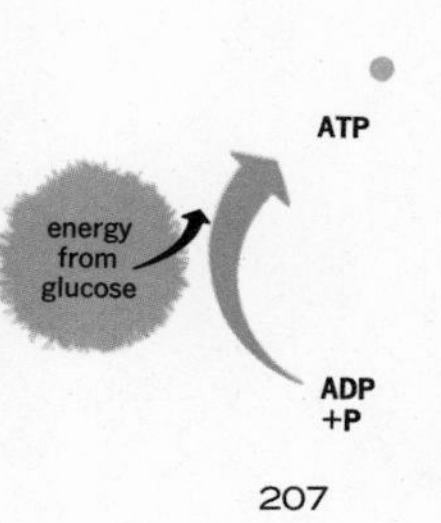

❶ What changes do you think have to take place? Why doesn't the cell use heat energy directly? Is there some real difference between the release of energy from a candle and the release of energy from food? Let children discuss these questions. It is unlikely that they will be able to hypothesize correctly, but they will be on the right track if they say that something goes on in the cells.

❷ ATP and ADP sometimes offer children difficulty in understanding what happens inside the cell. Write on the board:

A–P ~ P ~ P = ATP

and explain that the three phosphates are all alike and are joined as if by rubber bands. What happens when a rubber band breaks? (It snaps, releasing energy.) What happens if the last P breaks from the rest of the molecule? (It releases energy, leaving A–P ~ P and ~ P.)

Explain that APP (or ADP) is adenosine diphosphate and *di* means two P groups. What happens to the energy that is released? (It is used by the cells to do their work.)

❸ Let the children study the second half of the diagram on this page. When glucose, a kind of sugar, is oxidized, its energy connects the P group to ADP so that the molecule becomes ATP again with all the stored energy it needs. It's as if a new rubber band replaced the broken one.

❶ Notice that this is where the kind of sugar called **glucose** comes in. The cell now needs energy to build up ATP. How does the cell get energy for building up ATP? It oxidizes glucose that it takes in.

There is a kind of merry-go-round here, isn't there? The ATP breaks down into pieces. As it does so, it yields ❷ energy for the cell's work. Then the ATP builds up again from its pieces. The energy for building up the ATP is taken from glucose. Now the ATP is ready to break down again.■ This merry-go-round is called an **energy cycle.**

■

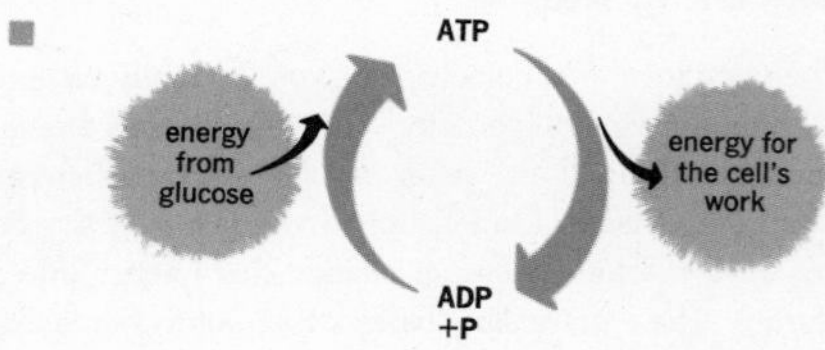

We can write the energy cycle in equations like this:

ATP ⟶ ADP + P + energy for the cell's work

ADP + P + energy from glucose ⟶ ATP

You can see that this energy cycle can keep going around and around, as long as the cell takes in glucose and has ❸ work to do.

Of course, these pictures show an imaginary model. A cell does not look like this. However, the cell does behave as if it had an energy machine inside it. It does make use of ATP to get energy.

Scientists know what ATP looks like in a test tube. It is a powdery, yellowish substance. They know what glucose looks like, too. It is a powdery, white substance. But scientists don't know yet just how energy comes out of breaking down ATP.

Scientists do know that it is the cell that does the job. The work of a living thing is done by its cells.

Continuing Lesson Cluster 2

❶ Glucose is the form of sugar in many fruits, grapes especially. But it is also the main nutrient carried by cells after food has been changed by digestion and enters the bloodstream (See Unit Six). It is this glucose that gets into cells, is oxidized, and releases energy.

❷ What, basically, do you think the cell does? Perceptive children may correctly infer that it changes the energy in food by oxidizing it in the cell and then releasing it for motion of the body, for sensing the environment, and for other functions of the organism.

❸ Do cells ever have no work to do? For example, when you are asleep, do you need energy? (yes—for breathing, heart beat, getting rid of wastes of oxidation) Why is an adequate diet necessary? Let children speculate what would happen to the cell energy process if a person had no food for a number of days.

Supporting Statement: The cell is the unit within which energy from the environment is changed into energy for the work of cells.

❶ BEFORE YOU GO ON

A. Check your understanding of the concepts of this section. Which ending would you choose for each statement below?

1. The main substance oxidized in the cell is
   a. glucose b. starch

2. For the cell to have energy for its work, it must first build up
   a. glucose b. ATP

3. Energy that cells can use comes from the breaking down of
   a. ATP b. ADP

4. When oxidation takes place
   a. energy is released
   b. there must be a flame

5. The statement that fits the main concept of this section is
   a. The cell's energy process is a molecule.
   b. The cell's energy process is a cycle.

B. Write a paragraph or two on this topic: "ATP—Why My Life Depends on It."

❷ USING WHAT YOU KNOW

1. When ATP breaks down,
   ATP ⟶ ? + P
2. When ATP is built up,
   ADP + ? ⟶ ATP
3. A cell must have energy to build up ATP. What main food substance supplies the energy?

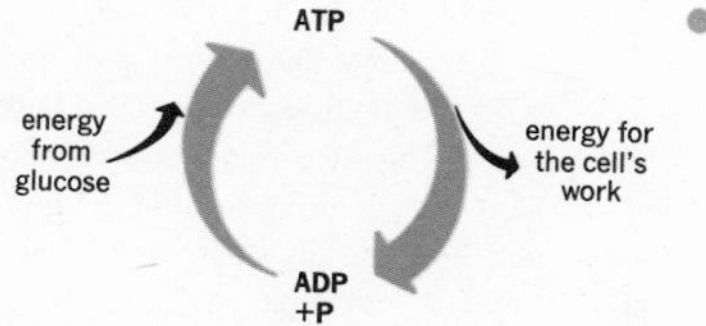

A LOOK AHEAD

This is a simple diagram. ● But it is important. It is a diagram of something going on in you right now—the cell's energy cycle. The process is not completely understood. Of course, the diagram is much too simple. But if you understand this simple diagram, you are at the beginning of your understanding of a most important activity in living things.

Let us see what is inside a cell.

209

VERIFYING PROGRESS

In methods of intelligence

Children can *demonstrate* their understanding of the ATP–ADP cycle by *inventing* and *constructing* models. They may draw the cycle, model it in clay, use colored beads and wire, balloons and wire, felt, or whatever medium interests them. They then *explain* their models.

VERIFYING PROGRESS

❶ Before you go on. Children *demonstrate* understanding of the cell energy process by *identifying* suitable endings to statements and *explaining* the importance of ATP.

A. 1. a 3. a 5. b
   2. b 4. a

B. Children should *demonstrate* understanding of how energy going into body cells is changed to energy used by these cells in their activities.

❷ Using what you know. Children *analyze* and complete word equations and *identify* the food substance that supplies the energy to build up ATP.

1. ADP 2. P 3. glucose

UNIT FIVE

Unit Concept-Statement: The cell is the unit of structure and function in living things.

LESSON CLUSTER 3
GETTING INSIDE A CELL

Teaching background. 3 T-225

Concept-seeking. Children become aware of the basic structure of a body cell and how the cell membrane makes possible the interchange of substances with the cell's environment.

Operations. Children *investigate* the structure of the cell by viewing some of their cheek cells under a microscope and *investigate* the action of a cell membrane.

Methods of intelligence. Children *observe* and *analyze* the structure of the cell. They *demonstrate* a function of the cell by making a model of a cell and its membrane.

Useful materials: Potato, marble, teaspoon.

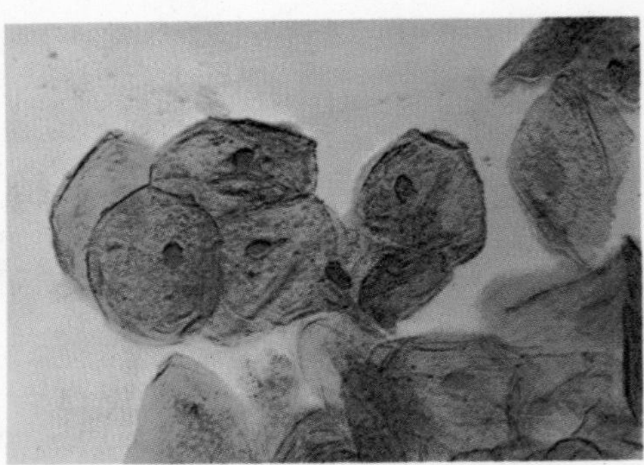

3. Getting Inside a Cell

Bend your finger—once again.

What is happening in the cells of the finger to make it possible for the finger to move?

To move that finger, your body cells are breaking down ATP and yielding energy. To build up the ATP so that it can be used again, cells are breaking down food substances. The food yields energy to build up the ATP. This breaking down and building up again is the cell energy cycle. (You may unbend your finger now.)

The cell energy cycle goes on in *all* cells. In every cell in your body, ATP is being broken down to ADP and ADP is built into ATP right now.

Inside Cells

❶ These flat, odd-shaped bodies are cheek cells.■ They are very small. How many cheek cells do you think it would take to stretch across the circle at the end of this ❷ sentence? ○

210

Introducing Lesson Cluster 3

Ask every child to bend his finger as the text suggests. How were you able to do this? Were only cells in your finger used? If others were used what were they? Children may be able to trace the action from the sound of your voice to the ear to the brain and then to the finger. All kinds of cells were used. How many cells had to have energy in order to bend your finger? When children start thinking about this question, they may be surprised.

Developing the lesson

❶ The cells in the picture are stained with iodine and magnified about 250 times.

❷ Let children speculate on the number of cheek cells that would fit into the circle. (For your information, about 30 cheek cells would fit into the circle. These cells are, however, relatively large: the circle would contain about ten times as many, or 300, white blood cells.)

Supporting Statement: Plant and animal cells have basically similar structures.

Have you observed that each of these cells has a dark spot in the middle? This spot is the **nucleus.** Around the nucleus is more material. It is called **cytoplasm** (sī′tə·plaz′əm). Around the cytoplasm is a very thin skin. This skin is the **cell membrane.**

❶ A cheek cell looks different from a yeast cell. But both cells have a nucleus, cytoplasm, and a cell membrane.

The nucleus, cytoplasm, and cell membrane are important parts of these cells. To see these parts clearly, make a model. You will need a potato and a marble.

Cut the potato in half. With a spoon, hollow out a small ❷ space in each half. Put the marble in this space.

The marble is a model of the nucleus of a cell. The white part of the potato stands for the cytoplasm. The skin stands for the cell membrane. ● Of course, this model doesn't act as a cell does. However, you can easily observe some cheek cells of your own, if you have the use of a microscope. To learn how to use a microscope, try the investigation on the next two pages. Then, to see cells for yourself, try the investigation on page 214. INVESTIGATE

❶ Let children turn to the pictures of yeast cells on pages 202 and 204 to compare them with the cheek cells. What do you notice about the nucleus when the yeast cell divides? (It divides, too.)

❷ Children may make potato-marble models of cells either in class or at home. They may make and attach labels for the "nucleus," "cytoplasm," and "cell membrane." What kinds of fruits could be used as cell models? (peach, apricot, avocado, date, etc.) What would the pit represent? (the nucleus) the pulp? cytoplasm) the skin? (cell membrane)

Performance objectives. Children *construct* slide preparations by placing 2 hairs in a drop of water on a slide and lowering a cover slip over it; they *demonstrate* the use of a microscope by placing in focus, under low power and high power, the slides they have prepared.

Useful materials: Some similar materials are available in CLASSROOM LABORATORY: PURPLE.

AN APPRENTICE INVESTIGATION into Using a Microscope

Needed: a microscope, slides, cover slips, medicine dropper

❶ First, let's examine a microscope. ■ The upper lens, the one you look through, is called the eyepiece. The lower lenses are called objectives. There is a number on the top of the eyepiece of ❷ this microscope: "10X." Each of the objective lenses is marked with a number also. One lens is marked "10" and the other lens is marked "20." These numbers indicate the magnifying power of these lenses. The eyepiece magnifies 10 times. The objective lenses magnify 10 times and 20 times.

How much can this microscope magnify? Multiply the number on the eyepiece by the number on the objective being used. For the low-power objective, marked 10, this is 10 × 10, or 100. Thus, the microscope magnifies 100 times. Multiply the number on the high-power objective marked "20" by the number on the eyepiece: 10 × 20 is 200. ❸ Thus, the microscope magnifies 200 times. (Some microscopes magnify different amounts than these.)

The wheel at the side of the microscope is for focusing. When you turn the wheel, the distance between the objective lens and the object being observed changes. The mirror is reflecting light onto the object being examined.

eyepiece
objective lenses
focusing wheel
mirror
foot

Methods of Intelligence: Using a Tool

Scientists, you recall, strengthen their observations by using tools. Some tools, like the microscope, extend the power of the eye to observe.

Perhaps the easiest way to begin using the microscope is by looking at some of your own ❹ hairs. Follow these steps.

❺ —Take up a little water in the medicine

212

Continuing Lesson Cluster 3

❶ There are many variations in design among microscopes. Have children identify the parts of the one they will use by comparing it with the photograph.

❷ Be sure children check the magnifications of the eyepiece and objective on their instruments.

❸ Suppose a microscope has an eyepiece marked 10X, a low-power objective marked 15X, and a high-power objective marked 20X. How many times does the microscope magnify under low power? (10 × 15 = 150) under high power? (10 × 25 = 250)

❹ Slides and cover slips should be clean, as smudges or pieces of lint will obscure objects viewed under the microscope. Clean slides and cover slips with rubbing alcohol and lens tissue. Let them dry in the air by placing them on paper toweling. Handle clean slides and cover slips by their thin edges, as in the photograph on page 213.

❺ Children should avoid placing too much material, or material that is too thick to let the light through, on a slide. A "hair or two" is literally the best procedure.

Supporting Statement: Plant and animal cells have basically similar structures.

dropper. Put a small drop on a slide.

–Put a hair or two in the drop.

–Touch a cover slip to the edge of the drop of water.

–Gently lower the cover slip onto the drop. The hairs are now mounted on a slide and ready to be examined.

❶ –Swing the low-power lens under the eyepiece until it clicks into place.

–Put your eye to the eyepiece. Turn the ❷ mirror toward a window or a light so that light is reflected into the microscope. You will see a circle of light in the eyepiece.

–Take your eye from the eyepiece. Put the slide under the clips on the stage so that it is held firmly. Place the slide so that the hair is in the light from the mirror.

❸ –Turn the wheel so that the low-power objective moves slowly down toward the slide. Stop when you see the lens is about 1/8 of an inch from the slide.

–Now put your eye to the eyepiece and turn the wheel the other way so that the lens moves up, away from the slide. *Be sure to turn the wheel so that the lens moves away from the slide.* If you turn the wheel the wrong way, you may run the objective into the slide, break the cover slip and the slide–and scratch the lens. Turn the wheel until the hair is in focus, sharp and clear.

❹ –Try moving the slide around with your fingers carefully, while looking through the eyepiece, to see other parts of the drop.

❺ –To look at the hair through the high-power objective, swing the high-power objective around until it clicks into place under the eyepiece. It will be very nearly in focus. Move the wheel *very carefully,* for the high-power objective is very close to the cover slip and slide!

–Before you remove the slide, raise the tube and swing back to low power again. Rinse the slide and cover slip and dry with tissue paper.

Learn to use the microscope–by using it. How does it extend your field of observation?

213

❶ A microscope is an easily damaged instrument. Before children view the slides they have made, run through a demonstration on the use of the microscope. First the tube should be raised as high as it will go. Determine which way the tube moves, upward or downward, as the adjusting wheel is turned. If several groups are working with a microscope, see that they understand this motion. With the tube up as high as it will go, let the children learn how to swing the low-power objective into place.

❷ The microscope should be placed so that a source of light will be reflected by the mirror through the hole in the stage. Children should move the mirror until they see a clear spot of reflected light through the eyepiece.

❸ Children should be cautioned not to lower the tube so far that it crashes into the cover glass. A scratch on the lens ruins the microscope.

❹ After children have examined a hair, they may repeat the procedure with paper, cloth, string, salt, sand, animal fur, etc. before they attempt the use of the high-power lens.

❺ Caution children to watch carefully from the side as they swing the high-power lens into place. If the lens looks as if it may not clear the slide, the tube should be raised until it does clear.

Unit Concept-Statement: The cell is the unit of structure and function in living things.

Performance objectives. Children *construct* stained microscope slide preparations of material from the insides of their cheeks; they *demonstrate* the use of a microscope by placing these slides in focus; they *describe* the appearance of a cheek cell and *identify* the cell nucleus.

Useful materials: Some similar materials are available in CLASSROOM LABORATORY: PURPLE.

AN APPRENTICE INVESTIGATION into Your Cheek Cells

❶ **Needed:** a microscope, a glass microscope slide, a cover slip, a weak solution of iodine, a clean medicine dropper, a clean toothpick

Put a drop of water on the center of the glass slide. Gently scrape the inside of your cheek with the side of the clean toothpick. A whitish mate- ❷ rial will collect on the toothpick. The material is made up of cells from your cheek.

Mix this material in the drop of water. ■ To see the cells more clearly under the microscope, ❸ stain them. Add just one drop of the weak iodine solution to the drop of water on the slide. ● Place ❹ a cover slip over the drop.

Place the slide under the lens of the microscope. The shapes are cells from the skin of your cheek. ▲ Can you observe a dark spot in ❺ each cell? It is the nucleus of that cell, stained by the iodine solution.

Methods of Intelligence: Inferring

❻ Let the drop of water on the slide dry and observe what happens to the cells. What will you find? How does your inference extend your understanding?

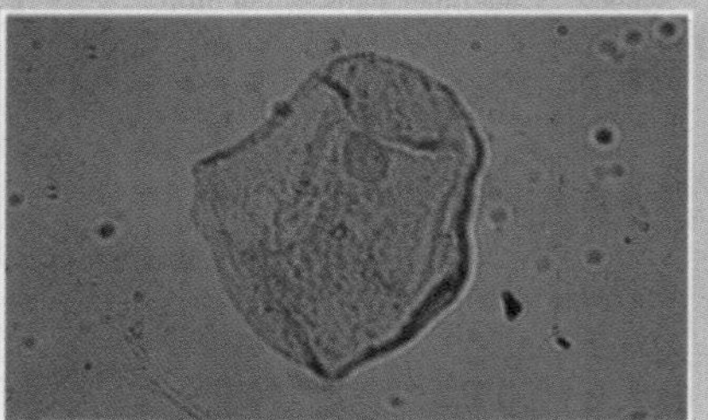

214

Continuing Lesson Cluster 3

❶ To prepare the iodine solution, mix equal parts of tincture of iodine and water.

❷ Dead cells children remove from inside their cheeks will come off quite easily and harmlessly with gentle rubbing with the flat end of a toothpick.

❸ Caution children against using too much water. One *small* drop is ample. The amount of iodine solution needed will cling to the tip of a toothpick.

❹ Children should place one edge of the cover slip in the liquid and gently drop it. When this is done correctly, there will be no air bubbles on the slide. If, however, children do have air bubbles on their slides, do not let them confuse these with the cells they are looking for. An air bubble has a heavy, dark, circular outline that is quite unlike the cell in the photograph on this page.

❺ How are the cells you see like yeast cells? (same three basic parts) How are they different? (Yeast cells are somewhat balloon-shaped; cheek cells are flat and irregular.)

❻ From their knowledge of the shriveling effect of drying on the leaves of a plant, children may infer that cells will also shrivel when allowed to dry.

Supporting Statement: Plant and animal cells have basically similar structures.

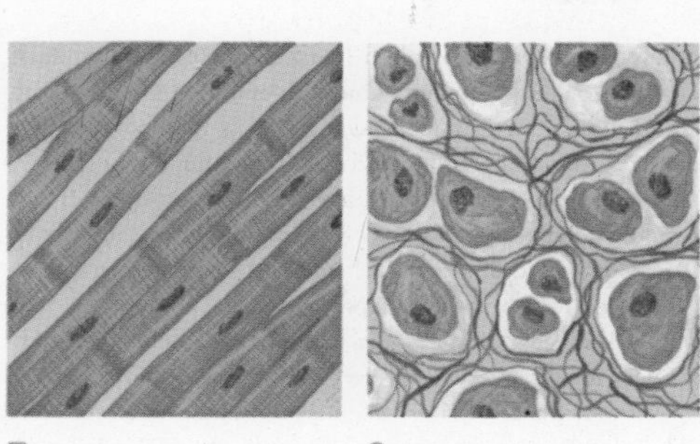

■ ●

❶ **Your Tiny Energy Machines**

Feel a muscle in your arm. There are millions upon millions of muscle cells in your muscles. One kind of
❷ muscle cell looks like this. ■ Touch your ear. There are
❸ millions of cells there, too. Some of them look like this. ●
If you could look into your blood, you would find more mil-
❹ lions of cells. ▲ In your brain are still more millions of
cells. ◆ *You are made up of many kinds of cells.*

These cells certainly look different. They *are* different, for they do different work. Yet each has a nucleus,
❺ cytoplasm, and cell membrane. (Red blood cells have nuclei before they enter the blood stream.)

◆ ▲

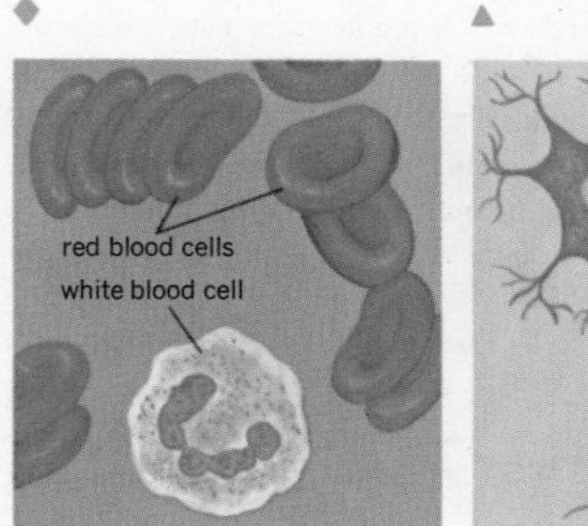

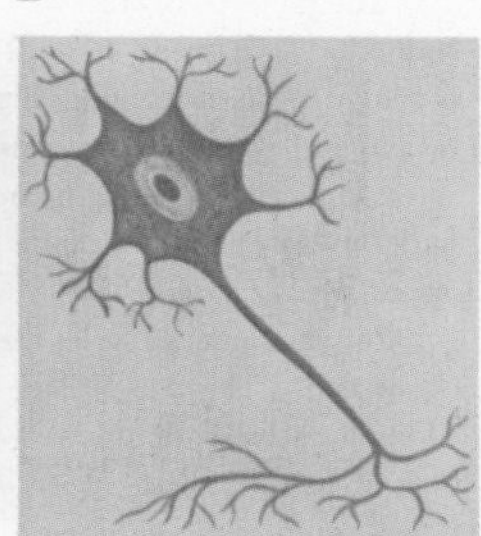

Useful materials: Prepared, stained slides of human or animal tissues, microscope.

❶ Prepared, stained slides of human or animal tissues can be used to study various types of cells under the microscope.

❷ The muscle cells pictured are the type found in skeletal muscles attached to bones in the arms, legs, head, and trunk of the body.

❸ The cells pictured here are cartilage cells of the type found in the tough, flexible tissue of the ears and nose.

❹ If you have a microscope, and if your school nurse or doctor is willing to prepare blood smears of children (who would need written permission from home), a lesson centered on the study of these would be of great interest. As an alternative, children can examine beef blood from a butcher shop.

❺ In the pictures on this page children will realize that there are many variations in the basic plan of the cell. What seems to be the general shape of a muscle cell? (long, stringy)

In the pictures of the (cartilage) cells in the ear and the (nerve) cell in the brain, what parts do you notice besides the nucleus, cytoplasm, and cell membrane? (clear areas and stringy material around the ear cartilage cells; branched twig-like ends on the nerve cell) What part is missing from the red blood cells? (nucleus)

Unit Concept-Statement: The cell is the unit of structure and function in living things.

Most other many-celled living things, besides yourself, are also made of many kinds of cells. An onion, frog, spider, cat, or tree, for instance, has cells that look different ❶ and do different work. And just like your own cells, the cells of other living things have their likenesses. If you could examine the cells of a bit of cat muscle, or the leaf of a tree, you would find that each cell has a nucleus, cytoplasm, and a cell membrane, just as your cells do.

These cells are alike in other ways, too. Food substances go into every cell. Oxygen goes into every cell. In every cell the food substances are broken down and yield energy. This energy is used to build up ATP. In every cell, ATP breaks down and yields energy for that cell's work.

So each cell has a tiny energy machine. You use the energy in your cells every moment, for play and work and growth. You are using the energy of your cells right now, ❷ to read these words. How else are you using energy?

Getting into a Cell

Now, here is a puzzle. You know that substances go into a cell and provide it with energy. Oxygen goes in, for example. Sugar goes in. So do other food substances. Substances come out of a cell, too.

How do substances get in and out of a cell?

The pictures of cells which you have seen show that each cell is sealed inside its cell membrane much as a potato is sealed in its skin. Do you think that substances can get ❸ in and out of the potato skin? Explain why you think so.

Do substances get in and out of a cell membrane? To find out for yourself, make the model cell shown on the opposite page. MODEL

In your model cell, the gelatin represents the cell's cytoplasm. The plastic bag stands for the cell membrane. The clay stands for the cell nucleus. Use this cell for the next investigation on page 218. It will show you something that a cell membrane can do. INVESTIGATE

216

Continuing Lesson Cluster 3

❶ Children can get a preview of the appearance of some plant cells by looking at the pictures on pages 221 and 223. If you have prepared slides of plant cells, you may want to let children compare these with human and animal cells at this time.

❷ Encourage children to list as many ways as they can in which they are using energy as they read the page: for breathing, sitting up, digesting food, keeping their eyes open and moving, building ATP, thinking, keeping warm, heart beating, blood circulating, making new cells, etc.)

❸ Children may speculate on the question in the text, but unless they investigate the passage of materials through a potato skin they have little evidence upon which to hypothesize. They may have observed that the iodine solution stained the nucleus inside a cheek cell. They can make an inference, but it should be tested. **How could you investigate the question?** (Place a potato in a jar of water colored with 2% tincture of iodine. After a lapse of time, open the potato and see if dye has penetrated the skin. The starch inside the potato will be bluish black, near the skin at least, if the iodine solution went through the skin.)

Supporting Statement: Plant and animal cells have basically similar structures.

MAKING A MODEL
The Cell Membrane

Needed: clear gelatin, some starch, cologne, 3 or 4 small plastic bags (sandwich size), string, modeling clay, scissors

❶ Boil 1 cupful of water and stir in a packet of gelatin. This will dissolve the gelatin. Then add ❷ ½ cupful of cold water. Add a teaspoonful of starch and a teaspoonful of cologne. Stir to mix with the gelatin.

Pour some of this mixture into a plastic bag. An amount about the size of a Ping-Pong ball will do. Add a small, round piece of clay about the size of a pea. Tie the bag tightly with string so that it has the shape of a ball. There should be as little air as possible in the bag. Cut away the unused part of the bag with scissors.

Make 3 or 4 of these cell models, so that you can try several investigations. Let the gelatin ❸ cool and harden overnight in the plastic bags.

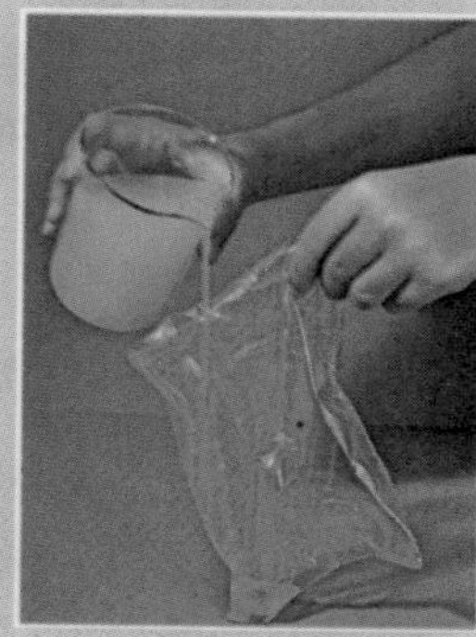

Methods of Intelligence: Inventing A Model

How could you use a dried prune as a model of a cell? What parts of a cell could the different ❹ parts of the prune stand for? Invent a way of showing that certain substances can pass through the "cell membrane" of your model cell.

Now go back to MODEL *on page 216.*

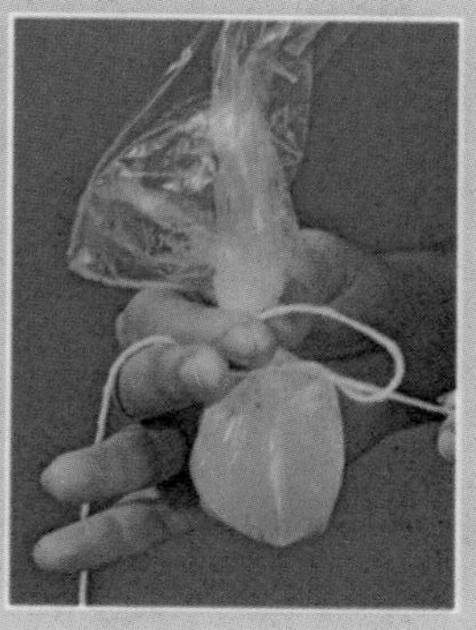

217

Performance objectives. Children *construct* a model of a cell, using a mixture of water, gelatin, starch, cologne, and a small piece of clay, letting the mixture congeal inside a sealed plastic bag.

Children *identify* parts of the model similar to a cell, such as the gelatin mixture for cytoplasm, the plastic bag for the membrane, and the clay for the nucleus.

Advance preparation. If you wish to have children volunteer to bring some of the materials needed for the investigations on pages 217 and 218, write a list of these materials on the board several days in advance: thin plastic sandwich bags, plain, unflavored gelatin, cologne, starch.

Useful materials: Instead of clay, children may use a marble or other small spherical object to represent the nucleus. Thin wire bag-ties may be substituted for string. Some similar materials are available in CLASSROOM LABORATORY: PURPLE.

❶ To avoid lumps, children should soften the gelatin before adding it to boiling water. Sprinkle the gelatin into a small glass of cold water and let stand for a few minutes. Add this mixture to the boiling water.

❷ Again to avoid lumps, mix the starch with a little warm water before adding to the gelatin mixture.

❸ To get the bags to gel, put them in a refrigerator or in a large bowl lined with ice cubes.

❹ The skin of a dried prune can stand for the cell membrane, the prune pulp for the cytoplasm, and the pit for the nucleus. To show that substances pass through the cell membrane or skin of the prune, children might leave the prune in a dish of water. Observe what happens. (prune plumps up) Why? (Water has entered the prune.)

Unit Concept-Statement: The cell is the unit of structure and function in living things.

Performance objectives. Children *demonstrate* how a cell membrane will allow certain materials to pass through, by using a cell model, placing it in iodine solution, causing the starch inside the bag to turn blue-black.

Children *describe* that the iodine solution passes into the cell model, but starch did not come out, since the iodine solution outside the model did not turn blue-black.

Useful materials: In addition to items listed under "Needed," pink litmus paper and baking soda should be provided. Some similar materials are available in CLASSROOM LABORATORY: PURPLE.

AN APPRENTICE INVESTIGATION into What a Membrane Does

Needed: a gelatin cell model, iodine solution, a bowl or jar, water

Fill the jar about $\frac{1}{4}$ full with warm water. Add just enough iodine solution to turn the water a light tan. ■ Place the gelatin cell model in the jar. ●

These are the photographs of one trial. What ❶ has happened to the cell model? ▲

How can this happening be explained? Reason with us this way. Iodine turns starch blue, and then black. Which liquid turned blue, the one inside the membrane or the one outside? Which substance must have moved through the membrane, then, the starch or the iodine? ❷

Methods of Intelligence
Inferring from the Use of a Model

Place another cell model in a dish of clear water. After a few hours, take out the cell model. Smell the water in the dish. What has happened ❸ to the cologne in the plastic bag?

If you want to investigate further, try this. Make a gelatin cell model, but this time add a teaspoonful of baking soda instead of starch. Does the soda move through the plastic membrane? ❹ How would you know? (Remember that pink litmus turns blue in the presence of baking soda.)

■

IODINE SOLUTION

●

▲

218

Continuing Lesson Cluster 3

❶ The whitish-colored gelatin turns blue-black.

❷ Since the material inside the plastic bag "membrane" turned blue-black, the liquid containing iodine outside the "membrane" must have moved through the "membrane."

❸ The cologne has moved through the plastic bag "membrane" and into the water.

❹ Children should test the water with pink litmus before placing the cell model in it. What happens? (no color change) What is this procedure called? (using a control) They should then put the soda-containing model in the water, and later test the water with litmus. What happens (pink litmus turns blue) What do you infer? (that soda has passed through the plastic "membrane")

Supporting Statement: Plant and animal cells have basically similar structures.

The Important Membrane

Everyone knows what happens to a lump of sugar at the bottom of a glass of water. The sugar dissolves in the water. But not everyone realizes how this happens. As the sugar
❶ **dissolves,** it *spreads* through the water. No stirring is needed! If it is given enough time, the sugar will spread through every bit of the water.

When a substance spreads in this way, we say that the substance **diffuses.** Sugar diffuses through water. Oxygen diffuses through water. Carbon dioxide diffuses through water. In fact, if a substance dissolves in a liquid, it can diffuse through the liquid.

Iodine diffused through the water in the investigation into the model cell. The iodine spread into all parts of the water in the jar. Since iodine dissolves in water, this is what you would expect. But something else also happened. The starch *inside* the model cell membrane turned blue. *This evidence shows that iodine diffused through the membrane.* The iodine diffused through the plastic membrane almost as if the membrane weren't there!

Scientists have discovered, after much investigation, that only substances that dissolve can pass through membranes. Oxygen dissolves in water, and oxygen diffuses easily through a cell membrane. Carbon dioxide dissolves in water and diffuses easily through a cell membrane. So does glucose. Most compounds and elements that dissolve in water can go through cell membranes by diffusion. But what about a substance like starch?

❷ Starch does *not* dissolve in water. As the investigation showed, starch does *not* diffuse through the plastic membrane of the model cell.

The plastic bag is only a model of a cell membrane. It acts like a real cell membrane in one way only. Some substances diffuse through it and some do not. However, it does show us an answer to our puzzle. This is how certain substances can enter and leave a cell—they are able to pass through the cell membrane by diffusion.

219

VERIFYING PROGRESS

In methods of intelligence

Children can *investigate* substances that contain starch by *testing* with iodine solution. Have them mix tincture of iodine with an equal volume of water and use a drop of this mixture for each test. Set out on numbered squares of wax paper small pinches of white powders such as cornstarch, soda, powdered sugar, flour. **Which powders contain starch? How do you know?** (Those that contain starch turn blue-black when iodine is added.)

Children may find out whether frankfurters, hamburgers, and sausages are padded with starchy breading. (Caution children not to eat the iodine stained meat afterwards.)

Useful materials: Drinking glasses, salt, starch, paper-towel filters.

❶ Have on your desk two glasses of water, into one of which you have dissolved a teaspoonful of salt. **Which glass contains the salt?** (don't know) **How can you find out?** (taste) **How can you separate the salt from the water?** (Children may suggest filtering, or evaporation.) To prepare a filter, fold an 8-inch square of paper toweling into a triangle, and then fold the triangle in half. Open out and tape where needed to get a filtering cone. Let them try the procedures, and see for themselves which works. **Why can't the salt be separated by filtering?** (A dissolved substance is spread out into particles too small to be caught by the filter.)

❷ Have on your desk two glasses of water, into one of which you have stirred a teaspoonful of cornstarch. **Which glass contains the starch?** Children should easily see that starch does not dissolve as does salt—the evidence for this is that particles of starch are visible even after thorough mixing with water. **Can you separate the starch from the water by filtering?** Let children predict, then try it. **How is a cell membrane like a filter?** (Like a filter, the cell membrane keeps some particles out and lets others through.) **What is the difference between the two kinds of particles?** (One difference is size.)

UNIT FIVE

Unit Concept-Statement: The cell is the unit of structure and function in living things.

❶ BEFORE YOU GO ON

A. Check your understanding of the concepts of this section. Which ending would you choose for each statement below?

1. A substance placed near a cell did not get into the cell. It was kept out of the cell by the
a. cytoplasm
b. cell membrane

2. Substances get into a cell by the process of
a. oxidation
b. diffusion

3. The statement that fits the main concept of this section is
a. Plant and animal cells have parts that are mainly alike.
b. Plant and animal cells have parts that are entirely different.

B. Write a paragraph or two on this topic: "The Importance of the Cell Membrane."

❷ USING WHAT YOU KNOW

1. Name the parts of this cell. ■

2. A test tube is filled with water and glucose. A membrane is fastened over the mouth of the tube. Then the mouth of the tube is placed in a jar of water. What might you expect to find in the water in the jar after a while? Why?

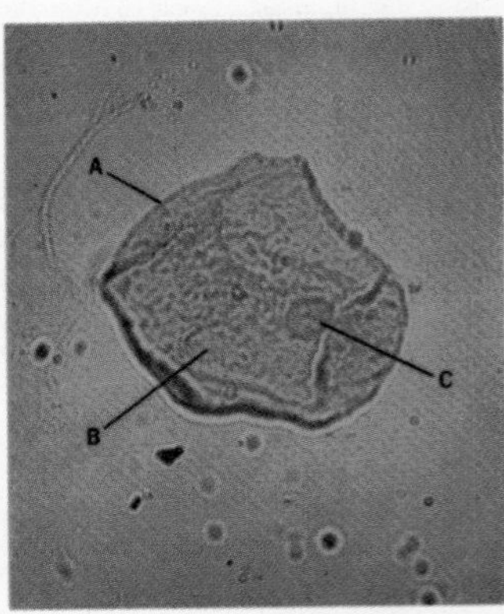

■

A LOOK AHEAD

Suppose you could look at a tiny part of a frog under the microscope. What might you find? Cells!

Suppose you took a tiny part of a fish and placed it under a microscope. What would you find?

Suppose you did the same to an oak tree. At this point in your study, could you form a theory on the make-up of living things? State your theory. Will it hold up? Will it be supported by the evidence?

VERIFYING PROGRESS

❶ Before you go on. Children *demonstrate* understanding of the similarities in plant and animal cells by *identifying* suitable responses to open-ended questions; they *explain* the function of the cell membrane.

A. 1. b 2. b 3. a

B. Children's responses should include its function of letting some substances into the cell and other substances out.

❷ Using what you know. Children *identify* the parts of a cell; they *predict* the diffusion of glucose through a membrane, and *explain* their prediction.

1. nucleus, cytoplasm, cell membrane

2. The glucose will enter the water in the jar and spread through it. This happens because glucose dissolves in water and is made up of fairly small molecules. Thus it is able to diffuse through a membrane.

4. Cells in a Plant

Place an onion on top of a jar filled with water up to the bottom of the onion. ● Keep the jar in a cool place, out of the sunlight. In a few days, green shoots and roots will sprout from the onion bulb, and you can examine the green
❶ plant cells under a microscope.

●

What Makes It Green?

Under a high-power lens, you can't miss seeing, inside the cells, tiny green bodies shaped like basketballs. ▲ They give the plant its green color. They are called **chloroplasts** (klôr′ə·plasts). *Chloro* means *green*. *Plast* means *body*.

❷ Now look at some cells from the bulb of the onion. ♦ As you might expect, there are no chloroplasts. The bulb is not green.

Chloroplasts are found in cells of many different plants.

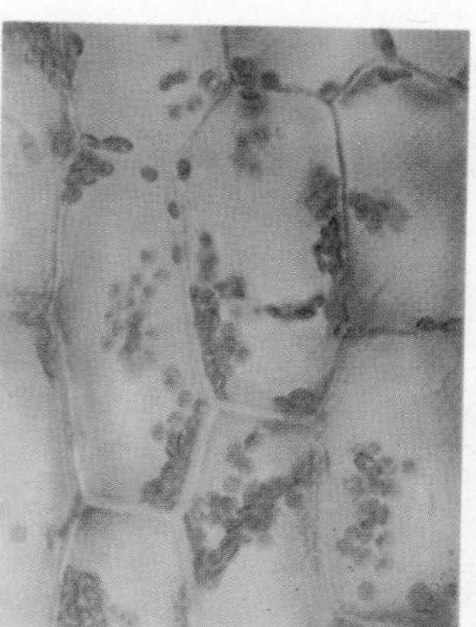

▲

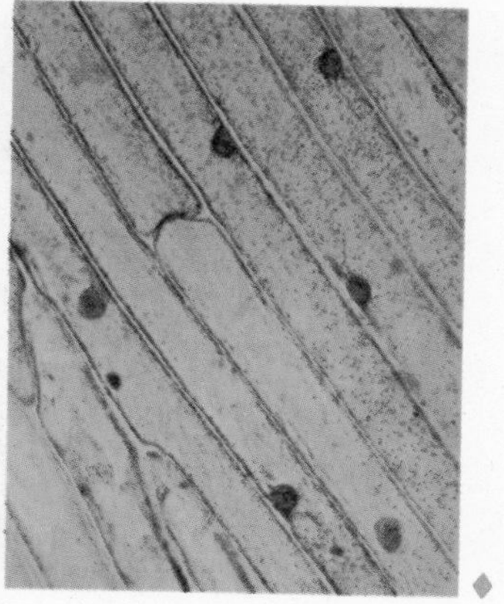

♦

221

LESSON CLUSTER 4
CELLS IN A PLANT

Teaching background. 4 T-226

Concept-seeking. Children become aware of the differences between plant and animal cells and of the special functions of the parts of the cell.

Operations. Children *probe* plant cell structures and the skeleton of a leaf.

Methods of intelligence. Children *analyze* their observations of different plant cells and *infer* that though they have basically similar cell structures they have different functions that serve the entire plant.

Useful materials: Pictures of different plant and animal cells, microprojector, celery.

Introducing Lesson Cluster 4

If possible, project slides of various plant and animal cells on the wall with a microprojector. Be sure to say whether cells are from plants or animals. If you have a collection file of pictures of plant and animal cells, these may be passed around.

What differences do you observe between plant cells and animal cells? Children may observe that some plant cells have green bodies in them. However, point out that not *all* plant cells have these green bodies.

Children may observe differences in form and shape, but the significant difference is a cell wall that seems to give plant cells a more rigid and less flexible structure than animal cells. If children do not proffer similar observations, let the differences await development in the lesson.

Developing the lesson

❶ Have children make the thinnest possible slice of the green shoot. This is most easily done by tearing towards or away from you along the parallel veins of the leaf. The translucent edge will make the best slide.

❷ Children should peel the brown skin off the onion and gently pull off a piece of the thin white outer skin with a tweezer. In the photograph, have children identify the brown-stained nuclei in the onion bulb cells. How can you make your onion slide look the same? (stain with iodine)

Unit Concept-Statement: The cell is the unit of structure and function in living things.

Cells That Work Underground

Here is a picture of a young bean plant, about two weeks old.■ The leaves are green. The roots are whitish. Where would you expect to find chloroplasts? In the
❶ green leaves, of course, not in the roots.

Look at the drawing of the cells in the root.■ They are magnified many times. See the fingerlike part on one cell. This single cell is a **root hair.**

❷ You know that roots anchor the plant to the soil. But root hairs are special kinds of cells. Each root hair takes in water and minerals from the soil. However, this is not all that the cells in the roots do. The plant uses the water and the minerals from the soil. These root hair cells do their work underground.

Look at the different parts of the bean plant as they are
❸ seen under the microscope. The bean plant is a living thing. It is made of cells, as you would expect. There is something more. There are different kinds of cells in different parts of the plant. See how the cells in the root, stem, and leaf, for example, are different from one another.

■

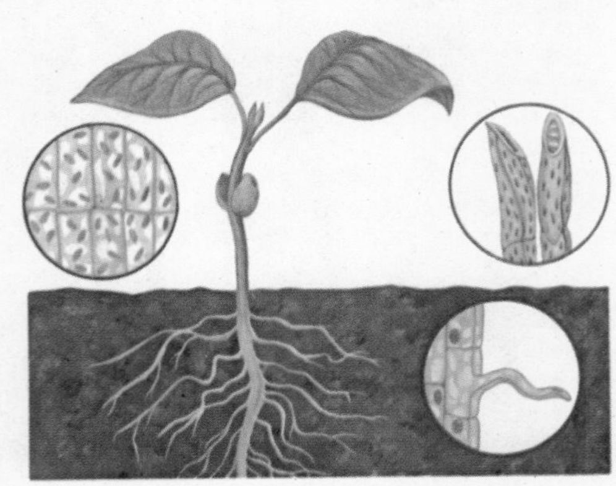

Continuing Lesson Cluster 4

❶ Can anyone explain what the chloroplasts do in the green leaf? From earlier work, children may recall that chlorophyll is the green coloring in chloroplasts, and that chlorophyll has an essential role in the process of food-making (*photosynthesis*) in green plants.

❷ Look at a pinch of salt, a mineral. What must happen to a mineral in the soil before it can get through a cell membrane? (dissolve) Dissolve a teaspoonful of salt in water. Can you see it now? Can you feel it? Dissolved minerals are carried through the roots of the plant into the stems.

In the drawing, notice the tube-like opeings in the tops of the cells in the stem. Without water a plant cannot make food. Without minerals a plant may be weak and spindly.

❸ The magnified sections are: top left, cells in leaf; top right, cells in stem; bottom right, cells in root hair.

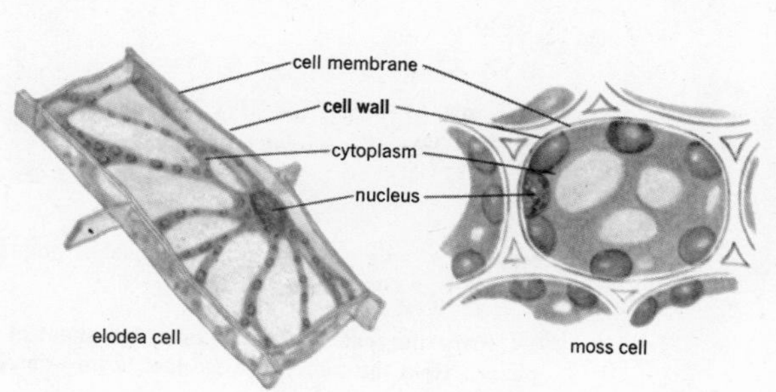

Look closely at these pictures of an elodea cell and a moss cell. ● Notice that a green plant cell has a nucleus, cytoplasm, a cell membrane, and chloroplasts. Chloroplasts have different shapes.

Do you observe something new about these cells? It may help if you compare them with the body cells on page 215. Do you observe that these plant cells have *thick* ❶ *sides?* You may have thought that this was simply a thick cell membrane—but it is not. It is something that the cells on page 215 do not have at all. It is a **cell wall.** The cell membrane is still there, inside the cell wall. *Plant cells have cell walls.* Animal cells do not have cell walls.

The cell walls of a plant are made of **cellulose** (sel′yə·lōs). ❷ Wood, for instance, is mainly cellulose. When wood is burned, it is mainly the cellulose in millions of plant cells that is burning. The fluffy boll of a cotton plant is mainly cellulose, and so is a cotton dress or shirt. The paper on which these words are printed is made from dead cell walls, the cellulose of plants.

❸ It seems that the *structure* of a plant cell, the way it is built, has something to do with its work. Root cells have a different structure and do different work than cells in a leaf.

Without cellulose, a tree or other woody plant could not stand erect. See for yourself how cellulose in the veins of a leaf forms a support for a leaf. Try the investigation on the next page. INVESTIGATE

❶ What can animals do that plants cannot do? (move around) How do you think a cell wall helps plant cells give the plant a structure? (provides support)

What two things do leaf cells have that animal cells do not have? (chloroplasts, cell walls) Must a plant cell have chloroplasts in it? (No; there are root cells, and there are some plants, like yeast, that do not have chloroplasts.)

❷ Bring in a stalk of celery, cut it into half-inch pieces, and distribute a piece to each child. Let them pull a fiber from the side of the piece. What do you think makes this string tough? (cell wall, cellulose) Let children chew the piece of celery. What happens to it? Can you chew it up so that it is soft like a piece of bread that you chew? (no) Why not? (The cellulose fibers do not break down.)

❸ What else besides cellulose might give structure to a plant cell? (water) If children need a hint, ask: What causes a plant to wilt? (lack of water)

Performance objectives. Children *construct* a "rubbing" of a leaf, by placing a leaf face down under a sheet of paper, and rubbing a crayon over the outline of the raised parts of the underside of the leaf.

Children *describe* that the leaf's skeleton is made of cellulose and gives the leaf strength and stiffness.

Useful materials: Hand lens (optional), microscope and slides. Some similar materials are available in CLASSROOM LABORATORY: PURPLE.

AN APPRENTICE INVESTIGATION into the Skeleton of a Leaf

Needed: a large leaf from a tree, a sheet of white paper, a crayon ❶

Place the leaf face down under the sheet of paper. Hold the paper and the leaf down firmly so that they can't move. ❷

Rub the broad edge of the crayon over the surface of the paper, above the leaf. Use long, quick strokes. ■ As the crayon crosses the raised parts of the leaf, it will outline them on the paper. ● ❸ This is called "making a rubbing." A kind of skeleton of the leaf will be outlined on the paper.

What is a leaf's skeleton made of? It is made mainly of cellulose. The cellulose skeleton of a leaf helps to give it strength and stiffness. ❹

Methods of Intelligence
Extending Observation with a Tool

Place a thin piece of cellulose under a microscope. With your teacher's help, cut a thin slice from a leaf. (Try to make the slice thin enough to see light through it.) Be sure your slice includes one of the leaf's veins. Place the slice on a microscope slide and examine with the 20X objective in position. Recall that the microscope magnifies 200 times with the 20X objective. Can you see cell shapes? ❺

224

Continuing Lesson Cluster 4

❶ It will be more interesting if several kinds of leaves are used, one kind for each group of children.

❷ The ribs, or veins, are on the underside of the leaf to keep it rigid and exposed to the maximum amount of sunlight. Hence, the veins, when placed as directed, will offer a rough surface that will reproduce the crayon marks.

❸ Light pressure will probably give a better picture of the veining than a heavy stroke. Several trials may be made to show the different effects.

❹ Where will the chloroplasts be found—in the veins or between the veins? (between the veins) Children can test this response by examining the leaf and its veins with a hand lens. There may be some green color in the veins, but it will be much less than in the soft parts of the leaf.

❺ A torn edge of the leaf offers a better opportunity for seeing cells. Some children may find something interesting in their specimens. It will look like a tiny opening with sausage-shaped cells around it. These openings are *stomata* that let air into the leaf. This is how the plant takes in carbon dioxide and releases oxygen. The cells around the opening are guard cells that can open or close to regulate the interchange of carbon dioxide and oxygen, and to permit water vapor to go out.

❶ BEFORE YOU GO ON

A. To help you in seeking the concept of this section, draw 2 cells, a green plant cell and an animal cell. How are these cells different? How are they alike?

B. The statement that fits the main concept of this section is

a. The parts of cells in plants and animals have special uses.

b. The parts of cells in plants are the same as the parts of cells in animals.

C. Write a paragraph or two on this topic: "Differences Between Green Plant Cells and Animal Cells."

❷ USING WHAT YOU KNOW

1. Here is a picture of 2 cells from a single plant.■ Which cell would you expect to find above ground, perhaps in a leaf? Which one would you expect to find in part of a plant underground? Why?

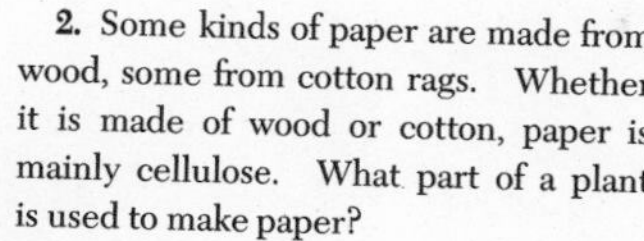

2. Some kinds of paper are made from wood, some from cotton rags. Whether it is made of wood or cotton, paper is mainly cellulose. What part of a plant is used to make paper?

3. Which parts of a tree contain chloroplasts: the roots, the trunk, or the leaves? Explain your answer.

INVESTIGATING FURTHER ❸

You know that the cellulose in a leaf's skeleton (that is, the *veins* of the leaf) helps keep the leaf stiff. To find out about another way in which the veins of the leaf serve a plant such as celery, try this.

Add ink to a glass of water until it is deeply colored. Place a fresh, leafy stalk of celery in the water. After a day or so, what do you observe in the veins of the celery leaves?

Now cut across the stalk of the celery and examine the cut surface. What do you conclude?

■

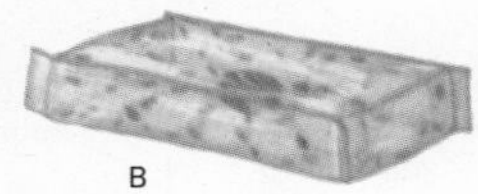

A LOOK AHEAD

You have studied cells in animals and cells in plants. How many different kinds of cells have you examined?

These cells are samples from different living things. On the basis of these samples, can you come to a theory about the structure of living things? Why or why not?

225

VERIFYING PROGRESS

In methods of intelligence

Children can *demonstrate* their understanding of plant and animal cells by *constructing* diagrams of each, *naming* the parts, and *distinguishing* those that are not common to both kinds of cells.

Children may be encouraged to draw large diagrams of plant and animal cells. Suggest they use colored crayons to distinguish the parts and to label each part. Labels for parts not common to each may be circled or printed with a different color from those common to both.

VERIFYING PROGRESS

❶ Before you go on. Children *analyze* and *describe* the likenesses and differences in plant and animal cells.

A. Differences: plant cells have a cell wall and may have chloroplasts; animal cells have neither; cellulose occurs only in plant cells. Likenesses: Both have a cell membrane, cytoplasm, and a nucleus.

B. a

C. Description will include differences under A.

❷ Using what you know. Children *analyze* plant cells and *infer* commercial uses of plant cells and functions of different cells within a growing plant.

1. The cell with the chloroplasts would be in the leaf, the one without would be underground. Chloroplasts are needed if the plant is to make food. Food-making also requires sunlight.

2. The woody part, chiefly the stem of a fibrous plant like cotton or the trunk of a tree; that is, the cell walls.

3. Leaves, because they make the sugars that are stored (as starches) in the green plant.

❸ Investigating further. Children *observe* the action of a dye in the celery stalk and *infer* that tubes in a plant carry water and dissolved substances throughout the plant. Color will appear in the leaf veins. Children should *infer* that dots of color on the cut ends are tubes that carry liquids.

LESSON CLUSTER 5
A WHOLE SKIN

Teaching background. 5 T-226

Concept-seeking. Children become aware that living cells are continually reproducing themselves.

Operations. Children *probe* into cell division as a means by which cells reproduce themselves.

Methods of intelligence. Children *observe* drawings of plant and animal cells dividing, *analyze* descriptions of cell division, and *infer* that this process is related to growth and repair of tissues, and that different cells in an organism have different functions.

Useful materials: Scissors, piece of cloth or paper.

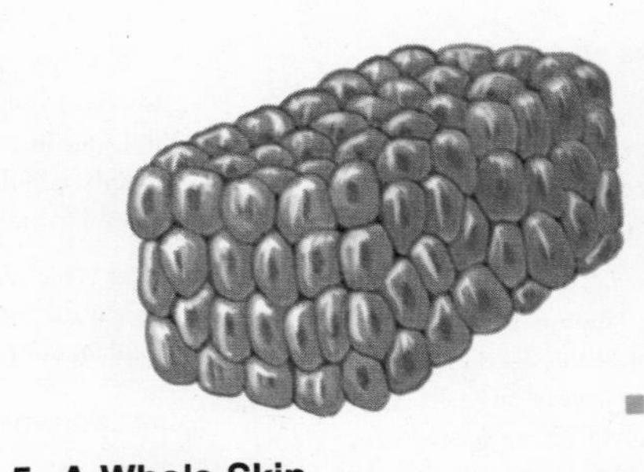

■

5. A Whole Skin

By now you must have had many cuts. Yet your skin is whole. Skin heals.

What happens when skin heals? Scientists have found out that healing is mainly the work of cells. For healing to take place, more skin has to be made. Since skin is made up of cells, more skin cells must be produced. Cells can produce more cells, as you know. In other words, cells can reproduce.

●

▲

◆

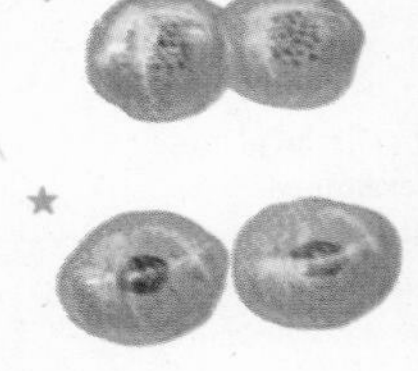

★

How Skin Cells Reproduce

Under the top layer of your skin are cells shaped like grapes. These skin cells fit together like this. ■

Each of these skin cells has a nucleus, cytoplasm, and a cell membrane—as most cells do. ● These cells reproduce to form more skin cells.

When the time comes for one of these cells to reproduce, the nucleus starts to divide in two. ▲ Then the cell pinches in the middle. ◆ ❶

Finally, there are two skin cells made from one cell. Each new cell has its own nucleus. ★ The cell has reproduced itself by **cell division.**

Each new cell can also reproduce by cell division. The cells under the skin on each side of a cut make new cells by cell division. The new cells close up the cut. ◈ ❷

226

Introducing Lesson Cluster 5

Cut a slit in the edge of a piece of cloth or in a sheet of paper. How can we put these together again? (sew or tape the edges) If you get a cut in your skin, what happens? (It heals up.) The cloth (or paper) is made of cells, isn't it? Why didn't it heal up? Children should infer that only living cells can heal up by themselves. How do you think living cells can do this? Let children hypothesize before beginning the lesson.

Developing the lesson

❶ Trace with the children the reproduction of one skin cell into two. What do you see happening in the second drawing of a cell? Children should observe that the nucleus is dividing. Actually, the content of the nucleus duplicates itself before it divides, so that both cells have a complete nucleus. What is taking place in the third drawing? (The content of each nucleus is coming together and a new membrane seems to be forming in between.) That this happens, children will find evident in the last drawing. The cells then grow to the size of the original cell.

❷ What happens when you get a cut? (bleeds, scab forms) Children may ask about the healing process. Substances in the blood cause a scab to form, sealing the edges of the cut. Underneath the scab, cells are able to divide, come together and form new skin. Then the scab falls off and in a few days not even a scar remains, unless the cut was deep.

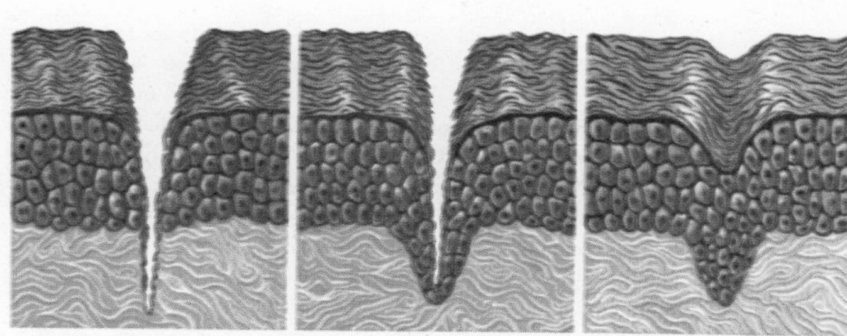

A Cut in a Tree

1 Have you ever noticed how a tree heals a cut in its bark?

Beneath the bark of a tree are layers of cells called the 2 **cambium** (kam′bē·əm). The cambium is made up of cells that divide easily. One of these layers reproduces to heal a cut in the bark. After a year or two, or longer, the cut is covered with new bark.

Like skin cells, cambium cells reproduce by cell division. However, if you could watch cambium cells dividing, you would see that they divide a little differently than skin cells do. The cambium cell is a cell from a plant, not an animal. The nucleus of the cell becomes two nuclei. A 3 new cell wall then grows inside the plant cell. This new wall divides the cell in two. Each new cell grows until it is the same size as the old cell was. Then it, too, reproduces by cell division.

Dividing Cells

Cell division is going on in every living thing. Cells divide very fast in living things that have just been formed. 4 In a frog's egg that is growing into a tadpole, the cells are dividing quickly. The cells of the robin growing inside the egg are also dividing quickly. And the cells of the rabbit inside its mother are dividing quickly.

227

1 If trees or shrubs on the school grounds were pruned the previous season, a brief trip to a specimen you have selected for observation will be an experience for the children. When a branch has been cut close to a main branch or trunk, wood can be observed beginning to close over the place where the cut was made.

2 If possible, display the cut end of a section of a branch $2\frac{1}{2}$ to 3 inches in diameter. A freshly cut branch will be better than a dried one, but either will do. Let children examine and identify bark and cambium. Call attention to the rings, and explain that these show the growth made in one year by the outer cambium cells. The inner part of the branch is entirely made of cellulose and no longer is growing. Each year the inner cambium layer becomes wood. Inside the cambium are the tubes that carry food and water. Recall the tube in the celery if you followed the suggestion on page 225.

3 Encourage comparison of plant cell division with cell division in the skin.

4 Why do you think the cells are dividing so rapidly? (The frog, robin, and rabbit are growing.) What do you think will be the main function of cell division when these animals are grown up? (repair)

Unit Concept-Statement: The cell is the unit of structure and function in living things.

VERIFYING PROGRESS

In methods of intelligence

Encourage children to *design* and *build models* of cells reproducing. Clay can be used to show yeast cells budding. A small box with a cardboard division to stand for the wall between newly-formed cells can represent plant cells. A plastic bag tied at the center and at its open end can represent a pair of newly formed animal cells. The plant cell and animal cell models can have gelatin for cytoplasm and split peas for nuclei. Children should be urged to think of other model materials on their own.

All around you, as you read this, cells are reproducing in living things. Cells are reproducing in you.

There are differences, however. For instance, cells reproduce in a radish and in yeast. A radish, however, has many different kinds of cells. Yeast has only one kind of cell. A radish is a **many-celled** living thing. A yeast is a ❶ **single-celled** living thing. In some way, reproduction in a many-celled living thing makes different kinds of cells. Reproduction in a single-celled living thing makes just one kind of cell.

It is an astonishing difference. Not only are cells in a many-celled living thing different, but they do different things.

❷ **BEFORE YOU GO ON**

A. Check your understanding of the concepts of this section. Which ending would you choose for each statement below?

1. A cell reproduces by the process of
a. diffusion
b. cell division

2. The result of cell division is 2 cells that are
a. very much alike
b. very different

3. The cells in a tree that divide when the bark repairs itself are
a. leaf cells b. cambium cells

4. A cell that doesn't pinch in when it divides is a
a. skin cell b. cambium cell

5. The statement that fits the main concept of this section is
a. Cells have walls.
b. Cells reproduce themselves.

B. Write a paragraph or two on these topics: "How Cells Divide" and "What Would Happen If Cells Did Not Divide."

A LOOK AHEAD

The body grows. The body repairs itself. How?

Suppose you cut your skin. You have seen how the skin would repair itself—some of its cells would divide to make new skin cells.

In the next section, we will take a close look at some one-celled animals. How do they grow? How do they reproduce?

228

Continuing Lesson Cluster 5

❶ Why do you think a plant has several kinds of cells? (leaves to make food, bark or outer skin for protection, stems for support and carrying food and water, roots for anchorage and intake of water and minerals) Why do you, a many-celled living thing, have so many kinds of cells? (You have to eat and digest food, have an outer covering for protection, be able to use your muscles, be able to sense environment, etc.) Recognition of cell differences is all that is needed at this time. The human body systems will be developed in the next unit.

VERIFYING PROGRESS

❷ **Before you go on.** Children *demonstrate* understanding of cell structure and function by *identifying* appropriate endings for open-ended statements, by *describing* cell functions, and by *drawing an inference*.

A. 1. b 3. b 5. b
2. a 4. b

B. Children give evidence of understanding the diagrams on pages 226 and 227. They *infer* that without division there would be no growth or repair.

Supporting Statement: A single cell may function as a complete organism or have special functions in many-celled organisms.

6. Just One Cell

If you go for a walk in the woods, take along a small, covered, plastic jar. When you come upon a stream or a pond, scoop up some of the water. Get some water plants and mud, too.

Bring the jar to class and place it where it will be at room ❶ temperature and out of the sun. Add to the water a bit of hard-boiled egg yolk, about the size of a pea. Or add 10 grains of rice. **Bacteria,** tiny plantlike organisms, will use these substances to grow and to reproduce. The bacteria are food for some one-celled animals that live in ponds.

At first, the pond water in your jar may be fairly clear. ❷ A few days after the food is added, the water will become cloudy with bacteria. Soon after that, the water will swarm with tiny animals just large enough for you to see them with your eye.

In a Drop of Water

Look at the amazing world in a drop of pond water.■ In a drop that might spread out no larger than a dime, dozens of different animals are scurrying about, feeding and

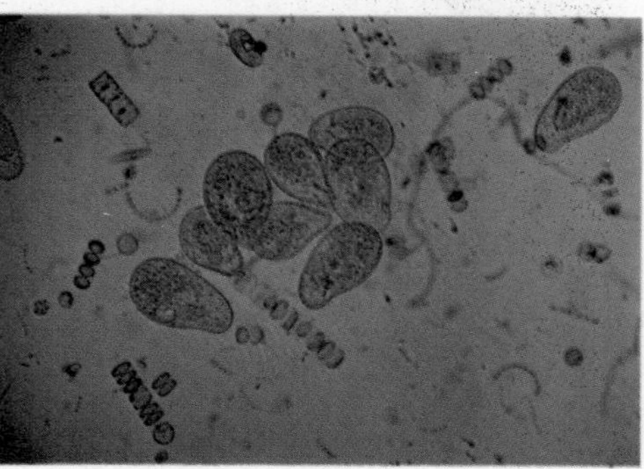

229

LESSON CLUSTER 6
JUST ONE CELL

Teaching background. 6 T-226

Concept-seeking. Children become aware that some single cells can carry on all the functions of a complete organism and that other cells are specialized in function for the activities of many-celled organisms.

Operations. Children *investigate* single-celled organisms in a drop of pond water.

Methods of intelligence. Children *observe* a variety of living things in a drop of water, and *infer* that a sincle cell can carry on all the life activities of a complete plant or animal.

Useful materials: Hardboiled egg yolk or uncooked rice grains, pond water.

Introducing Lesson Cluster 6

Since you will need pond water for the investigation in this lesson cluster, it is useful to begin with it. You may wish to have children collect a few plastic containers of pond water from a stream in advance of the lesson, with an adult accompanying them. Or you may obtain it yourself.

Present a container of pond water. What do you think is in the water? Some children, from earlier work, may know the water has living things in it.

If there are animals in the water, what will they need to grow? (food, oxygen) If there are green plants, what will they need? (light, water, and carbon dioxide) If there are plants that are not green, what will they need? (food)

Developing the lesson

❶ Proceed to add food to the water, as directed in the text. If there are only a few living things in the jar, what will the food do for them? (make them reproduce)

❷ Develop the idea of a food chain. Where did the egg yolk come from? (chicken) Where did the chicken get food? (green plants) Where do the bacteria get food? (egg yolk, or rice) You may need to explain that rice comes from a green plant. If there are animals in the jar, where will they get their food? (bacteria) This chain can be diagrammed on the chalkboard.

Unit Concept-Statement: The cell is the unit of structure and function in living things.

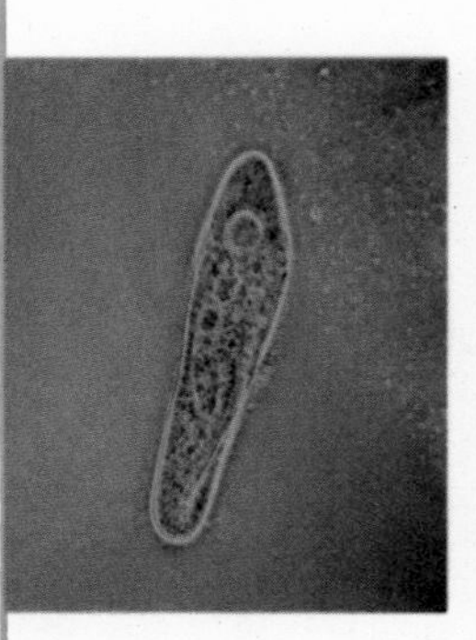

reproducing. The paramecium (par′ə·mē′shē·əm), shaped like a slipper, twists and turns and darts from place to place at tremendous speed.■ It moves by waving the hairlike structures on its body, which are called **cilia** (sil′ē·ə). The cilia push against the water like oars. They also steer bits of food into the paramecium's mouth. ❶

The ameba does not have any cilia. It moves about in a different way. The ameba bulges out at one point into a kind of finger. The finger grows as the ameba's cytoplasm flows into it. Thus, the ameba moves in the direction of the finger. It can swallow a smaller animal or a plant by flowing around and over it.● ❷

Euglena (yoo·glē′na) has a long, delicate whip on its front end.▲ By lashing this whip, the animal slowly moves ❸ forward. At the same time, the euglena's body turns and twists, as does the paramecium when it swims.

The stentor (sten′tôr) sways from side to side and can shrink down to hide where it is standing. The stentor's cilia fan water and food into its cell shaped somewhat like a ❹ trumpet.◆

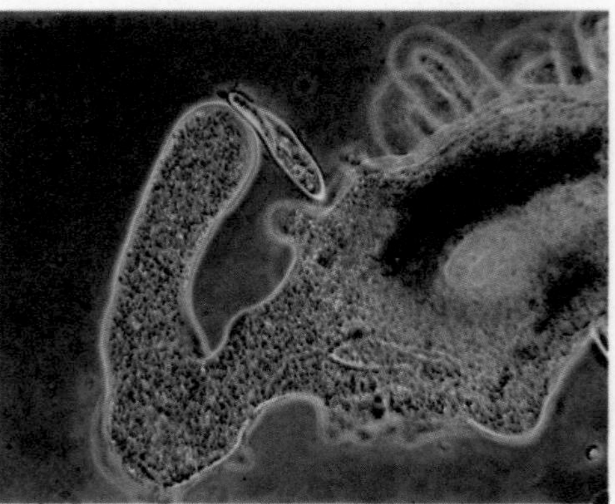

Continuing Lesson Cluster 6

❶ You may wish to point out the paramecium's "mouth." It is on the lower right side of the paramecium in the picture. Children may recognize the "mouth" by the white line entering the side of the animal and running down into its "heel."

❷ What animal is the ameba in the picture about to swallow? (a paramecium) What animal does the ameba seem to have swallowed? (another paramecium)

❸ Some scientists classify the euglena as a plant; others as an animal. Why might it be called a plant? What might the green bodies be in the euglena in the photograph? (chloroplasts) Where else did you see chloroplasts? (in green leaves) Euglena can move around like an animal and take food into its body. It can also use light to make food as a plant does.

❹ The stentor often attaches itself by its "stem" to a bit of debris.

Supporting Statement: A single cell may function as a complete organism or have special functions in many-celled organisms.

These are only a few of the animals that can be seen in a drop of pond water. Like the animals in a forest or jungle, they feed on one another. They feed, grow, and reproduce in their own little world. And animals are not the only kinds of tiny living things you may see in pond water. There are many microscopic plants, as well. Some of these tiny plants are green, and others have no color.

You can get a better look at the living things in your jar of pond water by doing the investigation on the next page.

INVESTIGATE

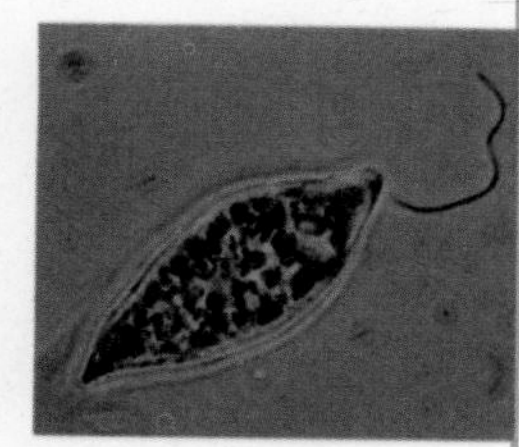

▲

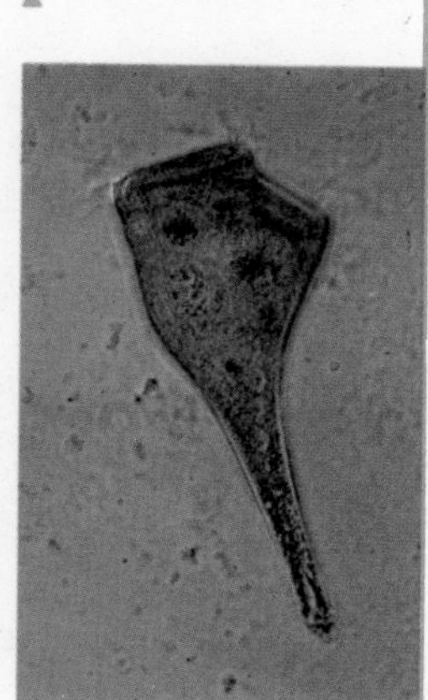

◆

One Cell Can Be Enough

Think of a mouse and a paramecium.

A mouse is a complete living thing, an **organism.** It is ❶ an organism made up of millions of cells: muscle cells, nerve cells, blood cells, and many other kinds of cells. A mouse is a many-celled organism.

A paramecium is a complete living thing, too. A paramecium is an organism, but it is made up of just *one* cell. A paramecium is a single-celled organism. One cell carries on all its body functions. Just as one cell carries on all the ❷ body functions of a yeast, a single-celled plant, one cell does the same for a paramecium, a single-celled animal.

What is the difference between a single-celled animal, like a paramecium, and a single animal cell, such as a muscle cell in the mouse?

The paramecium can get its own food. The muscle cell in the mouse depends on blood to bring it food. The single cell of the paramecium moves about on its own. But the single muscle cell of a mouse moves along with millions of other muscle cells.

Free-living animals that are single-celled carry on all life activities in one cell. *A single-celled animal is a complete organism.* But a muscle cell is only one kind of cell in a many-celled animal like the mouse. *In a many-celled* ❸ *animal, a single cell is only part of the organism.*

231

❶ The key concept term ***organism*** may be new to some children. Developing the concept that the cells mentioned are organized to do certain things may help children to understand the term.

❷ Children may have observed that animals in the drop of pond water moved away from objects they touched. A paramecium may change direction, a stentor may shrink if something touches it, or an ameba may send out a "finger" in another direction. Although these animals have no nerves, they are sensitive to their environment.

❸ A number of organisms have been discussed in this lesson. As you name each one, have children develop a classification of them as follows:

SINGLE-CELLED MANY-CELLED

How are the single-celled organisms able to live? (One cell performs all life activities.) How are cells in the other group different from those in a single-celled organism? (They are organized for specific functions; all cells work together so that the organism can carry on its life activities.)

Performance objectives. Children *demonstrate* how to place a cover slip on a drop of pond water on a microscope slide, without trapping air bubbles under the cover slip.

Children *describe* the movement and feeding of life in a drop of pond water, using a microscope to observe.

Children *distinguish* between life found in a drop of pond water and life in water from the surface of pond mud, by using a microscope to observe.

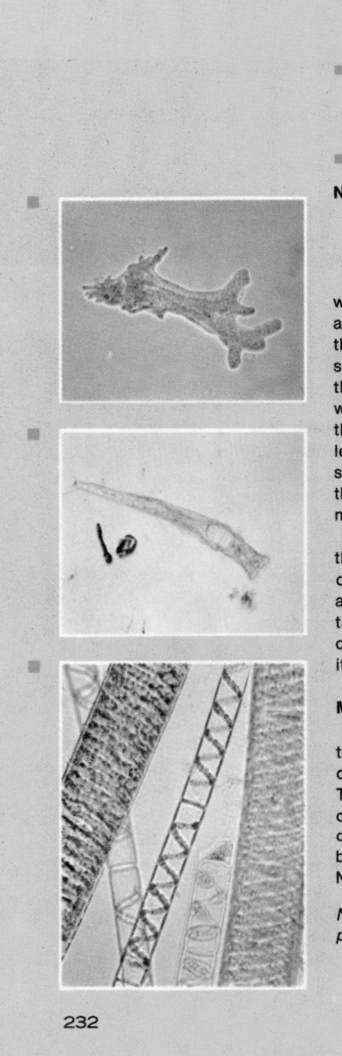

AN APPRENTICE INVESTIGATION into Life in a Drop of Pond Water

Needed: a microscope, 2 glass slides, 2 cover slips, a medicine dropper, a small jar of pond water, mud from a pond ❶

With the medicine dropper, take some pond water from the surface of the jar. Place a drop on ❷ a slide. Try to place a cover slip on the drop so that no air bubbles are trapped under the cover slip. (Don't be discouraged if you don't succeed the first time—it takes practice.) The cover slip will flatten the drop for better viewing and prevent the lens from getting wet. Put the slide under the lens. Bring the microscope lens down close to the slide. Then put your eye to the eyepiece and move the lens *up and away* from the slide to focus the microscope.

Study the living things in the drop. Are any of them like those shown in the illustrations here and on the previous page? Observe how they move ❸ and how they feed. Place a drop of water from the surface of the mud on a slide. Cover it with a cover slip. Explore it. Are there living things in it that you did not see in the first drop? ❹

Methods of Intelligence: Consulting Authorities

Perhaps you can make drawings of the living things you see under the microscope. Then try to decide which are plants and which are animals. To find out whether your observations are correct, compare your drawings to the drawings of one-celled living things in a book such as *Protozoology*, by Richard R. Kudo, published by C. C. Thomas, New York, 1966. Is Dr. Kudo an authority? Why? ❺

Now go back to "One Cell Can Be Enough" on page 231.

Useful materials: Some similar materials are available in CLASSROOM LABORATORY: PURPLE.

Continuing Lesson Cluster 6

❶ If you started a culture of pond-water animals as suggested on page 229, children should be able to see microscopic organisms in the drop of water.

❷ For review of microscope technique, refer back to page 212 if necessary.

❸ The slide may need to be moved very gently until an organism appears. The organisms may tend to move toward the edge of the cover slip or gather around a piece of debris in the drop.

❹ Animals and plants that use light, like euglenas and algae, are more likely to be found at the surface. Other organisms, such as amebas, may be found nearer the bottom.

❺ Why is a recent book in science probably a better authority than an older one on the same subject? (One reason is that scientists build on the work of others.)

Supporting Statement: A single cell may function as a complete organism or have special functions in many-celled organisms.

Single-celled animals belong to a group known as **Protozoa** (prō′tə·zō′ə). The ameba is a protozoan; it belongs to the Protozoa. The stentor and the euglena, and other one-celled animals, are protozoans. In fact, there are more than 15,000 different kinds of protozoans, or single-celled animals.

❶ BEFORE YOU GO ON

To gain a better understanding of the concepts of this section, answer these questions.

1. What are the differences between a single animal cell, such as a cheek cell, and a single-celled animal, such as an ameba?

2. What are the differences between a many-celled organism, such as a mouse, and a single-celled organism, such as a paramecium?

3. The statement that fits the main concept of this section is

a. A single-celled animal is a complete organism, but a single animal cell can carry on all life activities by itself.

b. A single-celled animal is a complete organism, but a single animal cell is only part of an organism.

❷ USING WHAT YOU KNOW

1. Which of these two cells is *part* of an organism? Which is a *complete* organism?

muscle cell   euglena

2. Are these 2 living things the same or different? How?

single animal cell
single-celled animal

❸ INVESTIGATING FURTHER

To see some single-celled green plants, try this. In a park or woods, find some tree green, which usually grows on the north sides of trees.

Take some tree green back to the classroom and place a bit of it in a drop of water on a slide. Add a cover slip and examine under the microscope. You may want to sketch what you see.

A LOOK AHEAD

When man invented microscopes, the fascinating world of single-celled plants and animals became visible. Microscopes have made it possible for us to learn many things about *all* living things. We have begun, for example, to understand how organisms reproduce themselves. Let's see how.

233

VERIFYING PROGRESS

❶ Before you go on. Children *demonstrate* understanding of single-celled and many-celled organisms by *describing* similarities and differences.

1. A single animal cell carries on certain functions in a larger organism; a single-celled animal performs all life functions with the single cell.

2. A mouse has many kinds of cells, each with a different function. A paramecium has one cell that performs all the life functions.

3. b

❷ Using what you know. Children *analyze* and *distinguish* between single cells and organisms.

1. Muscle cell is part of an organism; euglena is a complete organism.

2. A single animal cell is part of an organism; a single-celled animal is a complete organism. They are alike in structure, but differ in the functions they perform.

❸ Investigating further. Children collect tree green, *observe* it under the microscope, *identify* single cells, and *infer* they are plant cells because they contain chloroplasts. Tree green, or *pleurococcus,* is found on trees in moist places or in a moist atmosphere. The single cells grow in patches. What are the cells—plants or animals? (plants) How do you know? (They contain chloroplasts and have cell walls.)

LESSON CLUSTER 7
LIKE BEGETS LIKE

Teaching background. 7 T-227

Concept-seeking. Children become aware that there is a pattern of cell structure that is passed on from cell to cell through cell division.

Operations. Children *probe* into the multiplication of similar cells by fission.

Methods of intelligence. Children *analyze* the structures in dividing cells, *infer* that the structures duplicate themselves, *consult evidence* to seek an explanation for this event, and begin to *construct a theory* to explain the inheritance of traits by an organism.

7. Like Begets Like

Spallanzani, the Italian scientist, seemed to be doing something silly. He would put a drop of water on a glass slide. Then another drop on another slide. Then another . . . and another . . . and another . . . .

But Spallanzani had a concept that had come out of many observations. He reasoned this way. Where do single-celled organisms come from? If he could only get just *one* organism in a drop of water! Then he would be able to watch it closely and perhaps find out. So he put drop after drop of water on slides. At last, he caught just one single-celled organism in one drop.

He watched the organism carefully through his microscope. It began to pinch in the middle. The pinch deepened. The organism pinched into two organisms! So that was the way it reproduced! One divided into two. Then two could divide into four. Four could divide into eight, and so on. No wonder the water was so crowded with organisms since they could divide so quickly. Of course, you know this already. But scientist Spallanzani was working in the year 1750. His discovery was a great one.

1 This is an ameba dividing in two. ■ When amebas are well fed, they can reproduce themselves. An ameba

■

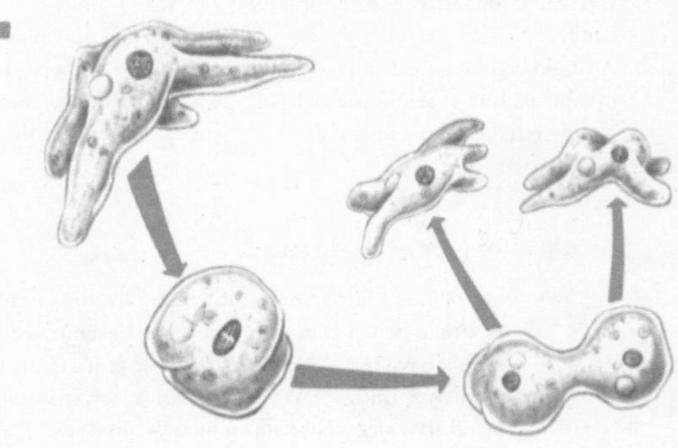

234

Introducing Lesson Cluster 7

How many parents does a puppy have? How many does a kitten have? How many do you have? How many does an ameba have? What makes you think so? It is quite possible you will have disagreement. Some children will argue the obvious, while other children may reason that single cells divide and that single cells are complete organisms. Maybe they can just divide. How would you find out? Accept any hypotheses and then let children read the text about Spallanzani's experiments.

1 When an ameba divides, what difference will there be in the two new amebas? (none) Why? Children should reason that the daughter cells have nothing in them except what was in the single parent cell.

Supporting Statement: The pattern of a living thing is passed along to its young by duplication of DNA and chromosomes.

swimming about becomes pinched in the middle. In a few hours, there are two amebas, looking just like each other. ❶ This kind of cell division is called **fission.** Protozoans generally reproduce this way—by fission. Fission means "splitting apart."

Setting the Pattern

By fission, one protozoan produces two protozoans. They are like each other and like the parent. They are alike because of tiny bodies called **chromosomes** (krō′mə• ❷ sōms). The chromosomes set the pattern and make the young protozoans look like the old ones.

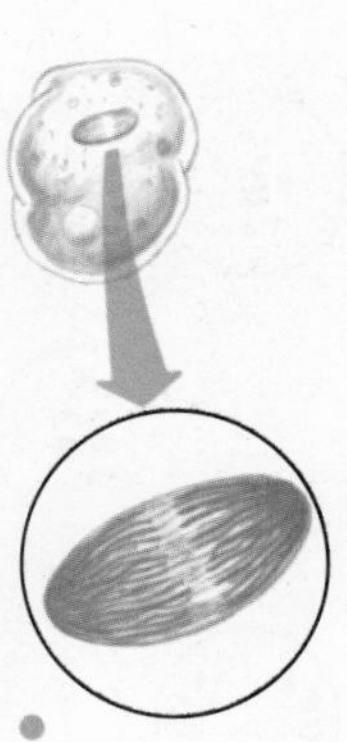

Suppose that you could examine the nucleus of an ameba as it is dividing. Within it you would find these threadlike bodies. ● These are the chromosomes. Because of them, an ameba looks like an ameba. The chromosomes of an ameba have a substance in them that sets the pattern for the way the animal gets its shape and its other parts. How do scientists know that the chromosomes set the pattern? They have managed to change the substance in some chromosomes and have then seen the organism change.

In *your* cells there are chromosomes. Your chromosomes have a substance in them that is somehow responsible for your characteristics. Your chromosomes set the pattern for the way you get the shape of your face and the color of ❸ your eyes, your hair, and your skin. Your chromosomes set the pattern for the kind of nose, lungs, heart, and brain you will have.

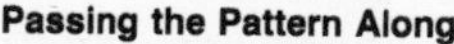

Passing the Pattern Along

How are characteristics handed along from parent to offspring?

When a protozoan divides, its nucleus divides too, as you know. Before the nucleus divides, however, the chromosomes inside the nucleus become two, just alike. We

Developing the lesson

❶ Refer children to the budding yeast cell on page 204. How is this budding different from the fission of an ameba? (A new part grows from the yeast plant; the ameba splits in half. Why is the yeast bud exactly like the parent plant? (comes from the one cell) Refer to the dividing plant cell on page 227. How is this division like that of the ameba? (The cell divides in two.)

❷ Call attention to the drawing. What do you see happening in the nucleus? (The strings seem to be moving apart.) After children have recognized these as ***chromosomes,*** ask: What would happen if half the chromosomes were passed on to each new cell? (Soon there would be no more to distribute.) Scientists have observed that in fact there are just as many chromosomes in each of the new cells as there were in the original one. How could this happen? Children should infer that each chromosome becomes two and that they then separate to form two new nuclei.

❸ Let children recognize that their body cells divide in much the same way as the cells of an ameba. How children get their individual traits will be discussed in the next lesson cluster.

Unit Concept-Statement: The cell is the unit of structure and function in living things.

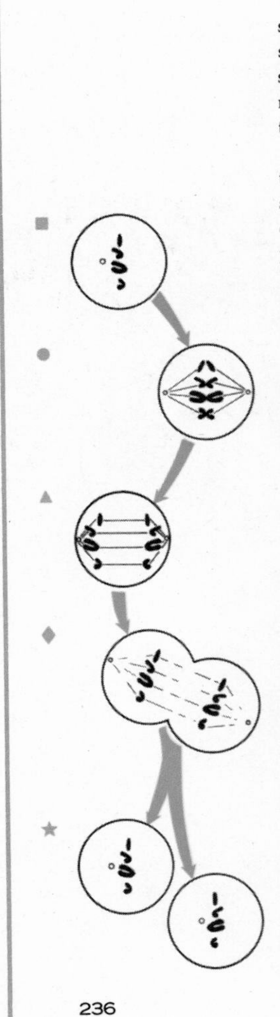

say they *duplicate* themselves. When this happens, the substance in each chromosome also duplicates itself. This ❶ substance is called **DNA.** (Its chemical name is deoxyribonucleic [dē·ok′se·rī bō·nōō·klē′ik] acid, but you don't need to remember that at this point.)

Suppose a protozoan has four chromosomes shaped like these.■ Each chromosome duplicates itself. Now there are four *pairs* of chromosomes.● When the protozoan divides, each offspring gets one chromosome from each pair.▲ Thus each offspring gets four chromosomes just like the parent's chromosomes.◆ Each of the four chromosomes has the DNA of the parent. The two offspring are twins.★

When the protozoan divides, the two new protozoans have equal numbers of chromosomes. Each protozoan has the *same* kind of chromosomes. Each has the *same* DNA. So the young protozoans are twins.

A paramecium actually has 16 chromosomes. Different living things have different numbers of chromosomes. A ❷ vinegar fly has 8 chromosomes. An onion has 16 chromosomes. You have 46 chromosomes.

The study of chromosomes is one of the most important tasks of scientists. There is a great deal still to be discovered about how chromosomes duplicate themselves. For instance, no one yet knows *how* the DNA in a chromosome helps to make a brain, or an eye, or eye color. The evidence is, however, that the chromosomes are responsible for the patterns of living things. The chromosomes of an apple tree make it produce apples, not pears. The egg of a hen produces a chick, not a duckling or a turtle. Whatever it is that sets the pattern for a chick is in the DNA within the chromosomes of the egg. Thus the pattern is set—within the environment in which the organism lives. And the pattern is handed along from parent to offspring, by duplication of the DNA in the chromosomes. ❸

You have seen some evidence for this conclusion. To collect more evidence, try the Search On Your Own on the next page.

236

Useful materials: Toothpicks, string of different colors, saucers.

Continuing Lesson Cluster 7

❶ Children who inferred that chromosomes duplicated themselves now have their inference confirmed.

❷ Children should not jump to the conclusion that the more chromosomes a cell has, the more complex the organism is. A crayfish has more than 200 chromosomes. Some plants have few, others have many.

Children might model the division of a cell with 8 chromosomes by using toothpicks or bits of string of different colors, or both. Have them use a saucer to represent the nucleus. They can duplicate each "chromosome" by adding an identical toothpick or bit of string to the "nucleus." Then they can divide the "chromosomes" and place them on different saucers.

❸ What does "the environment in which the organism lives" mean? Children may be able to infer that an apple tree does not develop to its best in poor soil; that a duck doesn't grow well if its food is scarce or poor in quality. That is, environment determines whether the pattern of the chromosomes develop to their full potential.

Supporting Statement: The pattern of a living thing is passed along to its young by duplication of DNA and chromosomes.

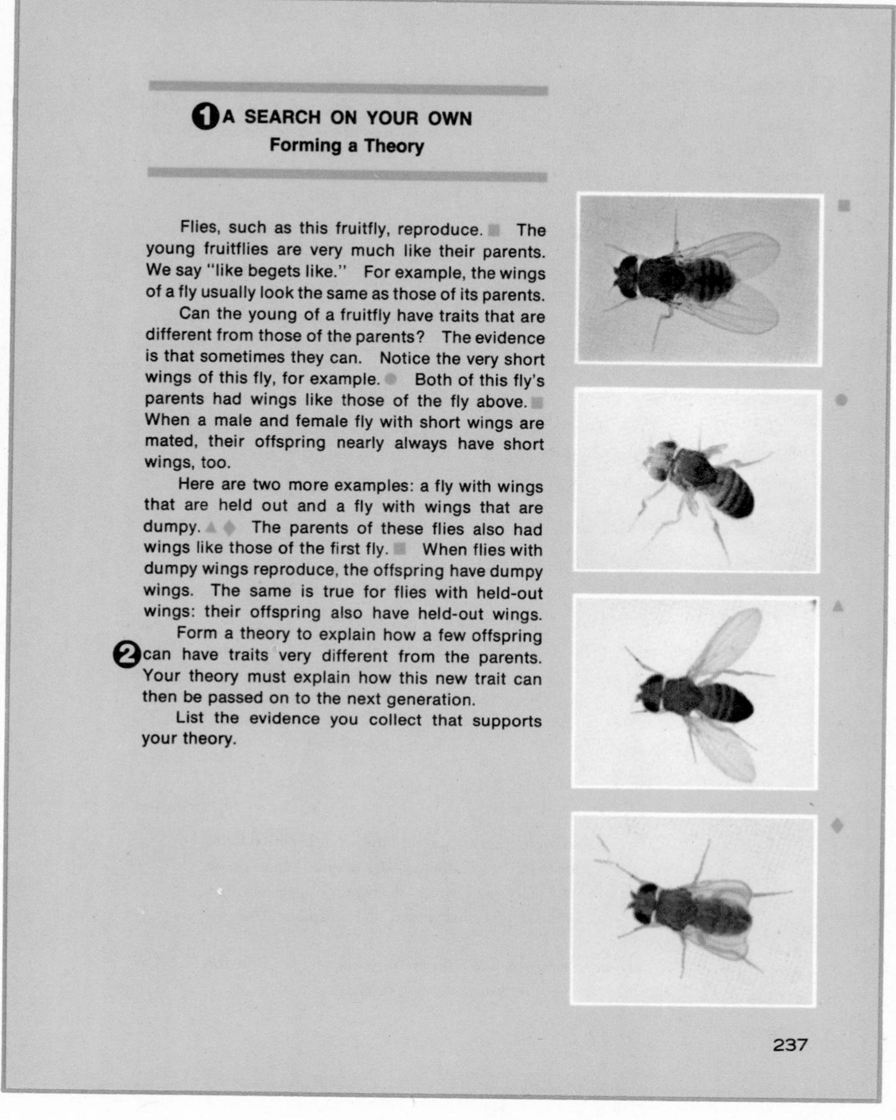

❶ **A SEARCH ON YOUR OWN**

Forming a Theory

Flies, such as this fruitfly, reproduce. ■ The young fruitflies are very much like their parents. We say "like begets like." For example, the wings of a fly usually look the same as those of its parents.

Can the young of a fruitfly have traits that are different from those of the parents? The evidence is that sometimes they can. Notice the very short wings of this fly, for example. ● Both of this fly's parents had wings like those of the fly above. ■ When a male and female fly with short wings are mated, their offspring nearly always have short wings, too.

Here are two more examples: a fly with wings that are held out and a fly with wings that are dumpy. ▲ ◆ The parents of these flies also had wings like those of the first fly. ■ When flies with dumpy wings reproduce, the offspring have dumpy wings. The same is true for flies with held-out wings: their offspring also have held-out wings.

Form a theory to explain how a few offspring ❷ can have traits very different from the parents. Your theory must explain how this new trait can then be passed on to the next generation.

List the evidence you collect that supports your theory.

237

VERIFYING PROGRESS

A search on your own. Children *seek evidence* for the inheritance of traits by offspring of two parents, *analyze* the evidence, and attempt to *construct a theory* to explain inheritance of traits.

❶ This Search will require interested children to do research in the library on inheritance of traits and on mutations. They might look up the work of Gregor Mendel on dominant and recessive traits, the work of cattle breeders, and the development of seedless oranges. For the fruit fly, the work of Herman Muller with X-rays will offer useful evidence.

❷ The theory should include some reference to inheritance of mutant traits and methods by which these traits can be passed on to offspring. Grafting (seedless oranges) and breeding for pure traits should also be reported. For additional information, children may refer to *Concepts in Science* BROWN.

Unit Concept-Statement: The cell is the unit of structure and function of living things.

❶ BEFORE YOU GO ON

Check your understanding of the concepts of this section. Which ending would you choose for each statement below.

1. A paramecium divides by
   a. budding b. fission

2. The paramecium, a single-celled animal, divides in two to reproduce itself. It has 16 chromosomes. Each single-celled animal that is produced has
   a. 8 chromosomes
   b. 16 chromosomes

3. Each of the two offspring from one parent paramecium has an amount of DNA that is
   a. the same b. different

4. The substance that makes an apple tree produce apples, not pears, is
   a. DNA b. ATP

5. The statement that fits the main concept of this section is
   a. The pattern of a living thing is passed along to its young by duplication of DNA and buds.
   b. The pattern of a living thing is passed along to its young by duplication of DNA and chromosomes.

❷ USING WHAT YOU KNOW

1. What is the difference between budding and fission? Include a drawing in your answer.

2. Suppose paramecia divide by fission once a day. Starting with one paramecium, how many paramecia would there be in 10 days?

3. What is meant by "like begets like"? Give examples, using a
   yeast cell
   robin
   paramecium

INVESTIGATING FURTHER

Perhaps you would like to read more about chromosomes. Where would you look? in the dictionary? in an encyclopedia? in a book on biology? Biology is the science in which living things are studied.

A LOOK AHEAD

You have some information on how a single-celled living thing reproduces itself. It divides—by fission. In so doing, it passes on chromosomes to its offspring. These chromosomes carry the traits that make the offspring like the parent.

Thus, like begets like. In the next section, see how this applies to some other kinds of living things.

238

VERIFYING PROGRESS (cont.)

❶ **Before you go on.** Children *demonstrate* understanding of inherited patterns by *identifying* suitable completions to open-ended statements.

1. b 3. a 5. b
2. b 4. a

❷ **Using what you know.** Children *distinguish* between budding and fission, *analyze* questions, and *predict* an outcome or *state* examples to support a concept.

1. Children's drawings should resemble yeast on page 204 and cell division of ameba on page 234.
2. 1024 paramecia.
3. Offspring are like the parents. Yeast and paramecium cells have a single parent; a robin has two robins as parents, male and female.

Supporting Statement: When a many-celled organism develops, the egg cell grows into many more cells of many different kinds.

8. From One Cell

You know that a chicken, a frog, or a robin is made up of millions upon millions of cells. All these animals are made up of organs such as the heart, brain, and lung. If you could examine a bit of any of these organs under the microscope, you would find them made up of cells.

Would you, however, believe that all cells in each of these animals came from an egg? To start with, a chicken's egg is one large cell. Did you know that? So is a frog's egg. So is the egg of a bird like this cardinal. ■

Surely, this is a remarkable happening when you stop to think of it: a bird—warm and full of movement—coming from a single cell.

❶ How does a single cell produce many different cells? You can see for yourself how this happens if you can get ❷ some frog's eggs. INVESTIGATE

239

LESSON CLUSTER 8
FROM ONE CELL

Teaching background. 8 T-228

Concept-seeking. Children grow in awareness of how a fertilized egg cell divides and becomes an organism having traits from two parents.

Operations. Children *investigate* the development of a frog's egg into a frog and *probe* into the development of a chicken and a horse from fertilized eggs.

Methods of intelligence. Children *observe* the development of fertilized frog's eggs, and *infer* that the egg divides into structures differentiated in function; they *apply* the knowledge acquired to *analyze* the development of a chicken and a horse, and *conclude* that the traits of the parents determine those of the offspring.

Useful materials: Egg, saucer.

Introducing Lesson Cluster 8

Break an egg into a saucer and let children examine it. What parts do you see? (white, yolk, and white spot on yolk) What do the white and yolk contain? (food for developing the chick) the white spot? Children may infer that the white spot contains the cell nucleus. In an egg that has been fertilized, the nucleus has already begun to divide before the egg is laid. Thus, the white spot of a fertile egg contains a group of cells that will grow into a chick.

Developing the lesson

❶ Let children hypothesize before starting the investigation.

❷ Preparing for the investigation, you may be able to collect frog's eggs from a pond if the season is right. Or you may purchase them from a biological supply house in early spring. Fertilized frog's eggs look like black dots in masses of jelly.

It is a good plan to organize a schedule for regular care of the developing eggs, observation time, and recording.

For instructions on the care of frog's eggs, see pages 6–7 in *A Sourcebook for Elementary Science*, by Hone, et al., Second Edition, Harcourt Brace Jovanovich, Inc., 1971.

Unit Concept-Statement: The cell is the unit of structure and function in living things.

Performance objectives. Children *describe* the growth and development of a frog, by observing frog's eggs in an aquarium as they develop, hatch into tadpoles, and develop into frogs.

Children *describe* that the frog begins its life as a single cell which develops and multiplies by cell division, begins to form structures, such as eye and tail, then legs and gills, and finally develops into an air-breathing frog.

AN APPRENTICE INVESTIGATION into the Growth of a Frog

Needed: frog's eggs in pond water, an aquarium with growing plants, a hand lens

In the early spring, the female frog lays her eggs in bunches in a pond. The male frog spreads sperm cells over the mass of eggs. After a sperm ❶ enters an egg, the egg can develop. If you live near a pond, collect some eggs that are ready to ❷ develop. They will have black dots in the egg mass.

Bring some eggs to class in some of the pond water in which you found them. If you separate ❸ a few eggs from the larger mass, you can watch a single egg develop.

First, the egg cell divides into two. ■ It ❹ divides again and again. It forms a ball of cells. ●

The ball of cells lengthens. It changes its shape. Finally, the beginnings of a tail can be seen. ▲

The tail gets longer, and legs show. Gills form and grow. They begin to take in oxygen from the water. The egg cell has become a tadpole. ◆ ❺

The tadpole's hind legs develop first. ★ Later, its front legs develop. ◆

The tail gets shorter and disappears. The tadpole becomes a frog that lives on land. ● The ❻ single cell has become millions of different cells.

Methods of Intelligence
Interpreting Observations

How long does it take the egg to develop into a tadpole? How long does it take the tadpole to develop into a frog?

What is the size of the egg? What is the size of the hatching tadpole? How do you explain the difference in size between the egg and the tadpole? ❼

How do you explain the change of the tadpole into a frog?

Courtesy Carolina Biological Supply Company

240

Continuing Lesson Cluster 8

❶ Sperm are tiny whiplike cells much smaller in size than the egg cell. Until a sperm enters an egg cell, the egg will not develop; it is not fertilized. If separate egg and sperm cells do not unite, both will die after a time.

❷ Frog's eggs will be floating on and just below the surface of the water. Toad's eggs are laid in long strings and will be found near the bottom of the pond.

❸ Include a few green plants in the water with the eggs, to help supply oxygen. Also bring back an extra supply of pond water to add to the eggs as the original water evaporates. Tap water is not suitable. (Children should keep the water in the aquarium about six inches deep.) Try to keep the water cool (around 59° to 65°). Leave uncovered in a light place, but avoid direct sunlight.

Supporting Statement: When a many-celled organism develops, the egg cell grows into many more cells of many different kinds.

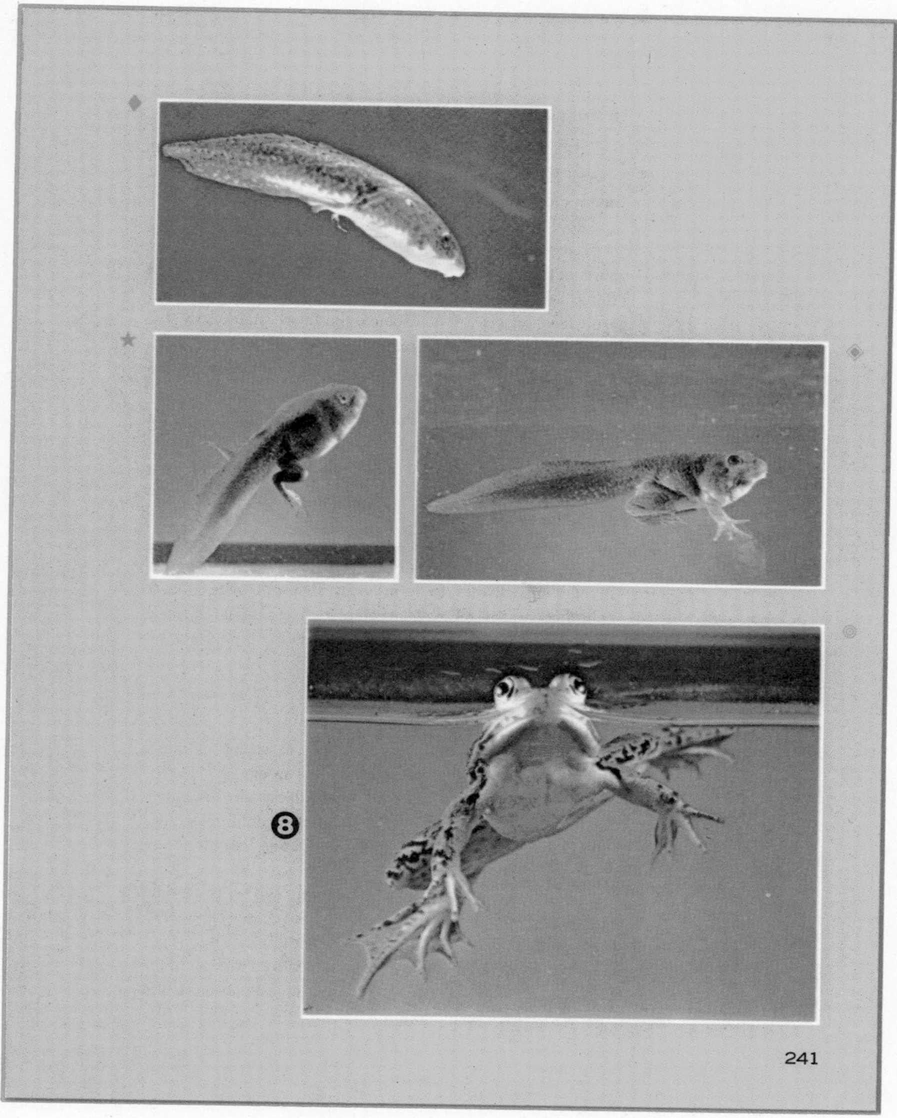

❹ It is likely that the eggs children find will have already started to divide. Have them use a hand lens to observe whatever cell division they can. After a while, discard all eggs that are not developing or have turned gray or white.

❺ Once the tadpoles develop, you will have to add food to the water. Bits of raw liver, cooked spinach, boiled lettuce, and tiny pieces of hard-boiled egg yolk are what some tadpoles like. After the tadpoles have eaten, use a dip tube to remove left-overs.

❻ Children may want to make a terrarium including growing plants, a mossy land area, bits of trees and rocks, and a pool of water for the frogs or toads. If you are raising toads, you will have to include insects and perhaps worms in their diet.

❼ The time of development will vary. Have children keep records so they can answer these questions. They should observe the changes in size and development and interpret these changes as reproduction of various kinds of cells from the original fertilized egg.

An interesting and complete illustrated book that will be helpful in raising frogs is *The Frog Book*, by Mary C. Dickerson, Dover (paperback), 1969.

❽ The species of frog in the photograph is *Rana pipiens*, commonly known as the leopard frog or meadow frog.

Unit Concept-Statement: The cell is the unit of structure and function in living things.

A Frog Develops

The egg of a frog is just one cell. However, it is a
❶ special kind of cell. When the egg cell begins to divide, it doesn't form more egg cells. *The egg cell forms many different kinds of cells.* It forms skin cells, muscle cells, bone cells, nerve cells, blood cells. These cells form the different parts of the frog's body. The different parts do the different things a living thing has to do to live. These different parts
❷ are called organs. For instance, the heart is an organ that pumps blood. The intestine is an organ that digests food. The lungs, the liver, and the brain are other organs of the body. Each organ does a special kind of work.

However, all these different organs begin with the same cell. All begin with the dividing egg cell.

We have a word that you know well for this forming of more and different cells. Yet you may not have thought of the word in this way. This forming of more cells and different cells is growth.

The frog begins as one egg cell. That cell divides and divides and divides to form many different cells. These cells form organs. Finally, a complete living thing is formed, an *organism.* It has grown from one cell.

A Chick Grows

What happens inside a hen's egg to change it into a living bird? Scientists have watched as an egg cell divides.

❸ When the egg is laid, the single cell has already begun to divide into many cells. Two days later, different groups
❹ of cells appear. ■ Four days later, a beating heart is pump-
❺ ing blood. ●

Can you see the beginnings of legs and wings, 9 days
❻ later? ▲ On the 13th day, you can see the chick's feathers. ◆
❼ The chick is almost fully formed by the 16th day. ★

On the 21st day, the young chick pecks its way out of the
❽ egg. ◈ It is not yet ready to fly. In fact, a chicken is a bird that does not fly very well.

242

Continuing Lesson Cluster 8

❶ Do you know what this specialized kind of cell is called? (a fertilized egg cell) What is a fertilized egg cell? (an egg cell which has combined with a sperm cell)

What is special about this kind of cell? (It came from the cells of two parents.) Children, recalling cell fission, may wonder whether it has *twice* the number of chromosomes. Explain that the cell is special because sperm and egg cells have only half as many chromosomes as other body cells. Then the fertilized egg cell has the same number as each parent has in its body cells. What does this suggest about the DNA? (half from each parent cell) This is why an organism looks like both parents. This is why you look a little like both your mother and father.

❷ Why do these parts develop as they do? (chromosomes and DNA)

❸ How is the chicken egg you eat different from the one that hatches into a chick? (Chicken eggs sold in stores are usually unfertilized eggs. Thus, the egg you eat has not been fertilized and the cell has not begun to divide. The egg that has started to divide before it is laid is fertilized.)

Supporting Statement: When a many-celled organism develops, the egg cell grows into many more cells of many different kinds.

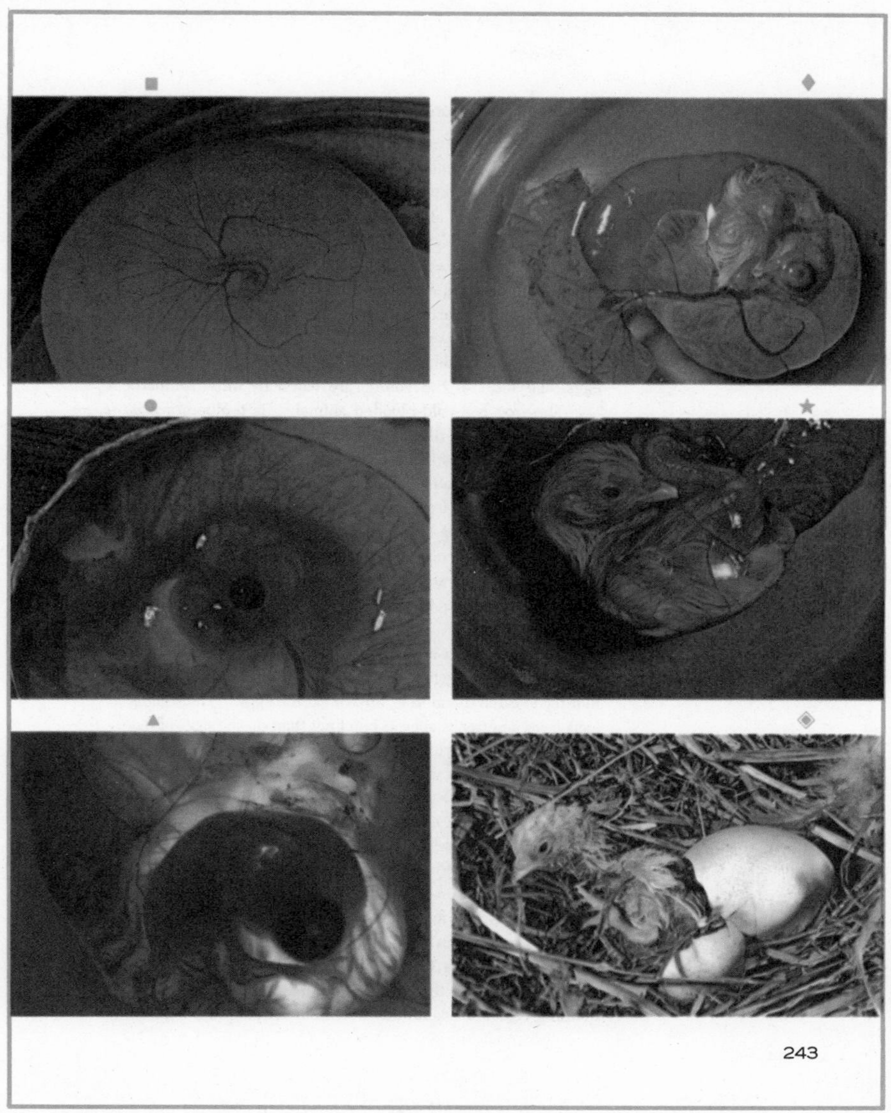

❹ In photograph ■, the early embryo of the chick is shaped somewhat like a question mark. Blood vessels radiate from the embryo over the egg yolk. **What do you think is the function of the blood vessels?** (to bring food from yolk to the developing chick)

❺ The head of the chick embryo in photographs ● and ▲ is much larger than the rest of its body. Children should be able to identify the chick's well-developed eye. The eye is not, however, as large as it seems: the pictures have been magnified several times.

❻ Children will notice in the photograph that the chick's feathers are now well developed, that the body of the chick is now bigger than its head, but that the eye is still out of proportion. **What do you infer about the rates of growth of the various parts of the chick?** (At any given time, some parts are growing faster than others.)

❼ A chick at the stage shown in photograph ★ will cheep inside of the egg from time to time.

❽ The just-hatched chick is still damp. It will acquire a downy look after drying in the air.

VERIFYING PROGRESS

In methods of intelligence

After children have studied these pages, let them *analyze* and *distinguish* differences between the development of the offspring of frogs, robins, and mammals (such as the horse). For example: How are the numbers of each maintained? (*frogs:* lay many eggs and a few survive; *birds*: parents take care of eggs and of young after hatching; *mammals*: young develop inside mother and have parental care after birth)

■

Protecting the Young

In early spring, robins build their nests. A male robin and female robin collect twigs and mud and build a nest shaped like a bowl. ■ (Other birds build other kinds of nests. The robin always builds a robin's nest, not an oriole's or an eagle's nest.) In the nest, the female robin lays from 4 to 6 blue eggs. ❶

While a robin's egg is developing, it is kept warm and protected by the parents. How different this is from what happens to a frog's eggs! Frogs do not protect their eggs. Their egg cells divide and develop in the water. Most of the eggs, and most of the young, are eaten by other animals.

The frog is a cold-blooded animal. Its temperature is nearly the same as the temperature of its surroundings. A frog's egg can develop in water that changes temperature. It doesn't have to be kept at an even temperature. However, a long freeze may kill frogs' eggs.

A bird is a warm-blooded animal. Its body temperature is about 104° Fahrenheit. Its eggs have to be kept at a fairly even temperature. The robin sitting on the eggs supplies warmth for the young birds developing inside the eggs.

Have you seen a male robin standing guard while the female sits on the eggs? He will chase off birds and animals that try to catch the mother bird or eat the eggs. The robin's eggs have a better chance of hatching than do the eggs of the frog, because they are protected by the parents.

●

The young of some animals have even better protection, ❷ because the eggs develop inside the mother. The eggs of an animal such as a mouse, a rabbit, a horse, or an elephant begin to divide inside the mother's body. ❸

Within a female horse, for example, dividing cells form the different organs of a young colt's body. Inside its mother's body, the forming colt is protected from harm. It gets food substances and oxygen from its mother. It also gets the substances from its mother that its dividing cells must have in order to grow and divide. ● The wastes from dividing cells are taken away by the mother's body.

244

Continuing Lesson Cluster 8

❶ What differences are there between a robin and a frog? (Frogs lay eggs in water, robins build nests and protect the eggs until the young are ready to fly and be grown robins.) You may wish to state that a frog lays hundreds of eggs while a robin lays only a few eggs. What do robins provide for their eggs that frogs do not? (protection as they grow into adult organisms)

❷ Why are eggs that develop inside an organism better protected than those of a frog or a bird? (Children can infer that animals that like frogs' eggs will eat them without difficulty, since the eggs are unprotected; that animals that like birds' eggs must drive away the parents. In the case of animals whose eggs develop within the female parent, the mother must be captured and killed in order to kill the offspring.)

❸ Children can properly infer that the female horse's (mare's) egg cells were fertilized by a male horse's (stallion's) sperm cells. The offspring develops, and the colt, when it is born, is ready to feed and walk around in a few hours.

Supporting Statement: When a many-celled organism develops, the egg cells grow into many more cells of many different kinds.

After the colt is born, its mother nurses it with milk. It ❶ keeps on growing. In time, it becomes full-grown.

Scientists have watched many kinds of cells dividing. But how can one egg cell form many different kinds of cells? So far scientists have found out very little about this. They know even less about how such cells join together to form different organs!

There is still a great deal for scientists to find out.

❷ **BEFORE YOU GO ON**

A. Check your understanding of the concepts of this section. Which ending would you choose for each statement below?

1. The egg cell of an animal such as the grass frog or the robin divides to produce many cells. These cells are
a. all the same b. not all the same

2. The egg cell of an animal such as a bird or a frog develops first into a
a. ball of cells b. layer of cells

3. The process by which an egg cell forms more cells is
a. growth b. oxidation

4. Unlike frogs and birds, some animals develop from the egg
a. outside the mother
b. inside the mother

5. The statement that fits the main concept of this section is
a. When a many-celled organism develops, the egg cell grows into many more cells that are all alike.
b. When a many-celled organism develops, the egg cell grows into many more cells of many different kinds.

B. Write a paragraph or two in answer to this question: "How does an egg produce a complete living thing?"

A LOOK AHEAD

The many-celled animal begins its life when the egg begins to divide. But the egg doesn't divide into more cells exactly like the egg.

The egg divides into different cells—different for each different part of the body.

The liver has many cells that are different from those of the heart. So does the kidney.

However, parts of the body do work together.

245

VERIFYING PROGRESS

In methods of intelligence

If any of the children has a pet dog, cat, hamster, or other animal that has had offspring, let him report his observations of his pet families. The children's report can include answers to such questions as: How did the mother care for her young? Which parent did the offspring look like? How soon did the young open their eyes? move about like the parents? begin to feed from a dish instead of nursing?

Children may *synthesize* their findings as they *conclude* that parental care is an adaptation that enables organisms to survive.

❶ From what does the mother make its milk? (from food it eats) What is the food? (green plants) How does the colt get energy and matter for growth and activity? (Food provides matter for new cells and energy for cell division.)

VERIFYING PROGRESS

❷ **Before you go on.** Children *demonstrate* understanding of the growth of a many-celled organism from a single cell by *identifying* suitable completions for open-ended statements, and by *describing* the growth of a single cell into a many-celled organism.

A. 1. b 3. a 5. b
2. a 4. b

B. Children should give evidence of understanding that a fertilized egg divides into different kinds of cells that have special functions within the complete organism.

UNIT FIVE

Unit Concept-Statement: The cell is the unit of structure and function in living things.

LESSON CLUSTER 9
FROM EARTH INTO CELL

Teaching background. 9 T-229

Concept-seeking. Children become aware that all cells are composed of compounds formed from elements in earth, air, and water.

Operations. Children *investigate* the cells to determine the basic compounds of which they are made.

Methods of intelligence. Children *observe* the result of testing substances derived from plants and animals; *distinguish* among proteins, carbohydrates, fats, minerals, and vitamins; and *infer* that all living cells consist of elements chemically combined to form these compounds.

9. From Earth into Cell

A seed of wheat is planted. The soil is watered. The seed cells start dividing. Roots grow down. Through the root hairs, substances in the soil enter the plant. A stalk rises above the soil and puts out leaves. Through the leaves, gases in the air enter the plant. The seed has become a wheat plant.

Where does a plant get the substances that enable it to grow? The substances come from the soil and from the air. So the plant must have in it some elements and compounds from the Earth's crust. And it must have some elements and compounds from the air as well.

When soil is watered, the water dissolves elements and compounds in the soil. Many of these dissolved elements and compounds get into a plant cell. Elements and compounds in the air pass into plant cells, too. So a cell may have many different elements and compounds in it.

Inside the cell, food substances are oxidized as part of the cell's energy process. As this happens, many new compounds are formed.

1 The living stuff in cells—such as this desmid, photographed just as it was reproducing—is made up of various elements and compounds. ■ What kinds of compounds are there in the cells? To see for yourself, try the investigation on the opposite page. INVESTIGATE

■

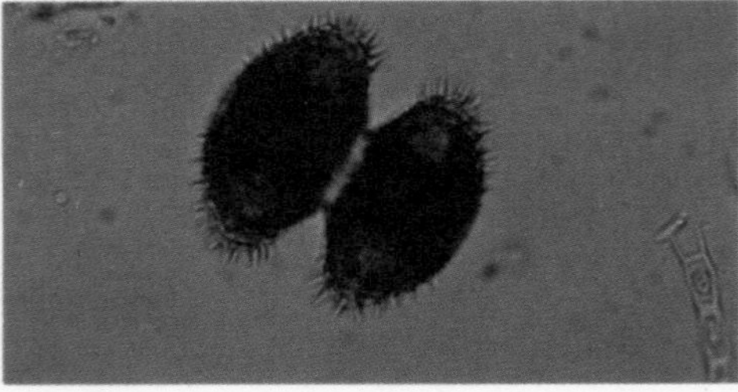

Introducing Lesson Cluster 9

Present a plant growing in a pot of soil. What do we know about this plant? As children mention growth, reproduction, foodmaking, and so on, write these on the chalkboard, or let each child write his own response to form a list. You may wish to ask some of the following questions if children do not mention something toward which the question is directed: What are the parts of a plant? (leaves, stem, roots, etc.) What does each part do? (*leaves:* make food; *stem:* supports leaves and conducts liquids between leaves and roots; *roots:* anchor whole plant and take in water and minerals from soil) Where does the plant get the substances it needs to grow? (air, soil) What does each plant part consist of? (cells)

What does every part of your body consist of? (cells) How are your cells different from a plant's cells? (Our cells cannot make their own food.) How do your cells get food? (eventually from plants through vegetables and meat products)

Finally, after children have told what they know about green plants, as well as their uses to us, ask: What do you think cells are made up of? Children may or may not think of elements or compounds. If they do, ask: What kind of compounds? In any event let them hypothesize and then read the page in preparation for investigation.

Developing the lesson

1 Children may not recognize that the desmid is a single-celled green plant, a microscopic alga that lives in water.

Supporting Statement: The living stuff of a cell contains elements that are found in the Earth's crust.

AN APPRENTICE INVESTIGATION into Testing for Compounds in Cells

Needed: a bowl, 2 sheets of aluminum foil, a feather, some hair, dry cereal, a pat of butter, a peanut, a glass plate, brown wrapping paper, matches

Put aluminum foil on the bowl as shown. ■ Place the feather on the foil. Your teacher will light the feather. Notice the strange smell as the ❶ feather burns. This smell is one test for protein. Protein contains the elements nitrogen, oxygen, carbon, and hydrogen.

Watch as your teacher burns some hair on the foil. What is its odor? What does this tell you ❷ about the substances in hair?

Notice that the feather turns black as it burns. This is a test for the element carbon.

Place cereal flakes on the foil. Your teacher will light them with a match. Hold the glass plate over the flakes as they are burning. What collects ❸ on the glass? ● What color do the burning flakes turn? What do your observations tell you about the substances in cereal flakes?

Rub some butter on the brown paper. It makes a shiny spot, through which some light can pass. ▲ This is a test for fat. Rub the peanut ❹ on the brown paper. What do you observe? What do you conclude?

Methods of Intelligence: Predicting

Shape some aluminum foil into a cup. Put a small lump of sugar in it and hold the cup over a flame with a pair of pliers or tongs. Predict what ❺ will happen.

■

●

▲

247

Performance objectives. Children *describe* compounds in living cells, by *observing* the odor and color as protein substances are burned, the formation of carbon and water as carbohydrates are burned, and the shiny spot on brown paper as substances containing fat are rubbed on it.

Useful materials: Some similar materials are available in CLASSROOM LABORATORY: PURPLE.

❶ The odor is similar to ammonia, a compound containing nitrogen. Nitrogen is one of the four elements in all proteins—nitrogen, hydrogen, oxygen and carbon combine in a number of different ways, resulting in a number of different proteins.

❷ Children should infer from the odor that hair is made up of protein.

❸ Since water collects on the plate, children can infer that the cereal contains hydrogen and probably oxygen, although some children may think oxygen came from the air. The black color is evidence of carbon.

❹ The peanut will make a shiny spot, evidence that it contains fat. Do not let children conclude that peanuts contain only fat. Peanuts and peanut butter are excellent sources of plant protein.

❺ Children learned in Unit Three that sugar is a combination of carbon, hydrogen, and water. They therefore should predict the formation of water and carbon. The sugar will first melt (turn liquid) and then, as water evaporates, turn black. A plate held over the cup will collect droplets of water. When only carbon is left in the cup, children can scrape some of it off and feel it with their fingers.

Children may be interested to know that in cooking sugar may be melted until it turns light brown and then used in making caramel sauce and cake frostings. They may have eaten this sauce on molded custard desserts.

Unit Concept-Statement: The cell is the unit of structure and function in living things.

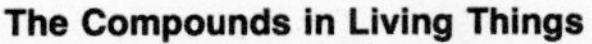

The Compounds in Living Things

❶ Living things have a good deal of **protein** in them. Proteins are compounds made up of carbon, hydrogen, oxygen, and nitrogen. (Some proteins contain sulfur and phosphorus as well.) Meat, fish, shrimp, oysters, eggs, peanuts, beans, chicken, turkey, milk, and cheese are foods that are rich in protein. ■

A test for protein is its smell when a substance containing it burns. If a feather or some hair is burned, the odor of burning protein can be detected.

Another group of compounds found in living things are the **carbohydrates** (kär′bō·hī′drāts). Carbohydrates are made up of carbon, hydrogen, and oxygen. They do *not* have nitrogen in them, as the proteins do. When carbohydrates are completely burned, carbon dioxide and water are produced. If the carbohydrates are incompletely burned, black carbon remains and may be seen.

Starches and sugars are carbohydrates. As you know, starch turns blue-black when iodine is placed on it. Test for starch with iodine. Potatoes, rice, bread, sugar, molasses, candy, fruits, cereal, cookies, spaghetti, macaroni, grits, and corn are among the many foods that are rich in carbohydrates. ●

Not all compounds that turn black and give off water when burned are carbohydrates. Some are **fats.** Butter is a fat. Nuts have fat in them. So do meat, eggs, cheese, shortening, and milk. Oil made from olives, corn, cottonseed, soybeans, peanuts, and other plants are fats. Cells make fats, and living things have fat in them. Here are some foods rich in fat.

Fats are compounds of hydrogen, carbon, and oxygen, as are carbohydrates. But these elements are combined in different ways in fats and in carbohydrates. The number of carbon, hydrogen, and oxygen atoms in the molecules differs. The arrangement of atoms differs, too.

When a feather or some hair is burned, ashes are left. When a bone or some wood is burned, ashes are left. The ash is made up mainly of **minerals** found in living things.

248

VERIFYING PROGRESS

In concept-seeking

Let children *test* for starch by adding tincture of iodine to bits of foods. Have them select some samples that they *predict* will show a positive result and others that will show a negative result. Their samples might include: bread, raw or cooked potato, sugar, salad oil, boiled rice, milk, peanut butter, sliced apple, orange juice, etc. Among the samples that contain starch, some will turn darker blue than others when iodine is added. Thus, children may *conclude* that some "starchy" foods contain more starch than others.

Continuing Lesson Cluster 9

The food groups illustrated on this page and the next should not be confused with the "Basic Four" food groups, developed as a nutrition index by the U. S. Department of Agriculture. These four are: the milk group, the meat group, the vegetable and fruit group, and the bread and cereal group.

❶ Children may be interested to classify, according to the food groups in the textbook, the kinds of food they eat in one day. These groups are often collectively called *nutrients*. Encourage children to list the foods they ate the day before. When the day's list is completed, have them attempt to classify each food in one or more of the five food groups. They should be made aware that one food may contain two or more nutrients. For example, beef pie would contain protein, carbohydrates, fats, minerals, and vitamins.

EXTENDING THE LESSON

Ask children to find out: Which food group is most important for growth? (proteins) Which groups supply mainly energy? (carbohydrates and fats) Why are vitamins and minerals important? (They regulate body processes—for details, see a junior high school science text.) Why can't we live without water? (The substances in cells are in a water suspension or solution.)

Supporting Statement: The living stuff of a cell contains elements that are found in the Earth's crust.

The minerals are salts, like common salt, or compounds of calcium and phosphorus. They enter the plant through its root hairs. Besides salt itself, fruits and vegetables are rich in minerals. Fruits and vegetables, as well as many other foods (such as meat, milk, whole wheat, and butter) are also
❶ rich in **vitamins.**

The minerals in living things are almost always dissolved in water. In fact, a cell may be as much as $\frac{99}{100}$ water. Different kinds of living things may have different amounts
❷ of water. For example, an egg has much less water in it than has a plum. And a watermelon has much more water than has a peanut.

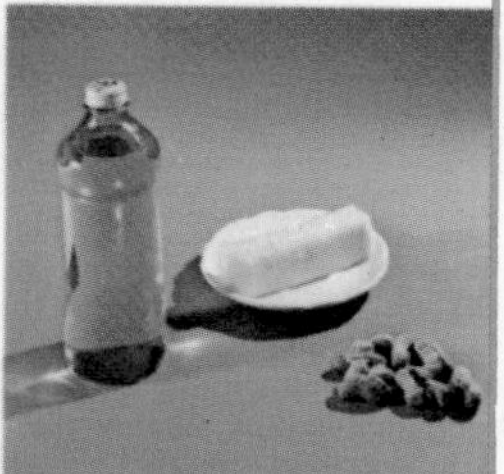

In the living stuff in a cell, there are six main kinds of compounds:

proteins	minerals
carbohydrates	vitamins
fats	water

Let's go a little further. What makes up all elements and compounds? What are the building blocks? Atoms, of course. Atoms are the building blocks of living things, as they are of all matter. In a cell, atoms are combined into different kinds of molecules.

Many scientists call cells the building blocks of living things. Certainly the cell is the center of the process that gives us energy. Isn't a cell also like a tiny factory? It breaks down some substances and puts together other substances.

Scientists still know very little about just how a cell does all these things. There is a great deal yet to be found out.

But scientists have come to understand one very important concept. They have come to know that living things have ways to get the matter from which they make the
❸ compounds in cells. What is this source of matter?

The source of the matter used by living things is the *environment:* the Earth. Because of this man has come upon a great problem. To understand this problem, you may want to try the Search On Your Own on the next page.

249

❶ Vitamins are often lost by overcooking or by cooking in too much water that is then poured down the drain, carrying the vitamins. Different vitamins aid the body in using foods for different purposes.

❷ What foods can you think of that have a lot of water in them? (fruits such as apples, melons, oranges, grapefruit; vegetables such as celery, radishes, potatoes, lettuce, tomatoes)

❸ How does the cell take in matter? For example, what are the ways a cell in a plant leaf might get matter? (Roots take in water with dissolved minerals from the soil; leaves take in carbon dioxide from the air.) How does an animal take in matter from the Earth? (by eating plants or other animals that have eaten plants)

Unit Concept-Statement: The cell is the unit of structure and function in living things.

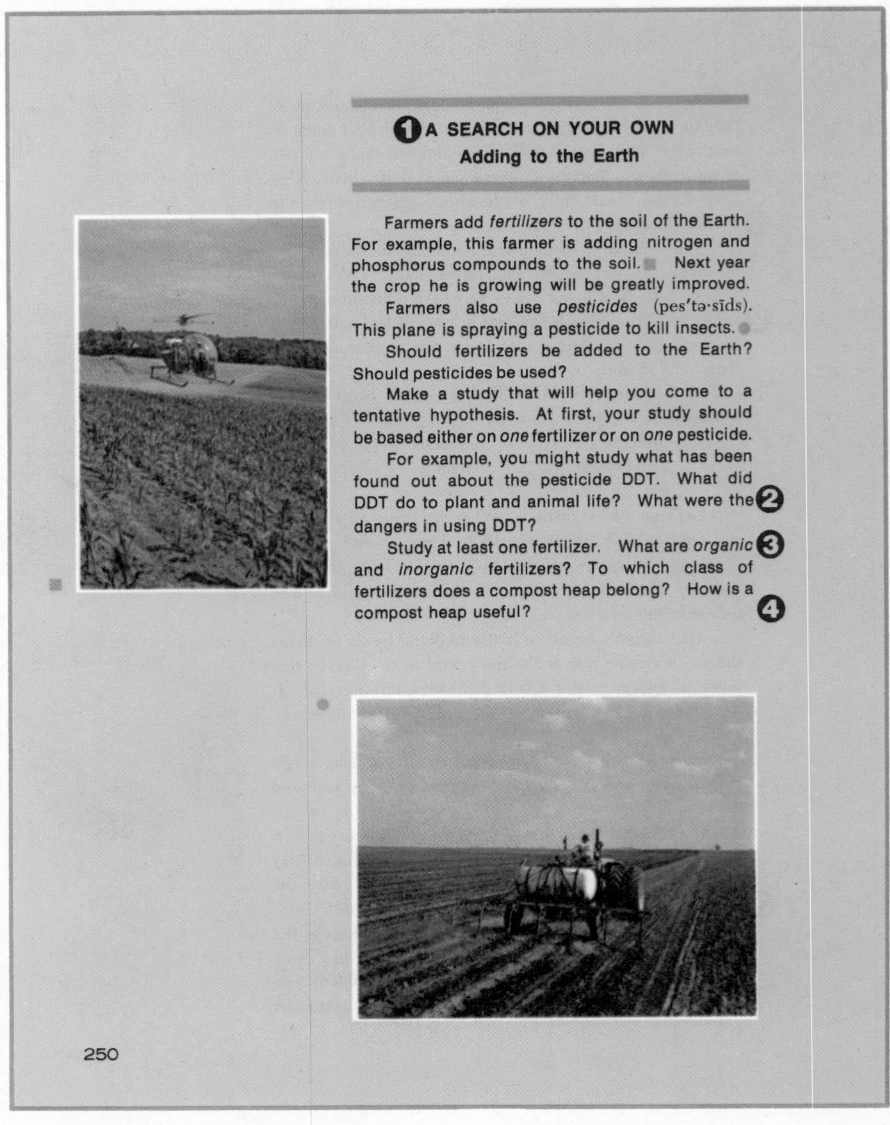

❶ A SEARCH ON YOUR OWN

Adding to the Earth

Farmers add *fertilizers* to the soil of the Earth. For example, this farmer is adding nitrogen and phosphorus compounds to the soil. ■ Next year the crop he is growing will be greatly improved.

Farmers also use *pesticides* (pes′tə·sīdz). This plane is spraying a pesticide to kill insects. ●

Should fertilizers be added to the Earth? Should pesticides be used?

Make a study that will help you come to a tentative hypothesis. At first, your study should be based either on *one* fertilizer or on *one* pesticide.

For example, you might study what has been found out about the pesticide DDT. What did DDT do to plant and animal life? What were the ❷ dangers in using DDT?

Study at least one fertilizer. What are *organic* ❸ and *inorganic* fertilizers? To which class of fertilizers does a compost heap belong? How is a compost heap useful? ❹

250

VERIFYING PROGRESS

❶ **A search on your own.** Children *investigate* pesticides and fertilizers and *hypothesize* about the wisdom of their use.

❷ Although DDT *does* destroy harmful insects, it also destroys useful insects like the honeybee. DDT is a chemical poison. Crops sprayed with DDT can be harmful to animals or human beings that eat them. It may not do immediate harm, but it can build up in body cells until it is dangerous. DDT can be carried into lakes and rivers where it gets into the bodies of fish, becomes concentrated, and makes them unsafe to eat.

❸ An organic fertilizer consists of humus made from the return of decayed plant and animal matter to the soil. Inorganic fertilizers are chemical compounds.

❹ A compost heap is a pile of organic material that is allowed to decay until it forms humus rich in minerals from decomposed bodies or wastes of plants and animals. It is used to return minerals to soil from which they had been removed by growing plants.

Unit Concept-Statement: The cell is the unit of structure and function in living things.

❶ **BEFORE YOU GO ON**

Check your understanding of the concepts of this section by answering these questions.

1. What are the main kinds of compounds found in cells?

2. What are some kinds of food that contain each of these compounds?

3. What are the building blocks of these compounds?

4. How can you test for some of these compounds?

5. The statement that fits the main concept of this section is
   a. The living stuff of a cell contains elements that are found only in organisms.
   b. The living stuff of a cell contains elements that are found in the Earth's crust.

❷ **USING WHAT YOU KNOW**

Glucose is a kind of sugar. Like all sugars, glucose is a carbohydrate. Would a test for protein work on glucose? Why? Would a test for fat work on this sugar? Why?

❸10. The Main Concept Likenesses in Living Things

FOCUS ON THE CONCEPT

It took many years of work to find out that living things are made up of cells.

About 300 years ago, an English scientist named Robert Hooke was looking at all sorts of things through a new invention called the microscope. He examined the point of a needle, the edge of a razor, linen cloth, snow, bubbles, plants, seeds, insects, fleas, molds, and many other things. (The first microscopes were sometimes called "flea glasses," because people liked to look at fleas through them.) Hooke examined some cork, and was amazed and delighted to see that it was made up of little boxes. ■ He called the boxes *cells.* He was looking at cell walls, really, for in cork the inner cell materials have disappeared. Only the cell walls are left.

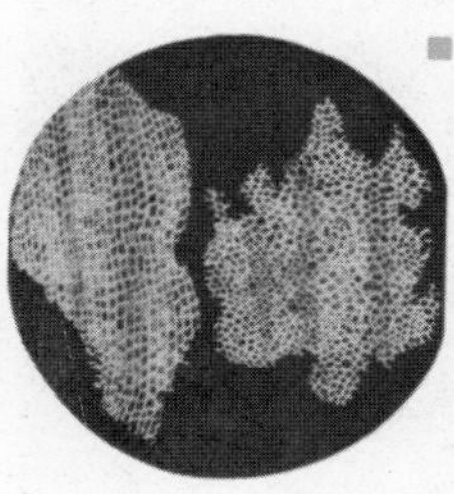

251

LESSON CLUSTER 10

THE MAIN CONCEPT: LIKENESSES IN LIVING THINGS

Teaching background. T-224–228

Concept-seeking. Children strengthen their awareness of the concept that the cell is the unit of structure and function in living things.

Methods of intelligence. Children *analyze* evidence of cell structure and function and *synthesize* it into a broad unifying concept.

❶ **Before you go on.** Children *demonstrate* understanding of essential compounds useful to cells by *analyzing* questions and *naming* the composition or uses of these compounds.
1. Proteins, carbohydrates, fats, minerals, vitamins, and water.
2. *Proteins:* meat, milk, fish, etc.; *carbohydrates:* candy, cake, bread, etc.; *fats:* butter, margarine, salad oil, etc.; *vitamins:* fruits, vegetables, etc.; *minerals:* most foods; *water:* all foods.
3. atoms
4. Ammonia odor from burning proteins; carbon and water from burning carbohydrates; shiny spot on paper from fats.
5. b

❷ **Using what you know.** Children *analyze* questions and *apply* tests to *distinguish* among proteins, carbohydrates, and fats.

Glucose will not give off an ammonia odor when burned, nor will it leave a shiny spot when rubbed over paper.

❸ Let children begin by reading this page. What concept do you have that Hooke could not have had when he first looked at cork? (All living things are made of cells.)

Unit Concept-Statement: The cell is the unit of structure and function in living things.

It took almost 200 years of work after Robert Hooke's ❶ discovery to convince scientists that *all* living things are made of cells, and that cells do the work of a living thing.

We have come to a deeper understanding of the concept of **life:**

Living things are made up of cells.

This understanding tells much about the common likenesses in all living things.

In 1839, two German scientists, M. J. Schleiden and Theodor Schwann, stated their famous cell theory. Their cell theory was that all living things are made up of cells. Today, more than a hundred years later, we know that cells are the building blocks of living things. We know more.

The Energy Cycle in the Cell

We know that each cell is a kind of energy machine. Inside a cell, ATP is broken down to yield energy for the cell's work and growth. Then the ATP that has been broken down is built up again. The energy to build up the ATP comes from glucose and other food substances. ❷

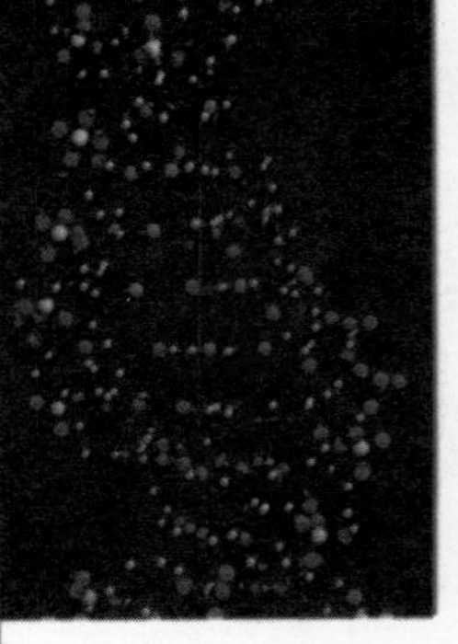

We know also that cells are made up of elements and compounds found on the Earth. Cells take in these elements and compounds from soil, water, and air.

All living material within the cell is not the same. When you eat food, your cells make more of *you*. When a cat eats food, its cells make more cat cells. The cells in a bean plant make more bean cells.

We are all different. Yet we are alike too, for we have the same kinds of cells. Each of us has muscle cells, nerve cells, blood cells, skin cells, and bone cells. Each of us has these different kinds of cells grouped in tissues and in organs.

Cells are the building blocks of living things. Within a cell of each living thing are chromosomes. Within each chromosome is the substance DNA. (Here is a model of a ❸

252

Continuing Lesson Cluster 10

❶ What kind of search had to take place before it could be accepted that all living things are made of cells? (search for hidden likenesses in all kinds of plants and animals) Encourage children to look up and report on the lives of M. J. Schleiden and Theodor Schwann. They may be especially interested in the initial opposition to the cell theory and the length of time it took for it to be accepted.

❷ Why is ATP such an important substance? (It enables cells to change energy in glucose into other forms of energy for the cell's and the body's activities.)

❸ Why was the discovery of the DNA molecule important? (It helped to explain how traits of parents are inherited by their offspring.)

part of a DNA molecule. ■) DNA has in it the pattern of that living thing. When a cell begins to divide, to reproduce, its chromosomes duplicate themselves. As the chromosomes duplicate themselves, so does their DNA. Thus, living things receive the ability to develop characteristics carried by their parents.

You have come to understand an important concept about **living things:**

The cell is the basis for the activities of all living things.

This concept is stated another way: *The cell is the unit* ❶ *of structure and function in living things.* This statement is known as the cell theory. What does structure mean? What does function mean? How are living things alike? ❷ Does the cell theory explain the facts as you know them?

FOCUS ON THE SCIENTIST'S WAYS

From your study of science this year, you know that "hidden likenesses" means likenesses that are not seen at first. In other words, as we examine things we find that likenesses, which are at first hidden, become open.

For example, you examined rocks in an earlier unit. At first it seems as if every rock is different. Then you begin to group them. You find their likenesses. You group some rocks as sedimentary, some as igneous, others as metamorphic. As you do this, you begin to see one of the ways of the scientist: he groups things by their likenesses.

You recognize that all rocks are made up of matter. From your knowledge of the make-up of matter, you search for still further likenesses. The rocks, you find, are all made up of elements and compounds. Then you seek ❸ further into their hidden likenesses and find that, like all matter, the elements in the rocks of the Earth are made up of atoms. And atoms, in turn, are made up of protons, neutrons, and electrons.

253

❶ Structure refers to the size and shape of an organism and the way its parts are built and fit together. Function refers to the activities of an organism or the use of any of its parts. Living things, both plants and animals, have cells with basic similarities of nucleus, cytoplasm, and cell membrane.

❷ Discussion of this final question should reveal understanding of the difference between fact and theory. A fact is a confirmed observation—something that is observed again and again and found to be the same. A theory is a logical explanation of a group of related facts, which can be discarded or changed if new facts are discovered. Children can agree that the cell theory is a logical explanation. They may recall, however, that scientists are still seeking fuller explanation of just how ATP and DNA function in a cell. They should not conclude that the cell theory explains life, but rather that it describes living things.

❸ Why do scientists search for hidden likenesses? Discussion should reveal that understanding of similarities among what is known helps to explain what is not yet known or only imperfectly understood.

Unit Concept-Statement: The cell is the unit of structure and function in living things.

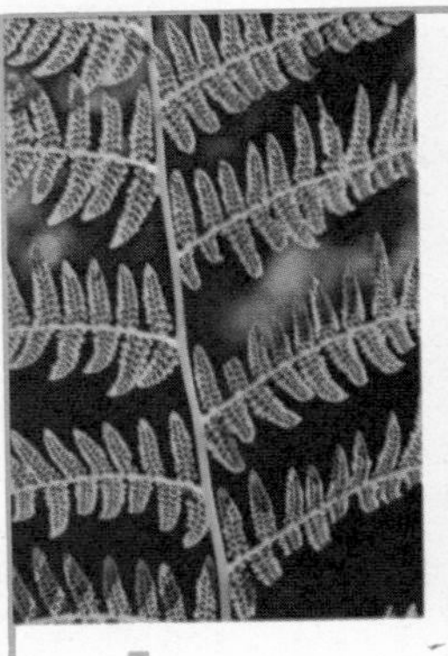

Now you have looked at living things, and seen that these have their hidden likenesses, also. Think of how different two living things, such as a porpoise and a fern, can appear. ■ ● Yet you know that both of these, like most living things, are made up of cells. And the cells, in turn, have similar parts: nucleus, cytoplasm, cell membrane.

Clearly, one of the main methods of intelligence of the scientist is to seek out hidden likenesses. When he does so, he can put the objects or events he studies into groups. In grouping them, he puts together those objects or events that ❶ are related.

A Student of Science and Scientists

The scientist who used the phrase "hidden likenesses" is Jacob Bronowski. ▲ Bronowski is a man who thinks about the way people work. He has long been interested in the way scientists try to uncover hidden likenesses.

In studying scientists, Bronowski was interested in the values that make men scientists. A value is a human behavior which is prized. Thus honesty is a value; so is courtesy. ❷ Which value do scientists prize most?

Dr. Bronowski thinks scientists prize most the behaviors that lead to truth. Put another way, truth is their highest ❸ value. Do you agree with this? Are there other values scientists prize?

254

Continuing Lesson Cluster 10

❶ What happens when a scientist discovers an unknown object or a new event? How can he find out a great deal about it? (He looks for something in it which is common to known objects or events; when he finds it, he can explain structure or function or both—at least in part.)

❷ Let children discuss what the term *value* means to them. Probably they will first think of financial value—a price set on an object or on something done. You may wish to rephrase the question: What do you think is worthwhile in your life? (It may be something that gives satisfaction, and it may be evaluated in terms of a price, too.) What do you value most in your friends? in your family?

❸ What are some behaviors that led us to seek concepts in science this year? Children should mention several methods of intelligence they have used—testing a hypothesis, making careful observations, making precise measurements, keeping accurate records, analyzing problems, and so on.

Unit Concept-Statement: The cell is the unit of structure and function in living things.

Focusing on the Main Concepts

❶ **TESTING YOURSELF**

A. Test your understanding of important concepts in this unit by answering these questions.

1. Here are pictures of some common cells. ■ Which cells are from a plant? which from an animal? Explain your answers.

■

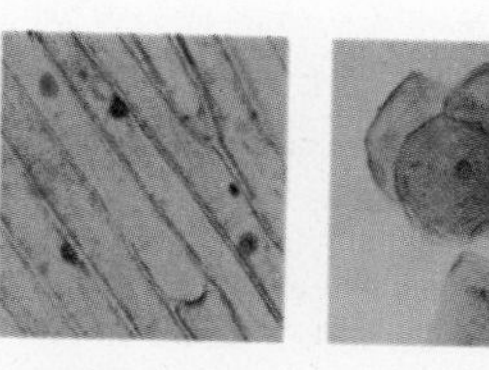

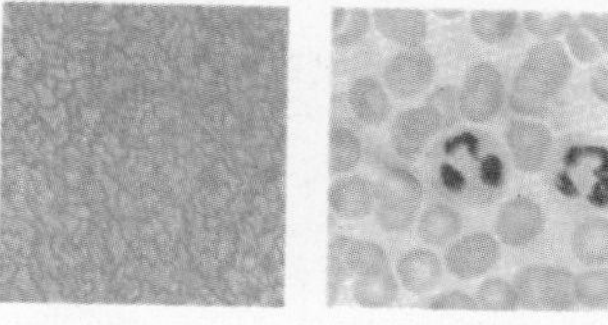

2. a. What is *wrong* in this diagram of a dividing cell? ●

b. Why is the diagram wrong?

●

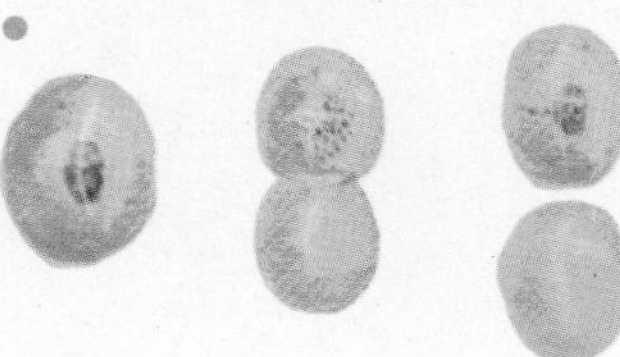

3. Here is a diagram of a dividing cell and its chromosomes. ▲ What is *wrong* here? Why is it wrong?

▲

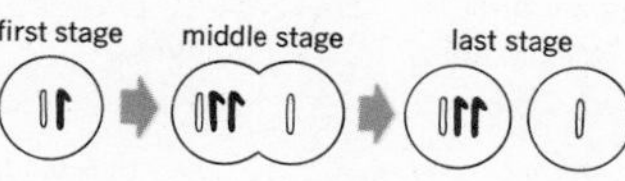

4. Put a lump of sugar in some water and leave the solution open to the air. After a while, bubbles of gas come from the water. From what you have learned in this unit, try to answer these:

a. What might the bubbles be?

b. How could you test your guess? (Hint: Yeasts and molds float about in the air.)

❷ **B.** Test your knowledge with this quick check.

1. A part that is not found in an animal cell is the

a. nucleus
b. cell membrane
c. cell wall
d. cytoplasm

2. A part of a cell that many plants have but that a cell in a chicken does not have is the

a. nucleus
b. cell membrane
c. chloroplast
d. cytoplasm

3. The part of the egg cell that has in it the pattern of growth of the entire living thing

a. cell membrane
b. cell wall
c. chloroplast
d. chromosome

255

VERIFYING PROGRESS

❶ **Testing yourself.** A. Children *analyze* substances, and *describe* or explain their interpretations.

1. *top* (left to right): plant cell (onion), animal cell (cheek); *bottom* (left to right) plant cell, (green leaf), animal cell (blood) Plant cells have rigid cell walls and animal cells do not.

2. One new cell has no nucleus. When a cell divides, its nucleus also divides.

3. New cells should have chromosomes identical with the original cell. Chromosomes duplicate themselves, and one of each pair is included in the new cells.

4. a. carbon dioxide

b. Let some of the gas bubble through limewater. If it turns milky, it is carbon dioxide.

B. Children *identify* suitable responses to open-ended questions.

1. c 2. c 3. d

UNIT FIVE

Unit Concept-Statement: The cell is the unit of structure and function in living things.

❶ 4. The substance ATP, in the cell, has mainly to do with

a. energy c. size
b. shape d. color

5. The living thing that is *not* like the other three is

a. paramecium c. stentor
b. ameba d. yeast

6. The statement that fits the main concept of this unit is

a. The cells of all living things are all alike.
b. The cell is the basis for the activities of all living things.

❷ **INVESTIGATING FURTHER**

1. Some foods are sold dehydrated—that is, the water in the cells of the food has been removed. How could you use this fact to find out about how much water was originally in the cells of some plants?

Cut some ½-inch cubes out of an apple. Slowly dehydrate them with heat. How can you find out how much water they lose?

2. What is a good way of growing the single-celled animal, the paramecium?

The best way to get some paramecia is to collect a pint of pond water in the spring or summer. Add to the water a bit of hard-boiled egg yolk the size of a pea. Crumble the egg yolk between your fingers as you drop it in the water.

Bacteria will grow on the food of the egg yolk. The paramecia will feed on the bacteria. Paramecia have been grown on rice and on wheat, as well as on egg yolk.

How will you know when the paramecia are growing best? We suggest you count them. A paramecium is large enough to be seen with a 200X microscope. One way to find out when the paramecia are growing best is to count how many are in a drop of the water.

Plan your investigation. Perhaps you would like your teacher to read over your plan. Share your findings with your classmates.

3. In the spring, the toad lays its eggs in still water in long strings, rather than in bunches like the frog. Collect some toad's eggs and watch them develop. Keep a record of their growth in drawings.

How does the growth of the toad compare with that of the frog?

4. Study the growth of a plant from seed to complete organism. One way to do this is to soak a dozen bean seeds or corn grains overnight. Then plant them between a blotter and the glass in a jar. Keep the blotter damp.

256

VERIFYING PROGRESS (cont.)

❶ **Testing yourself** (cont.)
4. a 5. d 6. b

❷ **Investigating further.** Children *analyze* situations, *hypothesize* or *predict*, *design* investigations to *test* hypotheses or predictions, *observe* what takes place, and *make inferences* from the results.

1. Weigh the food to be tested before and after dehydration. Children infer that the difference is the weight of water lost.

2. The plan should include taking a drop of water from the same place in the pond water over a period of eight or ten hours. Each drop should be placed on a slide with a cover slip, and all paramecia seen should be counted. The slide should be moved slowly so that the whole area of the drop is observed. (Since paramecia are lively animals, it may be necessary to let them slow down by waiting four or five minutes after making the mount.) Drops should be examined at regular intervals, say every hour, and a count recorded. (The area of the drop can be determined by placing it in a circle of Vaseline before lowering the slide.)

3. Children's observations should include the growth of eggs, the tadpole stage, and the resorption of the tail—all as in the frog.

4. In the drawing, the embryo plant consists of a primitive root and shoot—with two tiny leaves—growing between the large bean halves (cotyledons) that contain the food supply. The cotyledons gradually shrivel as the growing embryo uses the food stored in them. The leaves will turn green as they are exposed to sunlight.

Each day, take a bean apart. Draw the steps in the growth of a bean. The first drawing might look something like this bean seed, a day after being soaked. ●

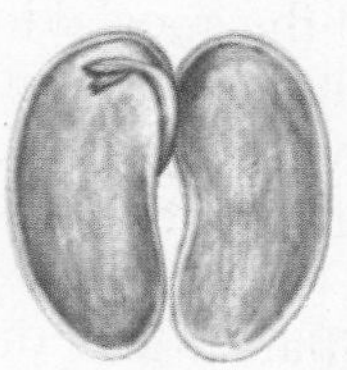

●

Search out the parts of the plant you see here. What does each part become as the plant grows? What does it look like the 3rd day? the 4th? the 5th? the 6th?

FOR YOUR READING

1. *Adventures with a Hand Lens,* by Richard Headstrom, published by Lippincott, Philadelphia, 1962. This interesting book will help you get practice in using a magnifying glass.

2. *Mighty Human Cell,* by Patricia Kelly, published by John Day, New York, 1967. This book begins by describing cells in general and the ways in which they are alike. The book then introduces you to the various kinds of special cells and the work that they do.

3. *A World in a Drop of Water,* by Alvin Silverstein published by Atheneum, New York, 1969. By using a microscope, you will be able to observe the life cycle of the ameba and other single-celled animals.

4. *New Worlds Through the Microscope,* by Robert Disraeli, rev. ed., published by Viking, New York, 1960. The author tells you what to look for, how to mount specimens, and how to interpret what you see.

5. *From One Cell to Many Cells,* by George Zappler, published by Messner, New York, 1970. If you have a microscope, you will be able to observe the cells of an onionskin, and single-celled animals found in pond water. Also, you are told how to watch the development of frogs' eggs into tadpoles and then into frogs.

6. *Cells: Building Blocks of Life,* by Alvin Silverstein, published by Prentice-Hall, Englewood Cliffs, New Jersey, 1969. After reading this book, you will understand that the cell is the basic unit of life and also how it works and grows.

7. *Window Into An Egg; Seeing Life Begin,* by Geraldine Flanagan, published by Young Scott Books, New York, 1969. Remarkable photographs let you watch how a hen's egg grows and develops into a baby chick.

UNIT SIX

WE STUDY MAN—FITNESS TO THE ENVIRONMENT

Basic behaviors sought: Children *measure* respiration rates and *order* them from slowest to fastest; they *compare* breathing rates before and after exercise, *infer* that the interchange of gases in breathing is related to activity, and *predict* that the respiration rate will increase after exercise.

Children *investigate* changes of starch to sugar in the presence of saliva, *hypothesize* that during digestion complex food substances are reduced to simpler substances, and infer that these simpler substances are oxidized to release energy.

Children *identify* cell structures and *distinguish* the relationship of structure to function. They *probe* the structure and function of the major organ systems of the body, *analyze* the functioning of each system, and *infer* that anything that affects any organ affects the whole body.

A VIEW OF THE UNIT

Man is a living thing, an organism. As such, he is interdependent with his environment—physical, chemical, and biological. His survival, and well-being, in the environment depends upon his adaptation to it. When we study the structures and functions of the human body we are probing man's fitness to the environment.

One basic function for which the body is adapted by its structure is the exchange of oxygen and carbon dioxide gases with the environment. Man's respiratory system is equipped to take oxygen from the air and to return carbon dioxide to the air. Green plants take carbon dioxide from the air, and return oxygen to the air. This oxygen-carbon dioxide cycle is a basic process that affects all animals and plants and is an important example of their interdependence with one another and with the environment.

Another basic function for which the human body is adapted is the digestion of food substances taken in from the environment. Molecules of most nutrients must be broken down into smaller molecules before they can enter the cells. That is, foods must be digested. And one of the body's main adaptations that make digestion possible is its production of substances known as enzymes. The production of enzymes is one of many ways in which man's digestive system is equipped to break down nutrients.

After oxygen is brought into the lungs and after foods are digested—a process that is completed in the small intestine—the oxygen and digested foods must be distributed to all the cells of the body. This distribution is one of the special jobs of the circulatory system. In the lungs, oxygen diffuses into the blood in capillaries which join to form veins to the heart. In the small intestine, digested foods diffuse into capillaries and into lymph vessels, as well. From both the capillaries and the lymph vessels, digested foods are eventually delivered into veins that enter the heart. Thus, both oxygen and nutrients in forms that the cells can use are distributed as the heart pumps blood through arteries to all parts of the body. The distribution of other substances, such as hormones and antibodies, and the collection of wastes such as carbon dioxide and urea, are also carried out by the circulatory system. The actual removal of these wastes from cell activities is a function of the excretory system.

Man's skeletal system, and his system of skeletal muscles, adapt him for a remarkable variety of bodily movements. At the joints, ligaments tie bones together. Tendons attach muscles to bones in such a way that movement at joints can occur when muscles contract. Muscles work in pairs; when one muscle of a pair contracts, the other relaxes.

Man's nervous system enables him to sense and respond to stimuli of many kinds, both within his own body and in the environment. Sensory nerves transmit messages from sense organs to the brain and spinal cord, and motor nerves transmit messages from these centers of control to muscles and glands. The nervous system can be compared to an elaborate communications network, somewhat like a telephone exchange, but one that has literally billions of possible connections. Man's capacity for abstract thinking, reasoning, and speech give him unique advantages in relating to his surroundings. When we consider that these abilities depend upon the functions of man's brain, it is difficult to overestimate the role of the nervous system in man's fitness to the environment.

1 The make-up of air and the oxygen-carbon dioxide cycle

Clean, dry air consists of about 78% nitrogen, 21% oxygen, 0.04% carbon dioxide, and 0.9% rare gases (argon, neon, etc.). These percentages are on a volume basis. Air that is untreated to remove moisture varies in its composition—the water vapor content of air can be as much as 1%, on a day of average temperature and humidity. Pollutants such as carbon monoxide, sulfur dioxide, and soot do not change the percentage composition of air appreciably; however, even tiny amounts of such substances in the air can be harmful.

The air that we exhale contains less oxygen (about 16%) and more carbon dioxide (about 4%) than the air we inhale. There is also more water vapor in exhaled air than in inhaled air, since exhalation is one way the body excretes excess water.

Not only man, but all animals and plants generally use oxygen for the oxidation of glucose—a part of the energy process in their cells. Carbon dioxide is given off as a by-product of this oxidation. But green plants also use up carbon dioxide, in the process of photosynthesis, and give off oxygen as a by-product. The amount of oxygen given off by green plants is more than the amount their cells need for the energy process. The net result is that plants, generally, take in carbon dioxide from the air and return oxygen to it. Animals, and nongreen plants, generally, take in oxygen from the air and return carbon dioxide to it. This interchange of oxygen and carbon dioxide with the air is the oxygen-carbon dioxide cycle.

2 Digestion and the role of enzymes

Digestion is the process by which the body changes the foods we eat into substances that can enter the cells. Most of the nutrients in our food must be broken down in some way before they can pass from the digestive tract into the blood.

Chewing and mixing are among the mechanical parts of digestion. Another part of digestion is the breaking down, or emulsification, of fats into small droplets that are suspended, but not actually dissolved, in water. Enzymes act upon the large, insoluble molecules of starches, proteins, and fats, breaking them down into small, soluble molecules. The enzyme ptyalin, for example, in the saliva, begins to break down starch in the mouth. The enzyme pepsin, secreted by the stomach, helps break down protein molecules.

In the small intestine, many more enzymes are at work upon nutrients of all kinds. When completely digested, a nutrient has been changed to a form in which it can pass through the intestinal walls into the blood stream, and from the blood into cells all over the body.

3 Tissues in the human body

The main kinds of human body tissues are blood, connective, supportive, muscle, nerve, covering, and glandular. The term "tissue" usually refers to a group of body cells all doing the same kind of work. But tissues can, and often do, contain nonliving components—such as hair.

Blood tissue contains red blood cells, which carry oxygen from the lungs to the body cells, and white blood cells, which attack disease bacteria. These two kinds of cells float in the plasma, a colorless liquid. Also floating in the plasma are the blood platelets, which play a key role in the clotting of blood at the site of an injury. The plasma itself transports digested foods, hormones, wastes, antibodies, and other substances which are dissolved in the plasma.

Connective tissues in the body include ligaments and tendons, which connect bone to bone and muscle to bone in the body. Supportive tissues include cartilage and bone, both of which help support and shape the body.

There are three kinds of muscle tissues: voluntary muscle, heart muscle, and smooth muscle. Voluntary muscle tissue consists of striped, or striated, cells. They make up the muscles that can be moved at will—those attached to the bones of the head, limbs, and trunk of the body. Heart muscle tissue is striped too, but is branched. It has the ability to contract and relax rapidly, again and again. Smooth muscle tissue has no stripes. It contracts and relaxes slowly, and is responsible for the movements of organs such as the stomach, intestines, and blood vessels, which are not under voluntary control.

Nerve tissue is made up of three principal types of nerve cells, or neurons: sensory neurons, associative (connective) neurons, and motor neurons. Sensory neurons conduct impulses from nerve endings in the skin or sense organs to the spinal cord or brain. Motor neurons conduct impulses from the spinal cord or brain to muscles or glands, which respond to the messages received. Associative neurons in the spinal cord and brain help make possible a huge variety of connections between sensory and motor neurons.

Covering tissue includes not only the skin, but the linings of the nose, mouth, windpipe, digestive tract, and urinary tract. Organs made up largely of gland tissue include the salivary glands, pancreas, liver, reproductive glands, and endocrine (hormone) glands.

4 The body's organ systems

Cells are organized into tissues, tissues into organs, and organs into organ systems. All together, the organ systems make up the complete organism, that is, the living human body.

A. *The Digestive System.* In the mouth, the food is chewed and mixed with saliva. Then it passes through the esophagus to the stomach, where muscles squeeze and churn the food, mixing it with gastric juice. Now in liquid form, the food passes into the small intestine, where pancreatic juice, bile from the liver, and intestinal juices complete digestion. Digested food is absorbed by the villi, small projections in the lining of the small intestine. In the large intestine, much water is absorbed into the blood, and undigested solids are collected; these solids pass on to the rectum, from which they pass out of the body.

B. *The Respiratory System.* When we inhale, the air passes through the nose and into the windpipe, which branches into two bronchial tubes. In turn, the bronchial tubes branch again and again, so that the lungs are made up of many air tubes with many branches. The smallest branches are microscopic in size and end in air sacs.

In the mechanics of breathing, the muscular diaphragm, which separates the chest cavity from the abdominal cavity, plays a key role. Each time we inhale, the muscles of the diaphragm contract, and the diaphragm moves down. At the same time, muscles attached to the ribs also contract so that the ribs are lifted. These motions increase the amount of space between the lungs and the wall of the chest cavity. As the lungs expand to fill this space, air pressure within them is lowered. Thus, air rushes in until the air pressure inside the lungs is equalized with the air pressure outside the body. When we exhale, the muscles in the diaphragm and between the ribs relax, causing the ribs to swing down and the diaphragm to push up. These motions create a pressure inside the lungs that is greater than that outside the body, so that air rushes out until the pressure is again equalized.

C. *The Circulatory System.* One way to get a quick overall view of the body's circulatory system is to trace the path of the blood as it moves through the heart and the body's network of blood vessels. Begin with the dark red (deoxygenated) blood in the right auricle. As a valve opens, the blood flows into the right ventricle. Then the valve between auricle and ventricle closes. Next, a valve between the ventricle and the pulmonary artery (to the lungs) opens, and the blood flows into the lungs. In the capillaries of the lungs, red cells give up their carbon dioxide and take on oxygen. As it becomes oxygenated, the blood changes color from dark red to bright red.

Returning from the lungs through large veins the bright red blood enters the left auricle. A valve opens and the blood passes into the left ventricle. The valve between the auricle and ventricle closes and the blood is pushed out through the aorta, the body's largest artery. Through large arteries that branch from the aorta to all parts of the body, the blood flows into smaller and smaller arteries that end in capillaries. There, oxygen and nutrients are delivered to the cells, and carbon dioxide and other wastes are picked up. As it loses its oxygen, the blood again becomes dark red. The blood now flows into veins, which carry it back towards the heart. The largest veins enter the right auricle, and the round trip is complete.

D. *The Muscular System.* The skeletal muscles of the body, those attached to the bones, do the work of voluntary body movements. These muscles work in pairs. For example, the biceps, on the front of the upper arm, is paired with the triceps, on the back of the upper arm. When the biceps contracts, the triceps relaxes, and the arm is bent at the elbow. When the triceps contracts, the biceps relaxes, and the arm is straightened.

E. *The Skeletal System.* The body contains 206 bones, many of which work together to give the body its erect position and to permit the motion of many parts in many directions. Many bones also protect important body parts. The vertebrae, for example, are connected by joints that make it possible to bend the back. At the same time, these bones protect the soft, delicate spinal cord that runs through them. Another function of some bones is the production of red blood cells inside the marrow.

There are several types of joints: hinge (as in the knee or the tip of a finger), ball-and-socket (as in the shoulder or hip), gliding (as in the wrist and jaw), pivot (as in the neck) and immovable joints (as in the skull). Many joints have more than one kind of action: the neck is a hinge as well as a pivot, for example.

F. *The Nervous System:* A nerve cell is made up of a cell body plus nerve fibers that are sometimes several feet in length. The cell bodies are usually located in the brain or spinal cord, and bundles of the long fibers make up the sensory and motor nerves that thread the parts of the body where voluntary muscles and sense organs are located. These nerves belong to the central nervous system through which conscious reactions to the environment are made.

The autonomic nervous system works largely automatically. The cell bodies of its nerve cells are located in two chains of ganglia, one on each side of the spine, and bundles of the fibers make up nerves to the internal organs. The brain has three main parts: the cerebrum, cerebellum, and medulla. The cerebrum has particular areas in which conscious activities are controlled. For example, there are areas that control sight, hearing, smell, speech, memory, thinking, and muscular movements. The cerebellum helps in balance and in the coordination of muscles. The medulla controls the heartbeat, breathing, and some reflexes such as sneezing and blinking.

G. *The Excretory System.* For their life activities, all the cells of the body need food and oxygen. As by-products of their use of food and oxygen, and from the breakdown of worn out parts, cells give off wastes. If these wastes are not to poison the body, they must be excreted.

Among the principal wastes produced by the breakdown of proteins in the body is urea, a compound containing nitrogen. As the blood passes through the kidneys, some two million tiny "filters" remove from the blood most of the urea (and other wastes containing nitrogen), excess salts, and some water. This mixture of substances makes up the urine, which flows through the ureters to the bladder for storage. When the bladder is emptied, the urine passes out through the urethra.

The lungs have sometimes been considered as an organ of excretion, although they belong to the respiratory system. It is through the lungs that a waste, carbon dioxide, is removed from the body.

The skin, too, can be thought of as an excretory organ. Some urea and salts, and much water pass out of the body through the sweat glands. The loss of water through the sweat glands, however, also has the important function of helping to maintain a constant body temperature. The evaporation of perspiration on a hot day helps remove excess heat from the body.

Tobacco, Alcohol, and Other Drugs. The effects of tobacco, alcohol, and other drugs on the human body and mind have been the subject of much scientific research. There is evidence, for example, that even small amounts of alcohol can impair the reflexes of the driver of a car to a dangerous extent. It has been shown that even moderate habitual cigarette smoking may be linked to heart disease or to cancer. As for the heavy, long-continued use of alcohol and tobacco, the majority of medical and social scientists are in agreement: serious, and often fatal, disease is likely to result.

Research in the area of drug abuse has become increasingly important in recent years. Some of the findings have been confirmed again and again, and accepted by most scientists. For example, codeine and cocaine are prescribed by doctors at times to relieve pain, but if overused, they are dangerously habit-forming. Heroin is extremely habit-forming. Heroin, LSD, and many other drugs may have long-lasting effects on the DNA in certain of our body cells. Marijuana and hashish often affect judgment and may lead to the use of more dangerous drugs. Any drug used without a doctor's prescription may harm the body in some way.

Other findings have been controversial. For up-to-date information, readings in the books on drugs listed on page T-294, and in current periodicals, are recommended.

SUPPLEMENTARY AIDS

All films and filmstrips are in color. All films are accompanied by sound; filmstrips are accompanied by sound only if so designated. Names and addresses of producers and distributors are on page F-29.

Filmstrips

The Bones and Muscles (44 frames), #400159, McGraw-Hill. Explains the structure, function, and proper care of bones and muscles.

The Circulatory System (39 frames), #400158, McGraw-Hill. Explains the structure, function, and proper care of the circulatory system.

Finding Out How Your Body Is Protected (41 frames), #434-7, SVE. Explains the skeleton and the skin.

The Digestive System (41 frames), #400160, McGraw-Hill. Explains the structure, function, and proper care of each part of the digestive system.

Human Body Framework (50 frames), #570-6, SVE. Describes the structures that provide form and support for the body and the functions of the body's muscular system.

Human Digestive System (36 frames), #570-1, SVE. Shows how food is changed to forms that the body can assimilate.

Human Respiratory System (28 frames), #570-2, SVE. Shows that oxygen, supplied through respiration, replaces carbon dioxide in the body cells.

The Nervous System (45 frames), #400155, McGraw-Hill. Explains the structure, function, and proper care of the nervous system.

The Respiratory System (40 frames), #400154, McGraw-Hill. Reveals that the respiratory system supplies the body with oxygen and removes carbon dioxide, and that any condition that impairs this function affects the whole body.

Films

About the Human Body (15 min.), Churchill. May be used as an introduction to the workings of the human body, or as a review of the body systems. Animation allows the student to visualize the actual functioning of parts.

Muscles and Bones of the Body (11 min.), #1291, Coronet. Emphasizes the importance of the muscles and bones to the internal and external functioning of the human body by showing how the tendons, joints, muscles, and bones of the skeleton work together smoothly, as a unit.

Your Body Grows (11 min.), #1686, Coronet. Shows that body growth takes place in tiny units called cells; that growth does not occur everywhere in the body at the same time or speed; and that growth is regulated by our glands.

Science Reading Table

All About the Human Body by Bernard Glemser, Random House, 1958. The anatomy and physiology of the body are described in simple terms. Good diagrams enhance the narrative and accurate concept development. (Average)

Blood by Herbert Zim, Morrow, 1968. This is a fine description of the composition of blood and the processes by which the body makes use of it. Several other topics are included: the use of vaccines and antibiotics, the various blood groups, and the Rh factor. (Average)

The First Book of the Human Senses by Gene Liberty, Franklin Watts, 1961. Describes what our many senses are, what they do, and what they do for us. Includes many more senses than the familiar ones of sight, hearing, touch, smell, and taste. (Average)

For Junior Doctors Only by Helen Jill Fletcher, Bobbs-Merrill, 1961. Provides basic facts about the structure and functions of the human body. Conveys a sense of appreciation of the wonderful design of the body and responsibility of individuals to keep it in good working order. (Average)

The Human Body: Its Structure and Operation by Isaac Asimov, Houghton Mifflin, 1963. An interesting account which describes the skeleton, muscles, the major systems of the body and their functions. (Advanced)

The Human Body: The Skin by Katherine Elgin, Franklin Watts, 1970. In this well-written and concise book, the author explains why children have freckles, why the skin tans under the sun, why the skin color of some people is darker than others, why the lips are red, how the surface of the skin increases with age, and how perspiration and oil are given off by the skin. Good illustrations and an index are included. (Average)

Science Experiences: The Human Senses by Jeanne Bendick, Franklin Watts, 1968. A well-illustrated book encouraging observation and investigation of the senses. Includes an explanation of how the eye works and the role of the reflexes in the use of the senses. (Easy)

The Story of Your Blood by Edith Weart, Coward-McCann, 1960.

The Story of Your Bones by Edith Weart, Coward-McCann, 1966.

The Story of Your Brain and Nerves by Edith Weart, Coward-McCann, 1961.

The Story of Your Respiratory System by Edith Weart, Coward-McCann, 1964.

These four books give the reader a good overview of the different functions of the circulatory system, the skeleton, the control system of the body, and the respiratory system. They are all illustrated with clear drawings and contain glossaries to explain technical terms. (Average)

What You Should Know About Drugs by Dr. Charles W. Gorodetzky and Dr. Samuel T. Christian, Harcourt Brace Jovanovich, 1971. A factual "tell it like it is" book about many kinds of drugs. The authors define "drug" as "any substance that affects living matter." Many color photographs, tables of slang-terms, and an extensive index. Also, quotations from youngsters undergoing treatment. An excellent source for children, teachers, and parents. (Average)

What You Should Know About Drugs and Drug Abuse by Dr. Harvey Greenberg, Four Winds Press, 1971. A comprehensive guide which includes a detailed chapter on drug laws. Informative but without preachy overtones. (Average)

Why You Are You by Amram Scheinfeld, Abelard-Schuman, 1958. Consists of introductory treatment of heredity and genetics. Excellent beginning reading on these complicated subjects. (Average)

An Analysis of Behaviors in Concept-Seeking*

Conceptual Scheme D: Living things are interdependent with one another and with their environment.

Unit Concept-Statement: Living things are adapted by structure and function to their environment.

Lesson Cluster titles in blue are essential to guide concept-seeking toward the Unit Concept-Statement and to enrich the Conceptual Scheme (*see page F-23*).

Lesson Cluster and Supporting Statement	*Operations Basic to Concept-Seeking**	*Methods of Intelligence (Processes and Behaviors)*
1. A Deep Breath Animal life depends on an interchange of oxygen and carbon dioxide within the body.	**Measuring** childrens' respiration rates; **ordering** the rates from slowest to fastest	**Comparing** breathing rates at rest and after exercise; **inferring** that interchange of oxygen and carbon dioxide in breathing is related to activity; **predicting** that the respiration rate will increase after exercise
2. Before We Can Use Food Food substances must usually be digested before they can diffuse into cells of the body.	**Investigating** the breaking down of starch into sugar in the presence of saliva	**Observing** changes of starch to sugar in the presence of saliva; **hypothesizing** that during digestion complex food substances are reduced to simpler substances; **inferring** that these simpler substances are oxidized to release energy
3. Some Important Cells and Their Work Cells are grouped into tissues that have specific functions.	**Probing** into the different cells in the body and their organization into tissues that perform specific functions	**Analyzing** various cells of the body; **identifying** their structures; **distinguishing** the relationship of structure to function
4. Within the Body An organism is adapted by organ systems to perform its life functions.	**Probing** into the structure and function of the major systems of the body	**Analyzing** the functioning of each organ system in terms of the operation of the entire body; **inferring** that anything that affects any organ of the body affects the whole body
5. The Main Concept: Fitness to the Environment Living things are adapted by structure and function to their environment.	Children **synthesize** their understanding of the organization of a living thing for carrying out its life functions; they **conclude** that it is through its functions and structures that an organism is adapted to its environment.	

** A concept is synonymous with the corresponding operations. In turn, operations are served by relevant methods of intelligence.*

UNIT SIX

WE STUDY MAN— FITNESS TO THE ENVIRONMENT

Teaching background. "A View of the Unit" T-291

Concept-seeking. Children begin to become aware that an organism's body has a specific structure and certain functions that enable it to live in its environment.

Operations. Children *investigate* a few functions of a living animal.

Methods of intelligence. Children *observe* some of an animal's functions (such as moving about) and its conditions (such as bodily warmth); they *infer* that other living things, themselves included, have similar functions and conditions; they *conclude* that all the cells in the body must work together.

Useful materials: Gerbil or other small warm-blooded pet; cage, food and water as required by the animal.

Introducing the unit

Ideally, a live animal should be available for observation by sight and touch. It need not be a gerbil, but may be a hamster, guinea pig, white mouse, rabbit, kitten, or even a bird such as a parakeet. If a child can bring such a pet to class, so much the better. This child can respond to the questions that are surely to be raised by other children: **What does (the animal) do?** (eats, sleeps, runs around the exercise wheel) **What does it eat? Where does it sleep? What does it feel like?** (If the animal can be held and the owner permits it, children will notice the animal's body warmth.)

If no one in the class can contribute a pet for observation and you have none you can exhibit, use a vicarious approach. Have children who have had experiences with pets try to describe them. You may need to cue them with some of the questions above, but once discussion has begun, children will ask many questions.

Children usually love all kinds of pets, cold-blooded ones (fish, turtles, earthworms, ants) as well as the more touchable warm-blooded ones. If they bring a cold-blooded pet to class, postpone any discussion of why it feels cold and focus on the ways in which the animal's body and activities resemble those of human beings.

Unit Concept-Statement: Living things are adapted by structure and function to their environment.

UNIT SIX

We Study Man–Fitness to the Environment

❶ Observe a pet gerbil in his cage. Watch him eat his meal. Later he runs on his exercise wheel. How does the energy in his food turn ❷ into the energy which he uses to run?

Hold the gerbil in your hands. ■ Notice how ❸ warm his body is. Perhaps you can feel his heart beating.

Your body is warm, too, and your heart beats. ❹ How does the food turn into heat to warm the body? Why must the heart beat for the body to stay alive and healthy?

You can see that your many cells must somehow be able to work together. How they do this is ❺ the story of this unit. To start the story, take a deep breath and let it out. Turn the page.

259

❶ Gerbils like to eat seeds and bits of leaves. **What does the animal's food provide?** (energy) **How is its energy used?** (for the activity of moving around, among other things) If another pet is available, ask the same questions.

❷ Let children speculate. Record the more disparate hypotheses on the board for later evaluation.

❸ If possible, let a few of the children hold the animal they are observing. (If a bird, it can perch on a finger.) The animal should not be handled by too many children. Usually a volunteer will be very gentle with the animal and can report to the others. The warmth of the animal–and probably its heartbeat as well–will be very evident.

❹ **How have you found out that your body is warm like (the pet's)?** (taking temperature, touching cold objects or even cold-blooded animals) **Why do you think the heart must keep beating regularly to keep you alive and healthy?** (Again let children speculate and perhaps place disparate hypotheses on the board for later evaluation.)

❺ As the children take a breath and let it out, ask: **What do you think has happened in your cells in this short time?** After their responses, you are launched into this unit.

Unit Concept-Statement: Living things are adapted by structure and function to their environment.

LESSON CLUSTER 1
A DEEP BREATH

Teaching background. 1 T-291

Concept-seeking. Children become aware of the differences in the composition of inhaled and exhaled air.

Operations. Children in the class *measure* their respiration rates and *order* them from slowest to fastest.

Methods of intelligence. Children *compare* breathing rates at rest and after exercise and *infer* that interchange of oxygen and carbon dioxide in breathing is related to activity. They *predict* that the respiration rate (oxygen-carbon dioxide interchange) will increase after exercise.

Useful materials: Candle, candle holder or saucer, matches.

100 quarts of air that is **inhaled** contains	100 quarts of air that is **exhaled** contains
about 78 quarts of nitrogen	about 78 quarts of nitrogen
about 21 quarts of oxygen	about 16 quarts of oxygen
about 4/100 quart of carbon dioxide	about 4 quarts of carbon dioxide
about 1 quart of water vapor and other gases	about 2 quarts of water vapor and other gases

1. A Deep Breath

By the time you have finished reading this sentence, every person on Earth will have taken a breath of air.

We all have to breathe. What are we doing when we breathe? We are taking in molecules from the environment, molecules to be used as building blocks. More than that, we are giving out molecules as well. When we breathe in, or *inhale*, molecules are taken in. When we breathe out, or *exhale*, we return molecules to the environment. But the air we exhale is not the same as the air we inhale.

Why is this so? Let's see what happens when we breathe.

The Part of Air We Use

We inhale and exhale air. What do we do with this air
1 when we have it in our bodies? Here is some evidence. More than a thousand people were examined to get this evidence.

260

Introducing Lesson Cluster 1

What do you think is in the air your (pet) breathed in? What is in the air you breathe in? Children who have studied the diagram at the top of the page may have some good ideas. Call attention to the diagram. How much nitrogen is there on each side of the diagram? (same) What seems to happen to oxygen? (Five quarts in 100 seems to have been used.) Carbon dioxide? (increases 100 times) Water vapor? (twice as much) How can you account for the difference? Let children speculate.

Developing the lesson

1 The evidence in the diagram is that in our bodies oxygen decreases and carbon dioxide increases. What must have happened? (Somehow carbon in the body must have combined with oxygen from the air.) How? This is the thrust of the lesson cluster.

Supporting Statement: Animal life depends on an interchange of oxygen and carbon dioxide within the body.

Let us compare the fresh air and the exhaled air. The fresh air that was inhaled contained about 78 quarts of nitrogen gas. So did the exhaled air. Nothing happened to the nitrogen, it seems.

Now look at the oxygen inhaled and exhaled. The air inhaled contained about 21 quarts of oxygen. The air
1 exhaled, however, held only 16 quarts of oxygen. About 5 quarts of oxygen were taken from the air in breathing. The evidence is that oxygen is used during breathing.

With carbon dioxide, the opposite happens. There is very little carbon dioxide in the air we breathe. Thus, very little carbon dioxide was inhaled, about $\frac{1}{100}$ of a quart. Yet the exhaled air contained about 4 quarts of carbon dioxide gas. The evidence is that carbon dioxide is produced during breathing. About one hundred times more carbon dioxide is exhaled than is inhaled.

At this rate, it would seem that the oxygen would soon
2 be used up. Carbon dioxide would fill the air. Why doesn't this happen? At the same time that you are exhaling carbon dioxide, green plants are using it and are, in turn, giving off oxygen gas. In this way, the carbon dioxide and oxygen in the air remains about the same. We keep exchanging molecules with the plants.

261

VERIFYING PROGRESS

In methods of intelligence

To help determine children's progress in analysis and inference, put these word equations on the board:

carbon dioxide + water + energy → sugar (glucose) + oxygen

sugar + oxygen → carbon dioxide + water + energy

What happens in the first equation? (sugar is built up) In the second? (sugar is broken down) What else is needed in the first? (energy goes in) What happens to this energy in the second? (released for work of cells)

1 At this point, children receive confirmation of their hypotheses. Oxygen is used, and carbon dioxide is produced. If children have previously investigated the burning of a candle, have them recall what happens—or light a candle now. What do you notice? (heat, light) Explain. (Carbon in the candle combines with oxygen to form carbon dioxide; during this change, energy stored in the candle is released as heat and light.) When you petted the (animal), what did you notice? (heat) Where could it have come from? (Children should infer that oxygen combined with carbon from somewhere to produce carbon dioxide and release energy in the form of heat.)

2 In what ways other than breathing is oxygen in the air used? (Children should be able to cite burning of fires and rusting.) Is the oxygen permanently lost? (no) Why not? (Most of it becomes carbon dioxide which green plants must have to store energy.) What happens then? Some children may recall that green plants use carbon dioxide (and water) in making food, in which energy is stored, and that oxygen is given off as a byproduct of this process (photosynthesis). What does it mean when we say that we keep exchanging molecules with plants? (Molecules of carbon dioxide that human beings and animals give off are taken up by plants, while molecules of oxygen that plants give off are taken up by human beings and animals.)

UNIT SIX

Unit Concept-Statement: Living things are adapted by structure and function to their environment.

What part of the air we breathe do we use? It is clear that we take oxygen from the air as we breathe. ■ Of course, this fact fits in with something else we know, that ❶ our cells use oxygen. Our cells combine oxygen with food substances. The oxygen that our body cells use in their work is taken from the air we breathe.

The rate at which people inhale and exhale has been studied by scientists. They have found that most boys and ❷ girls your age inhale (and exhale) about 16 to 18 times a minute. Some inhale more slowly, from 12 to 15 times a minute. Most adults inhale about 15 times a minute. How many times do you inhale in a minute? Do your classmates inhale at the same rate? See for yourself. Try the investigation on the opposite page. INVESTIGATE

You know that when you breathe you take in air from which your body takes oxygen for its needs. What about the other substances in the air you breathe? Some of these, ❸ such as nitrogen, are not used by the body directly from the air. But they do not do the body any harm, either. Are there substances in the air that *can* do harm if you breathe them? If you want to look into the question now, turn ahead to the Search on Your Own on page 294.

■

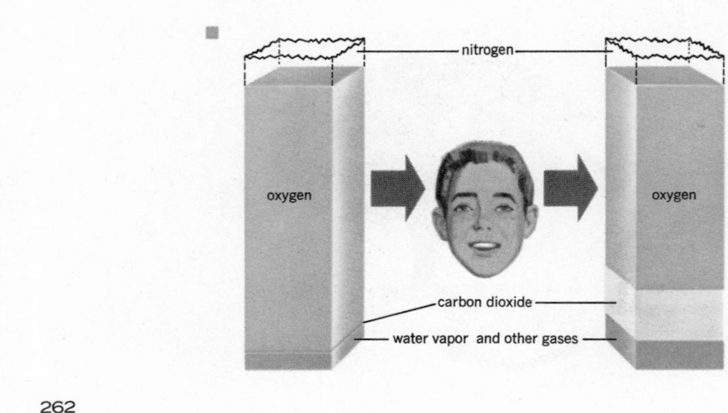

262

Continuing Lesson Cluster 1

❶ From the diagram on page 260, it is clear that we take from air about 5% of its oxygen. The principal food that gets into the blood stream is glucose, a very simple sugar, sometimes called "blood sugar." (Glucose has the formula $C_6H_{12}O_6$.) It is glucose that gets into the cells as food. It is oxygen that changes glucose in the cells. **What happens during this change?** Let children hypothesize. They should also infer that oxygen combines with glucose, and that carbon dioxide is released.

❷ **Why do you suppose scientists might be interested in rate of breathing?** Encourage children's hypotheses which will be partially confirmed by the investigation and the next lesson cluster.

❸ Children are likely to ask about the work of nitrogen. Recall the glowing-splint test for oxygen. In air, the splint burns more slowly than in pure oxygen, because nitrogen in the air slows the rate of combustion. If children ask about smog, dust, or pollution—as they may well do—encourage those interested to start the Search (on page 294) and be ready to report their findings in a few weeks. It's best to set a time so that the Search progresses on schedule before interest lags.

Supporting Statement: Animal life depends on an interchange of oxygen and carbon dioxide within the body.

AN APPRENTICE INVESTIGATION into Rate of Breathing

❶ **Needed:** a clock or watch

Do this investigation with your classmates. Have one person act as timekeeper, to signal the beginning and end of one minute of time. During this minute, silently count the number of times you ❷ inhale. Inhale and exhale just as you do usually. Enter in a table like the one shown the number of times that you inhaled during the minute.

Now compare your rate of breathing with your classmates. Fill in your table by asking those who found that they inhaled 11 or fewer times per minute to hold up hands. Write in the number. Then observe how many breathed 12 to 15 times per minute, and so forth.

Now you can use this information to answer these questions about your class.

—Does everyone inhale at the same rate?

—What is the slowest rate? How many pupils ❸ are in this group?

—What is the fastest rate? How many pupils are in this group?

—Which group has the most pupils in it?

Times I Inhaled in One Minute ________

Times Inhaled in One Minute	*Number of Pupils*
11 or fewer	________
12 to 15	________
16 to 18	________
19 to 21	________
22 or more	________

Methods of Intelligence: Predicting

Predict what your breathing rate will be after some ❹ exercise. ■ (Not more than one minute.) Test the prediction. What is your control?

263

Performance objectives. Each child measures his breathing rate by counting the number of times he inhales in one minute. He *distinguishes* his breathing rate from those of his classmates by comparing his rate with theirs. The children together *construct* a table of the breathing rates of the members of the class, indicating the number of pupils who inhale at each rate.

❶ The timepiece should have a second hand for precision in measuring one minute.

❷ It is important to avoid giving the impression that one child is competing against the class. Make it clear that each child is trying to find his own rate of breathing, and that this rate is normal for him. Since some children may increase or decrease their breathing rate due to self-consciousness, it may be well to make two or three trials to strike an average.

❸ Quite possibly few or no children will be in either the "11 or fewer" or "22 or more" groups. Probably most of the children will be in a middle group. Do not let slow breathers or rapid breathers become concerned. You can point out the differences in rates of breathing are perfectly normal. (Some persons are shallow breathers and others are deep breathers; some have greater lung capacity than others. How fast a person breathes is related to his need for oxygen for the work of cells.)

❹ Mild exercise, rather than strenuous, for one minute only is desirable. It is easier to control and no strain on an ailing child will result. Instead of "running in place," as pictured, children may want to do some form of calesthenics they are accustomed to doing. The ascertained breathing rate at rest is the control that determines variation after exercise.

Unit Concept-Statement: Living things are adapted by structure and function to their environment.

❶ BEFORE YOU GO ON

A. Check your understanding of the concepts of this section. Which ending would you choose for each statement below?

1. When we breathe in, we
   a. inhale
   b. exhale

2. People inhale and exhale at
   a. the same rate
   b. different rates

3. The amount of nitrogen we inhale and the amount we exhale are
   a. about the same
   b. very different

4. The amount of oxygen we inhale, compared with the amount we exhale, is
   a. larger
   b. smaller

5. The amount of carbon dioxide we inhale, compared with the amount we exhale is
   a. larger
   b. smaller

6. The statement that fits the main concept of this section is
   a. When you breathe, your body exchanges oxygen and carbon dioxide with its environment.
   b. When you breathe, your body exchanges oxygen and glucose with its environment.

B. Write a paragraph or two in answer to this question: "What Happens to the Air We Inhale?"

❷ USING WHAT YOU KNOW

1. A candle is placed inside a jar of fresh air. Another candle is placed in a jar of exhaled air. Do you think both candles will burn for the same length of time? What is the reason for your answer?

2. A boy went to the chalkboard and breathed on it. A dark spot appeared on the board. It soon disappeared. What was the dark spot? What made it?

3. A girl's rate of breathing was faster after she had been running for 10 minutes than it was after she had been resting for ten minutes. Explain why.

A LOOK AHEAD

You are dependent on your environment for the air you breathe. Mainly you use the oxygen in the air. The cells in your body must have oxygen to do their work. Your body is well-fitted to the task (the function) of using oxygen. But your body can't live on oxygen alone. What else does it need?

VERIFYING PROGRESS

❶ **Before you go on.** Children *identify* the appropriate completion for open-ended statements that *describe* what happens when they inhale and exhale.

A. 1. a 3. a 5. b
2. b 4. a 6. a

B. Children's responses.

❷ **Using what you know.** Children *analyze* situations and *demonstrate* understanding of the composition of inhaled and exhaled air.

1. Fresh air contains more oxygen than exhaled air. (If children try this as an investigation, they should *infer* that both jars should be of the same capacity.)
2. The dark spot was water which condensed on the board from water vapor in the boy's breath. It disappeared when the water evaporated.
3. More energy is needed for running. Energy is supplied when oxygen combines with glucose in the body cells. If more energy is needed, more oxygen is needed. To get more oxygen, one breathes faster. Therefore, the girl breathes faster after running.

Supporting Statement: Food substances must usually be digested before they can diffuse into cells of the body.

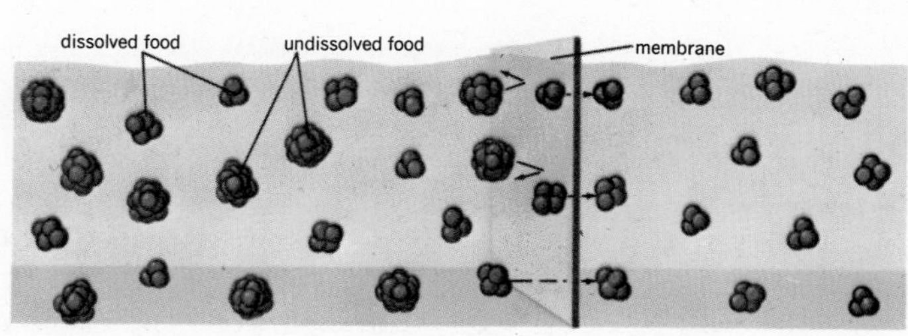

2. Before We Can Use Food

It is hard to believe that an apple or a piece of chicken or a jelly sandwich can get into our body cells. Yet we know that the elements and compounds in what we eat do get to all our cells. We know, too, that to get into a cell the elements and compounds must pass through a membrane. Let's see how this happens.

❶ Which burns faster in a furnace, large pieces of coal or small pieces? Small pieces burn faster, of course. Oxygen can get at small pieces quickly and combine with them. Which then would be acted on faster chemically, large pieces of food or small pieces? Small pieces, certainly. Our food is, in fact, broken down into small pieces. The first part of the body to break down food is the teeth.

Still, it is not enough to have the food in small pieces. To get into the cells, the elements and compounds in food must pass through membranes. The only compounds that can pass through membranes are compounds dissolved in water. *The food substances must be changed into compounds that dissolve in water.* ❷

Let's take an example. Starch is a food substance. It does not dissolve in water. In the body, however, starch is changed into compounds that do dissolve. How is starch changed? See for yourself in the investigation on the next page. INVESTIGATE

265

LESSON CLUSTER 2
BEFORE WE CAN USE FOOD

Teaching background. 2 T-291

Concept-seeking. Children become aware that our food must be broken into simple substances that can pass through membranes of the cells in our bodies.

Operations. Children *investigate* the breaking down of starch into sugar in the presence of saliva.

Methods of intelligence. Children *observe* changes of starch to sugar in the presence of saliva and *hypothesize* that during digestion complex food substances are reduced to simpler substances; they further *infer* that these simpler substances are oxidized to release energy.

Useful materials: Paper towels, salt, tape, two small jars or tumblers, water, soda crackers.

Introducing Lesson Cluster 2

Fold an 8-inch square of paper towelling into a triangle and then fold the triangle in half. Open out and tape where needed to get a filtering cone. Prepare two such cones. Set one on each of two jars.

Place a teaspoonful of salt in one cone in one jar. **What do you think will happen if you pour this half-cupful of water into the filter?** Let children hypothesize; then have a volunteer pour the water. The water drains through the filter; the salt gets wet but much of it stays caked in the bottom of the filter. Let children see how much of the salt remains undissolved.

Place another teaspoonful of salt into a half-cupful of water. **What do you think will happen when you pour this mixture into the filter?** Let children hypothesize and then pour the mixture. **How do you account for the difference?** (When salt is mixed with water, the particles become small enough to pass through.) At this point, children should have some idea of what digestion involves: breaking food down into small bits and mixing with water, so that the bits can go through a membrane.

Developing the lesson

❶ **Who has built a fire in a fireplace or at camp? Which catches fire more quickly, twigs or logs?** (twigs)

❷ **In the diagram, what is the difference between "undissolved food" and "dissolved food"?** ("Dissolved food" consists of smaller particles; only these go through the membrane.)

Performance objectives. Children *demonstrate* how starch is changed to sugar by using Benedict's solution to show the absence of sugar in a starch mixture, the absence of sugar in saliva, and the presence of sugar in a starch mixture to which saliva was added and allowed to stand ten minutes.

Children *describe* the result as produced by the action of a substance in the saliva (an enzyme) on the starch causing a change to sugar.

AN APPRENTICE INVESTIGATION into How Starch Is Changed

Needed: starch, warm water, Benedict's solution, 2 test tubes, a glass, a beaker, 2 labels, a teaspoon, burner

Stir a level teaspoonful of starch into a glass ❶ of warm water. It will make a cloudy mixture, since starch does not dissolve in water.

Label one test tube number 1, the other number 2. Pour in the mixture so that each tube is one-third full. ■

To test tube 1 add about a teaspoonful of saliva ❷ from your mouth. To test tube 2 add about a teaspoonful of warm water.

After about 10 minutes, add a teaspoonful of Benedict's solution to each tube. ● Heat the tubes in the beaker of water. *Benedict's solution will change color if sugar is present.* What happens as the water boils? ▲

At the beginning, there was *no sugar* in the Benedict's solution, in the starch, water, or saliva. Does either test tube contain sugar now? ❸ If so, where did the sugar come from?

Methods of Intelligence: Using a Control

Put the same amounts of starch mixture in two test tubes. Add saliva to both tubes. Put one tube in a refrigerator. Put the other in a glass of warm ❹ water. After 10 minutes, test both tubes with Benedict's solution. What do you find? How do you explain this?

266

Useful materials: Some similar materials are available in CLASSROOM LABORATORY: PURPLE.

Continuing Lesson Cluster 2

❶ Children may need instruction in how to level a teaspoonful of starch with a knife blade or tongue depressor.

❷ If the same teaspoon is used to add water after adding saliva, be sure the spoon is well rinsed.

❸ The blue color of Benedict's solution has changed toward a rusty brown. It may vary from yellow or orange to brick red depending on various factors. This result shows that the test tube with starch and saliva now contains some sugar. Children should be able to infer that this happened only because saliva was present, since the contents of the tubes were otherwise identical.

❹ The starch-water mixture should be made with cool water at the same temperature in each tube. After 10 minutes, addition of Benedict's solution should reveal sugar in the warmed test tube, and none, or very little, in the refrigerated test tube. Children should infer that heat is a condition that favors the changing of starch to sugar in the presence of saliva. To set up a control, another test tube at room temperature would be desirable.

Supporting Statement: Food substances must be digested before they can diffuse into cells of the body.

Making Large Molecules into Small Ones

❶ **Saliva** (sə·lī′və) is the liquid you find in your mouth when you think of a good meal. It is the liquid that moistens your food as you eat. Saliva does more for you than just moisten your food, however.

Saliva changes starch. It changes starch into compounds that dissolve in water and can pass through membranes. When you take a bite of a sandwich, your teeth chew the food into small pieces. The saliva in your mouth can get at these pieces easily. The saliva begins to break down some of the sandwich—mainly the starch.

What does saliva do to starch? Saliva is largely water, but there is a substance in saliva that breaks down starch. This substance is called an **enzyme** (en′zīm). The enzyme in saliva breaks down starch into malt sugar. That is, it breaks down some of the large food molecules into smaller molecules. ❷ The molecules of malt sugar are later changed to a sugar made of even smaller molecules, which can pass through cell membranes.

Of course, we eat other food substances besides starch. We eat meat, butter, milk, fruit, and so forth. Most of the foods we eat contain carbohydrates, proteins, and fats. They are the kinds of food materials that provide the molecules the body needs. In other words, we eat carbohydrates and proteins and fats. Most of these must be broken down into ❸ molecules that can pass through membranes. Other enzymes do these jobs.

When food is broken down by enzymes, we call the process **digestion** (di·jes′chən). Digestion means breaking down food into compounds that do dissolve. Mostly digestion means breaking down very large molecules into smaller ones.

Where does digestion take place? In your mouth, stomach, and intestine. It is taking place right now. Enzymes are at work in your stomach and intestine. They are breaking down large molecules of the food you have eaten into smaller ones.

267

❶ What does it mean when your mouth waters? How can you explain it? If children have difficulty responding, suggest sights, sounds, tastes, or smells in the kitchen just before meal time. What do you think saliva does? Summarize responses on the board. (keeps mouth moist, mixes with food when chewed, changes starch to sugar, helps keep teeth clean)

❷ The maltose into which starch is broken down has the same chemical formula as sucrose, ordinary table sugar. Put on the chalkboard:

sucrose: $C_{12}H_{22}O_{11}$
maltose: $C_{12}H_{22}O_{11}$
glucose: $C_6H_{12}O_6$

When maltose combines with one molecule of water (H_2O), two glucose molecules are formed.

Have children count the atoms in the molecules represented by these formulas. (sucrose and maltose, 45; glucose, 24) Point out that the size of a molecule is related to the number of atoms in it, and that the simpler the structure, the more readily the molecule can pass through a membrane.

❸ You have seen that starch is changed by an enzyme in saliva into maltose. Why do you think other enzymes would be needed to break down other carbohydrates, fats, and proteins? (They are different molecules, and thus have different structures.)

Unit Concept-Statement: Living things are adapted by structure and function to their environment.

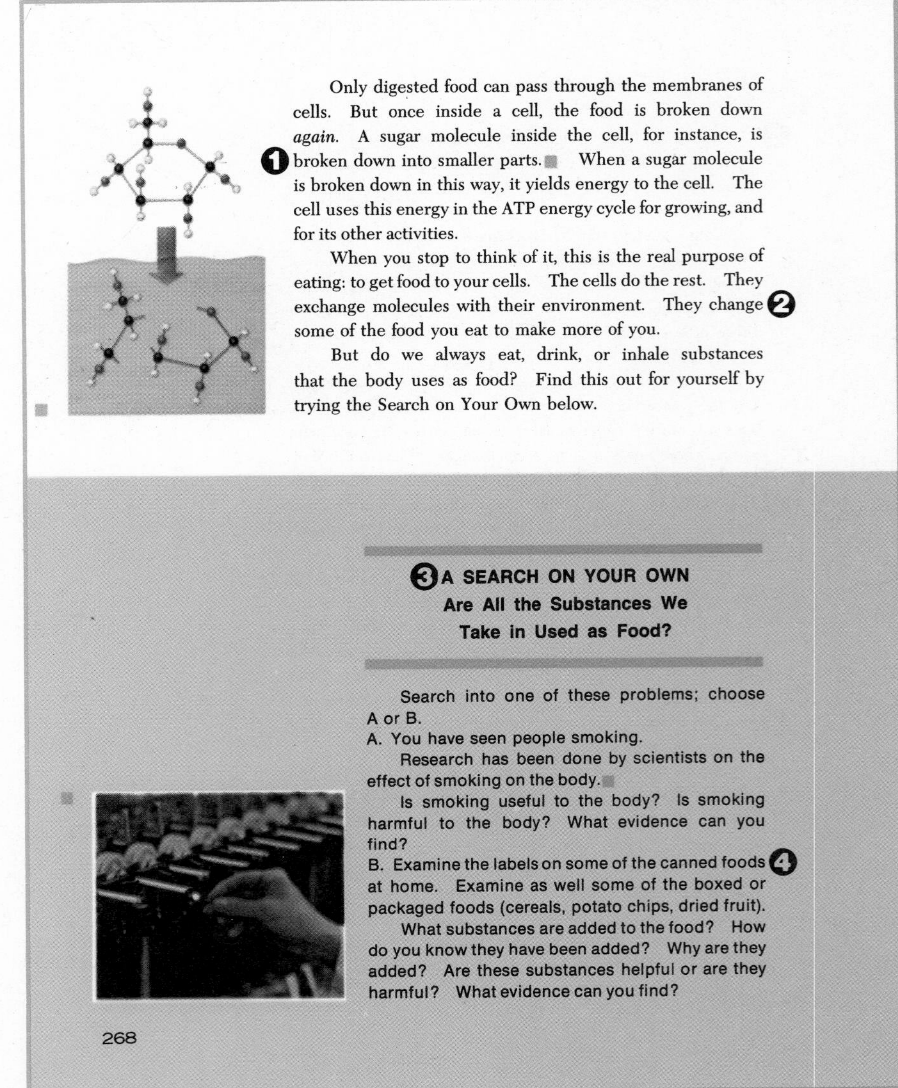

Only digested food can pass through the membranes of cells. But once inside a cell, the food is broken down *again.* A sugar molecule inside the cell, for instance, is ❶ broken down into smaller parts. When a sugar molecule is broken down in this way, it yields energy to the cell. The cell uses this energy in the ATP energy cycle for growing, and for its other activities.

When you stop to think of it, this is the real purpose of eating: to get food to your cells. The cells do the rest. They exchange molecules with their environment. They change ❷ some of the food you eat to make more of you.

But do we always eat, drink, or inhale substances that the body uses as food? Find this out for yourself by trying the Search on Your Own below.

❸ A SEARCH ON YOUR OWN
Are All the Substances We Take in Used as Food?

Search into one of these problems; choose A or B.

A. You have seen people smoking.

Research has been done by scientists on the effect of smoking on the body.

Is smoking useful to the body? Is smoking harmful to the body? What evidence can you find?

B. Examine the labels on some of the canned foods ❹ at home. Examine as well some of the boxed or packaged foods (cereals, potato chips, dried fruit).

What substances are added to the food? How do you know they have been added? Why are they added? Are these substances helpful or are they harmful? What evidence can you find?

268

Continuing Lesson Cluster 2

❶ Have children recall that in molecuar models such as those in the diagram here, black represents atoms of carbon; red, oxygen; and yellow, hydrogen. Count the atoms of each kind in the molecule at the top and then write a formula for it. ($C_6H_{12}O_6$) Some children may recall that this is the formula for glucose, the kind of sugar molecule that is simple enough to enter a cell. What is happening to the glucose molecule here? (being broken down inside the cell)

❷ What is the molecular exchange? (Blood brings to the cells oxygen from air and glucose from food and takes away wastes, such as water and carbon dioxide.) Place on board:

glucose + oxygen → water + carbon dioxide

What's missing from this equation? (release of energy)

VERIFYING PROGRESS

❸ **A search on your own.** Children *investigate* problems that are current in the news media, *seek evidence,* and *order* it in a reasoned report.

Why is it useful to gather evidence on smoking? on food labeling? These questions should lead to the concept that intelligent decisions on actions should be based on scientifically supported evidence rather than upon social acceptance or special pleading.

❹ Children who undertake Search B should be especially referred to library references on activities of the Federal Food and Drug Administration (FDA).

Supporting Statement: Food substances must usually be digested before they can diffuse into cells of the body.

❶ BEFORE YOU GO ON

A. Check your understanding of the concepts of this section. Which ending would you choose for each statement below?

1. To break down food substances in the mouth, stomach, and intestine, the body uses
a. oxygen b. enzymes

2. When large molecules of food are broken down in the intestine, we say the food is
a. digested b. burned

3. The molecules that have been broken down can then
a. pass through membranes
b. digest enzymes

4. One example of digestion is the breaking down of
a. starch into sugar
b. sugar into starch

5. The statement that fits the main concept of this section is
a. Before food can be used by cells in our bodies, it must be cooked.
b. Before food can be used by cells in our bodies, it must be digested.

B. Write a paragraph or two on this topic: "What Happens to Food in the Mouth, Stomach, and Intestines?"

❷ USING WHAT YOU KNOW

If a boy gulps his food in large chunks, what advice would you give him? What reasons would you give him for your advice?

❸ INVESTIGATING FURTHER

You know what one enzyme in saliva does. In the library, find out what the following enzymes do in your body: pepsin, in the stomach; trypsin, in the intestine.

A LOOK AHEAD

Oxygen is needed by the body. So is food.

Unlike oxygen, however, food must be digested. That is, it must be broken down into small molecules. These molecules can then pass through the membrane of the intestine. In this way, they reach your blood—and every part of your body.

What are the different kinds of cells in your body that receive and make use of oxygen and food? Turn to the next section.

269

VERIFYING PROGRESS (cont.)

❶ **Before you go on.** Children *demonstrate* understanding of the need for digestion of foods by responding to questions.
A. 1. b 2. a 3. a 4. a 5. b
B. Children's responses.

❷ **Using what you know.** Children *apply* their knowledge of digestion to an everyday situation.

Chew your food longer before swallowing it. Smaller pieces are more easily acted on by enzymes in saliva. Food is better made ready for passing through membranes.

❸ **Investigating further.** Children *seek evidence* and *distinguish* among the work of different enzymes and *describe* their action in digestion.

Pepsin breaks down large protein molecules into smaller molecules. Trypsin breaks down these smaller molecules into even smaller ones (amino acids) which can be absorbed into the blood.

Unit Concept-Statement: Living things are adapted by structure and function to their environment.

LESSON CLUSTER 3
SOME IMPORTANT CELLS AND THEIR WORK

Teaching background. 3 T-291

Concept-seeking. Children become aware that different kinds of cells in the body have their specific functions.

Operations. Children *probe* into the different cells in the body and their organization into tissues that perform specific functions in the body.

Methods of intelligence. Children *analyze* various cells of the body; *identify* their structures, and *distinguish* the relationship of structure to function.

Useful materials: Bones, muscle meats (including heart), and organ meats (kidney, liver, pancreas, lung, etc.) from the butcher or from your own cleaning of a chicken, will make good display materials in this lesson cluster.

3. Some Important Cells and Their Work

■

You are alive because your cells are alive. However, ❶ some parts of your body are not made up of cells. Does it surprise you that some parts of your body are not alive?

Think of the last time you had a haircut. As your hair was cut you felt no pain. Hair is not alive. It does not ❷ take in oxygen or food substances. Notice how the dead cells of hair look under a powerful microscope.■ The cells around the *root* of a hair are alive, and they grow. This is what makes hair get longer. But hair itself is not alive.

Are there other parts of the body that can be cut without pain? The nails, of course. They are not alive.

When you are at the dentist's, it seems as if your teeth are very much alive! Yet it does not seem so when you brush your teeth, does it? The living cells in your teeth are not exposed. They are well protected. Your gums are lined with living cells, but each tooth is covered with a hard material that is not alive. This is called **enamel.** Inside each tooth, however, is the **pulp,** which contains blood vessels and a nerve.● The pulp is very much alive.

Where do parts of the body such as enamel and nails and hair come from? They are all made by living cells. There is another hard material in your body, made by cells, that is important to you. Bone is made by cells. Right now your cells are making more bone. This is one reason why you are growing taller.

●

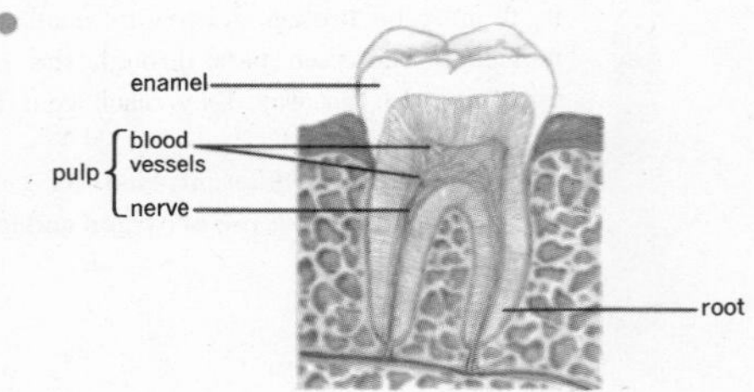

270

Introducing Lesson Cluster 3

❶ At this level, children have some knowledge that all living things are made of cells. You might ask children to work in pairs, each describing the different things the other child can do with his face. Allow three minutes for listing. (smile, frown, raise eyebrows, chew, smell, hear, feel, see, wiggle ears, etc.) How can we do all these things?

What structures, for example, do you use when you smile? (muscles) chew? (muscles and teeth) Ask similar questions for the other functions children list. What are the living structures of the body made of? (cells) Are they the same or different?

If necessary, review with children the similarities and differences among cells studied in Unit Five, by having them look at the illustrations on page 215 of their textbooks. What parts of the body are not alive? (hair, nails, enamel of the teeth, hard parts of bones, the outermost layer of skin, lining of mouth, etc.)

❷ What are some differences between something that is alive and something that isn't? (Living things can grow, take in food and air, reproduce, etc.) If an observant child says hair and nails must be alive because they grow, ask him to think of an explanation. (The cells from which these parts emerge are alive.)

Supporting Statement: Cells are grouped into tissues that have specific functions.

▲ 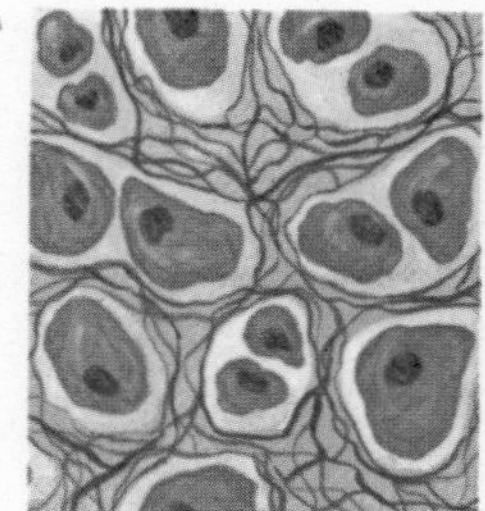 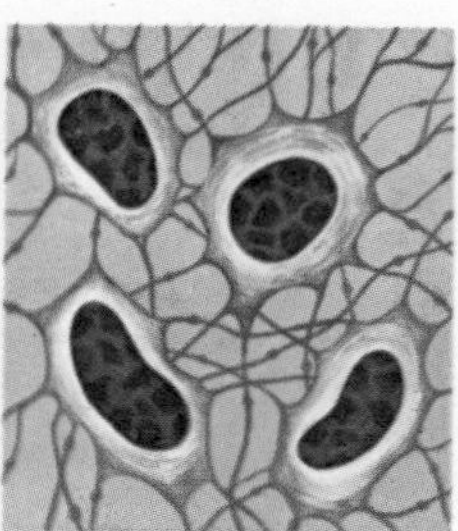 ◆

There are many different kinds of cells in your body, doing many different jobs. The cells that make bone, for ❶ instance, differ from the cells in a muscle. The cells in your brain differ from the cells at work in your blood. ❷ However, scientists have managed to classify or group cells, just as they have classified many things.

Let's look at some of these different groups of cells in your body and the jobs they do.

Cells That Support

Your ear doesn't hang down, does it? Why not?

Your ear is stiff and erect. Yet it has no bones in it. What holds it up?

Cells in the ear make a kind of material that supports the ear. This material is called **cartilage** (kär'tə·lij). Cells of the ear are surrounded by the cartilage they make. ▲ ❸ Cartilage gives the ear stiffness. Cartilage gives your nose its shape, too.

Another kind of **supporting cell** allows you to stand straight. You can stand because you have bones, which support your body. The bones are made by **bone cells** ◆ another kind of supporting cell. Bone cells might better be ❹ called bone-making cells. These cells make the hard bone that surrounds them.

271

VERIFYING PROGRESS

In concept-seeking

Children can evaluate their progress in *investigation* by *demonstrating* the digestion of protein in meat, as follows:

Add a meat tenderizer containing the enzyme pepsin to a little raw hamburger. What happens? (hamburger liquifies) Explain. (The molecule pepsin breaks down large, insoluble molecules of protein into small, soluble molecules.)

Useful materials: Wall chart, large diagram or model of a tooth.

❶ How do muscle cells do their work? (expand, contract, push, pull) bone cells? (support) Why would you expect muscle cells to be flexible and bone cells rigid? (These properties are necessary for the functions named.) How do brain cells work? (send messages through fibers) blood cells? (move all through body)

❷ How would you classify cells? (by likenesses of structure) Let children hypothesize to what extent structure determines function. Could a blood cell ever become a muscle cell? A class discussion using questions such as this can help make clear that structure is the classifying factor.

❸ If you have eaten chicken recently, perhaps you have noticed cartilage. Where? (at ends of bones in joints and at tip of the breastbone) What does it look and feel like? (nearly colorless, firm, very smooth, flexible) Cartilage is at the ends of our bones, too. What use do you think cartilage is between bones? (helps bones glide over one another at joints; acts as cushion to absorb shocks)

❹ In what other ways are bones important to you? (protection inside of body, anchorage for muscles that make movement possible, marrow for manufacture of blood cells)

Unit Concept-Statement: Living things are adapted by structure and function to their environment.

VERIFYING PROGRESS

In concept-seeking

Children may *investigate* the relationship of tendons and bones in a chicken foot, or the relationship of ligaments, tendons, muscles, and bones in a lamb shoulder joint, if you can obtain these specimens from a local butcher. (1) Trim the cut end of the chicken foot enough to expose the whitish tendons. Let children pull the tendons one by one. What do you observe? (Some tendons bend the toes, and others straighten them.) What part of the chicken leg does your hand, doing the pulling, take the place of? (muscles)
(2) The school nurse can help children identify the various parts of a lamb joint. Let children predict what movement of the joint will result from pulling different tendons, then test their predictions.

There are other cells that provide support. Feel your knee just below the kneecap. There is a tough band there, ❶ called a **ligament** (lig′ə·mənt). A ligament is built of strong fiberlike cells. ■ It joins one bone to another. Now feel inside of your elbow as you bend your arm. There is another tough connecting band there. This one is a **tendon** (ten′dən), a band of cells that joins bone to muscle. See if you can feel tendons in your ankle.

Cells That Move Your Body

Move your fingers, bend your arm, turn your head. **Muscle cells** are at work. There are many different muscles in the body, several hundred of them, in fact. Each one of ❷ these muscles is made up of many cells working together.

Here is one kind of muscle cell. ● When you lift a finger or move an arm or leg, this kind of muscle cell is in action. The muscles made up of these cells do what you command them to do. In other words, muscle cells of this kind are *under your control.*

❸ Here is a second kind of muscle cell. ▲ This kind is *not under your control.* Can you cause the muscle cells of your intestine to digest your food or stop digesting it? No. These muscle cells work without your commanding them.

■

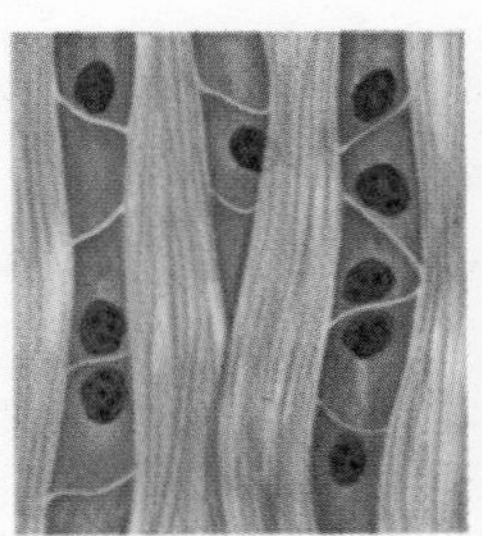

●

272

Continuing Lesson Cluster 3

❶ How does a ligament differ from cartilage? (A ligament ties bones together; cartilage is attached to the ends of bones.) Let children volunteer other parts of the body where they can feel ligaments and tendons. Why do we group these four types of cells as supporting cells? (All are related to bones; all help hold the body in shape and position.)

❷ What different kinds of muscles can you think of besides those that move your arms, head, torso and legs? Children should be able to think of heart, stomach, and other internal muscles.

❸ The illustration at the lower right on this page shows voluntary muscle tissue that makes up skeletal muscles. Have children compare this drawing with two kinds of involuntary muscle tissue at the top of page 273: intestine (left) and heart (right). Children should be able to identify the cell membrane, cytoplasm, and nucleus in the intestinal muscle and the nuclei in the cells of the other two types.

How do these three kinds of cells differ in appearance? (Voluntary muscle and heart muscle cells are tightly bound together and have "stripes"—crosswise on the voluntary muscle cells and in two directions on the heart cells; intestinal cells are separated and have no "stripes.")

Children should realize that the differences in structure of the three kinds of muscle cells are reflected in the differences in function.

Supporting Statement: Cells are grouped into tissues that have specific functions.

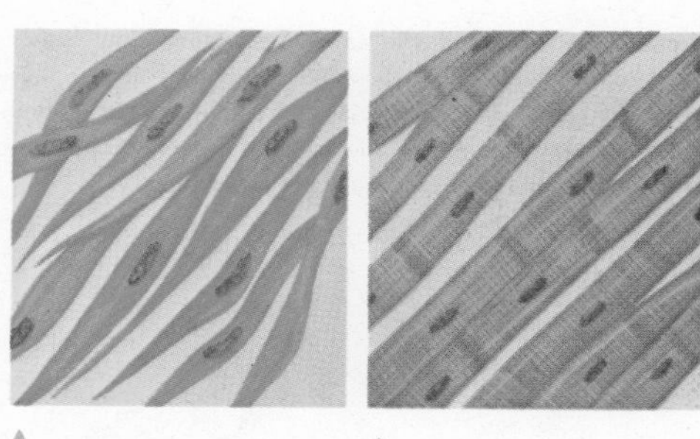

▲ ◆

❶ The muscles of your heart are not under your control either. ◆ Your heart beats without your thinking about it. But as you can see, these heart muscle cells and the muscle cells of the intestine look different. They do different kinds of work. The heart muscles are made up of the third kind of muscle cell.

Heart muscle cells and intestinal muscle cells are not under the control of your brain. Most of the muscle cells in your arms, legs, face, and tongue are under the control of your brain.

Cells That Cover

A sheet of cells covers you from head to foot. These **covering cells** are skin cells. ★

So long as the covering cells of the skin are unbroken, **bacteria** cannot get into the body through the skin. Bacteria are tiny organisms that may cause illness. When the skin is ❷ broken, more skin cells grow to knit covering cells together again. Thus the opening in the covering cells is closed.

★

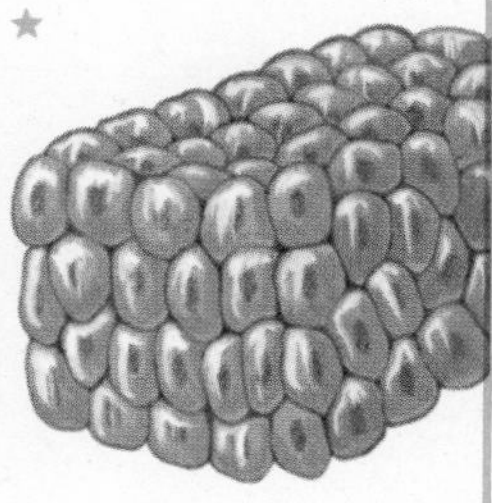

There are covering cells on the *inside* of your body, too. For example, the inside of the stomach and intestine is covered with cells. As you saw in Unit Five (page 214), the inside of your mouth is covered with cells. The inside of your nose, too, and other breathing organs, are covered with

❶ Why is it desirable that our heart muscles are not under conscious control? (If we had to be aware of our heart's beating all the time, we could not think about other things, and we could never go to sleep.) What if you had to tell your stomach and intestinal muscles to work or stop working? Encourage children to imagine the difference if many of the body's unconscious functions required conscious thought.

❷ Why should we take good care of our skin? You might mention that some infections and allergies attack the skin: athelete's foot, some kinds of itches, poison ivy, etc.

Unit Concept-Statement: Living things are adapted by structure and function to their environment.

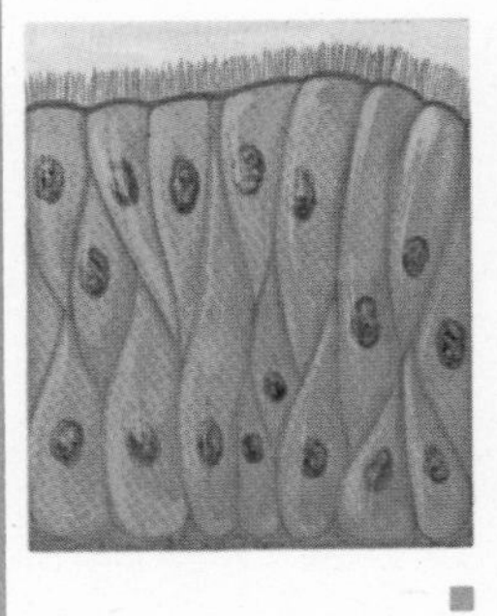

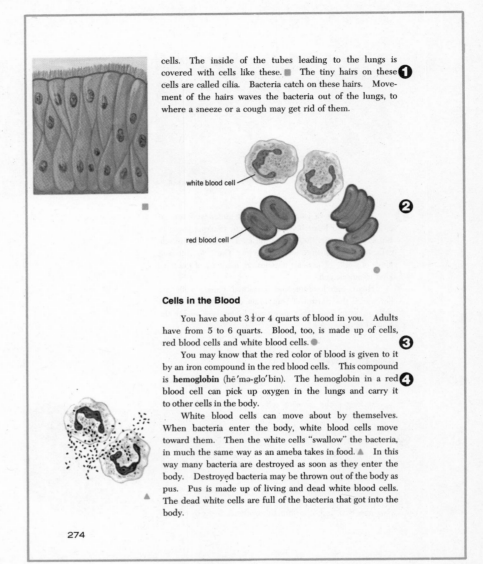

cells. The inside of the tubes leading to the lungs is covered with cells like these. ■ The tiny hairs on these ❶ cells are called cilia. Bacteria catch on these hairs. Movement of the hairs waves the bacteria out of the lungs, to where a sneeze or a cough may get rid of them.

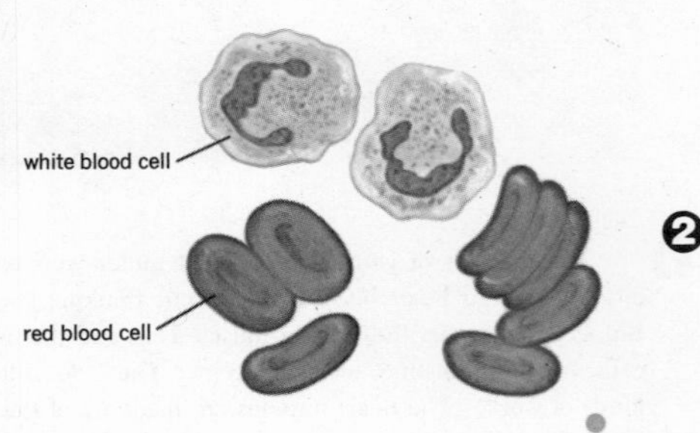

❷

Cells in the Blood

You have about 3½ or 4 quarts of blood in you. Adults have from 5 to 6 quarts. Blood, too, is made up of cells, red blood cells and white blood cells. ● ❸

You may know that the red color of blood is given to it by an iron compound in the red blood cells. This compound is **hemoglobin** (hē′mə·glo′bin). The hemoglobin in a red ❹ blood cell can pick up oxygen in the lungs and carry it to other cells in the body.

White blood cells can move about by themselves. When bacteria enter the body, white blood cells move toward them. Then the white cells "swallow" the bacteria, in much the same way as an ameba takes in food. ▲ In this way many bacteria are destroyed as soon as they enter the body. Destroyed bacteria may be thrown out of the body as pus. Pus is made up of living and dead white blood cells. The dead white cells are full of the bacteria that got into the body.

274

Continuing Lesson Cluster 3

❶ How are the tiny hairs inside the windpipe, the cilia, different from the hair on the head? (The cilia are living and moving parts of the cells; the hair on our head is not living.)

❷ Have children identify the parts of the cells in the diagram. (nucleus, cytoplasm, cell membrane, cilia)

❸ The darker color in the white cell is a nucleus—shaped differently from nuclei in other kinds of cells they have studied.

❹ Hemoglobin can also carry carbon monoxide—a poisonous gas that is present in the exhaust from automobiles. Hemoglobin picks up carbon monoxide more readily than it picks up oxygen. You may have heard of someone who was killed by carbon monoxide poisoning. How might this happen? (Carbon monoxide mixed with air enters the lungs, where hemoglobin picks up the carbon monoxide *instead of* oxygen: thus, cells are deprived of oxygen.) Can you smell the oxygen in the air? (no) Point out that carbon monoxide is odorless too. How, then, would you know if there were a dangerous amount of carbon monoxide in a closed garage when the engine of the car is running? (You wouldn't.) Impress upon the children that this is why one must *never* run a car engine while the garage door is closed.

Supporting Statement: Cells are grouped into tissues that have specific functions.

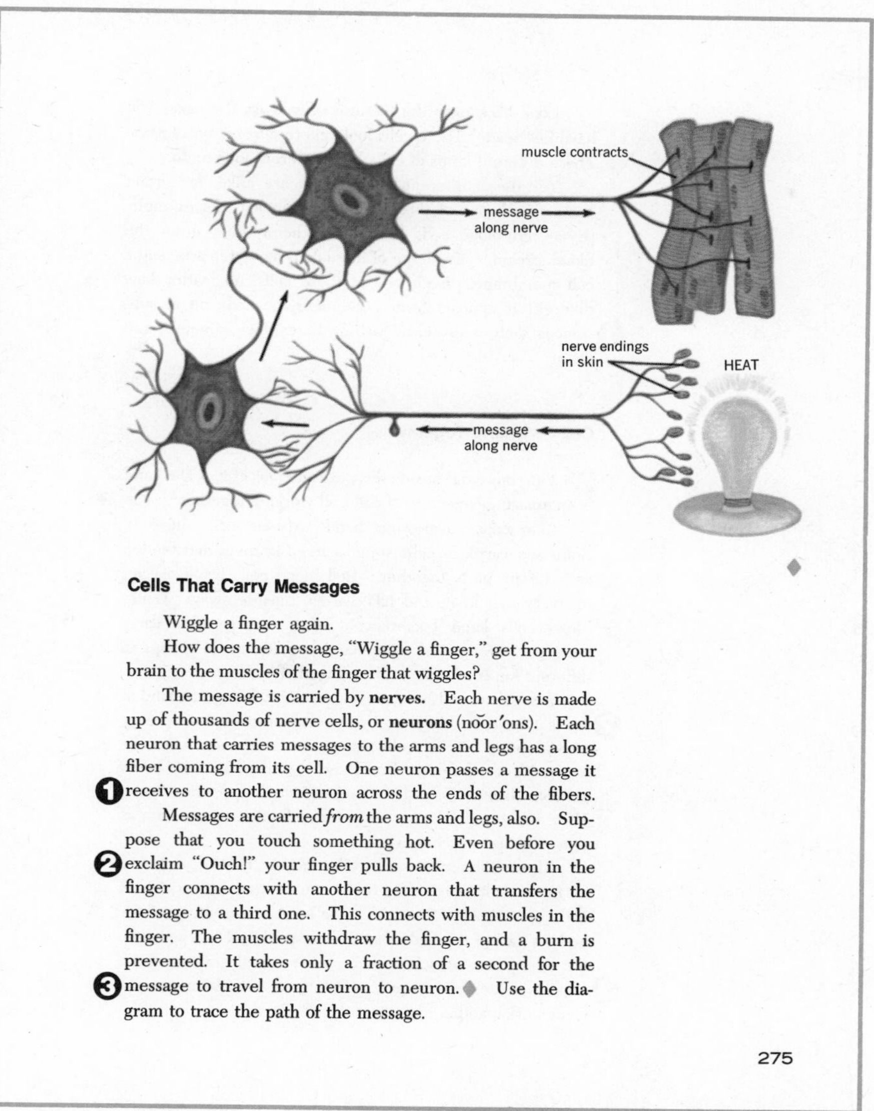

Cells That Carry Messages

Wiggle a finger again.

How does the message, "Wiggle a finger," get from your brain to the muscles of the finger that wiggles?

The message is carried by **nerves.** Each nerve is made up of thousands of nerve cells, or **neurons** (no͝or′ons). Each neuron that carries messages to the arms and legs has a long fiber coming from its cell. One neuron passes a message it ❶ receives to another neuron across the ends of the fibers.

Messages are carried *from* the arms and legs, also. Suppose that you touch something hot. Even before you ❷ exclaim "Ouch!" your finger pulls back. A neuron in the finger connects with another neuron that transfers the message to a third one. This connects with muscles in the finger. The muscles withdraw the finger, and a burn is prevented. It takes only a fraction of a second for the ❸ message to travel from neuron to neuron.◆ Use the diagram to trace the path of the message.

275

❶ Let's say that you are playing catch. A message from your brain goes along a ***neuron*** from your brain, and you hold your hand up to catch the ball coming to you. ***Nerves*** from your eye give your brain a message of the flight of the ball. The brain interprets this and sends a message to your arm. This is a conscious (voluntary) reaction.

❷ Have children follow the path of the message from a hot object touched by the fingers, as pictured in the diagram. The message of heat (or pain) goes up the arm to the spinal cord, across a connecting neuron, and back down the arm to muscles in the arm and fingers; and the muscles receiving the message contract and pull the arm away. This is an automatic reaction—although the same voluntary muscles are used. The message also goes to the brain along another nerve and interprets the message as a burn.

❸ Let children note the three kinds of nerve cells or ***neurons.*** The one that carries a sensation message has its nucleus along the ***nerve*** fiber. The nucleus of the other two neurons is the dark part inside the main part of the cell. Both the neuron that receives the message and the one that transmits it have long fibers. The type of neuron that connects other neurons is usually in the spinal cord or the brain.

Unit Concept-Statement: Living things are adapted by structure and function to their environment.

Look back over the pictures of cells on the pages you have just read. These cells look different from one another. These different kinds of cells have different jobs to do.

Yet these different-looking cells are alike, in certain ways. Each one of these cells has a nucleus, for example. (Even red blood cells have nuclei before they enter the blood stream.) Each one of these cells has cytoplasm, and a cell membrane. Each one of these cells, no matter how different it appears from other cells, is made up of sub-
❶ stances such as proteins, carbohydrates, fats, minerals, and water.

Cells Working Together

Put your hand beside this page and look at it. The hand is an amazing collection of cells, all working together.

Skin cells cover your hand. Muscle cells move it. Bone and cartilage cells support it. Ligament and tendon cells tie its parts together. Red blood cells bring oxygen to every cell in it, and take carbon dioxide away. White blood cells keep bacteria out of it. Nerve cells carry messages through it. Your hand is made up of groups of different kinds of cells working together.

A group of cells of the same kind and doing one kind of
❷ job is a **tissue** (tish′o͞o). Muscle cells, for example, make up *muscle tissue.* Nerve cells make up *nerve tissue.* The cells in the blood make up *blood tissue.* Cells that make bone, cartilage, ligaments, and tendons are called *supporting tissue.* They support the body. And the cells that cover, such as skin cells, are *covering tissue.*

These different tissues work together, too. Your lungs, for instance, have covering tissue, muscle tissue, blood tissue, and nerve tissue. Recall that the lungs are an organ of the body, a part of the body that does a special job. The lungs, the liver, the stomach, and the heart are all organs. Each
❸ organ is made up of tissues. Each tissue is made up of cells. Cells work together in tissues and in organs.

Useful materials: Microscope, dissecting needles.

Continuing Lesson Cluster 3

❶ What are the elements in proteins? (carbon, oxygen, hydrogen, nitrogen) carbohydrates? (carbon, oxygen, hydrogen) fats? (carbon, hydrogen, oxygen) water? (hydrogen, oxygen) What are some minerals in cells? (iron, phosphorus, calcium, sodium, etc.) What evidence do you have that there are different kinds of proteins and carbohydrates in cells? (There are several kinds of sugar, such as glucose and sucrose or table sugar; several kinds of fats, such as butter and salad oil; and several kinds of protein foods, such as milk, eggs, and meat, which would seem to contain different proteins.)

❷ If possible, plan to show and discuss samples of tissue from the butcher shop, perhaps with the cooperation of the school nurse. Good examples are: bone, cartilage, ligament, tendon, muscle, heart, stomach, or small intestine. Samples from a steer, hog, or sheep are good to examine; or use parts from a chicken or turkey.

❸ If you have a microscope and dissecting needles, you may wish to tease apart some tissue and mount it on slides and cover slips for children to examine. Children can then more easily identify the differences in cells that make up different tissues. Examine under low and high power.

Supporting Statement: Cells are grouped into tissues that have specific functions.

1 BEFORE YOU GO ON

A. Here are drawings of some cells like those in your body. See how many you can recognize. Try to tell what parts of the body they come from, and what work they do.

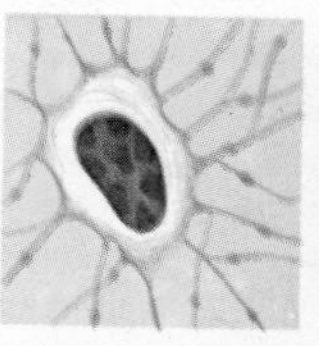

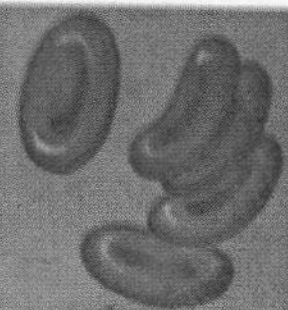

B. The statement that fits the main concept of this section is

a. The unit of structure and function in the body is the molecule.

b. The unit of structure and function in the body is the cell.

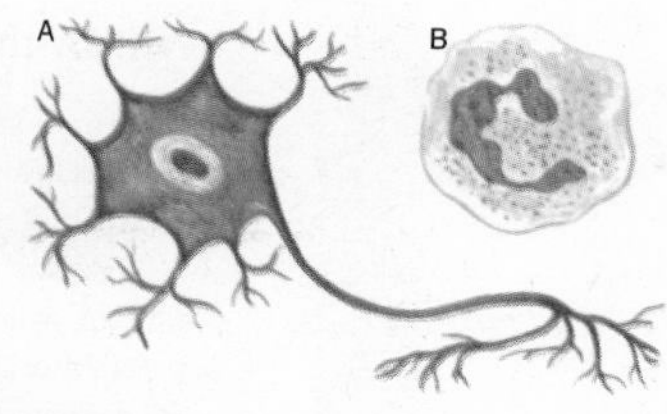

USING WHAT YOU KNOW 2

Here are drawings of two cells found in a rabbit.

1. What tissues do they come from?
2. What does each cell do?

INVESTIGATING FURTHER 3

If you have a microscope, look for tissues in an onion plant. Peel off a layer of the onion bulb that is so thin you can see light through it. Place on a slide, add a drop of water and a cover slip, and examine under low and high power of the microscope. Do the same with a thin bit of the green leaf of the onion plant. After you have examined the tissues mounted in water, add a drop of iodine to each specimen. What parts of the cells seem to take up the most iodine?

A LOOK AHEAD

Your body is made up of many different kinds of living cells, all working together and keeping you alive and well. Cells make up tissues. Tissues make up organs. Organs work together. You have begun to collect some evidence that the body is well fitted for its work. In the next section, you can collect some more evidence.

277

VERIFYING PROGRESS

1 Before you go on. Children *identify* cells and the parts of the body in which they are found, *describe* their functions and *identify* the concept of the section.
A. *Top left:* bone cell; in bones; support the body or protect inside organs. *Top right:* skin cells; cover body; keep out bacteria and regulate water loss in perspiration. *Lower left:* muscle cells in intestine or stomach; keep organ contracting to help digest food. *Lower right:* red blood cells; in blood; carry oxygen to cells.
B. b

2 Using what you know. From their knowledge of human body cells and their function, children *infer* that similar cells in a rabbit will have similar functions: they *identify* pictured cells and *describe* their location and function.

A is a nerve cell; it aids in transmitting messages. **B** is a white blood cell; it destroys harmful bacteria.

3 Investigating further. Children *investigate* plant cell structure by examining plant tissues under the microscope. After staining the mounts, they *observe* a dark part of the cell and *infer* it is the nucleus.

LESSON CLUSTER 4
WITHIN THE BODY

Teaching background. 4 T-292

Concept-seeking. Children become aware of the major organ systems in the human body.

Operations. Children *probe* into the structure and function of the major organ systems of the body.

Methods of intelligence. Children *analyze* the functioning of each organ system in terms of the operation of the entire body, and *infer* that anything that affects any organ of the body affects the whole body.

4. Within the Body

Your body is built in a marvelous way. Its building blocks are billions of tiny cells, working together in tissues and in organs.

Organs work together too. Organs work together in teams called **organ systems.**

One organ system, for example, is made up of organs like the mouth, the stomach, and the intestine. The work of this system is digesting food, of course. Another organ system has to do with breathing. It is made up of organs like the nose, the throat, and the lungs, working together.

Organ systems form the body. The body is beautifully
1 organized to do a remarkable job.

In a way, we are putting the body together from its building blocks. See how the body's building blocks fit together: Atoms form molecules; molecules form cells.
2 For example, this is a smooth muscle cell from the stomach. ■ Cells form tissues. This is smooth muscle tissue in the stomach. ● Tissues form organs. The stomach, for example, is an organ. Organs form organ systems. The organ system shown here is the digestive system. ▲ Its job is digesting food, as you shall see.

3 Organs work together in teams. *How* do organs work together? What does each member of a team do? In the illustrations that follow, you can study some of the organ systems of the body, and see for yourself.

A. Digestion—Making Food Ready for Cells

Cells need food, but every cell in your body is wrapped in a membrane. To get into a cell, food substances must pass through that cell membrane. To pass through the mem-
4 brane, food must be broken down, that is, digested.

When food is taken into the *mouth*, the tongue and teeth break it up. At the same time, juice is poured on the food. This juice is saliva. Saliva comes from **glands** that open into

278

Introducing Lesson Cluster 4

What do you think happens to the meat, bread, catsup, and relish when you eat a hamburger or a hot dog? Let children describe their ideas in responses to these questions:

1. What happens in your mouth?
2. What happens in your stomach?
3. How do you think your sandwich has changed when it gets to the intestine?
4. How does it give you energy? When does it begin to do so? (when it gets to the cells) How does it get there? (by the blood)
5. What happens to parts that are not digested?
6. Why do you have to eat again a few hours later?

Encourage all kind of responses and discourage none.

Developing the lesson

1 What does it mean for a class club to be organized? (Certain persons have certain jobs.) What does it mean when body cells are organized into tissues? (Tissues work together.) When tissues are organized into organs? (Organs do certain jobs.)

2 Let the children study the page of diagrams. How is the single stomach muscle cell like all the cells in the stomach muscle tissue? (same shape, has nucleus) Be sure children realize that these cells are greatly magnified and cannot be seen in the organ labeled "stomach."

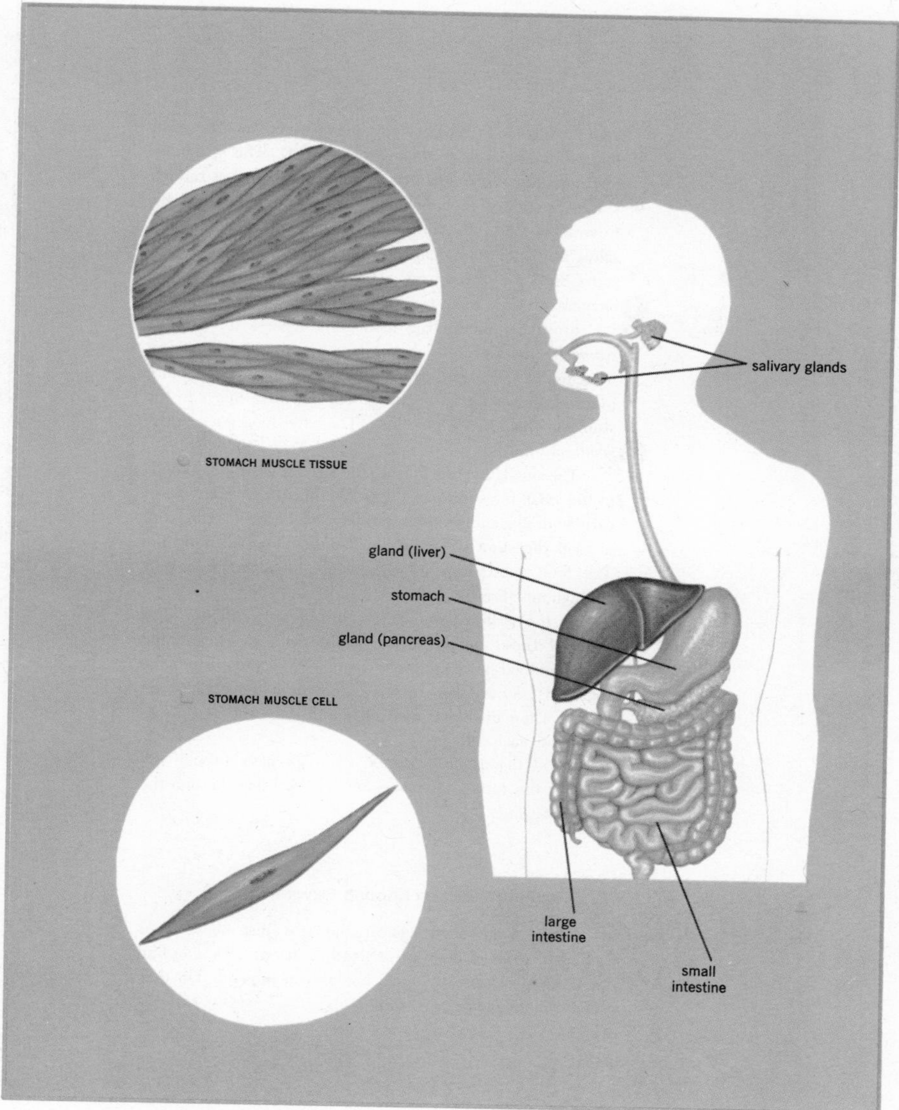

VERIFYING PROGRESS

In concept-seeking

To let children *investigate* the effect of saliva on food, have them collect ½ inch of saliva in a test tube. Let them place a bit of soda cracker moistened with water in another tube and then chew an equal sized piece until soft and place it in a third tube. Add Benedict's solution to all tubes and place them in hot water. What do you observe? (a reddish color in the third tube) What does this indicate? (Saliva changes something in the soda cracker.)

❸ On the diagram, let children observe that all the organs are connected. In a good organization, what do all members do? (work together) All the labeled parts are organs. What shows they must work together? (all connected)

❹ If you have a fine sieve, and a potato, how could you put the potato through the sieve? Let children hypothesize until someone suggests breaking the potato down by boiling it. Agree; then ask: How is food made smaller in the mouth? (chewing) How is it made softer? (saliva) Point out the location of the salivary glands on the diagram and explain one function of moistening food so that it is more like boiled potato.

the mouth. Close your eyes and imagine that you can taste your favorite food. You may imagine an ice cream cone, a hot dog with mustard, or whatever you like best. This imaginary food may cause saliva to flow in your mouth, just as though you had some real food in your mouth. The saliva helps you to swallow food. Swallow now and you will swallow some saliva sent into your mouth by the **salivary** glands. Saliva starts digestion of the food in the mouth, for it contains an
❶ enzyme. Saliva, then, is a digestive juice.

❷ From the mouth the food goes down a tube to the *stomach.* In the stomach the food is squeezed by strong muscles and broken up still more. Glands pour more digestive juices on the food. These digestive juices in the stomach break down proteins. Then the food goes to the
❸ *small intestine.*

The small intestine finishes the job of digestion. Glands
❹ in the small intestine make digestive juices that break down carbohydrates and proteins and fats still further. The work of food digestion is finally finished in the small intestine. The food substances are dissolved. Now they can pass through membranes.

In the wall of the small intestine are tiny tubes. The walls of these tubes are very thin membranes, and the dissolved food passes through them. From these tubes the digested food is taken by the blood to all the cells of the body. Then dissolved food passes through the cell membrane into each cell.

Food that is not digested does not pass through the walls of the tubes. It passes out of the body through the *large intestine.*

B. Breathing—Getting Enough Oxygen

Press your hand against the ribs just above your stomach. Take a deep breath and let it out. Do you find that the ribs seem to move out as you inhale? Do they seem to move in as you exhale?

Continuing Lesson Cluster 4

❶ An enzyme that salivary glands produce helps to break insoluble starch into soluble sugars. Saliva also helps to keep the tongue, lining of the mouth, and the tube to the stomach moist at all times. This moisture is an aid to taste and appĕtite as well as to digestion.

❷ If a child asks what the tube (gullet or esophagus) to the stomach is called, see if another child knows and can tell him before you supply the name; but do not require children to remember it.

Does the food just drop down this tube? Let children hypothesize, then say: Place your hand on your throat and swallow. What do you feel? This movement demonstrates that muscles are at work passing food from the back of the mouth to the stomach.

❸ What form do you think the food is in when it passes out of the stomach into the small intestine? (liquid) Why? (has been mixed, as if in a blender, with juices in mouth and stomach, squeezed and churned)

❹ The inside of the small intestine is somewhat like a turkish towel—very absorbent. Any soluble matter, now largely glucose and a number of other simple compounds, can pass through the thin membranes of the thread-like tubes directly into the blood stream.

Supporting Statement: An organism is adapted by organ systems to perform its life functions.

You might think that this movement happens because you breathe. But this is not so. Just the opposite is true. You breathe partly because of this movement! Let's look at a model and see what happens.

❶ This bottle has a sheet of rubber for a bottom. The balloons are attached to glass tubing that is open to the air at the top. Notice what happens when the rubber sheet is pulled down. More air has entered the balloon. When the rubber sheet is pulled down, the space around the balloons becomes larger. Now the air pressure in the bottle is lower. The air outside the bottle has more pressure. It rushes into the balloons, and the balloons expand.

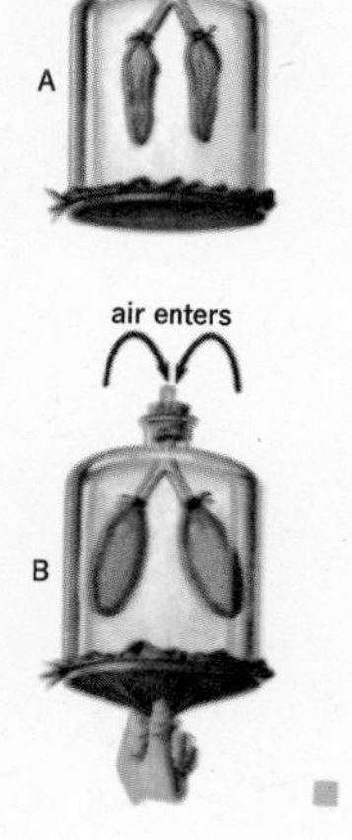

Strange to say, this is a model of what is happening inside you now as you breathe. The balloons are like your lungs. Think of the glass bottle as the ribs and muscles surrounding your lungs. The stretched sheet of rubber is ❷ like your **diaphragm** (dī′ə·fram). The diaphragm is a sheet of muscles below the lungs.

Recall what happens when the rubber sheet across the bottom of the bottle is pulled down. The muscles of the diaphragm can make the diaphragm move down, rather like ❸ the rubber sheet. When the diaphragm moves down, the space around the lungs becomes larger. Air rushes into the lungs just as it rushed into the balloons. The lungs expand.

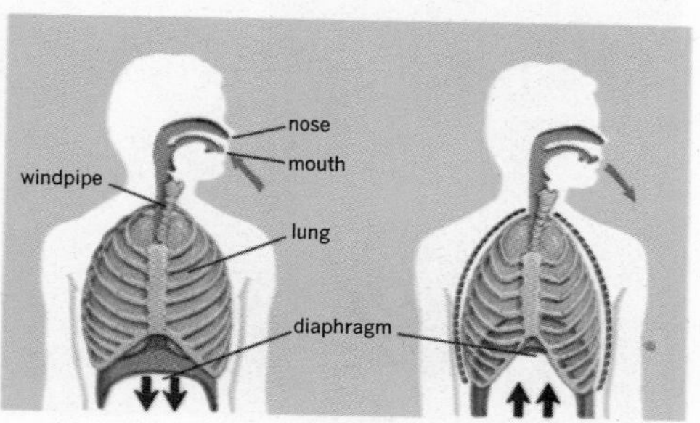

281

Useful materials: Bell jar, single-holed stopper to fit jar, Y-tube (or straight glass tube), two balloons, rubber sheeting, string.

❶ It is fairly easy to develop a working model of the illustration. If a bell jar is not available, use any transparent plastic bottle and cut off the bottom with a hot knife. A Y-tube is not necessary, but the imagery of two lungs is improved if you can obtain one. A "single-lung system" can be demonstrated with a single tube through a cork with a firmly attached balloon and a flexible sheet, preferably rubber. Encourage a child or several children to demonstrate and explain the model.

❷ What happens when your diaphragm muscles move up? (Air is breathed out.) If children have built a model, let them demonstrate what happens when they push up on the rubber.

❸ Encourage children to compare the diagram at the bottom of the page with the model. Which part of your respiratory system is not shown by the model? (nose)

When the diaphragm moves down, under the lungs, the ribs and muscles around the lungs move outward at the ❶ same time. This is the movement you can feel as you inhale with your hands on your ribs. It makes the space around the lungs larger still.

Then the diaphragm moves back up. The ribs and ❷ muscles around the lungs move inward. The space around the lungs becomes smaller. Air is squeezed out of the lungs. The lungs contract, and you exhale. The organs of breathing make up the **respiratory** (ri·spīr'ə·tôr'ē) **system.**

Now let's follow the path of air from outside the body into the lungs. Air enters through the nose and travels down the windpipe. In the lungs the air becomes moist. Oxygen in the air dissolves in the moisture. Then this oxygen passes through the thin membrane of the lungs into the ❸ blood. The blood carries the oxygen to every cell.

In each cell, oxygen combines with food substances. Water and carbon dioxide are produced. These substances ❹ pass from the cell into the blood. Now the blood carries carbon dioxide back to the lungs. The carbon dioxide passes through the membranes in the lungs. The air in the lungs now has more carbon dioxide. We exhale this air.

282

Continuing Lesson Cluster 4

❶ Encourage each child to place a hand under his rib cage on either side and observe the muscular movement as he exhales and inhales.

❷ **Do you pull air in and push it out?** If some children respond affirmatively, refer again to the model and try to develop that it is the difference between outside-the-body air pressure and inside-the-body air pressure that causes the interchange. Air moves from a high pressure region to a low one, and the diaphragm is a muscle for changing pressure.

❸ **How can the blood carry oxygen?** (Red cells have an iron compound called hemoglobin that attracts oxygen to the red cells.)

❹ **How does the blood get rid of the carbon dioxide produced by the cells?** (Most is picked up by red blood cells and exchanged for oxygen in the lungs.) **What happens to the water?** (exhaled) If children do not recall that their breath has water vapor, have them verify by breathing against a cold surface such as a pocket mirror.

Supporting Statement: An organism is adapted by organ systems to perform its life functions.

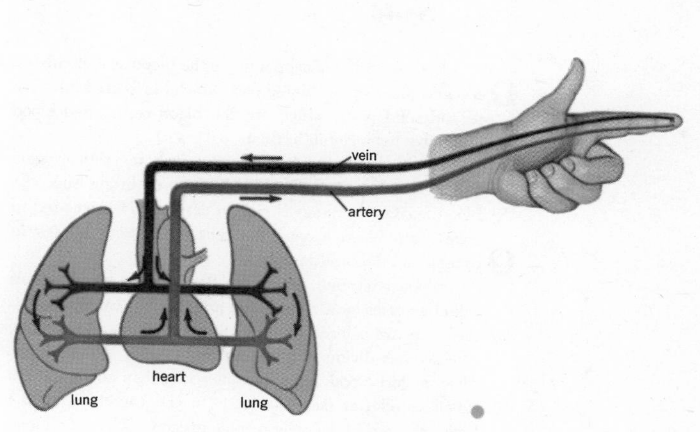

C. Circulation—Getting Substances to Cells

❶ Feel your pulse. Place the fingers of your right hand on the edge of your left wrist. ■

What is the beat you feel? It is the surge of your own blood being pumped through your body. The bundle of muscles that is your heart is expanding and contracting, pumping blood. Each time your heart contracts, it forces blood into the **blood vessels**, tubes that carry the blood. The beat that you feel in your wrist is due to the contraction of your heart.

❷ The blood you feel pulsing in your wrist is on its way to the fingers of your left hand. Trace the blood's path as shown in the diagram and see. ●

From your finger the blood goes to your heart. The heart pumps the blood to the lungs. From the lungs the blood goes back to the heart. Again, the heart pumps the blood, this time out to the finger. From the finger the blood goes back again to the heart. Around and around, the blood **circulates** (sûr′kyə·lāts). This system of the heart and the blood vessels is the **circulatory** (sûr′kyə·lə·tôr′ē) **system.**

283

VERIFYING PROGRESS

In concept-seeking

Children may *investigate* their pulse rates at rest and after exercise. They will need a watch or clock with a second hand, and may work in groups of three: one to be the subject whose pulse is being taken, one to keep time, and one to write down the results.

Have children design their own procedures and get your approval before carrying them out. Children should be commended if they suggest counting the pulse more than once and using an average count.

After results are in, ask: Why does the heart beat faster when you exercise? (You need more oxygen in order to produce the extra energy it takes to move your muscles.)

❶ Let each child find his own pulse as directed, and mark the exact spot with his ball-point pen. To demonstrate the rhythm of the heartbeat, each child can place the head of a thumbtack on the marked spot after inserting the point of the tack through the end of a paper match. Of course, the hand must be held palm up and the wrist held level. The swaying of the match with the beat of the heart provides a graphic image of the heart-beat. What makes the match-stick move back and forth? (expansion and contraction of the heart muscles)

❷ Children need training in reading diagrams. Have them start tracing from either lung, beginning with the red lines. Explain that the bright red line refers to blood rich in oxygen. Where does the blood get the oxygen? (lungs) Where does it go? (heart) Then where? (finger) Why is the return line dark red? (Oxygen has been given up, carbon dioxide has been taken in.) Where does this blood go? (heart and out to lungs) What happens there? (Carbon dioxide is given up, oxygen is taken in.)

Let's see what is happening to the blood as it circulates.
❶ Blood is made up of a liquid part, which has food dissolved in it, and solid parts, which are the blood cells. Red blood cells have hemoglobin in them.

In the lungs the hemoglobin combines with oxygen. When this happens, the blood becomes bright red. So blood leaving the lungs is rich in oxygen and bright red in color. But blood leaving the cells of the body is poor in
❷ oxygen and dark red in color.

Blood is carried away from the heart in blood vessels called **arteries** (ar'tər·ez). The arteries that carry blood to the lungs are colored dark red in the diagram on page 283. The arteries divide into smaller and smaller blood vessels. The smallest blood vessels are no wider than a hair and are called **capillaries** (kap'ə·ler'ēz). In the capillaries in the lungs, the red blood cells receive oxygen. Thus, the blood changes color, from dark red to bright red. ■ This bright
❸ red blood goes through blood vessels called **veins** (vānz) back to the heart.

Arteries carry bright red blood from the heart to all
❹ the other organs of the body, except the lungs—to the kidneys, intestines, arms, legs, brain, and so forth. The arteries all over the body divide into smaller and smaller blood vessels, ending in capillaries, just as they do in the lungs. But the blood going into the capillaries in your finger, for instance, is bright red. ● In these capillaries, the red blood cells pass oxygen to other cells. The same thing happens in capillaries in other parts of the body. Now the blood has less oxygen and is dark red. It flows from the capillaries into
❺ veins, which go back to the heart. On each round trip, then, the blood exchanges material with the cells.

As you can see in the drawing on the opposite page,
❻ your body is threaded through with blood vessels. ▲ Arteries lead from the heart to all organs. Veins lead from the organs to the heart. Try tracing the circulation of blood from the heart to the brain, from the heart to a toe. No matter how long the path or how many turns it makes, it is like the circulation to your finger.

284

Continuing Lesson Cluster 4

❶ What two things are in the blood that all body cells must have? (food and oxygen) Why do cells need oxygen? (to combine with food when it reaches cells and to release energy)

❷ If you cut yourself in two places and the blood was bright red in one place and dark red in another, what would you infer about the blood from each cut? (bright red: oxygen-rich; dark red: full of carbon dioxide)

❸ How can you now explain why you saw two colors of blood when you cut yourself in two places? (Blood on its way from the lungs to the body cells is oxygen-rich; blood on its way from the body cells back to the lungs is full of carbon dioxide.)

❹ Why do you think arteries do not carry bright red blood from the heart to the lungs? (The blood is on the way from the body, where it has picked up carbon dioxide given up by the cells, to the lungs, where it will give up carbon dioxide and pick up oxygen.)

❺ If an artery goes to the body from the heart, why is the blood bright red? (It has picked up oxygen from the lungs, passed through the heart and still has its oxygen.) When the artery branches into capillaries, what happens to the oxygen? (goes to cells on the way) Why does the blood become darker as it flows into veins? (picks up carbon dioxide)

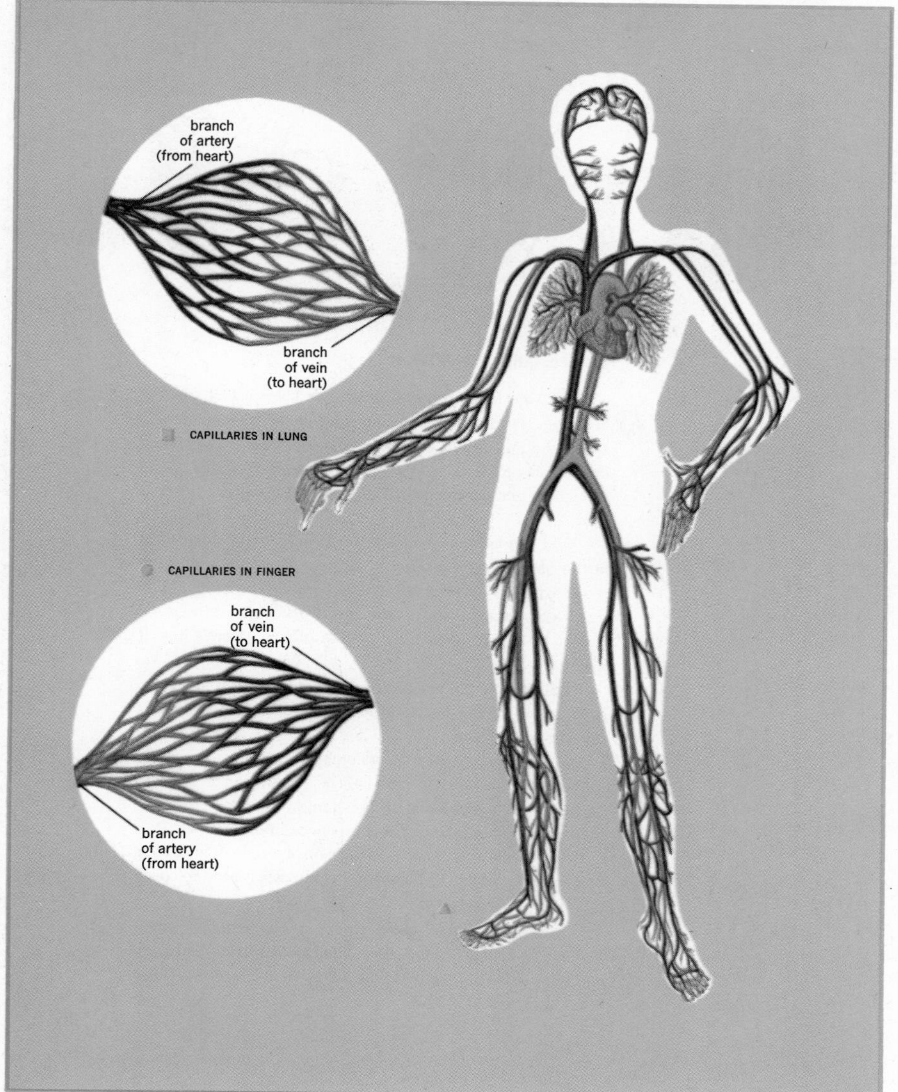

EXTENDING THE LESSON

If you have a low-power microscope and a goldfish, children can watch blood circulating in the capillaries of the fish's tail. Wrap the fish in wet cotton and lay it in a shallow saucer of water. Place the saucer on the stage of the microscope, and focus on the thinnest part of the tail, which is outside the cotton. Children should be able to see many criss-crossed tiny tubes—the capillaries. Some of the red blood cells coursing through will move in one direction, some in another. (Be careful not to keep the fish out of water too long.)

6 Encourage children to "read" the diagram. **What do the dark and bright red colors indicate in the top circle?** (Arteries from heart to lungs carry blood with a large amount of carbon dioxide. As the blood goes back, it has a high oxygen content.) **How is this different from the bottom circle?** (The artery from the heart carries oxygen-rich blood to the body. The blood gives up oxygen and picks up carbon dioxide through the capillaries in the finger, changes color, and returns to the heart. Then it goes to the lungs.)

Now encourage children to start with the intake of oxygen from a lung into the blood. **What color will this blood be?** (bright red) Let them trace possible routes of bright red blood to the head, an arm, a leg, and then trace dark red blood back to the heart and out to the lung. **Why do you think there are so many capillaries in the lungs?** Perceptive children may infer that this is the center of interchange of oxygen and carbon dioxide.

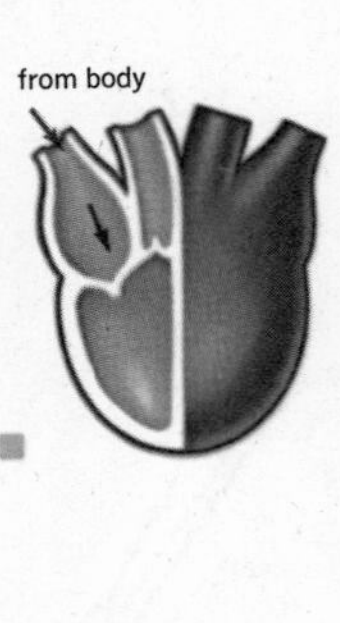

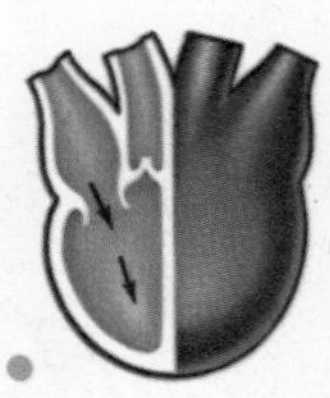

D. Circulation—The Heart

Put your hand over your heart. What is it that you feel ❶ beating? Powerful muscles of your heart are contracting and expanding and forcing blood through your body. They do this about 70 times every minute, on the average. The expanding and contracting of the muscles cause the heart to beat.

Did you notice, when you were studying the circulation ❷ of the blood, that the heart pumps the blood *twice* on each round trip? The heart pumps the blood to the lungs. The heart also pumps blood to the rest of the body at the same time. In fact, the heart is a double pump. Here's how it works.

Let's follow the action of one side of the heart at a time. Blood flows to the heart through the veins. This blood is ❸ called venous blood.

Part of the venous blood enters a space in the heart called the right **auricle** (ôr′i·kəl). ■ This venous blood is dark red in color, because it is coming from all parts of the body except the lungs. Thus, it is poor in oxygen.

The blood stays in this auricle, on the right side of your heart, for a moment. Then the blood passes into the space called the right **ventricle** (ven′trə·kəl). ●

Now comes one of the two pumping movements, which you feel as a single heartbeat. The right ventricle contracts ❹ and squeezes the blood into a blood vessel leading to the lungs. ▲

286

Continuing Lesson Cluster 4

❶ It is not always easy to feel the heartbeat in this way—an alternate way is to locate the pulse in the artery of the neck about an inch below the ear lobe.

❷ If children do not recognize that the blood traveled twice through the heart from the lungs to the body and back to the lungs, encourage them to retrace the circulation in the diagram on page 285.

❸ In this series of six diagrams, children should be made aware that the drawings are shown as if the person owning the heart is facing the reader. Therefore, the right side of the heart in the drawing will be at the left.

❹ **Why doesn't the blood flow back from the *ventricle* to the *auricle*?** Refer children to the white flaps between the auricle and the ventricle. When the muscle of the ventricle contracts, the pressure of the blood in the ventricle closes the flaps and opens another set of flaps so that the blood is squeezed out to the lungs. The flaps are known as ***valves.***

Supporting Statement: An organism is adapted by its organ systems to perform its life functions.

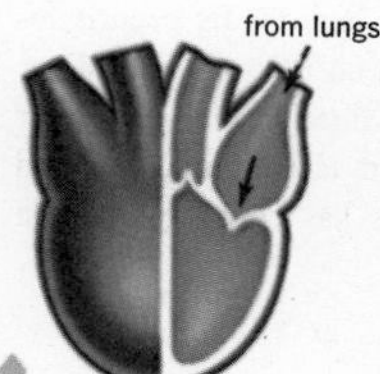

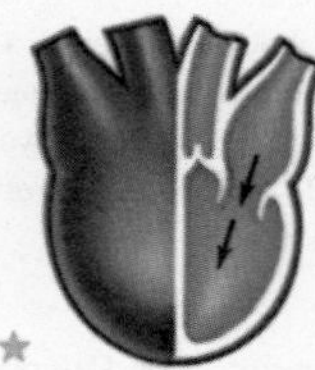

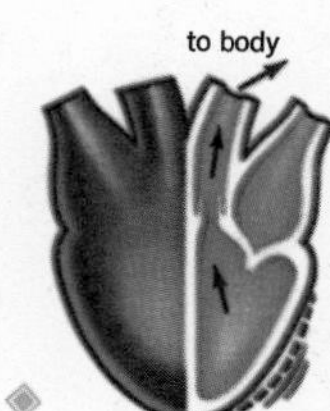

❶ In the lungs, as you know, the blood becomes rich in oxygen. From the lungs bright red blood returns to the left auricle of the heart. ◆ From the left auricle blood goes to the left ventricle. ★ The powerful muscle of the left ventricle contracts. Bright red blood surges from the heart into arteries leading to all parts of the body. ◈

As you see, the heart really is a double pump. The left auricle and left ventricle make up one pump, sending blood to the body. The right auricle and the right ventricle make up the other pump, sending blood to the lungs. Both pumps work at the same time, of course, and in step. ◎ As the right ventricle contracts, the left ventricle also contracts.

Each of these four spaces inside the heart has its own work to do, then, as shown below:

Right auricle	Receives venous blood from the body
❷ Right ventricle	Sends the venous blood to the lungs
Left auricle	Receives oxygen-rich blood from the lungs
Left ventricle	Sends the oxygen-rich blood to the body

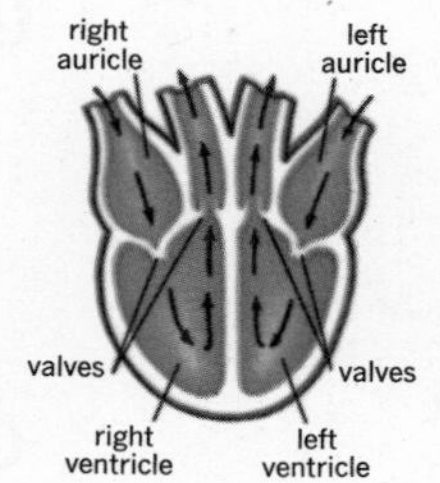

When a ventricle contracts, why isn't the blood forced back into the auricle it came from? Notice the **valves** that separate the auricles from the ventricles. Each valve is like a gate that allows blood to pass in one direction only. When a ventricle contracts, the valve to the auricle closes. The blood cannot back up into the auricle, and instead surges into the arteries.

287

❶ It may be useful for children to make another tracing of circulation through the diagram on page 283. Trace also the action in the heart as blood comes from the lungs and is sent out to the body in the same fashion as on the opposite page.

❷ Try to have the children relate the right side of the heart to venous blood and the left to oxygen-rich blood. **What does venous blood carry?** (carbon dioxide) **Oxygen-rich blood?** (oxygen) However, they should not infer that each side of the body has separate systems. Blood from either the right or left side of the body may enter the right auricle, but the right ventricle will always send blood to the lungs. Blood from the lungs will always enter the left auricle, but this blood may go to any part of the body. Trace the circulation again, using the diagram on page 285.

Unit Concept-Statement: Living things are adapted by structure and function to their environment.

❶ Your heart is a remarkable organ. Its ventricles contract about 70 times in a minute, on the average. How many times have they contracted thus far in your life? About every 60 seconds your blood is sent once around your body. How many round trips has your blood made ❷ since this time yesterday?

E. Movement—The Muscles

Bend your knee. Lift a book. Walk. You do these ❸ things without thinking about them. Your muscles are at work.

What are muscles like? How do they work together? Where are the main muscles of the body? You can see some of the answers to these questions in the drawing on the opposite page. (Muscles are red; tendons and ligaments are ❹ white.) ■ Your body is clothed in muscles. They crisscross and overlap in many directions, as you see. It would be almost impossible to move if all of your muscles did not work together!

Look at this drawing of the muscle called the **biceps** (bī seps) in your arm. ● Move your arm back and forth and ❺ feel your biceps getting thicker and thinner. When the cells of the muscle shorten, the whole muscle shortens, or contracts. Muscles exert a force when they contract. They pull the bones to which they are attached.

Notice how the muscles in the shoulder crisscross and overlap. They enable the arm to move in all directions—up, down, sideways.

The muscle in the calf of the leg is powerful. It raises the heel, and with it some part of the weight of the body. ❻ See how the end of the muscle is attached to the bones of the ankle by a very strong tendon.

There are many different muscles, as you can see. Yet all are alike in this way: Each muscle is made up of a bundle of long muscle cells. ▲ The bundle is bound together by a tough membrane. All of your muscles make up your **muscular system.** Your body is clothed in muscles.

288

Continuing Lesson Cluster 4

❶ If you can get an untrimmed beef heart from the butcher, it may be dissected to give the children a view of the interior chambers and valves. (Be sure the heart has not been trimmed so that all four chambers will be visible.) Unless you have done dissection work, you may wish to enlist the aid of the school nurse or a biology teacher or a student taking biology in a local college. Have children relate the internal structure of the heart to the diagram on page 287.

❷ In 11 years a normal heart will beat 11 (years) × 365 (days) × 24 (hours) × 60 (minutes) × 70 (beats per minute) = 404,712,000 times. In 24 hours, at the rate of one round trip a minute, the blood will make 24 × 60 = 1440 round trips.

❸ Children should not be given the idea that walking or lifting are automatic acts. Were you always able to walk? (no) How does it happen that you can now? (We learned when we were very young.) Some children may have had a broken limb or known someone who has. Let him tell how he had to learn to use his muscles again.

❹ What makes up all the muscles in the drawing? (cells) Let children look back to page 272. Let the children compare the drawing there with the photograph on page 289. Which of the cells there are muscle cells that move the parts of the body? (the ones with lines crossing them) The muscle cells make up muscle tissue.

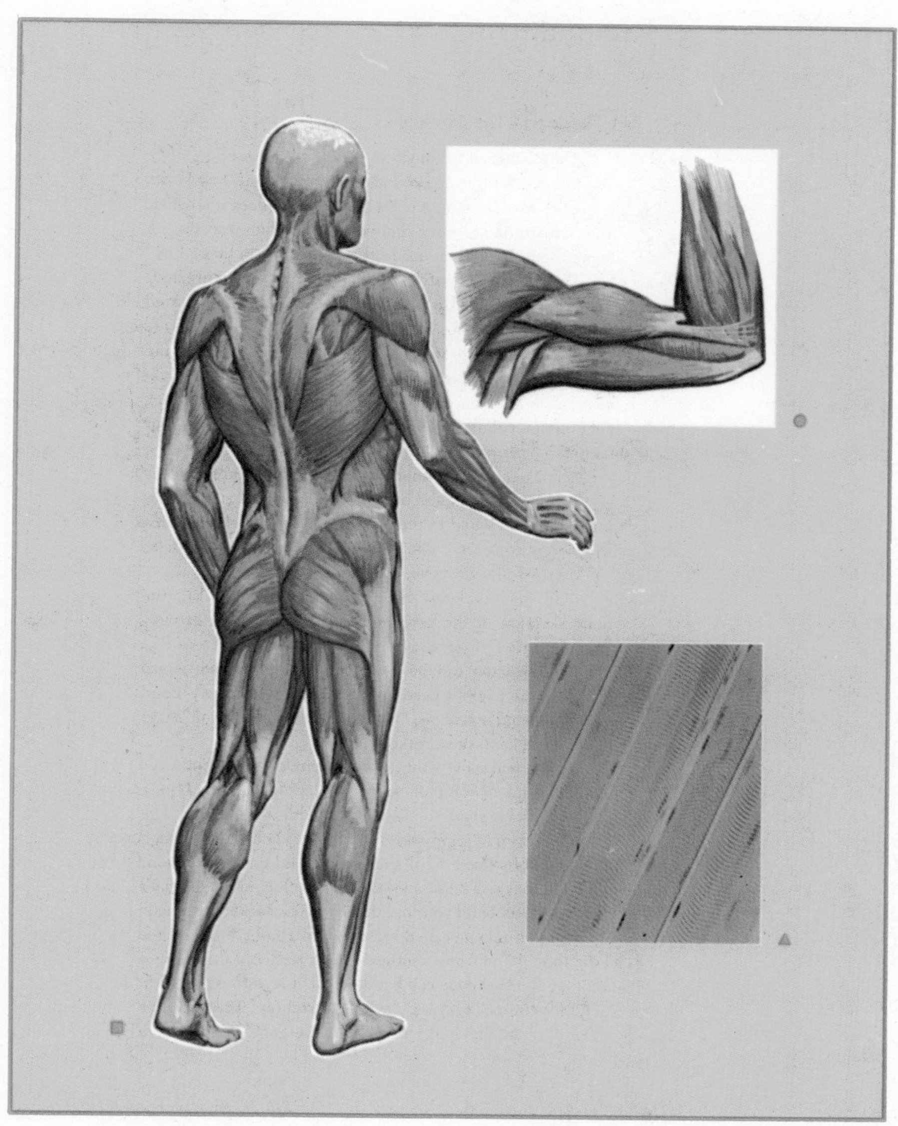

What do you think the ligaments and tendons do? (attach muscles to one another and to bones) If children do not at first respond in this way, help them to interpret the drawing.

5 You have felt your biceps contract when you pull your arm up. What happens to the biceps when you put your arm down? (relaxes, gets longer) Call attention to the muscle attached to the under part of the arm. What do you think happens to this muscle when you put your arm down? (contracts) When you pull your arm up? (relaxes) See if the children can infer that muscles work in pairs to produce motion.

6 Why would an injury to the large tendon connecting the calf muscle to the knee and ankle bones cripple a person? (He would not be able to walk with that leg because he could not push with his foot against the ground.) Tendons and muscles work closely together to give movement to the body.

F. Support—The Skeleton

Think yourself fortunate to have a skeleton.

Some creatures do not have inside skeletons, you know. ❶ A beetle, for example, has no bones. Nor does a jellyfish. Such creatures are very limited in what they can do. A living thing that has an inside skeleton is not so limited.

Have you ever watched a high building being erected? Steel columns and girders are put in place first, making a kind of skeleton building. In fact, the columns and girders are the skeleton of the building. They support its floors and walls and give it strength to stand erect. Your skeleton does much the same for you. It is the framework to which your organ systems are attached. All the bones in your ❷ body are parts of your **skeletal** (skel′ə·təl) **system.** ■

The skeleton does more than support the body. Look at the muscular system again (page 289) and notice how muscles are attached to the skeleton. Muscles exert a force when they contract. The body moves because the muscles are fastened to, and move, the bones.

The steel skeleton of a skyscraper is rigid. But the bony skeleton of the body can move about in an extraordinary number of ways! How is this managed?

The skeleton can be moved because you have **joints.** They are the places where two bones come together. Bend your knee, and notice the ***hinge joint*** in it. ● Can you locate ❸ other hinge joints in your skeleton?

If you will move your arm in a circle, you can observe another kind of joint of your skeleton in action. It is a *ball-and-socket joint.* ▲ The ball, on the end of the arm bone, can turn in any direction in the socket in the shoulder. ❹ Where else is there a ball-and-socket joint on the skeleton?

You have a backbone that holds you erect. What's more, you can bend your backbone. Your backbone is made up of pieces of bone called **vertebrae** (vûr′tə·brā). ◆ Notice ❺ how they fit into one another. Each vertebra can move a little, so the backbone can bend. Still, it is a strong support.

Notice the opening in the vertebra. Through this opening runs the spinal cord, or nerve cord. Even when

Continuing Lesson Cluster 4

❶ **How does a beetle differ from a jellyfish?** Children may be able to mention that a beetle has a hard outer covering; a jellyfish has no hard parts, although its body parts are enclosed in a membrane that gives the jellyfish shape.

How are these animals limited by not having a skeleton? (size, ability to move rapidly in certain ways, not as strong as a skeletoned animal, etc.)

❷ **What important function of the skeleton did you meet when you studied muscles?** (permits many kinds of motion)

❸ Children should mention that the elbow and the fingers have hinge joints. **Why do you say so?** (The joints can move in only one direction.) If children are skeptical, let them try to move a finger tip sideways without moving the joint at the base of the finger.

❹ Children should clearly see the ball-and-socket joint where the thigh bone joins the body skeleton. **Why is it useful to have a hinge joint in the knee and not a ball and socket? What would happen to your walking if your knee could move in any direction? Why is a ball and socket joint useful in the hip?** (We can turn quickly in any direction by being able to step sideways, at an angle, or forward.)

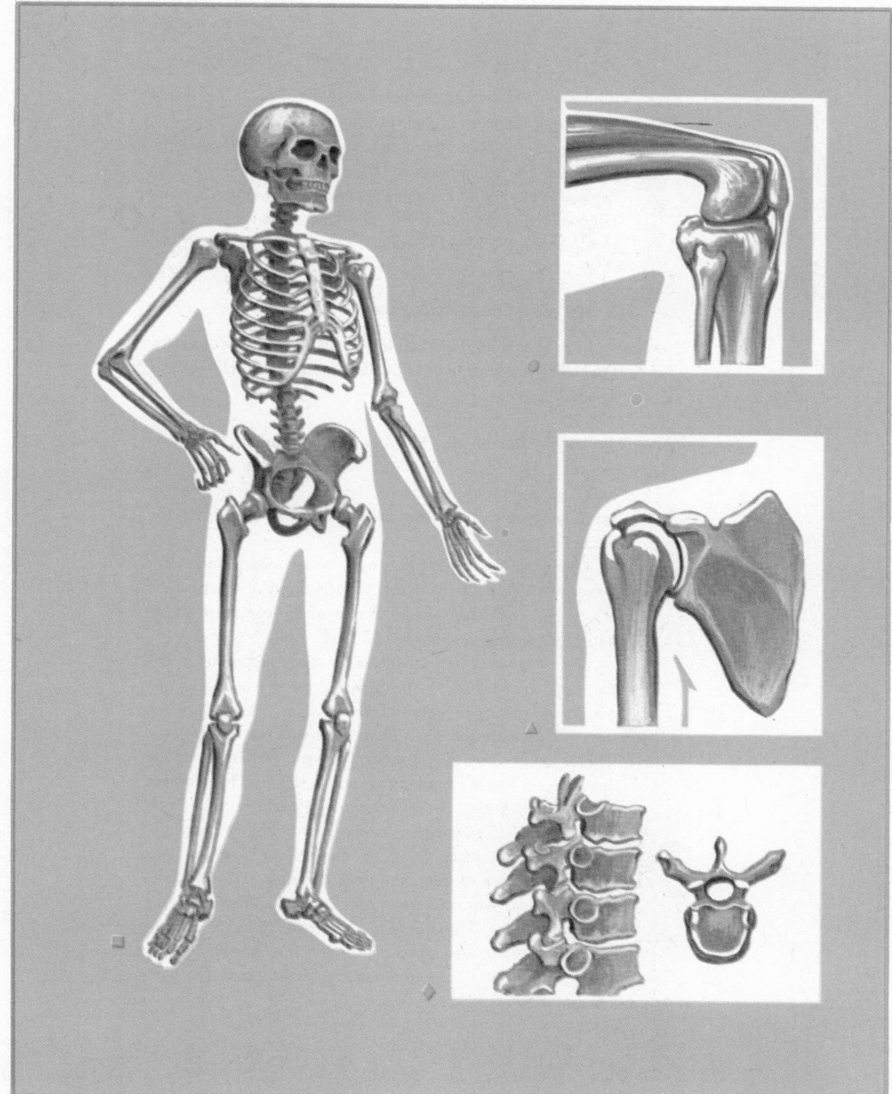

VERIFYING PROGRESS

In concept-seeking

Children may *investigate* motions they make and *identify* two other kinds of joints. Nod your head up and down: What kind of joint motion is this like? (hinge) Rotate your head in a circle: What joint motion is this like? (ball and socket) Actually, the second vertebra below the skull has a pivot on the top which permits all these motions. It is called a *pivot* joint.

In the drawing, notice that the wrist is composed of several small bones. Hold your forearm rigid with one hand while you move your wrist: How many directions can you move it? Children should *observe* that the bones glide over one another. These are *gliding* joints. Where else will you find gliding joints? (ankle) The lower jaw acts like a hinge but it also permits sideways motion by gliding.

❺ The vertebrae act as gliding joints and are connected by disks of cartilage that act as shock absorbers, when you jump for example. Why is this arrangement useful? (One can bend and turn the back a little.)

Unit Concept-Statement: Living things are adapted by structure and function to their environment.

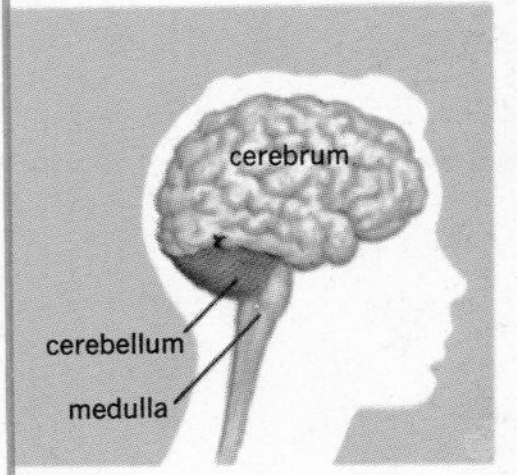

the backbone bends, your spinal cord is well protected inside the bony framework of the vertebrae.

Here is yet another important task that the skeleton performs. As all cells do, red blood cells die and have to be replaced. Inside some bones is **bone marrow** (mar'ō). The bone marrow manufactures new red blood cells to be ❶ circulated in the blood stream.

G. Nerves – Coordinating the Body

■ Try this. Take a pencil in your hand. Close your eyes. Feel what you have in your hand. You can still tell that it is a pencil.

How can you tell?

In the tips of your fingers are nerve endings like those shown on page 275. These nerve endings join together to make up a **sensory** (sen'sər·ē) **nerve.** The sensory nerves carry messages about the pencil in your hand from the fingers to the brain.

Sensory nerves of the eyes sense light and carry ❷ messages to the brain, which forms a kind of "picture" of what you see. The sensory nerves of the ear sense sound and carry messages about sound to the brain.

Some sensory nerves, especially those beginning in the legs and arms, lead to the spinal cord in the backbone. So do some sensory nerves from muscles. And there are ❸ nerves that carry messages *from* the spinal cord to muscles. These nerves are called **motor nerves.** When a muscle receives a message from a motor nerve, the muscle contracts.

The brain itself is divided into parts, each with its work. ❹ The **cerebrum** (ser'ə·brəm) is the part of the brain where thinking takes place. ■ The **cerebellum** (ser'ə·bel'əm) controls muscles so that they work together. The **medulla** (mə·dul'ə) is very important, too; from it and to it go the nerves that control breathing and heartbeat.

Your brain and spinal cord are the center of your **nervous system.** Your nervous system keeps all the parts of your body working together.

Continuing Lesson Cluster 4

❶ Not all bones contain bone marrow in which red blood cells are made. The main bones are the vertebrae, hip-bones, skull, and certain bones of the chest. Recall that red blood cells have a nucleus while in the marrow but lose it when they become mature cells and enter the blood stream.

❷ If children ask how we perceive light, let them look at the sensory nerve endings on page 275. There are endings in the back of the eye (retina) which are stimulated by differences in wavelength of light. These endings go to the optic nerve which carries the message to the brain. The brain interprets the message. In the ear, the nerve endings are sensitive to vibrations that produce sounds. The brain interprets the message sent from the inner ear along the hearing nerve.

❸ Review the diagram on page 275 and the teaching notes accompanying it so that children recall how nerves in the spinal cord permit almost instant reaction. This act is called a reflex.

❹ The *cerebrum* is the center of conscious thought. Why are the *cerebellum* and the *medulla* so important? See if children can infer that telling every single muscle how to work or telling the heart when to beat would be impossible. (These parts enable us to do automatic acts, or acts that are essential to living.)

H. Excretion—Getting Rid of Wastes

When you breathe on a mirror, moisture collects on the glass. This means that your body is getting rid of water as well as carbon dioxide when you breathe out. The water
1 and carbon dioxide are waste substances produced by your body.

Where do these wastes come from? Remember that carbon dioxide and water are produced in your cells as oxidation goes on. When these wastes are given off, we say that **excretion** (iks·krē′shən) is taking place. In other words, cells excrete carbon dioxide and water.

It is just as important for a cell to excrete waste substances as to take in food substances. If either function
2 stops, the cell dies.

Let's look at some of the ways in which the body gets rid of wastes. Carbon dioxide and water, for instance, leave the body through the lungs. The lungs are organs of excretion, biologists say.

The skin is also an organ of excretion. You notice this particularly on hot days when sweat flows freely. This means that the body is excreting wastes through the sweat glands in the skin. ● Notice the coiled shape of the gland. It excretes not only water which helps to cool your body, but substances such as salt. Only the salt that the body does not use is excreted.

3 The kidneys are another organ of excretion. Organs that work together to get rid of body wastes make up the

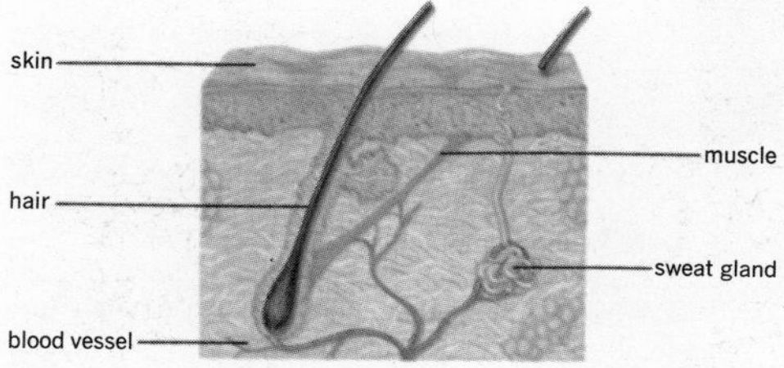

1 If water is a waste product of the body, why do we drink so much of it? When oxygen combines with food in cells, not enough water is given off for all our needs. We need extra water to help dissolve food substances and to keep the amount of water in the blood stream constant. We also lose water by perspiration which helps keep body temperature constant.)

2 Why would the cell die if it could not excrete its water and carbon dioxide wastes? Children may hypothesize that too much waste matter can "crowd out" the food and oxygen that cells need to stay alive.

3 What is the difference between the skin and lungs as organs of excretion and the kidneys as organs of excretion? (The kidneys' main function is to excrete water and dissolved excess salts; the skin functions mainly as covering tissue and an organ for regulating body heat and only incidentally as an organ of excretion; the lungs interchange oxygen and carbon dioxide.)

Unit Concept-Statement: Living things are adapted by structure and function to their environment.

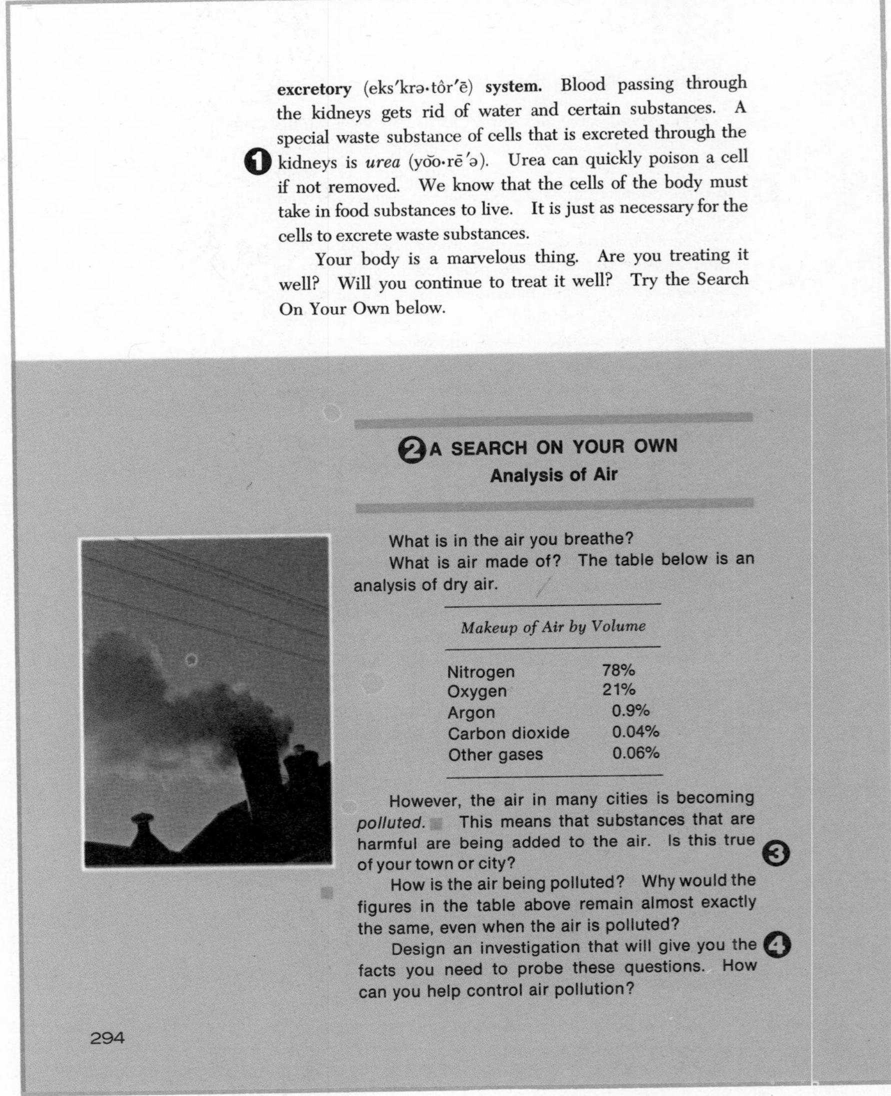

excretory (eks′krə·tôr′ē) **system.** Blood passing through the kidneys gets rid of water and certain substances. A special waste substance of cells that is excreted through the
1 kidneys is *urea* (yo͞o·rē′ə). Urea can quickly poison a cell if not removed. We know that the cells of the body must take in food substances to live. It is just as necessary for the cells to excrete waste substances.

Your body is a marvelous thing. Are you treating it well? Will you continue to treat it well? Try the Search On Your Own below.

2 **A SEARCH ON YOUR OWN**
Analysis of Air

What is in the air you breathe?

What is air made of? The table below is an analysis of dry air.

Makeup of Air by Volume

Nitrogen	78%
Oxygen	21%
Argon	0.9%
Carbon dioxide	0.04%
Other gases	0.06%

However, the air in many cities is becoming *polluted.* This means that substances that are harmful are being added to the air. Is this true of your town or city? 3

How is the air being polluted? Why would the figures in the table above remain almost exactly the same, even when the air is polluted?

Design an investigation that will give you the 4 facts you need to probe these questions. How can you help control air pollution?

294

Continuing Lesson Cluster 4

1 Children may ask what urea is. It is an organic compound containing nitrogen and is the main waste product from the breakdown of proteins in the cells.

VERIFYING PROGRESS

2 **A search on your own.** Children *investigate* the content of the air environment, *identify* products of pollution, and *infer* that pollution must be controlled and kept well within safety levels for good health.

3 Children may look for evidence of smog, smoke from chimneys and from exhausts of trucks and automobiles, strong and unpleasant odors. Pollution adds matter to the air but does not change the normal percentages of gases in the air.

4 Children may also conduct an investigation of the chimneys and smokestacks in their neighborhood that are pouring out heavy smoke. They can also estimate the number of cars in the downtown sections of one town as compared to another. They can help control air pollution by seeing to it that their own families and friends do not add poisonous substances to the air.

Supporting Statement: An organism is adapted by organ systems to perform its life functions.

❶ BEFORE YOU GO ON

Check your understanding of the concepts of this section.

1. Name the organs shown in the diagram. ■

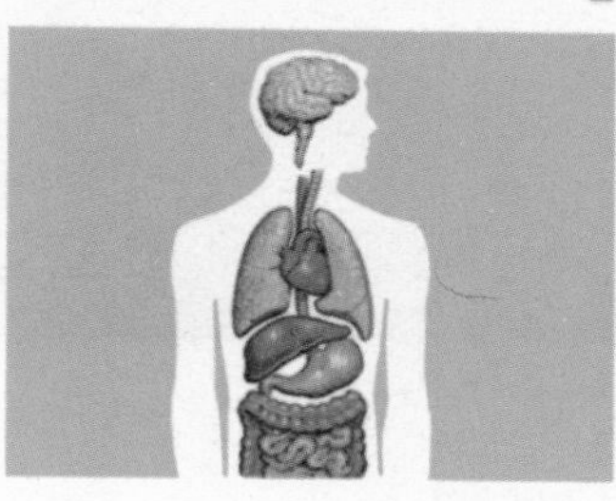

2. Write a sentence or two about the work of each organ named.

3. The statement that fits the main concept of this section is
   a. The functions of the body are carried out by organs that are grouped together in tissues.
   b. The functions of the body are carried out by organs that are grouped together in organ systems.

❷ USING WHAT YOU KNOW

1. Here is a diagram of some organs in the body of a rat. ● Can you identify them?

2. What is the function of each of these organs?

3. How is the rat fitted—by its structure—to live in its environment?

❸ INVESTIGATING FURTHER

Perhaps you have done the Search on page 268. Clearly, people who smoke are taking in substances not needed for their growth.

What other substances are not needed for growth? For example, are certain drugs needed?

The answer to this question may not be clear. Doctors prescribe certain drugs to persons who are ill. Other drugs are illegal, and they are sold to persons by criminals to make money for themselves. These drugs are dangerous, even if used once.

Some drugs you might find out about are codeine (kō′dēn), cocaine (kō·kān′), marijuana (mar′ə·wä′nə), heroin (her′ō·in), hashish (hash′ēsh), and LSD. Perhaps you have heard of others. Peryou believe alcohol is a drug.

Which of these drugs are useful to the body? In what way? Which drugs are harmful to the body? In what way? What is your evidence?

● 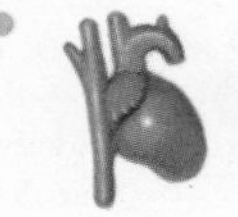 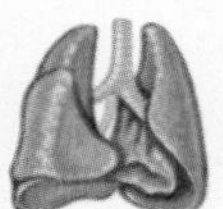

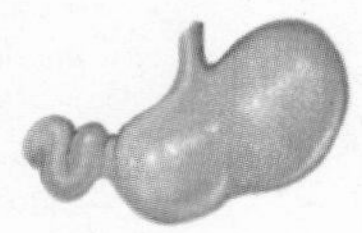

VERIFYING PROGRESS

❶ Before you go on. Children *demonstrate* their understanding of body systems by *identifying* organs in a diagram and completing open-ended statements.

1. For the brain, have children compare their responses with diagram on page 292; for the digestive system, page 279; for the lungs, page 281; for the heart, page 287.

2. Cerebrum: controls thought; cerebellum: coordinates muscles; medulla: regulates heartbeat and other functions that occur without conscious thought; heart: pumps blood to all body cells; lungs: take in oxygen and give off carbon dioxide and water; liver: aids in digestion. Stomach: continues digestive process; small intestine: completes work of digestion; large intestine: collects solid waste.

3. b

❷ Using what you know. Children *apply* their knowledge of human organs to *identify* similar organs and *describe* their functions in another mammal.

❸ Investigating further. Children *consult authorities* on the uses and abuses of drugs; they *analyze* and *synthesize* the information obtained. For a summary of basic facts about drugs, see the Teaching Background for this lesson cluster.

UNIT SIX

Unit Concept-Statement: Living things are adapted by structure and function to their environment.

LESSON CLUSTER 5
THE MAIN CONCEPT: FITNESS TO THE ENVIRONMENT

Teaching background. T-224–228

Concept-seeking. Children increase awareness that living things are adapted by structure and function to their environment.

Methods of intelligence. Children *synthesize* their understanding of the organization of a living thing for carrying out its life functions; they *conclude* that it is through its functions and structures that an organism is adapted to its environment.

Useful materials: Paper skeleton, box or bowl of sugar, potted plant, rock, brick, piece of wood.

5. The Main Concept Fitness to the Environment

FOCUS ON THE CONCEPT

Look at this bowl of sugar. Take away a spoonful of sugar, and what remains is still a bowl of sugar. Why? A bowl of sugar is just a collection of tiny lumps. Taking away a part of the collection makes no difference to the rest.

Now look at a living thing—yourself, for instance. Your skeleton is not just a collection of bones. The bones are
1 joined together, one working with another. Your skeleton is a wonderful structure. What is its function?

Your digestive system is not just a collection of parts. Food tube, a stomach, and intestines work together. Food taken into the mouth is made ready for the stomach; food in the stomach is made ready for the intestines. The parts of the digestive system work together.

Your cells are grouped in tissues, tissues are grouped in organs, organs are grouped in organ systems. Cells, tissues, and organs work together, all doing their jobs—their

296

Introducing Lesson Cluster 5

Display a box or bowl of sugar, a potted plant, a rock, a brick, and a piece of wood. Which of these are living? non-living? How do you know? Let children discuss their ideas briefly before they go on to read the text.

Developing the lesson

1 Hang up a paper skeleton such as you find in dime stores at Halloween, or have children look again at the drawing of the skeleton on text page 291. Why do we say the skeleton is not just a collection of bones? (The bones are all joined together in ways that give support, protect internal organs, and make motion possible.)

Unit Concept-Statement: Living things are adapted by structure and function to their environment.

functions. All the parts of the body work together. Each organ and each structure depend on every other organ. *The body is organized.*

1 Indeed, every living thing is organized—for living. If some part is taken away, what remains is somehow changed. If some part of the sugar in the bowl is taken away, however, the sugar that remains is *not* changed.

Think of a frog. Its parts are organized for living. But if the frog's heart stops, the frog can no longer carry on its life activities or **life functions.** It is no longer organized for the work of living. The frog no longer has the structures it needs for life. Therefore, it no longer can function. Its heart can no longer carry on the function of pumping blood to the cells. Then the cells get no oxygen and no food. The body gets no energy. The frog dies. Its life activities stop. It is no longer fitted to the environment. Fitness to
2 the environment surely means that all life activities go on.

The parts of a plant are organized for living, too. What happens if a plant's roots are damaged? The plant is no longer organized to do the work of a plant. It cannot carry
3 on its life activities properly.

Any living thing is organized. It is organized to carry on its life activities. The loss of any part makes a difference. The bits of sugar in a sugar bowl are not organized in this way at all, as you can see. The loss of part of the sugar makes no difference in what remains. The sugar in the bowl remains sugar.

A living thing is organized to carry on its life activities. But we must add one more thing. A living thing is organized to live in a certain kind of **environment.** It is fitted to the environment. These damsel fish and sea anemones (ə·nem′ə·nez), for example, are adapted for life in the water.

A fish can live in water. It can make use of oxygen dissolved in water, and its tail and fins enable it to move about in water. We say that a fish is **adapted** to live in water. This means that its organ systems are organized for life activities in the environment. Thus, a fish has organ systems that adapt it to live in a water environment.

VERIFYING PROGRESS

In methods of intelligence

If you have pictures of tropical region and desert, of forest and meadow, of valley and mountain top that clearly show differences in the kinds of plants and animals found there, let children use these to *demonstrate* their understanding of adaptation.

Children may use the pictures to arrange a bulletin board display. (The amount of moisture and the mean annual temperature are thought to be factors in the distribution of living things in these life zones.) How is a palm tree adapted for life in a warm region but not in a cold one? How is a cactus adapted to hot, dry regions?

1 Place these headings on the chalkboard: ORGANIC, INORGANIC, ORGANIZED FOR LIVING, NOT ORGANIZED FOR LIVING.

How would we arrange the things on display under these headings?

ORGANIC: sugar, wood
INORGANIC: rock, brick
ORGANIZED FOR LIVING: plant
NOT ORGANIZED FOR LIVING:
sugar, rock, brick, wood.

2 Now let children verify, and, as needed, correct the lists from the text reading. What other organic substances do you see in the classroom or through the window? (cotton and wool clothing, rubber bands and erasers, writing paper in books, etc.) Inorganic substances? (glass, concrete, metal paper clips, buttons, etc.)

Have children add the substances they can see and classify to the chalkboard lists. Let them do the same for the living things that are in view. (grass, trees, fish in classroom tank, etc.)

3 If possible and seasonable, take the class on a ten-minute trip around the school grounds. Ask the children to show you a plant. Pick a leaf. Is this a plant? Why not? Pull a weed or bunch of grass, roots and all. Why is this not a plant? (It will die, removed from soil, moisture, and nutrients.) How is it different from a potted plant? (The latter has its environment.)

UNIT SIX

Unit Concept-Statement: Living things are adapted by structure and function to their environment.

1 The fish is adapted to a water environment. Man is adapted to a land environment. Every living thing is adapted to the environment in which it lives. It is adapted by its structure, by its organs, to live in its environment.

Whenever you see a living thing and want to understand its way of life, ask yourself these questions:

How is this living thing organized by structure to carry on its life activities? What sort of environment does it live
2 in? How is it adapted to its environment?

Robins, oak trees, roses, dandelions, dogs, fishes, frogs—every living thing lives in an environment to which it is fitted.

This concept of **adaptation** is clear:

Each living thing is fitted or adapted by structure and function to its environment.

Put it another way: The way a living thing is organized fits it to live in a special environment.

FOCUS ON THE SCIENTIST'S WAYS

Have you ever had "shots" against polio? Perhaps you know that Jonas Salk developed the vaccine you were given. Dr. Salk's work in developing the polio vaccine was a great achievement. Many people have heard of Jonas Salk, but not as many have heard of John Enders. ■ Yet without the work of Dr. Enders, there could have been no Salk polio vaccine. What did Dr. Enders do? He worked for many years to grow the polio virus alive. In other words, Dr.
3 Enders did *basic* research for the prevention of polio, and Dr. Salk used or *applied* the results of Dr. Enders. Scholars who study the ways of scientists sometimes divide the work they do into these two kinds: basic and applied.

Doctors are experts in applied science. They use, or apply, the work of basic research to the healing of man. After years of investigation, a team of researchers discovered the structure of hemoglobin. Remember that hemoglobin is the substance in red blood cells that carries oxygen to the

Continuing Lesson Cluster 5

1 You have seen how your body structure has adapted you to live in your environment. Which environments could you not live in—at least, not without special equipment? (air, water)

This offers an opportunity to review man's special structures and adaptations. Children now need to see that each living thing, as a total organism, is adapted to live in its own special kind of environment.

2 What animals can live in water or air? If the classroom has an aquarium, a goldfish is a good starter for observation of how animals are adapted to special environments. Ask the children to suggest the life functions of a fish. How is it adapted by structure to carry on these functions in the water?

3 Discuss the difference between basic and applied science. What does the worker in basic science do? What does the worker in applied science do? Place children's responses under the headings BASIC and APPLIED on the chalkboard.

Who works more with concepts? (basic) Who works more with tools? (applied)

cells of the body. Without enough hemoglobin, a person is said to have *anemia* (ə·nē′mē·ə). When a person has anemia, his cells can't get enough oxygen. The research on hemoglobin is basic science. How can doctors apply the basic work?

Let's look at another example of basic science—the work ❷ of Charles Drew. Dr. Drew did research on the liquid part of the blood, the *plasma* (plaz′mə). Transfusions of blood or of blood plasma are often necessary to save the life of a sick or injured person. Doctors who use transfusions are applying the basic research done by Dr. Drew in this field.

Other fields of science also have workers in basic and applied science. The basic work of Isaac Newton, for example, has been applied by the engineers who send astronauts to the Moon. Could the work of exploring the Moon have been done unless basic science had been joined to ❸ applied science? Whose work is more important—the work of those who do basic research or the work of those who apply the research?

❶ What is the evidence that Dr. Enders and Dr. Drew used tools? (Both are seen at work with microscopes.) Workers in basic science, and not only those in applied science, then, use tools.

❷ Children interested in Dr. Drew will enjoy *Black Pioneers of Science and Invention,* by Louis Haber, Harcourt Brace Jovanovich, 1970.

❸ Have children recall (Unit One) that men like Newton (who worked mainly with concepts) are sometimes described as *scientists* to distinguish them from men like von Braun (who apply science concepts) who are sometimes described as *engineers.*

Encourage discussion of the questions in the text. Children will probably conclude that the work of *both* the men and women who do basic research and those who apply the research is important.

Unit Concept-Statement: Living things are adapted by structure and function to their environment.

Focusing on the Main Concepts

❶ TESTING YOURSELF

A. Test your understanding of important concepts in this unit by answering these questions.

1. Here is a list of three types of cells. Two of them belong to the same kind of tissue; one does not. Which one does not? What is the reason for your choice?

cell of skin — muscle cell
cell inside the cheek

2. Cells form tissues. Tissues form organs. Organs form systems, such as the nervous system.

From the following list of cells, choose at least three cells you expect to find in one tissue. What is the tissue? What is the reason for your choice?

red blood cell	tendon cell
bone cell	neuron
white blood cell	muscle cell
ligament cell	cartilage cell

3. At least three of the organs below are found in one system. What is the system? What is the reason for your choice?

heart	large intestine
salivary gland	brain
stomach	small intestine
lungs	diaphragm

4. Imagine a red blood cell in a vein of your left leg. Trace the travels of that red blood cell from the left leg and back again.

❷ B. Test your knowledge with this quick check.

1. Blood with the most oxygen will be found in blood vessels
a. in the intestine
b. going to the lungs
c. in the legs
d. coming from the lungs

2. Proteins, fats, and carbohydrates in food enter the mouth. They enter the blood completely digested in the
a. mouth — c. large intestine
b. stomach — d. small intestine

3. Enzymes help in the digestion of food. The importance of digestion is that it gets the molecules of food into the
a. blood — c. cells
b. bones — d. intestines

4. The statement that fits the main concept of this unit is
a. The human body is the only living thing fitted to its environment.
b. Every living thing is adapted to the environment in which it lives.

FOR YOUR READING

1. *A Drop of Blood,* by Paul Showers, published by Thomas Y. Crowell, New York, 1967. This book will help you understand the blood and how it functions. It contains many helpful pictures.

300

VERIFYING PROGRESS

❶ Testing yourself. A. Children analyze situations and apply their understanding of the structure and functions of the human body.
1. muscle cell; both the other kinds are part of covering tissue
2. bone, cartilage, and tendon; all found in supporting tissues
3. salivary gland, stomach, large intestine, and small intestine; all part of the digestive system
4. The blood cell would go through veins until it reached the right auricle of the heart; then it would go, in turn, to the right ventricle, an artery to a lung, a capillary in the lung, a vein to the left auricle, the left ventricle, and through arteries back to the left leg.

❷ B. Children *demonstrate* their understanding of concepts of the unit by *identifying* correct endings to statements.
1. d 2. d 3. c 4. b

Unit Concept-Statement: Living things are adapted by structure and function to their environment.

2. *Hear Your Heart,* by Paul Showers, published by Thomas Y. Crowell, New York, 1968. In this book, the author of *A Drop of Blood* tells you about your heart. He describes the size and shape of your heart, the heartbeats of persons of different ages, and how the veins and arteries function.

3. *Your Body and How It Works,* by Patricia Lauber, published by Random House, New York, 1962. You have already learned a good deal about how your body functions. With this book you can continue your study of the body's major systems.

4. *The First Book of the Human Senses,* by Gene Liberty, published by Franklin Watts, New York, 1961. To learn more about how you sense your environment, try this interesting book. How we hear, see, and feel are carefully explained.

5. *Vaccination and You,* by Daniel Cohen, published by Messner, New York, 1969. This is an interesting story of vaccination as it has developed through the years. You find out why you should be vaccinated for certain diseases.

❶ INVESTIGATING FURTHER

Do you grow steadily or in spurts? Do you grow the same amount every month? Or do you suddenly shoot up every three months or so? Investigate yourself.

You can investigate the weekly changes in your height or weight for a period of 6 months. Recording your changes will be important because you will want to compare your growth with others. You might record the changes in a *graph,* like this. ■ The lower line marks the date. The line on the left marks the weight.

This graph is the record of one particular boy.

How much did he weigh on the first day of February? How much did he weigh on the first day of March? Has he gained weight?

What would a graph of *your* growth look like?

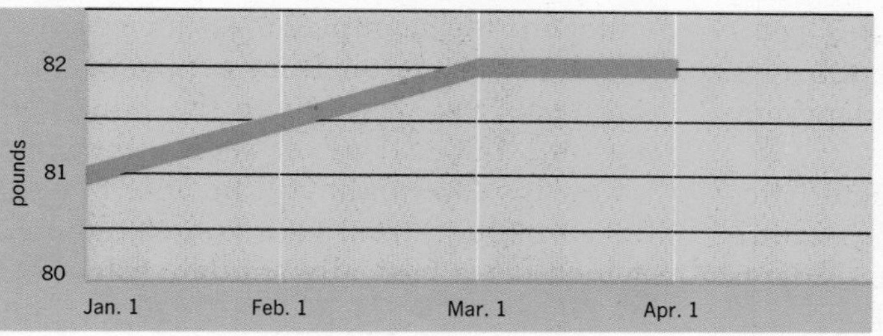

❶ Investigating further. Children *measure* their weight or height over a period of time, record their data in a graph, and *compare* the graphical record of their growth with one illustrated in the text.

Some children may find that they grow steadily; others, in spurts. Some may gain only a pound or two in three months; others considerably more than two pounds. Children should realize that their own rate of growth may differ from that of others and still be normal.

UNIT SEVEN

WE PROBE THE STORIES IN THE EARTH

Basic behaviors sought: Children *investigate* evidence in fossils, and *probe* the relationships between structure and function; they *compare* fossil bones with the structure of a present-day animal, and *infer* that structure adapts an animal to function in a given environment.

Children *analyze* the fossil and *infer* that the age of fossils can be determined by studying the rock layers in which they are found; they *infer* that the dating of fossils enables us to order them in a sequence and determine adaptations of animals to changes in the environment.

Children *observe* how a fish is adapted to life in water; they *infer* that animals in the past, as in the present, had structures that adapted them for living in a water environment. They *investigate* the role of temperature in the environment, *compare* temperature changes in water and air, and *infer* that water is a safer environment than land; they *compare* the adaptations of amphibians and reptiles for land living and *theorize* that inability to adapt may lead to extinction.

Children *seek evidence* of the characteristics of mammals, *observe* the steady body temperature of man, and *infer* that warm-bloodedness adapts mammals to a variety of environments. They *construct theories* in an attempt to *explain* the evidence of change on Earth over millions of years.

A VIEW OF THE UNIT

In past ages of the Earth's history there lived many kinds of plants and animals that no longer exist. A major source of evidence that forms of life on the Earth have changed is the fossil record laid down in sedimentary rocks. On the basis of what they know about the relation of structure and function in living animals, scientists assemble skeletons from fossil bones and make inferences about the structures and functions of other body parts. One example of a particularly complete fossil record is that of the horse.

Direct fossil evidence for the very first living things is lacking. Many scientists believe, however, that the earliest organisms lived in the water. Very primitive forms of life do appear in the fossil records of the Proterozoic Era, an age in the Earth's history that has been dated at over 600 million years ago. In the fossil records from that time onward, structural changes can be traced—from invertebrates to vertebrates in the water, to the appearance on the land of amphibians, reptiles, birds, and, eventually, mammals. At every period, adaptation to the environment can be seen. There have been many hypotheses and theories to account for the changes in the adaptations of living things through the ages as you will read in detail on page T-343. The universality of change itself, however, in living things as well as in matter and energy throughout the Universe, is clear.

1 Assembling fossil skeletons

Scientists who specialize in the study of the Earth's history based upon rock formations and the fossils they contain are known as paleontologists, as we saw in Unit Two (T-59). Putting together bones of ancient animals is a special skill of the paleontologist—a skill that depends upon his knowledge of the structures of animals now living.

If you are familiar with the structure of a chicken, for example, it is not very difficult to assemble a skeleton from a pile of chicken bones. Suppose you were given the bones of a robin, or an owl, but had never seen either of these kinds of birds. You might still be able to put their skeletons together, from your knowledge of the chicken, which has a basically similar structure.

The paleontologist trying to assemble the bones of a dinosaur is in a somewhat similar situation. He has never seen a living dinosaur, and may never even have seen any bones of the same kind of dinosaur he is putting together. But he has studied the skeletons of modern lizards and other reptiles, and the general body plan of a dinosaur is similar enough to these animals to give him many clues.

2 Dating fossils and the history of the horse

Digging up the bones of an ancient animal and putting them together is an important aspect of paleontology, but it is also important to determine how long ago the animal lived. The main way to determine the age of a fossil embedded in rock is to find the age of the rock itself. Radioactive dating is often used for this purpose. As we saw in Unit Two (T-60), some substances are radioactive.

Uranium-238 is radioactive, is found in many rocks, and has an exceptionally long half-life—$4\frac{1}{2}$ billion years. The half-life is the time in which half of the radioactive atoms in a sample will decay. When uranium-238 decays, a special kind of lead is formed. By determining the amount of that kind of lead in a layer of sedimentary rock, scientists have a way of dating the rock. The larger the proportion of lead to uranium-238, in the rock, the older the rock is assumed to be.

Using radioactive dating and other methods, paleontologists have gathered evidence that has enabled them to assign ages to different kinds of rock layers. These ages are called Eras, and each Era is divided into Periods, as shown in the Geologic Time Scale on the next page. The Periods in the most recent Era, the Cenozoic, are further divided into Epochs. When the rock in which a given fossil was found has been placed in the Geologic Time Scale, we have an estimate of the age of the fossil itself.

Fossils of the four-toed, fox-sized dawn horse have been found in rocks of the Eocene Epoch, and have been dated at about 60 million years ago. Fossils somewhat like those of the dawn horse, but larger, and with three toes instead of four, have been found in rocks of the Oligocene Epoch. The Oligocene horses have been dated at about 40 million years ago. Fossils of a horse found in rocks of the Miocene Epoch, have been dated at about 30 million years ago. The Miocene horse was larger, still, than the Oligocene horse, and also had three toes—but two of these did not reach the ground. And in rocks of the Pleistocene Epoch, dated at 1 million years ago up to the present, fossils have been found that are essentially the same as the skeleton of a modern horse. Recent Epoch horses all have just one toe—a hoof, actually.

The fossils themselves are evidence; they may be observed and their observation confirmed. The explanation that modern horses are descended from the dawn horse (or, perhaps, from an animal related to the dawn horse) is a theory. (For further discussion of theories that have been advanced to explain the fossil evidence of the horse and other organisms, see page T-343).

3 Life in the waters: from the beginning to the present

Scientists believe the Earth is at least $4\frac{1}{2}$ billion years old, and some think it may be as old as 10 billion years. Hypotheses about the date of the first living things on the Earth vary, too. There is evidence for the existence of life as far back as the Archeozoic Era. (At this point, and whenever Eras or Periods are mentioned during the remainder of the unit, you will find it useful to refer to the Geologic Time Scale on the following page.) The first known fossils of primitive invertebrates date from the Proterozoic Era, over 600 million years ago. But the very first living things may have left no traces at all, partly because they were probably no larger than a single cell and might have contained no hard substances that lend themselves to preservation. There is, however, good reason to believe that whatever the first living things were like, they probably lived in the water.

Fossils of primitive invertebrates somewhat like sponges and jellyfish begin to appear in the Proterozoic Era. The earliest fossil algae are found in rocks of this Era, too.

During the Cambrian Period, trilobites began to flourish. These aquatic invertebrates were usually one or two inches in length, but sometimes longer than 20 inches. They had segmented bodies, and in other ways resembled modern arthropods—a group that includes shrimp, spiders, and insects. Trilobites were the dominant animal form until the middle of the Paleozoic Era; then they became extinct at the end of the Era.

Ostracoderms, a kind of armoured fish, are the first vertebrates for which there are good fossil records. They date from the Ordovician Period. These early fishes, like modern lampreys, were jawless and had cartilage skeletons. The earliest known bony fishes, with jaws, lived in the Silurian Period. Fishes were the dominant form of animal life during the Devonian Period—the so-called Age of Fishes. Their adaptations to water life included gills, fins, and streamlined bodies similar to those of present day fish.

The first known land plants appeared during the Silurian Period; by the time of the Devonian Period, they were well established and widespread.

4 Animal life on the land

Modern amphibians, such as the frog, spend part of their lives in the water and part on the land. In a sense, they represent a bridge between life in the water and life on the land, and they may be the direct descendants of the first vertebrates to take up life on the land. These may have been the ancient lobe-finned fish, which, like the lungfish, had a swim bladder that became a simple kind of lung. Fossils of the first amphibians date from the Devonian Period.

GEOLOGIC TIME SCALE

Era	*Period*	*Epoch*	*Approximate Time*	*Plants*	*Animals*	*Climates*
CENOZOIC	Quaternary	Recent		Herbaceous plants dominant. Decrease of trees.	Man dominant. Insects abundant. Many large mammals extinct.	Changes of seasons and climate zones as we know them today.
		Pleistocene	2 million years ago			
	Tertiary	Pliocene	13 million years ago	Herbaceous plants numerous. Grasslands on increase.	Mammals abundant.	Cooler climates well-established away from equator.
		Miocene	25 million years ago	Forests shrinking. Beginnings of grasslands.	Increase of mammals.	Climates cooling and becoming less humid.
		Oligocene	36 million years ago	Tropical forests throughout world.	Appearance of modern mammals.	Warm and humid climates still prevalent.
		Eocene	58 million years ago	Spread of angiosperms.	Archaic mammals.	Climate zones established.
		Paleocene	63 million years ago	Rise of modern angiosperms.	Expansion of mammals.	Climate zones first appear.
MESOZOIC	Cretaceous		135 million years ago	Spread of flowering plants. Decrease of gymnosperms.	Decrease of reptiles. Climax of dinosaurs, later extinct. First modern bony fish.	Generally warm and humid climates, but some variation.
	Jurassic		180 million years ago	First flowering plants. Gymnosperms and cycads dominant.	First birds and mammals. Giant dinosaurs abundant.	Worldwide warm and humid climates.
	Triassic		230 million years ago	Increase of gymnosperms. First cycads.	First dinosaurs. Appearance of mammal-like reptiles.	Worldwide tropical and subtropical climates.
PALEOZOIC	Permian		280 million years ago	Decrease of ancient plants. Seed ferns disappear.	Expansion of primitive reptiles.	Variable climates. Glaciers in southern hemisphere.
	Carboniferous		345 million years ago	Primitive gymnosperms. Tropical fern forests. Club mosses, horsetails, and seed ferns.	First reptiles. Amphibians dominant on land. Expansion of insects.	Climate warm and humid throughout world.
	Devonian		405 million years ago	First extensive vascular land plants.	First amphibians. First insects. Age of Fish.	Quite warm uniform climate, but some drying out.
	Silurian		425 million years ago	First known land plants.	Extensive spread of invertebrates.	Slight cooling and extensive drying toward end of period.
	Ordovician		500 million years ago	No known land plants. Marine algae widespread.	Earliest known fish.	Uniformly warm climate.
	Cambrian		600 million years ago	Marine algae, fungi, and bacteria.	Appearance of many marine invertebrates.	Climate becoming warmer.
PROTEROZOIC			???	Earliest fossil algae.	First known fossils. Primitive Invertebrates	Cool climate with glaciers earlier.
ARCHEOZOIC				No known plant fossils.	Evidence of life, but no recognizable fossils.	? ? ?

The first known reptiles appeared during the Carboniferous Period, while ancient amphibians were the dominant form of animal life. Forests of huge, ancient seed ferns were the dominant form of plant life at that time. Reptiles were better adapted for life on the land than were the amphibians; and in time, the reptiles became dominant. During the Permian period, primitive reptiles became more abundant, and during the Triassic Period, the first dinosaurs appeared. Gymnosperms, a group of plants that include modern pines and firs, were better adapted for life on land than ferns. Thus, the gymnosperms became the dominant plants.

The first birds and mammals appeared while the dinosaurs were flourishing. It was not until after the Age of Dinosaurs, which covered the whole Mesozoic Era and came to a climax in the Cretaceous Period, that mammals began to increase and develop significantly. But increase they did, and the Cenozoic Era became the Age of Mammals.

5 The adaptations of mammals and theories of change

The earliest mammals were small, but some of their adaptations for survival on the land were superior to those of the huge dinosaurs that dominated the land when mammals first appeared.

Mammals are warm-blooded, for example; this adaptation makes it possible for an animal to be just as active in cold weather as in warm weather. The care that mammals give their young, including feeding by means of mammary glands, is another advantageous adaptation.

Man, too, has a fossil record. Some fossils of man have been dated as far back as over a million years ago—in the Pleistocene Period.

The fossil records are impressive evidence that life on the Earth today is not the same as it was at many different times in the past. And if past organisms are the ancestors of present ones, there must be a way in which hereditary characteristics can change. The evidence indicates that this is true. Changes known as mutations have been observed to take place, in which mutant offspring have traits unlike those of either parent or any known ancestor. If the change is a true mutation, the new trait may be inherited by succeeding generations. From what we know about heredity, it is clear that mutations involve some sort of change in the DNA of the chromosomes.

Darwin's Theory of Natural Selection indicates that inheritable changes in organisms do take place through small variations. The original form of his theory, of course, was published in 1859 before the term *mutation* was in use, and before either chromosomes or DNA had been discovered. In brief, the assumptions of the theory as first stated by Darwin are as follows:

1. The number of organisms that a favorable environment can support is limited.
2. Organisms vary widely. They vary in the traits that adapt them to the environment.
3. Those organisms whose variations best adapt them to the environment tend to survive.

In short, the environment selects those organisms best adapted to it. This selection is known as natural selection; hence the Theory of Natural Selection. The Theory of Natural Selection is based in part on the fossil evidence.

Many theories beside the one of Charles Darwin have been proposed to explain the existence of animals and plants and fossils as we now see them. This section contains a brief summary of the most important of these theories, with some comments upon Darwin's own theory.

Until Darwin published his *Origin of Species* in 1859, the most widespread explanation of the existence of living creatures was some variant of the theory of divine special creation. In Christian countries the vast majority of people believed the account of creation given in Genesis, the first book of the Bible. Genesis states that God created the heaven and the earth and all living creatures in six days. God, according to Genesis, created each kind of animal and plant. It was believed that these kinds had remained constant up to the present day. People saw that animals and plants were amazingly well adapted for their ways of life and they believed this could happen only through the handiwork of God. Many of the greatest thinkers during the seventeenth, eighteenth, and early nineteenth centuries believed this doctrine, including Sir Isaac Newton. It is still supported by some groups, notably among them the various groups of Creationists.

During the eighteenth century, however, evidence of fossil remains grew rapidly. Fossils seemed to be the remains of animals and plants which had once lived on the earth. The fossil record indicated that new forms of life had come into existence and that many forms of life had become extinct. But this evidence did not influence most biologists to give up the special theory of creation. They believed that God had caused certain catastrophes, such as the great flood described in Genesis, and that these catastrophes had caused some forms of life to disappear. After each catastrophe, God created new forms of life which took the place of the older forms that had disappeared. This theory of a succession of special creations was popularized by Georges Cuvier (1769–1832), the great anatomist. Cuvier was probably the most respected biologist of his time. Because of his influence, in the fifty years before Darwin's *Origin of Species,* more biologists believed Cuvier's theory of a succession of special creations of life than any other theory.

Charles Darwin's theory of evolution was, of course, much different from the theories of special creation described above. But it is essential to understand that Darwin's Theory of Natural Selection, the mechanism of evolution, was a theory of how one species could change into another. Natural selection does not account for the actual origin of life in the first place. In the last sentence of the *Origin of Species* (Sixth Edition), Darwin speaks of life "having been originally breathed by the Creator into a few forms or into one." Thus Darwin believed in divine special creation for the *origin* of life; but he believed natural selection explained how the original form or forms of life changed into the species of animals and plants we observe today. The difference between Darwin's theory of evolution and the theories of special creation may be simply stated. The Creationists believed that the Creator made all the kinds of life and that these kinds had remained true to type over the years. Darwin believed that the Creator made only one or a few forms of life which had changed through evolution by natural selection into the species observable today.

Charles Darwin's *Origin of Species* stirred two major reactions. First, the book convinced most biologists that evolution of species had actually occurred. Second, it aroused opposition to his Theory of Natural Selection. In the fifty years following the first publication of the *Origin of Species,* a number of biologists, though agreeing with Darwin that species had evolved, proposed other mechanisms of evolution to replace the theory of natural selection. Three major alternatives to Darwin's theory of natural selection were proposed.

1. *Lamarckism,* or the inheritance of acquired characteristics. Jean Baptiste Lamarck (1744–1829) was a French biologist who lived a generation before Charles Darwin. He believed strongly, as Darwin did later, that the animals and plants he observed had evolved from earlier, more primitive forms. He noticed that if an animal or plant were removed from its usual surroundings and put into a different environment, it would develop physical characteristics in conformity with the new environment. For example, people who are blinded often develop their sense of hearing to a higher degree than other humans. Lamarck believed that the newly acquired characters could be passed on to the following generations because the internal organization of the organism was altered. Thus the evolution of one form of life into another proceeded by the inheritance of acquired characters.

Lamarck's theory of evolution gained little attention until Darwin convinced biologists that evolution of species had occurred. Then some of the biologists who found the Theory of Natural Selection repugnant turned to the inheritance of acquired characteristics as the mechanism of evolution. Lamarckism was a popular theory in the late nineteenth century, especially among biologists in the United States. During the twentieth century much evidence accumulated against the theory, but as late as the mid-1950's the inheritance of acquired characteristics was considered by Russian biologists to be the primary mechanism of evolution.

2. *Orthogenesis,* or directed evolution. Some biologists disliked Darwin's Theory of Natural Selection because it depended upon the chance hereditary variations which appeared in a population. But the process of evolution appeared to have purpose. Thus these biologists thought evolution must be a directed process and tried to eliminate the factor of chance. They proposed that the variations which appeared in a population were not random but were directed by God or by a nonmaterial biological force. They pointed to fossil remains of some grazing animals that had developed horns of a prodigious length. The fossil record showed that these animals at one time had relatively short horns, but that the horns got longer and longer over a period of time until the animals died out, presumably because they could no longer defend themselves. This example indicated that the variations were directed, but in the wrong direction for survival. One major fact of evolution which the upholders of orthogenesis believed they could explain was why organisms had become more and more complex during the process of evolution. It was because evolution was directed by a nonmaterial force guiding the production of variations. The theory of orthogenesis attracted much attention in the late nineteenth century, and appealed to many philosophers as well as biologists. Interest has

declined in this theory in the twentieth century. There are still some important recent thinkers, among them Father Teilhard de Chardin, who strongly support the theory of orthogenesis.

3. *Heterogenesis,* or evolution by large mutational leaps. Darwin's theory of evolution rested upon the belief that natural selection acted upon very small variations. Thus the process of evolution was slow and gradual. Even some of Darwin's closest friends, including Thomas H. Huxley ("Darwin's bulldog") and Francis Galton (Darwin's cousin), thought that evolution proceeded by large discontinuous leaps. They pointed to such examples as the origin of the Ancon sheep, a variety with very short stubby legs. One of them had appeared suddenly in a flock of normal sheep. By breeding from this one unusual individual, breeders produced a whole new variety of sheep with short legs in only a few generations.

The adherents of heterogenesis claimed that natural selection could not be effective when acting on only the very small variations, as Darwin believed. In 1901 the Dutch biologist Hugo de Vries published a book in which he presented what he believed were examples of large mutational leaps. He had actually observed the creation of the new true breeding varieties among his stocks of *Oenothera Lamarckiana,* the evening primrose. DeVries' book attracted so much attention from biologists that until about 1920 Darwin's theory of natural selection was less popular among biologists than de Vries' theory of mutational leaps. But it was discovered that de Vries was mistaken in his examples. His new varieties were shown to be semi-permanent hybrids. Furthermore, some biologists performed experiments which strongly supported Darwin's belief that the selection of small variations could change a species. Thus, by about 1920, most biologists had come back again to Darwin's Theory of Natural Selection as the mechanism of evolution.

Especially in the twentieth century, many biologists and chemists were unhappy with Darwin's suggestion that the Creator had breathed life into one or a few forms of life. They wanted to prove that life could have evolved on the earth without the direct help of the Creator. In 1938 a Russian scientist, A. I. Oparin, published a book in which he proposed a theory of chemical evolution which might have taken place on the surface of the earth and which could have led to the first forms of life on this planet. Since the time Oparin published this book, other possibilities for the chemical evolution of life have been proposed. Moreover, some scientists believe that the first forms of life on earth came from outer space on a meteorite.

At the present time, it would be fair to state that the great majority of biologists believe that there was a chemical evolution on the earth which led to the first forms of life, and that Darwin's Theory of Natural Selection accounts for the subsequent evolution of species. This does not mean that the other theories which account for the existence of plants and animals and fossils are undeserving of attention. Popularity of a theory among scientists is not an entirely accurate guide to its truth. If it were, then Darwinism would have been proved false in the early years of the century.

SUPPLEMENTARY AIDS

All films and filmstrips are in color. All films are accompanied by sound; filmstrips are accompanied by sound only if so designated. Names and addresses of producers and distributors are on page F-29.

Filmstrips

Collecting and Interpreting Fossils (58 frames, sound), #10952, EBEC. Shows some techniques for removing fossils from rocks; how to make molds of fossil footprints; how we use fossils to discover what past environments were like.

Fossils and Organic Change (33 frames, sound), #10955, EBEC. Traces the fossil history of Eohippus and its descendants; demonstrates that changes in body structure can probably be correlated with changes in the way of life.

Fossils and Prehistoric Environment (38 frames, sound) #10955, EBEC. Shows that fossils can reveal the environments and geography of the past, for example, the position of a prehistoric shoreline.

Fossils and the Relative Age of Rocks (51 frames, sound), #10953, EBEC. Reveals that layers of sedimentary rock that cover much of the Earth are like pages of a diary that nature has been keeping for hundreds of millions of years.

How Fossils Are Formed (38 frames, sound), #10951, EBEC. Explores some of the conditions under which organisms or their traces have been preserved for millions of years through fossilization.

How We Know About Life Long Ago (41 frames), #431-4, SVE. Introduces the world of fossils, and how they help us reconstruct the past.

Hunting Fossils (44 frames), #431-5, SVE. Shows how fossils are formed; how to identify them; where they can be found; how they are removed, preserved, recorded, and assembled.

Mammals Inherit the World (44 frames), #431-3, SVE. Shows, with photographs from museums, the development of different kinds of mammals from the Age of Reptiles.

Prehistoric Animals (42 frames), #400354, McGraw-Hill. Presents a brief picture history of plants and animals, beginning 500 million years ago and ending when a mammal called man appeared on Earth.

Stories That Fossils Tell (40 frames), #431-6, SVE. Traces the development of plants and animals known today—the horse, camel, elephant.

Up Through the Coal Age (44 frames), #431-1, SVE. Traces the development of life in the oceans and the emergence of land animals and plants.

When Reptiles Ruled the Earth (40 frames), #431-2, SVE. Shows earlier reptiles as reconstructed from fossils—plant-eating and flesh-eating dinosaurs, sea reptiles, air reptiles.

Films

The Dinosaur Age (14½ min.), BFA. Presents the Age of Dinosaurs through the work of museum paleontologists as they discover the fossil remains of a giant reptile and reconstruct its skeleton.

Fossils Are Interesting (11 min.), BFA. Shows how fossils are formed, how they may be found, and how they help to tell us the story of the Earth's past.

The History of Living Things (13½ min.), #1649, Coronet. Shows how scientists infer the history of living things from fossil evidence; how scientists tell age of fossils by location of rock in which they are found, by radioactivity of elements in the rock, and by analysis of the fossils themselves.

Prehistoric Animals (13 min.) Fleetwood. Traces the evolution of life with examples of animals in the major evolutionary steps. Includes plants and their part in evolution.

Science Reading Table

After the Dinosaurs by Carla Greene, Bobbs-Merrill, 1968. A useful book about the animals that flourished after the dinosaurs became extinct. (Average)

Ancient Elephants by William E. Scheele, World Publishing, 1958. A surprising amount of information about extinct mastodons and mammoths has been learned from fossils and cave paintings.

Answers About Dinosaurs and Prehistoric Mammals, by Frederick Smithline, Grosset, 1968. Typical questions about these prehistoric animals are answered in this easy-to-read book. (Easy)

Bone for Bone by Margaret Cosgrove, Dodd, Mead, 1967. Reveals likenesses and differences in the anatomy of vertebrates and how these comparisons contribute to our understanding of animals. (Advanced)

Dinosaur Hunt by George O. Whitaker and Joan Meyers, Harcourt Brace Jovanovich, 1965. An absorbing account of Mr. Whitaker's discovery of the first complete skeletons of Coelophysis, a small dinosaur, their removal and shipment for display at the American Museum of Natural History. (Intermediate)

Dodos and Dinosaurs by Dorothy E. Shuttlesworth, Hastings House, 1968. Describes fossils of extinct birds and reptiles, and how museum exhibits of these are prepared. (Advanced)

The Earliest Americans by William E. Scheele, World Publishing, 1963. Describes people who inhabited North America thousands of years before the Indians. Methods and techniques of archeological exploration are interwoven with the account. (Average)

In the Days of Dinosaurs by Roy Chapman Andrews, Random House, 1959. The discovery of fossil remains of dinosaurs is highlighted by the author's account of his exploration in the Gobi Desert. (Easy)

On the Face of the Earth by Marion Gill MacNeil, Henry Z. Walck, 1959. Describes the lengthy evolution of the Earth and its living things. (Average)

Science Explorer: Roy Chapman Andrews by Jules Archer, Messner, 1968. An interesting account, for able readers, of this dedicated explorer's more exciting adventures and spectacular discoveries. Should inspire readers with an understanding of some of the satisfactions of devoting one's life to a search for scientific knowledge. (Advanced)

The Secret Story of Pueblo Bonito by Mary Elting and Michael Folsom, Harvey House, 1963. A thought-provoking account of archeological findings at an old Indian town in New Mexico. The reader is challenged to consider from artifacts the lives of the inhabitants and, particularly, to deduce why the village was abandoned after being occupied for centuries. With many illustrations. (Average)

A Star in the Sea by Alvin and Virginia Silverstein, Warne, 1969. The life cycle of a starfish is vividly and dramatically told. The competitive nature of the tide-pool and the many hazards of survival are described. The illustrations are particularly delightful. (Easy)

The Story of America's Horses by Louis Taylor, World Publishing, 1968. In the early days in America, the horse was considered only for his utilitarian uses. As horses were needed for other tasks, the role of the horse changed, and horses were bred to fit these modifications. This is a good combination of history and horse lore, enhanced by excellent illustrations. (Average)

The Story of Dinosaurs by Stanley and Barbara Brown, Harvey House, 1958. Principally, a comprehensive portrayal of the dinosaurs at the time of their greatest development, with many illustrations. (Average)

What Is a Dinosaur? by Daniel Q. Posin, Benefic Press, 1961. The book describes dinosaur-fossil discoveries, outstanding characteristics of dinosaurs, and Earth changes which contributed to their extinction. (Easy)

An Analysis of Behaviors in Concept-Seeking*

Conceptual Scheme F: Living things are in continuous change.
Unit Concept-Statement: Over the ages, living things have changed in their adaptation to the changing environment.

Lesson Cluster titles in blue are essential to guide concept-seeking toward the Unit Concept-Statement and to enrich the Conceptual Scheme (*see page F-23*).

Lesson Cluster and Supporting Statement	*Operations Basic to Concept-Seeking**	*Methods of Intelligence (Processes and Behaviors)*
1. A Story About Bones Animals in the past were adapted to their environment.	**Probing** the relationship between structure and function by investigating evidence in fossils	**Analyzing** fossil bones; comparing them with the structure of a present-day animal; **inferring** that structure adapts an animal to function in a given environment.
2. Only Sixty Million Years Ago Changes in structure enable organisms to adapt to changing environments.	**Probing** the record of rock layers and obtaining evidence of changing environments and changing life forms	**Analyzing** the fossil record; **inferring** that the age of fossils can be determined by studying the rock layers in which they are found; **inferring** that dating of fossils enables us to determine adaptations of animals to changes in the environment
3. Life in the Ancient Waters Early animals were adapted to the seas.	**Probing** into the structures that have adapted organisms for living in a water environment in the past and the present	**Observing** how a fish is adapted to life in water; **inferring** that life began in the water millions of years ago and gradually developed adaptations to survive in a water environment
4. First Steps on Land Some sea animals changed and became adapted for land living.	**Investigating** the role of temperature in the environment; **probing** evidence of the changing life forms prior to the appearance of mammals	**Comparing** changes in temperature in water and air; **inferring** that the land is less safe than water as an environment for life; **comparing** the adaptations of amphibians and reptiles for land living
5. Up to Now Mammals have developed complex adaptations to the environment.	**Probing** into the various adaptations of mammals; **investigating** the advantages of a steady body temperature in relation to the temperature of the environment	**Seeking evidence** of the characteristics of mammals; **observing** the steady body temperature of man; **comparing** the changes on Earth over millions of years; **theorizing** in an attempt to explain the evidence of change
6. The Main Concept: Changes in Fitness to the Environment Over the ages, living things have changed in their adaptation to the changing environment.	Children **analyze** and **synthesize** evidence of change into a unifying concept of adaptation of organisms to their environments.	

* *A concept is synonymous with the corresponding operations. In turn, operations are served by relevant methods of intelligence.*

UNIT SEVEN
WE PROBE THE STORIES IN THE EARTH

Teaching background. "A View of the Unit" T-340

Concept-seeking. Children begin their search into the changes in life and environment during the Earth's history.

Operations. Children *probe* the appearance of the bones of an ancient animal as compared to those of a modern one.

Methods of intelligence. Children *seek evidence* from data and *state a hypothesis* to be tested.

Introducing the unit

Suppose you saw a dog burying a bone. Then a few days later you dug up that bone. How much would you know about what happened? How would you know it? (direct observation) Now suppose you dug somewhere else and again dug up a bone. Would you know what kind of a bone it was? (not unless it was like a bone you had seen) How did the bone get where you found it? Let children discuss. They cannot know it was buried by a dog, much less by a particular dog. However, they might *infer* that a dog buried the bone because that's what dogs do. Observation is direct evidence; inference relates an observed fact with indirect evidence. Encourage children to think of other situations in which fact and inference are related.

Unit Concept-Statement: Over the ages, living things have changed in their adaptation to the changing environment.

UNIT SEVEN

We Probe the Stories in the Earth

The man in this picture is almost 6 feet tall. The bones making up the skeleton of the animal were found in rocks known to be 160 million years old.

Here is the same man with his hand on the thigh bone of a present-day horse. ■

1 You may want to think of these pictures as **data.** "Data" means "given." When you are presented with data, you are being given some information. In the data here, there is information about the bones of an ancient animal compared with those of a modern one.

What do you infer from this data? What hypothesis might you make? As you study this unit, see how your hypothesis stands up.

■

1 What data is given in the pictures? (size of man, size of bones) Where do you think the large bones are on display? (museum) How do you know? (display cases in a large room) How about the small picture? (We can't know where the bones are on display. We have only the stated fact that the bones are those of a horse.)

What kind of animal is in the large picture? If children say it is a dinosaur, ask whether this is a fact or an inference. Unless they have actually seen this skeleton of Tyrannosaurus in the Museum of Natural History in New York City, they must respond that, for the time being, it is an inference.

2 Children may infer, and state as a hypothesis, that ancient animals were larger than modern animals. (This will not prove to be true—because a modern blue whale is larger than the largest dinosaur was. Also, there were many tiny ancient animals.)

Another hypothesis children may make is that dinosaurs died out long ago. Still another hypothesis, based on the size of the bones of the dinosaur and the horse, is that some dinosaurs were many times larger than our horse, and that the horse has larger bones than the man. Children may draw other inferences and state other hypotheses. Place these on the board for testing against the evidence they will gather.

UNIT SEVEN

Unit Concept-Statement: Over the ages, living things have changed in their adaptation to the changing environment.

LESSON CLUSTER 1
A STORY ABOUT BONES

Teaching background. 1 T-340

Concept-seeking. Children become aware, through fossils, of adaptations of animals of the past.

Operations. Children *probe* the relationship between structure and function by investigating evidence in fossils.

Methods of intelligence. Children *analyze* fossil bones, *compare* them with the structure of a present-day animal, and *infer* that structure adapts an animal to function in a given environment.

Useful materials: Pictures of models of dinosaurs, toy dinosaurs.

1. A Story About Bones

A scientist from a natural history museum was talking to a fifth-grade class.

"A farmer wrote a letter to us at the museum. He told us he had found a strange bone, a bone as long as he was tall. It sounded to us as if he had discovered a fossil bone of one ❶ of the huge reptiles, the dinosaurs. We decided that we'd better go and see. So we sent out a team of scientists to look.

"Early in the morning, five of us started to work. We studied the place where the farmer found the bone. ■

"Carefully we began to shovel away the soil and pieces of sedimentary rock. Then one digger gave a shout—another fossil bone had been discovered. Now we chipped rock more carefully and gently brushed away the rock chips so that no part of the bone would be broken. ●

304

Introducing Lesson Cluster 1

What is the largest animal you have ever seen? Do you think there were ever any larger animals? Most children will be familiar with dinosaurs. If any have toy dinosaurs, or pictures or models of prehistoric animals, encourage them to bring them to class and tell what they know about the life and times of the dinosaur. If no children have models or pictures, try to have some available to display.

How big was the dinosaur? What did it eat? What was the land like when it lived? What was the climate like? Why aren't there any more dinosaurs?

If children cannot respond to these questions now, encourage them to gather evidence as they progress through this unit.

Developing the lesson

❶ What is a fossil? (the remains of a plant or animal. A fossil may also be an imprint of a plant or animal left in a rock or in hardened earth.)

Supporting Statement: Animals in the past were adapted to their environment.

"Soon it was lunch time, but no one wanted to stop. By two o'clock we had uncovered three more bones! We stopped at last to eat and to rest. Then we went back to digging.

"Whenever we found a bone, we photographed it where it lay. We took many notes—for instance, on how deep the
❶ bone was and the kind of rock layer in which we found it. We marked each bone. The marks and photographs and notes helped to show us which bones belonged where when we got them to our laboratory.

"We spent several months in that farmer's field and collected many bones. We packed them very carefully for the trip to our laboratory in the museum. ▲ ◆

"In the laboratory our real job began, putting the bones together. It was really exciting. What would the animal look like?

"We spent a whole year studying and putting together
❷ the fossil bones we found in that field. Some bones were in pieces. We put them together. Some parts were missing.

▲ ◆

Useful materials: Seashell such as clam, mussel, or scallop; small bone or bone fragment; Vaseline; plaster of Paris; foil food tray, milk carton, or small box lined with foil.

❶ What important methods of the scientist can you find on this page? (careful recording by notes and photographs, careful handling of the fossils) Why were these records so important? (They told where the bones were found. The depth at which they were found might be a clue to their age; records of the way the bones were found would be helpful in putting the bones together later, etc.)

❷ The children might enjoy making models of fossils. One easy way is to use a seashell (like a clam, mussel, or scallop shell) and modeling clay. Children should mold the clay around the outside of the shell and then remove the shell. The impression of the shell is the model fossil—really a fossil imprint. Greasing the shell with Vaseline will make removal easier.

Another way to make a fossil is to cover a small bone or bone fragment with Vaseline and partially embed it in plaster of Paris that has been mixed to the consistency of heavy cream. When the plaster hardens, the bone can be removed. The impression left is a fossil model. For a mold, children may use a foil food tray, a milk carton, or a small box lined with tin foil or waxed paper to hold the liquid plaster.

1 We used plaster to make the missing parts. We could do this because we knew the shapes of the bones. Finally the whole skeleton of the animal was put together. It is quite a skeleton, as you can see from the picture. It must have been a fine animal."

2 Bones and Their Meaning

Look at this picture of an animal that fossil-hunting 3 scientists put together. When they were scattered, the bones seemed to have no meaning. When they were studied carefully and put together, the bones became the 4 skeleton of the ancient reptile Brontosaurus (bron·tə·sôr′əs).

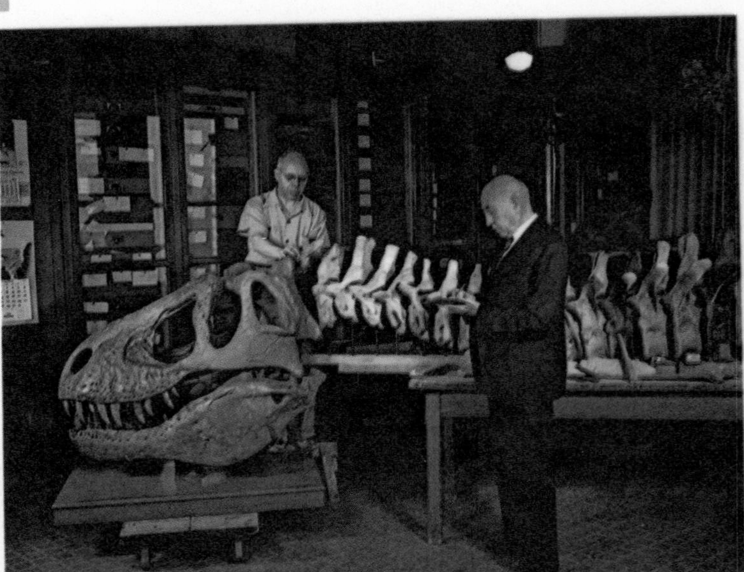

Continuing Lesson Cluster 1

1 How do you think the scientists were able to know what the missing parts looked like? (They had to infer from the bones they had or from the bones of other animals with a similar structure.)

2 Write the title of this section on the board. What do these words mean? How can bones have meaning? What kind of meaning might they have? Let children speculate. Some valid responses are: Bones tell us the means of support for the animal, the shape of the animal, its size, how it moved, what it ate, how many legs, eyes, claws the animal had, etc. What are the facts? (bones and their shape) What are the inferences we can draw? (how the structures aided the animal in its activities)

3 Why do you think it took fifteen years to put together a skeleton of Brontosaurus? (slow, delicate work, with time for frequent reference to similar parts of related forms)

4 If you or the children have pictures or other models of Brontosaurus, place them on display. Let children measure off 70 to 80 feet—the length of a full-grown Brontosaurus. If our classroom is 25 feet wide how many classrooms would have to be put together to exhibit Brontosaurus? (a little over three)

Brontosaurus weighed around 38 tons. A ton is 2,000 pounds. How many boys and girls weighing 100 pounds each would equal the weight of one Brontosaurus? (The number of 100-pound boys and girls in one ton is 20. The number equalling Brontosaurus in weight is: 20 × 38 = 760!)

Supporting Statement: Animals in the past were adapted to their environment.

Brontosaurus was a type of dinosaur that lived on the Earth about 150 million years ago. The name Brontosaurus means ❶ "thunder lizard."

When Brontosaurus was alive, many other reptiles lived on Earth. The remains of the dinosaurs, however, became fossils. From these fossils, scientists are building up a ❷ picture of the world in which the dinosaurs lived.

How do scientists go about putting bones together to make an animal they've never seen? To get an idea of how this is done, try putting some bones together. Try the investigation on the next page. INVESTIGATE

❶ The name "dinosaur" comes from two Greek words—*deimos* meaning "terrible" and *saurus* meaning "lizard." Dinosaur is the group term; each type of dinosaur was named as a kind of lizard by changing the prefix. Brontosaurus was called the thunder lizard, possibly because its tremendous weight would have caused the ground beneath it to rumble as it walked.

❷ When Brontosaurus lived in the western United States, the region was a humid swamp with a lush growth of green plants. Scientists believe that Brontosaurus was a plant-eater, and that it was at home both in water and on land. The swamps of its day provided it with plenty of food. Living part of the time in the water could have been useful to Brontosaurus. Water has a buoying effect, so that its great weight would put less of a strain on its body system than continental land-living. Of course we don't know; we can only infer that Brontosaurus was adapted by his structures to both land and water environments.

Performance objectives. Children *order* the arrangement of the bones of the leg of a chicken, when given the separated bones. They *identify* the ball on the end of the thigh bone and the socket of the hip bone.

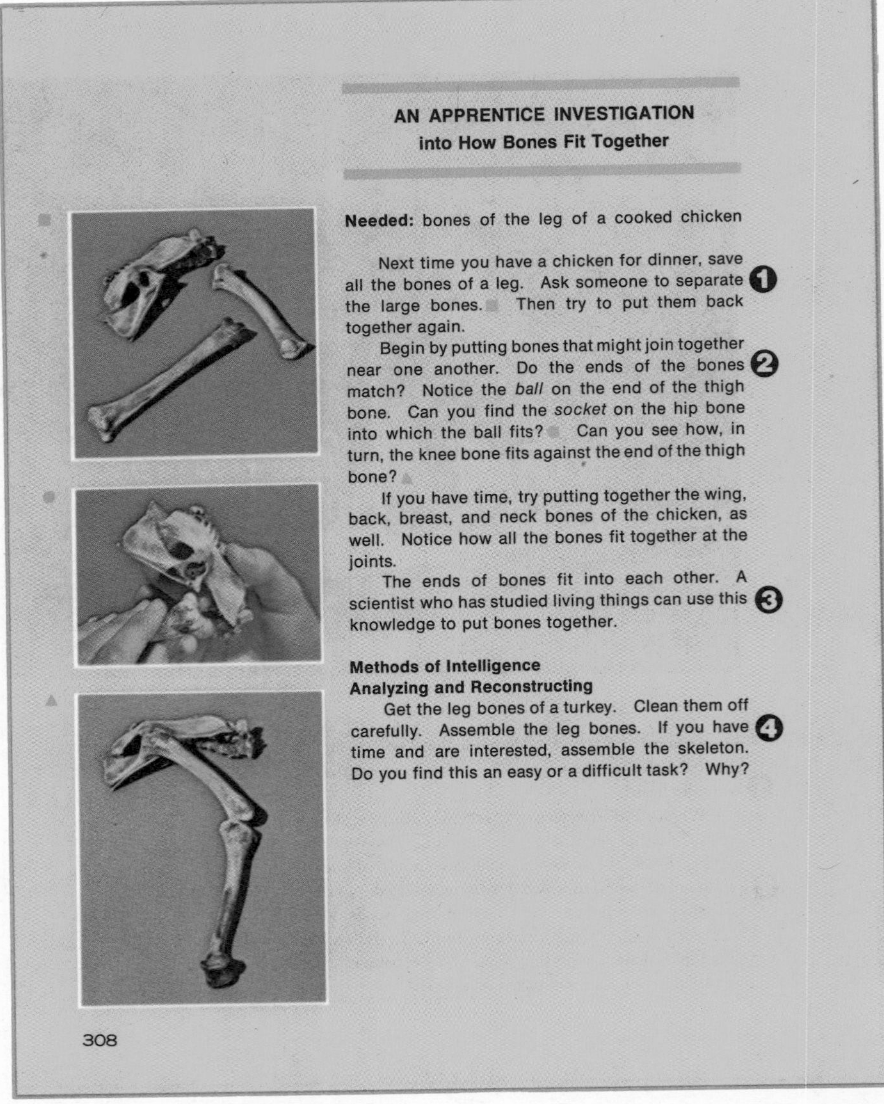

AN APPRENTICE INVESTIGATION into How Bones Fit Together

Needed: bones of the leg of a cooked chicken

Next time you have a chicken for dinner, save all the bones of a leg. Ask someone to separate the large bones. Then try to put them back together again. ❶

Begin by putting bones that might join together near one another. Do the ends of the bones match? Notice the *ball* on the end of the thigh bone. Can you find the *socket* on the hip bone into which the ball fits? Can you see how, in turn, the knee bone fits against the end of the thigh bone? ❷

If you have time, try putting together the wing, back, breast, and neck bones of the chicken, as well. Notice how all the bones fit together at the joints.

The ends of bones fit into each other. A scientist who has studied living things can use this knowledge to put bones together. ❸

Methods of Intelligence
Analyzing and Reconstructing

Get the leg bones of a turkey. Clean them off carefully. Assemble the leg bones. If you have time and are interested, assemble the skeleton. Do you find this an easy or a difficult task? Why? ❹

308

Continuing Lesson Cluster 1

❶ To make bone separation easier and to remove fat and remaining meat, it is advisable to simmer the bones in water for 30 minutes to an hour. If boiling is not practical, use a stiff brush and running water to clean bones.

❷ If this investigation is to be done by several groups of children, it is essential that the bones from one chicken be kept separate from those of another. Differences in the size of the chickens may make the bone relationships seem uncertain for children.

❸ How would a scientist use his knowledge of bone structure to fit bones together? (Ball-and-socket bones fit together; knee and thigh bones move back and forth like a hinge. If the bones do not permit the rotary motion of ball-and-socket joints or back-and-forth motion of hinge joints, they do not fit together.)

Other bones are joined for other functions. For example, the bones of the backbone permit a certain amount of twisting motion.

❹ Preparation of turkey bones for assembly is identical with that for chicken bones. Let children compare the assembled leg bones of turkey with those of chicken bones. From bones alone, how might you tell a chicken leg from a turkey leg? (turkey legs larger, otherwise similar in function) Only the most persistent child will be able to assemble the bones of an entire fowl. Gluing should be done with proper ventilation, as glue, especially plastic glue, can have harmful effects when its fumes are breathed.

Supporting Statement: Animals in the past were adapted to their environment.

The Importance of Structure

The shape of a bone and the way it fits another bone is called its *structure*. Look at the bone structure of a cat, a dog, and a man. ■

Observe how neatly the bones fit into each other. Notice how the structure of one bone differs from another, ❶ depending on the job each does.

Put your right hand on your left shoulder. Wave your left arm about. Your shoulder has a ball-and-socket joint. Now put your hand on the left elbow. Bend the arm up and down. You can see that the ball-and-socket joint of your shoulder has a different way of working from that of the elbow ❷ joint. Each of these joints has a special structure.

Scientists have studied the bone structure of animals now alive to help understand the structure of animals that lived long ago. Animals now alive often have much the same bone structure as animals of the past. By knowing about structure, some scientists can put together a whole animal skeleton from a pile of bones.

Scientists have been able to put together animals (and plants) from their remains. In this way, they have been able to build up pictures of life in the past. Scientists have ❸ found the remains of the ancient world in fossils. Many of these fossils formed in the sediment that was laid down under water millions of years ago.

■

cat

dog

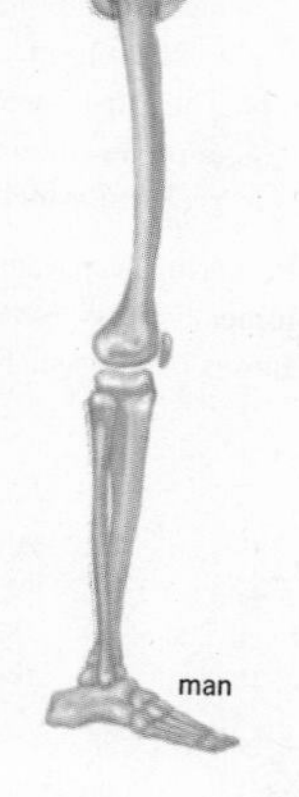

man

309

VERIFYING PROGRESS

In concept-seeking

Children can *probe* the relation of structure to function in bones by studying discarded X-ray photographs provided by the school nurse or a family doctor. Taping the photographs lightly to a window pane will reduce handling and permit better viewing by all the children.

❶ What does a bone in a chicken leg do? (enables chicken to walk around) What does a bone in its wing do? (enables it to fly) Why will the structure of leg bones and wing bones be different? (serve different functions)

Now let the children look at the illustrations of the leg bones of a cat, a dog, and a man. What do the hind legs of a cat and dog enable it to do? (run, walk, spring, but cats and dogs walk on four feet) Why do you think man's leg bones are different? (He walks erect.) What can you infer about the functions of the bones in man as compared with the cat and dog? (They differ, fitting man to his activities in his environment.)

❷ After children have tried the motions suggested, ask them to move their hands up and down from the wrist and then from side to side. How is this motion useful? Let them move their heads from side to side, nod up and down, and then look to the left at the ceiling and right to the floor. How are these motions useful? Children should infer that joint structure differs and that each structure aids them in functioning in their environment to move, sidestep dangers, play baseball or swing a tennis racket, and a host of other activities.

❸ How are fossils formed in sediments under water? Review fossil formation from Unit Two (page 64).

❶ **BEFORE YOU GO ON**

A. Check your understanding of the concepts of this section. Which ending would you choose for each statement below?

1. Parts of ancient animals found in the Earth are
 a. fossils
 b. rocks

2. The shape of a bone and the way it fits into another bone is its
 a. function
 b. structure

3. The living things that are no longer found on the Earth are the
 a. dinosaurs
 b. sharks

4. The statement that fits the main concept of this section is
 a. The structure and function of an animal's bones adapt it to its environment.
 b. The structure and function of an animal's bones adapt it to the rocks in which they are found.

B. Write a paragraph or two on this topic: "How Scientists Know Which Bones of a Fossil Fit Together."

❷ **INVESTIGATING FURTHER**

1. Ask a butcher to give you a leg bone from a sheep or calf. Study the ends of the bone carefully. What can you determine about the shape of the ends of the other bones of the leg, hip, or foot of the animal? How do you think the bones fit into one another?

2. Ancient ferns often formed coal. If you live near a coal yard, ask a foreman if you can look for fossil prints in the coal. Collect these prints and learn to know some of the plants that lived about 300 million years ago.

Why not make a collection of models of fossil animals? You may make them of plaster, or soap, or perhaps whittle them out of wood. The pictures in this section of the book may help you in making your models. You might also use the pictures in a book like *Fossils*, by Frank H. T. Rhodes and others, published by Golden Press, New York, 1962. Plastic model kits of ancient animals are helpful for learning about bone structure.

If you live near a museum, you may be able to make models of real fossils. You and your classmates might enjoy making a little museum of fossil animals and plants.

A LOOK AHEAD

Fossils are formed in the Earth. We know they are the remains of plants and animals that lived long ago.

How old are fossils? What is the evidence? Let's see.

VERIFYING PROGRESS

❶ **Before you go on.** Children *demonstrate* understanding of structures of animals by *identifying* suitable completions to open-ended statements.

1. a 2. b 3. a 4. a

❷ **Investigating further.** Children *demonstrate* understanding of bone structure as it relates to the life activities of an animal by *drawing inferences* from partial evidence of single bones or of fossil prints.

1. If this is a thigh bone, one end will have a ball on it. Children infer that it fits into a socket and permits rotary motion. The other end will have a groove between two mounds of bone. Another bone must fit into the groove and work like a hinge. From the location of this bone in the animal, they infer how the end of the lower bone must fit the foot bones in the animal. If only the lower bone is available, similar inferences should be drawn about the fitting together of the bones.

2. Models, from whatever source, should demonstrate the relationship between structure and function.

2. Only Sixty Million Years Ago

Certainly these animals look quite different. The small animal is about the size of a fox. Notice its toes and
1 its front legs. Now notice the legs and toes of the fine racehorse. The legs of the racehorse are sturdy. Its hooves can travel fast over rough ground. It can carry a man.

Strangely enough, the small animal is also a horse. However, it lived about 60 million years ago. Since that
2 time, many changes have taken place. From those changes came the horse that we know today.

The story begins with the discovery of some fossil
3 bones. When scientists had put the bones together, made a skeleton, and clothed it as if it had muscles, skin, and hair, they saw a small animal.

How do scientists know the animal looked like this? Hunters of fossils are great detectives. They can build an entire animal from bones. By studying the structure of living animals, scientists know how much muscle a bone can carry. A small bone doesn't carry as much muscle as a large bone. Little by little, a picture of the animal is built up.

311

LESSON CLUSTER 2

ONLY SIXTY MILLION YEARS AGO

Teaching background. 2 T-340

Concept-seeking. Children become aware of how the records of sedimentation and fossilization enable us to reconstruct life in past environments.

Operations. Children *probe* the record of rock layers and obtain evidence of changing environments and changing life forms.

Methods of intelligence. Children *analyze* the fossil record and *infer* that the age of fossils can be determined by studying the rock layers in which they are found; they further *infer* that dating of fossils enables us to order them in a sequence and determine adaptations of animals to changes in the environment.

Useful materials: Picture of alligator (or crocodile) and horse.

Introducing Lesson Cluster 2

Show a picture of a crocodile or alligator and ask children to compare the size with that of the skeleton of Brontosaurus. After comparison, explain that the crocodile (or alligator) is related to Brontosaurus, perhaps even that Brontosaurus was its ancestor of 60 million years ago. Then show a picture of a horse, asking: How big do you think horses were 60 million years ago—or were there any? After hypotheses, let children compare the pictures at the foot of the page.

Developing the lesson

1 Children will not be able to count the toes on the fox-sized horse, but they will be able to see that it has no hooves; they should see resemblances in head, tail, and the general way in which its limbs are articulated in comparison with the modern horse.

2 What could have happened over these many years to change the little horse into the big horse of today? Let children hypothesize. Briefly, through hereditary change, development may have taken place in body structure that better adapted the horse to its environment. These changes were inherited and gradually, as other changes in heredity came about, made the horse what it is today. Scientists call these changes successful mutations that are inherited by the offspring.

3 What do scientists find when they dig up fossils? (bones) What do they do when they draw a picture of skin, muscles, brain, and hair color? (make inferences, use imagination)

Unit Concept-Statement: Over the ages, living things have changed in their adaptation to the environment.

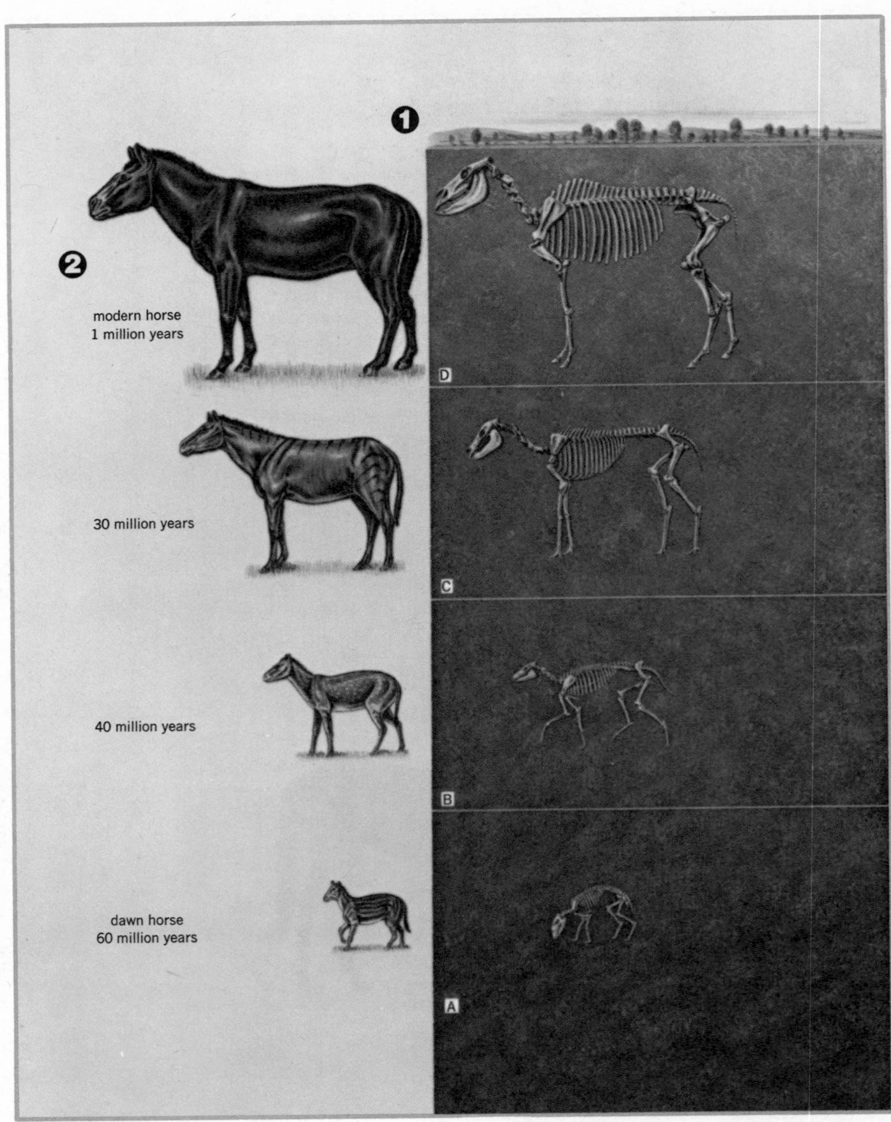

Continuing Lesson Cluster 2

The drawings on this page should be considered in relation to the text on page 313, but it is useful to give children an opportunity to "read" the drawings and try to interpret them first.

❶ What do you infer from the landscape above the brown layers with skeletons? (depths of soil in which the skeletons were found) Which layer has the oldest skeleton? (A)

How long has the modern horse looked much the same as it does today? (1 million years) Looking only at the skeletons, what changes in structure can you see? (Head gets larger, front legs support the frame differently, bones become heavier, rib-cage gets larger, hind legs get heavier and straighter, toes become hooves, etc.)

❷ Now look at the artist's drawings. What differences do you observe between horse A and horse D? (size, proportions) What relationships can you see between the reconstructed full-grown horse and the fossil skeleton? (heavier body, more muscled limbs, larger head, etc.) If children remark about the color of the hide, explain that scientists do not know. The soft parts of an organism do not become fossils.

Supporting Statement: Changes in structure enable organisms to adapt to changing environments.

The Story of the Horse

The animal pictured turned out to be a kind of horse. It was the beginning, or dawn, of the kind of animal we know as the horse. You could, then, call it the dawn horse.

As soon as the first dawn horse was found, the search ❶ was on for more. Scientists searched sedimentary rock layers like the layer in which the dawn horse had been found. They found other fox-sized fossil horses in that kind of sedimentary layer. In the picture opposite, the sedimentary layer of the dawn horse is called layer A.

Scientists searched the next sedimentary layer, the one laid down on top of layer A. It is layer B in the picture. There they found more bones of horses. But these horses were larger than the dawn horses! More than that, these ❷ horses walked on three toes. The dawn horse had walked on four toes.

As they searched the sedimentary layers from the oldest layer (A) to youngest layer (D), fossil-hunting scientists found larger and larger horses. The smaller horses were found in the older layers, laid down long ago. The larger horses were found in the younger layers, the layers laid down more recently. What did all this mean? It meant something simple but astonishing. *It meant that the horse had changed over the years.*

In 60 million years, the horse having the size of a fox changed to the horse we know today. It changed in other ways as well, as the pictures show. Notice how the head changed. Did it become larger or smaller? Look at the feet. The dawn horse, in layer A, had four toes on each foot. Twenty million years later, the horse in layer B had three toes. After another 10 million years, the horse in layer C had only one toe—a hoof—as does the modern horse in layer D.

Try this. Put your hand on a table. Raise your hand ❸ until only the nail of your middle finger rests on the table. Now your hand and arm are supported on that nail. Perhaps something like this happened to the horse. Over the

313

VERIFYING PROGRESS

In concept-seeking

How do sedimentary rocks date living things of the past? Children can *probe* this question with a 15-inch-thick stack of newspapers. From top to bottom, the stack represents 150 million years on a scale of 1 inch = 10 million years. What do the layers of newspaper represent? (sedimentary deposits) Where in these layers would dinosaurs be found? (6 to 12 or 14 inches down) Where would the first dawn horse fossils be found? (about 6 or 7 inches down) What can we infer from the "sedimentary layers" of newspaper about when the dawn horse first appeared in Earth's history? (The dawn horse lived 60–70 million years ago, at about the same time the dinosaurs were dying out.)

❶ How do fossils get into sedimentary rock? Have children recall the formation of this kind of rock (Unit Two). A horse that drowned would be covered with water; bacteria and water animals would eat its flesh, and sediment would cover its bones. Horses of the same kind—or period of sedimentation—would be found in the same sedimentary layer.

❷ How many years seem to have passed before the three-toed horse appeared? (20 million) Children may ask why scientists dug in the older layer first rather than in the top layer. The answer is perhaps that erosion by wind and rain had washed away the three top layers in the region the dawn horse was found. Other regions had layers D, C, and B still in place. The layers could be dated in other ways.

❸ What might be an advantage to a horse having only a hoof instead of toes? (feet would be better protected for running faster to escape enemies, could travel better in rocky areas in search of food, etc.)

EXTENDING THE LESSON

Encourage children to look up and report on the different kinds of modern horses. If possible, they should bring in pictures of the horses for display. Also, if any of the children have ridden a horse, they may describe the various gaits of the horse—walk, trot, canter, gallop, and pace.

If it is practicable, take the class to a stable or a farm to observe how the horse is well adapted for the purposes for which it has been bred.

Unit Concept-Statement: Over the ages, living things have changed in their adaptation to the changing environment.

years, the front foot of the changing horse seems to have lifted up on the middle toe and rested on the nail. The hoof of a horse is a kind of thickened nail.

This has been the story of how one kind of animal changed. Scientists have been able to uncover many other stories, showing changes in many other animals and in plants, too. Fossils of camels have been found in Wyoming. They show the camel was once the size of a sheep! We know that the elephant was once very different from the elephant ❶ of today. Birds were also different from the birds of today. Reptiles have changed, too.

How do we know how long ago these fossil horses lived? ❷ Let us see how we learn the age of a fossil.

The Age of a Fossil

❸ Look at these layers of sedimentary rock. ■ Can you tell one layer from another? Yes, for one sedimentary layer does differ from another.

■

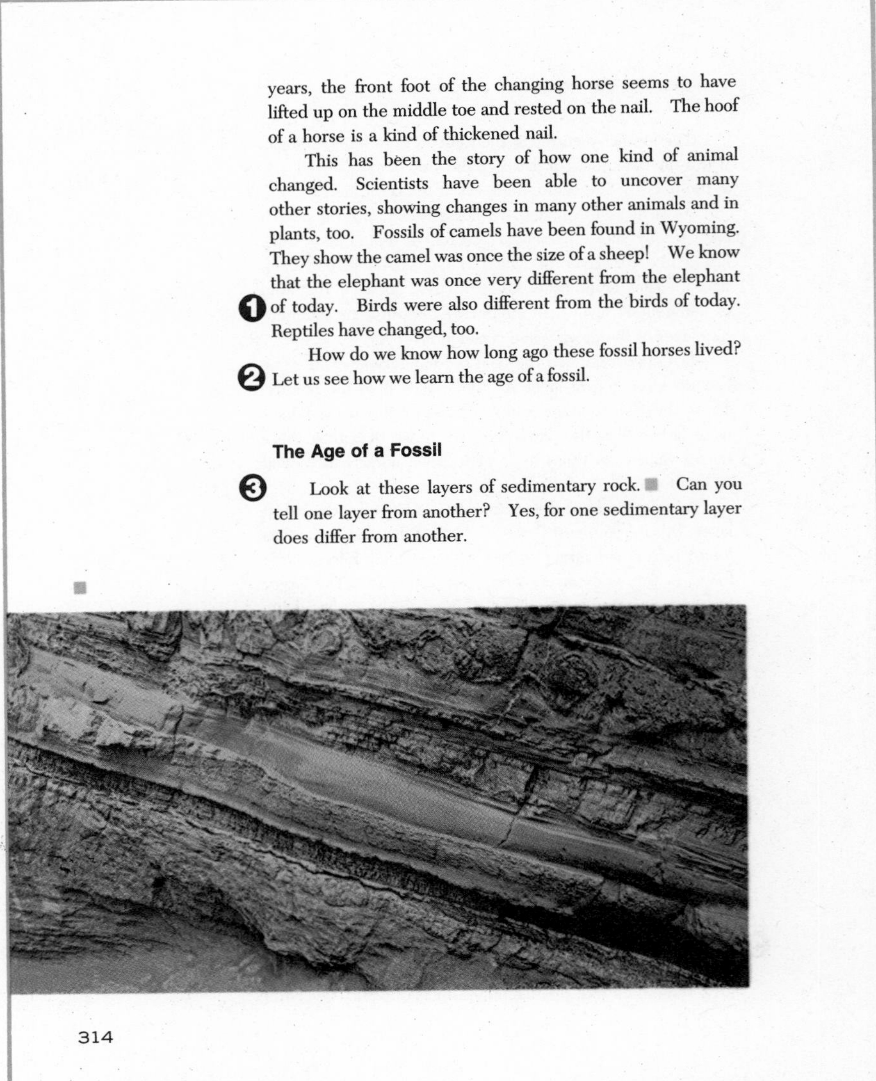

Continuing Lesson Cluster 2

❶ What reason can you suggest that camels, elephants, and birds changed over millions of years, just as the horse did? Children should freely speculate, but you can guide them by such questions as: What happens during a very cold winter to plants in a garden? (Some die that would have lived through a warm winter; the more hardy survive.) What would happen to certain animals if food suddenly became scarce and they didn't have enough to eat? (Only those best adapted—or lucky—would survive.)

❷ Let children hypothesize. If you live in an area where snow is familiar to the children, you might suggest a snowstorm as a model. It would go something like this: Suppose after an inch of snow has fallen, you throw out some sunflower seed for the birds. It snows and covers the seed. Then you throw out cracked corn and it starts sleeting. By the next morning, eight inches of snow have fallen on the sleet. You throw out some more seed and it snows for another hour. If you know that it has been snowing an inch an hour for twelve hours, how can you tell how long ago you first threw out the sunflower seed? the cracked corn? (Measure how many inches the different seeds are from the surface of the snow.)

Children should be able to infer that sedimentation is like a snowstorm. If you can find the rate of sedimentation, you can find the age of a fossil.

❸ You may wish to interpret the coarser layers in the picture as gravel and sand, and the smooth layer as silt and clay.

Supporting Statement: Changes in structure enable organisms to adapt to changes in environment.

In some layers are formed substances that are colored red, or yellow, or brown. Different chemical elements and compounds color the sediment. Iron compounds, for instance, may color sediment red. Soil has color. There are red soils, black soils, brown soils. There are sands of different colors, as well. Thus, sedimentary rock layers may be colored differently.

To know which layer is oldest, you must know which was laid down first. If the layers are in the order in which they settled down, then the bottom layer is the oldest.

Scientists have discovered a kind of clock in the Earth. The element uranium in the Earth is slowly breaking down.
❶ As this happens, the uranium is turning into lead. How fast uranium changes into lead has also been found out. The substance uranium, then, is a kind of clock, keeping time in the rocks. The uranium clock doesn't tell time in hours, like an ordinary clock. It tells time in millions of years.

Suppose a fossil-hunting scientist finds a piece of rock with both uranium and lead in it. He knows that the lead in the rock came from uranium. He can figure out how long it took for uranium to change into that much lead. Since the uranium began changing when the rock was formed, he knows about how old the rock is.

From the uranium clock, and from other evidence,
❷ scientists have an idea of how old the Earth is. The Earth is thought to be at least 4½ billion years old.

Here is still another way of finding out the age of rock. Sometimes scientists can discover how long it takes for
❸ sediment to build up a certain thickness. For instance, in a certain place sediment may take 500 years to form 1 inch of rock. Suppose that the rock is 1,000 inches thick. Then it must have taken about 1,000 times 500 years to form, or 500,000 years.

Scientists do have ways of finding out how old sedimentary rock layers are. *When the age of a sedimentary layer is known, then the age of the fossils in the layer is known, too.* This is how scientists know that the dinosaur

315

Useful materials: Quart milk carton or gallon tin can, brad or large needle for punching hole, water.

❶ As children may recall from Unit Two (page 78), uranium is radioactive. By chemical analysis, scientists determine that a sample of rock has a certain amount of radioactive uranium and a certain amount of lead that is the product of radioactive disintegration of that uranium. Scientists know how long it takes for a given amount of lead to form from a given amount of uranium. They can therefore calculate how long this rock must have been in existence for it to have its relative proportions of lead and uranium.

❷ Uranium dating has been useful in judging the age of the Earth. More useful in judging the age of fossils has been the faster rate of disintegration of radioactive potassium or radioactive carbon (carbon-14). Reports of these methods of dating might be made by interested children.

❸ If it takes 10 years to form 1 inch of sedimentary rock, how many years would it take to lay down the mile-deep sedimentary layers such as those exposed by water eroding the Grand Canyon? (63,360 inches [5,280 feet per mile × 12 inches per foot] × 10 years per inch = 633,600 years.)

To draw an analogy, let children punch with a brad or large needle a small hole in a quart milk carton or a gallon tin can, fill the container with water, and record the time it takes for half of the water to drip out. If it takes 6 hours, how old is the accumulated water in the pan? (6 hours) The analogy might further be refined by measuring the time it takes for specific depths of water in the pan to accumulate.

Unit Concept-Statement: Over the ages, living things have changed in their adaptation to the changing environment.

VERIFYING PROGRESS

In concept-seeking

You may know of sedimentary rock layers in your area. They are often exposed in road cuts through hills to reduce the grade of the road. If possible, arrange a field trip to view exposed sedimentary layers in a road cut, quarry, or other excavation. If a child has a camera, a photograph of the exposed sedimentary layers can be an extra dividend for the display board. After the field trip, have children *demonstrate* their understanding of sedimentation by *explaining* how deposition occurred and can be interpreted.

pictured on page 307 lived about 150 million years ago and that the dawn horse lived about 60 million years ago.

Finding the age of a rock layer isn't always easy. Sometimes the earth's crust heaves up and the sedimentary rock ❶ layers are lifted, split apart, tilted. ■ Huge pieces are separated. The layers are no longer in order or in the place where they were laid down. Even so, scientists may manage to fit the puzzle together.

No man ever saw the dawn horses alive. Yet we believe that 60 million years ago the dawn horses roamed and grazed in the forests of what is now North America. Scientists infer this from the evidence of many fossils that have been found in sedimentary rock.

316

Continuing Lesson Cluster 2

❶ The sandstone cliffs in the photograph form part of the Captital Reef National Monument in southern Utah. In the foreground, rock layers are exposed by erosion and tilted upward towards the bluffs. The bluffs show deposition of sediment in the visible colored layers and erosion in the *scree* deposition at the base. The bluffs were harder than the surrounding land and were not readily worn away. They therefore tell a story.

Supporting Statement: Changes in structure enable organisms to adapt to changing environments.

1 BEFORE YOU GO ON

A. Check your understanding of the concepts of this section. Which ending would you choose for each statement below?

1. The modern horse came from an animal that was about the size of
a. a fox
b. an elephant

2. Scientists can build up an entire animal from a few bones because they have studied animal
a. structure
b. environment

3. The older sedimentary layers have in them animals that came
a. earlier
b. later

4. Scientists may be able to tell the age of a rock layer by means of the element
a. uranium
b. helium

5. From their studies, scientists think that the age of the Earth is at least 4½
a. thousand years
b. million years
c. billion years

6. The statement that fits the main concept of this section is
a. Changes in the structures of animals took place in the past very slowly.
b. Changes in the structures of animals took place in the past very quickly.

B. Write a paragraph or two on one of these topics: "The History of the Horse" or "How We Tell the Age of a Fossil."

2 USING WHAT YOU KNOW

1. Recall the changes in the foot of the horse over the ages. How might a foot with a hoof be more useful on land than a foot with several toes?

2. The fossils of a certain fish are generally older than the fossils of a certain amphibian. Would you expect to find the fossils of these amphibians in sedimentary layers above or below those of the fish?

3 INVESTIGATING FURTHER

Many museums have collections and exhibits of fossils. If there is such a museum near where you live, why not visit it?

A LOOK AHEAD

Scientists who have studied fossils are agreed that they are very old. The fossils of the first horse are calculated to be at least 60 million years old. Suppose we look into life in the waters—next.

317

VERIFYING PROGRESS

1 Before you go on. A. Children *demonstrate* understanding of how to interpret the record in the rocks by *identifying* suitable completions to open-ended statements.

1. a 3. a 5. c
2. a 4. a 6. a

B. On either topic, children *demonstrate* understanding that changes in structure of animals, in relation to changes in the physical environment, help the animals to survive.

2 Using what you know. Children *analyze* situations and *predict* outcomes.
1. A hoof might provide protection against stony areas, be more useful in defense against predators, or give greater take-off and running speed to escape predators. Any or all of these responses exhibit conceptual understanding of successful adaptations.
2. The longer ago the animal lived, the more likely it is that its fossils will be in older layers of sedimentary rock.

3 Investigating further. Children can plan in advance for a visit to an exhibit. Encourage them to make a list of questions on which they would like information. In this way, questions will be more easily answered by the museum personnel.

Unit Concept-Statement: Over the ages, living things have changed in their adaptation to the changing environment.

LESSON CLUSTER 3
LIFE IN THE ANCIENT WATERS

Teaching background. 3 T-341

Concept-seeking. Children develop awareness of the development of complex structural adaptations among animals in the ancient seas.

Operations. Children *probe* into the structures that have adapted organisms for living in a water environment in the past and the present.

Methods of intelligence. Children *observe* how a fish is adapted to life in water; they *infer* that life began in the water millions of years ago and gradually developed structural and behavioral adaptations to survive in a water environment.

■

3. Life in the Ancient Waters

We can go back in time still further.

Let's go back before the dawn horse, before dinosaurs. Let's go back to the time when there was no life at all on land. However, there was life in the waters. How can scientists put together a picture of life in those ancient waters? There are, after all, the sedimentary rocks and fossils found in them.

The early living things that dwelt in the waters may have looked like these single-celled animals and plants. ■ There were no cod or salmon, no porpoises or whales. Only very simple, single-celled living things swarmed in the warm waters, at first.

●

Somehow, from the simple, single-celled animals came the larger, many-celled animals. In time, the seas held not only single-celled living things, but many-celled living things. There were sponges, jellyfish, and many kinds of wormlike animals. These were all animals without backbones, or **invertebrates.** ● ❶ ❷

There was also a strange animal that is no longer around. It was the trilobite (trī′lə·bīt). The trilobite, too, was an invertebrate (without a backbone), in spite of its bony appearance. We know it from its fossils. ▲

318

Introducing Lesson Cluster 3

Ask children to imagine a world in which there were no plants on land, no animals—nothing but bare rocks. There was water, however, in vast seas that covered about three-quarters of the Earth's surface. In this water, there lived large numbers of single-celled organisms. Would you expect to find fossils? (no) Why not? (Single-celled organisms have no solid parts.)

What do you think life was like a half billion years ago? Let children speculate, then begin reading.

Developing the lesson

❶ Let children compare the two illustrations on their textbook pages. What differences do you observe? (Single-celled organisms look a lot simpler in structure than the fossil trilobite.) The top photograph shows single-celled plants and single-celled animals (protozoa) which were able to perform all the functions that enabled them to exist in the early environment.

❷ How were invertebrates different from single-celled animals? See if children can infer that the invertebrates had more cells and that these cells were adapted for special functions of the entire organism. Do not expect children to arrive at conclusions, but encourage hypothesizing.

Supporting Statement: Early animals were adapted to the seas.

There must have been a time when the ancient waters ❶ were almost crowded with trilobites. Scientists believe this is so because many ancient sedimentary rock layers contain many, many fossils of trilobites.

A Backbone Appears

In the older layers of sedimentary rock the fossils are all invertebrates. There were invertebrates that we know ❷ today; clams, starfish, and huge squidlike animals.

Then, in a higher layer of rock, there was a great find. ❸ It was the fossil of an animal with a backbone, a **vertebrate!** This vertebrate was a fossil fish, not more than a foot long, called the ostracoderm (os·trak′o·dûrm). Unlike any fish alive today, the ostracoderm was covered with hard plates of bone. The fish at the center of the picture at the top of the next page is an ostracoderm. This small armored fish is important because ostracoderms may have been the ancestors of the kinds of fishes we know today.

❶ You may wish to introduce the term "extinct," although it is not used in the text. When we say that the trilobite is extinct, we mean that it has died out. What causes can you think of that might have made the trilobite become extinct? (lack of food, changes in temperature, larger animals that ate the trilobites)

❷ Children should be able to recognize jellyfish, clams, scallops and starfish in the picture. On what do you think these animals fed? (on tiny animals in the water or on green plants which children should recognize in the picture)

❸ How would a backbone be useful to an animal? (would give support to its body, so that it could move more easily, could grow larger)

❶ The fishes in the early waters were not as they are now. But the ancient fishes lived much as fishes do today. They fed on smaller fishes and invertebrates. Most of all, they fed on the green, red, and brown algae (simple sea plants). These plants have changed little since ancient times. The plants of the sea haven't changed as much as the ❷ animals.

The story of the ancient waters that scientists are piecing together seems to be this:

In those ancient seas, single-celled animals gave rise to many-celled animals. The earliest many-celled animals were invertebrates. There were jellyfish, starfish, crab and ❸ lobsterlike animals, clams, and squid, to name a few.

Somehow, in those ancient waters, one kind of invertebrate gave rise to a vertebrate. From this vertebrate came the early **fishes.** The early fishes seem to have been the earliest vertebrates. The armored fishes gave rise to the bony fishes. These bony fishes were not very different from the fishes found in our waters today.

Fishes are particularly well fitted to live in water, or nicely adapted to live in water, scientists say. Indeed, fishes are so ❹ well adapted to live in water that they have become the main vertebrates of the sea. Why were fishes so successful in becoming the main vertebrates of the sea? You can study their adaptation, or fitness for life in the water, in the investigation on the next page. INVESTIGATE

Continuing Lesson Cluster 3

❶ As children study the drawing, let them observe that there are several different fishes. (This plural is used when referring to different kinds of fishes. If one catches 20 flounder, the collective plural, fish, is used.) All the fishes in the drawing are armored; the ostracoderm is the large one in the center.

❷ Some algae are single-celled plants that float on the top of the water. Other kinds of algae are much larger—like the seaweed in the photograph.

❸ Although they live in the water, lobsters, crabs, clams, jellyfish, starfish, and squid are not really fishes. They belong to other groups: animals with saclike structures (coelenterates); animals with stony shells (mollusks); animals with jointed legs (arthropods); animals with spiny skins (echinoderms). The true fishes all have backbones.

❹ Let the children try to name some of the structural adaptations of fishes before they go on.

Supporting Statement: Early animals were adapted to the seas.

AN APPRENTICE INVESTIGATION
into the Adaptations of the Fish

1 **Needed:** an aquarium tank, sand, water plants, goldfish or guppies, and, if possible, water from a pond, well, or stream

Put about 2 inches of sand on the bottom of the tank. Add water to a level about an inch below the top of the tank. Let the sand settle, then plant the
2 water plants. ■ Let the aquarium stand in medium light for a week. Then you can put in the fish. Feed the fish every 2 days.

Methods of Intelligence
Observation and Inference

Here are four life activities: movement, getting
3 food, getting air, reproduction. How is the fish adapted to carrying on these life activities in its special environment?

Performance objectives. Children *construct* an aquarium system by establishing a tank containing water, sand, plants, and fish. They *describe* the adaptation of a fish for such life activities as movement, getting food, getting air, and reproduction, by observing fish in an aquarium and making inferences from their observations.

Useful materials: Fish food; a few snails, to serve as scavengers in the aquarium.

1 If you have an established aquarium in the classroom, it can be used for observations, while a spare aquarium tank may be prepared by some of the children for the experience.

2 Two purposes are served by letting the aquarium stand. One is to permit water purifiers, such as chlorine, to evaporate, if tap water is used. The other is to permit the water plants to become established. The plants, as they grow, will return oxygen to the water for the fish to breathe. When feeding the fish, remove any uneaten food after ten minutes to avoid fouling the water. A few snails will help keep the water clear, for they are scavengers that clean up wastes.

3 Let children observe the first three life activities and draw inferences on the fishes' adaptation. If goldfish are used, it is unlikely that children will observe reproduction. The female goldfish lays eggs which develop into baby fish. Guppies are born alive, and, with luck, the birth of baby guppies may be observed. The baby guppies will need to be removed to another tank, for guppies will eat their own offspring.

Unit Concept-Statement: Over the ages, living things have changed in their adaptation to the changing environment.

The Fitness of a Fish

Observe a fish and you will see that it is adapted for life in the water. Its body glides easily through the water. Its fins and tail push it through the water. Most important, the fish can get oxygen gas dissolved in water. Let a glass of cold water stand in a warm place. Soon bubbles of air that was dissolved in the water appear. A fish gets its oxygen from such dissolved air. ❶

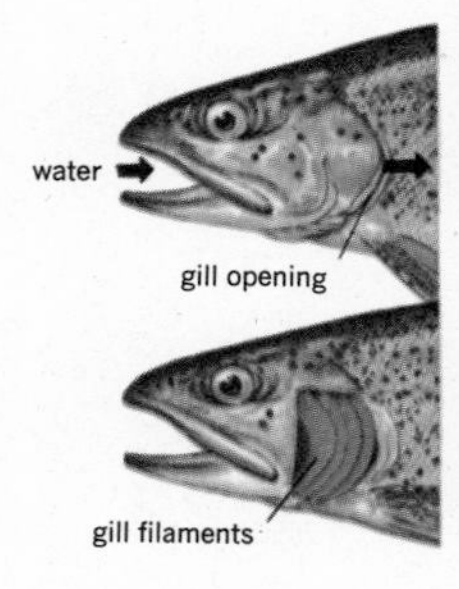

The fish takes oxygen from water by means of its **gills.** The fish gulps in water through its mouth. As the water passes over the gills, oxygen enters the gill filaments. Then the water flows out through a slitlike opening. This opening is usually covered by the gill cover. In the drawing at the top, the arrows show the direction in which the water flows. In the bottom drawing, the gill cover has been cut away, showing the gill filaments. ❷

Thus the fish is adapted to life in water by its structure. It is the structure of an organism that adapts it for life in its special environment.

The fishes of the ancient waters had adaptations for living in water. These adaptations made the fishes very successful animals in their environment. Soon they filled the ancient seas. ❸

However, there is still much to be known about life in the ancient waters. There is still much to find out. For instance, scientists don't know just how these changes happened. They do know that these changes took millions of years. The fishes didn't appear suddenly. Other animals gave rise to the ostracoderm. Then the ostracoderm changed slowly.

Many pieces of the puzzle are still missing. However, from the evidence we have, this much is clear. More and more living things became fitted to live in the seas. The waters became filled with life as living things changed in their fitness to live and multiply in the seas. We begin to see that life forms have changed during the millions of years living things have been on Earth. ❹

Continuing Lesson Cluster 3

❶ How is the fish adapted for movement in water? (streamlined shape, scales, fins, and tail for motion and balance)

❷ How is the fish adapted for getting air? Why do you think the fish's gills are red? Children should be able to infer that only a thin membrane separates the blood vessels from the water in which oxygen is dissolved. Oxygen passes through this membrane into the blood. How do you get oxygen from the air? (through the lungs)

❸ As fishes became the most successfully adapted animals in the water environment, what happened to those less well adapted? (Many became extinct.) Children often do not realize that other living things are part of an animal's environment. How might the successful adaptation of fishes have affected the environment of the trilobite, causing it to become extinct? Speculation can suggest several reasons: The temperature of the water or the amount of salt in it may have changed, favoring the fishes; fishes may have eaten the trilobites or the food they ate; possibly the trilobites couldn't stand the competition and died out. The important point is that children realize we have little evidence of what happened and can only infer or theorize.

❹ What evidence can you cite that living things have changed? (fossils of extinct animals) Would a statement about how they changed be evidence or theory? (theory) When can theories change? (when more evidence is found that the original theory cannot explain)

Supporting Statement: Early animals were adapted to the seas.

❶ BEFORE YOU GO ON

A. Check your understanding of the concepts of this section. Which ending would you choose for each statement below?

1. The earliest living things lived
a. in water b. on land

2. The earliest living things were made of
a. only one cell b. many cells

3. The older sedimentary rocks contain the fossils that are
a. older b. younger

4. The earliest vertebrates were the
a. sponges b. fishes

5. To be adapted to an environment means to be
a. fitted to it b. born in it

6. The statement that fits the main concept of this section is
a. Vertebrates in the early seas gave rise to invertebrates.
b. Invertebrates in the early seas gave rise to vertebrates.

B. Write a paragraph or two on this topic: "Ancient Life in the Seas."

❷ USING WHAT YOU KNOW

Bone develops from cartilage. The bones of a newborn child are soft. They have cartilage in them. Later the cartilage will become hard bone.

The early fishes may have had skeletons of cartilage. Sharks have skeletons of cartilage. Cod have skeletons of bone. Which do you think came earlier, fishes like sharks or fishes like cod?

❸ INVESTIGATING FURTHER

Vertebrates have backbones made up of vertebrae. In what ways are the vertebrae of various animals alike? In what ways are they different? To find out, compare the backbone of a fish with that of a chicken. A butcher may be able to give you single vertebrae from other animals, as well. Soak the bones until they are clean. Then, if you like, label your specimens and put them on display in the classroom.

A LOOK AHEAD

The waters have been filled with different kinds of animals—at different times. First, there were animals without backbones. Then—animals with backbones, the fishes.

One time—long, long ago—the waters gradually became dominated by fishes.

Then came the first step on the land—by some animals from the waters.

VERIFYING PROGRESS

In methods of intelligence

Children *demonstrate* the concepts of this lesson by *describing* ancient life in drawings or *constructing models.*

Children may draw or paint forms of life in the ancient waters and in the waters of today. They may need to consult encyclopedias or biology books.

Using modeling clay, children may make a model of a trilobite or of an ostracoderm or other ancient fish. For comparison, they may also model a horseshoe crab—a modern animal somewhat like the trilobite—or a modern fish.

Let the children exhibit and *explain* their drawings and models.

VERIFYING PROGRESS

❶ Before you go on. A. Children *demonstrate* understanding of change in the early seas by *identifying* sentence completions for open-ended statements.

1. a 3. a 5. a
2. a 4. b 6. b

B. Children's responses should include the concept of life changing over millions of years.

❷ Using what you know. Children *analyze* evidence presented and *infer* from it that the shark may have come before the cod.

❸ Investigating further. Children *investigate* likenesses and differences in the backbone of a fish and a chicken. They *compare* structures and *infer* that the differences adapt the animals to their special environment. For example, the chicken's backbone has vertebrae that provide support for wings for flying and legs for walking, and flexibility for turning the body. Both have a hollow for the nerve cord. Other answers are possible.

LESSON CLUSTER 4
FIRST STEPS ON LAND

Teaching background. 4 T-341

Concept-seeking. Children become aware of the changes that made it possible for animals to become adapted to life on land.

Operations. Children *investigate* the role of temperature in the environment and *probe* evidence of the changing life forms prior to the appearance of mammals.

Methods of intelligence. Children *compare* changes in temperature in water and air, and *infer* that the land is less safe than water as an environment for life; they *compare* the adaptations of amphibians and reptiles for land living and *theorize* that inability to adapt to the changing environment may result in extinction of life forms.

4. First Steps on Land

Long, long ago a sea animal left the water for the land. It was probably a fish of some sort. Of course, learning to live on land didn't happen suddenly. It probably took millions of years. Even so, it was a great adventure, for surely the water was a safer place to live than the land.

Does it surprise you that water may be safer than land? The investigation on the opposite page will give you a clue as to why this is so. INVESTIGATE

From Water to Land

❶ One reason why the water is a safer place than the land for living things is that *water changes temperature slowly.* The sea never gets as hot as a desert, or as cold as the Antarctic. Animals and plants on land may have to stand burning heat in the summer or icy cold in the winter. When the Sun's heat is too great, animals and plants on land may dry out. Have you ever seen a field of parched corn? Drying out is dangerous for living things. Plants and animals in the sea do not dry out.

In spite of that danger, the adventure happened. Some-
❷ time in the ancient past, a kind of fish developed a way to crawl out on land. There, it could make use of new supplies
❸ of food not available to water dwellers.

What a strange creature the first land animal must have been! Fossil evidence makes scientists think that the creature may have looked part fish, part salamander. No such animal is alive today. However, there are fishes now alive which crawl out on land and breathe air for a short time, like the lungfish. For such animals to be able to live on land for long, they would have to change. They would, for instance, have to develop legs, instead of fins, for moving about. They would also have to develop lungs, instead of gills, for breathing. What sort of creatures could these have been?

324

Introducing Lesson Cluster 4

Which do you think is a safer environment for living things—the land or the sea? What are some conditions that make one environment safer? less safe? If children do not mention temperature as a factor, let the investigation come as a surprise. Instead of discussion you may wish to read the two paragraphs with the children and begin with the investigation.

Developing the lesson

❶ After the investigation, ask: How do you think fish can live when a lake freezes? Children may not know that there is water under the ice and that it is above the freezing point. How do plants survive a freezing winter? (Some are adapted to the cold; others make seeds that are dormant during the winter.) Why is water so necessary to plants and animals on land? (Without water, plants cannot make food, and all animals need water for their cells to do work.)

❷ In what ways isn't a fish adapted for land living? (It cannot crawl or walk, cannot take oxygen from air.) There is a walking catfish that uses its strong fins to propel itself over the land. It can apparently store enough oxygen to let it stay out of water for 15 minutes or longer.

❸ What must have happened earlier for food to be available on land? (Plants must have started to grow on the soil.)

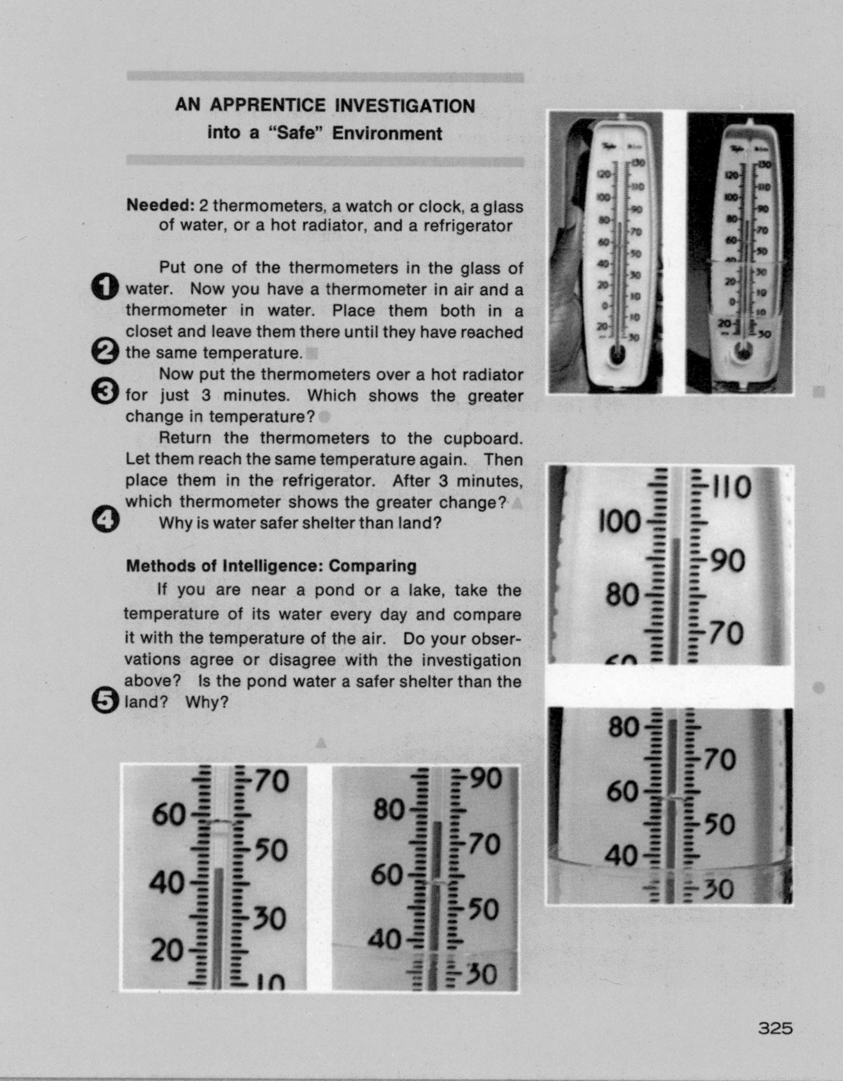

AN APPRENTICE INVESTIGATION into a "Safe" Environment

Needed: 2 thermometers, a watch or clock, a glass of water, or a hot radiator, and a refrigerator

Put one of the thermometers in the glass of ❶ water. Now you have a thermometer in air and a thermometer in water. Place them both in a closet and leave them there until they have reached ❷ the same temperature.

Now put the thermometers over a hot radiator ❸ for just 3 minutes. Which shows the greater change in temperature?

Return the thermometers to the cupboard. Let them reach the same temperature again. Then place them in the refrigerator. After 3 minutes, which thermometer shows the greater change?

❹ Why is water safer shelter than land?

Methods of Intelligence: Comparing

If you are near a pond or a lake, take the temperature of its water every day and compare it with the temperature of the air. Do your observations agree or disagree with the investigation above? Is the pond water a safer shelter than the ❺ land? Why?

325

Performance objectives. Children *demonstrate* that the temperature of water changes less rapidly than the temperature of air, by using thermometers to measure changes in air and water as sudden changes of environmental temperature occur. They *describe* the activity as an example of why a water environment can be safer than the land.

Useful materials: some similar materials are available in CLASSROOM LABORATORY: PURPLE.

❶ Results will be more rapid if the temperature used is close to room temperature.

❷ The temperature in different parts of the room may vary. Children should therefore have all their thermometers in the same place. A closet is likely to have a constant temperature.

❸ If you do not have a warm radiator, substitute another heat source. An electric food-warming tray would be ideal.

❹ Observations should result in the inference that water is less subject to temperature variation than air.

❺ Observations should agree with the investigation. In terms of temperature extremes, water is safer than land. However, children should also realize that water is not necessarily as safe as the land for animals adapted to breathing air. Many land animals and some sea animals—such as the seal and the whale—are able to swim and make use of the "safer" environment.

Unit Concept-Statement: Over the ages, living things have changed in their adaptation to the changing environment.

Early Life on Land

In an early age the land was moist and warm. Ferns as tall as trees grew in it. They shielded animals on the land from the Sun's heat.

❶ Do these animals remind you of any animals today? ■
❷ These early animals were **amphibians,** as are today's frogs, toads, and salamanders. An amphibian is an animal that lives both in water and on land.

For many millions of years, the ancient amphibians lived in the warm, moist forests, and were kings of the land. But the amphibians did not rule forever.

❸ The Great Reptiles Arrive

Nothing remains the same. The Earth changes. Plants and animals change. As millions of years passed, the amphibians changed. There came amphibians whose bodies

■

Continuing Lesson Cluster 4

❶ The large animal in the picture is an Eryops. The smaller one is a Diplovertebron. Have children study the legs and the shape of the head and then respond to the question. Frogs, toads, and salamanders are common amphibians. A child may also think of the alligator—a reptile, as he will shortly discover.

❷ The term amphibian comes from the Greek words *amphi* meaning "both" and *bios* meaning "life." An amphibian, then, lives two kinds of life. What are the two kinds of life a frog lives? (in water as a tadpole; both in water and on land as a frog) Why don't you find amphibians in dry areas? (Eggs with no shell are laid in water; young develop in water.)

Children may not know that amphibians must keep their skins moist, because some of their breathing takes place through the skin.

❸ Where would you have expected to find ancient amphibians? (near water) Why do you think they were kings that ruled the land? Children should not take "kings" and "rule" literally; rather, they should infer that the amphibians were the best adapted for land living, grew large and powerful, and were probably for a long time the only animals that could walk on the land.

Supporting Statement: Some sea animals changed and became adapted for land living.

could stand more drying out. They had tougher skin. In time, somewhere on land, amphibians gave rise to the early reptiles. So scientists infer from the evidence.

❶ The first **reptiles** were strange creatures, to be sure. But they did look somewhat like modern reptiles such as the alligator and the crocodile. One early reptile may have ❷ looked like this.

Reptiles are better fitted than amphibians to live on land. An amphibian, you may remember, has a moist skin through which it can breathe. A reptile's skin, however, has scales which help keep it from drying out. A reptile breathes with lungs and does not have a moist skin for ❸ breathing.

A reptile, moreover, lays eggs with tough shells and lays them on land. The shells keep the young inside them from drying out. An amphibian lays eggs that have no ❹ shells on them and lays them in water.

327

VERIFYING PROGRESS

In methods of intelligence

Children *demonstrate* their understanding of the Age of Reptiles by *building a model* in the form of a diorama. Light-blue construction paper or water-colored paper may be curved for a background. Use modeling clay for the animals and plants. They may be supported from above with thread.

If feasible, a class or individual trip to a greenhouse can be made to note the general effect of moisture and temperature on green plants. The Age of Reptiles experienced a similar "greenhouse" effect.

❶ The term *reptile* comes from a Latin word that means "crawling."

What reptile do you know that has no legs and moves by crawling? (snake) What reptile do you know that walks on short legs? (alligator)

❷ The large brown reptile is a Dimetrodon, and the purplish one is an Edaphosaurus. Children interested in knowing more about these animals can refer to an encyclopedia or other references on prehistoric reptiles.

❸ What big advantage does a dry, tough, scaly skin give the reptile? (It can travel farther from water and live there; internal water does not evaporate through the skin so rapidly.) Children may also mention that the reptiles can go farther than an amphibian can for food, and that they can get water from the plants or animals they eat.

❹ What advantage is there in the reptile's tough-shelled egg? (It doesn't need to be kept moist, eggs can be hidden in sand rather than in water; young reptiles in ancient times may have had fewer enemies and were better able to develop.) Let children compare the adaptations of reptiles for land living to those of amphibians.

The children who prepare the diorama should *explain* it in detail, with others acting as critics or commentators on the accuracy of the information.

UNIT SEVEN

Unit Concept-Statement: Over the ages, living things have changed in their adaptation to the changing environment.

You already know something of the early reptiles, the dinosaurs. Think how huge and terrifying some of them must have been to the smaller animals. Some were 18 feet tall! There were dinosaurs of many different kinds.
1 Some ate meat, like the Allosaurus (al′o·sôr′əs) in the center of this picture. Others, like the Stegosaurus (steg′ə·
2 sôr′əs) at the top, ate plant foods.

Some reptiles were able to fly. They did not fly with feathered wings, however. They had a sheet of skin stretched over the arms and toes.

Continuing Lesson Cluster 4

1 What shows that Allosaurus in the center of the picture was a meat-eater? (It is eating the remains of an animal; also, it has sharp teeth and claws for tearing flesh.) Allosaurus means "leaping lizard." Why do you think scientists gave it this name? (Fossil bones showed strong hind limbs and short fore limbs.) What leaping animals do you know that have similar structures for leaping? (frogs, kangaroos, etc.)

2 Stegosaurus means "roof lizard." What do you see in the picture that might account for the name? (bony plates on its back) How might these have been a good adaptation for this plant-eating animal? (Possibly they protected it from a leaping animal like Allosaurus which might have leaped on its back and torn it apart.)

EXTENDING THE LESSON

What's wrong with this? A fossil hunter found a stone diary in a sedimentary layer with dinosaur bones. It told how a caveman hunted dinosaurs. For dinner his wife gave him an omelet of dinosaur eggs with a side order of Stegosaurus steak. How many false statements are in this story? Children should cite at least five errors or improbabilities which they can challenge using their present concepts of the ancient environment.

Supporting Statement: Some sea animals changed and became adapted for land living.

❶ Some of the early reptiles left the land and lived in the water. These sea reptiles still breathed by means of lungs. When one came to the surface, it took a great gulp of air which lasted it for some time. In the picture, the long-❷ necked animal that has come up for air is a Pliosaurus (plī′o·sôr′əs). The animal that has just caught a fish is named Placodus (plak′ə·dəs). Notice how the bodies of all these water reptiles have become streamlined, and their feet ❸ have become flippers. These creatures were strong and fast and must have ruled the early waters. However, most reptiles lived on land. And, as you see, some even left the land and took to the air.

Scientists have called this ancient age, some 160 million years ago, the Age of Reptiles.

❶ What reptiles living today spend much of their time in the water? (turtles, crocodiles, alligators)

❷ What adaptations for water living do these sea reptiles have? (flippers or legs for better swimming) Why are they not called fishes? (breathe through lungs, can rest on the shore)

❸ Since these are classed as reptiles, how would they reproduce offspring? (laying tough-shelled eggs on land)

The Death of the Dinosaurs

The powerful dinosaurs ruled over all. They roamed the land. Some of them lived on plants. Some lived on meat and fought and killed each other for food.

All the time the land was becoming drier. Tree ferns **1** became scarce, for they grew only where the land was wet and warm. Then the huge reptiles began to die out. In time, over millions of years, the dinosaurs disappeared. Why?

Perhaps the land became too dry. Perhaps the food gave out. Perhaps the dinosaurs fought so much that they killed each other off. (You may want to look into this question in the Search On Your Own on page 332.)

Some ancient relatives of the dinosaurs didn't die out, however. Some of them must have been ancestors of reptiles living today. Our lizards are related to the king dinosaurs.

Then came a great event. Toward the end of the Age **2** of Reptiles, birds and mammals began to appear.

The story in the sedimentary rocks gives us an idea of **3** what the first **bird** we know of looked like. The fossil of this

330

Continuing Lesson Cluster 4

1 How do changes in the environment affect living things? Suggest changes in the seasons and their effect on plants. If it becomes too hot or too cold, too wet or too dry, what happens to plants? (many die) How would the disappearance of many plants affect the food supply of animals? Be sure that children are aware that we don't know why the dinosaur died out. We infer that climate may have had something to do with it, because we can see the effect of climate on living things today.

2 Children should not get the idea that birds and mammals appeared only after the smaller dinosaurs and the ancient reptiles died out. Actually, for a while, they lived together, the birds and mammals slowly developing and the smaller dinosaurs and ancient reptiles slowly dying out.

3 The bird shown in the pictures on these pages is the Archeopteryx, the oldest fossil of a bird that man has found.

Have children compare the reconstructed Archeopteryx on the opposite page with the picture of the fossil. What parts can you identify? What new adaptation did the Archeopteryx have? (wings for flight; feathers)

Supporting Statement: Some sea animals changed and became adapted for land living.

❶ bird looks like this. ■ Scientists think that when it was alive it had scales like a reptile and some feathers. ●

It was very different from the birds of today.

Along with the first bird came other animals especially well adapted to living on land—mammals. The mammals were to rule the world, as you shall see.

But before you go to a further study of the stories in the earth, a few questions seem to be in order:

Is the story of the dinosaurs complete? Why don't
❷ we find one huge dinosaur alive today?

Are living things disappearing today? Why? Try the Search On Your Own on the next page.

331

❶ Children may be interested in a theory of how wings developed. There were many reptiles smaller than the dinosaurs. Some, through a change in inheritance, were able to climb trees and get out of reach. The ones best adapted to tree-climbing survived, and their offspring inherited this ability. Then, perhaps some of these tree-climbers, by another inherited change, began to jump from tree to tree or from a tree to the ground. Some were better at it than others, and they survived. Perhaps they inherited a web-like skin on their front feet that allowed them to soar farther. This ability helped more of them to escape. Sometime something must have changed so that scales became feathers. Again, this was a useful adaptation. (If you examine the foot part of a chicken, you will observe it is covered with scales like those on a reptile.)

❷ Let children discuss these questions and make their own hypotheses.

Unit Concept-Statement: Over the ages, living things have changed in their adaptation to the changing environment.

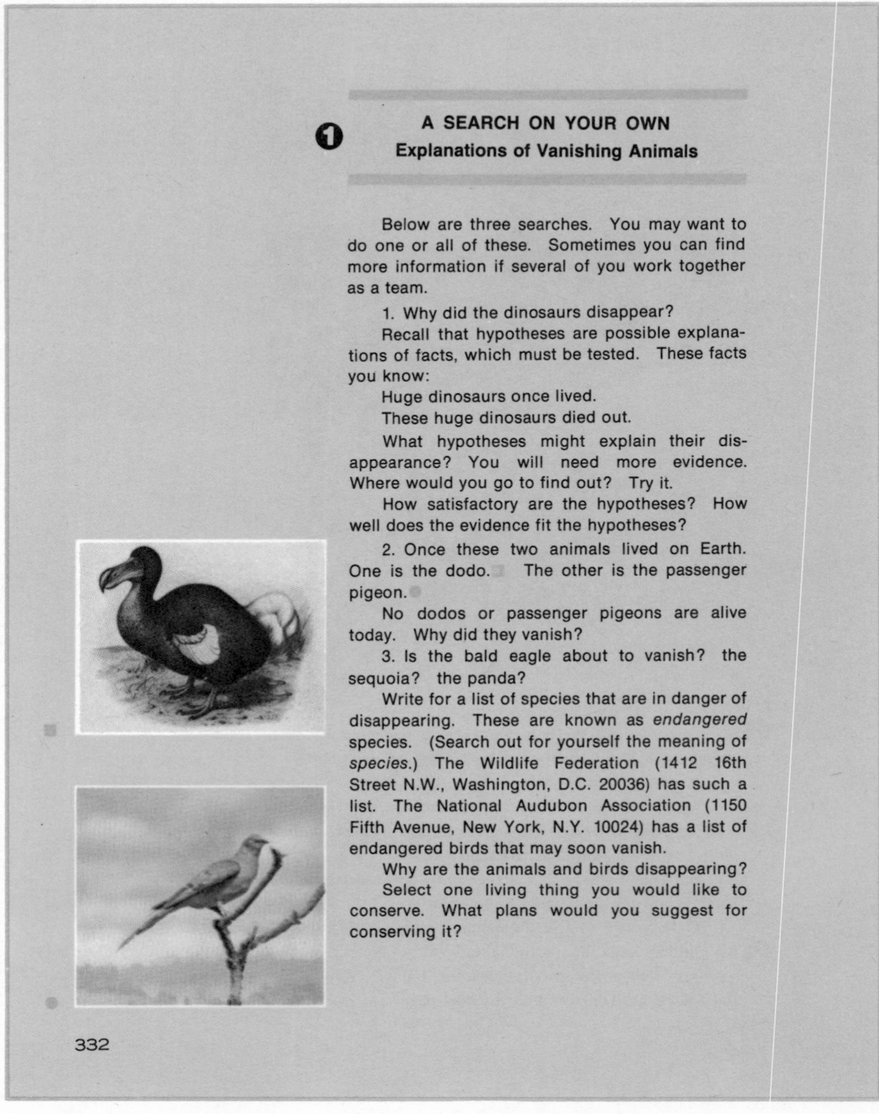

A SEARCH ON YOUR OWN
Explanations of Vanishing Animals

Below are three searches. You may want to do one or all of these. Sometimes you can find more information if several of you work together as a team.

1. Why did the dinosaurs disappear?

Recall that hypotheses are possible explanations of facts, which must be tested. These facts you know:

Huge dinosaurs once lived.

These huge dinosaurs died out.

What hypotheses might explain their disappearance? You will need more evidence. Where would you go to find out? Try it.

How satisfactory are the hypotheses? How well does the evidence fit the hypotheses?

2. Once these two animals lived on Earth. One is the dodo. The other is the passenger pigeon.

No dodos or passenger pigeons are alive today. Why did they vanish?

3. Is the bald eagle about to vanish? the sequoia? the panda?

Write for a list of species that are in danger of disappearing. These are known as *endangered* species. (Search out for yourself the meaning of *species*.) The Wildlife Federation (1412 16th Street N.W., Washington, D.C. 20036) has such a list. The National Audubon Association (1150 Fifth Avenue, New York, N.Y. 10024) has a list of endangered birds that may soon vanish.

Why are the animals and birds disappearing?

Select one living thing you would like to conserve. What plans would you suggest for conserving it?

332

VERIFYING PROGRESS

1 A search on your own. Children *hypothesize* about the extinction of forms of animal life, *seek evidence* that attempts to explain this event, *infer* the need for conservation, and *design a plan* for saving a species.

All children should be encouraged to do some research into the important question of conservation. They can begin by obtaining evidence from the encyclopedia and other references about the dinosaurs, the dodo, and the passenger pigeon. Then they should consult references on endangered species.

For any one child to pursue the entire Search is asking a great deal. It is suggested that each child select an animal or plant and find out all he or she can about its adaptations to its environment, threats to its survival, and so on. When the information is gathered, it can be pooled in a class discussion with accompanying illustrations when available.

In this way all members of the class will benefit from the Search, and it can be accomplished in about one week. In writing for information, one well-phrased letter will be more likely to get an immediate response than letters from each child.

Supporting Statement: Some sea animals changed and became adapted for land living.

❶ BEFORE YOU GO ON

A. Check your understanding of the concepts of this section. Which ending would you choose for each statement below?

1. The environment in which the temperature changes slowly is
a. land
b. water

2. The first land vertebrates may have come from a kind of
a. insect
b. fish

3. The earliest vertebrates to live on land probably were the
a. reptiles
b. amphibians

4. The amphibians probably gave rise to
a. birds
b. reptiles

5. The reptiles probably gave rise to the birds and the
a. mammals
b. trilobites

6. The statement that fits the main concept of this section is
a. The first animals adapted for land living may have come from ancient sea animals.
b. The first animals adapted for land living may have come from ancient birds.

B. Write a paragraph or two on this topic: "The First Land Animals."

❷ USING WHAT YOU KNOW

1. Why can't a salamander or a frog survive if the environment dries out? (*Some hints:* Fishes take in oxygen that is dissolved in water. The skin of a salamander is moist.)

2. The eggs of fishes and amphibians are laid in water. Those of reptiles are laid on land.

Why can't the eggs of fishes and salamanders develop on land? Why do the eggs of reptiles have a better chance of developing?

3. Why do the eggs of reptiles have a better chance of hatching than do the eggs of amphibians or fishes?

A LOOK AHEAD

Animals conquered the land. Life was everywhere. Just as fishes adapted to the waters, so amphibians adapted to the land.

And then came the rule of the reptiles. There were the huge dinosaurs. Then the first strange birds appeared. And then? What life forms developed?

333

❶ Before you go on. Children *demonstrate* understanding of adaptations of the early land animals by *identifying* suitable completions to open-ended questions.

A. 1. b 3. b 5. a
2. b 4. b 6. a

B. Children should include evidence of adaptations to the environment.

❷ Using what you know. Children *analyze* questions and situations and *infer* or *explain* outcomes.

1. Salamanders and frogs can take dissolved oxygen from water through their skins. Although they have lungs, they also breathe through their skin.

2. The eggs of fishes and salamanders have no shells. Their eggs must be laid in water to keep them from drying out. Also, the temperature of the egg in water remains more constant than it would on land.

Reptiles lay eggs with tough, leathery shells. The eggs are laid on land, and therefore cannot be eaten by fish (although they can be eaten by other animals). Also, a reptile's eggs are fertilized inside the reptile, before being laid. Each egg has the chance to develop into a new reptile.

3. The shell protects the young from drying out; the eggs are better hidden in the sand than in the water and are less likely to be eaten.

Unit Concept-Statement: Over the ages, living things have changed in their adaptation to the changing environment.

LESSON CLUSTER 5
UP TO NOW

Teaching background. 5 T-343

Concept-seeking. Children become aware of the adaptations that fit mammals to survive in a wide variety of environments.

Operations. Children *probe* into the various adaptations of mammals and *investigate* the advantages of a steady body temperature in relation to the temperature of the environment.

Methods of intelligence. Children *seek evidence* of the characteristics of mammals, *observe* the steady body temperature of man, and *infer* that warm-bloodedness adapts mammals to a variety of environments. They *compare* changes that have taken place on Earth over millions of years and *construct a variety of theories* in an attempt to *explain* the evidence of change.

5. Up To Now

What did the first mammals look like? We don't know exactly. However, we do have an idea, based on fossil evidence discovered in the rocks.

1 The early mammals had fur or hair, as all mammals do. The evidence suggests that they were small animals. They were probably not very different from the shrews we have today. The shrew is a mouselike mammal with a long
2 pointed snout. ■ Some early mammals may have laid eggs,
3 like the duckbilled platypus. ● The duckbill lives in

334

Introducing Lesson Cluster 5

A useful way to begin and also to give children an insight into classification is to have as many pictures as possible of all kinds of animals, both present-day and prehistoric. You might enlist the help of children the day before you begin this lesson. Have them bring animal pictures from magazines which you can shuffle and hold up or pass out to small groups.

Ask children to sort out the mammals. What makes you think these are mammals? If children challenge the sorting, ask: Which one do you think is not a mammal? Why?

Developing the lesson

1 What advantage does fur or hair give a mammal? (It keeps its skin warm, and protects its body from cold.) Children should infer that fur or hair is one of the differences that separates mammals from other animals. The main difference, however, is that the mother mammal feeds her young with her own milk. The milk comes from her mammary glands.

2 Children should realize that the photograph of the shrew has been enlarged. Shrews are tiny creatures, ranging in size from $2\frac{1}{2}$ to 6 inches long. The smallest species of shrew weighs less than a penny. The blades of grass in the picture should give a clue to the actual size of the animal.

3 The duckbill platypus is about 2 feet long, including its 6-inch tail.

Supporting Statement: Mammals have developed complex adaptations to the environment.

Australia. It lays eggs that have shells around them.

After the young of the duckbill hatch out of their eggs, they are fed with a strange milk made by the mother. Most people would not recognize it as milk. It is more like very thin white of egg. Is the duckbill part reptile? It would ❶ be better to say that it is an egg-laying mammal which hasn't changed much over millions of years.

Protecting the Young

The eggs of reptiles of long ago hatched outside the reptile's body, as do the eggs of most reptiles living now. Often the eggs were eaten by other animals. Sometimes the eggs dried up in the heat or froze in the cold. One way or another, the eggs of reptiles were exposed to many dangers. But the eggs of mammals are protected inside the mother's ❷ body. This is one way in which mammals are well adapted to living on land.

The young of many mammals are born almost ready to take care of themselves, except for getting food. For example, a young horse can stand up and walk only a few minutes after birth. ▲

▲

❶ Only two kinds of mammals lay eggs. They are the duckbill platypus and the spiny anteater. Both are native to Australia.

❷ How is a baby that is developing inside its mother adapted to all kinds of environments on land? (While the baby is inside the mother, it doesn't matter what the environment outside the mother is like—unless it is bad for the mother—because the baby is specially protected.) Actually it is the mother that *is* the environment for the internally developing baby mammal.

■

❶ There are some mammals today whose young are born not fully developed. Even if you haven't visited Australia, you know of the kangaroo, a mammal that carries its young in a pouch. ■ The young of the kangaroo are born blind and without fur. Quickly they climb into the mother's pouch. There they are kept warm, and there they are fed with the mother's milk. After a few months in the pouch, they begin to look like kangaroos. The young kangaroos climb out of the mother's pouch to hop about. Whenever there is danger, they scamper back into the pouch. The mother protects them in this way until they can care for themselves.

The young of mammals are fed and taken care of by the mother for a longer time than are the young of any other kind of living thing. This mother bear, for example, cares
❷ for her cubs for 2 years after their birth. You can see that the young of mammals have a better chance of growing up than the young of reptiles.

The young of birds and mammals are protected until they can take care of themselves. Birds build nests and feed their young. Young mammals develop within the mother and are fed until they can feed themselves and hide from their enemies. The young of most fishes, amphibians,

336

Continuing Lesson Cluster 5

❶ This is a good time to make use of the reading table. The librarian may be able to assist you in supplementing the books you have with others or with nature magazines that tell how animals protect their young. Let children select books or articles and allow for a free browsing period followed by reports.

❷ How might a bear care for her young cubs? (feed them, see that they don't hurt themselves, see that they don't get lost, fight animals that might attack them, set an example of how a bear should live, teach them things, give them love and affection)

Supporting Statement: Mammals have developed complex adaptations to the environment.

and reptiles are at the mercy of their enemies. Fishes eat the young of the other fish just hatched. Frog tadpoles are food for other animals. Young snakes are eaten by birds.

The young of mammals and birds are protected, kept warm, and fed. This is an adaptation to the environment that ❶ has made mammals and birds successful. There is an adaptation which helps adult birds and mammals survive, too—their steady body temperature.

Fishes, amphibians, and reptiles are **cold-blooded.** ❷ That is, their body temperature changes with that of the environment. But birds and mammals are **warm-blooded.** A warm-blooded animal has a steady body temperature. The investigation on the next page will help you understand this adaptation. INVESTIGATE

Changes in Living Things

Ancient living things that lived in the water changed into forms that could live on land. Cold-blooded living things may have given rise to warm-blooded living things that could keep a steady body temperature. Living things that laid their eggs outside the body may have given rise to living things whose eggs developed inside the body. ●

❶ How are mammals and birds especially well adapted to their environment? (protection of young, even body temperature)

What difference do these adaptations make in the chances of survival of these two animal groups? (The animals are less likely to die out, more likely to become a dominant group within their special environments.)

❷ If the water that a fish is swimming in is 35°, what do you think the temperature of the fish is? (around 35°) If another fish is swimming in water that is around 70°, what will the temperature of this fish be? (around 70°) If the fish from the 35° water swims into the 70° water, what will happen to its temperature? (It will rise to around 70° if it stays in this water for awhile.)

What would your temperature be in 70° water? (around 98.6°, which is normal human body temperature) Don't expect children to know this temperature, however, as it will first be introduced in the investigation.

Unit Concept-Statement: Over the ages, living things have changed in their adaptation to the changing environment.

Performance objectives. Children *demonstrate* the body's adaptation for maintaining a steady temperature by measuring body and air temperatures, indoor and outdoor, once a day for a week, showing that the temperature of the body fluctuates very little compared to air temperature outside the body.

Children *construct* a table of the temperature readings collected, indicating the day of the readings and air and body temperatures both outdoors and indoors.

Useful materials: Alcohol or other disinfectant for oral thermometer. Thermometers are available in CLASSROOM LABORATORY: PURPLE.

Day	Air Temperature	Body Temperature
OUT-OF-DOORS		
1	39° F	98.5° F
2	29° F	98.4° F
3	29° F	98.6° F
4	26° F	98.8° F
5	32° F	98.3° F
INDOORS		
1	69° F	98.5° F
2	75° F	98.4° F
3	72° F	98.6° F
4	68° F	98.8° F
5	65° F	98.3° F

AN APPRENTICE INVESTIGATION into a Steady Temperature

Needed: a clinical thermometer (oral) and an air thermometer ❶

Take the temperature of your classroom with the air thermometer. As you do so, take your own temperature in the classroom with the clinical thermometer. Before using the clinical thermometer, dip it in alcohol and wash it off under cold running water. Then shake it until the temperature reads 97° or less. Be careful not to break the thermometer! Place the bulb of the thermometer under your tongue and keep it in the mouth for about 3 minutes.

Next, take the temperature out-of-doors with the air thermometer. At the same time take your ❷ own temperature out-of-doors.

Take these temperature readings at the same time each day for a week and record them. You will be able to see how your temperature was affected by the temperature of the environment.

A student in a northern state recorded these temperatures during a week in January in one trial.

What do you conclude from these observations, and your own, about body temperature? What is one of man's most important adaptations to his ❸ environment?

Methods of Intelligence: Comparing

With your teacher's permission, exercise for a minute or so, until you feel warmer than you were. Take your temperature. Rest for several minutes, until you feel cooler. Take your temperature again. ❹ What happens to your temperature? Why?

Now go back to "Changes in Living Things" on page 337.

338

Continuing Lesson Cluster 5

❶ *Warning:* Do not allow any child to use a thermometer that has not been disinfected. Consult your school nurse (from whom you may probably borrow a thermometer) and follow her instructions for disinfecting the thermometer after use by one child and before use by another.

❷ Temperatures should be taken at the same time each day because body temperature may vary normally over a 24-hour period, as well as from day to day as shown in the table.

❸ Children should conclude that their temperature is not changed by the environment. This fact, called being "warm-blooded", is a useful adaptation to the environment. Cold-blooded animals slowly adjust their body temperature to the environment. A too-rapid change may cause many of them to die.

❹ *Caution:* To prevent children from carrying out procedures hazardous to health, have them check their plans with you before doing this part of the investigation. Children should find that man's temperature remains constant because he is warm-blooded.

What keeps man's temperature at about 98.6°? (the energy that is released inside his body from the food he eats)

Supporting Statement: Mammals have developed complex adaptations to the environment.

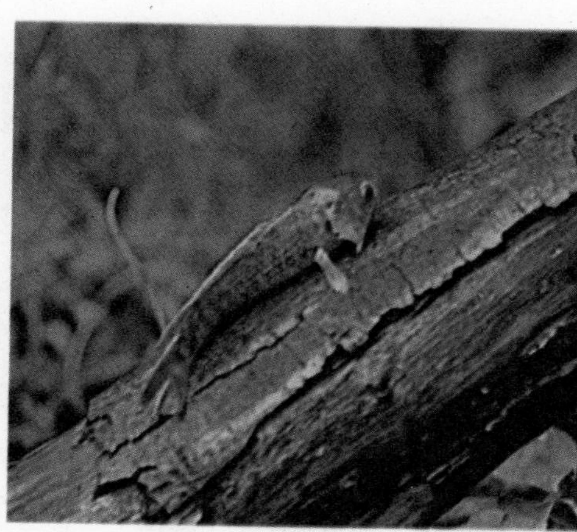

Organisms adapted to life in water gave rise to organisms adapted to life on land. Over millions of years, many, many changes in structure took place in the fishes. Some of these changes were in the fins. The fins of
1 certain fishes changed to a kind of flipper-foot. Those fishes that didn't develop the flipper-foot stayed in the seas. Those fishes that did develop it could try the land. ■

Of course, these early land animals developed other adaptations, such as lungs. How do these changes come
2 about? The changes take place first in the chromosomes. You may recall that chromosomes are the bodies in the cells responsible for the characteristics we inherit. The changes in the chromosomes came before the changes in the structure of living things. Before the toes of the horse became a hoof, changes took place in the chromosomes within the horse. After millions of years, horses with hooves survived and horses with toes did not. The horses with toes, then, were probably not as well fitted for the environment. What other explanation can you think of?

1 How did the flipper adapt these fish to the land? (Since most animals have to walk or crawl around on land—or else fly—the flipper helped these fish to crawl on the land.)

2 What molecule in the chromosomes determines changes? (DNA) If a change takes place, what happens in the offspring? (change in some of its characteristics) When is the change important? (when it results in better adaptation) Are small changes or large ones more likely to be passed on? (Small; large ones are more likely to make the organism unfit for its environment.)

Unit Concept-Statement: Over the ages, living things have changed in their adaptation to the changing environment.

Once upon a time (but this is not a fairy tale) huge mammoths, with long hair and curved tusks, plodded across ❶ what is now Nebraska. ■ Early man hunted the mammoths. Now only their fossils remain.

However, the mammals we know today—dogs, cats, tigers, horses, camels, elephants, and all the rest—have taken the place of those vanished mammals of long ago.

When man came, he found coal, oil, iron, copper, silver, and gold. Great forests were his, and rich soil. The rivers, lakes, and seas teemed with life.

Man is here. He depends on the Earth's soil and ❷ forests. He depends on the Earth's minerals and water and air. He depends on his brain to use the riches of the Earth. He also depends on his brain to find out more about his planet. How is he doing it? See for yourself.

340

Continuing Lesson Cluster 5

❶ What animals do the mammoths in the picture remind you of? (elephant) How does the mammoth differ from the elephant? (Its tusks curl outward and the elephant's tusks are straight. The mammoth has thick hair all over its body; the elephant does not.) Why would woolly hair be a disadvantage to a modern elephant? (too hot)

The woolly mammoth lived about 12,000 years ago, at a time when great glaciers extended down below Nebraska. Mammoths have been found preserved in ice in Siberia. From these frozen "fossils," man knows of its covering of wooly hair that adapted it for cold climates. Elephants of today live in tropical climates.

❷ What adaptations does man have that enables him to make use of his environment? Children should be able to infer that these include his brain, erect posture, ability to speak, hand structure, care of offspring, etc.

Supporting Statement: Mammals have developed complex adaptations to the environment.

A SEARCH ON YOUR OWN

Man and His Environment

❶ Study the reports of man's activities. Unlike other living things, man reports his activities to others. He talks and writes. He reports activities on TV, in newspapers, and in magazines.

How wise is man in using the land and the waters? What is he doing to conserve his inheri-
❷ tance—or to destroy it?

Choose one of these parts of the environment for study:

- —soil (farm land, as well as land on which we build)
- —water (rivers, lakes, oceans)
- —air (everywhere)
- —forests (timber and recreation)
- —minerals (oil, coal, copper, and so forth)

Or, if you wish, choose one of these ways in
❸ which man is damaging his environment:

- —pollution (What is happening to our air, water, soil?)
- —pesticides (How are they harming the environment? How and when are they useful?)
- —cities (How well are they being planned to give a good environment? How do cities affect the lives of people?)

You should seek to answer this question: Is man conserving the environment he shares with other living things?

What will be your part in conserving your
❹ environment? Plan one act of conservation in which you can take part.

341

VERIFYING PROGRESS

A search on your own. Children *probe* into activities peculiar to man, *analyze* information and data about his environment, infer that man's use of his environment is not always beneficial to him and to other forms of life, and *design a plan* for conserving the environment.

❶ Children should look for articles and books on ecology.

❷ Children should infer that the total environment includes man. They should therefore consider both the use and misuse of natural resources and the effects of each. For example: If forests are cut down, what may happen to wild life, lakes, rivers, soil, and man's own enjoyment or profit from the environment?

❸ Let children consider what happens if pollution kills off fish and wild life, if pesticides are not selective yet long-lasting, if cities destroy the natural habitats of plants and animals—and what the results of these effects on the environment and on man himself will be.

❹ After children have gathered such evidence as they can obtain, let them draw up a plan. You may wish to forward to the proper authorities the results of thoughtful studies by the children, including a covering letter explaining the work of your science class on the project.

Unit Concept-Statement: Over the ages, living things have changed in their adaptation to the changing environment.

VERIFYING PROGRESS

In methods of intelligence

Children can *demonstrate* understanding of adaptations by *seeking* and *ordering* evidence about the largest animals known on Earth.

Let children find out what is the largest animal that has ever lived. After they find out, they can make a short report about the animal. They should include whether the animal is living or extinct, whether it is a fish, an amphibian, a reptile, or a mammal, and anything else that they find interesting. (The largest animal that has ever lived is the whale. A blue whale can grow to be bigger than the largest dinosaur and an elephant put together. Whales are living today and they are mammals.)

❶ BEFORE YOU GO ON

Check your understanding of the concepts of this section. Which ending would you choose for each statement below?

1. The young of the duckbill hatch out of
   a. eggs
   b. a pouch

2. One adaptation that made mammals more successful in surviving than reptiles was that mammal young were protected inside
   a. the mother
   b. eggs

3. Another adaptation that fitted mammals for success on land was their
   a. changing body temperature
   b. steady body temperature

4. Changes in the structure of living things came about
   a. after changes in their chromosomes
   b. before changes in their chromosomes

5. Early man once hunted
   a. dinosaurs
   b. mammoths

6. The statement that fits the main concept of this section is
   a. The living things that have been most successful in their adaptations are the reptiles.
   b. The living things that have been most successful in their adaptations are the mammals.

❷ USING WHAT YOU KNOW

1. Is there any place in the world where mammals cannot be found? Where on Earth might it be difficult to find mammals?

2. Compare the adaptations of mammals with the adaptations of reptiles.
   a. Why can mammals live in very cold regions while reptiles generally cannot?
   b. Why do the eggs of mammals have a greater chance of survival than the eggs of reptiles?

❸ INVESTIGATING FURTHER

With the permission of your teacher, prepare two bulletin board displays on
   a. the mammals of Australia, such as the pouched or egg-laying mammals.
   b. the mammals of Africa, such as the chimpanzees, gorillas, or monkeys.

Several students might work together as a committee in collecting information and pictures and preparing the display.

342

VERIFYING PROGRESS (cont.)

❶ Before you go on. Children *demonstrate* understanding of the adaptations of mammals by identifying suitable completions to open-ended questions.

1. a	3. a	5. b
2. a	4. a	6. b

❷ Using what you know. Children *analyze* the adaptations of mammals and *infer* that these adaptations fit mammals for survival in their environment.

1. It would be difficult to find mammals high in the air because mammals do not fly so high, or at the depths of the sea where lung breathing is not possible.

2. a. Mammals can maintain body heat with adequate food; reptiles would freeze to death at temperatures below the freezing point.

b. Except for two species of egg-laying mammals, all eggs of mammals develop within the body at a constant temperature and have full protection as long as the mother is not injured; reptile eggs are subject to changes in the physical environment and to eating by predators.

❸ Investigating further. Children, by gathering information and pictures for display, *describe* and *group* different kinds of mammals.

Unit Concept-Statement: Over the ages, living things have changed in their adaptation to the changing environment.

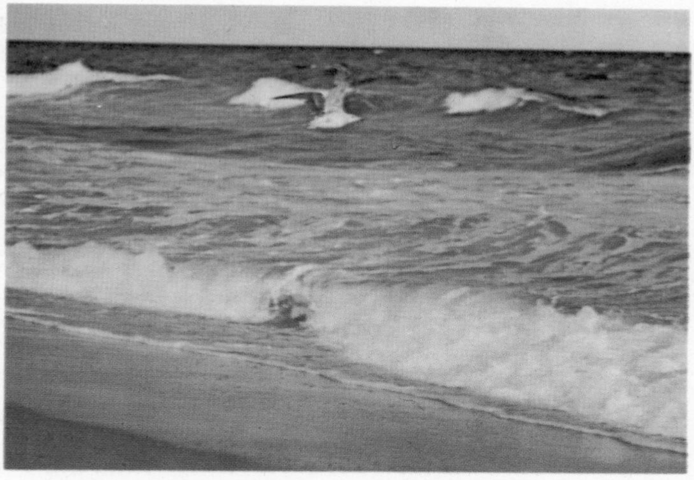

6. The Main Concept Changes in Fitness to the Environment

FOCUS ON THE CONCEPT

We have added to our story of the changing Earth. From what evidence they have, scientists think that there was a time when the Earth was just a ball of hot matter revolving around the Sun. As the ball cooled, the mixture of gases that surrounded it cooled, too. The water vapor in that atmosphere cooled and began to rain down. It was a long rain, thousands of years long, scientists think. From it came the early oceans.

Volcano after volcano burst out of the young Earth, as melted rock came bubbling to the surface. The crust slowly cooled. The rock began to weather and break down,

343

LESSON CLUSTER 6
THE MAIN CONCEPT: CHANGES IN FITNESS TO THE ENVIRONMENT

Teaching background. T-340–346

Concept-seeking. Children seek to understand the large concept that living things have changed over the ages as they adapt to changing or different environments.

Methods of intelligence. Children *analyze* and *synthesize* evidence of change into a unifying concept of adaptation of organisms to their environments.

Introducing Lesson Cluster 6

Let children speculate on what the Earth may have been like before there were oceans with living things in them and birds flying above them. What was probably needed before plants could grow? (water, suitable temperature) before animals could develop? (food—made by green plants) Children may have various speculations. Accept them without comment, but some children may keep the discussion going on the evidence of the preceding lessons.

Or ask: What one word would you use to describe the physical environment of the Earth and life on it over the ages? (interdependence) Have they always been the same? (No; changes have happened.)

Developing the lesson

You may wish to continue discussion with the following questions:

What would life have been like if nothing had changed? What would life have been like if things stopped changing at any one point? Why did living things change? (Their environment changed and they had to change in order to survive.)

Unit Concept-Statement: Over the ages, living things have changed in their adaptation to the changing environment.

❶ cracked by heat and cold. Erosion began. Weathered rock was carried down into the ocean, where the first sedimentary rocks began to form.

There was no life on Earth.

Slowly, year after year, the sediment streamed into the ocean to form rock. The rock layers became thicker and thicker, heavier and heavier, pressing on the material beneath them. Later, the Earth's crust was heaved up. Then these raised areas were worn down.

These things are still going on. Right now, sedimentary layers are pressing down. Right now, as this pressure slowly grows, the Earth's crust is being pushed up in places. Earthquakes and volcanoes show that the Earth is still changing. Erosion is still cutting down mountains and building up new ❷ land. Since the Earth is still a young planet, we think that these changes will go on for a long time.

And now we know that *plants and animals are changing, too.* We know it through evidence found by fossil-hunting scientists. They have found evidence which helps them understand what life was like on Earth as far back as 2 ❸ billion years ago. ■

■

Continuing Lesson Cluster 6

❶ Why was erosion of rock necessary before there could be living things? (Broken rocks provide anchorage for roots of plants, minerals for plants' food, etc.)

❷ The age of the Earth as a planet is thought to be at least 4.5 billion years. Children may think that this number of years is old. Scientists predict that the Sun will still be sending out energy for another 15 billion years. If we say that the life of the Sun is compared to 80 years of human life, children can appreciate that the Earth would be only just out of the teens.

❸ The fossil fern and the modern fern look very much alike. Evidence in the fossils show very little change. If we were to dig into older layers of sediment than those where these fossils were found and could find no ferns, what would you infer? (Some change had occurred at some time that allowed ferns to develop.)

Unit Concept-Statement: Over the ages, living things have changed in their adaptation to the changing environment.

The first plants in the seas and waters were simple flat-bodied plants. Then mosses and ferns covered the
1 warm, moist land. Tree ferns grew in forests. Finally, our present flowering plants – grasses, shrubs, and trees – came to be. Simpler plants, without roots, stems, leaves, or flowers, came first. Plants with different, more complex, structures came later.

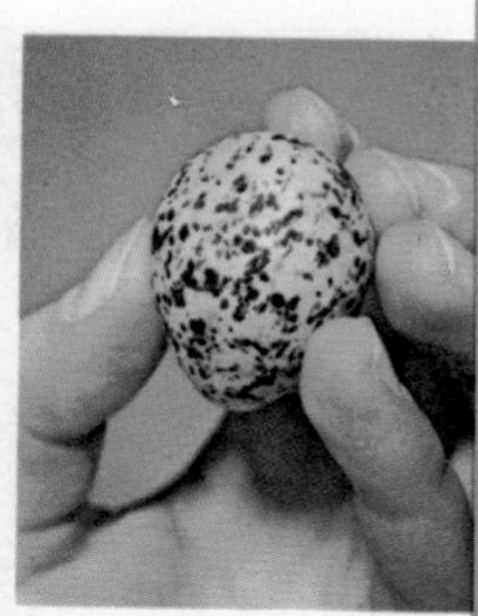

The single-celled animals were first in the early waters. Then the waters filled with simple invertebrates – sponges, jellyfish, worms, and starfish.

The trilobites, very much like our crabs and lobsters, came along next. Then came the squids and clams. All these appeared over many millions of years.

After the invertebrates came the first vertebrates, the fishes. Then one kind of fish crept up on land. From changes in this fishlike ancestor came the great amphibians. From changes in the amphibians came the great reptiles. These changes, too, took millions upon millions of years.

The story of changes in living things is also the story of new adaptations in living things. The fishlike ancestor that came out on land had developed – at least partly – new structures that fitted it or adapted it to live on land.

These adaptations for life on land appeared: eggs with a
2 hard cover. ● Lungs. Feathers. Fur. These adaptations meant that the living things were better fitted to live on land.

The first true land animals were the reptiles. The amphibians laid their eggs in water and lived part of their lives in water. But the reptiles were true land animals. The reptiles, especially the dinosaurs, ruled for a long time. They were in the air, on the land, and in the seas. From them, it seems, came birds and mammals.

In any event, the fossil evidence leads scientists to these explanations. Is there any other explanation that fits the evidence?

You have come then to know more about the concept
3 of change:

Throughout the history of the Earth, living things have changed.

1 How were the first plants adapted to their environment? How were the tree ferns adapted to their environment? Through discussion, children should come to realize, or infer from evidence they have studied, that each plant, in its time, was adapted to the environment. As the environment changed – both physically and biologically – some plants became less well adapted and died out, while others with better adaptations to the changed environment thrived.

Carry the discussion similarly to animals. To what extent were animals dependent on plants? (Entirely; only green plants make food.)

2 Let children review the adaptations of land animals and trace how certain adaptations made the animals more suited to dominate the environment.

3 It has been said that only change is constant. Let children cite evidence that change has been going on through the ages.

Unit Concept-Statement: Over the ages, living things have changed in their adaptation to the changing environment.

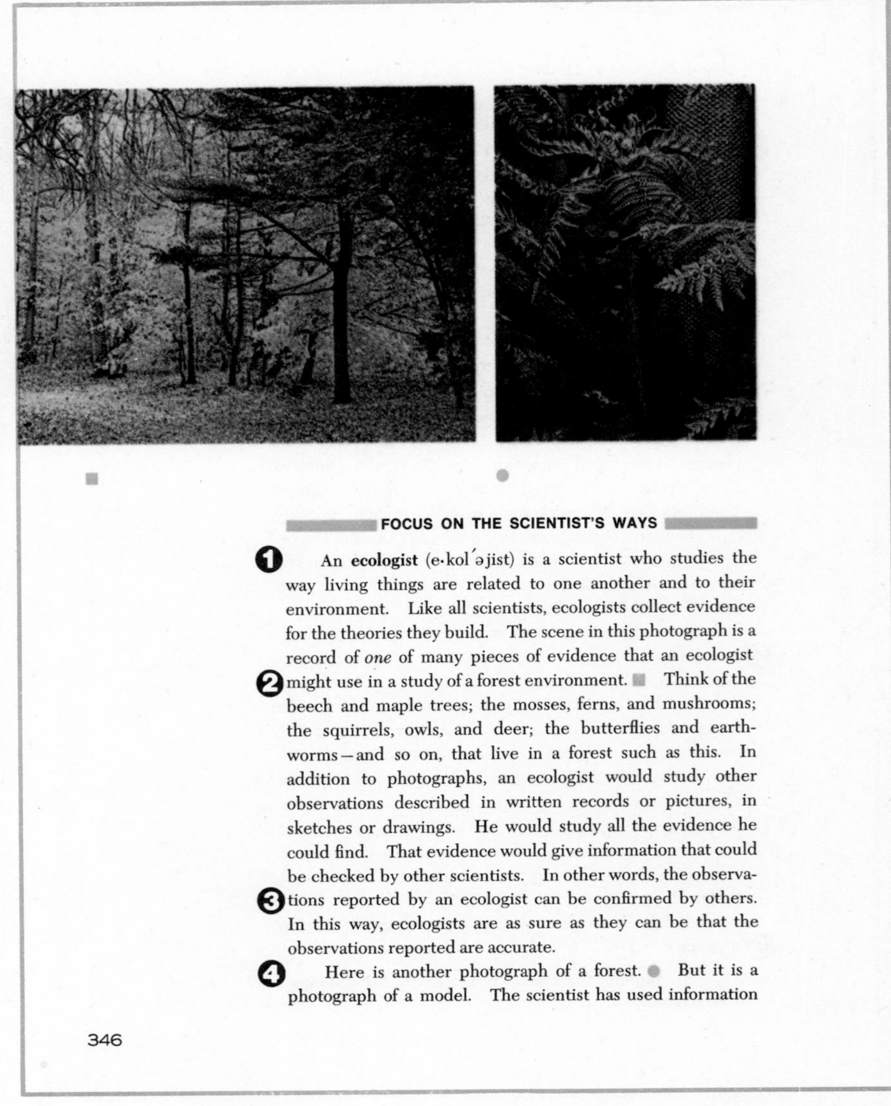

FOCUS ON THE SCIENTIST'S WAYS

❶ An **ecologist** (e·kolʹəjist) is a scientist who studies the way living things are related to one another and to their environment. Like all scientists, ecologists collect evidence for the theories they build. The scene in this photograph is a record of *one* of many pieces of evidence that an ecologist
❷ might use in a study of a forest environment. ■ Think of the beech and maple trees; the mosses, ferns, and mushrooms; the squirrels, owls, and deer; the butterflies and earthworms—and so on, that live in a forest such as this. In addition to photographs, an ecologist would study other observations described in written records or pictures, in sketches or drawings. He would study all the evidence he could find. That evidence would give information that could be checked by other scientists. In other words, the observa-
❸ tions reported by an ecologist can be confirmed by others. In this way, ecologists are as sure as they can be that the observations reported are accurate.

❹ Here is another photograph of a forest. ● But it is a photograph of a model. The scientist has used information

346

Continuing Lesson Cluster 6

❶ The term "ecology" comes from the Greek word *oikos*, which means "home."

❷ What kind of evidence might a scientist look for in this forest environment? Children should consider many things they have learned about the physical environment: the range of temperature and rainfall, the amount of humus on the floor of the forest, whether it was on high or low ground, and so on. Children should then consider the kinds of animals, what they used for food, whether there was water for them, the amount and kinds of cover, nesting places and so on.

❸ Of what use would all this information be? Scientists could infer relationships between plants and animals, predict the effects of changes (from lumbering or forest fire, for example) and make corrections if certain factors of the environment were to change drastically.

❹ How can an ecologist build a model of the environment from fossils? Children can infer that he knows something of the conditions of the environment from the type of fossil plant shown and the type of layers in which the fossils were found. That is, he can interpret evidence and put it together on the basis of comparative evidence from present living ecological communities.

Unit Concept-Statement: Over the ages, living things have changed in their adaptation to the changing environment.

supplied by fossil evidence to help him imagine how a forest of tree-ferns some 60 million years ago might have looked. A scientist interested in the ecology of the world in ancient times might use this picture to help imagine the environment of ancient animals such as dinosaurs. Would 1 you say that the information in this photograph is as accurate as that in the first one? Which photograph might be used as direct evidence? Which one would be thought of as an inference from the evidence?

Rachel Carson, Scientist-Writer

Rachel Carson was a scientist concerned about rela-2 tionships of living things to their environment. ▲ Miss Carson recorded the observations and conclusions of many ecologists in books such as *Edge of the Sea, Silent Spring,* and *The Sea Around Us.* Partly as a result of Rachel Carson's work many persons have become aware of environmental problems man has created for himself. If you want to read some of her writings for yourself, you might start with the special edition of *Edge of the Sea* for young people, published by E. M. Hale Co. (Eau Claire, 1955). Look for it in your school or public library.

▲

347

VERIFYING PROGRESS

In methods of intelligence

Children may *investigate* a forest, pond, park, or field environment; *observe* the forms of life from both direct evidence and indirect evidence (footprints, burrows, nests); *record* the evidence in photographs or sketches and written notes. Later they may *analyze* this evidence, and *describe* the ecological relationships they find. They can *interpret* whether the area is being conserved wisely and *construct a plan* for maintaining or improving it.

A field trip of the sort described can give children an opportunity to use the methods of intelligence that are characteristic of a scientist when he approaches a problem.

1 A photograph is an accurate record; a model can only be an interpretation of what this ancient forest might have looked like. The forest is direct evidence. The model is indirect evidence. Then the model is an inference. Scientists use fact (direct evidence) and can build models by inferring from such direct evidence what other facts (fossils) might reveal as indirect evidence of a whole ecology.

2 The recent concern about pollution and pesticides is due in part to Miss Carson's writings.

Unit Concept-Statement: Over the ages, living things have changed in their adaptation to the changing environment.

Focusing on the Main Concepts

1 TESTING YOURSELF

A. Test your understanding of important concepts in this unit by answering these questions.

1. Put these living things in order of their appearance on Earth.

a. trilobites
b. reptiles
c. mammals
d. fishes

2. How are mammals better adapted to live on land than amphibians?

3. Igneous rock was formed with great heat. Would you expect to find many fossils in igneous rock? Why?

B. Test your knowledge with this quick check.

1. The group of animals that came earliest in time is the

a. ostracoderms
b. dinosaurs
c. insects

2. The group of animals that came earliest in time is the

a. single-celled animals
b. backboned animals
c. many-celled animals

3. The group that came latest in time is the

a. birds
b. amphibians
c. fishes
d. mammals

4. The statement that fits the main concept of this unit is

a. Throughout the history of the Earth, living things have remained unchanged.
b. Living things of the past changed as they came to be fitted to changing environments.

2 INVESTIGATING FURTHER

1. Many different kinds of animals and plants have been formed in the $4\frac{1}{2}$ billion years the Earth has existed. There is a great variety in living things on Earth today.

Make a collection of one group of living things to show this great variety. You might make a collection, for example, of shells, leaves of trees, insects, feathers, or cocoons.

2. You can see that some of the living things around you are closely related. Others are related less closely. For instance, all dogs seem to be closely related. They have much the same structure. Although there are differences between a spaniel and a bulldog, still, both are dogs.

All flowering plants are fairly closely related. They have flowers and produce seeds. Can you separate the flowering plants into two groups? Try to do this by observing the way the seeds produce the young plants.

348

VERIFYING PROGRESS

1 Testing yourself. A. Children *analyze* questions and statements, and respond by *ordering* a sequence, *describing* a condition, and *predicting* an outcome.

1. a, d, b, c
2. Warm-blooded with steady temperature, not dependent on water for skin-breathing, young develop inside mother instead of from eggs laid in water, exercise parental care, none of which is characteristic of amphibians.
3. Igneous rock comes from within the Earth. Flowing hot lava that covered any plant and animal remains on the surface would destroy them.

B. Children *demonstrate* understanding of concepts of the unit by *identifying* suitable completions of open-ended statements.

1. a 2. a 3. d 4. b

2 Investigating further. Children *order* the variety of living things by *constructing* a collection. They *investigate* relationships in seed plants and *order* them into two large groups.

1. Children should limit their collection only to plants or to a single large group of animals.

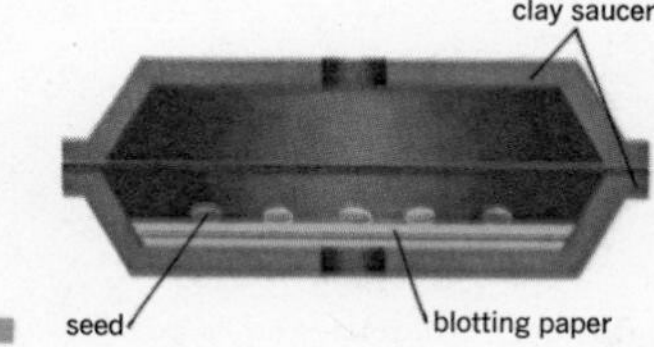

❶ Take many different seeds: bean, squash, wheat, oat, radish, corn, pea, sunflower, grass, and as many others as ❷ you can get. Put one clay saucer on top of another to make the moist chamber shown in the diagram. ■

The two blotters on the bottom saucer should always be kept moist. Soak all the seeds overnight in water, then place them in the moist chamber. They will germinate (jûr′mə·nāt). That is, they will produce young plants.

Observe the way seeds of flowering plants produce young plants. Can you ❸ separate them into two related groups?

FOR YOUR READING

1. *Famous Fossil Finds,* by Raymond Holden, published by Dodd, Mead, New York, 1968. Follow the adventures of fossil-hunting scientists like Roy Chapman Andrews. Find out, for instance, how dinosaur eggs were discovered.

2. *Wonders of Fossils,* by William H. Matthews, published by Dodd, Mead, New York, 1968. This book explains how fossils are formed.

3. *All About Horses,* by Marguerite Henry, published by Random House, New York, 1968. This is an interesting account of horses from the very first fossils of their ancestors to the horses of today.

4. *Dinosaurs and Their World,* by Lawrence Pringle, published by Harcourt Brace Jovanovich, New York, 1968. The book tells what the dinosaurs were, how their fossils were discovered, and where their fossils may be found today.

5. *Tales Told by Fossils,* by Carroll Fenton, published by Doubleday, New York, 1966. Fossil-hunting can be very interesting. This book tells you what can be learned through fossils.

6. *After the Dinosaurs,* by Carla Greene, published by Bobbs-Merrill, Indianapolis, Indiana, 1968. Read this book if you would like to know what animals roamed the Earth after the dinosaurs died out.

7. *From Bones to Bodies: a Story of Paleontology,* by William Fox and Samuel Welles, published by Walck, New York, 1959. You will learn how scientists find and test evidence of animals no longer living on Earth. You will also discover how scientists use living animals to understand structure of ancient ones.

❶ Children must keep a record of which seeds are which. They should make a labeled drawing of the name and location of each kind of seed in the germinating dish.

❷ These saucers are the kind used under clay plant pots and can be obtained in garden supply stores and nurseries, and in some hardware stores.

❸ Children will observe that some seeds, such as beans, split into two separate parts. Plants having this type of seed are *dicotyledons* (two seed leaves).

Plants from other seeds, such as corn, are *monocotyledons* (one seed leaf). Children will observe that some seeds have only one big part. The first leaves will grow from the whole seed without its splitting in two.

Concept Relationships: We are adapted to and interdependent with the continually changing matter and energy in the Universe.

A NEW VIEW OF CHANGE

Teaching background. For Units One through Seven, as indicated in Teaching Notes.

Concept-seeking. Children seek to relate concepts of change in matter, energy, and living things and become aware of their responsibilities in conserving the environment.

Methods of intelligence. Children *synthesize* concepts of change in the Earth's crust, bodies in space, living things, and the environment; they *analyze* and *describe* changes that man causes in his environment and in conclusion *state a plan* for assuming responsibility to conserve the environment.

A NEW VIEW OF CHANGE

We know that the Earth rotates on its axis.

We know that the Earth revolves in orbit around the Sun. We've become accustomed to the fact that our Earth is always on the move in space. We know ❶ too that our Sun is but one star among millions in our galaxy—and that this galaxy is moving in space.

We know, then, that everything moves in space. No planet, no star, stays in one place. Everything changes.

❷ Yet these changes do not frighten us, for we can predict them. We can predict where the Earth will be in its orbit at any moment. (How else could we hurl men into space and have them come back to Earth safely?) These changes seem to be going on in an orderly way. That gives us some confidence.

We see change going on elsewhere, too. Our Sun is not just a hot ball giving off light and heat. From its spectrum we have discovered that the Sun is almost all hydrogen and helium. Stranger still, the hydrogen is being changed into helium—and as this happens some of this matter is changed into energy. From this change comes the Sun's light and heat.

❸ The Sun is constantly changing. Its matter is being changed into energy. It is energy coming from the Sun that makes life possible on Earth. And scientists believe that the changing of matter into energy goes on in all the stars whose light we see.

The whole Universe is constantly changing.

Why should we be surprised at this? We live, after all, on a planet that is constantly changing. Here on Earth the day gives place to night, winter to spring, fair weather to foul weather. Mountains rise up,

350

Introducing the New View

❶ Are you moving while sitting still on a chair? (In relation to the chair, no; but in relation to space, yes.) In Unit One, (T–1–5) you studied the motion of the Earth and Moon around the Sun. What force pulled the bodies into an elliptical path around the Sun? (gravitation) The stars seem to be in a different position at different times of the year. Why? (The position of the Earth changes as it moves around the Sun. Even the stars move, too, as Unit One, T-48–49, tells us.)

❷ How does knowing this motion of bodies in space help us predict where the Moon will be at certain times—for example, how can scientists predict when to send a spacecraft to the Moon so that it can land exactly where they want it to, as Apollo 11 did on July 20, 1969? (The changes in motion follow the pattern predicted by Sir Isaac Newton in his laws of gravitation and motion.)

❸ When you play outdoors in the summer, what do you observe that tells you the Sun is changing? (Its energy makes you warm and may give you a sunburn.) How is this possible? (The fusion of hydrogen atoms into helium atoms gives off tremendous energy that travels through space.) Which bodies in space give off energy in this way? (all the stars) How do we know? (Evidence obtained by using the spectroscope shows that only glowing gases can give off heat and light, i.e., energy. All the stars show that atoms are fusing and giving off energy.) What does this tell us? (The stars are changing.)

Concept Relationships: We are adapted to and interdependent with the continually changing matter and energy in the Universe.

quickly like volcanoes, or slowly, like the Rockies, over
❶ millions of years. The mountains change again; water, wind, heat, and cold slowly break them down. The mountains are weathered and eroded, and the sediment which flows from them turns into sedimentary rock at the bottom of the sea. In this rock, we can read another story of change.

A Story of Change in the Rocks

No one has ever seen a live dinosaur.

❷ Yet, from the evidence, we know dinosaurs lived. They lived in an environment no longer found on the Earth. Why did they disappear? One hypothesis is that the environment changed—and the dinosaurs did not change fast enough to match the changes in the environment. Thus, no man ever saw live dinosaurs: they had left the Earth before man arrived. But the story of the dinosaurs is clear, in the sedimentary rocks. In the sedimentary rocks there is recorded a great story of change—for us to read.

Some 2 billion years ago, single-celled animals lived on the Earth. Over millions of years, Earth's animals were invertebrates. They swarmed in the oceans—there were no animals on land.

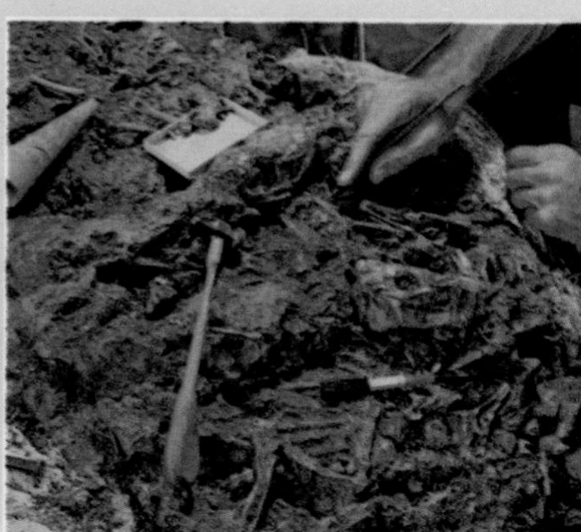

351

❶ In Units One (T-32–33) and Seven (T-389–90), you learned that the Earth began as a ball of hot gases that cooled gradually until the Earth's matter became solid rock, liquid water, and gaseous air. You learned, too, that the Earth and its matter are continually changing. What are some of these changes? How have they been important to living things in the past? How are they important today? Children should be able to cite the work of weathering, erosion, and mountain building in changing the Earth's surface.

❷ How is our knowledge of living things of the past related to changes in the Earth's surface? (As a result of sedimentation and mountain uplift, we can study fossils.) What do fossils tell us? (Organisms have changed.) What kind of changes took place in living things as the Earth changed? (adaptation) How did these changes happen? (chromosome changes) How is adaptation of structure for life in a changing environment another kind of change? (Its slow changes have led to our present living things from Earth's earliest single-celled organisms.)

A NEW VIEW

Concept Relationships: We are adapted to and interdependent with the continually changing matter and energy in the Universe.

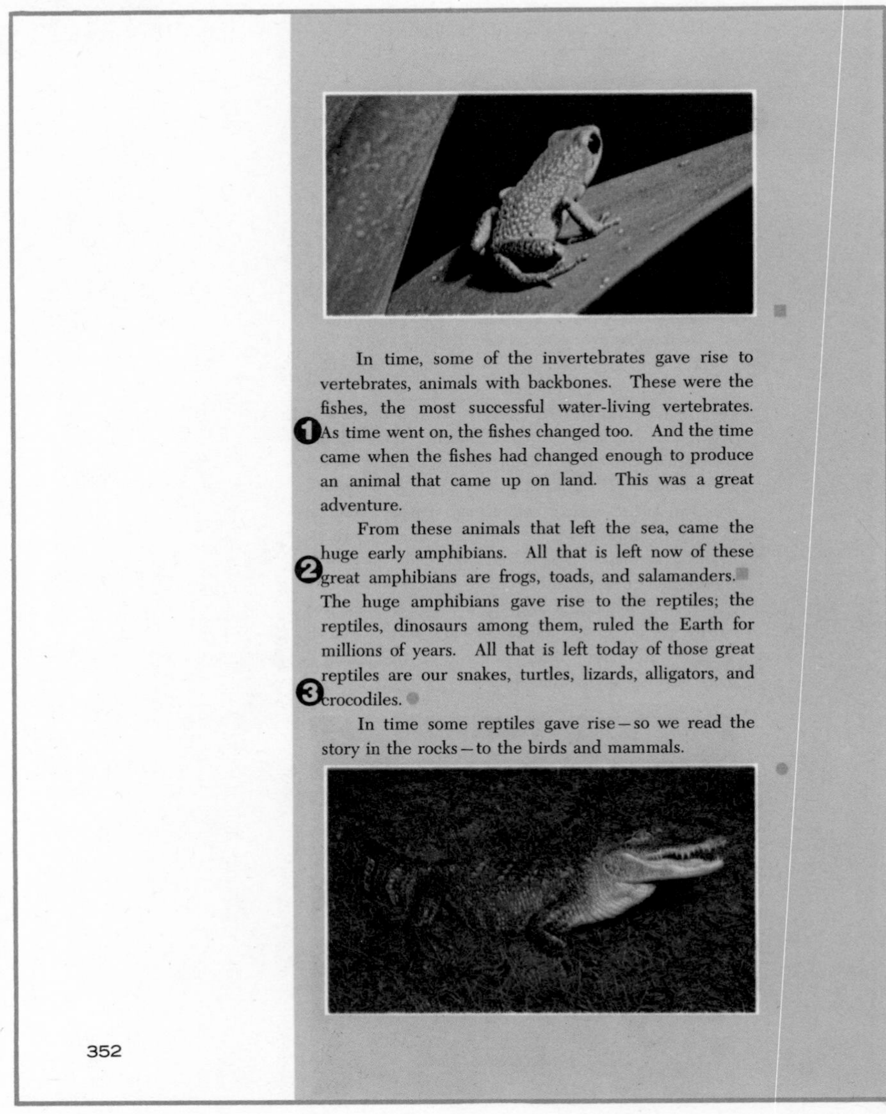

In time, some of the invertebrates gave rise to vertebrates, animals with backbones. These were the fishes, the most successful water-living vertebrates. ❶ As time went on, the fishes changed too. And the time came when the fishes had changed enough to produce an animal that came up on land. This was a great adventure.

From these animals that left the sea, came the huge early amphibians. All that is left now of these ❷ great amphibians are frogs, toads, and salamanders. The huge amphibians gave rise to the reptiles; the reptiles, dinosaurs among them, ruled the Earth for millions of years. All that is left today of those great reptiles are our snakes, turtles, lizards, alligators, and ❸ crocodiles.

In time some reptiles gave rise—so we read the story in the rocks—to the birds and mammals.

352

❶ How would a fish have to change in order to survive on the land? (develop legs, a skin that would resist drying out, lungs for breathing air, etc.)

❷ What changes have there been in amphibians since the time of the ancient ones? Have children compare the tree frog here, and the leopard frog on page 241, with the ancient amphibians on page 326.

❸ What changes have there been in reptiles since the time of the ancient ones? Have children compare the alligator here, and the turtle on page 337, with the reptiles on page 327.

Concept Relationships: We are adapted to and interdependent with the continually changing matter and energy in the Universe.

Man's Adaptation to His Environment

We know that a fish is adapted for life in the water. We know that a bird is adapted for life in the air. A tree is adapted to life on the land, and so are you.

Living things are adapted to their environment.

Early man was related to his environment in a simple way. He took the air, water, food, and shelter that were there and used them for his needs. He lived and multiplied. He spread to other environments. ❶ As man developed, his life became less simple. In some parts of the Earth to which he spread, for example, the climate was different from the places where he had lived before. Life became less simple, and man soon ❷ began to *change* the environment. What were some of these changes?

1. Man built farms to grow food. He developed fertilizers to grow more food. He used pesticides to control insects and other organisms that attacked his food.

2. Man built cities. In cities, man's life could de- ❸ velop in many new ways. As time went by, man built more and bigger cities.

353

❶ From their work in social studies, children should be able to offer examples of ways in which man's life in earlier times was simpler than it is today. You may want to stimulate discussion by such questions as this one: How did people travel in the 18th century (or whatever period the children may have studied)? Let them make comparisons with modern methods of travel—especially the automobile and airplane, but also including spacecraft to the Moon.

❷ Continuing with the train of thought begun above, ask: How have new ways of travel led man to change the environment? (Among the more obvious ways are: destruction of trees, etc. to build highways and airports, consumption of oil reserves for fuel, air pollution from engine exhausts, noise pollution from jet planes.)

❸ Again from their social studies, children may be aware of the economic and cultural advantages of building large cities. But for many children who live in a city, the effects of overcrowding and pollution of all kinds may be live issues they will want to discuss without much prompting.

Concept Relationships: We are adapted to and interdependent with the continually changing matter and energy in the Universe.

3. Man built machines and tools. In other words, he developed technology. With his machines and ❶ tools, man changed the environment more thoroughly and more quickly. To build more roads, houses, offices, and factories, for example, man now uses machines to clear trees from the land.

In these ways and others, man was not only adapting to the environment; he was modifying the environment for his own uses. Man is still changing the environment. But the changes he makes are not always wise. Because of this, the environment is not always an environment fit for life.

There are, for example, smog and dying lakes and overcrowding in cities. If you have done some of the Searches in this book, you know about other examples, too: fouled streams, eroded soil, harmful substances taken into the body, and so on. Man seems to be out of harmony with his environment.

But *you* are man. You—all of you—can use your knowledge to conserve the environment. To ❷ conserve the environment means to use it wisely, intelligently. Conservation (kon′sər·vā′shən), then, means the intelligent use of the environment.

❶ Encourage children who have seen bulldozers and other land-clearing machinery at work to describe their experiences. Who of you has seen men chopping down trees with axes? (perhaps none) Try to help children realize the relative speed and ease of bulldozing trees compared to cutting them down by hand. Another contrast between a newer, and faster, way to change the environment with an older one would be the use of dynamite instead of shovels to excavate for a road or building.

❷ What resources are renewable? Children who have done the Search on page 130 may recall that the following resources, if used or managed wisely, are renewable: soil, water, air, forests, wild life. What resources are non-renewable? (metals, minerals, and fossil fuels)

What are some methods of conservation? (Soil may be conserved by planting appropriate crops and by contour farming. Soil may be made by garden composting. Water may be conserved by wise use and recycling. Air may be filtered or kept free of aerial garbage. Forests may be reseeded; recreation areas may be used wisely and with respect. Non-renewables may be used wisely; some metals may be reclaimed.)

Concept Relationships: We are adapted to and interdependent with the continually changing matter and energy in the Universe.

We Live with Change

We study the changing Universe—its stars, its planets, its space. We study the changing Earth—its seasons, its weather, its moving surface. We study living things, and find change there too—from single-celled animals to many-celled animals, from invertebrates to vertebrates.

We see change everywhere. We have two great concepts that help us to understand this world in which we live:

The Earth and its living things are in continual change.
The Universe and its bodies are in continual change.

❶ We see change everywhere. But we find order in the changes. When these changes are regular and orderly, we can predict them. We can predict changes on the Earth. We are getting to know how to predict changes in living things. We're beginning to understand the orderly changes—such as this one—in the Universe. 

We know much. Yet what we know is very little compared to what we need to know. (And as we learn more, what we think we know changes!) Indeed, as we study changes in the world of matter and energy and living things, knowledge changes our lives. For we use the knowledge we gain by science to change the world we live in. As we change the world, we change the way we live.

We are also learning a great lesson. We are *re-*
❷ *sponsible* for this Earth and for its riches. We are *responsible* for keeping the environment healthy. We alone have this great task of conservation before us. What will happen to man—to us, to you—if we fail to conserve this Earth? ▲

355

VERIFYING PROGRESS
In concept-seeking

Children can *probe* problems of their environment by collecting local news stories that deal with soil and water conservation, protection of wildlife, and pollution of all kinds. Clippings can be used to make a bulletin board display or to provide data for a debate or panel discussion.

❶ Now that you have reviewed changes in the Earth and in living things, think of some ways in which we count on change in planning our lives. For example: How do you plan for changes in day and night? in the seasons? (Children may discuss the use of lights, heating and cooling devices, clothing, etc.)

How are you changing? (growing, learning new things)

Suppose the Earth's matter and energy never changed. For example: If ice did not melt, water did not evaporate, or water vapor condense, how would you and other living things be affected? (There would be no changes in the weather, and without such changes, there would be no rain. Without rain, the crops we now grow for food wouldn't grow, etc.)

❷ What are some ways in which you can be responsible? (Turn off water and electric appliances when not in use; put waste paper in proper containers; don't litter picnic sites or camping areas; return cans and bottles to collection centers, etc.) What is your community doing about air and water pollution? (regulating burning of leaves and trash, providing and caring for wildlife refuges, etc.)

KEY CONCEPT TERMS: A BEGINNING VOCABULARY FOR SCIENCE

To record what they have learned from their investigations, scientists use words that have the same meaning to every other scientist; that is, scientists try to use words accurately. You are building up a vocabulary of key concept terms of science during this year. You will, of course, want to use them properly. The first time a term is used with a special meaning for scientific communication, it is in boldface type in your textbook. In this vocabulary of key concept terms, a page reference is given to refer to if you need more information or examples of the meaning than are given here. In other words, the definition given may need filling out. As you study science, the terms you use will take on fuller meaning. A few terms you probably know from earlier work in science do not have a page reference; you should already know how to use these terms in their correct meaning. The index gives other page references.

PRONUNCIATION KEY

This key is the same as that used in *The Harcourt Brace School Dictionary.*

SYMBOL	KEY WORDS	SYMBOL	KEY WORDS	SYMBOL	KEY WORDS
a	*a*dd, m*a*p	o	*o*dd, h*o*t	u	*u*p, d*o*ne
ā	*a*ce, r*a*te	ō	*o*pen, s*o*	y	*y*et, *y*earn
ä	p*a*lm, f*a*ther	ô	*o*rder, j*aw*	zh	vi*s*ion, plea*s*ure
e	*e*nd, p*e*t	oi	*oi*l, b*oy*	ə	an unstressed vowel
ē	*e*ven, tr*ee*	o͞o	p*oo*l, f*oo*d		as in the words *a*bove,
i	*i*t, g*i*ve	o͝o	t*oo*k, f*u*ll		sick*e*n, clar*i*ty,
ī	*i*ce, wr*i*te	th	*th*in, bo*th*		mel*o*n, foc*u*s

acid, a compound whose water solution turns blue litmus pink, 132

action, a thrust or force acting in one direction that is equal to a thrust or force (reaction) acting in the opposite direction, 15

adapted, fitted to carry on life activities in a particular environment, 297

ADP, the part of the ATP molecule that remains after it has broken down to yield energy in the cell energy process, 207

aeronautics (âr′ə·nô′tiks), the science and art of designing, making, and flying aircraft, 47

alga (al′gə); *plural* **algae** (al′jē), a tiny green plant, generally single-celled, 55

amphibian (am·fib′ē·ən), an organism, such as a frog or salamander, adapted by structure to spending part of its life in water and part of its life on land, 326

artery (är′tər·ē), a blood vessel that carries blood from the heart to the body, 284

atmosphere (at′məs·fir), the layer of gases around the Earth; the air, 100

atoms, the building blocks of elements and compounds, 78

ATP, a large molecule in a living cell, which, when it breaks down chemically, yields energy for the work of the cell, 207; *see also* ADP

auricle (ôr′i·kəl), a part of the heart that receives blood from the body, 286

axis (ak′sis), an imaginary line through the center of a body, such as the Earth, around which the body turns, 158

bacteria (bak·tir′ē·ə), single-celled, nongreen plants, 229; some cause disease, 273

base, a compound whose water solution turns pink litmus blue, 132

biceps (bī′seps), a large muscle in the front part of the arm above the elbow, 288

bird, a warm-blooded animal that has feathers, lays hard-shelled eggs, and usually has the ability to fly, 330

blood vessel, any tubelike part in the circulatory system that carries blood, 283

bone cells, cells that make the substance of which bones are composed; bones give the body shape and support, 271

bone marrow (mar′ō), a tissue of soft cells and substances inside bones in which red blood cells are made, 292

cambium (kam′bē·əm), layer of living cells beneath the bark of a tree, 227

capillary (kap′ə·ler′ē), the smallest and narrowest of the blood vessels, 284

carbohydrate (kär′bō·hī′drāt), a compound of carbon, hydrogen, and oxygen, produced by living things; it has about twice as many hydrogen atoms as oxygen atoms; any sugar or starch found in living cells, 248

cartilage (kär′tə·lij), a substance made by cells that gives certain parts of the body support and flexibility, 271

cell, the smallest living part of a living thing, 202

cell division, method by which a cell divides to produce two similar cells, 226

cell membrane, the outer boundary of the living cell of an animal, 153; the inner boundary of a plant cell, 211

cellulose (sel′yə·lōs), substance that makes up the walls of plant cells, 223

cell wall, the outer nonliving boundary of a plant cell, 223

cerebellum (ser′ə·bel′əm), the part of the brain that is the center for control of the movement of muscles, 292

cerebrum (ser′ə·brəm), the part of the brain which is the center of thinking, imagining, 292

chemical change, any change in which a substance is broken down or built up into other substances. In a chemical change, atoms of the substance (or substances) become joined in a different way, 149

chemical reaction, a chemical change; term usually used by scientists for a chemical change that they understand exactly and for which an equation describes what takes place, 139

chemical test, a means of identifying the chemical properties of substances, thus making it possible to classify them, 132

chloroplast (klô·r′ə·plast), a tiny green body in most green plant cells, 221

chromosome (krōm′ə·sōm), a structure inside a cell nucleus, containing a substance that is basic to determining the characteristics of each new organism, 235

cilia (sil′ē·ə), tiny hairlike structures that enable certain single-celled animals to move about or to obtain food, 230; also on certain covering cells lining the body, as on the tubes to the lungs, 274

circulate (sûr′kyə·lāt), to move in a course that returns to its starting point, as the blood, 283

circulatory (sûr′kyə·lə·tôr′ē) **system,** the organs that work together to carry (circulate) the blood to and from body cells; the heart and blood vessels, 283

classify, to group objects by their likenesses

cold-blooded, having blood whose temperature changes with that of the surrounding air or water, 337

compound, any substance consisting of two or more kinds of atoms chemically combined, 122

contract (kən·trakt′), to change in such a way that less space is occupied

control, that part of an investigation that includes all conditions except the condition being investigated, 203

core, the central part of the Earth, 71

covering cells, the outer cells of a many-celled organism or of organs inside the organism, 273

crater (krā′tər), the opening at the top of a volcano through which lava may flow if the volcano is active, 76

crest, the top point of a wave, 168

crust, the firm, outer layer of the Earth, which may vary from 3 to 40 miles in thickness, 68

crystal (kris′təl), the tiny regular shapes in which the atoms of a solid are arranged, and by which the solid can be recognized

cytoplasm (sī′tə·plaz′əm), all the living matter outside the nucleus of a cell, 211

data (dā′tə), facts or figures; information, 303

diameter (dī·am′ə·tər), the distance from one side of a circle or sphere through its center to the other side

diaphragm (dī′ə·fram), a sheet of muscle below the lungs that, by expanding and contracting, enables the lungs to obtain oxygen from the air and return carbon dioxide (from the cell energy process) to it, 281

diffuse (di·fyo͞oz′), to mix or spread evenly throughout; to pass through a membrane, 219; the spreading of one substance evenly through another is **diffusion**

digestion (di·jes′chən), the breaking down in the body of complex food compounds that do not pass through a membrane into other compounds that do, 267

dissolve (di·zolv′), to mix one substance thoroughly in another substance, as sugar in water, 219

DNA, the substance in chromosomes that is basic to determining the characteristics of an organism, 236

earthquake wave, a regular wavelike motion transmitted through the Earth in all directions as a result of slipping of rock layers in one region, 66

ecologist (i·kol′ə·jist), scientist who studies the relationships between living things and their environment, 346

electron (i·lek′tron), a charged part of an atom that moves about the nucleus; electrons moving through a wire make up an electric current, 172

element (el′ə·mənt), a substance whose molecules consist of only one kind of atom, 122

ellipse (i·lips′), a closed curve flatter on two opposite sides and rounder on opposite ends, 29

enamel (in·am′əl), the hard, outer layer of the teeth, 270

energy (en′ər·jē), the ability to do work, the ability to set an object in motion

energy cycle, a continuous process in which energy is built up or stored, released, and built up again in a living cell; supplying of energy to build up ATP and the breaking down of ATP to yield energy, 208

environment (in·vīr′rən·mənt), the total surroundings of an organism, 297

enzyme (en′zīm), one of a group of substances made by cells in the body; certain enzymes (as pepsin, for instance) speed up digestion without themselves being changed permanently, 267

erosion (i·rō′zhən), wearing away of the Earth's surface by water and wind, 56

excretion (iks·krē′shən), the getting rid of wastes by the body, 293

excretory (eks′krə·tôr′ē) **system,** all the organs that work together to excrete wastes from the body, 294

expand, to change in such a way that more space is occupied

fact, a confirmed observation, 8

fat, a compound of hydrogen, carbon, and oxygen, existing as a molecule; fat molecules have many more hydrogen than oxygen atoms, 248

fault, a break across layers of the Earth's crust, 83

fish, a vertebrate with scales and fins, adapted to live in water, 320

fission (fish′ən), the splitting of the nucleus of an atom, 79; reproduction by division of a cell into two cells that are alike, as in ameba, 235

fluid (flo͞o′id), any substance that can flow

focus (fō′kəs), the place at which rays of light passing through a lens or reflecting from a mirror come to a point, 157

fold, a wavelike bend in rock layers of the Earth's crust, 82

force, any push or pull acting on an object, 5

fossil, the preserved remains or a print of a plant or animal that lived long ago, 63

friction, a force at the surface of an object that makes it hard to move another object across it, 20

fungus (fung′gəs), *plural* **fungi** (fun′jī), colorless plant that cannot make its own food but gets it from other organisms or their remains, 55

fusion (fyo͞o′zhən), the joining of atoms of one element to form atoms of another element; some of the mass is changed to energy, 180

galaxy (gal′ək·sē), a family of millions of stars in space revolving around a center, 43

gas, a state of matter in which a substance expands to occupy a space in which it is free to move

geologist (jē·ol′ə·jist), a scientist who studies the history and structure of the Earth's crust, especially as recorded in rocks, 54

geology (jē·ol′ə·jē), the study of the history and structure of the Earth, especially as recorded in rocks, 104

gill (gil), the organ in the fish that separates dissolved oxygen from water, 322

gland, one of many structures that make special substances the body needs, 278

glucose (glo͞o′kōs), a sugar; when glucose is oxidized in a cell, it yields energy to build up ATP from ADP, 208

gravitation (grav′ə·tā′shən), a force that attracts all objects (masses) in the Universe to one another; each mass tends to pull every other mass towards itself, 5

gravity (grav′ə·tē), the pull of the Earth's gravitation on an object, 5

hemoglobin (hē′mə·glō′bin), an iron compound in a red blood cell that enables the cell to carry oxygen to other cells in the body, 274

hypothesis (hī·poth′ə·sis), a possible explanation of an object or event, which must be tested

igneous (ig′nē·əs), formed by fire or heat, as certain kinds of rocks, 87

image, likeness of an object, as seen on a screen or reflected from a mirror, 157

inactive, describes an element that does not combine readily with other elements, 143

inertia (in·ûr′shə), the tendency of a body at rest to remain at rest, or in motion to remain in motion, 19

inference (in′fər·əns), the act of inferring; something inferred, 8

infer (in·fûr′), *past tense* **inferred,** to come to by reasoning, 8

infrared light, invisible band of light next to red in the visible spectrum, 166

interdependent (in·tər·di·pen′dənt), depending upon one another

invertebrate (in·vûr′tə·brit), an animal without a backbone, 318

joint, any place where two different bones are joined, usually permitting motion, 290

lava (lä′və), molten rock from within the Earth flowing from a volcano, 76

lichen (lī′kən), a double plant consisting of a fungus and an alga, able to live on bare rock, 55

life function, an activity necessary for the life of an organism, 297

ligament (lig′ə·mənt), a band of fiberlike cells that joins one bone to another, 272

light-year, the distance light travels in one year, 185

liquid (lik′wid), a state of matter in which a substance takes the shape of the part of the container into which it is placed

litmus (lit′məs) **paper,** a special paper used as a chemical test for acids or bases, 132

magma (mag′mə), melted rock within the Earth's mantle, 81

mammal, a warmblooded animal having hair or fur, whose young are fed milk made by the mother, 334

mantle, layer of rock about 1,800 miles thick, beginning below the Earth's crust, 71

many-celled, consisting of many cells organized to carry on the life activities of an organism, 228

mass, the amount of matter in an object, 8

matter, all substances of the Earth or space, or any part of them; any object that has weight or takes up space

medulla (mə·dul′ə), the part of the brain that controls breathing and heartbeat, 292

metamorphic (met′ə·môr′fik), changed in form, refers to rock changed by heat within the Earth, 94

meteor (mē′tē·ər), a bit of matter from space that glows as it falls through Earth's atmosphere, 97

meteorite (mē′tē·ə·rīt′) a bit of matter that has fallen to Earth from space, 97

microscope (mī′krə·skōp), an instrument that magnifies very small and usually invisible objects, making them appear larger, and therefore visible to the eye

mineral (min′ər·əl), element or compound in the Earth's soil, water, or rocks, 86; also a salt of a metal such as sodium, calcium, or phosphorus as in living cells, 248

model, an example, or a reconstruction of an object that enables a person to explain or understand that object or a process connected with it

molecule (mol′ə·ky o͝ol), the smallest particle of a substance that still has the properties of that substance, 117

motor nerve, a nerve that carries impulses ("messages") from the brain or spinal cord to other parts of the body, 292

muscle cell, a cell that is able to shorten and lengthen, thus producing movement, 272

muscular (mus′kyə·lər) **system,** all the muscles in the body, 288

nerve, a bundle of neurons bound together and carrying messages to and from parts of the body, 275

nervous system, all the organs that together keep an organism in touch with its environment and enable it to react, 292

neuron (no͝or′on), a cell that carries impulses ("messages") from one part of the body to another; also known as a nerve cell, 275

neutron (no͞o′tron), one of the particles in the nucleus of an atom, 78

nucleus (no͞o′klē·əs), *plural* **nuclei,** the central part of an atom, 78; the central part of a living cell, 211

observe (əb·zûrv′), to make careful examination of, for scientific purposes, 8

orbit, the curving path that a moving body takes around another body in space, 18

organ, a part that carries on a special function within an organism

organism, any complete living plant or animal, 231

organ system, a group of organs working together as a main function of the organism, as in digestion, 278

oxidation (ok′sə·dā′shən), the combining of a substance with oxygen, 206

oxide (ok′sīd), a compound of oxygen and another element, 129

periscope (per′ə·skōp), a tube with mirrors (and sometimes lenses) so arranged that an observer can see over an object, 163

photosynthesis (fō′tō·sin′thə·sis), the process by which green plants use light energy in making carbohydrates

physical change, a change in the form of a substance without a change in its chemical properties, 150

planet, Earth or any of the other eight bodies of matter that revolve around the Sun

predict, to state an event before it happens, 13

prism (priz′əm), a device, such as a triangle of glass, which spreads light into a band of colors, 163

property, any characteristic that is generally true for a substance, and for which it can be tested, 117

protein (prō′tē·in), a compound of carbon, hydrogen, oxygen, and nitrogen and usually phosphorus and sulfur, formed by living things, 248

proton, one of the particles in the nucleus of an atom, 28

protoplanets (prō′tə·plan′its), the bodies of matter from which the planets formed (according to one theory), 26

protozoans (prō′tə·zō′ənz), single-celled animals, 233

pulp, the soft inner part of a tooth containing blood vessels and nerves, 270

radiation (rā′dē·ā′shən), the energy given off from radioactive atoms 79; also refers to the process by which energy travels through space

radioactivity, the slow breaking up of the nucleus of an atom; any element whose nucleus is breaking up is radioactive, 80

reaction (rē·ak′shən), a force equal and opposite to the action of another force (*see* action), 15; *see also* chemical reaction

reflected, bounced off an object, with a change of direction, as light from a mirror, 163

reproduce (rē′prə·do͞os′), to produce another cell like itself, or another organism like the parent organisms, 202

reptile (rep′til), a cold-blooded animal with scales. It lays soft-shelled eggs and breathes by means of lungs, 327

respiratory (ri·spīr′ə·tôr′ē) system, all the organs used in breathing, 282

revolution (rev′ə·lo͞o′shən), the motion of one body in space around another, as the Earth around the Sun, 24.

root hair, a hairlike cell of plant roots through which water and dissolved minerals from the soil enter a plant, 222

rotation (rō·tā′shən), the turning of a body around an imaginary line drawn through its center, 24

saliva (sə·lī′və), a digestive fluid made by glands in the mouth, 267

salivary (sal′ə·ver′ē) **gland,** a gland in the mouth that makes saliva, 280

satellite (sat′ə·līt), a natural object, such as the Moon, or a man-made object that revolves about a body in space, 23

sediment (sed′ə·mənt), particles of rock, soil, and other substances that settle out from the water which carries them, 62

sedimentary rock, rock formed from sediment, 63

seismograph (sīz′mə·graf), a device for recording earthquake waves, 66

sensory (sen′sər·ē) **nerve,** a nerve that carries messages from the body to the brain or spinal cord, 292

single-celled, an organism consisting of one cell able to carry on all life activities, 228

skeletal (skel′ə·təl) **system,** all the bones that support and protect the body and to which organ systems are attached, 290

solar (sō′lər) **system,** the Sun and its planets and other bodies that revolve around it

solid (sol′id), a state of matter in which a substance keeps a definite shape

spectrum (spek′trəm), a band of colors (light of different wavelengths) that is formed when light is passed through a prism, 279

spectroscope (spek′trə·skōp), a device used to analyze light from a glowing object to determine its composition, 176

stable, characteristic of an atom whose nucleus does not break up or change, is not radioactive, 29

structure (struk′chər), the way a cell, tissue, organ, or organism is built; also the way the parts fit together in a complete organism; also refers to the make-up of the atom

supporting cells, cells that give shape and support to the body, 271

technologist (tek·nol′ə·jist), someone who applies discovered concepts to the invention or improvement of materials or tools to do work, 47

tendon (ten′dən), a band of tough cells that joins bone to muscle, 272

theory (thē′ər·ē), a reasonable explanation of objects or events that seems to to fit the evidence about them that has been gathered, 24

thrust, the force that gives a rocket its forward motion, 3

tissue (tish′o͞o), a group of similar cells doing one kind of work, 276

ultraviolet (ul′trə·vī′ə·lit) **light,** invisible band of light next to violet in the visible spectrum, 166

valve (valv), a structure in the heart or veins that lets the blood flow in only one direction, 287

vein (vān), a blood vessel that carries blood from the body toward the heart, 284

ventricle (ven′trə·kəl), a part of the heart that pumps blood to the body, 286

vertebra (vûr′tə·brə), any of the small bones in the backbone which permit motion and through which the spinal cord passes, 290

vertebrate (vûr′tə·brāt), an animal with a backbone, 319

vitamin (vī′tə·min), one of many substances made by organisms and needed by cells for proper functioning, 249

volcano (vol·kā′nō), usually a mountain built up of lava and ash from within the Earth; a volcano begins with an opening in the Earth's crust, 76; *see also* crater

warm-blooded, having a constant warm body temperature regardless of surroundings, 337

wave, any regular back-and-forth or up-and-down motion that transmits energy through matter or through space; for example, a light wave or earthquake wave

wavelength, the distance between the top of one wave and the top of the next, 168

weathering (weth′ər·ing), breaking down of rock by heat, cold, and water, 55

weight, a measure of the force of gravitation acting on an object (a mass)

word equation, a statement in words of the substances taking part and of those produced in a chemical reaction; the substances are produced by breaking down a compound or by combining substances chemically, 123

INDEX